EIGHTH EDITION
GLOBAL EDITION

MARKETING
RESEARCH

EIGHTH EDITION
GLOBAL EDITION

MARKETING RESEARCH

Alvin C. Burns

Louisiana State University

Ann Veeck

Western Michigan University

Ronald F. Bush

University of West Florida

Pearson

Harlow, England • London • New York • Boston • San Francisco • Toronto • Sydney • Dubai • Singapore • Hong Kong
Tokyo • Seoul • Taipei • New Delhi • Cape Town • Sao Paulo • Mexico City • Madrid • Amsterdam • Munich • Paris • Milan

Vice President, Business Publishing: Donna Battista
Editor-in-Chief: Stephanie Wall
Editor-in-Chief: Ashley Dodge
Senior Sponsoring Editor: Neeraj Bhalla
Editorial Assistant: Eric Santucci
Managing Editor, Global Edition: Steven Jackson
Associate Acquisitions Editor, Global Edition: Ishita Sinha
Vice President, Product Marketing: Maggie Moylan
Director of Marketing, Digital Services and Products: Jeanette Koskinas
Field Marketing Manager: Lenny Ann Raper
Product Marketing Assistant: Jessica Quazza
Team Lead, Program Management: Ashley Santora
Team Lead, Project Management: Jeff Holcomb

Project Manager: Becca Groves
Project Manager, Global Edition: Sudipto Roy
Senior Manufacturing Controller, Global Edition: Trudy Kimber
Media Production Manager, Global Edition: Vikram Kumar
Operations Specialist: Carol Melville
Creative Director: Blair Brown
Art Director: Janet Slowik
Vice President, Director of Digital Strategy and Assessment: Paul Gentile
Manager of Learning Applications: Paul DeLuca
Full-Service Project Management, Composition and Design: Cenveo® Publisher Services
Cover Image: BestPhotoStudio/Shutterstock

Microsoft and/or its respective suppliers make no representations about the suitability of the information contained in the documents and related graphics published as part of the services for any purpose. All such documents and related graphics are provided "as is" without warranty of any kind. Microsoft and/or its respective suppliers hereby disclaim all warranties and conditions with regard to this information, including all warranties and conditions of merchantability, whether express, implied or statutory, fitness for a particular purpose, title and non-infringement. In no event shall Microsoft and/or its respective suppliers be liable for any special, indirect or consequential damages or any damages whatsoever resulting from loss of use, data or profits, whether in an action of contract, negligence or other tortious action, arising out of or in connection with the use or performance of information available from the services.

The documents and related graphics contained herein could include technical inaccuracies or typographical errors. Changes are periodically added to the information herein. Microsoft and/or its respective suppliers may make improvements and/or changes in the product(s) and/or the program(s) described herein at any time. Partial screen shots may be viewed in full within the software version specified.

Microsoft® and Windows® are registered trademarks of the Microsoft Corporation in the U.S.A. and other countries. This book is not sponsored or endorsed by or affiliated with the Microsoft Corporation.

IBM, the IBM logo, ibm.com, and SPSS are trademarks or registered trademarks of International Business Machines Corporation,registered in many jurisdictions worldwide. Other product and service names might be trademarks of IBM or other companies. A current list of IBM trademarks is available on the Web at "IBM Copyright and trademark information" at www.ibm.com/legal/copytrade.shtml.

Acknowledgments of third-party content appear on the appropriate page within the text.

Pearson Education Limited
Edinburgh Gate
Harlow
Essex CM20 2JE
England

and Associated Companies throughout the world

Visit us on the World Wide Web at: www.pearsonglobaleditions.com

© Pearson Education Limited 2017

ISBN 10: 1-29-215326-1
ISBN 13: 978-1-292-15326-1

British Library Cataloguing-in-Publication Data
A catalogue record for this book is available from the British Library

10 9 8 7 6 5 4 3

Typeset in Times LT Pro by Cenveo Publishing Services
Printed and bound by CPI Group (UK) Ltd, Croydon, CR0 4YY

Only we know how much our spouses, Jeanne, Greg, and Libbo, have sacrificed during the times we have devoted to this book. We are fortunate in that, for all of us, our spouses are our best friends and smiling supporters.

Al Burns,
Louisiana State University

Ann Veeck,
Western Michigan University

Ron Bush,
University of West Florida

Brief Contents

Contents

Chapter 7   Evaluating Survey Data Collection Methods   **170**

Preface to *Marketing Research,* Eighth Edition

What's New and What's Tried and True in the Eighth Edition?

■ *New! Ann Veeck, Co-author.* The eighth edition of *Marketing Research* heralds a significant change in authors. For the past seven editions, this textbook has been authored by Al Burns and Ron Bush. Ron shifted into retirement soon after the seventh edition was published, and Ann Veeck came aboard. Ann has impeccable credentials, including a Master of Marketing Research degree from the Terry College of Business at the University of Georgia. Ann has taught marketing research and used Burns and Bush textbook editions for a number of years. Ann's contributions appear throughout the eighth edition and especially in coverage of the marketing research industry, the marketing research process and problem definition, research design, secondary and packaged information, and qualitative research techniques. Ann is also on top of digital marketing research and big data analytics. Those adopters who have used previous editions of *Marketing Research* will nevertheless recognize coverage and contributions by Ron Bush and, while Ron is not an active writer of the eighth edition, we have retained his name as co-author for this reason. So the eighth edition of *Marketing Research* marks the transition of Burns and Bush to Burns, Veeck, and Bush, with the expectation that the ninth edition will be Burns and Veeck.

  Benefit: As a longtime user of *Marketing Research* and an accomplished teacher of countless marketing research students, Ann's contributions continue the tradition of intuitive and immediately understandable coverage of this subject matter.

■ *New! Big Changes in the Industry, Subtle Shifts in the Textbook.* Those of us in the marketing research business cannot help but notice the huge changes taking place. Big data and marketing analytics have arrived; social media marketing research practices are on the scene; qualitative research has become much more common; technological innovations happen daily; panels have become the way of surveys; data visualization, infographics, and dashboards are the preferred presentation vehicles. As seasoned marketing educators and perceptive textbook authors, we are well aware that instructors intensely dislike dramatic changes in new editions of textbooks they have used for some time. So, we have addressed the big changes in marketing research not with a major rewriting of the tried-and-true coverage in prior editions but with a more evolutionary approach by adding new sections, composing Marketing Research Insights as illustrations, and recasting some chapter sections to be consistent with current practice. We advise the adopters of the eighth edition to do as we do. When teaching marketing research to our own students, we use the textbook coverage as a springboard to current practices and examples that we glean by keeping up with *Quirk's Marketing Research Review*, *GreenBook*, and other marketing research industry news sources.

  Benefit: Adopters of the eighth edition will notice the modernization of coverage, but they will not be shocked or inconvenienced by huge changes in organization, topic coverage, and flow of material in the textbook.

■ *New! Digital Marketing Research.* We firmly believe that new technologies, principally computer-based innovations, are profoundly changing the practice of marketing research, and while we termed it *social media marketing research* and *mobile marketing research* in our previous edition, those terms do not completely capture what is happening. So, we have opted to use *digital marketing research* as our catchphrase, which we believe subsumes social media marketing and mobile marketing research, all technological shifts such as the huge popularity of online panels, the growth of Internet-based qualitative techniques, infographics, and so on. Thus, many of these are highlighted by Digital Marketing Research Applications in Marketing Research Insights throughout the book. Under the umbrella of digital media, many references will pertain exclusively to the subcategory of social media data (as in the section in Chapter 5 on social media as a form of secondary research) and will be labeled as such.

> *Benefit:* Students have the latest information on industry practices regarding technology's impacts on marketing research. Students will be able to appreciate how rapidly changing and evolutionary is the contemporary practice of marketing research.

■ *New! Big Data.* In the era of "big data," students need to be aware of traditional sources of data as well as exciting new sources. Chapter 5, Secondary Data and Packaged Information, now begins with an introductory section on big data that defines the phrase and explains why the multiplying types and volume of data are met with both anticipation and apprehension by marketing research professionals. One of these increasingly important sources of data is the user-generated data (UGD) that can be mined from social media websites; an extensive section on the use, as well as the strengths and weaknesses, of social media data has been added to Chapter 5. Another form of secondary digital data that is becoming increasingly useful is the Internet of Things (IoT), and a section on the future potential of these sources of "passive data" now concludes Chapter 5.

> *Benefit:* Students will have a better understanding of the current and potential use of emerging sources of data and how they can develop skills to be well equipped for careers in the marketing research industry.

■ *New! Updated Marketing Research Practical and Global Insights.* Marketing Research Insights—short illustrations and descriptions of marketing research practices—have been an integral part of *Marketing Research* from the first edition. In addition to the new Digital Marketing Research Insight element, we have retained those that have evolved over previous editions. Namely, Practical Marketing Research Insights and Global Marketing Research Insights appear in every chapter with fresh examples. These inserts help to illustrate concepts we discuss in the text or to introduce students to some unique application being used in practice. All of these are new and reflect current issues and practices in the industry.

> *Benefit:* Students are introduced to real-world applications in the marketing research industry. By focusing on four categories, students see how current issues that are important to the industry are being addressed by today's practitioners.

■ *New! Marketing Research Company Vignettes.* In past editions of *Marketing Research*, we leveraged the relationships we have developed in the industry by inviting key players to contribute a thumbnail company description or comment on a particular marketing research topic at the beginning of each chapter. With the eighth edition, all company vignettes are fresh. However, we opted, for the most part, to invite only the most innovative marketing research companies to contribute. Thus, we issued an invitation to companies identified in the *Top 50 Most Innovative Supplier Companies in Marketing Research* in the 2015 GreenBook Research Industry Trends Report. Several responded with thumbnail descriptions, photos of the CEO or other company principal, and company logo. With each one, curious students are encouraged to visit the company's website. Because most of these companies are innovative and cutting edge, they do not fit the "mold" of chapter coverage as did companies in past editions. Instead, instructors should treat these company vignettes as interesting success stories about contemporary marketing research practices.

> *Benefit:* Students get more than an academic perspective of marketing research. They benefit from reading about (and seeing, if they visit the websites) innovative marketing research practitioners solving real problems.

- *New! New End-of-Chapter Cases.* In many chapters, we provide new cases to reflect much of the current material in this eighth edition. We strive to make the cases interesting to the students and illustrate real-world applications. We have developed new short cases that are fictitious but written with a goal of stimulating students' interest and curiosity.

    Benefit: Students can apply concepts they have just learned in the chapter to a real-world setting. This allows students to see how valuable the information they have learned is in a practical example.

- *Tried and True! Retained Organization and Shorter Length.* With the previous edition, we responded to adopters' desires for a more concise approach. We reduced the number of chapters to 16 instead of the 20 or more chapters you'll see in many texts. We accomplished this aim by combining some chapters and streamlining the material. For example, we combined the chapters on steps in the research process and determining the problem into one chapter. This streamlined approach keeps the focus on the core lessons to be learned. Because this organization and shorter list of chapters proved successful both in terms of sales and adopters' comments, we have retained this format in the eighth edition.

    Benefit: The book is better synchronized with a 15- or 16-week semester. Students now have a comprehensive learning experience in a more manageable package.

- *Tried and True! Annotated Integration IBM® SPSS® Statistics software ("SPSS") 23.0.* This eighth edition is fully integrated with SPSS 23.0. We started this integration in 1995, and we enhance the integration of SPSS by offering your students step-by-step screen captures that help them learn the keystrokes in SPSS. This allows you to spend more time teaching what the analysis technique is, when to use it, and how to interpret it. Illustrated keystrokes for the latest edition of SPSS are presented in this text with clear, easy-to-follow instructions.

    Benefit: Students learn the latest version of SPSS, considered to be the "gold standard" among marketing researchers. By following our step-by-step screen captures, students will see the necessary menu operations and learn how to read SPSS output. Just by reading this book, they can learn a great deal about SPSS by "seeing" it operate before they get to a computer to practice.

- *Tried and True! Guidelines on Reporting Statistical Analyses to Clients.* We have noticed that after teaching our students to properly conduct a statistical analysis using SPSS, they have trouble when it comes to writing down what they have done. In our sixth edition, we added an element that would address this problem. We believe it is a significant improvement, and we have retained and streamlined it in the eighth edition. In our data analysis chapters, we include information on how to write up the findings for the client. We offer easy-to-follow guidelines and examples.

    Benefit: Most books teach data analysis. Students reading this book will benefit by not only knowing how to perform data analysis but also how to report what they find. This should make students better research report writers.

- *Tried and True (but tweaked)! Integrated Case.* Through our own teaching, we have found that an integrated case is an excellent teaching tool. One case example that develops over the semester allows students to see the linkages that exist in the real world all the way from formulating the problem through data analysis. Our integrated case follows a marketing research company project from start to finish. To freshen the integrated case, we changed the client company from Global Motors to Auto Concepts and modernized the automobile models being researched. The case focuses on a manager who must determine the type of automobiles the auto market will demand in the future. Students using this case will learn how to examine attitudes and opinions (for example, attitudes about global warming) that may influence consumer choice, how to determine the most preferred models, and how to identify market segment differences between the different models. Students are shown how SPSS tools can aid them in analyzing case data to make important decisions. The dataset is streamlined with fewer variables, and the "integrated" aspect has been cut back to nine end-of-chapter cases rather than one in every chapter. Of course, the dataset is used extensively in analysis chapters so students can replicate the examples and practice.

Benefit: The Auto Concepts integrated case offers the benefit of allowing students to examine the critical steps in a marketing research project and to more easily see how data are used to help managers choose from among decision alternatives.

- *Tried and True! Inclusion of Code of Ethics Passages as Ethical Marketing Research Insights.* A fourth Marketing Research Insight is entitled Ethical Consideration, which also harkens back to our text book's inception. In our previous edition, we decided to treat the topic of ethics the way it is treated in the industry, so we included excerpts from the *Code of Marketing Research Standards* as presented by the Marketing Research Association (MRA). We have long had a good relationship with the MRA, which has given us permission to present excerpts from the current standards. We continue this approach with the eighth edition. We understand that a textbook cannot teach someone to be ethical. Rather, we tie together issues of ethical sensitivity in the conduct of marketing research practices described in each chapter by specific reference to ethical code passages.

  Benefit: Students are introduced to areas of ethical sensitivity in the practice of marketing research using the actual codes/standards that practitioners use. As a result, students should have knowledge of potential "ethical dangers," whether as a future buyer or supplier of research.

- *Tried and True! YouTube Examples.* Current thinking on how millennial students approach their education emphasizes the importance of social media and Internet-based learning. With the previous edition, we experimented by searching for and including YouTube video references, and we have continued this learning resource in the eighth edition. YouTube references in the text provide useful insights ranging from problem definition to statistical analysis to report writing.

  Benefit: For students who like video learning, our YouTube references provide different perspectives and how-to insights on topics covered in the text.

- *Tried and True! Active Learning Challenges.* We innovated in the sixth edition with the inclusion of short exercises embedded at strategic points in each chapter where students are tasked with using the concept(s) they have just learned to experiment with or apply to some illustrative situation. We believe these exercises serve to solidify learning on the relevant concepts, and we have retained these Active Learning features in the eighth edition.

  Benefit: Active learning allows students to practice or apply some concept or technique they have just read about. Learning is facilitated by reading and then "doing."

- *Tried and True! Synthesize Your Learning.* We have also retained this feature from the sixth edition to help students synthesize the knowledge they have gained across several chapters. The exercises require students to go back to previous chapters and integrate material into answers for the exercise. The Synthesize Your Learning exercises are found at the end of sets of three or so chapters with the goal of showing how topics covered in these chapters work together to solve a marketing research case exercise.

  Benefit: This feature allows students to integrate material that is learned in "chunks" to see how the material is related. Students benefit by learning how integrated the marketing research process really is.

The Intended Market for This Book

When we first conceptualized this textbook in the early 1990s, we wanted to write it for undergraduate students who were taking marketing research for the first time. We saw other texts that were trying to be "all things to all people." Even though they were positioned as research texts for undergraduates, much of the material was advanced, and instructors either never used them or endured struggling students when covering these topics. This eighth edition, like its seven predecessors, was written specifically for undergraduate students who need a solid, basic understanding of marketing research. With so many marketing research tools that are easily accessible today, it is better to foster savvy do-it-yourself (DIY) generalists than to spawn marginally prepared technique specialists.

However, as is the case with all things marketing, our customers, both students and instructor-adopters, have changed. As we ourselves strive for perfection in our own educational pedagogies, so have we constantly sought to revise *Marketing Research* toward satisfying the requirements for success with (now) millennial student learners. With every edition, we have conscientiously tried to think about how to improve the presentations in the text so as to be intuitively understandable to the mainstream undergraduate student. Early editions of this textbook sought to equip marketing students with tools to be effective clients of marketing research services providers. Today the need is to provide marketing students with a basic knowledge of good marketing research practice that they will probably attempt to execute themselves. That is, we are now teaching the DIY generation of marketing research students.

Our Approach

Given our intended market, throughout all eight editions we strived to provide instructors with a book designed for undergraduates who wanted to know the "nuts and bolts" of marketing research. For example, our chapter on measurement teaches students the basic question formats, the scales of measurement, the primary uses of each type of scale, and the common methods used to measure popular constructs. It does not dwell on different forms of reliability and validity or the method used to develop valid and reliable multi-item scales. In our analysis chapters, we cover the basic "bread-and-butter" statistical procedures used to analyze data, but we do not cover multivariate techniques or nonparametric statistics in the book itself.

Our approach and writing style have probably been the two main reasons the book has been the market leader for well over two decades. Student evaluations indicate that we deliver on our intent to write at the level that people studying marketing research for the first time understand. We hope your teaching evaluations regarding the text will arrive at the same appraisal.

Recommended Prerequisites

To prepare for this course, we feel students should have taken an introductory course in marketing. We assume students know what we mean when we talk about marketing strategy and the elements of the marketing mix. Students having had an introduction to marketing course will better appreciate the role that marketing research plays in helping managers make better marketing decisions. We also recommend that students take an introductory statistics course prior to taking this course. It helps for them to know concepts such as the area under the normal curve, z scores, and the basics of statistical testing, including interpretation of p values. However, since we both have taught for many years, we are well aware that many students will not recall many of these concepts and, where necessary, we provide some review of these basics.

AACSB Guidelines

The Association to Advance Collegiate Schools of Business–International (AACSB), our accreditation society, influences us a great deal. We strive to keep current with AACSB's recommendations and guidelines, such as including material that will aid in your course assessment efforts, covering ethical issues, and pointing out global applications.

We include a number of items that should help in assessing your students' understanding of the course content. Each chapter begins with learning objectives. Embedded in each chapter are Active Learning exercises that allow students to apply the knowledge just acquired to some real-world resource. Synthesize Your Learning exercises in this edition require that students revisit chapters to integrate their knowledge from those chapters. For our test bank, Pearson has adopted guidelines established by AACSB. We discuss this in a following section.

Other Features in the Eighth Edition

- *Online Link to Careers in Marketing Research.* Some students will be interested in marketing research as a career. Beginning with the sixth edition and continued for the eighth, we provide an online Careers link. This gives us the opportunity to post new happenings in the industry as they occur. Students will find descriptions of positions, salary information, educational requirements, and links to actual position openings.

  There are some excellent master's programs in marketing research. Our Careers link also provides information on these programs. Go to **http://www.pearsonglobaleditions .com/Burns** and click on the link for the Companion Website for *Marketing Research*, eighth edition. When you open any chapter, you will see the list of links in the left margin. Click on "Careers."

  Benefit: Students have the most up-to-date information about careers.
- *Advanced Data Analysis Modules.* Even undergraduate students taking their first course in marketing research may need some knowledge of statistical analyses other than those we have provided in the text. Many times these issues arise as a result of a particular need associated with a real-world class project. We wanted to make some of these techniques available to you online, so we have written several additional data analysis modules. The emphasis in these modules is on explaining the basics of the analysis and when it is appropriate. We also provide an example. Topics covered are the following:
  - When to Use Nonparametric Tests
  - Nonparametric: Chi-square Goodness-of-Fit Test
  - Nonparametric: Mann-Whitney U Test
  - Nonparametric: Wilcoxon Test
  - Nonparametric: Kruskal-Wallis H Test
  - When to Use Multivariate Techniques
  - Factor Analysis
  - Cluster Analysis
  - Conjoint Analysis

    Students can access the modules by going to the textbook website and opening up any chapter. They will see a link to "Online Data Analysis Modules."
- *Datasets.* We offer datasets associated with our cases that can be downloaded. Of course, we provide the dataset for our integrated case, Auto Concepts. We also offer the L'Experience Félicité (formerly Hobbit's Choice) dataset for professors who wish to use this case. These datasets and the chapter locations of the relevant data analysis cases are as follows:
  - *Auto Concepts* (Auto Concepts.sav)—integrated case dataset used in Chapters 12–16

- *Auto Concepts Recoded* (Auto Concepts.Recoded.sav)—integrated case dataset with ordinal demographic variables recoded using midpoints of ranges to convert these variables to scales to be used as independent variables in multiple regression analysis
- *L'Experience Félicité Restaurant* (L'Experience.sav)— dataset for end-of-chapter cases used in Chapters 12–15.

To access these datasets, go to http://www.pearsonglobaleditions.com/Burns and click on the link for the Companion Website for *Marketing Research*, eighth edition. When you open any chapter, see the list of links in the left margin and click on "SPSS Student Downloads."

Instructor Resources

At the Instructor Resource Center, www.pearsonglobaleditions.com/Burns, instructors can easily register to gain access to a variety of instructor resources available with this text in downloadable format. If assistance is needed, our dedicated technical support team is ready to help with the media supplements that accompany this text. Visit http://support.pearson .com/getsupport for answers to frequently asked questions and toll-free user support phone numbers.

The following supplements are available with this text:

- Instructor's Resource Manual
- Test Bank
- TestGen® Computerized Test Bank
- PowerPoint Presentation
- Student Companion Website

Student Supplements

SPSS Student Assistant. With previous editions, we created the SPSS Student Assistant, a stand-alone tutorial that teaches students how to use and interpret SPSS. The SPSS Student Assistant may be downloaded from the Companion Website. Installation on a personal computer is simple, and the SPSS Student Assistant will reside there for easy, immediate access. The videos show cursor movements and resulting SPSS operations and output. There is a test for each Student Assistant session so that students may assess how well they have learned the material.

Go to http://www.pearsonglobaleditions.com/Burns and click on the link for the Companion Website for *Marketing Research*, eighth edition. When you open any chapter, see the list of links in the left margin and click on "SPSS Student Downloads" for more information.

Acknowledgments

Many people were involved in putting this eighth edition together. We are fortunate to have Pearson as our publisher. Over the years, we have been impressed with the professionalism and dedication of the people at Pearson and the people we worked with on this edition were no exception. We wish to thank our Senior Sponsoring Editor, Neeraj Bhalla, for his support and leadership. We have worked with Becca Richter Groves, Senior Production Project Manager, on several past editions, and we are grateful for her responsiveness and efficiency. This has been another successful collaboration with the Pearson team and we look forward to many more editions!

We have benefited from the input of Heather Donofrio, Ph.D., Business Communications, for several editions. Heather helped us keep the reporting, writing, and presentation chapter current. Ashley Roberts has worked behind the scenes for us on two previous editions. Parts of this eighth edition benefited greatly from the work of Ali Russo. We are fortunate to have these bright and enthusiastic people working with us.

We devote a major effort toward developing and maintaining relationships with our colleagues who practice marketing research. Their knowledge and insights are interwoven throughout these pages. Many of these people have been our friends for many years, and we appreciate their contributions. Professionals who contributed significantly to one or more of our eight editions include the following:

David Almy, CEO, Marketing Research Association

Eduardo Carqueja, NPolls

Kristen Darby, COO, Marketing Research Association

Andrea Fisher, Burke, Inc.

Raleigh Floyd, Nielsen

Chris Forbes, Research Reporter

Steven H. Gittelman, President and CEO, Mktg., Inc.

Erika Harriford-McLaren, Strategic and Corporate Communications Manager, ESOMAR

Lauren Hersch, Client Relationship Manager, IBISWorld

Kees de Jong, Vice Chairman of the Board, Survey Sampling International

Frankie Johnson, Research Arts

Shari Johnson, Business Librarian, University of West Florida

Jackie Lorch, Vice President, Global Knowledge Development, Survey Sampling International

Ramana Madupalli, Director, Master of Marketing Research Program, Southern Illinois University–Edwardsville

Jeff Minier, Co-President, GfK Kynetec

Leonard Murphy, Editor-in-Chief, *GreenBook*

William D. Neal, Founder and Senior Partner, SDR Consulting

Darren Mark Noyce, Founder and Managing Director, SKOPOS Market Insight

Kartik Pashupati, Research Manager, Research Now

Anne Pettit, Vice President, Conversition

Henry Schafer, Executive Vice President, The Q Scores Company

Jessica Smith, Vice President, Offline Client Services, Survey Sampling International

Eelco Snip, Market Intelligence Analyst, ESOMAR

Doss Struse, Managing Partner, Definitive Insights

Naoufel Testaouni, Mirametrix

Liz Tanner, Communications Director, Qualtrics Labs, Inc.

Leslie Townsend, President and Founder, Kinesis

Sima Vasa, Partner and CEO, Paradigm Sample

Mike Webster, Senior Vice President, Research Solutions, Burke, Inc.

Brendan Wycks, Executive Director, Marketing Research and Intelligence Association

Of course, we owe a debt of gratitude to our colleagues in academia who provide reviews of our work. Among the reviewers for the eighth edition were the following:

Linda Coleman, Salem State University

Michael Pepe, Siena College

Feng Shen, St. Joseph University

Minakshi Trivedi, State University at Buffalo

We also thank those who reviewed the previous seven editions of this book. Many of their suggestions and insights are still incorporated in this edition.

Manoj Agarwal, Binghamton University

Linda Anglin, Mankato State University

Silva Balasubramanian, Southern Illinois University

Ron Beall, San Francisco State University

Jacqueline J. Brown, University of Nevada, Las Vegas

Joseph D. Brown, Ball State University

Nancy Bush, Wingate University

E. Wayne Chandler, Eastern Illinois University

Tung-Zong Chang, Metropolitan State University

Kathryn Cort, North Carolina A&T State University

Thomas Cossee, University of Richmond

B. Andrew Cudmore, Florida Institute of Technology

Joshua Fogel, Brooklyn College

Yancy Edwards, University of South Florida

Eric Freeman, Concordia University

Anthony R. Fruzzetti, Johnson & Wales University

Stanley Garfunkel, Queensborough Community College

Corbett Gaulden Jr., University of Texas of the Permian Basin

Ronald Goldsmith, Florida State University

Ashok Gupta, Ohio University

Perry Haan, Tiffin University

Douglas Hausknecht, University of Akron

Stacey Hills, Utah State University

M. Huneke, University of Iowa

Ben Judd, University of New Haven

Karl Kampschroeder, St. Mary's University

James Leigh, Texas A&M University

Aron Levin, Northern Kentucky University

Bryan Lilly, University of Wisconsin

Joann Lindrud, Mankato State University

Subhash Lonial, University of Louisville

Gary McCain, Boise State University

Sumaria Mohan-Neill, Roosevelt University

Thomas O'Conner, University of New Orleans

V. Padmanabhan, Stanford University

Diane Parente, State University of New York, Fredonia

Jean Powers, Ivy Tech Community College

James A. Roberts, Baylor University

Angelina M. Russell, West Virginia University of Technology

Joel Saegert, University of Texas at San Antonio

Don Sciglimpaglia, San Diego State University

Srivatsa Seshadri, University of Nebraska at Kearney

Terri Shaffer, Southeastern Louisiana University

Birud Sindhav, University of Nebraska at Omaha

Bruce L. Stern, Portland State University

John H. Summey, Southern Illinois University

Scott Swain, Boston University

Nicolaos E. Synodinos, University of Hawaii

Peter K. Tat, University of Memphis

William Thomas, University of South Carolina

Paul Thornton, Wesley College

Jeff W. Totten, Southeastern Louisiana State University

R. Keith Tudor, Kennesaw State University

Steve Vitucci, University of Central Texas

Bernard Weidenaar, Dordt College

Carrie White, West Liberty State College

Beverly Wright, East Carolina University

Bonghee Yoo, Hofstra University

Eric Yorkston, Neeley School of Business, Texas Christian University

Charles J. Yoos II, Fort Lewis College

Heiko de B. Wijnholds, Virginia Commonwealth University

Xin Zhao, University of Utah

Zahir Quraeshi, Western Michigan University

Tom Mahaffey, St. Francis Xavier University

Finally, we wish to thank our spouses, Jeanne, Greg, and Libbo, respectively. Our spouses sacrifice much in order to allow us to work on our book. We are fortunate in that, for all three of us, our spouses are our best friends and smiling supporters.

Al Burns,
Louisiana State University

Ann Veeck,
Western Michigan University

Ron Bush,
University of West Florida

Pearson would like to thank the following people for their work on the Global Edition:

Contributors

Nina von Arx-Steiner, University of Applied Sciences and Arts, Northwestern Switzerland FHNW

Nils Magne Larsen, UIT—The Arctic University of Norway

Oh Yoke Moi, Taylor's University

Valdimar Sigurdsson, Reykjavik University

Jon Sutherland

Diane Sutherland

G. Swathy

Reviewers

Per Bergfors, Copenhagen Business School

Richard Beswick, SBS Swiss Business School

Amro Maher, Qatar University

Milena S. Nikolova, American University in Bulgaria

Hamed Shamma, The American University in Cairo

About the Authors

Alvin C. Burns, Professor of Marketing, is the former Ourso Distinguished Chair of Marketing/Chairperson of Marketing in the E. J. Ourso College of Business Administration at Louisiana State University. He received his doctorate in marketing from Indiana University and an M.B.A. from the University of Tennessee. Al has taught undergraduate and master's courses as well as doctoral seminars in marketing research for over 40 years. During this time, he has supervised a great many marketing research projects conducted for business-to-consumer, business-to-business, and not-for-profit organizations. His articles have appeared in the *Journal of Marketing Research*, *Journal of Business Research*, *Journal of Advertising Research*, and others. He is a Fellow in the Association for Business Simulation and Experiential Learning. He resides in Baton Rouge, Louisiana, with his wife, Jeanne.

Ann Veeck is Professor of Marketing at Western Michigan University. She received her Ph.D. in business, with a major in marketing and a minor in statistics, from Louisiana State University and her Master of Marketing Research degree from the University of Georgia. She has taught marketing research and related courses to thousands of undergraduate and M.B.A. students for over 17 years—using this marketing research text, of course. The main focus of her research is family and food consumption patterns in developing nations with an emphasis on China. She has also published extensively on best learning practices in marketing. She received the Haworth College of Business Teaching Award in 2013 and a national award for innovative teaching from the Marketing Management Association in 2012. Ann lives in Kalamazoo, Michigan, with her husband, Gregory Veeck.

Ronald F. Bush is Distinguished University Professor of Marketing, Emeritus, at the University of West Florida. He received his B.S. and M.A. from the University of Alabama and his Ph.D. from Arizona State University. With over 40 years of experience in marketing research, Professor Bush worked on research projects with firms ranging from small businesses to the world's largest multinationals. He served as an expert witness in trials involving research methods, often testifying on the appropriateness of research reports. His research is published in leading journals, including the *Journal of Marketing, Journal of Marketing Research, Journal of Advertising Research, Journal of Retailing,* and *Journal of Business,* among others. In 1993, he was named a Fellow by the Society for Marketing Advances. Ron retired in 2013, and he and his wife, Libbo, live on the Gulf of Mexico, although they may be anywhere in North America on an Air Stream trip.

1 Introduction to Marketing Research

Quirk's Marketing Research Media: Welcome to the World of Marketing Research!

Joe Rydholm is editor of Quirk's Marketing Research Media.

I started at Quirk's just about the time the Internet started changing all of our lives forever and it has been fascinating to see the marketing research industry react and adapt to all things online. Once traditional in-person focus groups and telephone and mail-based surveys were the gold standards. At first, the hue and cry was all about the Web-based methods' lack of statistical validity. While wrestling with that issue, the industry also struggled mightily to adopt old-style paper-and-pencil-based approaches to the digital age.

But one look at the array of tools available to researchers today will show you that the struggle was worth it. Thanks to the smartphone, myriad forms of in-the-moment research are now possible, from mobile ethnography to location-based surveys, giving marketers and researchers access to new and different types of insights.

Despite the outside impression of researchers as rule-following introverts, obsessed with getting the numbers to line up just so, the industry is full of smart, creative, and innovative people. So while big data and do-it-yourself research tools loom as two formidable threats to the traditional marketing researcher's job, the same adaptable, entrepreneurial spirit that enabled the transition from the pre-Internet days to the smartphone era will help current and future research professionals to keep delivering the insights to drive their organizations' strategic decisions.

About Quirk's

In the decades before he founded and began publishing *Quirk's Marketing Research Review* in 1986, Tom Quirk worked on all sides of the marketing research process as a corporate or client-side researcher and later as a research company executive. A firm believer in the merits of marketing research, he found himself regularly having to educate potential users of marketing research services on the value of investigating consumer wants, needs, and opinions and the various techniques that could be used to do so. Ever the entrepreneur, and seeing the need for a publication that would promote the use, understanding, and value of marketing research across all industries, he created *Quirk's Marketing Research Review*, a monthly trade magazine for marketing research clients and the vendors that partner with them.

Armed with a newly minted B.A. in journalism from the University of Minnesota, I interviewed with Tom in the summer of 1988 to become the magazine's second-ever editor-in-chief. I was impressed by his enthusiasm for marketing research and, perhaps more importantly, by his insistence that the articles in *Quirk's*, while generally aiming to promote the value of research, should be as objective, informative, and practical as possible. His aim was to show the many ways marketing research could be used and to give readers real-world, concrete examples of how the methods could be applied.

In the nearly 30 years since then, the staff and I have used Tom's words as a guide. From its beginnings as a monthly magazine, Quirk's Media now offers a feature-packed website and curates and produces marketing research–related content in a variety of forms, from e-newsletters to blogs and Webinars—all free of charge to qualified marketing research and insights professionals.

—Joe Rydholm

Source: Text and photos courtesy of Joe Rydholm and Quirk's Marketing Research Media.

Events in recent years have brought many changes to the world of business. As Joe Rydholm points out, these changes have profoundly influenced the marketing research industry. These are exciting times in marketing research! Globalization has added real meaning to the phrase "the business world." Digital and other technological innovations have allowed us to realize the promises of the "information age" in a few short years. New technologies continue to change the competitive landscape with much greater frequency than ever before. Digital media have expanded at unprecedented rates. Widespread adoption of mobile devices and apps provides consumers with information 24 hours a day. Many objects used by people collect and send information on an ongoing basis, creating the Internet of Things (IoT). Significantly, consumers have the power, through these online innovations, to create their own information, developing consumer-generated feedback in real time.

Marketing research provides managers with new information to help them make decisions.

© Peshkova/Shutterstock

The marketing research industry is changing rapidly.

This new era of big data and digital media not only challenges managers to keep pace but also to understand and respond to a changing world economy. Entire countries grapple with solvency. Political revolution has changed much of the world, and continued unrest threatens more change.[1] Businesses must anticipate what these changes will mean for their markets and capitalize on economic growth where it is occurring. Managers must determine what products to make or what services to offer, which methods of advertising are most effective, which prices will help their firm realize its target return on investment (ROI), and which distribution system will add the greatest value to the supply chain.

This is where marketing research becomes important. Marketing research is the process of gathering information to make better decisions. This book will help you learn the process of marketing research so that you will better understand how to use marketing research to develop actionable insights as you aim to manage in a world of unprecedented change.

1-1   Marketing Research Is Part of Marketing

To fully appreciate the role of marketing research, it is helpful to understand its role in and relationship to marketing. What is **marketing**? A short definition is "meeting needs profitably."[2] When Apple designed the iPad, it met a growing need among those seeking greater computer portability in a tablet format. Amazon has been successful in creating the first generation of online book readers with its Kindle tablets.[3]

The American Marketing Association offers a more detailed definition:

> Marketing is the activity, set of institutions, and processes for creating, communicating, delivering, and exchanging offerings that have value for customers, clients, partners, and society at large.[4]

The American Marketing Association defines marketing as the activity, set of institutions, and processes for creating, communicating, delivering, and exchanging offerings that have value for customers, clients, partners, and society at large.

Over recent years marketing thought has evolved to a service-centered view that (a) identifies core competencies, (b) identifies potential customers who can benefit from these core competencies, (c) cultivates relationships with these customers by creating value that meets their specific needs, and (d) collects feedback from the market, learns from the feedback, and improves the values offered to the public. Note that this view of marketing implies that firms must be *more* than customer oriented (making and selling what firms think customers want and need). In addition, they must *collaborate with* and *learn from* customers, adapting to their changing needs. A second implication is that firms do not view products as separate from services. "Is General Motors really marketing a service, which just happens to include a by-product called a *car?*"[5]

Modern marketing thought holds that firms should *collaborate with* and *learn from* consumers.

Our objective here is not to discuss how marketing thought is evolving but to emphasize a crucial point: To practice marketing, marketing decision makers need to make decisions. What are our core competencies? How can we use these core competencies to create value for our consumers? Who are our consumers and how can we collaborate with them? Managers have always needed information to make better decisions. In our opinion, to practice marketing well in today's environment requires access to more and better information. As you will learn, marketing research provides information to decision makers.

Crowdsourcing is the practice of obtaining services or ideas by asking for assistance from large groups of people, generally online communities.

The diffusion of digital media has created a culture that nurtures consumer collaboration. One important collaboration method is crowdsourcing. **Crowdsourcing** is the practice of obtaining services or ideas by asking for assistance from a large group of people, generally online

MARKETING RESEARCH INSIGHT 1.1 — *Digital Marketing Research*

Lego Crowdsources to Develop New Concepts

Lego is known throughout the world for the passion it inspires in consumers of all ages for its sets of building blocks. The Danish toymaker does not have official statistics of the demographics of its users, but the company estimates that up to half of the revenue at its stores may come from adult users, or AFoLs (Adult Fans of Lego).

To capitalize on the enthusiasm of its fans, Lego has created a web platform called "Lego Ideas," where consumers can post ideas for new concepts (see https://ideas.lego.com/). On this site, users post photos and descriptions of Lego projects they have built. If the concept receives 10,000 supporters within 365 days, it automatically qualifies for a review by the company's Lego Review Board. The website's clear and detailed rules for submitting a project ensure that only the best ideas are posted. For example, concepts involving torture, smoking, racism, or politics are prohibited.

If a concept makes it all the way through to production, the creator receives 1% of profits, five copies of the Lego set, and credit for being the creator. Consumer-inspired Lego sets that have made it all the way to store shelves include the Mini-Big Bang Theory and the Lego Bird Project. Lego Minecraft is one of the Lego Ideas that has been particularly successful,

Lego uses crowdsourcing to develop new product concepts.

leading to the production of multiple versions of Minecraft sets.

Lego Ideas is part of a broader social media strategy the company pursues that includes Facebook, Instagram, Twitter, LinkedIn, and other platforms. Lego's strategy is clearly working. Based on revenue and profits, Lego became the biggest toymaker in the world in 2014, surpassing Mattel.

Source: Grauel, T. (2014, November 28). Lego build adult fan base. *USA Today*. Retrieved from http://www.usatoday.com/story/news/nation/2014/11/28/lego-builds-adult-fan-base/19637025/, accessed August 24, 2015. Hansegard, J. (2015, February 25). Lego's plan to find the next big hit: Crowdsource it. *Wall Street Journal*. Retrieved from http://blogs.wsj.com/digits/2015/02/25/legos-plan-to-find-the-next-big-hit-crowdsource-it/tab/print/, accessed August 25, 2015. Dann, K., and Jenkin M. (2015, July 23). Back from the brink: Five successful rebrands and why they worked. The Guardian. Retrieved from http://www.theguardian.com/small-business-network/2015/jul/23/five-successful-rebrands-why-worked, accessed August 25, 2015. Petroff, A. (2014, September 4). Lego becomes world's biggest toymaker. *CNNMoney*. Retreived from http://money.cnn.com/2014/09/04/news/companies/lego-biggest-toymaker/, accessed August 24, 2015.

communities. Crowdsourcing via digital media is one of many new tools for marketing research. Marketing Research Insight 1.1 explains how the Danish toy company Lego uses crowdsourcing.

When firms make the right decisions, they produce products and services that their target markets perceive as having value. That value translates into sales, profits, and a positive ROI. However, we see many failures in the marketplace. Consultants Joan Schneider and Julie Hall state that they regularly hear from entrepreneurs and brand managers who believe they have come up with a revolutionary product. But Schneider and Hall state that these entrepreneurs almost never have done the research to confirm their grand expectations.[6] As an example, the firm Cell Zones thought it had the answer to cell phone privacy in libraries, restaurants, and so on by creating soundproof booths for private cell phone use. Had the company done the right research and noticed that people were using their new smartphones to text rather than talk, managers may have realized that talking in private was not a pressing need for consumers.

In many examples of failed products and services, managers could have avoided the associated losses if they had conducted proper marketing research. Many product extensions—taking a successful brand and attaching it to a different product—have also failed. Examples include McPizza, Colgate food entrees, BIC underwear, Coors spring water, and Harley-Davidson perfume. Negative reactions from consumers were responsible for removing the Ken doll's earring and taking Burger King Satisfries off the market.[7,8] Could these failures have been avoided with better research information?

Marketing Research on YouTube™ Learn how Lego products go from the idea phase to the shelves with help from consumers. Search "Lego Ideas Third Product Review 2014 Results" on **www.youtube.com**.

Marketing Research on YouTube™ See "10 Worst Product Flops" at **www.youtube.com**. Consider how these mistakes might have been prevented through improved marketing research methods.

Marketing Research on YouTube™ See consultants Schneider and Hall at www.youtube.com. Search "Lessons from New Product Launches—Cell Zone to iPad."

THE PHILOSOPHY OF THE MARKETING CONCEPT GUIDES MANAGERS' DECISIONS

A *philosophy* may be thought of as a system of values or principles by which you live. Your values or principles are important because they dictate what you do each day. This is why philosophies are so important; your philosophy affects your day-to-day decisions. For example, you may have a philosophy similar to this: "I believe that higher education is important because it will provide the knowledge and understanding I will need in the world to enable me to enjoy the standard of living I desire." Assuming this does reflect your philosophy regarding higher education, consider what you do from day to day. You are going to class, listening to your professors, taking notes, reading this book, and preparing for tests. If you did not share the philosophy we just described, you would likely be doing something entirely different.

The same connection between philosophy and action holds true for business managers. One of the most important philosophies managers have is that which determines how they view their company's role in terms of what it provides the market. Some managers have a philosophy that "we make and sell product X." A quick review of marketing history will tell us this philosophy is known as a *product orientation*. Another philosophy, known as *sales orientation*, is illustrated by the following statement: "To be successful we must set high sales quotas and sell, sell, sell!"[9] Managers who guide their companies by either of these philosophies may guide them right out of business. A much more effective philosophy—the marketing concept—is defined here by prominent marketing professor Philip Kotler:

The **marketing concept** is a business philosophy that holds that the key to achieving organizational goals consists of the company being more effective than competitors in creating, delivering, and communicating customer value to its chosen target markets.[10]

The marketing concept is a business philosophy that holds that the key to achieving organizational goals consists of the company being more effective than competitors in creating, delivering, and communicating customer value to its chosen target markets.[11]

For many years, business leaders have recognized that this is the "right" philosophy. Although the term *marketing concept* is often used interchangeably with other terms, such as "*customer orientation*" or "*market-driven*," the key point is that this philosophy puts the consumer first.[12]

What does all this mean? It means that having the right philosophy is an important first step in being successful. However, appreciating the importance of satisfying consumer wants and needs is not enough. Firms must also put together the "right" strategy.

THE "RIGHT" MARKETING STRATEGY

Strategy is another name for planning. Firms have strategies in many areas other than marketing. Financial strategy, production strategy, and technology strategy, for example, may be key components of a firm's overall strategic plan. Here, we focus on marketing strategy. How do we define marketing strategy?

A **marketing strategy** consists of selecting a segment of the market as the company's target market and designing the proper "mix" of product/service, price, promotion, and distribution system to meet the wants and needs of the consumers within the target market.

A marketing strategy consists of selecting a segment of the market as the company's target market and designing the proper "mix" of product/service, price, promotion, and distribution system to meet the wants and needs of the consumers within the target market.

Because we have adopted the marketing concept, we cannot come up with just any strategy. We have to develop the "right" strategy—the strategy that allows our firm to truly meet the wants and needs of the consumers within the market segment we have chosen. Think of the many questions we now must answer: What is the market, and how do we segment it? What are the wants and needs of each segment, and what is the size of each segment? Who are our competitors, and how are they already meeting the wants and needs of consumers? Which segment(s) should we target? Which product or service will best suit the target market? What is the best price? Which promotional method will be the most efficient? How should we distribute the product/service? All these questions must be answered to develop the "right" strategy. To make the right decisions, managers must have objective, accurate, and timely *information*.

It is equally important to understand that today's strategy may not work tomorrow because, as we noted at the beginning of this chapter, there is unprecedented change going on in the business environment. What new strategies will be needed in tomorrow's world? As environments change, business decisions must be revised on an ongoing basis to produce the right strategy for the new environment.

To practice marketing, to implement the marketing concept, and to make the decisions necessary to create the right marketing strategy, managers need information. Now you should see how marketing research is part of marketing; marketing research supplies managers with the information to help them make better decisions.

1-2 What Is Marketing Research?

Now that we have established that managers need information to carry out the marketing process, we need to define marketing research.

Marketing research is the process of designing, gathering, analyzing, and reporting information that may be used to solve a specific marketing problem.

Marketing research is the process of designing, gathering, analyzing, and reporting information that may be used to solve a specific marketing problem.

Thus, marketing research is defined as a *process* that reports information that can be used to solve a marketing problem, such as determining price or identifying the most effective advertising media. The focus then is on a process that results in information that will be used to make decisions. Notice also that our definition refers to information that may be used to solve a *specific* marketing problem. We will underscore the importance of specificity later in this chapter. Ours is not the only definition of marketing research. The American Marketing Association (AMA) formed a committee several years ago to establish a definition of marketing research:

Marketing research is the function that links the consumer, customer, and public to the marketer through information—information used to identify and define marketing opportunities and problems; generate, refine, and evaluate marketing actions; monitor marketing performance; and improve the understanding of marketing as a process.[13]

Each of these definitions is correct. Our definition is shorter and illustrates the *process* of marketing research. The AMA's definition is longer because it elaborates on the function as well as the *uses* of marketing research. In following sections, we will talk more about the function and uses of marketing research.

IS IT MARKETING RESEARCH OR MARKET RESEARCH?

Some people differentiate between marketing research and *market* research. Marketing research is defined the way we and the AMA have defined it in previous paragraphs. In fact, the Marketing Research Association (MRA) defines this term similarly as a process used by businesses to collect, analyze, and interpret information used to make sound business decisions and successfully manage the business. In comparison, some define market research as a subset of marketing research, using this term to refer to applying marketing research to a specific market area. The MRA defines **market research** as a process used to define the size, location, and/or makeup of the market for a product or service.[14] Having made this distinction, we recognize that many practitioners, publications, organizations serving the industry, and academics use the two terms interchangeably.

While the terms marketing research *and* market research *are sometimes used interchangeably,* market research *refers to applying marketing research to a specific market.*

THE FUNCTION OF MARKETING RESEARCH

The AMA definition states that the **function of marketing research** is to link the consumer to the marketer by providing information that can be used in making marketing decisions. Note that the AMA definition distinguishes between *consumers* and *customers*. The committee intended this differentiation between retail (or B2C) consumers and business (or B2B)

The function of marketing research is to link the consumer to the marketer.

Marketers use research to determine the value that consumers perceive in products.

customers. Some believe that having the link to the consumer by marketing research is more important today than ever. Having that link with consumers is crucial if firms are to provide them with the value they expect in the marketplace. Thanks to globalization, online shopping, and social media, consumers today have more choices, more information, and more power to speak to others in the market than ever before.

1-3   What Are the Uses of Marketing Research?

The AMA definition also spells out the different uses of marketing research. The three uses are (1) identifying market opportunities and problems, (2) generating, refining, and evaluating potential market actions, and (3) monitoring marketing performance. We explain each of these further in the following sections.

IDENTIFYING MARKET OPPORTUNITIES AND PROBLEMS

The first of these uses is the *identification of market opportunities and problems*. It is not easy to determine what opportunities are in the market. Although we can think of new product or service ideas, which ones are actually feasible? Which ideas can we accomplish, and which will mostly likely generate a good ROI? Often, after someone has found an opportunity by creating a highly successful product or service, managers ask, "Why didn't we see that opportunity?" Some marketing research studies are designed to find out what consumers' problems are and to assess the suitability of different proposed methods of resolving those problems. High gasoline prices and concerns about fossil emissions bothered consumers, so Toyota developed the Prius. Consumers wanted increasingly large TV screens to hang on their walls, so Samsung developed an ultra-thin, LED, large-screen TV. Consumers who did not have cable wanted to be able to buy HBO, so HBO developed HBO Now.

You would think that managers would always know what their problems are. Why would problem identification be a use of marketing research? Problems are not always easy to identify. Managers are more likely to always know the symptoms (sales are down, market share is falling), but determining the cause of the symptoms sometimes requires research. The identification of opportunities and problems is discussed in Chapter 3.

GENERATING, REFINING, AND EVALUATING POTENTIAL MARKETING ACTIONS

Marketing research can also be used to generate, refine, and evaluate a potential marketing action. Here "actions" may be thought of as strategies, campaigns, programs, or tactics. General Mills acquired Annie's Homegrown, an organic food company, in 2014 to meet a growing demand by consumers to have access to organic and natural foods. "Actions" of General Mills included *generating* the basic strategy to meet consumers' growing desire for organic foods, *refining* the Annie's brand by identifying ways to promote Annie's established products and develop new products that are consistent with the brand culture, and *evaluating* plans to market and grow the Annie's brand. Management can use marketing research to make better decisions for any and all of these actions.

We can think of "actions" as strategies, and strategies involve selecting a target market and designing a marketing mix to satisfy the wants and needs of that target market.

Marketing research is conducted in a variety of areas, including determining target markets and conducting product research, pricing research, promotion research, and distribution research.

Selecting Target Markets A great deal of marketing research is conducted to determine the size of various market segments. Not only are managers interested in knowing the size of the market segment that wants an all-electric vehicle but also they want to know if that segment is growing or shrinking and how well competitors are fulfilling the wants and needs of that segment. If research shows that a significantly large segment of the market has identifiable needs, the segment is growing; if its needs are either not being met or being met poorly by competition, this segment becomes an ideal candidate for a target market. Now the company must determine how well its core competencies will allow it to satisfy that segment's demand. Nissan very likely looked at the automobile market segments in terms of the number of miles driven in a day (we will consider this factor in Chapter 5 on secondary data). The company must have found a sizable segment that drives under 90 miles a day, because that is the range of its all-electric car, the Leaf.

Product Research Successful companies are constantly looking for new products and services. They know the lesson of the product life cycle: Products will eventually die. As a result, they must have a process in place to identify and test new products. Testing may begin with idea generation and continues with concept tests that allow firms to quickly and inexpensively get consumers' reactions to the concept of a proposed new product. Research studies are conducted on the proposed brand names and package designs of products before commercialization. Maritz Research conducts a *New Vehicle Customer Study*. The company has collected data over several years, and in recent years it has studied hybrids. Its market analysts know why drivers purchase hybrids, what makes them satisfied, what their expectations are for gas mileage and preferences for alternative fuels.[15]

Pricing Research When a revolutionary new product is created, marketers use research to determine the "value" consumers perceive in the new product. When cable TV was introduced, research was conducted to give the early cable providers some clue as to what people would be willing to pay for clear reception and a few additional channels. When cellular phones were introduced, much research was conducted to see what people would be willing to pay for (what was then) a revolutionary "portable" telephone. Marketing research is also conducted to determine how consumers will react to different types of pricing tactics such as "buy one, get one free" versus a "one-half-off" price offer. Using qualitative research in the form of asking potential buyers a series of open-ended questions—a qualitative research technique called "purchase story research"—a researcher found that the way a firm categorized its products negatively affected how B2B buyers had to use their purchase accounts. When items were recategorized, sales went up.[16]

Promotion Research As firms spend dollars on promotion, they want to know how effective those expenditures are for the advertising, sales force, publicity/PR, and promotional offers. Firms also conduct research on the effectiveness of different media. Is online advertising more cost-effective than traditional media such as TV, radio, newspaper, and magazine advertising? As an example of promotion research, Chobani launched a campaign, called "The Break You Make," in 2015 to increase awareness of the Chobani Flip, an afternoon snack yogurt. Research determined that the promotion was very successful, with sales of Chobani Flip up 300% over the previous year. As a result Chobani extended and expanded the campaign.[17]

Distribution Research What are the best channels to get our product to consumers? Where are the best dealers for our product, and how can we evaluate the service they provide? How satisfied are our dealers? Are our dealers motivated? Should we use multichannel distribution?

© 123rf

Marketing research is used to monitor marketing performance.

How many distributors should we have? These are but a few of the crucial questions managers may answer through marketing research.

MONITORING MARKETING PERFORMANCE

Control is a basic function of management. To assess performance on some variables, marketing research is often used. Sales information by SKU (stock-keeping unit) and by type of distribution, for example, is often gathered through tracking data collected at point-of-sale terminals as consumer packaged goods are scanned in grocery stores, mass merchandisers, and convenience stores. Scanner data allow managers to monitor their brands' sales as well as sales of competitors— and thus to monitor their market shares as well. Firms use marketing research to monitor other variables such as their employees' and customers' satisfaction levels. For example, the research firm MSR Group conducted a rolling tracking study measuring drivers of bank customer satisfaction. The nationwide study allows banks to identify factors that determine advocates and loyal, at-risk, and critical customer relationships.[18] Research firms such as the Nielsen Corporation and IRI monitor the performance of products in supermarkets and other retail outlets. They track how many units of these products are sold, through which chains, at what retail price, and so on. You will learn more about tracking studies in Chapter 5. Tracking social media, which has grown quickly the world over, is another means of monitoring market performance. Research firms have developed services that monitor what people are saying about companies, brands, and competitors.

IMPROVING MARKETING AS A PROCESS

Improving our understanding of the marketing process entails conducting research to expand our knowledge of marketing. Typical of such basic research would be attempts to define and classify marketing phenomena and to develop theories that describe, explain, and predict marketing phenomena. Marketing professors at colleges and universities and other not-for-profit organizations, such as the Marketing Science Institute, often conduct basic research and publish their results in journals such as the *Journal of Marketing Research* or the *Journal of Marketing*.

> Basic research is research that is conducted to expand knowledge rather than to solve a specific problem.

The aim of **basic research** is to expand our knowledge rather than to solve a specific problem. For example, research published in the *Journal of Marketing Research* may investigate the psychological process consumers go through in deciding how long to wait for a service to be provided. This research is not conducted for any specific company problem but rather to increase our understanding of how to satisfy consumers of services.[19] However, this basic research could be valuable to AT&T if the company were conducting an analysis of consumer reactions to different wait times in its stores, which may be a specific problem facing AT&T. Research conducted to solve specific problems is called **applied research**, which represents the vast majority of marketing research studies. For the most part, marketing research firms are conducting research to solve a specific problem facing a company. We will revisit the idea that marketing research solves specific problems a little later in this chapter.

> Applied research is research that is conducted to solve specific problems.

MARKETING RESEARCH IS SOMETIMES WRONG

Marketing research does not always provide management with the right answer. General Motors, for example, did research on what was to become the minivan—a small van that would be suitable for families—but the research did not convince the carmaker to produce a van. Shortly thereafter, Chrysler introduced the Dodge Caravan and Plymouth Voyager minivans, which turned out to be among the most successful models in automotive history.[20] A beer ad in the United Kingdom was deemed by marketing research to be inadequate, but management disagreed. When the ad ran, it was very successful.[21] The marketing research on the pilot of *Seinfeld* indicated the TV show would be a flop. Six months later, a manager questioned the accuracy of the research and

Marketing research is sometimes wrong.

gave the show another try. *Seinfeld* became one of the most successful shows in television history.[22] When Duncan Hines introduced its line of soft cookies, marketing research studies showed that 80% of customers who tried Soft Batch cookies stated they would buy them in the future. They didn't.[23]

Anyone who observes the marketplace will see products and services introduced and then taken off the market because they do not live up to expectations. Some of these failures are brought to market without any research, which increases their probability of failure. However, as we have learned, even when products are brought to market with the benefit of marketing research, the predictions are not always accurate, but this does not mean that marketing research is not useful. Remember, most marketing research studies are trying to understand and predict consumer behavior, which is a difficult task. The fact that the marketing research industry has been around for many years and is growing means that it has passed the toughest of all tests to prove its worth—the test of the marketplace. If the industry did not provide value, it would cease to exist. For each of the failed examples cited previously, there are tens of thousands of success stories supporting the use of marketing research.

Marketing Research on YouTube™ | Marketing research is not always correct. In the classic 1980's movie *Big*, Tom Hanks's character gives a toy company the insight it really needed—a kid's perspective! Go to **www.youtube.com** and enter "Tom Hanks in BIG 'I Don't Get It' by Therototube."

1-4 The Marketing Information System

Managers have recognized the importance of information as an asset to be managed for many years. The advent of computer technology in the 1960s allowed the dream of information management to become a reality. During the decades since, sophisticated management information systems have evolved that attempt to put the right information at the right time in the right format into the hands of those who must make decisions. Management information systems typically have subsystems to provide the information necessary for a functional area within an organization. Such subsystems are the accounting information system, financial information system, production information system, human resources information system, and marketing information system. Thus far, we have presented marketing research as if it were the only source of information. This is not the case, as you will understand by reading this section on marketing information systems.

Marketing decision makers have a number of sources of information available to them. We can understand these different information sources by examining the components of the **marketing information system (MIS)**. An MIS is a structure consisting of people, equipment, and procedures to gather, sort, analyze, evaluate, and distribute needed, timely, and accurate information to marketing decision makers.[24] The role of the MIS is to determine decision makers' information needs, acquire the needed information, and distribute that

An MIS is a structure consisting of people, equipment, and procedures to gather, sort, analyze, evaluate, and distribute needed, timely, and accurate information to marketing decision makers.[25]

information to the decision makers in a form and at a time when they can use it for decision making. This sounds very much like what we have been saying about marketing research—providing information to aid in decision making. Learning the components of an MIS will help to establish some distinctions.

COMPONENTS OF AN MIS

As noted previously, the MIS is designed to assess managers' information needs, to gather this information, and to distribute the information to the marketing managers who need to make decisions. Information is gathered and analyzed by the four subsystems of the MIS: internal reports, marketing intelligence, marketing decision support, and marketing research. We discuss each of these subsystems next.

Internal Reports System   Much information is generated in normal, daily transactions. When you make a purchase at a grocery store, management has a record of the SKUs you purchased, payment method, coupons or special promotions used, store location, and day of week and time of day. When that same grocery store orders supplies of foods, it has a purchase requisition and a shipping invoice from the supplier firm that ships the goods. Once all these forms of data are gathered, they serve as a source of information for managers. The **internal reports system** gathers information generated within a firm, including orders, billing, receivables, inventory levels, stockouts, and so on. In many cases, the internal reports system is called the accounting information system. Although this system produces financial statements (balance sheets and income statements, etc.) that generally contain insufficient detail for many marketing decisions, the internal reports system is a source of extreme detail on both revenues and costs that can be invaluable in making decisions. Other information is also collected, such as inventory records, sales calls records, and orders. A good internal reports system can tell a manager a great deal of information about what has happened in the past. When information is needed from sources outside the firm, marketing researchers must call on other MIS components.

> The internal reports system gathers information generated within a firm, including orders, billing, receivables, inventory levels, stockouts, and so on.

Marketing Intelligence System   The **marketing intelligence system** is defined as a set of procedures and sources used by managers to obtain everyday information about pertinent developments in the environment. Consequently, the intelligence system focuses on bringing in information generated outside the firm. Such systems include both informal and formal information-gathering procedures. Informal information-gathering procedures involve activities such as scanning newspapers, magazines, and trade publications. Staff members assigned the specific task of looking for anything that seems pertinent to the company or industry may conduct formal information-gathering activities. They then edit and disseminate this information to the appropriate members or company departments. Formerly known as "clipping bureaus" (because they clipped relevant newspaper articles for clients), several online information service companies, such as Lexis-Nexis, provide marketing intelligence. To use its service a firm would enter key terms into search forms provided online by Lexis-Nexis. Information containing the search terms appears on the subscriber's computer screen as often as several times a day. By clicking on an article title, subscribers can view a full-text version of the article. In this way, marketing intelligence goes on continuously and searches a broad range of information sources to bring pertinent information to decision makers.

> The marketing intelligence system is defined as a set of procedures and sources used by managers to obtain everyday information about pertinent developments in the environment.

Marketing Decision Support System (DSS)   The third component of an MIS is the decision support system. A **marketing decision support system (DSS)** is defined as collected data that may be accessed and analyzed using tools and techniques that assist managers in decision making. Once companies collect large amounts of information, they store this information in huge databases that, when accessed with decision-making tools and techniques (such as break-even analysis, regression models, and linear programming), allow companies

> A marketing decision support system (DSS) is defined as collected data that may be accessed and analyzed using tools and techniques that assist managers in decision making.

Marketing research can help retailers understand consumers' demand for delivery or pick-up services.

to ask "what if" questions. Answers to these questions are then immediately available for decision making. For example, salespersons complete daily activity reports showing customers they called on during the day and orders written. These reports are uploaded to the company databases routinely. A sales manager can access these reports and, using spreadsheet analysis, he or she can quickly determine which salespersons are at, above, or below quota for that day of the month.

Marketing Research System Marketing research, which we have already discussed and defined, is the fourth component of an MIS. Now that you have been introduced to the three other components of an MIS, we are ready to address a new question: If marketing research and an MIS are both designed to provide information for decision makers, how are the two different? In answering this question, we must see how marketing research differs from the other three MIS components.

 Active Learning

Use Google Alerts to Create Your Own Intelligence System

You can create your own intelligence system through Google, which offers a free service called Google Alerts (https://www.google.com/alerts). By entering key words, you will receive emails from Google Alerts whenever something appears with those key words. You can specify searching everything that appears on the Internet or limit results to search only blogs, videos, or books. What value would this be to you? If you have a paper to write for the end of term, this service will allow you to gather information all term as it occurs. Or, if you have an interview coming up, you may want to track the latest information about the company or industry. You will receive email results daily.

The marketing research system gathers information for a *specific* situation facing the company.

First, the **marketing research system** gathers information not gathered by the other MIS component subsystems: Marketing research studies are conducted for a *specific* situation facing the company. It is unlikely that other components of an MIS have generated the particular information needed for the specific situation. When Walmart was designing Walmart To Go, the retailer's online service that offers delivery or pick-up services in select markets, management had several service options available to offer customers. Could managers get information about what today's shopper will most prefer from the internal reports system? No. Could they get useful information from their intelligence system? No. Could they get information from their DSS? Not really. Marketing research can provide information to help Walmart understand what grocery delivery and pick-up services will be most appealing to today's consumers.

To consider another example, when *People* magazine wants to know which of three cover stories it should use for this week's publication, can its managers obtain that information from internal reports? No. From the intelligence system or the DSS? No. Filling this information gap is how marketing research plays a unique role in a firm's total information system. By providing information for a *specific* problem, marketing research provides information not provided by other components of the MIS. This is why marketing research studies are sometimes referred to as "ad hoc studies." *Ad hoc* is Latin for "with respect to a specific purpose." (Recall that earlier in the chapter when we defined marketing research, we said we would revisit the word *specific*. Now you see why we used that word in our definition.)

A final characteristic of marketing research differentiates it from the other MIS components. Although this difference does not justify the existence of marketing research in the MIS, it is notable. Marketing research projects, unlike the other components, are not continuous—they have a beginning and an end. This is why marketing research studies are sometimes referred to as "projects." The other components are available for use on an ongoing basis. However, marketing research projects are launched only when there is a justifiable need for information that is not available from internal reports, intelligence, or the DSS.

Summary

Globalization and digital innovations have dramatically changed the pace of change in the business world. Yet managers must still make decisions, and the role of marketing research is to provide information to help managers make better decisions. Because marketing research is part of marketing, to understand marketing research, we must understand the role it plays in marketing. The American Marketing Association (AMA) defines marketing as the activity, set of institutions, and processes for creating, communicating, delivering, and exchanging offerings that have value for customers, clients, partners, and society at large. There are new frameworks for understanding marketing. Advances in social media have increased the opportunities for marketers to "listen" to their consumers and even to collaborate with them. Firms are creating products, such as Adobe Social Analytics and Hootsuite, allowing managers to find out what consumers are saying about them on social media and helping those firms collaborate with their customers using social media. Marketers must "hear the voice of the consumer" to determine how to create, communicate, and deliver value that will result in long-lasting relationships with customers. Some firms "listen" to their customers and have success; others do not and experience product and service failures. There are many examples of product failures including Life-Savers sodas, Colgate food entrees, and Frito-Lay lemonade. In all these cases managers might have made better decisions with better information.

Because philosophies guide our day-to-day decisions, marketers should follow the philosophy known as the *marketing concept*. The marketing concept states that the key to business success lies in being more effective than competitors in creating, delivering, and communicating customer value to chosen target markets. Companies whose philosophy focuses on products and selling efforts do not tend to stay around long. If a firm's management follows the marketing concept philosophy, it develops the "right" strategies, or plans, to provide consumers with value. In short, to practice marketing as we have described it, managers need information to determine wants and needs and to design marketing strategies that will satisfy customers in selected target markets. Furthermore, environmental changes mean that marketers must constantly collect information to monitor customers, markets, and competition.

One definition of marketing research is that it is the process of designing, gathering, analyzing, and reporting information that may be used to solve a specific problem. The AMA defines marketing research as the function that links the consumer, customer, and public to the marketer through information—information used to identify and define marketing opportunities and problems; generate, refine, and evaluate marketing actions; monitor marketing performance; and improve the understanding of marketing as a process. Some differentiate between market*ing* research and *market* research. Marketing research is the broader of the two names and refers to the process of gathering, analyzing, and reporting information for decision-making purposes. Market research refers to applying marketing research to a specific market. However, in practice, the two names are often used interchangeably.

To link the consumer to the marketer by providing information to use in making marketing decisions is the function of marketing research. The uses of marketing research are to (1) identify and define marketing opportunities and problems; (2) generate, refine, and evaluate marketing actions; (3) monitor marketing performance; and (4) improve our understanding of marketing. Most marketing research that is conducted to solve specific problems is considered to be applied research. A limited number of marketing research studies conducted to expand the limits of our knowledge would be considered basic research.

If marketing research provides information to make marketing decisions, why should we also have a marketing information system (MIS)? Actually, marketing research is part of an MIS. Marketing research is only one of four subsystems making up an MIS. Other subsystems include internal reports, marketing intelligence, and decision support systems. Marketing research gathers information not available through the other subsystems. Marketing research provides information for the specific problem at hand. Marketing research is conducted on a project basis and has a beginning and end. The other MIS components operate continuously, 24/7.

Key Terms

Marketing (p. 34)
Crowdsourcing (p. 34)
Marketing concept (p. 36)
Marketing strategy (p. 36)
Marketing research (p. 37)
Market research (p. 37)

Function of marketing research
  (p. 37)
Basic research (p. 40)
Applied research (p. 40)
Marketing information system (MIS)
  (p. 41)

Internal reports system (p. 42)
Marketing intelligence system
  (p. 42)
Marketing decision support system
  (DSS) (p. 42)
Marketing research system (p. 44)

Review Questions/Applications

1-1. What is marketing? What is the relationship of marketing research to marketing?

1-2. Why is it important for decision makers to have philosophies? What is the marketing concept and what is its relationship to marketing research?

1-3. What is a marketing strategy, and why is marketing research important to strategy makers?

1-4. Define marketing research. What is the difference between marketing research and market research?

1-5. What is the function of marketing research?

1-6. Name four major uses of marketing research. Provide one example of each of the uses.

1-7. Which use of marketing research is considered basic research?

1-8. Give your own example to illustrate a marketing research study that may be used in (a) improving marketing as a process, (b) monitoring marketing performance, (c) generating potential marketing actions, and (d) identifying market opportunities and problems.

1-9. How would you distinguish between product and market-driven orientation? Which approach is more likely to be influenced by market research and why?

1-10. Distinguish among MIS (marketing information system), marketing research, and DSS (decision support system).

1-11. Why must modern marketers collaborate and learn from their consumers? What has increased the opportunities for marketers to collaborate with them?

1-12. Go online and search for leading marketing research companies. Look through their websites and blog sections. Identify and give examples of some case studies of their work mentioned on the blog.

1-13. A business is planning to expand internationally. They intend to gradually replace the existing arrangements and set up new offices and channels with distributors in the international market. Suggest what information the company's management would need to take these decisions. How can they gather and evaluate the necessary information? Will the information needs change from country to country?

1-14. In the following situations, what component of the marketing information system would a manager use to find the necessary information?

   a. A manager of an electric utilities firm hears a friend at lunch talk about a new breakthrough in solar panel technology she read about in a science publication.

   b. A manager wants to know how many units of three different products in the company sold during each month for the past three years.

   c. A manager wants to estimate the contribution to company return on investment earned by 10 different products in the company product line.

   d. A manager is considering producing a new type of health food. He would like to know if consumers are likely to purchase the new food, at which meal they would most likely eat the food, and how they would prefer the food to be packaged.

CASE 1.1

Anderson Construction

Larry Anderson is president of Anderson Construction. The firm had been in business for almost five years when the housing industry crashed with the Wall Street debacle of 2008. Although Anderson had quickly become profitable in the building business, it was a time when nearly everyone in construction was making profits, as the industry had been overinflated by a boom based on banking fees rather than real demand. To make a reputation, the company had invested heavily in the selection of a superior construction crew. Larry had followed a strategy of hiring only personnel with high levels of training and experience. This had given him the ability to be versatile. His well-experienced staff of employees gave him the ability to take on a variety of construction projects. By 2012, Anderson was one of the few firms left in town. Most construction firms had gone out of business trying to wait out the housing bust. Anderson had remained afloat with a few good employees and very limited demand among a few individuals who were interested in building custom homes. Because Larry had invested in his personnel with better pay and continuous training, he had many former employees who stayed in touch with him. These employees were eager to go back to work for Anderson and were biding their time in one or more part-time jobs.

Larry was not accustomed to doing marketing research. Starting his business at the time of an artificial building boom, he had what seemed like an endless supply of job opportunities on which to bid. The only research Larry had conducted during those formative years was exploration to find key personnel and to keep up with building materials and building code changes. Now, as Larry had only two custom-home jobs in the queue, he began to worry about how he could find more work for his construction crews. He wondered if marketing research would be of any help.

1. Explain why you think Larry should or should not look into doing marketing research.
2. In thinking about the components of a marketing information system, which components would you suggest Larry use and why?

CASE 1.2 INTEGRATED CASE

Auto Concepts

Nick Thomas is the CEO of Auto Concepts, a new division of one of the largest U.S. automobile manufacturers with multiple divisions representing several auto and truck brands. This company has been slowly losing market share to other competitors. Auto Concepts was created to develop totally new models that are more in tune with today's changing automobile market. A primary consideration in this development effort is the U.S. Department of Energy's Clean Cities Initiative that advocates the use of alternative automobile fuels such as propane, natural gas, biodiesel, electric, hybrid, and/or ethanol. At the same time, management believes that the Internet of Things (IoT) with its capabilities of safe mobile connections, self- or assisted-driving, infotainment, on-board diagnostics, and more will be a prominent part of future vehicles.

Nick Thomas knows he must come up with some innovations in automobile design and engineering, but he is not certain in which direction he should guide his division. Nick realizes that he needs to find out what consumers' attitudes are toward fuel prices and global warming. This knowledge will help him determine a direction for the company in terms of automobile design. Nick also needs more data on consumer preferences. Will they want to stay with today's standard compacts or hybrids, or might they be interested in radically different models that promise much higher fuel economies?

1. In the development of new automobile models, which of the following should Nick be primarily concerned with and why?
   a. Engineering and production feasibility
   b. The brand image of his division's parent U.S. automobile manufacturer
   c. Technological innovation
   d. Consumer preferences
2. Should Nick use marketing research?

2

The Marketing Research Industry

University of Georgia Terry College of Business: The Master of Marketing Research Program

Charlotte Mason, Marketing Department Head and MMR Program Director; C. Herman and Mary Virginia Terry Chair of Business Administration; Director, Coca-Cola Center for Marketing Studies

Fast-changing customer needs have caused companies to realize they must constantly be in touch with their customers. Further, the explosion of available consumer data has led businesses to develop and improve their capabilities to turn data into business actions. Businesses turn to the marketing research function, sometimes called consumer insights, to accomplish these goals. Consequently, those in the marketing research profession find that it is rewarding and fascinating as well as highly valued.

In the current business environment, *U.S. News & World Report* reports that the Bureau of Labor Statistics predicts a 31.6% employment increase between 2012 and 2022 resulting in 131,500 new marketing research job openings.

The University of Georgia's (UGA) Terry College of Business welcomed its first Master of Marketing Research (MMR) class in 1980. The MMR program was the first of its kind in the United States and is internationally regarded as the standard of comparison for such programs. Acknowledging the need for high-caliber marketing researchers, UGA faculty and leading marketing professionals have joined forces to develop a curriculum to prepare students for careers in marketing research. The coursework is designed to provide students with technical skills as well as an understanding of strategic marketing issues from both the client and supplier sides of the industry.

The industry has evolved with the ever-changing digital revolution, and the MMR program curriculum has evolved accordingly. Career opportunities today are practically limitless. Long-term prospects for MMRs are exceptional. Newly graduated MMRs move quickly into project manager, senior analyst, and marketing research or consumer insight manager roles. Many MMR alumni are now directors of consumer insights and analytics at client firms or senior vice presidents at suppliers and agencies.

Terry's MMR students surpass high entrance requirements and are immersed in a rigorous academic program including hands-on use of the same analytic tools and research methods used in the industry. The ultimate goal is to apply these methods to gain insights that guide business decisions. In addition to research methods, the MMR program emphasizes business applications to identify appropriate marketing strategy and tactics.

The Terry College of Business, located in Athens, Georgia, recently completed the first phase of its new Business Learning Community. Correll Hall houses all graduate programs. For more information, visit terry.uga.edu/mmr.

The MMR program gives students an understanding of data acquisition issues, analytic tools, and skills required for insight extraction and dissemination. MMR students learn how to design marketing research projects focused on specific business problems, analyze data using sophisticated statistical methods, prepare and present high-impact reports, and serve as market intelligence consultants to managers. The program maintains ties with many partner corporations who, as advisory board members, guide program content for standards and relevance. The program is structured to encompass the tools and techniques, business acumen, and "soft" skills necessary to succeed in the industry.

Terry MMR graduates are characterized by their industry knowledge and practical experience. A sense of collaboration is instilled in MMR students through numerous team projects. This prepares students to succeed in team environments. As a result, MMR graduates are highly sought by both marketing research suppliers and marketing research departments of major corporations. The program essentially has a 100% placement record. With 600 MMR alumni, the program's graduates hold many leadership positions in the marketing research/consumer insights industry. Many alumni maintain close ties to the program, providing a valuable network for themselves and new graduates. It's no wonder that the Terry College MMR program remains the leader in marketing research education.

—*Charlotte Mason*

Source: Text and Images by permission, University of Georgia Terry College of Business: The Master of Marketing Research Program.

Surveys were used in the early 1800s.

As the chapter's introduction notes, marketing research is a growing industry that can only be expected to gain importance as new forms of technology for gathering and analyzing information emerge. In 2015, *U.S. News & World Report* ranked the career of market research analyst as number one in "best business jobs."[1] After completing a course in marketing research, you may be interested in a career in this area. Serving as an introduction to the marketing research industry, this chapter will introduce several facets of the industry, including a brief history, the different types and sizes of some of the firms, the challenges to the industry, and the methods the industry uses for self-improvement. We will provide information about the industry's professional organizations as well as the Professional Researcher Certification (PRC) program, which is sponsored by the Marketing Research Association (MRA). Finally, we will examine the ethical issues facing the industry.

2-1   Evolution of an Industry

EARLIEST KNOWN STUDIES

People have been gathering information to be used for decision making since the earliest days of recorded history. As Lockley notes, "Even the Children of Israel sent interviewers out to sample the market and produce of Canaan."[2] In the United States, surveys were used in the early 1800s to determine the popularity of political candidates.[3] Political polling is a considerable part of marketing and opinion research today. The first known application of marketing research to a business marketing/advertising problem was conducted by the advertising agency N.W. Ayer & Son in 1879. In trying to put together a schedule of advertisements for its client Nichols-Shepard Company, a manufacturer of agricultural machinery, the ad agency sent a request to state officials and publishers throughout the United States asking for information about grain production.[4]

Robert Bartels, a marketing historian, writes that the first continuous and organized research was started in 1911 by **Charles Coolidge Parlin**, a schoolmaster from a small city in Wisconsin. Parlin was hired by the Curtis Publishing Company to gather information about customers and markets to help Curtis sell advertising space. Parlin was successful, and the information he gathered led to increased advertising in Curtis's *Saturday Evening Post* magazine. Parlin is recognized today as the "Father of Marketing Research," and the American Marketing Association (AMA) provides an award each year at the annual marketing research conference in his name.[5]

Charles Coolidge Parlin conducted the first continuous and organized research in 1911, when he was hired by the Curtis Publishing Company to gather information about customers and markets to help Curtis sell advertising space.

WHY DID THE INDUSTRY GROW?

By the 1920s more marketing research was being practiced in the United States. However, it was not until the 1930s that marketing research efforts became widespread as markets became more geographically diverse. Prior to the Industrial Revolution, businesses were located close to their consumers. In an economy based on artisans and craftsmen involved in barter exchange with their customers, there was not much need to "study" consumers. Business owners saw their customers daily. They knew their needs and wants and their likes and dislikes. However, when manufacturers began producing goods for distant markets, the need for marketing research emerged. Manufacturers in Boston needed to know more about consumers and their needs in "faraway" places such as Denver and Atlanta.

THE 20TH CENTURY LED TO A "MATURE INDUSTRY"

The 1900s saw the marketing research industry evolve. Researcher A. C. Nielsen started his firm in 1923. The Nielsen Company remains a prominent firm in the industry. In the 1930s colleges began to teach courses in marketing research, and George Gallup was designing surveys that could predict presidential elections. During the 1940s, Alfred Politz introduced statistical theory for sampling in marketing research.[6] Also during the 1940s, Robert Merton introduced focus groups, which today represent a large part of what is known as *qualitative marketing research.*

Computers revolutionized the industry in the 1950s.[7] Marketing research in the middle of the 20th century was dominated by small firms.[8] By the late 1950s and 1960s, marketing research was seen as indispensable for companies to track consumption changes in increasingly expanding markets. During this time, many client companies added marketing research departments and the number of supply-side companies also increased greatly. The development of computer technology in the 1970s led to the automation of data management and analysis for larger firms. In the 1980s, the innovation of personal computers brought computing technologies to companies of all sizes. The introduction of data automation to the marketing research industry led to the ability to gather and analyze data at much faster speeds.

In the 1990s and the 2000s, increased globalization and the growth of the Internet led to further dramatic changes in the marketing research industry. Marketing research supply-side firms established branches all over the globe, leading to mergers and acquisitions in the industry. As a result, a period of consolidation of companies took place, which has only recently begun leveling off. Meanwhile, the wide availability and convenience of the Internet transformed all phases of the research process, from data collection to analysis to reporting. Online surveys became the predominant form of questionnaire administration.

The marketing industry has continued to grow and mature. Today the industry includes a number of publicly held firms, as well as several professional organizations and a certification program. Later in this chapter, we will discuss the role of professional organizations and summarize the dynamics of industry revenues.

2-2 Who Conducts Marketing Research?

CLIENT-SIDE MARKETING RESEARCH

Any company seeking to understand its customers, distributors, competitors, or the environments in which they operate may conduct marketing research. Research that is conducted within an organization is called **client-side research**. Larger firms, such as those found in the *Fortune 500*, typically have a formal department devoted to marketing research. These departments may appear in organizational charts under a variety of names, such as consumer insights, but they serve the basic function of providing information to decision makers. Industries that tend to rely heavily on marketing research departments include consumer packaged goods (CPG), technology, advertising, banking and finance, pharmaceuticals and health care, automobile manufacturing, and retailing. Large firms that are recognized for having innovative approaches to marketing research include Procter & Gamble, Google, Unilever, General Mills, and Coca-Cola.[9]

> Client-side research is research that is conducted within an organization.

Medium-sized and smaller firms may assign one or more people to be responsible for marketing research. In these cases, the individual or team may actually conduct some of the research, but often their responsibilities lie in helping others in the firm know when to do research and in finding the right supplier firm to help conduct marketing research.

Do-it-yourself (DIY) research, which has been called the "democratization" of marketing research, is considered one of the most important emerging trends for client-side marketing research departments.[10] DIY marketing research has been facilitated by online access to secondary data and better knowledge of data analysis software such as SPSS.

> DIY marketing research, or do-it-yourself marketing research, refers to firms conducting their own marketing research.

DIY research can provide the information needed to solve the user's problem in a cost-effective way. An increasing number of tools are being developed for firms to conduct their own marketing research. Examples of DIY marketing research tools are online survey platforms (such as Qualtrics and SurveyMonkey), statistical analysis tools (such as SPSS, SAS, and R), social media monitoring tools (such as Hootsuite [see Chapter 5]), and data analysis and visualization *dashboards* (such as those offered by Burke and Tableau). Marketing Research Insight 2.1 introduces the Digital Dashboard, by Burke, Inc., as an example of online data tools.

MARKETING RESEARCH INSIGHT 2.1 *Digital Marketing Research*

Moving Beyond the Traditional Research Report: Digital Dashboard from Burke, Inc.

Michael Webster, Senior Vice President, Research Solutions

Burke, Inc., has developed an online reporting tool that allows clients to access and create reports that are updated in near real time as data are collected in the field. The Digital Dashboard® is a web-based application that can be accessed worldwide and enables users to create custom views of their data as well as access predefined reports. The flexibility of this application

allows users to analyze data themselves to help them make better decisions and ensure that everyone involved in the research project can interact with the data. Traditionally, the client did not see any data until all data were collected and analyzed and the final written report was prepared. Additionally, the traditional printed research report was not interactive. The manager who needed to examine the data differently than reported had to make a special request and wait for further processing. In many cases, the manager would forgo the additional work. The Digital Dashboard is an evolution in reporting that removes the barriers to further analyzing data that are present in traditional reporting methods. Like a driver monitoring a vehicle's

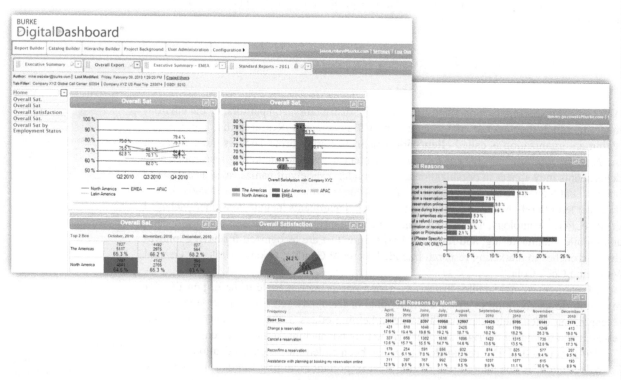

FIGURE 2.1 Digital Dashboard

dashboard for important information, clients using the Digital Dashboard can monitor the entire research project and input custom changes to make sure project results take them to the right destination—making the correct decision.

The Digital Dashboard is comprised of modules that allow the user to interact with data in multiple ways. The Report Builder module enables a user to create multiple charts and tables by following a guided wizard and to analyze and display data in the most meaningful way. These custom reports can then be shared with other users in the organization. Once shared, a user can continue to work with the report to meet specific needs. The Catalog Builder module enables a user to view respondent-level data. The user takes advantage of the same guided wizard available in the Report Builder to create views in this module as well. Data can be exported or scheduled to be delivered at regular intervals by email from this portion of the tool. The Project Background module provides a place for the client to communicate important details about the project and offer guidelines for interpreting the results. The Digital Dashboard can be used for online surveys as well as other data collection modes, such as telephone and mail surveys and mall-intercept surveys.

Visit Burke, Inc., at www.burke.com.

Mike Webster has played a leading role in bringing Burke Interactive to the forefront of Internet research. A key developer of Burke's Digital Dashboard, Webster has designed online reporting solutions for leading-edge clients in a wide variety of industries, including information technology, telecommunications, financial services, and consumer goods. He serves as Burke's resident expert on data collection and online reporting software, working with a variety of languages and platforms. His title is Senior Vice President, Research Solutions.

Source: Text and photos courtesy of Michael Webster, Burke, inc.

While DIY has its place, business owners and managers often do not have the time or expertise to feel confident about using DIY for important issues and will hire marketing research professionals to assist them with their information needs.

SUPPLY-SIDE MARKETING RESEARCH

Research that is conducted by an outside firm to fulfill a company's marketing research needs is called **supply-side research**. A firm that is engaged in supply-side marketing research is often referred to as an **agency**, or simply as a **supplier**. These firms specialize in marketing research and offer their services to buyers needing information to make more informed decisions. In most cases, client-side marketing researchers also purchase research from marketing research suppliers. General Motors, for example, while conducting research on electric cars, may hire a research firm in California to provide feedback from consumers who test-drive prototype cars. Large and small firms, for-profit and not-for-profit organizations, and government and educational institutions purchase research information from suppliers.

> Supply-side marketing research is research that is conducted by an outside firm hired to fulfill a company's marketing research needs. A supplier firm may be referred to as an agency or simply as a supplier.

2-3 The Industry Structure

FIRM SIZE BY REVENUE

Every year the American Marketing Association (AMA) publishes two reports on the marketing research industry on its website and in the publication *Marketing News*. The *AMA Gold Global Top 50* (formerly the *Honomichl Global Top 25*) report ranks the top marketing research firms in the world by revenue earned. These firms include proprietorships as well as international corporations with tens of thousands of employees. Table 2.1 lists the top 10 revenue-producing firms from the 2015 *AMA Gold Global Top 50* report.

As Table 2.1 indicates, a few firms dominate the industry in terms of size based on employees and revenues. The 26th firm in the report has revenues under $100 million. Still, there is extreme competition in the industry. Certainly, the larger firms have advantages, but many small firms develop new approaches and techniques and rely on talented personnel to

> To view the *AMA Gold Global Top 50* and the *AMA Gold Top 50* reports, go to the AMA website at www.ama.org and search "Top 50."

TABLE 2.1   **The Top 10 Global Marketing Research Firms**

Rank	Company	Headquarters	Website	Employees	Global Revenues
1	Nielsen Holdings N.V.	New York	Nielsen.com	42,000	$5,888,100,000
2	Kantar	London	Kantar.com	23,400	$3,389,200,000
3	IMS Health Inc.	Danbury, CT	IMSHealth.com	15,000	$2,544,000,000
4	Ipsos S.A.	Paris	Ipsos-NA.com	16,530	$2,276,600,000
5	GfK SE	Nuremberg	GfK.com	13,380	$1,985,200,000
6	IRI	Chicago	IRIWorldwide.com	4,547	$845,400,000
7	Westat Inc.	Rockville, MD	Westat.com	2,011	$582,500,000
8	dunnhumby Ltd.	London	dunnhumby.com	1,000	$462,000,000
9	INTAGE Group	Tokyo	Intage.co.jp	2,283	$402,000,000
10	Wood MacKenize	Edinburgh	WoodMac.com	957	$360,700,000

Source: Bowers, D. (2015, August). 2015 AMA Global Top 25 Research Report. *Marketing News*, pp. 35–75. See original article for complete details on revenues and other information. Reprinted with permission.

Full-service supplier firms have the capability to conduct the entire marketing research project for buyer firms.

Limited-service supplier firms specialize in one or, at most, a few marketing research activities.

Full-service supplier firms conduct a large variety of research.

be competitive with larger firms. The AMA also publishes the *AMA Gold Top 50*, listing successful U.S. marketing research firms (report available on the AMA website and published in *Marketing News*).

TYPES OF FIRMS AND THEIR SPECIALTIES

Firms in the research industry can be classified into two main categories: full-service and limited service firms. **Full-service supplier firms** have the capability to conduct the entire marketing research project for buyer firms. Full-service firms offer clients a broad range of services; they often define the problem, specify the research design, collect and analyze the data, and prepare the final written report. Typically, these are larger firms with the expertise and necessary facilities to conduct a wide variety of research that may range from qualitative studies to large international surveys to modeling effects of a proposed marketing mix. Most of the research firms found in the *AMA Global 25* and *AMA Top 50* are full-service firms.

Limited-service supplier firms specialize in one or, at most, a few marketing research activities. Firms can specialize in marketing research services such as online communities, questionnaire development and pretesting, data collection, or data analysis. Some firms specialize in specific market demographic segments such as senior citizens or Hispanics. Other firms specialize in different types of industries, such as airline, sports, or pharmaceuticals.

Major types of marketing research services are listed in Table 2.2. However, industry resources are available that provide a better understanding of the many different types of research firms and their specialties. Three professional organization that publish these listings are *GreenBook*, MRA's, *Blue Book*, and Quirk's, as showcased in the Active Learning Exercise, "Using the Marketing Research Directories."

INDUSTRY PERFORMANCE

How well has the marketing research industry performed in terms of revenues? ESOMAR, an international association of research

TABLE 2.2   Major Types of Marketing Research Services

Type	Description	Example Firms
Syndicated Data Services	Analyze the trends and consumer behavior within an industry and sold to many companies	The Nielsen Co., SymphonyIRI Group, Arbitron
Packaged Services	Use a proprietary process to conduct a service such as test marketing or measuring customer or employee satisfaction	GfK, Video Research LTD, Burke, Inc.
Online Research Specialists	Provide client services associated with measuring online consumer behavior and measurement or online data collection	Comscore, Inc., Harris Interactive, Knowledge Networks, Toluna, Mindfield Internet Panels, FocusVision
Customized Services	Provide services customized to individual clients' needs	All of the major firms can do this. Some examples include Burke, Inc., Kantar, Ipsos SA, Synovate, Maritz
Industry or Market Segment Specialists	Specialize in a particular industry or a market segment	IMS Health, Inc., Westat Inc., Latin Facts, Inc., Olson Research Group, Inc.
Technique Specialty		
a. Eye Tracking	Track eye movement to determine better package designs, advertising copy, etc.	The PreTesting Company
b. Mobile Research	Conduct research using mobile devices such as iPads or smartphones	Kinesis Survey Technologies, Cint+Mobile, NPolls
c. Sampling	Use different sampling methods to draw samples to suit client's research objectives	SSI, uSamp, Research Now, Peanut Labs
d. Neuroimaging	Observe brain activity as consumers are exposed to stimuli such as packages or ads	Neurofocus (Nielsen), Sands
e. Market Segmentation	Determine firms' target markets, locate these consumers, and determine other characteristics of these consumers such as media habits	ESRI, Nielsen Claritas
f. Social Media Monitoring	Monitor for relevant buzz over the social media and attach meaning for companies and their brands	Decooda, Conversition
g. Field Services	Collect data using a variety of methods: telephone, online, person to person, mall intercept	MktgInc., Readex Research, I/H/R Research Group, Focus Market Research, Irwin, Fieldwork, Schlesinger Associates

professionals, estimates worldwide revenues for the marketing research industry at more than $43 billion.[11] The AMA Gold Report states that the top 50 marketing research firms in the world brought in more than $28 billion in 2014.[12] According to the AMA report, the top 50 firms showed a healthy growth in revenues of 10.6% from 2013 to 2014. In 2014, the largest marketing research firm in the world by far was Nielsen Inc., with its $6.3 billion revenue accounting for over one-fourth (26.4%) of the top 50 firms' revenue. The report also showed a 7.9% increase in employees.[13]

The marketing research industry relies on derived demand. As client firms develop new products, expand into new markets, examine new opportunities, and develop and evaluate new promotional campaigns, they need information to guide their decisions. As the world economy continues to improve, client firms' businesses will grow and so will the revenues and profits of the marketing research firms that support them.

The largest marketing research companies are truly international. The top five companies each have offices or subsidiaries in at least 70 different nations.[14] Nielsen, the largest firm, has over 40,000 employees in more than 100 countries. Revenues vary around the world. North America has the largest market share (43%), followed by Europe (37%) and Asia Pacific.

 Marketing Research on YouTube™ To learn about a firm that specializes in eye tracking, go to www.youtube.com and type in "benefits of eye tracking."

 **Active Learning**

Using the Marketing Research Directories

Three major sources of online information can allow you to explore the many different types of research firms that operate worldwide.

GreenBook (www.greenbook.org). Many years ago the New York AMA chapter published a directory of marketing research firms in a book with a green cover. Now known as *GreenBook*, it remains a key resource of industry information. This website allows you to search for marketing research firms in several different ways. A number of specialties are listed, and you can also search by country, state, or metro area. Under "Market Research Specialties," you can search under "Business Issues," "Research Solutions," "Industries & Demographics," "Related Services & Software," or "International Expertise." These submenus list the many types of research and research firms in the industry. Click on a category that interests you to see the information available on each firm.

Blue Book (www.bluebook.org). *Blue Book* is a marketing research services and focus groups directory provided by the Marketing Research Association (MRA). The website allows you to search marketing research companies by state, by type of data collection, and by several different types of specialties. Spending some time to explore this website will allow you to gain an appreciation for the types of firms in the industry.

Quirk's Researcher SourceBook™ (www.quirks.com). Quirk's Marketing Research Media publishes an online directory that provides access to research firms from more than 7,000 locations. At the website, click "Directories" in the menu bar. You can then search for marketing research companies by geographical area, specialty, or type of industry.

By the time you finish this exercise, you will see that marketing research companies are involved in many areas, including mystery shopping, mock trial juries, behavioral economics, airport interviews, crowdsourcing, taste tests, copy testing, new product concept testing, competitor analysis, focus groups, brainstorming research, site selection, political polling, and in-store interviewing.

The fastest-growing regions of the world for marketing research are Africa and the Middle East. The five largest markets by country are United States (42%), United Kingdom (12%), Germany (8%), France (6%), and China (4%).[15]

2-4 Challenges to the Marketing Research Industry

With the fast speed of technological change, the marketing research industry is currently facing a number of important challenges. Three of those challenges include new and evolving sources of data and methodologies, the effective communication of results, and the need for talented and skilled employees. Each of these challenges will be discussed in the following paragraphs.

NEW AND EVOLVING SOURCES OF DATA AND METHODS

After many years of relative stability in marketing research methods, the industry is undergoing great change due to new sources of data and technology. Traditional methods of research included mail and telephone surveys to gather opinions and intentions. Next, syndicated data, focus groups and a host of other qualitative techniques, mall-intercept surveying, and marketing mix/brand equity modeling were added to the mix. In the 1990s, electronic surveys brought about significant change, with online panels becoming a primary source of data. And in recent years, *passive data*, or data that are gathered without overt questioning or other types of interactions with consumers, have become a new and valuable source of information (see Chapter 5).[16]

The new sources of data have created challenges for marketing research companies that want to take advantage of new technology. In a 2015 survey of marketing researchers by *GreenBook*, over half of respondents (56%) stated that methodologies are one of the biggest challenges that they face.[17] Data sources, such as social media websites, the Internet of Things (IoT), and new kinds of syndicated data, have the potential to provide valuable insights. However, the methodologies necessary to analyze the data are not easy to develop and learn. Some researchers believe that the marketing research industry has been adapting to new opportunities too slowly.[18] Older and established marketing research companies find it difficult to keep abreast of new technologies, and new, upstart marketing research companies cannot always deliver the insights that they promise. The industry must evolve or die.[19] Marketing Research Insight 2.2 outlines the different types of social media websites and the types of consumer research that they provide. Chapters 5 and 6 will report on types of quantitative and qualitative data and the methodologies needed to examine these data.

MARKETING RESEARCH INSIGHT 2.2   *Digital Marketing Research*

Types of Social Media That Provide Sources of User-Generated Content

Social media websites are an important source of consumer information. Following is a list of types of social media websites.

1. **Blogs**—Dated, online journal entries, usually focused on a particular topic. Examples: Blogger, WordPress
2. **Microblogs**—Short posts commenting on the user's activities. Examples: Twitter, Weibo, Tumblr
3. **Video Sharing Networks**—Websites or apps that allow the sharing of the user's videos online. Examples: YouTube, Vine, Vimeo
4. **Photo Sharing Sites**—Websites or apps that allow the sharing of the user's photos online. Examples: Instagram, Flickr
5. **Social Networks**—Websites that enable users to connect by creating personal information profiles, inviting friends and colleagues to access those profiles, and sending and receiving emails and instant messages. Examples: Facebook, WeChat
6. **Professional Networks**—Websites that enable users to connect by creating professional information profiles, inviting business colleagues to access those profiles, and sending and receiving emails and instant messages. Example: LinkedIn
7. **Product and Service Review Sites:** Websites that allow consumers to talk about and review their experiences

with a product or service. Examples: Yelp, Amazon, Angie's List

8. **Web-Based Communities and Forums:** Communities created online, often focused around a particular interest, whose members interact with each other online. Examples: Gala Online, College Confidential
9. **News Sharing Sites**—Websites that allow users to post and discuss news items. Examples: Digg, Reddit

© Syda Productions/Shutterstock

There are many different types of social media.

EFFECTIVE COMMUNICATION OF RESULTS

With the multiple new types of data and methods now in use, marketing researchers not only need to be skilled at gathering and analyzing data but also at communicating results effectively. Marketing researchers sometimes feel that they are not treated with respect by managers.[20] At the same time, marketing research clients often complain that researchers are not knowledgeable about their businesses.[21] In a 2015 survey by Quirk's, fully half of marketing research clients stated that they have had trouble with research suppliers who "did not take time to understand our business."[22] A need exists for marketing researchers who can dig deeper into data and who can deliver strategic insights with their results.[23]

In addition, there is an increasing demand that marketing researchers provide simple and straightforward reports that "tell a story" rather than give their clients lengthy, complex documents. Researchers are asked to present their results in unambiguous, understandable, easy-to-grasp reports.[24] Increasingly, researchers use "storytelling" techniques, along with pictures, videos, animations, and other visual and aural techniques, to deliver their results in compelling ways that will be remembered by management. Chapter 16 will discuss methods for presenting written and oral reports.

NEED FOR TALENTED AND SKILLED EMPLOYEES

Another challenge for the marketing industry is employing qualified individuals. As suggested by the first two challenges to the marketing industry, a 2015 survey by *GreenBook* notes a need for individuals who can combine tech savviness and analytical skills with the ability to synthesize data and communicate results in a compelling way. At the same time, the survey points to the need for people who have a good foundational understanding of the basics of research.[25] Some established marketing researchers complain that younger employees have not been trained in basic statistics and methodologies.[26] Only 4% of the members of ESOMAR, a global marketing research trade organization, are less than 30 years old versus 39% who are over 50 years old.[27] According to ESOMAR, very few people plan a career in marketing research while in college, but once they find themselves in that industry they are very satisfied.[28]

2-5 Industry Initiatives

The marketing research industry has been proactive in terms of self-improvement, largely through industry initiatives, extensive continuing education programs, and certification.

INDUSTRY PERFORMANCE INITIATIVES

Led by some active professional associations, several initiatives have been undertaken to improve industry performance. We summarize a few of these in the following paragraphs.

Best Practices The move toward Total Quality Management in the 1990s spawned an increase in companies' awareness of methods leading to improvement. One such method was spelling out best practices to help companies set benchmarks for performance in key areas. Many of the professional organizations serving the marketing research industry have a program of best practices. The MRA, for example, publishes best practices regarding issues such as privacy, calling cell phones, and online surveying.[29]

Maintaining Public Credibility of Research Researchers are concerned about the general public's trust of research information. Public disgust with telemarketing and political telemarketing known as "push polling"[30] is often inappropriately directed at marketing researchers. Several industry initiatives are directed at keeping the public informed about the value of research, the appropriateness of research methods, and the ethics the industry uses in collecting research information. The industry has fought to make **sugging**—or the practice of

Sugging, or "selling under the guise of research," is illegal. Frugging, or "fund raising under the guise of research," is unethical but not yet illegal.

"selling under the guise of research"—illegal. Telemarketers used sugging for years to entice the public into taking what they thought was an opinion survey but actually was a lead-in for a sales pitch. Though not illegal, the industry has fought the use of enticing unknowing consumers into taking a survey when the real intent is to raise funds. This practice is known as **frugging**, for "fund raising under the guise of research."

The Council of American Survey Research Organizations (CASRO) offers an online guide, "What Survey Participants Need to Know," to provide the public with information about the conduct and use of survey research.[31] The **Transparency Initiative** was launched in 2014 by the American Association for Public Opinion Research (AAPOR) to encourage the routine disclosure of methods used in research information that is released to the public.[32] As you will learn by taking this course, surveys can be conducted so that they deliberately lead to biased responses. It is important for the marketing research industry to discourage the practice of conducting biased surveys.

In 2003 the **National Do Not Call Registry** was established that allows U.S. residents to register their telephone numbers to be protected from receiving unsolicited telemarketing calls. Note, however, that unsolicited phone calls for the purpose of conducting surveys are exempt from the restrictions imposed by the Do Not Call Registry. In other words, researchers conducting surveys can still legally call U.S. residents.

The Transparency Initiative is a program by the AAPOR to encourage the routine disclosure of methods used in research that is released to the public.

Calling U.S. residents to conduct surveys is exempt from the Do Not Call Registry.

Monitoring Industry Trends For many years, *GreenBook* has monitored trends in the industry. Published annually as the *GreenBook Research Industry Trends (GRIT)* report, data are provided to the industry in terms of what techniques are being used as well as what drives their use. The report provides insights by contrasting supplier (marketing research firms) views on issues with buyer (client) views. The report examines perceived threats and attitudes toward changes in the industry, forecasts revenues, and profiles innovations. ESOMAR publishes an annual *Global Market Research* report that includes many measures of industry performance.

Improving Ethical Conduct The professional associations serving the marketing research industry have all established rules, standards, or codes of ethical conduct. These associations have been proactive in maintaining and updating these standards. For example, when the Internet made possible online surveys, the industry moved to adopt standards governing conduct in this area. Most industry codes of ethics are for the purpose of self-regulating professionals' behavior. In some cases associations may impose penalties, including censure, suspension, or expulsion. Certified professionals may lose their certification if they are found to have violated the granting association's standards. Each organization has its own standards, although some associations coordinate these codes of conduct. There are differences in the codes but also some commonalities among the major associations. Some of the most important marketing research codes are listed as follows:

I. Fair Dealings with Respondents
  a. Respondents should understand that they may elect to not participate in a research request. Participation is always voluntary and respondents should understand they have the right to withdraw or refuse to cooperate at any stage during the study.
  b. Respondent confidentiality must be maintained. Respondent identity should not be revealed without proper authorization.
  c. Respondents will be treated professionally. Should respondents be required to use a product or service, researchers will ensure that the product/service will be safe and fit for intended use and labeled in accordance with all laws and regulations.
  d. Respondents will not be given dishonest statements to secure their cooperation, and researchers will honor any promises made to respondents given to secure their cooperation.
  e. Special provisions are required for doing research on minors (under 18 years of age).

II. Fair Dealings with Clients and Subcontractors

a. All information obtained from clients shall remain confidential.

b. All research will be carried out according to the agreement with the client.

c. Client identity will not be revealed without proper authorization.

d. Secondary research will not be presented to the client as primary research.

e. Research results are the sole property of the client and will never be shared with other clients.

f. Researchers will not collect information for more than one client at the same time without explicit permission from the clients involved.

g. Clients will be provided the opportunity to monitor studies in progress to ensure research integrity.

h. Researchers will not ask subcontractors to engage in any activity that does not adhere to professional codes, applicable laws, or regulations.

III. Maintaining Research Integrity

a. Data will never be falsified or omitted.

b. Research results will be reported accurately and honestly.

c. Researchers will not misrepresent the impact of the sampling method and its impact on sample data.

IV. Concern for Society

a. Research released for public information will contain information to ensure transparency (i.e., disclosure of method of data collection, the sample frame, sample method, sample size, and margin of error, if appropriate).

b. Researchers will not abuse public confidence in research (e.g., no push polling).

c. Researchers will not represent a nonresearch activity (e.g., sales effort, debt collection) to be research for the purpose of gaining respondent cooperation.

You may want to see the entire standards of ethical conduct of some of these associations:

AAPOR (www.aapor.org): Go to Standards & Ethics.

MRA (www.marketingresearch.org): MRA Code of Marketing Research Standards.

CASRO (www.casro.org): Go to Resources, then The CASRO Code.

MRIA (www.mria-arim.ca): Go to Standards.

ESOMAR (www.esomar.org): Go to Knowledge and Standards.

MRS (www.mrs.org.uk): Go to Standards.

We will examine ethical issues in this book by highlighting a particular standard from the MRA's "Code of Marketing Research Standards" where it applies to the subject matter discussed in each chapter. This text also presents *Marketing Research Insights, Ethical Considerations,* such as Marketing Research Insight 2.3, which discusses the ethics of retailers using in-store video cameras to track customers.

Beyond the general standards, an issue that may pose an ethical problem for researchers is working on a project in which the outcome may not be in the best interests of society. Imagine, for example, that a client asks a researcher to help identify advertising messages that are persuasive in getting young teens to try their first cigarette. Or a firm might be asked to develop effective promotions to encourage children to eat more candy. The decisions researchers must make are sometimes difficult. This quandary is rarely discussed professionally.

Certification of Qualified Research Professionals Certification programs assure that certified individuals have passed some standard(s) of performance. Certification programs in accounting (CPA) and finance (CFA) and other professional areas in business have been in place for many years and give clients confidence in the credibility of those certified professionals.

MARKETING RESEARCH INSIGHT 2.3   *Ethical Consideration*

Video Surveillance Research: New Insights and the Ethics Involved

Monitoring and measuring "actual" consumer behavior has gained a more prominent role in marketing research in the retail industry lately. A key driving force is new or improved technology that opens up numerous opportunities to study consumer behavior in a store environment. Traffic counters, handheld shopping systems, beacons, radio frequency identification (RFID) tags, infrared sensing devices, and high-resolution video surveillance cameras are all examples of this technology. The value of the new technology lies in its ability to constantly deliver more accurate and non-disruptive accounts of how consumers behave in a store and how they react to marketing stimuli. By studying consumer activity (where customers go, their paths, their interactions with the store shelves, etc.), retailers can detect problems with store layouts, signage, product organization, and so on.

Since data from surveillance cameras gives retailers insights that are relevant for optimizing their store layout and merchandising approach, it is easy to see why many retailers are using video cameras to track and capture every detail about the customers in their store. However, this has raised ethical concerns. Many have expressed concerns about the increasing use of surveillance cameras in public places, especially when such use is concealed or when people being monitored cannot opt out. The European Society for Opinion and Marketing Research (ESOMAR), which has developed an international code for market and social research, advises market researchers to inform respondents of their intentions, except for instances where these techniques are openly used in a public place and where obtaining informed consent from individuals is beyond the bounds of possibility. Norway has specifically included the use of video surveillance cameras in its Personal Data Act, which categorizes any data acquired from the use of video cameras as a form of personal information.

Certain retailers use in-store cameras to track consumer behavior.

It does not matter whether the data is recorded, stored, or just streamed in real time, as the individual's face can be used to identify her or him and disclose personal information.

In most cases, authorities accept video surveillance as a theft-preventing measure. In European legislation, the legality of using video surveillance technology for other purposes is contingent on whether the data is important in terms of the performance of a task carried out in public interest. A legitimate cause might be that the results lead to ways to improve a customer's shopping experience. It would, for instance, be in the customer's own interest to spend less time navigating and searching for products.

Do more rewarding consumer experiences outweigh the ethical concerns? What do you think?

Sources: Kirkup, M. and Carrigan, M. (2000). Video surveillance research in retailing: Ethical issues. *International Journal of Retail and Distribution Management,* 28(11), 470–480; Burke, R. (2005). Retail shoppability: A measure of the world's best stores. *Indiana University.* Retrieved from www.kelley.iu.edu/CERR/files/shoppability.pdf; Williams, J. (2013, August 1). In-store cameras: From security aids to sales tools. INSEAD Knowledge. Retrieved from http://knowledge.insead.edu/innovation/technology-manufacturing/in-store-cameras-from-security-aids-to-sales-tools-2559; ESOMAR (2009), *Passive Data Collection, Observation, and Recording,* pp. 1–20; European Data Protection Supervisor (2010, March 17). *The EDPS Video-Surveillance Guidelines.* Retrieved from https://secure.edps.europa.eu/EDPSWEB/webdav/shared/Documents/Supervision/Guidelines/10-03-17_Video-surveillance_Guidelines_EN.pdf; Datatilsynet. (2015, January 10). Retrieved from https://www.datatilsynet.no/English/Regulations/Personal-Data-Act-/#Chapter 7.

In the United States, professionals may earn the **Professional Researcher Certification (PRC)**. You can read about the PRC in Marketing Research Insight 2.4. In Canada, the designation of Certified Marketing Research Professional (CMRP) is granted through the MRIA.

Continuing Education The marketing research industry does an exceptional job of providing conferences, workshops, courses, webinars, and many other forms of continuing education for industry professionals. All of the professional organizations listed offer programs designed to keep members up-to-date on skills needed in the industry. The Burke Institute, a division of Burke, Inc., has been providing high-quality training seminars since 1975. You can see the seminars the institute offers professionals at www.burkeinstitute.com.

The MRIA in Canada certifies researchers through the Certified Marketing Research Professional (CMRP) program. Read about the qualifications for this program at www.mria-arim.ca. Go to the link for Institute for Professional Development/Certification.

MARKETING RESEARCH INSIGHT 2.4   *Practical Application*

Professional Researcher Certification

Responding to a need to establish a credentialing program in the industry, several organizations, led by the Marketing Research Association, established a certification program for marketing researchers. The process took several years, and the program started in February 2005. The Professional Researcher Certification program (PRC) is designed to recognize the qualifications and expertise of marketing and opinion research professionals. The goal of PRC is to encourage high standards within the survey profession to raise competency, establish an objective measure of an individual's knowledge and proficiency, and encourage professional development. Achieving and maintaining PRC validates the knowledge of the market research industry and puts researchers in a select group of like-minded professionals. It's a visible badge of distinction, demonstrating professional skill, commitment, and dedication.

Requirements for Professional Researcher Certification

- A minimum of three years of industry experience in the marketing research industry
- 12 hours of PRC-approved training within the last two years
- Passing the PRC exam

- Renewal of the PRC requires 20 hours in PRC-approved training (18 in research; 2 in legal). Certifications must be renewed every two years.

You can read more about the PRC at www.marketingresearch.org/certification.
Source: Marketing Research Association, by permission.

2-6   A Career in Marketing Research

You may be interested in exploring a career in marketing research. A recent study by ESOMAR of young researchers found that new recruits to the marketing industry are overwhelmingly happy in their jobs. The young researchers described their jobs as "empowering" and "meaningful" and noted that "you get to make a difference."[33]

IBIS World predicts that the number of employees in the marketing research industry will expand at an average annual rate of 2.1% through 2020, with wages predicted to increase at an average annual rate of 2.5%.[34] The research industry workforce is expected to grow at an average annual rate of 2.1% to 154,250 employees. Similarly, total industry wages are expected to increase at an annualized rate of 2.5% to $7.3 billion over the same period.

Following graduation, some students go directly into a marketing research job with a bachelor's degree in marketing, statistics, business analytics, computer science, psychology, sociology, or another related field. Some marketing research jobs, particularly those in client-side companies, require a graduate degree for new employees who have no direct experience in the field. There are some excellent master's degree programs in marketing research. One of those master's program is the University of Georgia's Master of Marketing Research (MMR) program, which is profiled in the introduction to the chapter. You can find more information about programs that offer degrees in marketing research on the Quirk's Marketing Research Media website. Quirk's maintains a directory of colleges and universities that offer certificates, concentrations, programs, or degrees in marketing research. Quirk's website also provides an active job-posting service that allows you to explore the types and locations of current job openings in marketing research.

WHERE YOU'VE BEEN AND WHERE YOU'RE HEADED!

This concludes our two introductory chapters on marketing research. In Chapter 1 you learned how marketing research is defined and how it fits into a firm's marketing information systems. This chapter provided an overview of the marketing research industry. Now you should be familiar with the types and numbers of firms and the professional organizations that serve the industry. You've learned about issues facing the industry as well as the ethical issues that face all marketing researchers. Now, you are ready to learn about the 11-step process that characterizes marketing research. That process and its first steps are discussed in Chapter 3. Each of the remaining chapters addresses additional steps in the process.

There are many different directions you can take with your degree, such as going straight into the marketing research industry or going on to earn a master's degree in marketing research.

Summary

Gathering information dates back to the earliest days of recorded history. Surveys were used for politics in the United States in the early 1800s. The first known application of research to a business/marketing/advertising problem was conducted by an ad agency in 1879, and the first continuous, organized research was started in 1911 by Charles Coolidge Parlin. The industry began to grow in the early 1900s as the Industrial Revolution separated business owners from customers. Many developments occurred during the 20th century that allowed marketing research to evolve into a mature industry.

Marketing research may be divided into client-side research and supply-side research. Client-side research is marketing research that is conducted within and for a firm (such as research that is conducted by a marketing research department within a manufacturing firm). Supply-side research is research that is conducted by an outside firm to fulfill a company's marketing research needs. Firms that conduct supply-side marketing research are also called *agencies*, or simply *suppliers*. The industry is characterized by a few large firms and many small firms. The largest firms have revenues in the billions of dollars. Firms are classified as full-service or limited-service supplier firms. Several online directories are available to help clients locate marketing research firms.

The marketing research industry had total revenues of $43 billion in 2014. North America led the global market with the largest share of revenues (43%) by region, and the United States led all countries. Some of the fastest growth rates are in the Middle East and Africa.

Challenges facing the marketing research industry include keeping up with the many new sources of data and types of methods that have emerged in recent years. Other challenges include effectively communicating research results and hiring talented and skillful employees. The industry strives for self-improvement via efforts to identify and disseminate best practices, maintain public credibility of research, monitor trends, improve ethical conduct of members, support programs to certify professionals, and offer education programs. The marketing research industry offers excellent careers for recent college graduates.

Key Terms

Charles Coolidge Parlin (p. 50)
Client-side research (p. 51)
Do-it-yourself (DIY) research (p. 51)
Supply-side research (p. 53)
Supplier (p. 53)
Agency (p. 53)
Full-service supplier firms (p. 54)

Limited-service supplier firms (p. 54)
Sugging (p. 58)
Frugging (p. 59)
Transparency Initiative (p. 59)
National Do Not Call Registry (p. 59)
AAPOR (p. 60)
MRA (p. 60)

CASRO (p. 60)
MRIA (p. 60)
ESOMAR (p. 60)
MRS (p. 60)
Professional Researcher
    Certification (PRC) (p. 61)

Review Questions/Applications

2-1. Who is known as the "Father of Marketing Research" and why?

2-2. Why did marketing research expand by the 1930s?

2-3. What was the technology that revolutionized market research in the 1950s?

2-4. Define *client-side research*.

2-5. What are some advantages and disadvantages of DIY research?

2-6. Who are the buyers who purchase research information from suppliers?

2-7. What is common to most of the top-rated marketing research agencies in the world?

2-8. Describe limited-service supplier firms.

2-9. Explain the meaning of the statement that the "marketing research industry thrives off derived demand."

2-10. What began to drastically change the marketing research industry in the 1990s? Why?

2-11. Why is employing qualified individuals a challenge for the marketing industry?

2-12. Is it ethical for retailers to use video cameras in their stores to study the behavior of their customers? Explain.

2-13. Most marketing industry codes of ethics are for the purpose of self-regulation. What are the penalties that can be imposed in case these codes are breached?

2-14. Outline the marketing research code for *maintaining research integrity*.

2-15. Explain how market researchers can ensure that their research is in the interest of society.

2-16. What is the PRC, and what is it designed to do?

CASE 2.1

Heritage Research Associates

Tim Colley and John Williams had not been in business long as Heritage Research Associates, a small marketing research firm they started in their hometown. They were barely making ends meet by taking on very small accounts such as start-up retailers. Their marketing research experience was limited, but they knew the basics. Since they had not taken any specialized training beyond a college course in marketing research, they decided to join the Marketing Research Association. Tim explained, "We can tell clients we have the necessary credentials to be members of the most notable marketing research organization in North America." The partners thought this was a good way to persuade clients they knew what they were doing. They added the MRA logo to their promotional materials along with the line "Heritage is a Certified Member of the MRA." They used their limited funds to promote Heritage Research Associates and even took out a quarter-page ad in a national business magazine.

A phone call early one morning marked a real opportunity for Heritage. The potential client represented his organization as a "privately funded foundation that promoted business rights and the maintenance of a *laissez faire* pro-business environment." They were interested in Heritage doing some research that would disprove some university-sponsored research findings that had been in the news. The findings were unfavorable toward one of their prominent member industries. The caller stated, "Our patrons are upset that such erroneous information is being fed to the

American people, and we are quite prepared to fund additional research to clarify the facts. In fact, we are willing to fund several studies if we get the results we are looking for. Are you up to it?" Tim and John assured the caller that the foundation could be certain that Heritage Research Associates could deliver quality, objective research that would clear up any misconceptions in the minds of the public. The call ended with a promise to send the biased university research reports immediately. A second call was set up to follow in three days.

In the follow-up call the potential client got more specific. His foundation had hired some independent scientists who were willing to testify that certain environmental conditions were not being caused by the concerned industry group. "We have had little problem in getting three scientists, with doctoral degrees from well-known universities, to make statements affirming that firms in one of our major industry groups are not doing any significant harm to our environment." The client went on to say, "What we want now is a study from an independent research firm, such as Heritage, to report attitudes of consumers in terms of whether they are in favor of more industry regulation. We are willing to fund a small pilot study and, if we find Heritage is capable of delivering objective data, we are ready to sign on for a series of perhaps a dozen studies. Furthermore, we are well financed, and I am quite certain we can meet your bid to do this work." The caller went on to ask for a proposal that would outline methods to select the survey sample, research questions, and a sample analysis, including how Heritage would word the report. "Remember, we want this to be an independently prepared project using all your abilities to craft an objective research study," the client stated. Tim and John agreed to deliver a proposal within 10 working days.

Tim and John were thrilled that this opportunity had fallen to them. "Did you hear what he said in terms of 'being certain to accept our bid'?" John exclaimed. "He's telling us he is going to pay whatever we ask. This isn't a penny-pinching client."

Tim said, "Just a minute, though. He's talking about the studies *after* the pilot study. What if they don't like the first study? We won't ever get to the big accounts."

John agreed. "We've got to design a study they will like so we can get the additional work at a premium. This could set our little firm off in a totally new direction!"

"This can make us the most talked-about research firm in the world!" Tim said.

1. Do you think it is ethical to use membership in an association that doesn't require any demonstration of expertise to lead customers into thinking the membership conveys some automatic claim of competency?
2. Consult the MRA Code of Marketing Research Standards. Is the answer to question 1 covered? Explain.
3. What problems do you see in the future for Tim and John and Heritage Research Associates? Do you think they are likely to become the "most talked-about research firm in the world"?
4. Consult the MRA Code of Marketing Research Standards. Are there any standards that back up your answers to question 3?

3

The Marketing Research Process and Defining the Problem and Research Objectives

"WHERE WE ARE"

1 Establish the need for marketing research.

2 Define the problem.

3 Establish research objectives.

4 Determine research design.

5 Identify information types and sources.

6 Determine methods of accessing data.

7 Design data collection forms.

8 Determine the sample plan and size.

9 Collect data.

10 Analyze data.

11 Prepare and present the final research report.

General Mills: A Well-Defined Problem Is Half the Solution

Carrie Breisach is a Global Consumer Insights Manager at General Mills, Inc. Ms. Breisach has an M.B.A. from the University of Wisconsin-Madison and has 10 years of experience in the marketing research field.

It is an adage as old as scientific inquiry: A well-defined problem is half the solution. In Global Consumer Insights at General Mills, we partner with professionals in marketing, advertising, product development, and beyond to inform smart, consumer-first decisions. At times, the problems business partners bring us are vague, broad, difficult to tackle, and—all too often—urgent. The need for quick answers can entice us to jump into research design and execution so hastily that the results we get back will not really help answer the true question.

Instead, having the discipline to dig into the true business problem, including what has already been learned, explored, or decided, helps us as researchers to create a meaningful series of learning objectives and research questions. A good rule of thumb in the research design phase is "go slow to go fast." It is worth spending time in the beginning gaining clarity and alignment on the true problem and questions in order to facilitate meaningful learning that ultimately illuminates the path forward and enables better, faster decisions.

To illustrate, let's use the example of a recent consulting engagement our central Global Consumer Insights team took on with business partners on our Snacks team. They wanted help deciding where to focus next in building a pipeline of new products for a top-priority brand. The business team knew the consumer they were focused on and the brand was a given, but the possible product categories for innovation were nearly limitless. Should they create a new granola bar? A new cookie? New fruit snacks? New yogurt? What would be the next biggest opportunity for the brand?

Rather than jumping straight into "problem-solving mode," our central consulting team first reviewed the intake brief, a standardized template that captures the background, objective, key stakeholders, time line, and existing knowledge. The consulting team then set up a scoping meeting with the client team to talk through the brief and have conversations to clarify the scope, intended outcome, success criteria, and any other issues that might impact the project design. The consulting team then worked with internal subject matter experts to design the optimal research and learning plan, which they shared with the business team for feedback and alignment before starting the project.

In this example and so many others, the Global Consumer Insights team acted not just as research designers and executors but also as expert partners who can help a business team gain clarity on the real business issue and question that will unlock opportunity. In so doing, we were able to design an approach to help the team identify a robust pipeline of new product ideas to explore and further develop.

—*Carrie Breisach*

Source: Text and photos courtesy of Carrie Breisach and General Mills, Inc.

Visit General Mills at www.generalmills.com.

There are many facets to what we call marketing research, with many different research choices: forecasting models that predict sales of new products, measures of customer satisfaction, online communities to discover consumers' concerns, mobile surveys, and experiments to determine the most eye-catching package design, to name just a few examples. Researchers choose from many seemingly disorganized sets of alternative approaches in tackling a research project. Fortunately, there is a process, and understanding and adhering to that process will provide researchers with direction.

This chapter introduces the steps of the research process and then focuses on the first three steps in the process: establishing the need for marketing research, defining the problem, and developing research objectives. The chapter concludes with a discussion of the document that is usually prepared after the problem statement and research objectives have been defined: the marketing research proposal.

3-1 The Marketing Research Process

THE 11-STEP PROCESS

We, among many, believe the marketing research process should be viewed as a series of steps. Knowledge of these steps provides a road map for planning a research project. The value in characterizing research projects in terms of successive steps is twofold. First, the steps give researchers and others an overview of the process. Second, they provide a procedure in the sense that a researcher knows what tasks to complete and in what order.

Our introduction to these steps also provides a preview of what is in store for you in upcoming chapters of this book.

We identify the **11 steps in the marketing research process** in Figure 3.1:[1] (1) establish the need for marketing research, (2) define the problem, (3) establish research objectives, (4) determine research design, (5) identify information types and sources, (6) determine methods of accessing data, (7) design data collection forms, (8) determine the sample plan and size, (9) collect data, (10) analyze data, and (11) prepare and present the final research report. We will discuss each of these steps in the following section. As we summarize each step, we will briefly introduce vocabulary that is associated with the text. Those vocabulary words will be placed in *italics* to signal that we will define those words in more detail in later chapters in the text. But prior to introducing the steps, we should first consider some cautions associated with using a step-by-step approach to the process of marketing research.

CAVEATS TO A STEP-BY-STEP PROCESS

Why 11 Steps? There is nothing sacred about 11 steps. Although we conceptualize the research process as entailing 11 steps, others may present it in fewer or more steps. For example, the process could be distilled into three steps: defining the problem, collecting and analyzing data, and presenting the results. We think this short list oversimplifies the research process. On the other hand, the research process could be set out in 20 or more steps. In our opinion, this provides more detail than is needed. Eleven steps set out the process explicitly without being overly detailed. But you should know that everyone does not present the research process in the same way we present it here.

FIGURE 3.1 11 Steps in the Marketing Research Process

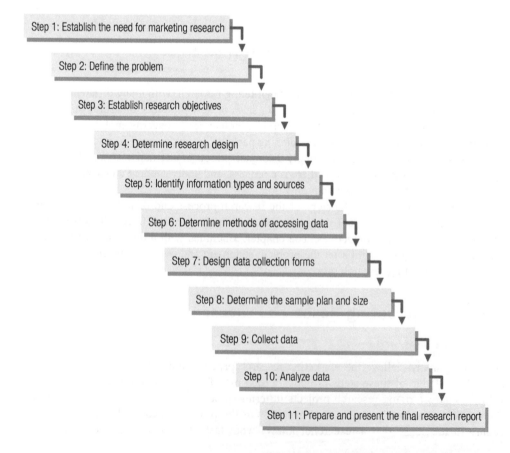

Step 1: Establish the need for marketing research

Step 2: Define the problem

Step 3: Establish research objectives

Step 4: Determine research design

Step 5: Identify information types and sources

Step 6: Determine methods of accessing data

Step 7: Design data collection forms

Step 8: Determine the sample plan and size

Step 9: Collect data

Step 10: Analyze data

Step 11: Prepare and present the final research report

Not All Studies Use All 11 Steps A second caution is that not all studies follow all 11 steps. Sometimes, for example, a review of secondary research alone may allow the researcher to achieve the research objectives. Our 11 steps assume that the research process examines secondary data and continues on to collect primary data.

Steps Are Not Always Followed in Order Our third and final caution is that most research projects do not follow an orderly, step-by-step process. In fact, the steps are often interrelated. Sometimes, after beginning to gather data, it may be determined that the research objectives should be changed. Researchers do not move like robots from one step to the next. Rather, as they move through the process, they make decisions on how to proceed in the future, which may involve going back and revisiting a previous step.

INTRODUCING "WHERE WE ARE"

Understanding the steps in the marketing research process establishes a foundation for learning to conduct marketing research. Knowledge of these steps helps researchers deal with the complex issues that arise in marketing research. We will examine some of those complexities in this text. To provide an aid in dealing with the rest of the course material, we introduce a new section at the beginning of every chapter, beginning with Chapter 4, called "Where We Are." As seen in Figure 3.2, this feature lists the 11 steps. The step that is presented in the current chapter you are reading will be highlighted. This way, even as you get immersed in the necessary details of marketing research, "Where We Are" is there to show you where the material you are reading fits into the overall framework of marketing research.

Now, let's look at our first step!

1 Establish the need for marketing research.
2 Define the problem.
3 Establish research objectives.
4 Determine research design.
5 Identify information types and sources.
6 Determine methods of accessing data.
7 Design data collection forms.
8 Determine the sample plan and size.
9 Collect data.
10 Analyze data.
11 Prepare and present the final research report.

FIGURE 3.2 "Where We Are"

At the beginning of every chapter, beginning with Chapter 4, the "Where We Are" feature lists the 11 steps of the marketing research process and highlights the step presented in each chapter.

STEP 1: ESTABLISH THE NEED FOR MARKETING RESEARCH

When managers must make decisions and they have inadequate information, this signals the need for marketing research. Not all decisions will require marketing research. Because research takes time and costs money, managers must weigh the value that may possibly be derived from conducting marketing research and having the information at hand with the cost of obtaining that information. Fortunately, most situations do not require research because, if they did, managers would be mired down in research instead of making timely decisions.

The need for marketing research arises when managers must make decisions and they have inadequate information.

A company's philosophy about the importance of research will be reflected in its policy regarding the use of marketing research. Managers must make a decision about the role they wish marketing research to play in their organization. Some managers simply do not believe in investing time and money conducting research, and they have a policy of not conducting marketing research. However, even the best decision makers cannot make good decisions without good information, and to rely solely on intuition in today's complex and rapidly changing marketplace is risky business.

Company policy regarding marketing research may also show a preference for the type of research management prefers. Some managers use focus groups extensively, some use online communities, and others rely on quantitative studies based on large samples. Some prefer to conduct most research in house; others prefer to hire marketing research suppliers to conduct most research. For a profile of a marketing research company that has developed an innovative solution for buying marketing research services, see Marketing Research Insight 3.1.

MARKETING RESEARCH INSIGHT 3.1   *Practical Application*

ZappiStore Provides a Self-Service Platform for Buying Research Services

Courtesy of ZappiStore

Ryan Barry is Senior
Vice President,
ZappiStore.

ZappiStore is the online research provider that is changing the way that companies are accessing insight. Businesses need to be increasingly responsive to shifts in the market and to the demand of ever tighter deadlines, but market research often fails to keep pace. ZappiStore provides an automated, self-service platform for buying high-quality research services—at lightning-fast speed and low cost.

ZappiStore's revolutionary system offers truly agile insight; no briefs and no proposals mean that you can test early and test often at key instances in the production process. The company has partnered with the world's leading research agencies to offer off-the-shelf products targeted at business issues from new product development, to package testing, creative testing, or social media monitoring.

Visit Zappistore at www.zappistore.com.

Source: Courtesy Ryan Barry.

Sometimes problems arise for which marketing research is not the best solution. The following sections describe four circumstances that indicate research is not the best option.

The Information Is Already Available Managers make many decisions. For routine decisions, most managers have the experience to act without any additional information. Remember, in well-established firms, managers have been intimately involved with their markets for many years. For many decisions, managers can rely on their base of acquired knowledge. When decisions require additional information, the firm may already have the necessary information. Prior to conducting research, managers should always ask: Do we already have the information? Other components of the marketing intelligence system (MIS) may be able to supply the data. Can the needed information be obtained from the internal reports system or from the decision support system (DSS)? All of these systems are ongoing sources of information. Marketing managers can quickly and inexpensively (low variable cost) access this information. Coca-Cola, for example, has an extensive database as part of its DSS. Managers at the large soft drink firm have ready access to data needed to forecast the effect on sales if they vary levels of ingredients in their products. When information is *not* available, the researcher should consider conducting marketing research.

The Timing Is Wrong to Conduct Marketing Research In cases when managers decide they need marketing research, time is critical. Consequently, time often plays a critical role in making the decision to use marketing research. Even though online research has sped up the marketing research process considerably, circumstances may dictate there is simply not enough time to conduct marketing research. As an example, let's assume that an auto manufacturer introduces a hydrogen engine that runs on water, and sales of the car are unprecedented in the history of this mode of transportation. Do other auto firms need to do marketing research to "see" what the market preferences are? Less dramatic examples include a new package design, new flavor, or new ingredient that causes breakthroughs in sales and market shares. Competitive firms need to react quickly.

Time may also be a factor for products that are nearing the end of their life cycle. When products have been around for many years and are reaching the decline stage of their life cycle, it may be too late for research to produce valuable results.

Costs Outweigh the Value of Marketing Research Marketing research should be seen as an investment. Managers should always consider the cost of research and the value they expect to receive from conducting it. Although costs are readily estimated, it is much more difficult to estimate the value research is likely to add. Sometimes it is obvious that the value of research is not worth the costs. One researcher reported that he advised his client, a pie manufacturer, not to pursue conducting research on understanding consumer pie buying in convenience stores. Why? The researcher had discovered that only 1% of pie sales were coming through convenience stores.[2]

Some recent work has attempted to generate heuristics to help determine the value of research. In a collaborative study by *Quirk's Marketing Research Review, Research Innovation,* and *ROI, Inc.,* 11 methods were developed to determine the return on investment in research. Some commonalities among the methods were the following:

a. All methods of measuring the value of research should explicitly link the research results to business impacts. In other words, a research study should not just conclude that alternative A produces more consumer satisfaction. Rather, the increase in consumer satisfaction should be linked to an impact such as greater customer retention or higher market share.

b. All methods of measuring the value of research should demonstrate that something happened as a result of the research that would not have happened otherwise and quantify the financial value of that difference. Or the metrics should demonstrate that risk was mitigated and quantify the financial value of that risk reduction.[3]

Although it is difficult to quantify value, some progress is being made among researchers to do a better job of helping clients evaluate research. If a researcher can show the sales volume impact for every 1% increase in consumer awareness, the researcher is in a much better position to help the client determine if research on awareness levels of new package designs is worth the cost.[4] Once a decision is made that research is needed, managers (and researchers) must properly define the problem and the research objectives.

STEP 2: DEFINE THE PROBLEM

Once a firm decides to conduct marketing research, the second step is to define the problem. This is the most important step, because if the problem is incorrectly defined, all that follows is wasted effort. Marketing research should only be conducted when firms need to make a decision and do not have the information available to guide decision making. At this stage, a *problem statement* should be developed that summarizes the problem succinctly. A later section of this chapter addresses issues that should be considered to properly develop the problem statement.

STEP 3: ESTABLISH RESEARCH OBJECTIVES

Research objectives tell the researcher exactly what information needs to be gathered and analyzed to allow managers to make decisions related to a problem. Research objectives need to be very clear, since they will determine the methods used and the content of the measurement instrument. We will revisit research objectives in greater detail later in this chapter.

STEP 4: DETERMINE RESEARCH DESIGN

The next step involves determining the research design. By *research design* we are referring to the research approach used to meet the research objectives. Three widely recognized research designs are *exploratory*, *descriptive*, and *causal*. *Exploratory research*, as the name implies, is a form of casual, informal research that is undertaken to learn more about the research problem, learn terms and definitions, or identify research priorities. Often exploratory research is conducted early on to help clients determine the research objectives. *Descriptive research* refers to research that describes the phenomena of interest. Many surveys are undertaken to describe things: level of awareness of advertising, intentions to buy a new product, satisfaction level with service, and so on. The final type of research approach is *causal research* design. Causal studies attempt to uncover what factor or factors *cause* some event. Will a change in the package size of our detergent cause a change in sales? Causal studies are achieved from a class of studies we call *experiments*. You will learn about these three research designs and when it is appropriate to use each in Chapter 4.

STEP 5: IDENTIFY INFORMATION TYPES AND SOURCES

Because research provides information to help solve problems, researchers must identify the types and sources of information they will use in step 5. Two types of information are *primary* (information collected specifically for the problem at hand) and *secondary* (information already collected).

Secondary information should always be sought first, since it is much cheaper and faster to collect than primary information and is sometimes superior to information that an individual firm is able to collect on its own. Much secondary information is available in published sources in the library and/or online and is either free or available for a small fee. Sometimes research companies collect information and make it available to all those willing to pay a subscription. This type of information is referred to as *syndicated data*; Nielsen Media Research's TV ratings, which report the numbers of persons who watch different TV programs, are an example of syndicated data. Secondary information is discussed further in Chapter 5. However, sometimes secondary data are not available or are inadequate, outdated, or insufficient. In those situations, primary data must be collected. Beginning with Chapter 6, the rest of this book covers how to gather, analyze, and report primary data.

Data can be collected by observing customers.

STEP 6: DETERMINE METHODS OF ACCESSING DATA

Data may be accessed through a variety of methods. Although secondary data are relatively easy to obtain, accessing primary data is much more complex. Some data are collected through observation of consumers. Some data are collected by monitoring information available online. Other data might be collected using surveys. Often multiple methods, called mixed methods, are used to acquire data. Data collection methods will be covered in detail in Chapter 7.

STEP 7: DESIGN DATA COLLECTION FORMS

Step 7 involves designing the form for data collection. If we communicate with respondents (ask them questions), the form is called a *questionnaire*. If we ask questions in a focus group, the form is called a *focus group guide*. In either case, great care must be given to design the form properly. This is one of the most important steps of the research process, since the quality of the data collection form determines the quality of the data gathered with that form. Questions must be phrased properly to generate answers that satisfy the research objectives and therefore can be used to solve the problem. The questions must be clear and unbiased. Care must also be taken to design the questionnaire to reduce refusals to answer questions and to get as much information as desired from respondents. Software is available to assist researchers in creating surveys, such as Qualtrics and SurveyMonkey. Most of these programs allow users to post the surveys online and, with a subscription service, the data are automatically downloaded into software such as Excel or SPSS as respondents complete the surveys. You will learn about preparing a questionnaire in Chapter 8.

STEP 8: DETERMINE THE SAMPLE PLAN AND SIZE

In many cases, marketing research studies are undertaken to learn about populations by taking a sample of that population. A *population* consists of the entire group about which the researcher wishes to make inferences based on information provided by the sample data. A population could be "all department stores within the greater Portland, Oregon, area," or it could be "college students enrolled in the College of Business at XYZ College." Populations should be defined by the research objectives. A *sample* is a subset of the population. *Sample plans* describe how each sample element, or unit, is to be drawn from the total population. The objectives of the research and the nature of the *sample frame* (list of the population elements or units) determine which sample plan is to be used. The type of sample plan used determines to what extent the sample is representative of the population.

As you will learn in Chapter 9, sample plans have become more complex as the best methods of communicating with people have changed. For example, not many years ago, about 96% of all U.S. households could be reached through a traditional land-line telephone. Today that number has dropped significantly. Researchers must use different methods to reach people who use cell phones exclusively.

Another issue is *sample size*. How many elements of the population should be used to make up the sample? The size of the sample determines how accurately your sample results reflect values in the population. In Chapter 9 you will learn how to determine the optimal sample size. Several marketing research companies, such as the firm Survey Sampling International, specialize in helping firms with the sampling process.

STEP 9: COLLECT DATA

In Chapter 11 you will learn what issues to consider in collecting data in the field to ensure the highest possible data quality. Errors in collecting data may be attributed to fieldworkers or to respondents, and they may be intentional or unintentional. Researchers should know the sources of these errors and implement controls to minimize them. For example, *fieldworkers*, the people who are collecting the data, may cheat and make up data they report as having come from a respondent. Researchers aim to minimize this possibility by undertaking a control referred to as *validation*. Validation means that 10% (the industry standard) of all respondents in a marketing research study are randomly selected, re-contacted, and asked if they indeed took part in the study. Companies that specialize in data collection are referred to as **field services firms**.

Field services firms are companies that specialize in data collection.

STEP 10: ANALYZE DATA

Marketing researchers transfer data from the data collection forms and enter the data into software packages that aid them in analyzing the data. In Chapter 12 you will learn how to manage quantitative data and how to conduct data analysis using IBM SPSS, the data analysis software you will be learning with this book. Also in Chapter 12, you will learn basic descriptive statistics and how to generalize values you generate from your sample data to the population. In Chapter 13 you will learn how to test for differences between groups. For example, are there differences in intention to buy a new brand between different groups? Determining relationships among variables are covered in Chapter 14. In Chapter 15 you will learn how regression analysis is used to predict a variable given what is known about other variables. The objective of *data analysis* is to use statistical tools to present data in a form that fulfills the research objectives. If the research objective is to determine if there are differences in intention to purchase a new product between four levels of income groups, data analysis would be used to determine if there are any differences in intention to purchase among the income groups in the sample and to determine if these differences actually exist in the population.

STEP 11: PREPARE AND PRESENT THE FINAL RESEARCH REPORT

The final step in the research process is preparing and presenting the marketing research report. The report is essential because it is often the client's only record of the research project. In most cases, marketing research firms prepare a written research report and also make an oral presentation to the client and staff. Traditionally, marketing researchers follow a fairly standard report-writing format. However, an emerging trend in marketing research is to present data using innovative methods that are more interactive. Regardless of reporting method, the most important criterion for reporting results is that it clearly communicates the research findings to the client. Methods for reporting results will be detailed in Chapter 16.

We've just outlined and briefly discussed the steps in the marketing research process. If the researcher and client exercise care, the research process will produce information that can be used to resolve the problem. The "Where We Are" feature at the beginning of each chapter will help you appreciate marketing research as a process as you delve into the details of each step. We have already discussed step 1 in the marketing research process in the preceding section. In the following sections, we will examine steps 2 and 3.

3-2 Defining the Problem

Defining the problem properly is *the* most important step in the marketing research process. The success of a marketing research project depends on properly pinpointing a problem to formulate the *problem statement*. We can properly follow all of the marketing research steps after defining the problem and get the correct answers, only to realize that we have been asking the wrong questions all along. If the problem is defined incorrectly, the rest of the steps in the research process will be fundamentally flawed. All of the time and money spent conducting the marketing research will be wasted.

When we refer to "the problem," our focus is on a situation that a manager or client is facing. **Problems** are situations calling for managers to make choices among decision alternatives. When managers make decisions, they do so to solve a problem. Sometimes these decisions are so routine and easily made based on past experience that we don't think of them as "problems." Nevertheless, choices must be made, and the manager must make the decisions. Managers must choose among alternatives to select new products, choose among advertising copy alternatives, determine the price of their products or services, and select dealers.

The marketing research process begins when a managerial problem or opportunity exists that demands action, but there is not enough information to know how to respond to the problem. This sets into motion a series of tasks that ultimately leads to establishing research objectives. As Figure 3.3 displays, there are five tasks to defining a marketing research problem. Each task is detailed in the following sections.

Defining the problem properly is the most important step in the marketing research process.

Problems are situations calling for managers to make choices among alternatives.

1. RECOGNIZE THE PROBLEM

A manager encounters a problem when he or she encounters a situation that is negative or potentially positive for the organization. These two sources of problems can be stated as the failure to meet an objective or the identification of an opportunity.

Failure to Meet an Objective We may recognize we have a problem when there is a gap between what was supposed to happen and what did happen—or when we fail to meet an objective.[5] For example, a retailer may experience a decrease in sales over previous periods, a website begins losing traffic, or an advertising campaign does not reach its expected level of awareness. That gap signifies what we normally think of when we use the term *problem*. We must now determine what course of action to take to close the gap between the objective and actual performance.

Identification of an Opportunity The second source of a problem is not often immediately recognized as a problem. An opportunity represents what might happen; the problem arises when an opportunity is lost—when there is a gap between what did happen and what could have happened. This situation represents a failure to realize a "favorable circumstance or chance for progress or advancement."[6] For example, a new use for a product is identified on social media, or those in a target market would like to have a service delivered to their doors. For our purposes, a **marketing opportunity** is defined as a potentially favorable circumstance in which a company can perform successfully. Google, for example, has millions of people using its services daily. There are many opportunities for Google to take advantage of this ready market. Google managers must make decisions about whether and how to take advantage of these opportunities.

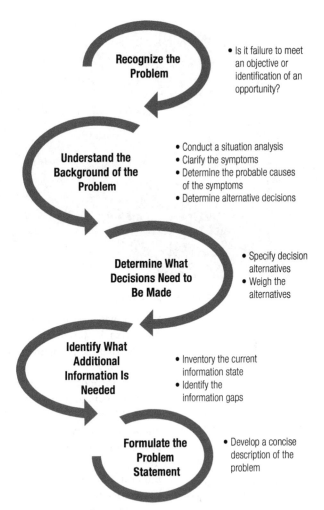

FIGURE 3.3 Process for Defining a Problem

A marketing opportunity is a potentially favorable circumstance in which a company can perform successfully.

Both of these situations—failure to meet an objective and identification of an opportunity—have the same consequence for managers: They must make decisions. Hence, we have what was defined earlier as a "problem." It is difficult to overstate the importance of recognizing a problem. Managers who do not recognize problems will not be in management for very long. Managers must be knowledgeable about objectives and performance. They should be setting objectives and have systems in place to monitor performance. This is sound management practice.

A function of an internal reports system, part of the firm's MIS (see Chapter 1), is to provide alerts when problems are emerging. Systems are now available to identify problems at an early point in time. For example, store-level versions of these systems alert managers to potential problems such as stockouts, which often double when stores run promotions. Other alerts make managers aware of promotions that are cannibalizing other products or indicate which geographical regions are responding or not responding to promotions. Early identification of problems can lead to managerial changes that can greatly improve bottom-line profits.[7]

How do managers recognize when they have an opportunity? There is much variability among firms in terms of ability to identify opportunities. Some firms have departments and formal procedures to ensure that opportunities are found and evaluated. These firms tend

The MIS can alert managers to potential problems such as stockouts.

A symptom is a change in the level of a key monitor that measures the achievement of an objective or a perceived change in the behavior of a market factor that indicates an emerging opportunity.

Marketing Research on YouTube™ For advice from Murphy Research on the initial steps of a new project, go to **www.youtube.com** and enter "4 Questions to Ask Before You Start a New Marketing Research Project."

A situation analysis is a form of exploratory research undertaken to gather background information and data pertinent to the problem area that may be helpful in properly defining the problem decision.

to rely on innovations to renew their life cycles and keep them competitive. Other firms empower their sales force and other front-line employees to identify problems.[8] Other companies only look at opportunities when they seem to "fall in their laps." When that happens, it may be too late; a competitor may already have an insurmountable head start. To capitalize on opportunities, companies must be proactive.

2. UNDERSTAND THE BACKGROUND OF THE PROBLEM

Sometimes managers call researchers when they sense something is wrong and they need help in diagnosing the situation. Managers may be aware of **symptoms**, which are changes in the level of some key monitor that measures the achievement of an objective (e.g., our measure of customer satisfaction has fallen 10% in each of the past two months). But that does not mean that the manager knows what the problem is. As a result, managers may not be sure what decision they should make, if any.

Other times managers have defined what they think the problem is and the decision that must be made to resolve it. In either scenario, the researcher has an obligation to be sure that the problem is defined correctly. This is particularly true when the researcher is called in by a manager who already has defined a problem in very specific terms. Researchers provide value at this point in the process by supplying a fresh view, unhindered by biases of recent events, trends, or influences that may have dominated the managers' decision-making process. It is important that researchers not simply be "order-takers" but instead use their experience and knowledge to advise managers on how to approach the problem.[9]

To understand the background of a problem, the researcher must conduct a situation analysis, clarify the symptoms of the problem, and determine the probable causes of the symptom. Each of these processes will be explained in the next sections.

Conduct a Situation Analysis As a first step to understanding the background of a problem, researchers should conduct a preliminary investigation called a situation analysis. A **situation analysis** is a form of exploratory research undertaken to gather background information and data that may be helpful in properly defining the problem decision. A situation analysis may reveal, for example, that the symptom of declining sales is more likely due to a problem with losing distributors than with ad copy. Researchers have a responsibility to ensure they are addressing the right problem, even when the problem has been previously defined by management.

A situation analysis may begin with the researcher learning about the industry, the competitors, key products or services, markets, market segments, and so on. The researcher should start with the industry to determine if any symptoms, to be identified later, are associated with the entire industry or only with the client firm. The researcher should then move to the company itself: its history, performance, products/services, unique competencies, marketing plans, customers, and major competitors.

The primary method of conducting a situation analysis is to review both *internal* and *external secondary data.* Other methods include conducting *experience surveys* (discussions with knowledgeable persons inside and outside the firm), *case analysis* (examples of former, similar situations), *pilot studies* (mini-studies that may reveal problem areas), and *focus groups* (small groups discussing topics such as the company's products or services).

Clarify the Symptoms When diagnosing a problem, symptoms are sometimes confused with problems. The role of a symptom is to alert management to a problem—that is, there is a gap between what should be happening and what is happening. A symptom may also be a perceived change in the behavior of some market factor that implies an emerging opportunity.

Researchers and managers must be careful to avoid confusing symptoms with problems. To illustrate, consider the classic statement: "We have a problem—we are losing money." The problem is not that "we are losing money." Rather, the problem may be found among all those factors that cause us to lose (or make) money. The manager, with help from the researcher, must identify all those possible causes to find the right problem(s). The managers must be aware that the symptoms are not the problem but are "signals" that alert us to a problem. As an example, when sales of portable radios, tape players, and TVs took off in the 1980s through the popular Sony series of Walkman and Watchman products, this should have served as a symptom that there was a basic market need for portability. Today that need has resulted in high demand for portability in terms of the many mobile devices available. In short, symptoms are not problems; their role is to function as a signal to alert managers to recognize problems.

The researcher should clarify the symptoms early in the research process. Are the symptoms identified properly? Companies vary greatly in terms of defining their objectives, monitoring their results, and taking corrective action. Does the company have an adequate system in place to identify symptoms? Are there other symptoms not identified? What are they? Are they accurate measures of performance? Are they reported in a timely fashion? Is there adequate screening of the environment to pick up on opportunities?

Next, researchers need to assess the symptoms themselves. Can the symptoms be verified by other factors that are identified in the situation analysis? Are the symptoms one of a kind? Are they likely to appear again? You are beginning to realize, no doubt, that the researcher acts much like a detective. It is the researcher's role to explore and to question with the aim of properly defining the problem. Once the researcher has validated the symptoms, he or she is now ready to examine their causes.

Determine the Probable Causes of the Symptom When the manager and researcher are in agreement about which symptom or symptoms are in need of attention, it is time to determine what could possibly cause the symptoms. There is usually some cause or causes for the change. Profits do not go down by themselves. Sales do not drop without customers doing something differently from what they have done in the past. Satisfaction scores do not drop without some underlying cause.

At this stage it is important to determine as many causes as possible. If only a partial list of causes is made, it is possible that the real cause will be overlooked, leading ultimately to an incorrect decision. To help visualize this process, let's look at an example of an apartment complex near your university. Let's assume management has been alerted to symptoms that show the occupancy rate declining from 100% to 80% over the last three semesters. After discussion with the researcher, all possible causes may be grouped in the following categories: (1) competitors' actions, which drew prospective residents away; (2) changes in the consumers (student target population); (3) something about the apartment complex itself; and (4) general environmental factors. The researcher should discuss all these possible causes with management. There may be several possibilities within each of these categories. For example:

1. Competitors might be reducing rents or "lowering price" by providing free services such as cable TV.
2. The number of students at the university may be declining.
3. The apartment building may not have been adequately maintained or might appear to be "aging" on the outside.
4. Financial aid may have decreased on campus, so that students are less able to afford off-campus housing.

The situation analysis should have identified these possible causes. After listing all possible causes under each one of the previously identified broad categories, the researcher and manager should narrow down the possible causes to a small set of probable causes, defined as the most likely factors giving rise to the symptom(s). In our apartment example, we can assume that the manager and researcher have eliminated many causes for the symptom. For example, there has been no change in financial aid, student enrollment is up, and the apartment building's appearance is on a par with, or even better than, competitors' apartments. After evaluating all the other possible causes, assume the researcher and manager have reduced the probable cause down to the competitors offering tenants free cable TV. Notice that something very important has happened: Management now has a decision to make!

Determine Alternative Decisions An important task in defining the problem is to determine what decisions managers need to make as a result of the problem. When the problem has been defined by management and the researcher has conducted a situation analysis, the researcher must make a decision as to whether the problem is defined correctly. If, according to the researcher, the problem is confirmed, we now need to determine what decision alternatives the manager needs to consider.

3. DETERMINE WHAT DECISIONS NEED TO BE MADE

The determination that the probable cause of the symptom is competitors offering free cable TV creates a decision for management. We see that we are now ready to specify the decision to be made. Management must decide what to do to win back market share, and as decisions consist of decision alternatives, managers must specify the decision alternatives.

Decision alternatives are all marketing action that the manager thinks may resolve the problem.

Specify Decision Alternatives Essentially, possible **decision alternatives** are all marketing action that the manager thinks may resolve the problem. Common examples are price changes, product modification or improvement, promotion of any kind, and adjustments in channels of distribution. During this phase, the researcher's marketing education and knowledge come into play fully. Often the manager and researcher brainstorm possible decision alternatives that may serve as solutions. It is important for the manager to specify as many as possible of the decision alternatives that might address the probable cause of the symptom. As Semon notes, "Unless the entire range of potential solutions is considered, chances of correctly defining the research problem are poor."[10]

Returning to our apartment complex example, assume the manager examines all types of decisions. One alternative is to offer what the other apartments are offering: free TV cable services. A second alternative is to try to gain a competitive advantage by offering free TV cable services plus wireless Internet. A third alternative is to continue as is without offering free services. Now the decision alternatives become clear. But what are the consequences of each particular decision alternative?

Consequences are the results of marketing actions.

Weigh the Alternatives **Consequences** are the results of marketing actions. To evaluate decision alternatives, we must speculate as to the consequences of selecting each alternative. What are the most likely consequences we can anticipate with each decision alternative? Will the decision alternatives affect sales? Product recognition? Market share? Note that we are *anticipating* a consequence. If we *know* the consequence, there is no need for marketing research. Assuming that we don't know the consequence, research on each alternative under consideration will help determine which decision alternative is the best choice.

Returning to our apartment complex example, it would seem reasonable for the manager to speculate that if free cable TV is made available for each apartment, the consequence of this alternative would be occupancy rates that are more than enough to offset the cost of providing the service. But we must ask: How certain is the manager that this will occur? Hasn't the manager made an *assumption* that providing free basic cable services will create a greater demand for the apartment complex?

Decision makers make assumptions when they assign consequences to decision alternatives. **Assumptions** are assertions that certain conditions exist or that certain reactions will take place if the considered alternatives are implemented. Assumptions deserve researcher attention because they are the glue that holds the decision process together. Given a symptom, the manager *assumes* certain causes are at fault. The manager further *assumes* that, by taking corrective actions (alternatives), the problem will be resolved and the symptoms will disappear. In our apartment complex example, the manager's assumption is that free cable TV will be a strong enough incentive to cause occupancy to increase at the apartment complex during the next academic year. Another assumption is that this demand will be so much greater than the demand for apartments without these services that the increase in the demand will more than offset the additional cost of providing cable. As we can see from Figure 3.3, our next step is to determine if we have adequate information on hand to make these assumptions. If we do not feel that information is adequate to support these assumptions, we will likely need new information. The new information will be gathered by conducting marketing research!

If the manager is completely certain that he or she has adequate information to support the assumptions, there is no need for research and the decision may be made. The problem may now be resolved by simply choosing the correct decision alternative. In this case we do not need marketing research, do we? However, if a researcher questions a manager about his or her beliefs regarding the consequences of certain proposed alternatives, it may turn out that the manager is not really as certain as he or she first seemed to be. It is imperative, therefore, that the manager's assumptions be analyzed for validity.

4. IDENTIFY WHAT ADDITIONAL INFORMATION IS NEEDED

The next task in properly defining the problem is to identify if additional information is needed. The researcher must assess the existing **information state**, which is the quantity and quality of evidence a manager possesses for each of his or her assumptions. During this assessment, the researcher should ask questions about the current information state and determine the desired information state. Conceptually, the researcher seeks to identify **information gaps**, which are discrepancies between the current information level and the desired level of information at which the manager feels comfortable resolving the problem at hand. Ultimately, information gaps are the basis for establishing research objectives.

Inventory the Current Information State An important question that should be asked at this stage is if the information already exists to make a decision. Recall from "Step 1: Establish the need for marketing research" that marketing research is only conducted when managers do not have the information they need to choose among decision alternatives. Thus, in defining the problem, managers must first determine what decisions they must make. Then they must ask if they have adequate information already available to make the decision. Managers should not conduct marketing research just "to know something," because marketing research takes time and money to conduct.

Identify the Information Gaps Now let's go back to the apartment complex situation and think about information gaps. Let's assume the manager feels quite confident about the accuracy of the information that competitors are offering free cable TV because they advertise this new feature and announce it with signs outside their apartment complexes. The researcher continues to test assumptions by asking: "How do you know that students will care about access to cable TV?" The manager responds: "Because there are great movies on these channels. My wife and I watch a movie almost every night."

"But, you don't have to study at night, and you are not involved in campus activities and a fraternity or sorority, are you? Plus students have access to television and movie programming

---

Assumptions are assertions that certain conditions exist or that certain reactions will take place if the considered alternatives are implemented.

Information state is the quantity and quality of evidence a manager possesses for each of his or her assumptions.

Information gaps are discrepancies between the current information level and the desired level of information at which the manager feels comfortable resolving the problem at hand.

from sources other than cable TV," the researcher counters. "How do you know that college students will want the cable?"

"I really don't know. I haven't even asked any of my own tenants how many of them subscribe to cable," the manager admits.

"Would knowing that information help you make the decision?" the researcher asks. "If none of them subscribe to cable, is it because they don't like cable TV or because they can't afford it? Or maybe they have access to Netflix or Amazon Prime and just watch films and TV shows on their computers."

By now the manager realizes that his "certainty" has turned into high "uncertainty." He has an information gap, and he needs more information to close this gap to make the right decision. This situation is not unusual. Like the apartment manager, many people make assumptions and are satisfied with those assumptions until they start asking hard questions. However, when the decision is important, it's wise to make the right decision alternative choice to solve that problem. In our example, the researcher has convinced the manager he needs more information to make sure his assumptions are correct. Now he needs to determine what information is needed to close the information gap.

5. FORMULATE THE PROBLEM STATEMENT

The problem statement is a concise description of the problem or opportunity that management is facing that requires research to make a decision.

Having gone through all of the tasks previously outlined, the researcher should be ready for the final phase of problem definition: developing a problem statement. The **problem statement** is a concise description of the problem or opportunity that management is facing that requires research to make a decision. The following are examples of problem statements:

- An apartment manager wants to increase the proportion of apartment occupancies per year at his apartment complex.
- A snack manufacturer seeks to increase sales by offering biodegradable packaging.
- An app developer hopes to increase downloads of her app.
- A retailer wants to understand the consequences of an increase in sales by baby boomers and a decrease in sales by millennials during the past 12 months.

Having defined a problem, the next step is to determine exactly what information is needed to solve the problem.

3-3 Research Objectives

A research objective is a goal-oriented statement or question that specifies what information is needed to solve a problem.

After establishing the need for marketing research and defining the problem, the third step of the marketing research process is to establish research objectives. What is a research objective? A **research objective** is a goal-oriented statement or question that specifies what information is needed to solve a problem. Research objectives should be clear, specific, and actionable. In other words, given the limitations of time, money, and technology, the research objectives should be obtainable through marketing research. The number of research objectives can be highly variable, depending on the problem statement, but a rule of thumb is to have three to six research objectives per research project. The research objectives can be formulated in terms of statements or questions, but they should be structurally consistent (all statements or all questions). Research objectives should specify from whom the information should be gathered and exactly what information is needed.

For example, suppose the American Red Cross has identified as an opportunity the potential to have more college students donate blood each year to increase the available blood supply. The problem statement of the American Red Cross would be as follows:

The American Red Cross wishes to increase the number of American university students who donate blood each year.

TABLE 3.1 **Formulating Research Objectives as Statements or Questions**

Problem Statement: The American Red Cross wishes to increase the number of American university students who donate blood each year.

Formulating Research Objectives as Statements	Formulating Research Objectives as Questions
To determine what college students see as the benefits of donating blood	What do college students see as the benefits of donating blood?
To determine what college students see as the obstacles to donating blood	What do college students see as the obstacles to donating blood?
To identify the incentives that would encourage students to donate blood	What incentives would encourage students to donate blood?
To distinguish the types of promotions that are most likely to attract college students	What types of promotions are most likely to attract college students?
To identify how the information defined from the previous statements varies according to the characteristics of college students, including gender, class standing, type of university attending, domestic versus international student, and geographical region.	How does the information defined from the previous questions vary according to the characteristics of college students, including gender, class standing, type of university attending, domestic versus international student, and geographical region?

The research objectives might be identified as follows:

- To determine what college students see as the benefits of donating blood.
- To determine what college students see as the obstacles to donating blood.
- To identify the incentives that would encourage students to donate blood.
- To distinguish the types of promotions that are most likely to attract college students.
- To identify how the information defined from the previous statements varies according to the characteristics of college students, including gender, class standing, type of university attending, domestic versus international student, and geographical region.

See Table 3.1 for a list of the same research objectives formulated as statements or questions.

USING HYPOTHESES

To guide the process of developing research objectives, research analysts sometimes propose hypotheses. **Hypotheses** are statements that are taken as true for the purposes of argument or investigation. In making assumptions about the consequences of decision alternatives, managers are making hypotheses. For example, a successful restaurant owner uses a hypothesis that he must use X amount of food in an entrée to please his customers. This restaurant owner bases his decisions on the validity of this hypothesis; he makes sure a certain quantity of food is served on every plate regardless of the menu choice. Businesspeople make decisions every day based on statements they believe to be true. They need to have confidence that their most important decisions are based on valid hypotheses. This is similar to our previous discussions about *assumptions*. Sometimes the manager makes a specific statement (an assumption) and wants to know if there is evidence to support the statement. In the instances in which a statement is made, we may use the term *hypothesis* to describe this "statement thought to be true for purposes of a marketing research investigation."[11]

Hypotheses are statements that are taken as true for the purposes of argument or investigation.

DEFINING CONSTRUCTS

An important part of developing research objectives is determining what type of information should be measured. When multiple characteristics are used to measure a concept, it is called a construct. A **construct** is an abstract idea or concept composed of a set of attitudes or behaviors that are thought to be related.

A construct is an abstract idea or concept composed of a set of attitudes or behaviors that are thought to be related.

Consider an example of managers faced with a decision involving four ads. They need to choose the best ad. But what is "best"? It is hard to write a research objective without defining this type of criterion. What information will tell us which ad is best? Is it the ad that is most memorable? Most relevant? Most believable? Least likely to be misinterpreted? Most likable? Most likely to produce a favorable attitude? Most likely to produce an intention to buy the advertised product?[12] These questions represent the different types of information we could collect; each is a separate construct. The following constructs have been mentioned: memory, relevance, believability, understandability, likability, attitude, and intention to purchase.

Variables are elements of a construct that can be measured or quantified.

For example, marketers refer to the specific instances of someone buying the same brand 9 out of 10 times as a construct referred to as "brand loyalty." Sometimes marketing researchers call the constructs they study *variables*. **Variables** are elements of a construct that can be measured or quantified. They are referred to as variables because they can take on different values—that is, they can vary.[13] (Constants do not vary.) A construct provides us with a mental concept that represents real-world phenomena. When a consumer sees an ad for a product and states, "I am going to buy that new product X," marketers would label this phenomenon as the construct called "intention to buy." Marketers use a number of constructs to refer to phenomena that occur in the marketplace. Marketing researchers are constantly thinking of constructs as they go through the problem definition process. Once they know the constructs to be measured, they can determine the proper way to measure that construct, which we discuss in the next section.

It is imperative to measure the right construct. Can you state the construct we have suggested to measure in the research objective for our apartment complex research project? We could call it "likelihood to rent," which is similar to "intention to rent." To illustrate why the selection of the right construct is important, let's assume we asked a sample of students to tell us what TV channels they currently "most prefer" to watch. Note that we would be measuring the construct "current preferences for TV channels." Can we make a decision based on this information? No, we can't, because students have only reported what they prefer to watch from what is currently available to them. Those who do not have access to cable, such as those being considered in our decision, will not list them, so we have no basis for making a decision as to how many students prefer them. Therefore, we can't make a decision because we measured the wrong construct. We really want to know if the presence of cable will affect their *likelihood to rent* our apartment.

What Is the Unit of Measurement?   Marketing researchers find constructs helpful because, once it is determined that a specific construct is applicable to the problem, there are customary ways of *operationalizing*, or measuring, these constructs. The research objective should define how the construct being evaluated is actually measured. These definitions are referred to as *operational definitions*. An **operational definition** defines a construct, such as intention to buy or satisfaction, in terms of the operations to be carried out for the construct to be measured empirically.[14]

For example, let's take the construct "intention to buy." (This is essentially the same as our "likelihood to rent" example.) This construct should represent a person's likelihood to purchase or patronize a particular good or service, such as renting an apartment. Because few people know with 100% certainty that they will, or will not, purchase something, we measure this construct using a scaled response format—that is, a scale ranging from 1 to 5, 1 to 7, or 1 to 10. (We are not concerned about the number of scale units here; we are just illustrating that we should measure this construct using a scale of numbers, each representing a different likelihood.) This knowledge becomes useful in properly formulating research objectives. Researchers can access sources of information that provide them with operational definitions needed to measure many constructs.[15]

What is critical in the formulation of research objectives is that the proper unit of measurement be used for the construct. To answer what is "proper" we could ask: What unit of measurement will allow the manager to choose among decision alternatives? Let's suppose that the researcher and manager have agreed to make a decision based on a statistically significant difference between the *mean* likelihood to rent apartments with free cable TV versus free wireless Internet. By measuring likelihood to rent on a 1–5 scale for both apartments with free cable TV and Internet, we can calculate the mean score for each type of service. We can then determine if there is a significant difference between the two means. This should give us the basis for choosing between the two alternatives. What if we had decided to measure "likelihood to rent" by asking students: *If you have a choice between two similar apartments and one offers free cable (provide list of channels) and the other offers free wireless Internet, which would you rent?* Certainly we could do this, but asking the question this way will not allow us to calculate the means we said we needed to make our decision. Whatever unit of measurement is used, the researcher and manager must agree on it *before* defining the research objectives to ensure that the choice among alternatives can be made after the research project.

What Is the Proper Frame of Reference? Often we use *jargon*, terminology associated with a particular field. Researchers realize that, when they are formulating their research objectives, the information requested of respondents must be *worded using the respondent's frame of reference*. A pharmaceutical manager who is about to initiate a marketing research project with physicians as respondents thinks of a particular drug in terms of dosage, form, differentiating characteristics from the nearest competitor, and so on. On the other hand, the physicians from whom the research must gather information think first in terms of a patient's symptoms, disease severity, possible interaction with other drugs, willingness to comply with treatment, and so on. The pharmaceutical manager must think of the information needed in terms of the respondent-physicians' frame of reference, not his or her own.

If we apply this concept to our apartment complex example, we could say that television companies often speak of "basic," "advanced basic," and "premium" channels. Consumers do not think of TV channels in these same terms. Consumers know channels by their names, such as ESPN, CBS, Golf, SHOWTIME, Adult Swim, or HBO. This is why it is important in our example to provide consumers with the actual channels provided so that they can make an informed decision without having to guess what channels they might have with an apartment that comes equipped with free TV cable.

3-4 Action Standards

We started this discussion by addressing different sources of problems (failure to meet objectives and opportunities) and the systems needed to recognize those problems. We then looked at problem definition and stated that problems must be couched in terms of decisions, and decisions must be couched in the form of decision alternatives. We addressed two different routes the researcher might take in defining the decision alternatives. We then discussed how decision alternatives contain assumptions and how managers may be uncertain about these assumptions. Uncertainty of assumptions creates information gaps, and research seeks to fill those gaps. The research objective specifies exactly what information the researcher must collect to fill the information gaps. Once this information is provided, the manager should be able to choose among the decision alternatives. But exactly how will that decision be made? What must the information look like for a certain alternative to be selected over others? This is the subject of the next section.

We've seen how the problem definition and research objectives development process proceeds using our apartment complex example. Next, it may be useful to determine an action standard. An **action standard** is the predesignation of some quantity of a measured attribute or characteristic that must be achieved for a predetermined action to take place. The purpose of the action standard is to define what action will be taken given the results of the research findings.[16] In other words, by specifying the action standard, managers will know, once they

An action standard is the predesignation of some quantity of a measured attribute or characteristic that must be achieved for a predetermined action to take place.

receive the information collected by the researcher, which decision alternative to select. In our apartment complex case, we have determined that one research objective should be to collect information that measures *the likelihood that students will rent an apartment that offers free cable TV in comparison to other alternatives*. Recall that we stated in our research objective that we would measure the construct "likelihood to rent" on a 5-point scale ranging from 1 = Very Unlikely to Rent to 5 = Very Likely to Rent. When we get our research results, how do we know whether to select from our three decision alternatives: (1) offer free basic cable TV, (2) offer free wireless Internet, or (3) do not offer either service?

From the research, we will derive three means: one for basic TV cable, one for free wireless Internet, and one for an apartment offering neither service. Recall that we are asking respondents to choose an apartment based on the provision of the three service options, with the assumption that all other factors are equal. Let's think about the three means and create a situation in which it is easy to make the decision: The wireless Internet mean is 4.8 (high likelihood) and the basic cable and no service are each 1.0 (very low likelihood), and the difference between these two means is statistically significant. Clearly, we should select the wireless Internet decision alternative.

The manager and researcher should try to determine, prior to collecting the data, at which point they would still make this decision. Let's assume they decide that if the wireless Internet mean is above 3.5 and is statistically different from a lower mean for TV cable or no service, they will still go with the decision alternative of wireless Internet. In other words, they believe that with any mean of 3.5 or above and with a mean for cable significantly (statistically) lower, the demand will be high enough to warrant the extra expense of providing the wireless service. A possible action standard that would warrant choosing neither would be that all means are *below* 2.0.

Action standards entail making important decisions before you collect information, and they serve as clear guidelines for action once the data have been collected. Ron Tatham, former CEO of Burke, Inc., stated: "Without action standards, managers will often say 'The results of the research are interesting. I learned a lot about the market but I am not sure what to do next.'"[17]

IMPEDIMENTS TO PROBLEM DEFINITION

As you can now appreciate, the process of defining the problem and research objectives is not simple. It takes time and serious interaction between clients and researchers. This creates a problem because clients are accustomed to dealing with outside suppliers efficiently, making certain not to divulge proprietary information. Some managers, accustomed to dealing with consultants, understand the necessity for serious communications with researchers. However, many managers fall short of appreciating the necessity of frank and detailed discussions during the marketing research process. Research projects have the greatest likelihood for success when the managers and researchers are in close communication throughout the research process.

Chet Kane refers to this problem in noting that managers often commission marketing research projects without being involved with them. He states that managers should not only be involved in designing the research but also should actually go out into the field and listen to some of the consumer responses firsthand. Had managers been more involved in the research involving "clear" products, they would have known that the positive findings of research for these products (clear beer, clear mouthwash, and clear cola) were based on the novelty or "fad" of the clear products. Had the managers been more involved with the research process, they might not have launched these new products, which failed in the marketplace.[18]

Often, to be effective, the marketing research process is slow. To repeat the statement of Carrie Breisach of General Mills from the introduction to this chapter: *It is worth spending time in the beginning gaining clarity and alignment on the true problem and questions in order to facilitate meaningful learning that ultimately illuminates the path forward and enables better, faster decisions.* Managers often are unaware of the need to work closely with the researcher, and this causes difficulties in identifying the real problem. Veteran researchers are well aware of this situation, and it is up to them to properly inform managers of their expected role and the importance of this initial step in the research process.

3-5 The Marketing Research Proposal

At some point early in the marketing research process, a contract is prepared. The **marketing research proposal** is the contract that documents what the marketing researcher pledges to deliver as a result of the marketing research process. When a client first contacts a marketing research supplier to conduct

Proposals should be professional looking, well written, and comprehensive.

research, the client will generally request a proposal prior to agreeing to work with the firm in a process called an **invitation to bid (ITB)** or **request for proposal (RFP)**. Often a client will request proposals from several suppliers before deciding which firm the client would prefer to hire to conduct the research. To ensure that their suppliers offer competitive prices and good quality, some companies even require that their managers acquire at least three bids prior to hiring a marketing research supplier. As such it is very important that the proposal be professional looking, well written, and comprehensive.

The proposal should very clearly define the problem and state the research objectives to be sure that the managerial client and the research firm are in agreement about the goals of the projects. Generally, the more details that the supplier can provide related to the problem background and the proposed methods for conducting the research, the more knowledgeable and capable the researcher will appear.

Even client-side marketing researchers who are planning to conduct research on behalf of their own companies are often required to submit proposals prior to conducting research. Their managers want to ensure that their money and their employees' time will be well spent before agreeing to a marketing research project. Sometimes the pool of money available for marketing research is limited and the marketing research department must compete on a company-wide level with other worthy projects to have their research projects funded.

> The marketing research proposal is the contract that documents what the marketing researcher pledges to deliver as a result of the marketing research process.
>
> Invitations to bid (ITBs) or requests for proposals (RFPs) are often used in the marketing research process. These are routinely used in all business sectors when a firm desires supplier firms to present proposals or bids.

ELEMENTS OF THE PROPOSAL

Following are the elements of the marketing research proposal and the types of questions that are answered through the proposal:

1. *Statement of the problem.* What is the overall problem that will be addressed? What are the decision alternatives that will be assessed through the research?
2. *The research objectives.* What information will be collected?
3. *The research method.* What methods will be used to conduct the research? Will the research be exploratory, descriptive, or causal? Will the research be qualitative, quantitative, or mixed method? What are the population, sample frame, sample size, sample method, incidence rate, and response rate? What will the measurement instrument look like? What methods will be used to analyze the data? Which, if any, subcontractors will be used for what services?

4. *Statement of deliverables.* How and when will the research results be communicated? A written report? An oral presentation? Will there be meetings with clients to discuss implementation issues?

5. *Cost.* What are the expenses for the project? Which expenses are paid in advance and on what dates? Which subcontractors are to be paid directly by the client?

6. *Timetable.* On what dates will the different stages of the research project be completed?

ETHICAL ISSUES AND THE RESEARCH PROPOSAL

The marketing research proposal process is an area where clients and researchers should be sensitive to ethical issues. Clients should not expect marketing research firms to provide value-added services prior to signing a contract. They should not provide one research company's proposal to other research firms for the purpose of competitive bidding. The research proposal, which may include many hours of work and contain details of proposed methods and cost structures, should be viewed as proprietary information.[19]

Some specific codes from the standards of the Marketing Research Association deal with issues related to the proposal:

Section A: All Marketing Research Association Members agree that they:

18. Work must be performed as specified in the agreement with the client.
19. … maintain trusted relationships with clients and research sponsors by keeping confidential all sensitive or proprietary research techniques, methodologies and business information. Maintain the confidential identity of clients and research sponsors. (MRA CODE OF MARKETING RESEARCH STANDARDS http://www.mra-net. org/resources/documents/expanded_code.pdf, page 7)

Summary

Although there is great variability in marketing research projects, there are enough commonalities among these projects to enable us to characterize them in terms of steps of the research process. The value in characterizing research projects in terms of successive steps is that (1) the steps give researchers and other parties an overview of the entire research process, and (2) they provide a procedure in the sense that a researcher, by referring to the steps, knows what tasks to consider and in what order. The steps are (1) establish the need for marketing research, (2) define the problem, (3) establish research objectives, (4) determine research design, (5) identify information types and sources, (6) determine methods of accessing data, (7) design data collection forms, (8) determine sample plan and size, (9) collect data, (10) analyze data, and (11) prepare and present the final research report.

The first step is determining the need to conduct marketing research. Can the needed information be obtained from the internal reports system? From the marketing intelligence system? From the decision support system? If these ongoing sources of information do not supply the needed data, marketing research may be needed. Sometimes the need to respond quickly to competition means there isn't time to conduct marketing research. Though placing a dollar figure on value is difficult, value can be estimated, and a more informed decision may be made justifying or not justifying marketing research.

Problems are situations calling for managers to make choices among alternatives. Research objectives state specifically what information the researcher must produce so that the manager can choose the correct alternative to solve the problem. Figure 3.3 depicts a process that may be used for defining the problem. There are two sources of problems. "Failure to meet an objective" arises when there is a gap between what was *supposed* to happen and what *did* happen. "Opportunity" refers to problems that arise when there is a gap between what *did* happen and what *could* have happened. Managers recognize problems either through monitoring control systems (in the case of failure to meet an objective) or through opportunity identification systems.

Symptoms are changes in the level of some key monitor that measures the achievement of an objective. Symptoms alert managers to both types of problems. The researcher is responsible for ensuring that management has properly defined the problem even in cases when management has already defined the problem through invitations to bid or requests for proposals. In many cases, a situation analysis is required to help define the problem.

When defining the problem, researchers must validate the symptoms that alerted management to the problem to ensure the symptoms are correctly reporting what they portend to report. Researchers should work with managers to determine *all possible causes* for the symptoms.

Researchers should work with managers to reduce all possible causes down to probable causes. The selection of a probable cause creates the decision. The decision itself must specify alternatives that may be used to eliminate the symptom. Researchers must work with managers to clearly state the decision alternatives and to determine the consequences of each alternative. Researchers should assess the assumptions managers have made in determining the consequences of each alternative. If the manager is certain about the assumptions made, a decision alternative may be selected without any further research. However, in most cases, managers are uncertain about their assumptions. Lack of sufficient information creates an information gap, which serves as the basis for establishing research

objectives. Sometimes hypotheses are stated to help to guide the development of the research objective.

A research objective is a goal-oriented statement or question that specifies what information is needed to solve a problem. Research objectives should be clear, specific, and actionable.

Action standards refer to the predesignation of some quantity of a measured attribute or characteristic that must be achieved for a research objective for a predetermined action to take place. Problem definition is sometimes impeded because managers fail to change their normal behavior of dealing with outside suppliers in an efficient manner during problem-solving situations.

Marketing research proposals are formal documents prepared by the researcher serving the functions of stating the problem, specifying research objectives, detailing the research method, stating the deliverables and costs, and specifying a timetable. There are ethical issues involved in submitting and evaluating a research proposal.

Key Terms

11 steps in the marketing research process (p. 68)
Field services firms (p. 73)
Problems (p. 74)
Marketing opportunity (p. 75)
Symptoms (p. 76)
Situation analysis (p. 76)
Decision alternatives (p. 78)

Consequences (p. 78)
Assumptions (p. 79)
Information state (p. 79)
Information gaps (p. 79)
Problem statement (p. 80)
Research objective (p. 80)
Hypotheses (p. 81)
Construct (p. 81)

Variables (p. 82)
Operational definition (p. 82)
Action standard (p. 83)
Marketing research proposal (p. 85)
Invitation to bid (ITB) (p. 85)
Request for proposal (RFP) (p. 85)

Review Questions/Applications

3-1. What are the steps in the marketing research process?

3-2. Are all 11 steps in the marketing research process used at all times? Why or why not?

3-3. Use an example to illustrate that the steps in the marketing research process are not always taken in sequence.

3-4. Explain why firms may not have a need for marketing research.

3-5. Why is defining the problem the most important step in the marketing research process?

3-6. Discuss why defining the problem is really stating the decision alternatives.

3-7. Explain why research objectives differ from the definition of the problem.

3-8. What is meant by the *problem*?

3-9. What is the research objective?

3-10. What are the two sources of marketing problems?

3-11. Explain how managers should recognize they have a problem.

3-12. What is the role of symptoms in problem recognition?

3-13. What is the role of the researcher when management has already defined the problem?

3-14. What is a situation analysis, and when would it likely be used in defining the problem?

3-15. What is the role of the researcher when management has *not* already defined the problem?

3-16. In what respect do researchers act much like detectives?

3-17. What is the difference between "all possible causes" and "probable causes"?

3-18. What is meant by *consequences* of the decision alternatives?

3-19. Explain why it is importance for managers to make assumptions in the process of defining a research problem.

3-20. Explain the information state when there are information gaps.

3-21. What is needed to close information gaps?

3-22. What is the role of a hypothesis in defining the problem?

3-23. What are some relevant factors in determining research objectives?

3-24. What role do constructs play in the problem definition/research objectives process?

3-25. What is an operational definition, and where would it likely be used?

3-26. What is an action standard?

3-27. Discuss how a researcher and a manager can foster a good working relationship in the process of defining the research problem and objectives.

3-28. What are the elements of the marketing research proposal?

3-29. Search the Internet for marketing research firms. Choose one of them. What is the range of services offered by it? What information does it require from potential clients in order to determine costs and timescales of research projects?

3-30. Formulate a problem statement and research objectives for the following situations:

a. A Chinese manufacturer wants to investigate whether or not Chinese nationals would be effective sales representatives in the European market.

b. A Japanese sushi chain wants to see if menu prices should be broadly equivalent to home prices for their new South Korean outlets.

c. A software manufacturer wants to gauge customer reaction to automated updates initiated without customer authorization.

d. An Indian tea cultivator wants to find out how to sell his premium tea blends directly to the UK market.

3-31. Use the Internet to look for templates and other aids that would help in creating a marketing research proposal. Analyze and assess five of them. In your view, are these standardized formats suitable for most instances? Do they contain all the elements required to create a successful research proposal? Explain how you would individualize the templates.

3-32. Observe a business in your community. Examine what it does, what products or services it provides, how it prices and promotes its products or services, and other aspects of the business. If you managed the business, would you have conducted research to determine the firm's products, design, features, prices, promotion, and so on? If you decide you would not have conducted marketing research in a given area, explain why.

CASE 3.1

Golf Technologies, Inc.

Golf Technologies, Inc. (GTI) relies on high-level scientific testing to design golf clubs that provide larger "sweet spots," resulting in fewer missed hits and maximum yardage. In the last year, GTI discovered a technical breakthrough in club design. Its newest clubs, for the same level of energy, hit the golf ball longer than any existing clubs on the market. CEO Harvey Pennick is very excited about this breakthrough and believes these clubs will create a new level of excitement and enthusiasm among players. Pennick is well aware that many club manufacturers tout "new scientific breakthroughs" with each year's new model clubs. He also knows that consumers have become fairly immune to these claims. He believes he must do something different to convince potential buyers that the newest GTI clubs actually do have a larger sweet spot and really do hit the ball farther. Armed with objective tests that prove these claims, Pennick and his marketing staff believe they need a highly credible golfer to be used in their promotional materials (TV ads, magazine ads, infomercials, and special event promotions). The credibility of the message in GTI's promotions will be critical if golfers are to really believe their claim of a breakthrough in club design.

Pennick's staff presents the two golfers whom they believe are the best known: Rory McIlroy and Bubba Watson. Both golfers are considered among the best in the world and have very high name recognition. However, both these golfers have exclusive contracts with other club manufacturers. Both contracts have buyout clauses so, if GTI is to hire either one of them, it will be expensive to buy out the existing contract and to offer enough money to attract one of these world-class golfers to be GTI's new spokesperson.

1. Assuming Pennick agrees with his staff on the choice of McIlroy or Watson, what now is Pennick's decision in terms of decision alternatives?

2. Assuming Pennick is not confident in his assumptions about the consequences of the outcomes associated with your decision alternative, what should Pennick consider doing?

3. If Pennick decides to conduct marketing research, write the research objective.

CASE 3.2 INTEGRATED CASE

Auto Concepts

Recall back in Case 1.2 that Nick Thomas, CEO of Auto Concepts, a new division of a large automobile manufacturer, has been slowly losing market share to other competitors. Auto Concepts was created to reclaim the manufacturer's highly competitive level in the auto industry by developing new models that are more competitive in today's new car market.

Auto Concepts now has five different models that are feasible in terms of engineering and production. Nick has assigned tentative model names to them.

1. "Super Cycle," one-seat all electric, mpg-e rating 125; estimated MSRP (manufacturer's suggested retail price) $30,000; range 200 miles.
2. "Runabout Sport," two-seat all electric, mpg-e 99; estimated MSRP $35,000; range 150 miles.
3. "Runabout Hatchback," two-seat gasoline hybrid, mpg-e 50; runs on battery for 50 miles and then switches to gas engine; estimated MSRP $35,000; range 250 miles.
4. "Economy Hybrid," four-seat diesel hybrid, mpg-e 75; runs on battery for 75 miles and then switches to efficient diesel engine; estimated MSRP $38,000; range 300 miles.
5. "Economy Standard," five-seat economy standard gasoline, mpg 36; runs on gasoline with computer control for maximum efficiency; estimated MSRP $37,000; range 350 miles.

Note: mpg-e is a measure of the average distance traveled per unit of energy used. It is the U.S. Environmental Protection Agency's measure of efficiency when alternative fuels (e.g., electricity) are used. It allows for a comparison of new energy propulsion with the fuel efficiency.

Nick knows no single model will have universal appeal to a huge market. Rather, different models will appeal to market segments, and Auto Concepts will be sharing those segments with other able competitors that are working just as hard to develop car models that satisfy consumer needs in those segments. In other words, Auto Concepts wants to reach target markets for the models it produces without wasting promotional dollars on those who aren't interested in the model. For example, if the company decides to produce a particular model, a decision must be made in terms of choosing among media types (TV, radio, magazine, newspaper, social media) in which to promote the product. Nick would like to know each market segment's media habits. Which TV show types do most people in each market prefer? Radio genres? Magazine types? Sections of local newspapers? Also, the marketing department has moved to spending large sums of the budget on online promotions. Nick wants to know which market segments he can reach through blogs, content communities such as YouTube, social network sites such as Facebook, and online games and virtual worlds.

Knowing that consumers like a particular medium is not enough. For example, Nick may learn that the target market for a particular model prefers one magazine type over another, but there are many choices of magazines within that type. Knowledge of the demographic profiles of the target market segments can be helpful in selecting one newspaper, one magazine, or one social medium for a selected market. Because all media provide information to potential advertisers on the demographics they reach, Auto Concepts should have a demographic profile of each market segment it attempts to target. To make the most of that information, the carmaker needs information on the demographics of those who most desire each model: gender, age, size of hometown or city, marital status, number of people in family, education, income, and dwelling type.

In terms of positioning the cars, Nick knows fuel economy will be the key motivator. In addition, he wants to know if appealing to consumers' concerns for global warming will have an impact on sales. Auto Concepts is making a major effort to reduce carbon emissions by moving to more efficient propulsion systems; should that effort be a prominent part of its positioning statement in promotions and, if so, for which models? Nick gets a lot of mixed information in the general information environment about global warming. He wants to know what consumers think about two issues: (1) Are consumers worried about global warming? (2) Do they believe gasoline emissions contribute to global warming?

Finally, there is the Internet of Things factor: What innovations do consumers expect and desire on their autos of the future? Do they wish for self- and/or assisted driving, types of infotainment, dashboard diagnostic features, or other smartphone driving aids?

Assume that Nick Thomas decides to conduct marketing research and that the marketing researcher agrees with the problems stated in this case.

1. State the problems.
2. Write the research objective for one of the problems defined in your answer to the first question.

4 Research Design

"WHERE WE ARE"

1 Establish the need for marketing research.
2 Define the problem.
3 Establish research objectives.
4 Determine research design.
5 Identify information types and sources.
6 Determine methods of accessing data.
7 Design data collection forms.
8 Determine the sample plan and size.
9 Collect data.
10 Analyze data.
11 Prepare and present the final research report.

Designing Research to Develop Great Ideas

Sven Arn, Managing Director and Partner, Happy Thinking People.

Founded in Munich, Germany (1989), Happy Thinking People is one of the world's leading independent qualitative marketing research and consulting companies. With offices in Berlin, Munich, Paris, Zürich, and Mumbai employing over 100 people, we have over 25 years of in-depth experience in understanding people across the globe and in helping our clients to build relationships between brands, products, services, and their customers that lead to business success.

We have provided qualitative research training for ESOMAR and BVM (the German Market Research Association) for over 15 years. In 2013 we were voted "Best in Class in Analysis" by the German Association of Market Researchers.

Happy Thinking People works for a wide range of clients and categories, focusing on four main areas: exploring markets, creating concepts, evaluating ideas, and brand consulting.

Exploring markets is about understanding people in the contexts, places, and situations in which they make their decisions. We have a range of innovative tools working across the blurring boundaries of online and offline from Brazil to Shanghai, from mobile ethnographies and online communities to behavioral semiotics.

Our concept development embraces the principles of co-creation but doesn't leave everything to the consumer. While being firmly anchored in directional insight, our experience and know-how pinpoint where to follow and where to disrupt consumer expectations. We have a strong portfolio of proprietary techniques involving storytelling and story changing, creative exercises, role playing, war games, and scenario building.

We approach idea evaluation to reflect the complexity of human decision making—without making results confusing. Our recommendations are always founded in understanding consumer reactions rather than just reflecting what people say.

Our brand consulting offer covers all the stages of the strategic process from insight identification through innovation, portfolio planning, and positioning to brand development.

In summary, "Happy Thinking" is the state that we believe leads to great ideas. We also believe that it makes sound business sense to involve consumers and our clients in an engaging discourse that encourages visionary thinking to develop ideas that make a real difference in people's lives.

—*Sven Arn*

Source: Text and photos courtesy of Sven Arn, Managing Director & Partner, Happy Thinking People.

HAPPY THINKING PEOPLE

THE PEOPLE UNDERSTANDING COMPANY

Visit Happy Thinking People at www.happythinkingpeople.com.

Once the problem has been defined and the research objectives have been established, the next step in the marketing research process is determining the research design. In this chapter, you will be introduced to three basic types of research design: exploratory, descriptive, and causal. Each serves a different purpose and relies on different methods. Each has its own set of advantages and disadvantages. Knowing the basic options for research design can assist a researcher in making appropriate decisions in advance of conducting a research project.

A research design is a master plan that specifies the methods that will be used to collect and analyze the information needed for a research project.

4-1 Research Design

Marketing research studies are carried out in many different ways. Some projects are food-tasting experiments held in kitchen-like labs; others are focus groups, ethnographic research, or large, nationally representative sample surveys. Some research objectives require only research, whereas others may require thousands of personal interviews. Researchers may observe consumers in convenience stores or conduct two-hour, in-depth, personal interviews in respondents' homes.

Each type of study has certain advantages and disadvantages, and one method may be more appropriate for a given research problem than another. How do marketing researchers decide which method is the most appropriate? After becoming familiar with the problem and research objectives, researchers select a **research design**, which is a master plan that specifies the methods that will be used to collect and analyze the information needed for a research project.

WHY IS KNOWLEDGE OF RESEARCH DESIGN IMPORTANT?

Knowledge of research design is important in developing an appropriate study to approach a problem or opportunity. David Singleton of Zyman Marketing Group, Inc., believes that good research design is the first rule of good research.[1] Why would a practitioner make such a statement? There are reasons to justify the significance placed on research design. First, we need to understand that even though every problem and research objective may seem unique, there are usually enough similarities among problems and objectives to allow us to make some decisions in advance about the best research design to use to resolve the problem. This means we can group or classify seemingly diverse types of research projects well enough to predetermine the most appropriate research design.

Early on in the research process, as the problem and research objectives are forming, researchers can begin to plan which research design will be most appropriate. What allows researchers to do this is the fact that basic research designs available to them can be successfully matched to a range of problems and research objectives. Once the researcher knows the basic research design, a series of advance decisions may be made to form a framework for the development of the research project. The research design for the project calls for detailing what steps will be necessary for the completion of a successful project.

For example, if a researcher knows that an exploratory research design is called for, he or she can start thinking of the different ways to carry out exploratory research given the unique characteristics of the particular project. A series of *focus groups* may be needed. Who will participate in the focus groups? How many focus groups will be conducted? What questions will be asked of focus group participants? What should be the outcomes of the focus groups? The research design will lay out these details. Or perhaps the researcher determines that a causal research design is needed. This sets the researcher off in a completely different direction of thinking about appropriate experimental designs. In this way, identifying the most appropriate basic research design and the characteristics of the design serves the researcher in the same way that a blueprint might serve a builder.

Knowledge of the needed research design allows advance planning so that the project may be conducted in less time and typically at a cost savings due to efficiencies gained in preplanning. Think about taking a long trip. If you have the ability to preplan, you can save yourself time and money. It works the same way in a research project. At this stage, researchers may also face ethical issues related to the research design. Some common ethical considerations are presented in Marketing Research Insight 4.1.

4-2   Three Types of Research Designs

Research designs are classified into three traditional categories: exploratory, descriptive, and causal. The choice of the most appropriate design depends largely on the objectives of the research. Three common objectives are (1) to gain background information and to develop hypotheses, (2) to measure the state of a variable of interest (for example, level of brand loyalty), or (3) to test hypotheses that specify the relationships between two or more variables (for example, level of advertising and brand loyalty).

MARKETING RESEARCH INSIGHT 4.1   *Ethical Consideration*

Planning the Research Design: Areas of Ethical Sensitivity

In most cases professionals know more about their fields than the clients who hire them. In fact, this knowledge is the reason we hire professionals. However, that imbalance of knowledge can cause serious ethical issues. In the marketing research industry, these issues may arise in the potential for researchers to take advantage of clients in the research design process.

Recommending a Costlier Design Than Needed Some research designs are simple, efficient, and much less costly than others. Exploratory research, for example, has these characteristics. A researcher could recommend a much more involved research design that takes more time and increases the cost to the client. Why would a researcher do this? If a researcher's fee is based on a percentage of costs of the project, then there is a built-in incentive to boost those costs. Or, if the researcher has an interest in a subcontracting research firm, there is an incentive to use the services of that firm whether needed or not. An egregious example of this ethical lapse is a researcher presenting secondary data as primary data collected by the researcher. The Marketing Research Association's (MRA's) Code of Marketing Research Standards, Section II 21, states that researchers "will, when conducting secondary research, inform clients of the source of secondary research and not misrepresent it as primary data."

Designing a Study in Which Data Are Collected for Multiple Clients A researcher could save data collection costs by collecting data for multiple clients at the same time. The MRA's Code of Marketing Research Standards, Section II 22, states that researcher must "be granted prior approval, if all or part of the work on a project is to be combined or syndicated with work for other clients, or if the same is to be subcontracted to another entity outside the researcher's organization."

Using Information Obtained for a Client in Another Research Project A researcher could design a research project so that a component of the project that reflects work already conducted and paid for by a previous client is presented as original work for the present client. The MRA's Code of Marketing Research Standards, Section II 24, provides that researchers "will ensure that research conducted is the property of the commissioning party or client(s). At no time may such research be shared with other entities without the express written permission of the original client(s)."

Over- or Underestimating Data Collection Costs As you will learn, data collection costs are strongly influenced by the incidence rate (the percentage of the population possessing the characteristics required to participate in a study). Incidence rates are high if the research design calls for interviewing "any adult over age 18." Incidence rates are low if the study requires "males, over 65, who take statin drugs but still have high cholesterol counts." The lower the incidence rate, the more persons are required to be contacted to find someone who qualifies for the study. As a result, low incidence rate studies can be very costly. The MRA's Code of Marketing Research Standards, Section II 34, states that researchers "will calculate research metrics such as incidence, performance measurements such as response rates, error measurements such as sample margin of error, and other formulas according to commonly accepted industry practices."

Wrongfully Gaining Respondent Cooperation to Reduce Costs A researcher could design a project in which respondent cooperation could be greatly increased by making promises to potential respondents without any intention of fulfilling those promises. The MRA's Code of Marketing Research Standards, Section I 8, requires that researchers will "make factually correct statements to secure cooperation, including for database/sample development, and honor all promises made to respondents including but not limited to the use of data."

Misrepresenting Sampling Methods Research design will include determining the appropriate sampling plan and sample size. Researchers should not use a sample plan that does not allow achievement of the research objectives of the study. Researchers should inform clients as to how the sample plan will result in a representative sample. Likewise, researchers should inform the client of the effect of sample size on the study's accuracy. Some sample plans are more costly than others, and more sample size means greater costs to clients. The MRA's Code of Marketing Research Standards, Section II 30, requires that researchers "offer guidance to clients as to the appropriateness of the methodology being employed and sample selected to the fullest extent possible on each project."

Adherence to ethical standards applies to many aspects of designing a research project, which is why the MRA and other professional associations develop and maintain codes of ethics and standards of conduct. Professionals who understand and comply with these standards serve their clients' interests fairly

and responsibly. Fortunately, 99% of marketing researchers are extremely ethical and follow their association's guidelines. The free market has a wonderful way of ensuring that those who aren't ethical do not stay around for long!

We strongly recommend that you visit the websites of the professional organizations identified in Chapter 2 and read their codes of conduct. The MRA posts its standards at http://www.marketingresearch.org (click the link to Standards).

Designing a research project may involve many ethically sensitive areas. Researchers learn how to treat clients ethically by being familiar with their association's codes and standards.

The choice of research design also depends on how much we already know about the problem and research objective. The less we know, the more likely it is that we should use exploratory research. Causal research, on the other hand, should only be used when we know a fair amount about the problem and we are looking for causal relationships among variables associated with the problem or research objectives. By reading this chapter you will better understand how different research objectives are best handled by the various research designs.[2]

RESEARCH DESIGN: A CAUTION

Before discussing the three types of research design, a warning may be in order against thinking of research design solely in a step-by-step fashion. The order in which the designs are presented in this chapter—that is, exploratory, descriptive, and causal—is *not* necessarily the order in which these designs should be carried out. In some cases, it may be perfectly legitimate to begin with any one of the three designs and to use only that one design. In many cases, however, research is an iterative process: By conducting one research project, we learn that we may need additional research, which may result in using multiple research designs. We could very well find, for example, that after conducting descriptive research, we need to go back and conduct exploratory research.

4-3 Exploratory Research

Exploratory research is unstructured, informal research that is undertaken to gain background information about the general nature of the research problem.

Exploratory research is unstructured, informal research that is undertaken to gain background information about the general nature of the research problem. By unstructured, we mean that exploratory research does not have a predetermined set of procedures. Rather, the nature of the research changes as the researcher gains information. It is informal in that there is no formal set of objectives, sample plan, or questionnaire. Often small, non-representative samples are used in exploratory research. Other, more formal, research designs are used to test hypotheses or measure the reaction of one variable to a change in another variable. Yet exploratory research can be accomplished by simply reading a magazine or even by observing a situation. Ray Kroc, the milkshake machine salesman who created McDonald's, observed that restaurants in San Bernardino, California, run by the McDonald brothers were so busy they burned up more milkshake machines than any of his other customers. Kroc took that exploratory observation and turned it into the world-famous fast-food chain. In another example, two eighth graders, Julianne Goldmark and Emily Matson, admired the hair accessories worn by characters on the television show *Gossip Girl* but were unable to find similar products in stores that were affordable. The duo began creating and selling their own hair accessories. They now have a business called Emi-Jay that makes about $10 million a year.[3]

Exploratory research is flexible in that it allows the researcher to investigate whatever sources he or she identifies and to the extent he or she feels is necessary to gain an understanding of the problem at hand. For example, a Wendy's franchisee went through his restaurant's cash register receipts, which were stamped with dates and times. He observed that weekday afternoons between 2:00 and 4:30 p.m. were his slack periods. He then initiated a mobile campaign for a free order of French fries during this time on weekdays. Traffic and sales went up. A University of West Virginia grad, Tom Petrini, attended a conference on sustainability. He noticed almost none of the attendees were drinking water from the reusable containers provided. When he asked them why, they told him there was no place to clean and refill the bottles. The company he started, Evive Station, provides free stainless steel containers and follow-up sterilization and refilling.[4]

Exploratory research is usually conducted when the researcher does not know much about the problem and needs additional information or desires new or more recent information. Often exploratory research is conducted at the outset of research projects. Chapter 3 discussed the use of a situation analysis to help clarify the problem. A situation analysis is a form of exploratory research.

USES OF EXPLORATORY RESEARCH

Exploratory research is used in a number of situations: to gain background information, to define terms, to clarify problems and hypotheses, and to establish research priorities.

Gain Background Information When very little is known about the problem or when the problem has not been clearly formulated, exploratory research may be used to gain the needed background information. Even the most experienced researchers often undertake some exploratory research to gain current, relevant background information. Exploratory research can offer breakthrough ideas and fresh insights that lead to strategic knowledge.

Define Terms Exploratory research helps to define terms and concepts. By conducting exploratory research to define a question such as "What is satisfaction with service quality?" the researcher quickly learns that "satisfaction with service quality" is composed of several dimensions—tangibles, reliability, responsiveness, assurance, and empathy. Not only would exploratory research identify the dimensions of satisfaction with service quality, but it could also demonstrate how these components may be measured.[5]

Clarify Problems and Hypotheses Exploratory research allows the researcher to define the problem more precisely and to generate hypotheses for the upcoming study. For example, exploratory research on measuring bank image reveals the issue of different groups of bank customers. Banks have three types of customers: retail customers, commercial customers, and other banks for which services are performed for fees. This information is useful in clarifying

Marketing Research on YouTube™ To see exploratory research in action, go to www.youtube.com and enter "brand exploratory research Giants game." An example of "man-on-the-street" interviews is shown.

Exploratory research is used to gain background information, to define terms, to clarify problems and hypotheses, and to establish research priorities.

the problem of the measurement of bank image because it raises the issue of identifying for which customer group bank image should be measured.

Exploratory research can also be beneficial in the formulation of hypotheses, which are statements describing the speculated relationships among two or more variables. Formally stating hypotheses prior to conducting a research study helps to ensure that the proper variables are measured. Once a study has been completed, it may be too late to state which hypotheses are desirable to test.

Establish Research Priorities Exploratory research can help a firm prioritize research topics. For example, examining user-generated feedback on review websites, such as Engadget or Yelp, may tell management where to devote attention. Business-to-business organizations often find interviews with salespeople helpful sources of future product and service concepts to pursue.

METHODS OF CONDUCTING EXPLORATORY RESEARCH

A variety of methods is available to conduct exploratory research. We will cover some of these in the section of this chapter that deals with qualitative research since the methods overlap. In this section we briefly discuss some commonly used methods for conducting exploratory research: secondary data analysis, experience surveys, and case analysis. Other methods common to both exploratory research and qualitative research are discussed in Chapter 6.

Secondary Data Analysis The process of searching for and interpreting existing information relevant to the research topic is called *secondary data analysis*. Analyzing secondary data is almost always an important part of a marketing research project. Secondary information is widespread and readily available. Thanks to the Internet and today's sophisticated search engines such as Google, you can conduct a search for secondary information on virtually any topic quickly and efficiently. The Internet and your library offer access to large amounts of secondary data, which include information found on websites and in books, journals, magazines, special reports, bulletins, and newsletters. An analysis of secondary data is often the core of exploratory research.[6] A search of secondary data or information may come in many forms. Many executives subscribe to journals or trade publications for their particular industry. By reviewing these publications, they are constantly doing a form of exploratory research—looking for trends, innovations, information about current or potential customers and competitors, the general economy, and so on. As Marketing Research Insight 4.2 outlines, social media websites can be an excellent source of data for exploratory research. We devote part of Chapter 5 to analyzing secondary data and some of its sources.

For some examples of secondary data often used in marketing research, see www.secondarydata.com, a website developed by Decision Analyst, Inc.

Experience Surveys **Experience surveys** refer to gathering information from those thought to be knowledgeable on the issues relevant to the research problem. This technique is also known as the **key-informant technique**. In the technology field, a **lead-user survey** is used to acquire information from lead users of a new technology.[7] A manufacturer of a new building material that provides greater insulation at less cost may call a dozen contractors, describe the new material, and ask them how likely they would be to consider using it on their next building. In other examples, nurses might be interviewed about the needs of hospital patients, and elementary teachers might be surveyed to gather information about types of products that might be developed to help children learn. Experience surveys differ from surveys conducted as part of descriptive research in that there is usually no formal attempt to ensure that the survey results are representative of any defined group of subjects. Nevertheless, useful information can be gathered by this method of exploratory research.

Experience surveys refer to gathering information from those thought to be knowledgeable on the issues relevant to the research problem. Experience surveys may also be called *key-informant* or *lead-user surveys*.

Case Analysis A review of available information about one or more former situations to gain understanding of a current research problem with similar characteristics is called a **case analysis**. Research situations typically have at least some similarities to a past situation.[8]

A case analysis is a review of available information about one or more former situations to gain understanding of a current research problem with similar characteristics.

MARKETING RESEARCH INSIGHT 4.2 *Digital Marketing Research*

Exploring Social Media Data

Social media websites are a powerful source of data for exploratory research. By providing access to the unfettered opinions of consumers, social media platforms offer an instant way to gain background information for a problem, to define terms, to clarify problems and hypotheses, and to establish research priorities. Many companies are aware of the value of using social media websites to gain marketing insights, but there is so much information out there. How can analysts use social media data to acquire strong and actionable insights from consumers? Following are the steps for analyzing social media data.

Step 1: Develop a Problem Definition and Research Objectives

As stated in Chapter 3, developing focused research objectives is a vital step in the research process. This guideline holds particularly true for social media analysis, where a clear direction is needed to make sense of the copious amount of data. Limiting the focus to a defined topic and specific objectives will make the analysis more manageable. Still, to take full advantage of social media data analysis, the research objectives should also allow for an element of discovery. The data may lead to unexpected places.

Step 2: Identify Key Search Terms

The identification of the proper key search terms is a crucial step to the successful analysis of social media data. The process is often an iterative process, with broader searches being followed by searches using combinations of terms or newly discovered synonyms or tangential phrases. Obvious terms to start a search include the product's brand name, competitors' brand names, and the product class. More exploratory analyses might investigate activities, events, and emotions related to a brand.

Step 3: Identify Social Media Data Sources

Identification of the most useful data sources is another important step to social media data analysis. Online tools, such as TweetDeck and Scout Labs, can aid in this process. Still, these tools can miss some important types of social media platforms. Finding the most current and germane websites is a moving target, since social media–oriented data sources ebb and flow in popularity. Although this makes the task of identifying the best websites from which to gather data more difficult, it also means that new forms of exciting and relevant user-generated feedback are emerging on an ongoing basis and can be uncovered with a bit of persistence.

Knowing the best data sources to use is a very important step in social media data analysis.

Step 4: Organize Data

Some of the most important user-generated data will not necessarily be in the form of text. Photos, videos, artwork, literature, and other forms of data might provide new insights into product feedback. As a result, organization of the data should be flexible and allow for diverse forms of media. A number of commercial services (for example, HootSuite and Radian6) and software (for example, NVivo) are available to assist in this process, as well as free online tools (such as SocialMention and Google Alerts). Or researchers can take more of a do-it-yourself approach to organizing data to ensure versatility and comprehensiveness.

Step 5: Analyze Data

Once the social media data have been gathered and organized, the data should be analyzed. First, the researchers should review the data thoroughly. As with all research, insightful analysis depends on a comprehensive knowledge and understanding of the data. Second, the analysts should begin identifying key themes that emerge from the findings—for example, key beliefs, ideas, concepts, definitions, or behaviors. The data should then be compared and categorized.

Step 6: Present Findings

Following analysis of the data, the findings will be presented in an oral and written presentation, using concrete examples and illustrations. Here is where social media data really stand out. Quotes can be presented from Twitter, reviews, and blogs. Photos found online can illustrate exactly where, when, and how a consumer is using a product or service. Consumer-produced videos can demonstrate perceived advantages and disadvantages of products.

Step 7: Outline Limitations

When using social media data, it is as important as with other research methods to outline the limitations of the research. Explicitly stating the problems and gaps encountered when gathering and analyzing the data will help to provide a more complete understanding of the findings.

Step 8: Strategize

As with all research, the final and most important step of the analysis is to use the finding to develop research-based, actionable recommendations related to the research objectives. Then, based on the project's results, the next stage of research should be planned.

Source: Veeck, A. (2013, October). Beyond monitoring: Analyzing the content of social media data. *Quirk's Marketing Research Review,* 74–77.

Even when the research problem deals with a radically new product, some similar past experiences may be observed. For example, when Apple introduced the iPad, this new device may have seemed revolutionary. However, Apple could refer to its experience with introducing the iPhone in 2007 when planning the strategy for introducing its new tablet. Then, as Apple introduced successive versions of the iPad, the company could examine the cases of the introductions of previous versions of the iPad to learn from mistakes and successes at the product introduction stage.

Case analysis can be a particularly useful technique for developing strategies to prevent and manage crises, since, by definition, crises occur on rare occasions. For example, an incident of adulterated milk in China in 2008 that led to the death of six infants and the illness of hundreds of thousands of other babies has been studied to prevent other disasters from occurring through supply chain management.[9] The 2009–2010 recall of Toyota automobiles with acceleration pedals that were susceptible to sticking has been examined to develop best practices for companies to communicate product failures to their customers.[10]

Focus Groups *Focus groups* are small groups brought together and guided by a moderator through an unstructured, spontaneous discussion for the purpose of gaining information relevant to the research problem. (We cover focus groups extensively in Chapter 6.) Focus groups are one of the most widely used exploratory techniques to gain greater understanding of a current problem or to develop preliminary knowledge to guide in the design of descriptive or causal research. For example, in 2015 a series of focus groups was conducted by the National Football League (NFL) in St. Louis, Oakland, and San Diego as part of a wider study to determine how fans would react to losing the professional football team that is currently based in their cities.[11]

To conclude, exploratory research in some form should be used in almost every research project. Why? First, exploratory research, particularly secondary data analysis, can be conducted efficiently through online and library resources. Second, compared to collecting primary data, exploratory research is inexpensive. Finally, exploratory research can often provide information that meets the research objectives or can assist in gathering current information necessary to conduct either a descriptive or causal design. Therefore, few researchers embark on a research project without first beginning with exploratory research.

Descriptive research is undertaken to collect data to examine the characteristics of consumers and/or markets.

4-4 Descriptive Research

Descriptive research is undertaken to describe answers to questions of who, what, where, when, and how. When we wish to know *who* our customers are, *what* brands they buy and in what quantities, *where* they buy the brands, *when* they shop, and *how* they found out about our products, we turn to descriptive research. Descriptive research is also desirable when we wish to project a study's findings to a larger population. If a descriptive study's sample is representative, the findings may be used to predict some variable of interest such as sales.

CLASSIFICATION OF DESCRIPTIVE RESEARCH STUDIES

Two basic types of descriptive research studies are available to the marketing researcher: cross-sectional and longitudinal. **Cross-sectional studies** measure units from a sample of the population of interest at only one point in time. A study measuring your attitude toward adding a required internship course to your degree program, for example, would be a cross-sectional study. Your attitude toward the topic is measured at *one point in time*. Cross-sectional studies are prevalent in marketing research, outnumbering longitudinal studies and causal studies. Because cross-sectional studies are one-time measurements, they can be described as "snapshots" of the population.

As an example, many magazines survey a sample of their subscribers and ask them questions such as their age, occupation, income, and educational level. These sample data, taken at one point in time, are used to describe the readership of the magazine in terms of demographics. Cross-sectional studies normally are designed to represent the population of interest and employ fairly large sample sizes, so many cross-sectional studies are referred to as *sample surveys*.

Sample surveys are cross-sectional studies whose samples are drawn in such a way as to be representative of a specific population. Prior to important elections, many sample surveys ask likely voters: "If the election were held today, which candidate would you vote for?" Such survey results are often featured in the news because they attract a lot of attention. The survey samples are drawn so that the news media may report that the results are representative of the U.S. population and that the results are accurate within a certain margin of error (very frequently + or −3%). To be able to report on the accuracy of sample surveys, researchers must plan exactly how the population will be sampled and how many people will be surveyed. You will learn about different methods of conducting samples and how to calculate margin of error in Chapters 9 and 10.

Longitudinal studies repeatedly measure the same sample units of a population over a period of time. Because longitudinal studies involve multiple measurements, they can be described as "movies" of the population. Longitudinal studies are employed by most of the largest companies that use marketing research. To ensure the success of the longitudinal study, researchers must have access to the same members of a sample, called a panel, so as to take repeated measurements. **Panels** are samples of respondents who have agreed to provide information or answer questions at regular intervals. Maintaining a representative panel of respondents is a major undertaking.

Several commercial marketing research firms develop and maintain consumer panels for use in longitudinal studies. Typically, these firms attempt to select a sample that is representative of some population. Firms such as IRI and Nielsen have maintained panels consisting of hundreds of thousands of households for many years. In many cases these companies recruit panel members so that the demographic characteristics of the panel are proportionate to the demographic characteristics found in the total population according to Census Bureau statistics. Sometimes these panels will be balanced demographically not only to represent the United States but also to allow representation of various geographical regions. In this way, a client who wishes to get information from a panel of households in the Northwest can be assured that the panel is demographically matched to the total population in the states making up the northwestern region. Many companies maintain panels to target market segments such as "dog owners" or "kids." Paradigm Sample offers a panel of 18- to 34-year-old mobile users through its IdeaShifters panel. B2B panels are also available allowing researchers to target populations such as building contractors, supermarket owners, physicians, lawyers, university professors, or government workers.

Cross-sectional studies measure units from a sample of the population at one point in time.

Sample surveys are cross-sectional studies whose samples are designed in such a way as to be representative of a specific population at a pre-determined margin of error.

Longitudinal studies repeatedly measure the same sample units of a population over a period of time.

Panels are samples of respondents who have agreed to provide information or answer questions at regular intervals.

 **Active Learning**

Omnibus Surveys

Let's learn more about omnibus surveys! Go to www.greenbook.org. At the top left, locate "Greenbook Directory." Under "Research Services," select the drop-down menu, and then scroll down and click "Omnibus Surveys." Besides "consumers," what other types of samples may be accessed using omnibus surveys? Go to some of the firms and read what they have to say about omnibus surveys. How long does it take them to get results back to clients?

Continuous panels are samples of respondents who agree to answer the same questions at periodic intervals.

Discontinuous panels vary questions from one panel measurement to the next.

Discontinuous panels, or omnibus panels, are samples of respondents who answer different questions on a regular basis over a period of time.

There are two types of panels: continuous panels and discontinuous panels. **Continuous panels** ask panel members the same questions on each panel measurement. **Discontinuous panels** vary questions from one panel measurement to the next.[12] Continuous panel examples include many of the syndicated data panels that ask panel members to record their purchases using diaries or scanners. The essential point is that panel members are asked to record the *same* type of information (for example, grocery store purchases) on an ongoing basis.

Discontinuous panels are sometimes referred to as **omnibus panels**. (*Omnibus* means "including or covering many things or classes.") They may be used for a variety of purposes, and the information collected by a discontinuous panel varies from one panel measurement to the next. How longitudinal data are applied depends on the type of panel used to collect the data. Essentially, the discontinuous panel's primary usefulness is that it represents a large group—people, stores, or some other entity—and its members are agreeable to providing marketing research information. Discontinuous panels, like continuous panels, are also demographically matched to some larger entity, implying representativeness as well. Therefore, a marketer wanting to know how a large number of consumers, matched demographically to the total U.S. population, feel about two different product concepts may elect to utilize the services of an omnibus panel. The advantage of discontinuous (omnibus) panels is that they represent a group of persons who have made themselves available for research. In this way, then, discontinuous panels represent existing samples of consumers that may be quickly accessed for a wide variety of purposes.

The continuous panel is used quite differently. Usually, firms are interested in using data from continuous panels because they can gain insights into changes in consumers' attitudes and behaviors. For example, data from continuous panels can show how members of the panel switch brands from one time period to the next. Studies examining the extent to which consumers are loyal to one brand versus buying different brands are known as **brand-switching studies**. Such studies can be invaluable to brand managers because cross-sectional studies that show changes in market shares between several brands can be misleading. We will illustrate this in Tables 4.1 and 4.2. Table 4.1 shows the results of two separate surveys conducted

Brand-switching studies are studies that examine the extent that consumers are loyal to one brand.

TABLE 4.1   **Results of Two Cross-Sectional Studies "Which Brand of Chocolate Chip Cookie Did You Most Recently Purchase?"**

Brand	Cross-Sectional Survey 1	Cross-Sectional Survey 2
Famous Amos	100	75
Pepperidge Farm	200	200
Nabisco	200	225
Total Families	500	500

TABLE 4.2 Results of Two Waves of a Longitudinal Study "Which Brand of Chocolate Chip Cookie Did You Most Recently Purchase?"

Wave 1 Brand	Wave 2 Brand			
	Famous Amos	**Pepperidge Farm**	**Nabisco**	**Totals, Wave 1**
Famous Amos	50	50	0	100
Pepperidge Farm	25	150	25	200
Nabisco	0	0	200	200
Totals, Wave 2	75	200	225	

six months apart. Let's assume you are the brand manager for Famous Amos chocolate chip cookies. We can see that both studies surveyed 500 families who were purchasers of chocolate chip cookies. In survey 1 Famous Amos had 100 families, and the other two brands had 200 and 200 respectively. (Please note these numbers are for illustration only; they do not reflect the true market shares of these brands.) What can we learn as the brand manager from one cross-sectional study? We now know that we are about 20% of the market and that our two competitors have about equal shares, each about 40% of the market. Now, let's look at another sample of 500 other families six months later as shown in cross-sectional survey 2. What can we learn? First, we see that Famous Amos's share has dropped! A brand manager should be very concerned about a drop in market share. Who is the culprit? If we compare the two cross-sectional studies, we see that Pepperidge Farm stayed the same at 200 families, but Nabisco climbed to 225 families. It would be quite natural to assume that Nabisco was eroding the brand share of Famous Amos. In this case, the Famous Amos brand manager would start examining Nabisco's marketing mix during the last few months. Has the competitor changed package design? Has it stepped up its promotion? Is it providing retailers with incentives?

Now, let us take a look at a longitudinal study with two waves of measurements, again six months apart. We will assume that the results (total families purchasing each brand) are exactly the same as we have in our two cross-sectional studies. But what will be different is how each family changed. Remember, with a continuous panel in a longitudinal study we ask the same family the same question with each administration, or wave, of the study. Look at the results in Table 4.2.

Notice that the totals for Wave 1 (green) and Wave 2 (blue) are exactly the same as the totals for the two cross-sectional studies shown in Table 4.1. However, the value of longitudinal data is reflected in the tan area inside of Table 4.2. Of the 100 families who bought Famous Amos cookies in Wave 1, 50 of them stayed with Famous Amos in Wave 2. Another 50 families switched to Pepperidge Farm. None of the Famous Amos families switched to Nabisco. Of the 200 Pepperidge Farm families in Wave 1, 25 switched to Famous Amos, 150 stayed with Pepperidge Farm, and 25 switched to Nabisco. Finally, of the 200 Nabisco families in Wave 1, all 200 of them stayed with Nabisco in Wave 2. This shows us how competition is affecting our brand. Pepperidge Farm, not Nabisco, is interacting with our Famous Amos cookie brand. More detailed data allow us to arrive at a more valid conclusion than we reached by first only considering the cross-sectional studies. As this example illustrates, the value of longitudinal information using continuous panels is that it allows brand managers to explore the dynamics among competing brands.

Another use of longitudinal data is that of market tracking. *Tracking studies* are studies that involve the monitoring of the same variables of interest—such as market share or unit sales—over time. By tracking sales by SKU over time, managers can learn a great deal about what is happening in the marketplace. We discuss tracking studies in more depth in Chapter 5.

Market-tracking studies are studies that monitor the same variables of interest over time.

4-5 Causal Research

Causal research is used to measure causality in relationships, such as "if *x*, then *y*."

Causality is a relationship in which one or more variables affect one or more other variables.

Causal research is used to measure causality in relationships, such as "if *x*, then *y*." **Causality** is a condition in which one or more variables affect one or more other variables. When conducting causal research, "if–then" statements become our way of manipulating variables of interest. For example, if the thermostat is lowered, then the air will get cooler. If I drive my automobile at lower speeds, then my gasoline mileage will increase. If I spend more on advertising, then sales will rise. Marketing managers are always trying to determine what will cause a change in consumer satisfaction, a gain in market share, an increase in website visits, or an increase in sales.

Prior to launching its new aspartame-free diet soda in 2015, PepsiCo conducted two years of research, including testing involving thousands of consumers, and was confident that its formula would be accepted by consumers.[13] Nevertheless, shortly after the introduction of the formula, the ratio of negative to positive comments on social media about the new Diet Pepsi was worse than is usually found with new products.[14] Understanding what causes consumers to behave as they do is extremely difficult. Nevertheless, there is a high payoff in the marketplace for even partially understanding causal relationships. Causal relationships are examined through the use of experiments, which are special types of studies.

EXPERIMENTS

An experiment is a type of study in which one or more independent variables are manipulated to see how one or more dependent variables are affected, while also controlling the effects of additional extraneous variables.

Independent variables are variables over which the researcher has control *and* wishes to manipulate to measure the effect on the dependent variable.

Dependent variables are variables that are measured in response to changes in independent variables.

Extraneous variables are all of the variables other than the independent variables that may have an effect on the dependent variable.

An **experiment** is a type of study in which one or more independent variables are manipulated to see how one or more dependent variables are affected, while also controlling the effects of additional extraneous variables. **Independent variables** are variables over which the researcher has control *and* wishes to manipulate. Broadly speaking, you can think of the 4 Ps (product, price, promotion, and place) as independent variables. Some examples of independent variables are level of advertising expenditure, type of advertising appeal (humor, prestige), display location, placement of website ads, method of compensating salespersons, price, and type of product. **Dependent variables**, on the other hand, are variables that are measured in response to changes in independent variables. Common dependent variables include sales, market share, customer satisfaction, sales force turnover, time spent on site, unique net profits, and RONW (return on net worth). Certainly, marketers are interested in managing these variables. Because managers cannot change these variables directly, they attempt to change them through the manipulation of independent variables. To the extent that marketers can establish causal relationships between independent and dependent variables, they can enjoy some success in influencing the dependent variables. Consider an analogy familiar to students: If you want to change your GPA (dependent variable), you must change certain independent variables such as amount of time devoted to study, class attendance, devotion to reading your text, and listening habits in the lecture hall.

Extraneous variables are all of the variables other than the independent variables that may have an effect on the dependent variable. To illustrate, let's say you and your friend wanted to know if brand of gasoline (independent variable) affected gas mileage in automobiles (dependent variable). Your "experiment" consists of each of you filling up your two cars, one with Brand A, the other with Brand B. At the end of the week, you learn that Brand A achieved 18.6 miles per gallon and Brand B achieved 26.8 miles per gallon. Does Brand B cause better gas mileage than Brand A? Or could the difference in the dependent variable (gas mileage) be due to factors *other* than gasoline brand (independent variable)? Let's take a look at what these extraneous variables may be: (1) One car is an SUV, and the other is a small compact. (2) One car was driven mainly on the highway, and the other was driven in the city in heavy traffic. (3) One car has properly inflated tires, whereas the other car does not. All these extraneous variables could have affected the dependent variable in addition to the brand of gas used.

Let's look at another example. Imagine that a restaurant chain conducts an experiment to determine the effect of supplying nutritional information on menu items (independent variable) on restaurant sales (dependent variable).[15] Management has a record of restaurant sales without menu-supplied nutritional information and then changes the menus (manipulates the independent variable) to include the nutritional information and measures sales once again. The experiment is conducted in one of the chain's restaurants. Assume sales increased. Does this mean that if the chain changes the menu information, then sales will increase in all its restaurants? Might other extraneous variables have affected sales? Could the following two variables have affected the restaurant's sales? (1) The restaurant selected for the experiment is located in a high-income area in California known for health spas and workout gyms; and (2) just prior to changing the menus, the FDA announced a study that caloric content for the same type of food had wide variation depending on the restaurant (coffee ranges in calories from 80 to 800 per cup; hamburgers range from 250 to over 1,000).

An example of an experiment is examining if listing nutritional information on menu items affects restaurant sales.

© Lightspring/Shutterstock

Yes, the clientele for the restaurant selected for the experiment could be unique, and a new, highly publicized study about nutritional information from a respected source, the FDA, could certainly have had an effect on the acceptance of the new menu information. In fact, it could have helped create "buzz" or positive WOM (word-of-mouth) influence. Both of these possible influences are likely extraneous variables that have an effect on the dependent variable but are not defined as independent variables. As this example illustrates, it is difficult to isolate the effects of independent variables on dependent variables without controlling for the effects of the extraneous variables. Unfortunately, it is not easy to establish causal relationships, but it can be done. In the following section, we will see how the design of an experiment allows us to assess causality.

EXPERIMENTAL DESIGN

An **experimental design** is a procedure for devising an experimental setting so that a change in a dependent variable may be attributed solely to the change in an independent variable. In other words, experimental designs are procedures that allow experimenters to control for the effects on a dependent variable by any extraneous variable. In this way, the experimenter is assured that any change in the dependent variable was due only to the change in the independent variable.

Let's look at how experimental designs work. First, we list the symbols of experimental design:

O = The measurement of a dependent variable

X = The manipulation, or change, of an independent variable

R = Random assignment of subjects (e.g., consumers, stores) to experimental and control groups

E = Experimental effect—that is, the change in the dependent variable due to the independent variable

An experimental design is a procedure for devising an experimental setting so that a change in a dependent variable may be attributed solely to the change in an independent variable.

A pretest is a measurement of the dependent variable that is taken prior to changing the independent variable.

When a measurement of the dependent variable is taken *prior to* changing the independent variable, the measurement is sometimes called a **pretest**. When a measurement of the dependent variable is taken *after* changing the independent variable, the measurement is sometimes called a **posttest**.

A posttest is a measurement of the dependent variable that is taken after changing the independent variable.

Control of extraneous variables is typically achieved by the use of a second group of subjects, known as a control group. By **control group**, we mean a group whose subjects have not been exposed to the change in the independent variable. The **experimental group**, on the other hand, is the group that has been exposed to a change in the independent variable. We shall use the following experimental design to illustrate the importance of the control group.

A control group is a group whose subjects have not been exposed to the change in the independent variable.

An experimental group is a group that has been exposed to a change in the independent variable.

Before-After with Control Group The **before-after with control group** design may be achieved by randomly dividing subjects of the experiment into two groups: the control group and the experimental group. If we assume that our restaurant chain has 100 restaurants spread around the country, we could easily randomly divide them into two groups of 50 restaurants each. Management already has a pretest measurement of the dependent variable on both groups by virtue of knowing sales volume prior to changing the menus. Next, the independent variable, adding the nutritional information to the menus, is changed only in the experimental group (50 restaurants). Finally, after some time period, posttest measurements are taken of the dependent variable in both groups of restaurants. This design may be diagrammed as follows:

$$\text{Experimental group } (R) \quad O_1 \quad X \quad O_2$$
$$\text{Control group } (R) \qquad\qquad O_3 \qquad O_4$$

where

$$E = (O_2 - O_1) - (O_4 - O_3).$$

By randomly (R) dividing our 100 restaurants into two groups—50 in the experimental group and 50 in the control group—the groups should be equivalent. That is, both groups should be as similar as possible, each group having an equal number of restaurants in high-income, middle-income, and low-income areas, and an equal number of restaurants in locales favoring exercising and nutrition concerns. The average age of the restaurants should be equivalent, the average square footage should be equivalent, the average number of employees should be equivalent, and the average sales should be equivalent. In other words, randomization should yield two groups of restaurants that are *equivalent* in all respects. An experimenter should take whatever steps are necessary to meet this condition if he or she uses this design. There are other methods for gaining equivalency besides randomization. Matching on criteria thought to be important, for example, would aid in establishing equivalent groups. When randomization or matching on relevant criteria does not achieve equivalent groups, more complex experimental designs should be used.[16]

Looking back at our design, the R indicates that we have randomly divided our restaurants into two equal groups—one a control group, the other an experimental group. We also see that pretest measurements of our dependent variable, restaurant sales, were recorded for both groups of restaurants, as noted by O_1 and O_3. Next, we see by the X symbol that only in the experimental group of restaurants were the menus changed to add the nutritional information for the menu items. Finally, posttest measurements of the dependent variable were taken at the same time in both groups of restaurants, as noted by O_2 and O_4.

Now, what information can we gather from this experiment? First, we know that $(O_2 - O_1)$ tells us how much change occurred in our dependent variable during the time of the experiment. But was this difference due solely to our independent variable, X? No, $(O_2 - O_1)$ tells us how many dollars in sales may be attributed to (1) the change in menu information *and* (2) other extraneous variables, such as the FDA publicizing the wide variation in nutritional values obtained in restaurant meals or just that more people decided to eat in restaurants during this time interval. Now, let us look at what is measured by the differences in sales among our control restaurants $(O_4 - O_3)$. Because it cannot account for changes in restaurant sales due to a change in menu information (the menus were not changed), then any differences in sales as measured by $(O_4 - O_3)$ must be due to the influence of all extraneous variables on restaurant sales. Therefore, the *difference* between the experimental group and the control group, $(O_2 - O_1) - (O_4 - O_3)$, results in a measure of E, the "experimental effect."

We now know that if we change menu information, then restaurant sales will change by an amount equal to E. We have, by using a proper experimental design, made some progress at arriving at causality. However, we should point out here, though we have established causality, it did not come without cost and complexity. Notice our experiment went from changing menus in 1 restaurant to 50 restaurants, and our total experiment involved 100 restaurants!

Often organizations use A/B testing to determine which of two or more alternatives involved in marketing a product is better, such as two pricing levels, two types of packaging, or two different brand names. **A/B testing** is testing two alternatives (A and B) to see which one performs better. A/B testing is often used to compare website designs to determine which design is more effective. Website traffic can be split between design A and design B, with an important measure, such as sales or repeat visitors, compared between the two websites to determine which design is superior.

> A/B testing is testing two alternatives (A and B) to see which one performs better.

As we noted earlier, there are many other experimental designs, and of course, there are almost limitless applications of experimental designs to marketing problems. Although we have demonstrated how valuable experimentation can be in providing knowledge, we should not accept all experiments as being valid. How we assess the validity of experiments is the subject of our next section.

HOW VALID ARE EXPERIMENTS?

How can we assess the validity of an experiment? An experiment is valid if (1) the observed change in the dependent variable is, in fact, due to the independent variable, and (2) the results of the experiment apply to the "real world" outside the experimental setting.[17] Two forms of validity are used to assess the validity of an experiment: internal and external.

Internal validity is the extent to which a researcher can be certain that a change in the dependent variable is actually due to the independent variable. This is another way of asking if the proper experimental design was used and if it was implemented correctly. To illustrate an experiment that lacks internal validity, let us return to our change in menu information example. Recall that we took the effort to expand our restaurants to 100 and randomly divided them into two groups to ensure that the experimental group and control group were, in fact, equivalent. What would happen if the researcher did not ensure the equivalency of the groups? Our experimental effect, E, could be due to the differences in the two groups (e.g., one group of restaurants was located in areas with clientele sensitive to nutrition). This difference in the groups, then, would represent an extraneous variable that had been left uncontrolled. Such an experiment would lack internal validity because it could not be said that the change in the dependent variable was due solely to the change in the independent variable. Experiments lacking internal validity have little value because they produce misleading results.

> Internal validity in an experimental study is the extent to which the researcher is certain that a change in a dependent variable is actually due to the independent variable.

External validity refers to the extent that the relationship observed between the independent and dependent variables during the experiment is generalizable to the "real world."[18] In other words, can the results of the experiment be applied to all the restaurants in the chain? There are several threats to external validity. How representative is the sample of test units? Is this sample really representative of the population? Additionally, there exist many examples of the incorrect selection of sample units for testing purposes. For example, some executives, headquartered in large cities in cold winter climates, have been known to conduct "experiments" in warmer, tropical climes during the winter. Although the experiments they

> External validity refers to the extent to which a researcher can be certain that a relationship observed between independent and dependent variables during an experiment would occur under real-world conditions.

conduct may be internally valid, it is doubtful that the results will be generalizable to the total population.

Another threat to external validity is the artificiality of the experimental setting itself. To control as many variables as possible, some experimental settings are far removed from real-world conditions.[19] If an experiment is so contrived that it produces behavior that would not likely be found in the real world, then the experiment lacks external validity.

TYPES OF EXPERIMENTS

Laboratory experiments are those in which one or more independent variables are manipulated and measures of the dependent variable are taken in an artificial setting for the purpose of controlling all extraneous variables that may affect the dependent variable.

We can classify experiments into two broad classes: laboratory and field. **Laboratory experiments** are those in which one or more independent variables are manipulated and measures of the dependent variable are taken in a contrived, artificial setting for the purpose of controlling the many possible extraneous variables that may affect the dependent variable.

To illustrate, let us consider a study whereby subjects are invited to a theater and shown test ads, copy A or copy B, spliced into a TV pilot program. Why would a marketer want to use such an artificial laboratory setting? Such a setting is used to control for variables that could affect the purchase of products other than those in the test ads. By bringing consumers into an artificial laboratory setting, the experimenter is able to control many extraneous variables. For example, you have learned why it is important to have equivalent groups (the same kind of people watching copy A as those watching copy B commercials) in an experiment. By inviting preselected consumers to the TV pilot showing in a theater, the experimenter can match (on selected demographics) the consumers who view copy A with those who view copy B, thus ensuring that the two groups are equal. By having the consumers walk into an adjoining "store," the experimenter easily controls other factors such as the time between exposure to the ad copy and shopping, as well as the consumers being exposed to other advertising by competitive brands. As you have already learned, any one of these factors, left uncontrolled, could have an impact on the dependent variable. By controlling for these and other variables, the experimenter can be assured that any changes in the dependent variable were due solely to differences in the independent variable, ad copy A and ad copy B. Laboratory experiments, then, are desirable when the intent of the experiment is to achieve high levels of internal validity.

There are advantages to laboratory experiments. First, they allow the researcher to control for the effects of extraneous variables. Second, compared to field experiments, lab experiments may be conducted quickly and with less expense. The disadvantage of laboratory experiments is the lack of a natural setting and, therefore, the concern that the findings do not generalize to the real world.

Field experiments are those in which the independent variables are manipulated and the measurements of the dependent variable are taken in their natural setting.

Field experiments are those in which the independent variables are manipulated and the measurements of the dependent variable are made on test units in their natural setting. Many marketing experiments are conducted in natural settings, such as in supermarkets, malls, retail stores, and consumers' homes. Let us assume that a marketing manager conducts a *laboratory* experiment to test the differences between ad copy A, the company's existing ad copy, and new ad copy B. The results of the laboratory experiment indicate that copy B is far superior to the company's present ad copy A. But, before spending the money to use the new copy, the manager wants to know if ad copy B will really create increased sales in the real world. She elects to actually run the new ad copy in Erie, Pennsylvania, a city noted as being representative of the average characteristics of the U.S. population. By conducting this study in the field, the marketing manager will have greater confidence that the results of the study will actually hold up in other real-world settings. Note, however, that even if an experiment is conducted in a naturalistic field setting to enhance external validity, the experiment is invalid if it does not also have internal validity.

The primary advantage of the field experiment is that of conducting the study in a naturalistic setting, thus increasing the likelihood that the study's findings will also hold true in the real world. Field experiments, however, are expensive and time consuming. Also, the experimenter must always be alert to the impact of extraneous variables, which are difficult to control in the natural settings of field experimentation.

The example we just cited of using Erie, Pennsylvania, for a field experiment would be called a "test market." Much of the experimentation in marketing, conducted as field experiments, is known as *test marketing,* which is discussed in the following section.

4-6   Test Marketing

Test marketing is the phrase commonly used to indicate an experiment, study, or test that is conducted in a field setting. Companies may use one or several test-market cities, which are selected geographical areas in which to conduct the test. There are two broad classes of uses of test markets: (1) to test the sales potential for a new product or service, and (2) to test variations in the marketing mix for a product or service.[20]

Although test markets are very expensive and time consuming, the costs of introducing a new product on a national or regional basis routinely amount to millions of dollars. The costs of the test market are then justified if the results of the test market can improve a product's chances of success. Sometimes the test market identifies a failure early on and saves the company huge losses. Other times a product tests well in a test market and then is introduced more widely. For example, Taco Bell tested a food item called a Quesalupa—a cross between a quesadilla and a chalupa—for two months in 2015 in 36 Toledo-area stores. The Quesalupa tested well in Toledo, so Taco Bell made the decision to launch the product nationally.[21]

Test markets are conducted not only to measure sales potential for a new product but also to measure consumer and dealer reactions to other marketing-mix variables. A firm may use only department stores to distribute the product in one test-market city and only specialty stores in another test-market city to gain some information on the best way to distribute the product. Companies can also test media usage, pricing, sales promotions, and so on through test markets. Products and services in both the consumer (B2C) and industrial (B2B) markets may be test marketed. Marketing Research Insight 4.3 describes the workings of a B2C test market in Germany.

TYPES OF TEST MARKETS

Test markets can be classified into four types: standard, controlled, electronic, and simulated.[22] Each is detailed in the following sections.

Standard Test Market   The **standard test market** is one in which the firm tests the product or marketing-mix variables through the company's normal distribution channels. A disadvantage of this type of test market is that competitors are immediately aware of the new product or service. However, standard test markets are good indicators as to how the product will actually perform because they are conducted in real settings.

Controlled Test Markets   **Controlled test markets** are conducted by outside research firms that guarantee distribution of the product through prespecified types and numbers of distributors. Companies specializing in providing this service provide dollar incentives for distributors to provide them with guaranteed shelf space. Controlled test markets offer an alternative to the company that wishes to gain fast access to a distribution system set up for test-market purposes. The disadvantage is that this distribution network may or may not properly represent the firm's actual distribution system.

Test marketing is conducting an experiment or study in a field setting to evaluate a new product or service or other elements of the marketing mix.

Test markets are classified into four types: standard, controlled, electronic, and simulated.

A standard test market is one in which the firm tests the product or marketing-mix variables through the company's normal distribution channels.

A controlled test market is one that is conducted by outside research firms that guarantee distribution of the product through prespecified types and numbers of distributors.

MARKETING RESEARCH INSIGHT 4.3   *Practical Application*

Looking over the Average German Consumer's Shoulder

The Average German Consumer

Hassloch, Germany, has been a permanent product test market for GfK, a marketing research institute, since 1986. Hassloch is considered to be representative of Germany in terms of its age distribution, population structure, buying power, and so on. Its geographic location allows it to have a unique combination of rural and urban lifestyles. All this makes the village an ideal market to test new products and to take important marketing decisions that are relevant for the entire German market.

The Mechanics

Seven supermarkets are involved in this project. Out of the total of 12,400 households, 3,400 are part of the panel and have been given a household card that has a chip. There are no questionnaires involved, and people taking part only use their smartcards at the time of check-out as every purchase is recorded. The 10 to 15 products that are tested in the select supermarkets are not disclosed. These products are placed on the shelves along with the rest of the supermarket's product range as a measure to make sure that the shopping conditions are genuine. GfK uses a system called GfK BehaviorScan to record this shopping behavior. In addition, GfK tests advertising by showing special television commercials to 2,500 households. By comparing the purchasing behavior of the participants and the control group, which consists of those who are exposed to the usual advertisements, GfK tries to determine whether the advertising campaign is working or not.

GfK tests new products in Hassloch to see if they will work in the German market.

The Impact

These tests have helped companies to gauge the sales potential of new products. Products like Pringles potato crisps, Dove soap, and Fairy Ultra dishwasher have been successfully tested and have worked in the German market. There are also tests that involve other elements of the marketing mix. For example, SO1, a marketing consulting company based in Berlin, tested a new type of discount coupon program to understand its effect on consumers' purchase behavior. The aim was to be able to offer discounts based on the shopping behavior of each consumer. Procter & Gamble tested two different TV commercials for their Always Ultra pads, and one of the commercials helped in doubling the sales figures.

Sources: Weichert, U. (2015, May 11). Jeder hat seinen Preis. *Technology Review*. Retrieved from http://www.heise.de/tr/artikel/Jeder-hat-seinen-Preis-2599605 .html; Die Welt. (2015, February 17). Neue Produkte auf dem Testmarkt in der Provinz. Retrieved from http://www.welt.de/regionales/rheinland-pfalz-saarland/ article137525493/Neue-Produkte-auf-dem-Testmarkt-in-der-Provinz.html; Waldherr, G. (2014, February). Das ist Deutschland. *Brandeins Wirtschaftsmagazin*. Retrieved from http://www.brandeins.de/archiv/2014/werbung/das-ist-deutschland/; Braun, C. (2015, December). *Goethe-Institute*. Retrieved from https://www.goethe.de/en/ kul/mol/20677297.html.

An electronic test market is one in which a panel of consumers has agreed to carry identification cards that each consumer presents when buying goods and services.

Electronic Test Markets **Electronic test markets** are those in which a panel of consumers has agreed to carry identification cards that each consumer presents when buying goods and services. These tests are conducted only in a small number of cities in which local retailers have agreed to participate. The advantage of the card is that as consumers buy (or do not buy) the test product, demographic information on the consumers is automatically recorded. In some cases, firms offering electronic test markets may also have the ability to link media viewing habits to panel members as well. In this way, firms using the electronic test market also know how different elements of the promotional mix affect purchases of the new product. Obviously, the electronic test market offers speed, greater confidentiality, and less cost than standard and controlled test markets. However, the disadvantage is that the test market is one more step removed from the real market.[23]

Simulated Test Markets **Simulated test markets (STMs)** are those in which a limited amount of data on consumer response to a new product is fed into a model containing certain assumptions regarding planned marketing programs, which generates likely product sales volume.[24] There are many advantages to STMs. They are much faster and only cost 5% to 10% of the cost of a standard test market. STMs are confidential; competitors are less likely to know about the test. The primary disadvantage is that STMs are not as accurate as full-scale test markets, as they are dependent on the assumptions built into the models.[25]

A simulated test market (STM) is one in which a limited amount of data on consumer response to a new product is fed into a model containing certain assumptions regarding planned marketing programs, which generates likely product sales volume.

SELECTING TEST-MARKET CITIES

Three criteria are useful for selecting test-market cities: **representativeness, degree of isolation**, and **ability to control distribution and promotion**. Because one of the major reasons for conducting a test market is to achieve external validity, the test-market city should be representative of the marketing territory in which the product will ultimately be distributed. Consequently, a great deal of effort is expended to locate the "ideal" city in terms of comparability with characteristics of the total U.S. (or any national) population. The "ideal" city is, of course, the city whose demographic characteristics most closely match the desired total market. For instance, R. J. Reynolds chose Chattanooga, Tennessee, to test-market its Eclipse "smokeless" cigarette because Chattanooga has a higher proportion of smokers than most cities, and R. J. Reynolds needed to test Eclipse with smokers.[26]

Marketing Research on YouTube™ To learn about McDonald's long process for testing products, go to **www.youtube.com** and type in "McDonald's Test Kitchen: Where Fast Food Is Born."

The ability to control distribution and promotion depends on a number of factors. Are distributors in the city available and willing to cooperate? If not, is a controlled-test-market service company available for the city? Will the media in the city have the facilities to accommodate your test-market needs? At what costs? All of these factors must be considered before selecting the test city. Fortunately, because city governments often consider it desirable to have test markets conducted in their city because it brings in additional revenues, they and local media typically provide a great deal of information about their city to prospective test marketers.

Three criteria useful for selecting test-market cities are representativeness, degree of isolation, and ability to control distribution and promotion.

PROS AND CONS OF TEST MARKETING

The advantages of test marketing are straightforward. Testing product acceptability and marketing-mix variables in a field setting provides the best information possible to the decision maker prior to actually going into full-scale marketing of the product. Test marketing allows for the most accurate method of forecasting future sales, and it allows firms the opportunity to pretest marketing-mix variables. On the downside, first, test markets do not yield infallible results. Second, competitors may intentionally try to sabotage test markets. For example, firms may flood a test market with sales promotions if they know a competitor is test-marketing a product.[27] Another problem with test markets is their cost. The costs of test markets involving several test cities and various forms of promotion can be extremely expensive. Third, test markets bring about exposure of the product to the competition. Competitors get the opportunity to examine product prototypes and to see the planned marketing strategy for the new product via the test market.

Finally, test markets may create ethical problems. Companies routinely report test-marketing results to the press, which allows them access to premarket publicity. But are negatives found in the test market always reported, or do we hear only the good news? Companies eager to get good publicity may select test-market cities that they feel will return favorable results. Perhaps the company already has a strong brand and market power in the market. Is this method of getting publicity ethical? There have been efforts to make reporting of test markets more candid.[28]

Summary

Research design refers to a master plan that specifies the methods that will be used to collect and analyze the information needed for a research project. There are three general types of research designs: exploratory, descriptive, and causal. The significance of studying research design is that, by matching the research objective with the appropriate research design, a host of research decisions may be predetermined. Therefore, a research design serves as a "blueprint" for researchers. Research designs are not carried out in a particular order; in fact, some projects may require only one form of research. But research is often an iterative process in which initial research indicates the need for additional studies, often of a different design.

Researchers are often much more knowledgeable of the marketing research process than managers. This imbalance of knowledge, which is not unique to marketing research, may lead to serious ethical issues. Ethical codes and standards developed by professional organizations prohibit such practices as designing research that is much more complex and expensive than needed.

Selecting the appropriate research design depends, to a large extent, on the research objectives and existing information about the problem. If very little is known, exploratory research is appropriate. Exploratory research is unstructured, informal research undertaken to gain background information; it is helpful for more clearly defining the research problem. Exploratory research is used in a number of situations: to obtain background information, to define terms, to clarify problems and hypotheses, and to establish research priorities. Reviewing existing literature, surveying individuals knowledgeable in the area to be investigated, relying on former similar case situations, and conducting focus groups are methods of conducting exploratory research. Exploratory research should almost always be used because it is fast and inexpensive; sometimes it resolves the research objective or is helpful in carrying out descriptive or causal research.

If concepts and terms are already known and the research objective is to describe and measure phenomena, then descriptive research is appropriate. Descriptive research is undertaken to measure the characteristics of consumers and/or markets and answers the questions of who, what, where, when, and how. Descriptive studies may be conducted at one point in time (cross-sectional study), or several measurements may be made on the same sample at different points in time (longitudinal study). Longitudinal studies are often conducted using panels. Panels represent sample units who have agreed to answer questions at periodic intervals. Continuous panels are longitudinal studies in which sample units are asked the same questions repeatedly. Brand-switching tables may be prepared based on data from continuous panels. Market-tracking studies may be conducted using data from continuous panels.

The second type of panel used in longitudinal research is the discontinuous panel. Discontinuous panels, sometimes called omnibus panels, are those in which the sample units are asked different questions each time they are surveyed. The main advantage of the discontinuous panel is that research firms have a large sample of persons who are willing to answer whatever questions they are asked.

Causal research is used to measure cause-and-effect relationships such as "if x, then y." Causal relationships may be discovered only through special studies called experiments. Experiments allow us to determine the effects of a variable, known as an independent variable, on another variable, known as a dependent variable. Experimental designs are necessary to ensure that the effect we observe in our dependent variable is due to our independent variable and not to other variables known as extraneous variables. The validity of experiments may be assessed by examining internal validity and external validity. Laboratory experiments are particularly useful for achieving internal validity, whereas field experiments are better suited for achieving external validity.

Test marketing is a form of field experimentation. Various types of test markets exist (standard, controlled, electronic, and simulated). Although test markets garner much useful information, they are expensive and not infallible. Test-market cities are selected on the basis of their representativeness, isolation, and the degree to which market variables such as distribution and promotion may be controlled.

Key Terms

Research design (p. 92)
Exploratory research (p. 94)
Experience surveys (p. 96)
Key-informant technique (p. 96)
Lead-user survey (p. 96)
Case analysis (p. 96)
Descriptive research (p. 98)
Cross-sectional studies (p. 99)
Sample surveys (p. 99)
Longitudinal studies (p. 99)
Panels (p. 99)
Continuous panels (p. 100)
Discontinuous panels (p. 100)
Omnibus panels (p. 100)
Brand-switching studies (p. 100)

Causal research (p. 102)
Causality (p. 102)
Experiment (p. 102)
Independent variables (p. 102)
Dependent variables (p. 102)
Extraneous variables (p. 102)
Experimental design (p. 103)
Pretest (p. 104)
Posttest (p. 104)
Control group (p. 104)
Experimental group (p. 104)
Before-after with control
  group (p. 104)
A/B testing (p. 105)
Internal validity (p. 105)

External validity (p. 105)
Laboratory experiments (p. 106)
Field experiments (p. 106)
Test marketing (p. 107)
Standard test market (p. 107)
Controlled test markets (p. 107)
Electronic test markets (p. 108)
Simulated test markets (STMs)
  (p. 109)
Representativeness (p. 109)
Degree of isolation (p. 109)
Ability to control distribution and
  promotion (p. 109)

Review Questions/Applications

4-1. What is research design?

4-2. Explain why it is important for marketing researchers to be knowledgeable of research design.

4-3. Discuss how research design can lead to ethically sensitive situations.

4-4. When might an organization use exploratory research?

4-5. In which type of research design would a lead-user survey be used?

4-6. Why do sample surveys have predetermined margins of error?

4-7. In what situation would a continuous panel be more suitable than a discontinuous panel? In what situation would a discontinuous panel be more suitable than a continuous panel?

4-8. What type of panel is an omnibus panel?

4-9. Explain why studies of the "if–then" variety are considered to be causal studies.

4-10. Define each of the following types of variables and give an example of each in an experiment designed to determine the effects of an advertising campaign: independent, dependent, extraneous, control group, and experimental group.

4-11. Explain the two types of validity in experimentation and also explain why different types of experiments

are better suited for addressing one type of validity versus another.

4-12. Distinguish among the various types of test marketing.

4-13. A newly established noodle house has suffered low sales lately. The owner of the noodle house wants to conduct research to collect information that will help him solve the problem at hand and design a workable strategy. Explain how the three types of research designs can be used in this case.

4-14. Can you identify research problems that might be addressed through a search of social media websites? What type of research design would you recommend for these problems?

4-15. Design an experiment. Select an independent variable and a dependent variable. What are some possible extraneous variables that may cause problems? Explain how you would control for the effects these variables may have on your dependent variable. Is your experiment a valid one?

4-16. Nan-Clean is a newly developed cleaning liquid for milk bottles that uses special enzymes to remove dirt effectively. Nan-Clean has been positioned as a product that is made of natural ingredients and is thus a more effective cleaning liquid than the other competing brand in the market. Design an experiment that compares Nan-Clean to the leading brand to determine which brand consumers consider more effective. Explain how the experiment can be conducted and assess its validity.

4-17. Artia Hunt is the CEO of a successful chain of coffee shops in the Midwest. Ms. Hunt would like to add a small selection of pastries to the current food offerings at her coffee shops. You have been hired to conduct an exploratory study using social media sources to develop an initial list of the types of pastries that should be considered for this new initiative. Based on Marketing Research Insight 4.2, outline the steps you will use to conduct this project and present the results of your research to Ms. Hunt.

4-18. Active-Ingredients, a company supplying baking ingredients to major hypermarkets, is facing intense competition from many local and foreign brands. Active-Ingredients is thinking of using a television set as a point-of-sale (POS) display at selected hypermarkets to advertise the different ingredients they are selling and demonstrate different ways of baking using their ingredients. Design an experiment that determines whether the installation of the television set next to the advertised products increases the sales of Active-Ingredients' products in the selected hypermarkets. Identify and diagram the experiment. Explain how the experiment is to be conducted and assess the validity of the experiment.

4-19. SplitScreen is a marketing research company that tests television advertisements. SplitScreen has an agreement with a cable television company in a medium-sized city in Iowa. The cable company can send up to four different television ads simultaneously to different households. SplitScreen also has agreements with three of the largest grocery store chains, which will provide scanner data to SplitScreen. About 25% of the residents have SplitScreen scan cards that are scanned when items are bought at the grocery store and that allow SplitScreen to identify who bought which grocery products. For allowing SplitScreen access to their television hookups and their grocery-purchase information, residents receive bonus points that can be used to buy products in a special points catalog. Identify and diagram an experimental design possible using the SplitScreen system. Assess the internal and external validity of SplitScreen's system.

CASE 4.1

Memos from a Researcher[29]

John Daniel, a researcher at Georgia Metro Research, made the following notes about several of his clients to you, a newly hired trainee who has just graduated from college:

Client A is a consumer packaged goods manufacturer with a well-established brand name. The client has focused on manufacturing and distribution for years while the marketing program has been set on "auto pilot." All had worked fine, though there was a hint of emerging problems when, in the preceding year, market share had fallen slightly. Now, our client has just reviewed the current market share report and notices that over the previous 12 months, the company's share has gradually eroded 15%. When market share falls, clients are eager to learn why and to take corrective action. In these situations we know immediately the problem is that we don't know what the problem is. There are many possible causes for this slippage. We need to determine the research design needed.

Second, Client B is a manufacturer of several baked goods products sold in grocery stores throughout the country. Marketing is divided into five regional divisions in the United States. The five divisions have had total autonomy over their advertising, though all of them have used TV advertising almost exclusively. Each division has tried several different TV ad campaigns; some were thought to be successful and others not as successful, but no one had ever formally evaluated the ad expenditures. A new marketing VP now wants to evaluate the advertising. She's interested in knowing not only the sales of the client's products sold during the different campaigns but also what happened to sales of competitors' brands. In this case, the client needs us to *describe* sales by SKU in the client's product category for each TV market and for each time period associated with each ad campaign. What research design do you recommend?

Finally, Client C is in a very competitive category with equal market share of the top three brands. Our client is convinced that it has changed every marketing-mix variable possible except for package design. Since the three competitive brands are typically displayed side-by-side, Client C wants us to determine what factors of package design (e.g., size, shape, color, texture) cause an increase in awareness, preference for, and intention to buy the brand. What do you recommend for the appropriate research design?

1. Describe what research design you would recommend for each client.
2. For each research design you selected for the three clients, discuss *why* you believe your choice of design is the correct choice.

5

Secondary Data and Packaged Information

"WHERE WE ARE"

1 Establish the need for marketing research.
2 Define the problem.
3 Establish research objectives.
4 Determine research design.
5 Identify information types and sources.
6 Determine methods of accessing data.
7 Design data collection forms.
8 Determine the sample plan and size.
9 Collect data.
10 Analyze data.
11 Prepare and present the final research report.

Hootsuite: Social Media Monitoring: Your Biggest Missed Opportunity?

Kristina Cisnero, Online Strategist, Hootsuite.

People are talking about businesses online right now. It could be in a positive way or a negative way, or they could just have a question. Regardless of how or why it happens, with social media you have an opportunity to listen, learn, and engage in those conversations.

Social media monitoring (also known as social listening) is all about gaining unique insight into customers, competitors, and industry influencers. By monitoring what people are saying on social media about business and the issues that affect it, firms can build a better relationship with their customers, get a leg up on their competitors, and improve their ROI.

Three Ways to Get the Most Out of Social Media Monitoring

1. ACQUIRE CUSTOMER KNOWLEDGE

A great way to obtain qualitative information about customers is through social media monitoring. Here are the kinds of insights you can gain by listening to customers on social media:

- The prevailing sentiment around brands and products
- The features or products customers are looking for from companies
- How to solve customers' problems

To get started on monitoring social media, you will need to have a social media monitoring tool. Once you're all set up, some examples of social media monitoring tactics you can use include the following:

- Monitor anyone mentioning a company's Twitter handle
- Create search streams for Twitter, Facebook, Google+, and Instagram to listen to people mentioning companies with positive or negative words or hashtags
- Start listening to customers (or future customers)

Visit Hootsuite at www.hootsuite.com.

2. GAIN A COMPETITIVE ADVANTAGE

Social media monitoring can also give you key information on competitors. This kind of intel will allow you to make strategic business decisions to always stay ahead of the competition.

To listen to what people are saying about competitors, use the tactics described earlier, but replace a business name with competitors' names as well as any of their product names. Social media marketing isn't all about promoting products. By solving people's problems before anyone else can, firms can gain new customers and also show current customers that they're there to help.

3. MONITOR BUSINESS INFLUENCERS

Most businesspeople who are savvy about using social media know it's important to listen to what customers and competitors are saying, but there's one group many leave out of their social media strategies: influencers. For businesses to be innovative and stay ahead of the curve, it is also important to listen to what thought leaders in their industry are saying.

Tools like the Hootsuite Syndicator can be used to follow influential executives, bloggers, and analysts on Twitter, Facebook, LinkedIn, and Google+ and see what they are posting on their websites. By doing this, companies can predict trends in their industry, position their company as an innovator, and improve their business.

—*Kristina Cisnero*

Source: Text and photos courtesy of Kristina Cisnero and Hootsuite.

A major reason that marketing research has never been a more exciting field is the new types of data that are now available for analysis. Grouped under the umbrella term *big data*, information is available from more sources than ever before—from government statistics to sensor data to tracking studies. As Kristina Cisnero from Hootsuite points out in the introduction, social media platforms are replete with insights about consumers and businesses.

You live in a world where secondary data are readily available and easily accessed. This chapter explores how secondary data are used, how we classify different types of data, what advantages and disadvantages such information sources offer, and where marketing researchers can find significant sources of secondary data. In addition, we introduce another type of information we call *packaged information* and examine its applications in marketing research. We end with a discussion of two powerful forms of digital data: social media data and the Internet of Things. The types of data and tools associated with managing data are changing quickly, and the more you keep abreast of these changes, the better equipped you will be to succeed in any professional position. As this chapter suggests, researchers who can combine data management and analysis skills with marketing knowledge are in great demand.

5-1 Big Data

Big data refers to large amounts of data from multiple sources.

Big data can be defined simply as large amounts of data from multiple sources. The term *big data* has been popularized in recent years in response to the numerous types and huge amounts of data to which companies now have access in real time. The phrase is often used to indicate alarm and apprehension about the enormous—and multiplying—amounts of data that are being created on an ongoing basis.[1] The *Wall Street Journal* estimates that in the 1950s, the insurance company John Hancock Mutual Life was one of the top storehouses of information, with a total of about 600 megabytes of data. Compare this to the 2010s, during which Facebook stores an estimated 100 additional petabytes daily.[2] The 2014 GreenBook Research Industry Trends Report (GRIT) survey found that managing big data is the number-one issue facing the marketing research industry.[3]

Sources of data can originate from many places, including from companies, sensors, retailers, trade organizations, governments, publishers, and social media. These data take many forms, both qualitative and quantitative, including text, photos, videos, business transactions, research data, and many other types of data. There is simply too much data available for any one company to exhaustively gather, store, analyze, and report. Decisions must be made about what data to collect and how to analyze the data to find trends, patterns, and relationships among data from multiple sources. The advent of big data has created great challenges for marketing researchers. Effective use of multiple sources of data requires having the resources and talent available to retrieve, store, integrate, analyze, and report the data.

Access to big data also creates great opportunities. Proper management of big data has the potential to increase productivity for companies significantly. To illustrate, Marketing Research Insight 5.1 focuses on how the tennis industry is using analysis of big data to improve match performance and spectator experience.

Given the large amounts of data available, researchers need to be strategic about their use. The optimal use of big data begins by following the research steps outlined in Chapter 3. First, researchers must be sure that the problem statement and research objectives have been carefully defined. You should never begin a data analysis project without knowing what the ultimate goals are. Next, researchers must decide what data are needed to solve the problem and reach the objective. And, finally, researchers must determine if they need to collect the data themselves or if the data already exist. Secondary data that already exist and have been gathered by somebody else are the focus of this chapter. The following section will clarify the differences between primary and secondary data.

Primary data refer to information that is developed or gathered by the researcher specifically for the research project at hand.

Secondary data have previously been gathered by someone other than the researcher and/or for some other purpose than the research project at hand.

5-2 Primary Versus Secondary Data

Data needed for marketing management decisions can be grouped into two types: primary and secondary. **Primary data** refers to information that is developed or gathered by the researcher specifically for the research project at hand. **Secondary data** have previously been gathered by someone other than the researcher and/or for some other purpose than the research project at hand. In this chapter we discuss secondary data in a form we call packaged information. After this chapter, much of the remainder of this text is devoted to teaching you how to collect and analyze primary data.

MARKETING RESEARCH INSIGHT 5.1 *Practical Application*

Big Data Shapes Tennis

Tennis has been a bastion of tradition for many centuries. Traditionalists view it as a one-on-one game in which coaches should not be allowed to intervene during a match. The player's approach and coach's approach have traditionally been guided by experience rather than data. However, in the last few years, bodies governing the sport of tennis have been re-evaluating this view. They have started adopting data analytics tools by using state-of-the-art equipment to make tennis matches more competitive and the spectator experience more exciting.

Women's Tennis Association and SAP

In 2015, SAP and the Women's Tennis Association (WTA) revolutionized on-court coaching possibilities by giving coaches a tablet that provides real-time data and which can be used to analyze the player's performance during a live match. The tablets can display real-time data from the official electronic scoring system as well as "Hawk-Eye," a ball-tracking system that is used in over 80 tennis tournaments worldwide. With this technology in hand, coaches can base their instructions on performance data like serve direction, shot placement, and techniques used by the opponent. Players are allowed to use the data during practice, helping them to further develop their performance and game strategies for future matches.

Wimbledon and IBM

The Championships, Wimbledon—the oldest and most prestigious Grand Slam tennis tournament in the world—utilizes data analytics in order to increase its fan base and fan community engagement. The IBM SlamTracker provides real-time match statistics and in-depth analysis of the game to the spectators. Users around the world can access this on Wimbledon's official website, where they are provided with real-time match data in a highly visual and compact style. What also appeals to the fans is that the system provides predictions on how the matches will develop by digging into eight years of Grand Slam's historical data.

Wimbledon also uses IBM Streams, which is a tool that compares live match data with each player's previous record at Wimbledon and automatically notifies the content team of the All England Lawn Tennis and Croquet Club (AELTC), the organizer of the Grand Slam tennis tournament, whenever a new record is set or is about to be set. This allows Wimbledon officials to break news faster than ever before, improve the broadcasting content, and drive greater fan engagement. Furthermore, the AELTC's team monitors social media conversations and tailors the content on its website and social media accordingly in order to improve the experience of its fan base across the world.

Wimbledon uses big data to make matches more competitive and to improve spectator experience.

Sources: Perrotta, T. (2015, August 4). Tennis gets hip to this whole "stats" thing. *Wall Street Journal.* Retrieved from http://www.wsj.com/articles/tennis-gets-hip-to-this-whole-stats-thing-1438715814; SAP News (2014, October 21). SAP and WTA transform women's tennis with new on-court coaching technology platform. Retrieved from http://news.sap.com/sap-and-wta-transform-womens-tennis-new-court-coaching-technology-platform/; Tabbitt, S. (2013, October 31). It's an ace: IBM SlamTracker lights up Wimbledon. *The Telegraph.* Retrieved from http://www.telegraph.co.uk/sponsored/sport/rugby-trytracker/10410268/slamtracker-wimbledon-tennis.html; IBM (2016, January 11). Wimbledon 2015, Real-time analytics helps share the moments that matter with tennis fans worldwide. Retrieved from http://www-03.ibm.com/software/businesscasestudies/bn/en/corp?synkey=X289813W52111E44; Baldwin, C. (2014, June 17). Wimbledon to analyse social interactions at tennis championship. *Computer Weekly.* Retrieved from http://www.computerweekly.com/news/2240222797/Wimbledon-to-analyse-social-interactions-during-tennis-championship.

As commercial firms, government agencies, or community service organizations conduct surveys, record transactions, or conduct business activities, they are creating a written record of these activities. When consumers register their automobiles, interact on social media platforms, make a purchase in a store, or search for a product online, this information is stored. If the information is made available for other purposes, it becomes secondary data. The sources of secondary data have grown greatly in recent years.

USES OF SECONDARY DATA

There are so many uses of secondary data that it is rare for a marketing research project to be conducted without including some of this information. Certain projects may be based exclusively on secondary data. The applications of secondary data range from predicting broad changes in a region's "way of life" to specific applications, such as selecting a street address location for a new car wash. Suggested applications for secondary data include forecasting economic trends analyzing the competition, choosing international markets to enter, understanding consumer concerns during a crisis situation, and many others. Secondary data might provide marketers with the information about demographics that they need to help forecast the size of the market in a newly proposed market territory.

A researcher may use secondary data to determine the population and growth rate in almost any geographical area. Government agencies often use secondary data to guide public policy decisions. For example, the Department of Education needs to know how many five-year-olds will enter the public school system each year. Health care planners need to know how many senior citizens will be eligible for Medicare during the next decade. Sometimes secondary data can be used to evaluate market performance. For example, since gasoline and fuel taxes collected per gallon are available in public records, petroleum marketers can easily determine the volume of fuels consumed in a county, thus making market share calculations easy and reliable. Articles are written on virtually every topic, and this storehouse of secondary data is available to marketers who want to understand a topic more thoroughly.

A wealth of secondary data is available concerning the lifestyles and purchasing habits of demographic groups. Because the people in these demographic groups tend to make similar purchases and have similar attitudes, they have been scrutinized by marketers. For example, one important means of analyzing people is by age. Age groups include the Baby Boomers (born between 1946 and 1964[4]), Generation X (born between about 1965 and 1979), and the Millennials or Generation Y (born between about 1977 and 1994). Born in 1995 or later, those in Generation Z are already having a large impact on the market, not only through their own technologically savvy habits but also through their influence on their families' meals, clothes, and electronic and entertainment purchases.[5] The demographic "grandparents" represents one-fourth of the U.S. population and spends about $55 billion a year on their grandchildren.[6] Secondary data also may be used to assess how a geographical area is changing. Figure 5.1 shows the number of inhabitants of Colorado Springs, Colorado, and population changes in the city from the 2000 Census to the 2010 Census. Notice that, while the population has increased in all age brackets, the largest increase is in the age group 55–74.

FIGURE 5.1 Census Data May Be Used to Assess Changes in Age Distribution for a Market

Source: Created by Ali Russo with data from the 2010 Census.gov website.

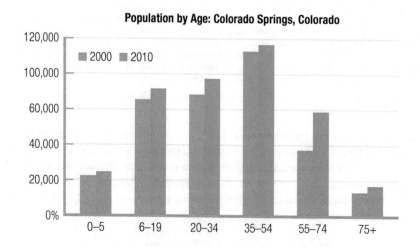

5-3   Classification of Secondary Data

INTERNAL SECONDARY DATA

Secondary data may be broadly classified as either internal or external. **Internal secondary data** are data that have been collected within a firm. Such data include sales records, purchase requisitions, invoices, and complaints. Obviously, a good marketing researcher always determines what internal information is already available. You may recall from Chapter 1 that we referred to internal data analysis as being part of the internal reports system of a firm's marketing information system (MIS). Today a major source of internal data is databases that contain information on customers, sales, suppliers, and any other facet of business a firm may wish to track.

Internal secondary data are data that have been collected within a firm.

Before we discuss internal and external databases, we should understand that a **database** refers to a collection of data and information describing items of interest.[7] Each unit of information in a database is called a **record**. A record could represent a customer, a supplier, a competitive firm, a product, or an individual inventory item, for example. Records are composed of subcomponents of information called **fields**. As an example, a company with a customer database would have *records* representing each customer. Typical *fields* in a customer database record would include name, address, telephone number, email address, products purchased, dates of purchases, locations where purchased, warranty information, and any other information the company considered useful.

A database refers to a collection of data and information describing items of interest.

Internal databases are databases consisting of information gathered by a company, typically during the normal course of business transactions. Marketing managers normally develop internal databases about customers, but databases may be kept on any topic of interest, such as products, members of the sales force, inventory, maintenance, and supplier firms. Companies gather information about customers when they inquire about a product or service, make a purchase, or have a product serviced. Companies use their internal databases for purposes of direct marketing and to strengthen relationships with customers, which is referred to as **customer relationship management (CRM)**.[8]

Internal databases consist of information gathered by a company, typically during the normal course of business transactions.

Internal databases can be quite large, and dealing with the vast quantities of data they contain can pose a problem. **Data mining** is the name for software that helps managers to make sense out of seemingly senseless masses of information contained in databases.[9] **Micromarketing** refers to using a differentiated marketing mix for specific customer segments, sometimes fine-tuned for the individual shopper.[10] Databases and data mining make micromarketing possible. An example is the pop-up ad you may see online after searching for a product.

Data mining software helps managers make sense out of seemingly senseless masses of information contained in databases.

While databases can be quite large and complex, even the simple databases in small businesses can be invaluable. Kotler and Keller describe five ways that companies use their databases:

Micromarketing employs a differentiated marketing mix for specific customer segments, sometimes fine-tuned for the individual shopper.

1. To *identify prospects*, such as sorting through replies to company ads to identify customers who can be targeted with more information
2. To *decide which customers should receive a particular offer*, such as sending a cross-selling suggestion two weeks after a sale
3. To *deepen customer loyalty* by remembering customer preferences and sending appropriately customized materials reflecting those preferences
4. To *reactivate customer purchases*, such as automatically sending out a birthday card
5. To *avoid serious customer mistakes*, such as charging a fee to one of the firm's largest customers.[11]

Databases can tell managers which products are selling, report inventory levels, and profile customers by SKU. Coupled with geodemographic information systems (GIS), databases can provide maps indicating ZIP codes in which the most profitable and least profitable customers reside. Internal databases, built with information collected during the normal course of business, can provide invaluable insights for managers.

What companies do with information collected for their internal databases can present ethical concerns. Should your credit card company share the information on what types of

MARKETING RESEARCH INSIGHT 5.2   *Practical Application*

Your Supermarket Is Spying on You

Tesco, one of the biggest supermarket retailers in the United Kingdom, has a well-developed customer loyalty card—Club-card. Customers can accumulate one point for every pound that they spend; effectively it is a 1% discount. However, these deals are sent to customers in the form of personalized offers based on their previous purchases. Periodically, Tesco offers extra points if customers buy certain brands or product categories. The cards are also used to attract infrequent customers back to the stores.

The value of the card for the supermarket goes far beyond rewarding customers. Each time a card is swiped or scanned, it helps the supermarket to collect information about the shopping habits of the customer. How do supermarkets analyze transactional behavior and use it to drive sales? The answer is RFV (recency, frequency, and value) analysis. This approach is used to group customers according to scores that are given to each of them on the basis of how often they shop, how many individual items they purchase each time, and how much they spend. This approach to market segmentation provides a framework that helps the supermarket to analyze consumer behavior.

While the reward side of the equation benefits the customer, the other side is all about RFV analysis and using that information to direct marketing efforts towards certain customers at personalized levels. Customers are segmented by age, gender, and other criteria and can be identified by their relationship with certain clusters or types of products that they buy

on a regular basis. This way, someone who buys pasta will be given offers on pasta sauce and, someone who buys a cat litter box will be given offers on cat food.

Shopping preferences are also tracked. The store identifies customers who pick almost the same basket of goods each time they shop. Some customers might only be attracted to special offers and would buy discounted products in bulk. Another group might only buy luxury brands and never purchase own-label products. Tesco uses this understanding to provide personalized offers and "tempts" each group with relevant mixes of coupons and bonus point deals.

If a customer does not have a loyalty card, the supermarket can still track him or her when a card payment is made. Supermarkets, in any case, supplement their own data collection with government data and credit reports. By using this broad range of data, supermarkets are able to make informed decisions and devise workable operational and marketing strategies. The data is used to better understand consumer needs and assist supermarkets in deciding store locations, placement of advertisements, which brands to offer, and how much to stock.

Tesco is one of a number of marketers who are refining their ability to micromarket, targeting each consumer with promotional materials customized for them specifically. Ostensibly, this could make the customer's shopping experience better, but are these practices of collecting data about customers without their consent ethical?

Source: Davis, G. (2013, July). Analysis: Loyalty cards—How retailers are using the data. *Retail Week.* Retrieved from http://www.retail-week.com/sectors/grocery/analysis-loyalty-cards-how-retailers-are-using-the-data/5050868.fullarticle; Hobbs, T. (2015, October 9). Is Tesco clubcard still relevant? *Marketing Week.* Retrieved from https://www.marketingweek.com/2015/10/09/is-tesco-clubcard-still-relevant/; Ferguson, F. (2013, June 8). How supermarkets get your data—and what they do with it. *The Guardian.* Retrieved from http://www.theguardian.com/money/2013/jun/08/supermarkets-get-your-data.

goods and services you bought with anyone who wants to buy that information? Should your Internet service provider be able to store information on which Internet sites you visit? As more consumers have grown aware of these privacy issues, more companies have adopted privacy policies.[12] Marketing Research Insight 5.2 illustrates how collecting data on consumers can raise ethical concerns.

EXTERNAL SECONDARY DATA

External data are data obtained from outside the firm.

External data are data obtained from *outside* the firm. Knowing where to find information is a valued skill in the workplace. In the following sections we will introduce some sources of secondary data, but we barely scratch the surface in terms of introducing you to secondary data sources that will be beneficial to you in your career. Take the opportunity you have in college to develop this skill. Your university librarians can be a great resource. Table 5.1 lists

TABLE 5.1 Secondary Information Sources for Marketing

I. Business Source Directories

Encyclopedia of Business Information Sources (Gale, Cengage Learning)—Published annually, this resource indexes almost 11,000 sources of business, finance, and industrial subjects.

BRASS Business Guides (BRASS, RUSA, American Library Association)—Maintained and updated by business information professionals at research universities, these online guides provide links and information for sources on an array of business topics including a list of the Outstanding Business Reference Sources awarded annually by the American Library Association.

Directory of Business Information Sources (Grey House Publishing)—Published annually and containing almost 24,000 entries, this resource indexes thousands of associations, publications, trade shows, databases, and websites.

II. Articles

ABI/Inform Complete (ProQuest)—Comprehensive collection of other ABI/Inform products (Global, Trade and Industry, Dateline, and Archive). There are over 2,200 full-text scholarly journals along with thousands of business titles in trade publications, news outlets, and reports from publishers like Business Monitor International, Economic Intelligence Unit, First Research, and the *Wall Street Journal*.

Business Abstracts with Full Text (H.W. Wilson, Ebsco)—Over 450 full-text business publications including many top peer-reviewed journals.

Business Collection (Gale, Cengage Learning)—Over 2,900 full-text business publications including 390 peer-reviewed journals, news sources, and reports from publishers like Economic Intelligence Unit and AII Data Processing. There are also Business Insights products from Gale that include the article content in addition to reports and company and industry information.

Business Source Complete (Ebsco)—Expansion of Ebsco's Business Source Premier. Nearly 2,000 full-text scholarly journals including *Harvard Business Review*. Also includes trade publications, news outlets, and reports from publishers like Marketline, Barnes Reports, Bernstein, and CountryWatch.

Factiva (Dow Jones)—Full-text articles from thousands of major news sources including Dow Jones, Reuters, *Financial Times*, Bloomberg, and the *Wall Street Journal*.

LexisNexis Academic (LexisNexis, Reed Elsevier)—Thousands of news article sources and access to reports from Hoovers, Business Monitor International, Morningstar, and Standard & Poor's.

III. Dictionaries and Encyclopedias

Brands and Their Companies (Gale, Cengage Learning)—Published annually, this directory provides company, product, and industry information for active and inactive brands from public and private companies.

Dictionary of Advertising and Marketing Concepts by Arthur Asa Berger (Left Coast Press, 2013)—Over 100 entries and essays on concepts, theories, and key people in marketing.

A Dictionary of Marketing by Charles Doyle (Oxford University Press, 2011)—Over 2,600 entries on modern and historic marketing concepts along with appendixes, notably including a time line of marketing.

Encyclopedia of Global Brands, 2nd Ed. (St. James Press, 2013)—Update of the *Encyclopedia of Consumer Brands* (St. James Press, 2005) with 269 entries on major global brands including an overview of each brand's history, performance, key competitors, industry analysis, and prospects.

Encyclopedia of Major Marketing Strategies (Gale, Cengage Learning, 2013)—This third volume is the continuation of the *Encyclopedia of Major Marketing Campaigns* series and contains detailed entries for 100 marketing campaigns in the early 2010s.

Wiley International Encyclopedia of Marketing (Wiley, 2011)—This six-volume set contains 360 entries in the areas of marketing strategy, marketing research, consumer behavior, advertising and integrated communication, product innovation and management, and international marketing.

IV. Marketing Directories

Advertising Redbooks (Red Books, LLC)—Formerly published as the *Advertising Redbooks* series, this database provides a directory by company or agency of advertising campaigns, including budgets by media type. There is also a live listing of marketing job prospects, movement of key people in the industry, and campaigns available for bid.

Complete Television, Radio & Cable Industry Directory (Grey House Publishing)—This annual directory, formerly published as the *Broadcasting and Cable Yearbook* (ProQuest), has entries on television, cable, and radio outlets in the United States and Canada along with rankings of top markets and programs.

(continues)

TABLE 5.1   Secondary Information Sources for Marketing (*continued*)

GreenBook (New York AMA Communication Services, Inc.)—An online directory of marketing research companies.

Advertising & Branding Industry Market Research (Plunkett)—Published as an annual almanac and available in print, ebook, or online, this source contains an industry analysis and profile of about 400 top companies in advertising.

Standard Rate and Data Service (Kantar Media SRDS)—This database is a directory of outlets for digital media, consumer and business magazines, direct marketing, newspapers, radios, and TV and cable. Local outlets are searchable by DMA. Entries include pricing, consumer analysis, and circulation. An additional section, Local Market Audience Analyst, contains Experian Simmons lifestyle and Nielson PRIZM segment information by DMA.

V. Statistics and Reports

American Consumers Series (New Strategist Press)—A series of books with in-depth consumer spending, demographic, and lifestyle statistical analysis.

DemographicsNow (Gale, Cengage Learning)—Allows for tabular and GIS mapping of demographic, consumer expenditure, Experian Simmons consumer study, and Experian Mosaic lifestyle segmentation data. Additionally includes a directory for people with income and household value information, a directory of small businesses with revenue, asset, and employment data, and business site prospecting statistical tools.

eMarketer (eMarketer)—Research on online marketing trends and emerging technology. Free daily newsletter provides highlights from recent reports.

LexisNexis Academic (LexisNexis, Reed Elsevier)—Company Dossier search has a directory of public and private companies including small businesses with employment, revenue, and asset data. The database also indexes thousands of domestic and foreign news sources.

Market Share Reporter (Gale)—Published annually, this report aggregates market share data and revenue figures for brands, companies, and services from industry sources.

Mediamark MRI + (GFK Mediamark Research and Intelligence)—This survey of 25,000 U.S. households gives indexes for consumer demographics, brand decisions, media use, and lifestyle behaviors.

Mintel Reports (Mintel Group)—Market research reports by industry published periodically and available for the United States and globally. Additional reports include demographic segment analysis and reports on cultural trends.

Nielson (Nielson Company)—Measures consumer media use and purchasing decisions on an individual level. PRIZM, P$YCLE, and ConneXions segmentation splits customers into target groups and details consumer and lifestyle decisions, financial behavior, and technology use typical of the group. Data available on a global level.

Passport GMID (Euromonitor International)—Formerly the Global Market Information Database, this source provides industry, consumer, and company trend and market share analysis available globally.

Reference USA (Infogroup)—Directory of businesses, including small businesses, and people and households with income, household value, and lifestyle information.

Simmons OneView (Experian)—Formerly Choices3, this database provides full access to Simmons consumer survey data covering lifestyle, media habits, and category and brand choices.

Simply Map (Geographic Research, Inc.)—Statistical mapping tool with official data. Add-ons include D&B company databases, Experian Simmons, Nielson, EASI, and Mediamark MRI data.

Statista (Statista)—Private and official statistics available in general-interest areas with a strong focus on company and industry sources. Statistics searchable as individual tables as well as collections of topical reports. Data available on domestic and global levels.

Courtesy of LuMarie Guth, Business Librarian, Western Michigan University.

many of the major sources that are most useful in marketing research. Most of these resources are online, although some are also available in print. Your university library may provide access to many of these sources.

The following sections introduce three sources of external data: (1) *published sources*, (2) *official data*, and (3) *data aggregators*.

Three sources of external data are (1) *published sources*, (2) *official data*, and (3) *data aggregators*.

Published Sources   **Published sources** are those sources of information that are prepared for public distribution and are normally found in libraries and online. Trade and professional associations publish information to meet the needs of specific industries, such as the food industry (e.g., the National Grocer's Association [NGA]) and the professional cleaning industry (e.g., the Worldwide Cleaning Industry Association [ISSA]). As detailed in Chapter 2, the marketing research industry has a number of associations that regularly print periodicals and annual reports, including Quirk's, ESOMAR, and *GreenBook*. A number of business journals, magazines, and newspapers, such as the *Wall Street Journal*, the *Economist*, *Bloomberg Businessweek*, *Fortune*, and *Forbes*, are available online, in libraries, and in stores. Academic journals, including the *Journal of Marketing Research*, the *Journal of Business Research*, the *Journal of International Business*, the *Journal of Consumer Research*, and the *Journal of Macromarketing*, publish evidence-based research studies related to marketing. Books with helpful information related to best practices in the research industry are published frequently. Many marketing research firms publish secondary information in the form of books, newsletters, white papers, special reports, magazines, or journals. Marketing research firms may post white papers on many topics on their websites. For example, see www.burke.com and under the "About" tab go to "Literature Library" to see reports on topics such as industry trends and best practices in research methodology.

> Published sources are those sources of information that are prepared for public distribution by trade associations, professional organizations, companies, and other entities and can be found in libraries and online.

Official Statistics **Official statistics** contain information published by public organizations, including government institutions and international organizations. Official statistics are both qualitative and quantitative and include information related to demographics, economic development, education, consumption patterns, health, education, the environment, and many other topics. Many international organizations offer statistics for free online, including the World Health Organization (WHO), the Organization for Economic Co-operation and Development (OECD), the World Bank, and the International Monetary Fund. Almost every country in the world gathers official statistics, generally using rigorous methods, and most make them available to the public. As one example, the National Bureau of Statistics of China publishes nationwide data annually on numerous topics, such as basic demographics by county and city, education levels, access to water, appliance penetration, and many other factors. China's national statistics are available online for every year since 1996 in both Chinese and English (www.stats.gov.cn).

> Official statistics are information published by public organizations, including governments and international organizations.

Since the passage of the **Open Data Policy** in 2013, the United States, by federal law, makes all data collected by the government "open by default," except for personal information or data related to national security. The website www.data.gov includes almost 200,000 datasets from 170 organizations. Free public data have been organized or merged to produce profitable companies (e.g., Garmin and Zillow) and apps (e.g., Citymapper).[13]

> The U.S. Open Data Policy makes all data collected by the government "open by default," except for personal information or data related to national security.

 **Active Learning**

Use data.gov to Explore U.S. Official Statistics

Investigate all the free data that are collected by U.S. government agencies and now are available by law due to the U.S. Open Data Policy. Go to www.data.gov. The website states on its opening page: "Here you will find data, tools, and resources to conduct research, develop web and mobile applications, design data visualizations, and more."[14] Note the number of topics represented, including agriculture, business, consumer, manufacturing, and many others. Click on "consumer" and then "apps." You will see the many apps that have been developed using these freely available data. Type "family" in the search box and note the many available datasets related to "family." This is just a small representation of the large number and wide variety of datasets available. Although these data are in and of themselves interesting, the main challenge for marketing professionals is to seek out relationships among these data that provide new insights.

For more information about the Open Data Policy, go to www.youtube.com and enter "Open Data Changes Lives."

Data aggregators are services or vendors that organize and package information on focused topics.

In a later section, we will provide a more in-depth introduction to one source of U.S. official statistics, the American Community Survey. We have chosen the American Community Survey because it is an excellent example of the rich resources of information that are available online for free.

Data Aggregators   **Data aggregators** are services or vendors that organize and package information on focused topics. Some of these services are available free of charge, but most are available from commercial sources. Examples of these services are IBISWorld, Factiva, Ebsco, and ProQuest. Business databases make up a significant proportion of these services. Most of the data sources in Table 5.1 could be called data aggregators. Your university library probably provides you with free access to many data aggregators.

5-4   Advantages and Disadvantages of Secondary Data

ADVANTAGES OF SECONDARY DATA

The advantages of secondary data are that secondary data can be obtained quickly and inexpensively, are usually available, enhance primary data collection, and can sometimes achieve the research objective.

The advantages of secondary data are, for the most part, readily apparent. There are five main advantages of using secondary data: (1) Secondary data can be obtained quickly; (2) compared to collecting primary data, secondary data are inexpensive; (3) for almost any application, some secondary data are readily available; (4) secondary data may enhance primary data by providing a current look at issues, trends, yardsticks of performance, and so on that may affect the type of primary data that should be collected; and (5) secondary data may be all that are needed to achieve the research objective. For example, a supermarket chain marketing manager wants to allocate TV ad dollars to the 12 markets in which the chain owns supermarkets. A quick review of secondary data shows that retail sales of food are available by TV market area. Allocating the TV budget based on the percentage of food sales in a given market would be an excellent way to solve the manager's problem and satisfy the research objective.

DISADVANTAGES OF SECONDARY DATA

Although the advantages of secondary data almost always justify a search of this information, there are caveats associated with secondary data. Five of the problems associated with secondary data include incompatible reporting units, mismatch of the units of measurement, differing definitions used to classify the data, timeliness of the secondary data, and lack of information needed to assess the credibility of the data reported. These problems exist because secondary data have not been collected specifically to address the problem at hand but have been collected for some other purpose.

Incompatible Reporting Units   Secondary data are provided in reporting units, such as, in the case of area units, county, city, metro area, state, region, ZIP code, and other statistical areas. A researcher's use of secondary data often depends on whether the reporting unit matches the researcher's need. For example, a researcher wishing to evaluate market areas for the purpose of consideration for expansion may be pleased with data reported at the county level. A great deal of secondary data is available at the county level. But what if another marketer wishes to evaluate a two-mile area around a street address that is proposed as a site location for a retail store? County data would hardly be adequate. Another marketer wishes to know the demographic makeup of each ZIP code in a major city in order to determine which ZIP codes to target for a direct-mail campaign. Again, county data would be inappropriate. Although inappropriate reporting units are often problems in using secondary data, more and more data are available today in multiple reporting units, such as data at the more refined ZIP + 4 level.

Mismatched Measurement Units   Sometimes secondary data are reported in measurement units that do not match the measurement unit the researcher needs. For example, a researcher may wish to compare the average income of households in urban areas in Turkey and China. If income is reported in one nation as annual income after taxes and in the other nation as monthly income before taxes, household income will be very difficult to compare.

Unusable Class Definitions The class definitions of the reported data may not be usable to a researcher. Secondary data are often reported by breaking a variable into different classes and reporting the frequency of occurrence in each class. For example, suppose a source of secondary data reports the variable of household income in three classes. The first class reports the percentage of households with income from $20,000 to $34,999, and the third class reports the percentage of households with incomes of $50,000 and over. For most studies, these classifications are applicable. However, imagine you are a manufacturer of high-end plumbing fixtures looking to expand the number of distributorships. You have learned that your dealers are most successful in geographical areas with average household incomes above $80,000. You need another source of information since the available source of secondary data only reports household incomes of $50,000 and over. What would a researcher do in this situation? Typically, if you keep looking, you can find what you need. There may be other sources of secondary data in other categories.

Outdated Data Sometimes a marketing researcher will find information reported with the desired unit of measurement and the proper classifications; however, the data may be outdated and no longer reliable. Some secondary data are published only once. However, even for secondary data published at regular intervals, the time that has passed since the last publication can be a problem when applying the data to a current problem. The researcher must assess the usefulness of the available data.

> Five of the problems associated with secondary data include incompatible reporting units, mismatch of the units of measurement, differing definitions used to classify the data, timeliness of the secondary data, and lack of information needed to assess data credibility.

5-5 Evaluating Secondary Data

The advice that you can't believe everything you read holds true for marketing research. You must carefully assess the quality and validity of secondary data in deciding whether to use it as a basis for making decisions. Caution is especially in order with Internet sources because few quality standards are applied to most Internet sites. To determine the reliability of secondary information, marketing researchers must evaluate it. If the information is not available to examine the reliability of the data, the source cannot be trusted. Trustworthy sources will almost always have comprehensive details related to the methods used to collect their data.

The following sections offer five questions that are useful in evaluating secondary data.

WHAT WAS THE PURPOSE OF THE STUDY?

Studies are conducted for a purpose, and sometimes readers do not know the true purpose. Some studies are conducted to "prove" some position or to advance the special interest of those conducting the study. In the 1980s environmentalists became concerned over the growing mountains of disposable plastic diapers that had all but replaced cloth diapers. More than a dozen state legislatures were considering various bans, taxes, and even warning labels on disposable diapers. Then "research studies" were produced whose "purpose" was to evaluate the environmental effects of disposable versus cloth diapers. The "new" research purported to "prove" that cloth diapers, by adding detergent by-products to the water table, were more harmful to the environment than the ever-lasting plastic disposables. Soon after several of these studies were made available to legislators, the movement against disposables was dead. However, further scrutiny might have called these findings into question. Procter & Gamble, which owned the lion's share of the market for disposable diapers, commissioned the consulting firm of Arthur D. Little, Inc., to conduct one of the studies. Another study that favored disposables was conducted by Franklin Associates, whose research showed disposables were not any more harmful than cloth diapers. But who sponsored this study? The American Paper

Institute, an organization with major interests in disposable diapers. Not all "scientific" studies touted in this debate supported the use of disposable diapers. A 1988 study characterized disposable diapers as "garbage" contributing to massive buildups of waste that were all but impervious to deterioration. Who sponsored this study? The cloth diaper industry![15]

Another example of the need to consider the source of data involves a "study" reported by the news media citing the terrible condition of roads and bridges in the United States. Who sponsored the study? An organization representing road and bridge construction companies. It may well be that the study was objective and accurate. However, users of secondary information should be well aware of the *true purpose* of the study and evaluate the information accordingly.

WHO COLLECTED THE INFORMATION?

Even when you are convinced that there is no bias in the purpose of the study, you should question the competence of the organization that collected the information. Organizations differ in terms of the resources they command and their quality control. How can you evaluate the competency of the organization that collected the data? First, ask others who have more experience in a given industry. Typically, credible organizations are well known in those industries for which they conduct studies. Second, examine the report itself. Competent firms almost always provide carefully written and detailed explanations of the procedures and methods used in collecting the information cited in the report. Third, contact previous clients of the firm. Have they been satisfied with the quality of the work performed by the organization?

Be wary of using information just because it is available on the Internet. The "information superhighway" is a rich source of all sorts of information but, as we have noted previously, the objectivity and reliability of all these data are not guaranteed. An emerging trend is the *crowdsourcing* of data. For example, one interesting application of crowdsourcing is the collection of geographic data, as highlighted in Marketing Research Insight 5.3. Although crowdsourcing can actually improve the quality of some types of data, in other cases crowdsourced data can be unreliable. Again, always check carefully what methods were used to collect data.

WHAT INFORMATION WAS COLLECTED?

Many studies are available on topics such as economic impact, market potential, and feasibility. But what exactly was measured in these studies that constitute impact, potential, or feasibility? Studies may claim to provide information on a specific subject but, in fact, measure something quite different. Consider the example of two studies offering differing results on the number of businesses in each county as a basis for projecting sales for a B2B service. A key question in evaluating the differing data was how the number of businesses was measured. In one report, each existing business location counted as a business, resulting in a high count, as one business may have had a dozen distribution outlets. Another report counted only the business and not its outlets. This resulted in a low count of "number of businesses." Is this distinction important? It may or may not be, depending on how the study's user intends to use the information. B2B service providers would need to assess if their service could be sold to each individual distribution outlet or only to the parent company. The important point is that users should discover exactly what information was collected!

HOW WAS THE INFORMATION OBTAINED?

You should be aware of the methods used to obtain information reported in secondary sources. What was the sample? How large was the sample? What was the response rate? Was the information validated? As you will learn throughout this book, there are many alternative ways of collecting primary data, and each may have an impact on the information collected. Remember that, even though you are evaluating secondary data, this information was gathered as

MARKETING RESEARCH INSIGHT 5.3   *Digital Marketing Research*

Crowdsourcing Geographic Knowledge

Crowdsourcing is a business model in which products or services are developed by soliciting contributions from a large group of people rather than from traditional employees or suppliers. Crowdsourcing typically integrates the efforts of many self-identified volunteers or part-time workers. Each contributor, acting on his or her own initiative, contributes to a small piece that can be synthesized into a larger whole to achieve a greater result.

Crowdsourcing is different from outsourcing in that a task is accomplished by an undefined public rather than being commissioned from a specific, named group or an established business supply chain. Compared to the traditional business model, significant changes, such as reduced costs, accelerated speed, unexpected/surprising innovations, more flexibility/scalability, and enhanced diversity/public participation, have been documented using crowdsourcing. There is also a general consensus among marketing researchers that crowdsourcing is an effective marketing tool because consumers are much more prone to use certain products or services when they are involved in the development of those products or services.

One interesting area for the application of crowdsourcing is the production of geographic knowledge via volunteered geographic information (VGI). VGI refers to geographic information acquired and made available to others through the voluntary activity of individuals or groups with the intent of providing information about the geographic world. The growth of VGI in the past 10 years is a result of several related technological advances and scientific practices, such as web 2.0, geoweb, spatial media, neogeography, citizen science, crowdsourcing, and open science.

VGI can be used to augment existing geospatial databases of various kinds. The OpenStreetMap (OSM) is perhaps the best example of geospatial framework data collected by volunteers. OSM is a collaborative global effort to produce a detailed, full-coverage digital map of the world's road networks (and some other features) through voluntary effort. Volunteers use global positioning systems (GPS) and satellite imagery to capture the locations of transportation infrastructure and topographic features. Once compiled, these data are available to the public as maps that can be viewed online and downloaded. The open access to these data stands in stark contrast to the limited accessibility and high costs of geographic data from many national mapping agencies and corporations.

The OSM data production approach has proved to be valuable. For instance, OSM volunteers leapt into action in the aftermath of the earthquake in Haiti to create the maps and digital geographic information needed to plan the response and recovery. Informal gatherings of volunteers were held in many places, at which digital geographic information was compiled from available online sources. Within days a detailed, open, free digital map was available that was quickly adopted by relief agencies.

One of the most exciting aspects of VGI is the ability to produce data on any theme or phenomena of interest, including information that has not previously been recorded. An emerging source of VGI may exist due to the increasing popularity of Apple iHealth, Google Fit, Jawbone UP, and other products that produce personal health data (such as heart rate, calories, and weight) that are geo-tagged. Although these types of data are private, they could become a gold mine for health-related research if consumers are willing to forgo privacy concerns to share their personal data.

—Courtesy of Dr. Daniel Sui

About Daniel Sui

Dr. Daniel Sui is an Arts and Sciences Distinguished Professor and Professor of Geography at the Ohio State University. Dr. Sui's 2012 book *Crowdsourcing Geographic Knowledge: Volunteered Geographic Information in Theory and Practice* (co-edited with Sarah Elwood and Michael Goodchild) provides a comprehensive overview of the phenomenon of VGI.

Dr. Daniel Sui, Arts and Sciences Distinguished Professor and Professor of Geography at the Ohio State University.

primary data by some organization. Therefore, the alternative ways of gathering the data had an impact on the nature and quality of the data. It is not always easy to find out how the secondary data were gathered. However, as noted previously, most reputable organizations that provide secondary data also provide detailed information on their data collection methods.

HOW CONSISTENT IS THE INFORMATION WITH OTHER INFORMATION?

In some cases, the same secondary data are reported by multiple independent organizations, which provides an excellent way to evaluate secondary data sources. Ideally, if two or more independent organizations report the same data, you can have greater confidence in the validity and reliability of the data. Demographic data for metropolitan areas (MAs), counties, and most municipalities are widely available from more than one source. If you are evaluating a survey that is supposedly representative of a given geographic area, you may want to compare the characteristics of the sample of the survey with the demographic data available on the population. If you know that, based on U.S. census data, a city's population is 45% male and 55% female and a survey that is supposed to be representative of that city reports a sample of 46% males and 54% females, then you can be more confident in the survey data.

It is rare that two organizations will report exactly the same results. In assessing differing data, the magnitude of the differences is a good place to start. If all independent sources report very large differences of the same variable, then you may not have much confidence in any of the data. You should look carefully at what information was collected and how it was collected for each reporting source.

5-6　The American Community Survey

As an example of official statistics that are available for free, we will take a closer look at the American Community Survey (ACS), an offshoot of the American Census. The administration of the census of the U.S. population began in 1790. Prior to 1940, all U.S. residents had to answer all the questions the census used. In 1940, the long form—a longer questionnaire that goes out to only a sample of respondents—was introduced as a way to collect more data more rapidly and without increasing the burden of all respondents. By 2000, the long form went to one in six housing units. As a result, much of the census data are based on statistical sampling.[16]

The 2010 U.S. Census departed from tradition and only collected data using the short form. This was done in an effort to get more accurate counts, and we now know that the 2010 Census was very accurate.[17] The short form asks only for name, sex, age, date of birth, race, ethnicity, relationship, and housing tenure. Data from the long form are still needed but are now collected through the *American Community Survey*. For many years the census has been the backbone of secondary data in the United States. Marketers use the information in many ways, and marketing research firms have developed many products to aid in the use of census data. You can learn more about the 2010 Census at the official website: http://2010.census.gov.

The **American Community Survey (ACS)** may represent the most significant change in the availability of secondary data to be used for marketing research purposes in several decades. The U.S. Census Bureau created the ACS in 1996 to collect economic, social, demographic, and housing information as part of the Decennial Census Program. The survey is designed to help update Decennial Census data by collecting information on a small percentage of the population in all counties, American Indian Areas, Alaska Native Areas, and Hawaiian Home Lands on a rotating basis using a sample. The main advantage is that the ACS provides data annually instead of once every 10 years. Since these data have the U.S. Census Bureau's "high marks" for reliable data *and* will be current, the ACS is a major secondary data resource for marketing researchers.

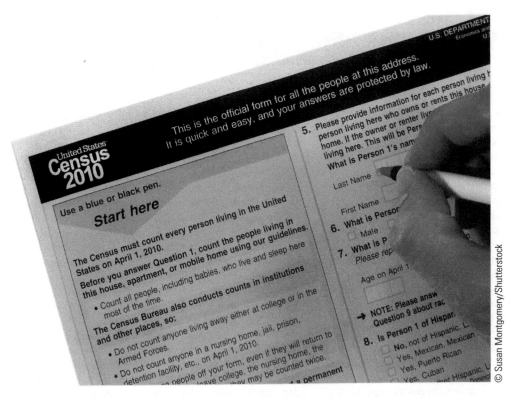

The 2010 U.S. Census departed from tradition and collected a limited amount of data using a short form.

In addition to providing new data each year, the ACS offers a measure of accuracy of the yearly estimates. To do this, the ACS relies on a sampling plan that involves surveying about 3 million Americans every year. Because a sample is used, data are reported with a margin of error, which is an estimate of the accuracy of the data. (You will learn about margin of error in Chapter 10.) For an example of how to use the ACS, see Marketing Research Insight 5.4.

5-7 What Is Packaged Information?

We are now ready to turn to a special form of secondary data. **Packaged information** is a type of secondary data in which the data collected and/or the process of collecting the data are prepackaged for all users. There are two broad classes of packaged information: syndicated data and packaged services.

SYNDICATED DATA

Syndicated data are a form of external secondary data that are supplied from a common database to subscribers for a service fee. Syndicated data are collected in a standard format and made available to all subscribers. Such information is typically detailed information that is valuable to firms in a given industry and is not available in libraries. Firms supplying syndicated data follow standard research formats that enable them to collect the same data over time. These firms provide specialized routine information needed by a given industry in the form of ready-to-use packaged data to subscribing firms.

As an example of syndicated data, Marketing Evaluations, Inc., offers several Q Scores services. The Q Score is the measure of the familiarity and appeal of performers in categories

Packaged information is a type of secondary data in which the data collected and/or the process of collecting the data are prepackaged for all users.

Two broad classes of packaged information are syndicated data and packaged services.

Syndicated data are a form of external data that are supplied from a common database to subscribers for a service fee.

MARKETING RESEARCH INSIGHT 5.4   *Practical Application*

Using the American Community Survey

The purpose of this exercise is to introduce the American Community Survey (ACS) and the American Factfinder, which is the tool used for searching data collected by the ACS.

Global Motors is considering adding a car model to its product mix that will be totally electric. Buyers will never have to buy gasoline. The cost to operate this vehicle will be about $0.02 per mile versus about $0.12 per mile for a gasoline vehicle. Global knows some manufacturers have an all-electric car, such as the Nissan Leaf. However, designers and managers at Global Motors believe they can gain a competitive advantage over these vehicles by building a car surface made of solar panels. Unlike other competitive vehicles that charge only when plugged into an electrical outlet, a car with a solar panel "skin" can absorb additional energy as long as the sun is out. This innovation is significant for another reason: If electric car owners charge their vehicles with electricity from a coal-powered electric plant (which powers the dominant percentage of U.S. power plants), the greenhouse gas emissions are still 0.8 pound per mile driven. While this is better than the 1 pound per mile for gasoline-powered emissions, it means the gas-free vehicles are far from "emission free."[18] A solar panel skin would help reduce the gas emissions, and the Global car would not only have greater range but also come closer to being a truly emission-free vehicle. However, the range of electric cars is still a major concern even with the ability of a constant charge using the solar panels. While the solar panels will help, they cannot keep up with the energy needed to propel the car even on a very sunny day. It is estimated that the range of this new car will be 125 miles, an improvement over other purely electric cars with a range of 60 to 100 miles.

Before proceeding with design, Global managers want to know if this car can be used for the bulk of commuter travel to and from work each day and still have sufficient range to run errands. If the majority of workers commute under 30 minutes each way, then the new car would have adequate range to get owners to and from work and run a few errands. Before going further with the concept of the new vehicle, secondary data may be assessed to answer the question, "What is the mean travel time, one way, for Americans to travel to work?" By retrieving ACS data via American Factfinder, managers quickly learn that the average time, in minutes, driven by Americans to work is 25.3. This is sufficient for them to continue with development plans for the new car.

After several months of concept testing using focus groups, a prototype vehicle is developed. The prototype meets all engineering and design expectations. Cost estimates for full-scale production put the cost of the car above a typical compact sedan, but the major selling point is that this price tag would be offset by reduced operating costs. Global would like to test-market 20 vehicles in a metropolitan statistical area (MSA) selected based, in part, on the percentage of the MSA's population that commutes less than 30 minutes. You can conduct this research yourself by using the following steps to access ACS data to evaluate the MSA of Jacksonville, Florida, on this criterion.

1. Go to www.census.gov and select the "Data" menu.
2. From the "Data Tools and Apps" menu, select American Factfinder and then "Advanced Search."
3. Select "Show Me All" and then "Topics."
4. In the dialog box that appears, select "People," then "Employment," and then "Commuting (journey to work)." It should appear as one of "Your Selections."
5. To select the Jacksonville, Florida, MSA, go to "Geographies" and select Metro/Micro statistical areas and scroll down until you find Jacksonville, Florida. Select "Jacksonville" and then "Add to Your Selection." Once you add this geography, close the dialog box and view the tables. Again, you will notice that you have several available to you.
6. Select the top table and find information about the "Travel Time to Work." Does Jacksonville, Florida, qualify for the test market based on this criterion?

The ACS provides data on commuting times for Americans.

© Christian Delbert/Shutterstock

such as actors, actresses, authors, athletes, and sportscasters. This information is used by companies to help them choose the most appropriate spokesperson for their company and by producers for casting television shows and movies. Performer Q is the service for ratings of approximately 1,800 performers. Data are available by demographic groups, and the company offers trends for many more personalities going back to 1964.[19] Meryl Streep and Tom Hanks, for example, are performers who maintain high Q Scores. The company even maintains ratings of deceased performers called Dead Q.[20] Data for performers studied are the same and are bought as a package by subscribers who typically include advertisers, TV and movie production companies, licensing companies, and talent and public relations companies. Data are collected two times a year for all performers based on a sample of nearly 2,000 persons. The Marketing Evaluations, Inc., site at www.qscores.com has information about the different Q Score studies that are available.

Another example of syndicated data is the Nielsen Ratings service, which measures TV audience size and viewer demographics for TV programs.[21] This information is packaged and made available to subscribers who typically include advertisers, ad agencies, TV production companies, networks, and cable companies. Nielsen's website, at www.nielsen.com, posts free, up-to-date Top 10 lists of TV programs, as well as other products, such as books, music, and video games.

As another example, Nielsen Audio (formerly Arbitron) supplies syndicated data on the number and types of listeners to the various radio stations in each radio market. This package of information helps advertising firms reach their target markets; it also helps radio stations define audience characteristics by providing an objective, independent measure of the size and characteristics of their audiences. With syndicated data, both the process of collecting and analyzing the data and the data themselves are not varied for the client.[22] Each subscriber buys the same "book" for each radio market.

PACKAGED SERVICES

The term **packaged services** refers to a prepackaged marketing research process that is used to generate information for a particular user. Unlike syndicated data, the data from a packaged service will differ for each client. Packaged services rarely provide clients with the same data. Rather, it is the process they are marketing. For example, a packaged service may measure customer satisfaction. Instead of a client firm trying to "reinvent the wheel" by developing its own process for measuring customer satisfaction, it may elect to use a packaged service to accomplish this aim. This is also true for several other marketing research services, such as test marketing, naming new brands, pricing a new product, or using mystery shoppers.

Esri's Tapestry Segmentation is such a service that uses a ready-made, prepackaged process to profile residential neighborhoods. This information is purchased by clients with the aim of better understanding who their customers are, where they are located, how to find them, and how to reach them. While the data will differ for each client, Esri's process for generating the data is the same for all clients.[23]

> Packaged services refers to a prepackaged marketing research process that is used to generate information for a particular user.

 **Active Learning**

Use Esri's Tapestry Segmentation to Learn About Your Neighborhood

Go to www.esri.com and click on the link to Products. Under "See All Products," you will find "Products A-Z." There you will find the website for the Tapestry Segmentation program, which has categorized every ZIP code according to the prevalence of one or more of the 65 different consumer types. Find out about your neighborhood by entering your own ZIP code. Does the description fit your perceptions of the types of people in your neighborhood?

5-8   Advantages and Disadvantages of Packaged Information

SYNDICATED DATA

Advantages of syndicated data are shared costs, high-quality data, and speed with which data are collected and made available for decision making.

One of the key advantages of syndicated data is *shared costs*. Many client firms may subscribe to the information; thus, the cost of the service is greatly reduced to any one subscriber firm. Second, because syndicated data firms specialize in the collection of standard data and because their long-term viability depends on the validity of the data, the quality of the data collected is typically very high. One final advantage of syndicated data is that the information is normally disseminated very quickly to subscribers; the more current the data, the greater their usefulness.

Disadvantages of syndicated data are that there is little control over the data collected, buyers must commit to long-term contracts, and competitors have access to the same information.

A primary disadvantage of syndicated data is that buyers have little control over what information is collected. Are the units of measurement correct? Are the geographical reporting units appropriate? A second disadvantage is that buyer firms often must commit to long-term contracts when buying syndicated data. Finally, there is no strategic information advantage in purchasing syndicated data because all competitors have access to the same information. However, in many industries, firms would suffer a serious strategic disadvantage by not purchasing the information. In addition, how well a firm uses information is as important as what information a firm can access.

PACKAGED SERVICES

Advantages of packaged services are the experience of the firm offering the service, reduced cost, and increased speed of conducting the service.

The key advantage of using a packaged service is taking advantage of the experience of the research firm offering the service. Imagine a firm setting out to conduct a test market for the very first time. It would take the firm several months to gain the confidence needed to conduct the test market properly. Taking advantage of others' experiences with the process is a good way to minimize potential mistakes in carrying out the research process. When a firm offers a packaged service, it has spent a great deal of time and effort in ensuring the process effectively delivers the information needed. In other words, it has worked out all the "bugs." A second advantage is the reduced cost of the research. Because the supplier firm conducts the service for many clients on a regular basis, the procedure is efficient and far less costly than if the buyer firm tried to conduct the service itself. A third advantage is the speed of the research service. The efficiency gained by conducting the service over and over translates into reduced turnaround time from start to finish of a research project. A fourth advantage is the ability to obtain benchmarks for comparison. A firm that offers a packaged service can use its experience to provide measures obtained from previous research to allow direct comparisons and make sense of results. For example, Nielsen BASES, a product concept testing service, claims that its 35+ years of experience involving 200,000 product concepts allows the firm to predict the probability of launching a new product successfully very accurately. These are all reasons why client firms are interested in packaged services, and because of these advantages, many marketing research firms offer packaged services.

Disadvantages of packaged services are the inability to customize services and the service firm not being knowledgeable about the client's industry.

One disadvantage of using packaged services is the inability to customize aspects of a project. Second, the company providing the packaged service may not know the idiosyncrasies of a particular industry; therefore, there is a greater burden on the client to ensure that the packaged service fits the intended situation. Client firms, being fully aware of the idiosyncrasies of their markets, need to be familiar with the service provided, including what data are collected on which population, how the data are collected, and how the data are reported before they purchase the service.

5-9   Applications of Packaged Information

Packaged information is useful in many marketing research decisions, such as measuring consumer attitudes and opinions, defining market segments, monitoring media usage and promotion effectiveness, and conducting market tracking studies. In the following section we illustrate these applications with examples of firms that provide the service.

MEASURING CONSUMER ATTITUDES AND OPINIONS

Marketers are always interested in consumer attitudes and opinions. At one time, the American public frowned on buying on credit. That attitude has certainly changed, as credit card ownership surged beginning in the 1970s. Marketers are interested in consumers' attitudes toward private brands versus national brands, the quality of products made in America and elsewhere, and claims of health benefits. Defense contractors are interested in the public's attitude toward war. Universities are interested in consumers' attitudes about the value of higher education. Manufacturers are interested in prevailing attitudes about pollution and government regulation. Research firms supply packaged services that measure and report attitudes and opinions on these issues and many more. Gallup, one of the oldest of these firms, has been tracking attitudes and opinions and monitoring changes for many decades.

MARKET SEGMENTATION

There are several marketing research firms that offer a packaged service of providing client firms with sophisticated methods of identifying members of their target market, locating these members, and providing information that will help develop promotional materials to efficiently reach these target markets. At the base of many of these services is geodemographics linking marketing information, such as consumer demographics, to specific geographical locations (latitude and longitude coordinates). **Geodemographics** is the term used to describe the classification of geographic areas in terms of the socioeconomic characteristics of their inhabitants. Aided by computer programs called *geodemographic information systems* (GIS), geodemographers can access huge databases and construct profiles of consumers residing in geographic areas determined by the geodemographer. Instead of being confined to fixed geographic reporting units such as a city, county, or state, geodemographers can produce this information for geographic areas thought to be relevant for a given marketing application.

Geodemographics is the term used to describe the classification of geographic areas in terms of the socioeconomic characteristics of their inhabitants.

MONITORING MEDIA USAGE AND PROMOTION EFFECTIVENESS

We have already mentioned the Nielsen Ratings for measuring TV audiences and Nielsen Audio (formerly Arbritron) for measuring radio listenership. Another example is measuring print media promotional impact. When promotional materials are placed in a newspaper, direct-mail piece, website, or magazine or on the package itself, marketers want to know what gets consumers' attention and what they think of the message. Packaged services are available to monitor the effectiveness of print media promotional messages. To measure reaction to print media, the SKOPOS service RepliKator allows consumers to electronically flip through the pages of a magazine or other printed material to resemble as closely as possible reading through a magazine. Then SKOPOS can measure what the reader recalled from having read the magazine. The marketing research supplier BrainJuicer specializes in measuring emotions evoked by advertising with its "Emotion-in-Action score."

Active Learning

Use BrainJuicer to Explore Emotional Reactions to Advertising

In 2014 and 2015, BrainJuicer was named the most innovative marketing research supplier in the world by industry peers.[24] To explore why, go to BrainJuicer's website at http://www. brainjuicer.com. Select the "Feel More" menu. Here you will find the top-ranked global advertising for the year in what BrainJuicer calls the Emotion-in-Action score. You can read on this page how BrainJuicer arrives at this score. Do you respond emotionally to the advertising that is ranked at the top for the year?

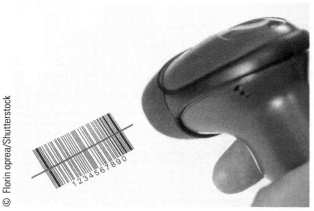

© Florin oprea/Shutterstock

Companies can purchase tracking data for particular categories of products and get up-to-date information about what brands are selling at which retailers at the SKU level.

Tracking studies are longitudinal studies that monitor a variable such as sales or market share over time.

Social media data, also termed user-generated content (UGC), are any information that is created by users of online systems and intended to be shared with others.

Social media monitoring, or social media listening, involves actively gathering, organizing, and analyzing social media data to gain consumer insights.

MARKET TRACKING STUDIES

Nielsen is the leader in the industry in terms of analysis of consumer purchase behavior. Nielsen **tracking studies** are longitudinal studies that monitor a variable such as sales or market share over time. Nielsen has two different methods of tracking the movement of goods at the retail level. First, consumers participating in a large panel group use a wand supplied by Nielsen to swipe the UPC barcode on goods they bring home. Data are uploaded to a Nielsen database. Second, Nielsen has agreements with many retailers to purchase data as products are scanned at checkout. The company augments these methods with in-store auditors to ensure they have a sample of stores that are representative. These methods give Nielsen the ability to offer a packaged service of key information to marketing managers. They can purchase tracking data for their category and get up-to-date information about what brands are selling at which retailers at the SKU level, and they can learn what their competitors are selling, which is key strategic information.

5-10   Social Media Data

One of the fastest-growing areas of marketing research involves the organization and analysis of social media data. A 2014 survey of marketing professionals found that almost half (46%) of marketing professionals currently analyze social media data and another one-third (31%) are considering using social media data in the future.[25] **Social media data**, also termed **user-generated content (UGC)**, are any information that is created by users of online systems and intended to be shared with others. Social media data may be considered a form of secondary data, since it is information that does not originate as a result of a marketing research project. In Chapter 6, we will discuss two additional forms of online research methods that can be considered primary data: marketing research online communities and online focus groups.

Social media information can take a number of forms, including photos, videos, comments, reviews, tweets, podcasts, pins, posts, ratings, emojis, likes, and blogs. As detailed in Marketing Research Insight 2.1 (Chapter 2), various types of social media platforms are host to this information, including blogs, microblogs, video-sharing networks, photo-sharing sites, social networks, professional networks, product and service review sites, web-based communities and forums, and news-sharing sites. **Social media monitoring**, also known as **social media listening**, involves actively gathering, organizing, and analyzing social media data to gain consumer insights. The timing of social media monitoring can vary. It may be focused on one period to solve a particular problem, conducted at regular intervals (for example, quarterly or annually), or be conducted on an ongoing basis.

TYPES OF INFORMATION

As Kristina Cisnero of Hootsuite states in the introduction, there are numerous types of information generated on social media that can be useful to businesses. For example, companies may learn through the Internet that their customers in different regions are using their products differently, leading to new advertising campaigns or product extensions. When Vegemite sales dropped in Australia, Kraft investigated social media websites to explore consumers' relationships with the yeast-based spread. Kraft learned from the social media platforms that

Australians were incorporating Vegemite in unusual food combinations according to their cultural backgrounds. This led to a successful ad campaign called "How do you have your Vegemite?" In addition, Kraft discovered that some Australians were mixing Vegemite with cream cheese. The result was a new popular product called Cheesybite.[26]

The following sections list some of the user-generated types of information that can be found on social media.

Reviews Consumers provide reviews for products and services on retailer (e.g., Banana Republic) and product or service specialty (e.g., Yelp) websites. These reviews offer context for internal data, such as sales and returns. Reviews can provide retailers and manufacturers early warnings and diagnoses of problems and successes. The consumers' comments also provide free promotion for the products and services that are reviewed, although this type of publicity may be unwanted when the reviews are not favorable.

Tips Often consumers use social media websites to share product- or service-related information with other consumers, such as troubleshooting information on products (e.g., solving software bugs), product demonstrations (e.g., showing products in action), pointers (e.g., best rooms to request in hotels), and warnings (e.g., don't buy this toy for larger dogs). Consumers also use social media to openly provide suggestions for companies. These can include ideas for new concepts and suggestions for improvements and additional features.

New Uses Consumers often share new uses for products, potentially leading to new ways to promote products. Examples might include new ways to use a food product in a recipe or unexpected uses for an appliance.

Competitor News Social media sites also provide a way to monitor perceptions of competitors' products, allowing direct comparisons of similar products and affording early warnings of advances in the industry.

ADVANTAGES AND DISADVANTAGES OF SOCIAL MEDIA DATA

Social media have a number of strengths as a source of marketing research data. First, and perhaps most important, is their currency. Social media can provide fast, immediate, up-to-the-minute feedback on any of the 4 Ps associated with a brand. Second, it is relatively inexpensive to access the data, although expertise is needed to organize and analyze the data properly. Third, social media data represent the unprompted, unfiltered, and authentic voice of the consumer. As such, social media sources can lead to new understandings that might not emerge through other types of research. Fourth, social media platforms provide one of the best means to trace trends and track big themes—that is, fears and aspirations—that influence consumers.

The use of social media data for marketing research also has quite a few disadvantages. First, the social media commenters may not represent a brand's target audience and, consequently, provide misleading feedback. Similarly, the most vocal consumers—whether advocates or critics of a brand—may have a more active voice and distort the conversation. Next, the demographic and geographic information of the consumers may not be identifiable or may be falsified, limiting its usefulness. In addition, some types of products, such as electronics and hotels, are more likely to be reviewed online, and some, particularly local products or low-penetration products, may not have a social media presence at all. Also, despite measures taken to prevent fraud by established websites, social media review websites can be subject to manipulation, whereby some reviews may be posted by individuals with ulterior motives. Finally, and most frustratingly, much of the material on social media is shallow, useless, offensive, or irrelevant. This means that a lot of content must be sifted through to find useful information.

TOOLS TO MONITOR SOCIAL MEDIA

A number of full-service research companies, such as Nielsen and Lieberman Research Worldwide, offer social media monitoring as a packaged service. Some research suppliers specialize in social media monitoring, including DigitalMR and Face. Some client companies, such as Meijer, the hypermarket chain, and Procter & Gamble, conduct much of their own social media listening. Companies and organizations that highly value social media data, such as Dell, the Red Cross, and Gatorade, set up "command centers," with multiple screens to monitor social media activity on an ongoing basis. Social media command centers can also be set up on a temporary basis to deal with a crisis or special event, such as the command center the National Football League set up for the 2015 Super Bowl in Phoenix, Arizona.

A number of tools and technology, some free or partially free and others with a price, have been created to aid in the monitoring of social media or web analytics. Examples include Radian6, Google Analytics, and Social Mention. Some companies, including Hootsuite and Sprout Social, offer social media dashboards with which to monitor multiple social media websites on one screen. Many of these services offer key metrics and summary information, such as word counts, volume, key words, and top influencers. For example, Social Mention, a social media search engine, provides a measure of **sentiment**, or the ratio of positive to negative comments posted about products and brands on the web. Still, no tool to aggregate social media data can replace the in-depth analysis of content that can be conducted by marketing research analysts who have a deep understanding of a brand, product, or company. See Marketing Research Insight 4.2 (Chapter 4) for an outline of the steps to use to analyze social media data.

> Sentiment is the ratio of positive to negative comments posted about products and brands on the web.

5-11   Internet of Things

To see an example of a social media command center, go to www.youtube.com and enter "Introducing Dell's Social Media Command Center."

An important emerging source of big data is called the **Internet of Things (IoT)** and is defined as the network of physical objects embedded with software or sensors that allow them to gather and send data. It is important to be aware of this data source because many research professionals believe that, as Kristin Luck, president of Decipher Market Research, stated, IoT "will radically transform our industry from relying heavily on primary data, to truly integrating passively collected secondary data."[27] In the future, it is believed that there will be more *things* providing data than people.[28] The Internet of Things will give people—and marketing researchers—greater access to computer intelligence through passive data. **Passive data** are defined as information that is collected without overt consumer activity.

A major category of objects that is part of the IoT, **wearables**, or **wearable technology**, are clothing or accessories that are equipped with computer technology or sensors that allow the collection and sharing of data. Wearables include smartglasses (e.g., Google Glass), fitness trackers (e.g., Fitbit), and smart watches (e.g., Apple Watch). In 2015 Ralph Lauren launched a "smart shirt," called the PoloTech, which is embedded with sensors to read vital signs like breathing and heart rate, stress level, and calories burned and will stream that information to an app. Next, the company is planning smart ties and smart suits.[29] Wearables turn people into walking, talking trails of data, all of which can be aggregated and analyzed with the proper technology and knowledge. These data can be particularly valuable to the health and the fitness industries, but information provided by wearables can be useful for any company that is tracking human behavior.

As more objects have sensors and the ability to share information, the information that is generated, along with the marketing research applications, will surely multiply. For example, if sensors were embedded throughout a store, data could automatically be collected related to the number of people who walked by the store, number of people who came into the store, number of people who bought something, aisles that people walked through, objects that

> The Internet of Things (IoT) is defined as the network of physical objects embedded with software or sensors that allow them to gather and distribute data.
>
> Passive data are information that is collected without overt consumer activity.
>
> Wearables, or wearable technology, are clothing or accessories that are equipped with computer technology or sensors that allow the collection and sharing of data.

people picked up, and many other types of information. Analysis of the data could be used to improve decision making related to retail layouts, stocking, pricing, promotional displays, and much more.

The Internet of Things offers real promise for greater automation of marketing research and exciting applications for the future. At the same time, the IoT raises concerns related to privacy and security that will need to be addressed. In addition, since the data from the IoT generally lack context, pairing passive data with qualitative data will be important. The topic of the next chapter is qualitative data.

 Marketing Research on YouTube™ | For further information about the IoT, go to **www.youtube.com** and enter "Data Security and the Internet of Things Deloitte University Press."

 Synthesize Your Learning

This exercise will require you to take into consideration concepts and material from the following chapters:

Chapter 1   Introduction to Marketing Research
Chapter 2   The Marketing Research Industry
Chapter 3   The Marketing Research Process and Defining the Problem and Research Objectives
Chapter 4   Research Design
Chapter 5   Secondary Data and Packaged Information

Drill Bits, Inc.

Bob Douglass owns a machine shop. Most of his work is local business, as machine shop work is labor intensive, and it is difficult to obtain large-quantity orders. Bob is considering branching out. For many years he has observed a couple of local manufacturers whose processes require them to make highly precise drills in metal. For example, the engine block cylinders they produce must be extremely precise for the engines to run at the required compression standards. To make such a precise drill, the drill bits can be used only a few times before they lose their original specifications. Then these expensive drill bits must be thrown away. Bob's customers have complained about this for years, and Bob has been working on a process to refurbish these throwaway bits back to their original specifications.

Finally, Bob has perfected this process. His local customers try out the refurbished bits and are ecstatic with the results. They can now get double the life or even more out of a drill bit. Bob knows his machine shop will soon be very busy from two local customers. To expand his business to accommodate a large volume of refurbishment business, he knows he will have to invest a large sum of money in expanding the building and the machinery needed for the process. But he has no idea of the volume of business to expect.

1. Looking back at Chapter 1, how would you describe the purpose of marketing research in terms of Bob's situation?

2. If Bob is interested in finding a marketing research firm in his state, describe how he might find marketing research firms by states using information contained in Chapter 2.

3. In Chapter 3 we discussed what the "problem" really is. What is Bob's problem?

4. If Bob just wants to know how many firms make engine blocks in the United States, what type of research design would best describe this activity?

5. What secondary source of information would Bob want to seek to achieve the goal stated in question 4?

Summary

Big data can be defined simply as large amounts of data from multiple sources. The term has been popularized in recent years in response to the numerous types and huge amounts of data to which companies now have access in real time. These data represent both opportunities and challenges.

Data may be grouped into two categories: primary and secondary. Primary data are gathered specifically for the research project at hand. Secondary data have been previously gathered for some other purpose. There are many uses of secondary data in marketing research, and sometimes secondary data are all that is needed to achieve the research objectives.

Secondary data may be internal, previously gathered *within* the firm for some other purpose. Examples include data collected and stored from sales receipts, such as types, quantities, and prices of goods or services purchased; customer names; delivery addresses; shipping dates; and salespeople making the sales. Data stored in electronic databases may be used for database marketing. Companies use information recorded in internal databases for purposes of direct marketing and to strengthen relationships with customers. The latter is a process known as customer relationship management (CRM).

External data are obtained from sources outside the firm. These data sources may be classified as (1) published sources, (2) official statistics, and (3) data aggregators. There are different types of published secondary data, such as trade association publications, periodicals, academic journals, books, marketing research company publications, and more. Official statistics are information collected by government organizations and international organizations. The United States by law makes all data collected by government "open by default," except for personal information or data related to national security. Data aggregators are services or vendors that organize and package information on focused topics.

Secondary data have the advantages of being quickly gathered, readily available, and relatively inexpensive; they may add helpful insights should primary data be needed, and sometimes secondary data are all that is needed to achieve the research objective. Disadvantages are that the data are often reported in incompatible reporting units, measurement units do not match researchers' needs, class definitions are incompatible with the researchers' needs, and secondary data may be outdated. Evaluation of secondary data is important; researchers must ask certain questions to ensure the integrity of the information they use.

The American Community Survey (ACS) is an example of free public data useful for researchers. The ACS makes U.S. data available on an annual basis instead of the 10-year interval required in the past to update census data. The ACS may represent the most significant change in several decades in the availability of secondary data to be used for marketing research purposes.

Packaged information is a type of secondary data in which the data collected and/or the process of collecting the data is the same for all users. There are two classes of packaged information. Syndicated data are collected in a standard format and made available to all subscribing users. Packaged services offer a standardized marketing research process that is used to generate information for a particular user.

Syndicated data have the advantages of shared costs of obtaining the data among all those subscribing to the service, high data quality, and the speed with which data are collected and distributed to subscribers. Disadvantages are that buyers cannot control what data are collected, must commit to long-term contracts, and gain no strategic information advantage in buying syndicated data because the information is available to all competitors.

Packaged services have the advantage of use of the supplier firm's expertise in the area, reduced costs, speed, and benchmarks for comparisons. The disadvantages of packaged services are that the process may not be easily customized and the supplier firm may not know the idiosyncrasies of the industry in which the client firm operates.

Four major areas in which packaged information sources may be applied are measuring consumers' attitudes and opinions, defining market segments, monitoring media usage and promotion effectiveness, and conducting market-tracking studies.

One of the fastest-growing areas of marketing research involves the organization and analysis of social media data. Social media data, also termed *user-generated content (UGC)*, is any information that is created by users of online systems and intended to be shared with others. Social media data provide many important forms of information including reviews, tips, new product uses, and competitor news.

An important emerging source of marketing research data is the Internet of Things (IoT), defined as the network of physical objects embedded with software or sensors that allow them to gather and send data. A major category of objects that are part of the IoT are wearables, or wearable technology, which are clothing or accessories that are equipped with computer technology or sensors that allow the collection and sharing of data. As more objects become equipped with sensors, the marketing research applications for the data will multiply.

Key Terms

Big data (p. 116)
Primary data (p. 116)
Secondary data (p. 116)
Internal secondary data (p. 119)
Database (p. 119)
Record (p. 119)
Fields (p. 119)
Internal databases (p. 119)
Customer relationship management (CRM) (p. 119)
Data mining (p. 119)
Micromarketing (p. 119)

External data (p. 120)
Published sources (p. 122)
Official statistics (p. 123)
Open Data Policy (p. 123)
Data aggregators (p. 124)
American Community Survey (ACS) (p. 128)
Packaged information (p. 129)
Syndicated data (p. 129)
Packaged services (p. 131)
Geodemographics (p. 133)
Tracking studies (p. 134)

Social media data (p. 134)
User-generated content (UGC) (p. 134)
Social media monitoring (p. 134)
Social media listening (p. 134)
Sentiment (p. 136)
Internet of Things (IoT) (p. 136)
Passive data (p. 136)
Wearables (p. 136)
Wearable technology (p. 136)

Review Questions/Applications

5-1. What are big data, and why do they represent both an opportunity and a challenge?

5-2. What should be kept in mind before beginning data analysis?

5-3. What are secondary data, and how do they differ from primary data?

5-4. Describe some uses of secondary data.

5-5. Describe the classifications of secondary data.

5-6. What is a database, and what are the components of a database?

5-7. Describe the different ways in which companies use their database.

5-8. What is meant by CRM?

5-9. How are databases useful for managers?

5-10. Give an example of a company that uses micromarketing and explain how.

5-11. Do you think Tesco's use of its database information in Marketing Research Insight 5.2 is ethical? Explain your answer.

5-12. Briefly explain the three different types of external data discussed in the chapter.

5-13. Name three sources of secondary data available to you through your school library.

5-14. What are the five advantages of secondary data?

5-15. Discuss the disadvantages of secondary data.

5-16. Which disadvantage of secondary data is resolved by geodemographics and why?

5-17. How would you go about evaluating secondary data? Why is evaluation important?

5-18. Describe the ACS in terms of the advantage it offers as well as how to retrieve data.

5-19. What is meant by packaged information?

5-20. What is syndicated data? Give an example of a company that supplies syndicated data and describe the information it provides.

5-21. What are packaged services? Give an example of a company that supplies a packaged service and describe the type of information it provides.

5-22. Esri's market segmentation service, Tapestry Segmentation, would be classified as which type of packaged information? Why?

5-23. What are the advantages and disadvantages of syndicated data?

5-24. What is the key difference between syndicated data and packaged services?

5-25. How can packaged information help in strategic marketing decisions?

5-26. Give examples of four types of user-generated information that can be found on social media.

5-27. What are the advantages and disadvantages of social media.

5-28. What is the Internet of Things?

5-29. Access your library's online databases. Describe how your library helps categorize the many databases to guide in your selection of sources appropriate for business.

5-30. Go online to your library's website. Can you locate a database that would be a good choice to find publications such as journal articles, trade publications, or newspapers? What are they?

5-31. Tracking studies are offered by many market research companies, and several use sophisticated software systems to carry them out. Research the typical areas examined in a tracking study. What value do such studies offer the client?

5-32. Refer back to Marketing Research Insight 5.4. Would Jacksonville, Florida, actually meet the criterion to be a test market? Cite the information on which you base your decision.

5-33. In the chapter we used an example of going to the Esri Tapestry Segmentation website for an Active Learning exercise. Go to those instructions. Enter your residence ZIP code and describe the inhabitants in terms of one or more of the consumer types available in the software.

5-34. Social media monitoring involves actively gathering, organizing, and analyzing social media data to learn about brands, products, and services. Choose a well-known brand in your own country or region and monitor social media sites at regular intervals over the next 24 hours to gain consumer insights. Comment on your findings.

5-35. How can companies use passive data collected from wearable technology?

CASE 5.1

The Men's Market for Athleisure[30]

Founded in 1998, Lululemon Athletica, the Canada-based maker of stylish, upscale workout clothes, had grown very quickly. A pioneer of the "athleisure" trend for women—that is, wearing casual clothing outside of the gym—Lululemon had been best known for its yoga pants. Lululemon had a thriving online business, as well as physical stores in the United States, Canada, Japan, and Australia. Although Lululemon's core strength had been its women's clothing, the company also sold men's clothing.

Lululemon's sales had grown rapidly, but the company faced some important challenges. First, other activewear companies, such as Nike Inc. and Under Armour Inc., had begun to directly compete with Lululemon in the athleisure market. Also, Lululemon had difficulty recovering from a 2013 controversy, in which the company had to recall a large number of black yoga pants because their fabric was too transparent. Chip Wilson, CEO of Lululemon, compounded the problem by offering the explanation that "frankly some women's bodies just don't actually work for it." Mr. Wilson resigned from Lululemon, and the company continued to grow under new leadership.

Lululemon has been pursuing the strategy of growing its male market. Despite Lululemon's association with women's clothing, men's clothing has had strong profits and some loyal customers. Your task is to consider what secondary sources can be used to examine Lululemon's current strength and potential in the men's athleisure market. Should Lululemon invest more resources into its men's market?

1. What internal secondary sources does Lululemon already have that the company could use to gain insights on its men's market? Be sure to consider supplier records, retail store records, website information, and sales force records.

2. Which external published sources and data aggregators have useful information about Lululemon's current position and the potential for the men's athleisure market? In your investigation, include the following:
   a. Business publications (e.g., *New York Times, Wall Street Journal, Forbes, Economist*, etc.)
   b. Trade and professional association information (e.g., athleticbusiness.com, wewear.org, etc.)
   c. Academic journals (search using your library's database of business journals)
   d. Industry information (check your library's sources, such as those found in Table 5.1)

3. Where does Lululemon currently have men's only stores? Use the American Community Survey to identify a promising metropolitan statistical area (MSA) for Lululemon to locate its next men's only store. Justify your decision.

4. Conduct an investigation of social media to examine user-generated content related to Lululemon.
   a. What are the trending topics on social media related to Lululemon? (Use a free social media aggregator, such as Addictomatic or Twazzup, to investigate.)
   b. What is the *sentiment* of the comments related to Lululemon? Compare the sentiment ratio of Lululemon to two of its competitors. What does that mean?
   c. What other sources of user-generated content can you find on social media? Do consumer perceptions appear to be supportive of sale of Lululemon's men's clothing? Explain.

5. Integrate your information from the preceding questions to determine whether or not Lululemon should invest more heavily in its men's market. Justify your response using information from your search of secondary data.

Sources: Beilfuss, L. (2015, September 10). Lululemon sales rise, gross margin declines. *Wall Street Journal*. Retrieved from http://www.wsj.com/articles/lululemon-quarterly-profit-slips-but-retailer-raises-full-year-guidance-1441882373; Petro, G. (2015, September 16). Lululemon, Nike and the rise of "Athleisure." *Forbes*. Retrieved from http://www.forbes.com/sites/gregpetro/2015/09/16/lululemon-nike-and-the-rise-of-athleisure/; Wallace, A. (2015, February 2). *New York Times*. Retrieved from http://www.nytimes.com/2015/02/08/magazine/lululemons-guru-is-moving-on.html?_r=0.

6

Qualitative Research Techniques

MTV: How MTV Uses Online Panels to Research Its Youth Audience

Alison Hillhouse, Vice President of Insights, MTV.

For over 30 years, MTV has continued to innovate for every new generation of youth—developing cutting-edge content from series to award shows to digital shorts to social media postings. It's crucial that MTV stays tapped into the psychographics and behaviors of youth today. And because of the impact of technology, youth culture is changing faster than ever. In fact, MTV's research shows that 84% of 20- to 24-year-olds agree that "teens today seem so different than when I was a teen." So MTV relies heavily on its research and insights team, MTV Insights, to keep constantly connected with this rapidly changing demographic.

One of the key methodologies MTV Insights employs to speak to its teen and 20-something audience on a daily basis is online panels. These panels are run via "Facebook Groups" and filled with a hand-selected group of articulate and culturally connected youth from across the country. On any given day, MTV will be posing questions to its panels about topics ranging from high school cliques to Tinder dating to start-up culture. And the panelists also proactively share trending topics from their social feeds, happenings from their high school and college campuses, and insight into their personal lives.

I find online panels to be the most valuable of all of our research methodologies. We establish relationships with our panelists and they feel committed to keeping us on top of trends and helping us understand their generation. It's a mutually beneficial arrangement for the panelists—they are compensated and also have a great experience to add to their resume. But their sense of commitment goes beyond the compensation. They genuinely like to help and be heard. I also frequently Facebook-message back and forth with several of the panelists. I call them my "high school best friends," as I truly feel like I know them and can depend on them.

The insights the panelists share feed into several research outputs that the MTV Insights team produces and shares with all of MTV—multimedia PowerPoint presentations, weekly newsletters, and video compilations of kids talking about their lives (panelists are asked to upload video responses of them talking about particular subjects). Once, MTV Insights took over a floor at MTV and created a multimedia exhibit called "High School Hallways" to bring the research to life, complete with a high school bedroom, party room, and social-media-detox tent. Sometimes findings from this research directly feed into show ideas, but mostly they are absorbed by MTV staff to help them develop a holistically better understanding of the people in the audience, what's important to them, and the kind of content they might be interested in consuming.

—Alison Hillhouse

Visit MTV at http://www. MTV.com.

Source: Text and photos courtesy Alison Hillhouse and MTV Networks.

ven as collecting many forms of quantitative data has become more automated and less expensive (see Chapter 5), qualitative research methods have retained their vitality in the marketing research industry. This is because qualitative research methods provide the context necessary to understand people's actions, opinions, and emotions. As you will learn, qualitative research delivers insights that are not found in quantitative research.

This chapter discusses how to distinguish between qualitative and quantitative research as well as the various methods used in conducting qualitative research. Each qualitative method has its place in the marketing research process, and each has its unique advantages and disadvantages as well. Because focus groups remain the most popular qualitative marketing research technique, an in-depth discussion of them is included. We begin with a discussion of quantitative, qualitative, and mixed methods research.

The means of data collection during the research process can be classified into two broad categories: quantitative and qualitative.

Quantitative research is defined as research involving the administration of a set of structured questions with predetermined response options to a large number of respondents.

6-1 Quantitative, Qualitative, and Mixed Methods Research

The means of data collection during the research process can be classified into two broad categories: quantitative and qualitative. There are many differences between these two methods, and it is necessary to understand their special characteristics to make the right selection. To start, we briefly define these two approaches, and then we describe mixed methods research.

Quantitative research is the traditional mainstay of the research industry, and it is sometimes referred to as "survey research." For our purposes, **quantitative research** is defined as research involving the administration of a set of structured questions with predetermined response options to a large number of respondents. When you think of quantitative research, you might envision a company that has a panel whose members complete

Online surveys are a form of quantitative research.

an online survey. That is, quantitative research often involves a sizable representative sample of the population and a formalized procedure for gathering data. The purpose of quantitative research is specific, and this research is used when the manager and researcher have agreed on the precise information that is needed. Data format and sources are clear and well defined, and the compilation and formatting of the data gathered follow an orderly procedure that is largely numerical in nature.

Qualitative research involves collecting, analyzing, and interpreting data by observing what people do and say.

Qualitative research, in contrast, involves collecting, analyzing, and interpreting unstructured data by observing what people do and say. Observations and statements are free-form or nonstandardized because questions and observations are open ended. Qualitative data can be categorized, but such data are not usually quantified. For example, if you asked five people to express their opinions on a topic such as gun control or promoting alcoholic beverages to college students, you would probably get five different statements. But after studying each response, you could characterize each one as "positive," "negative," or "neutral." This translation step would not be necessary if you instructed them to choose predetermined responses such as "yes" or "no." Any study that is conducted using an observational technique or unstructured questioning can be classified as qualitative research, which is becoming increasingly popular in a number of research situations.[1]

Qualitative research techniques afford rich insight into consumer behavior.

Why would you want to use such a "soft" approach? Often marketing researchers find that a large-scale survey is inappropriate. For instance, Procter & Gamble may be interested in improving its Ultra Tide laundry detergent, so it invites a group of age 30- to 45-year-old women to brainstorm how Ultra Tide could perform better or how its packaging could be improved or to discuss other features of the detergent. These ideas may have been the origins of Tide PODS or Tide To Go. Listening to the market in this way can generate excellent packaging, product design, or product positioning ideas. As another example, if the P&G marketing group were developing a special end-of-aisle display for Tide, it might want to test one version in an actual supermarket environment. It could place one in a Safeway grocery store in a San Francisco suburb and videotape shoppers as they encountered the display. The videos would then be reviewed to determine what types of responses occurred. For instance, did shoppers stop there? Did they read the copy on the display? Did they pick up the displayed product and look at it? Qualitative research techniques afford rich insight into consumer behavior.[2] An example of a company that makes extensive use of qualitative marketing research is the global home furnishings company Ikea (see Marketing Research Insight 6.1).

Our goal in this chapter is to emphasize the value of qualitative research techniques and the ability of qualitative research and quantitative research to work hand in hand. Although there are proponents of both qualitative and quantitative research, the majority of marketing researchers have adopted *mixed methods research*, also known as pluralistic or hybrid research. A 2015 survey of marketing research professionals found that more than two-thirds (69%) of marketing researchers use a combination of quantitative and qualitative research techniques, adopting their methods to the project at hand.[3] **Mixed methods research** is defined as the combination of qualitative and quantitative research methods with the aim of gaining the advantages of both. It is often said that quantitative data provide the "what," and qualitative data provide the "why."

Mixed methods research is defined as the combination of qualitative and quantitative research methods with the aim of gaining the advantages of both.

Mixed methods research can take a variety of forms. Traditionally, exploratory qualitative techniques precede quantitative techniques. For example, in-depth interviews of selected dealers or a series of focus group discussions with customers might be used to understand how a product or service is perceived in comparison to competitors. An observational study could be used to learn how customers use the product. These activities often help crystallize the problem or otherwise highlight factors and considerations that might be overlooked if the researcher had rushed into a full-scale survey.

The qualitative phase can serve as a foundation for the quantitative phase of the research project because it provides the researcher with firsthand knowledge of the research problem. Armed with this knowledge, the researcher's design and execution of the quantitative phase

MARKETING RESEARCH INSIGHT 6.1 — *Global Application*

Ikea Uses Qualitative Research to Develop New Markets

Ikea, the Swedish home furnishings company, makes extensive use of multiple forms of qualitative research, including observation and ethnography. As Ikea has expanded around the world, the company has conducted careful marketing research to understand the cultural nuances of its many markets. Before opening its first store in South Korea in 2014, Ikea studied the market for six years. *Fortune* magazine claims that "research is at the heart of Ikea's expansion."

Ikea uses observational research to understand consumers' experiences in their homes. In one exploration of how people use sofas, Ikea set up cameras in homes in Stockholm, Milan, New York, and Shenzhen, China. Among other findings, Ikea discovered that many people in Shenzhen sit on the floor, using the sofa as a backrest.

Ikea also makes extensive use of ethnographic techniques, with the *New Yorker* magazine calling Ikea "some of the world's foremost anthropologists of home life." Ikea employees conduct thousands of visits per year to consumers' homes to examine in what ways people are satisfied and frustrated with their furnishings.

In addition to visiting and monitoring homes, Ikea has purchased an apartment in Malmö, Sweden, to use as a "living lab." Ikea chose a smaller apartment, because the homes in Ikea's primary markets—emerging markets and large cities such as San Francisco and Boston—are getting smaller. Ikea invites families of diverse sizes and characteristics to live in the apartment for a couple of weeks at a time. The families are paid about $US 600 to participate in the project and given an iPad with an app that can be used to record their impressions. Among the products

Ethnographic research can involve observing consumers in their own homes.

being tested in this apartment are moveable walls and sliding power sockets.

A recent addition to Ikea's research department is an "innovation center" in Copenhagen, Denmark, called Space 10. Ikea invites innovators, including professors, students, artists, and designers, to Space 10 to collaborate on ideas.

Based on marketing research insights, Ikea produces about 2,000 new products and redesigns a year. Because of the careful research, it can take Ikea many years to design products. Among the products that Ikea has planned for the future is an electric bike.

Sources: Collins, L. (2011, October 3). House perfect: Is the IKEA ethos comfy or creepy? *New Yorker*. Retrieved from http://www.newyorker.com/magazine/2011/10/03/house-perfect; Hansegard, J. (2015, September 29). IKEA Tests Movable Walls for Cramped Homes. *Wall Street Journal*. Retrieved from http://www.wsj.com/articles/ikea-tests-movable-walls-for-cramped-homes-14www43546181; Kowitt, B. (2015, March 15). How Ikea took over the world. *Fortune*. Retrieved from http://fortune.com/ikea-world-domination/; Rhodes, M. (2015, November 24). The innovation lab: Where Ikea will get its next idea. *The Wired*. Retrieved from http://www.wired.com/2015/11/the-innovation-lab-where-ikea-will-get-its-next-big-idea/.

are invariably superior to what they might have been without the qualitative phase. As an example, *The Arizona Republic* newspaper has used online focus groups for brainstorming, and the outcomes of these sessions are then used to devise online surveys. Through this mixed methods approach, the Showtime network investigated the different lifestyle types of viewers of its *Nurse Jackie* show: those who watch on demand, those who prefer to watch live, those who use DVRs, and those who use a combination of the viewing platforms.[4] The on-demand and DVR viewers really valued the ability to pause, rewind, and re-experience; the live watchers eagerly anticipated the premiere shows; the DVR users had constraints and needed the convenience of recorded episodes; and the combination viewers had complicated schedules and used whatever platform worked that week.

In others cases, a qualitative phase is applied after a quantitative study to help the researcher understand the findings in the quantitative phase.[5] For example, after getting the results of a survey, a company might convene focus groups to gain a greater understanding of the survey findings. In another example, following a consumer segmentation study, researchers might then use in-depth interviews to develop rich profiles of each segment.

Qualitative and quantitative research can also be conducted simultaneously. For example, to test three new flavors of pastries, a baked goods company organized a series of focus groups across the United States. For each flavor, the focus group participants were asked to first privately taste and rate the flavor of the pastry on a number of characteristics and then discuss their reactions with other focus group participants. This method allowed the company to obtain independent ratings of their product concepts, supplemented with more details on how the participants arrived at their ratings. In addition, by monitoring the interactions among the focus group members, the company could observe how perceptions of the pastry flavors might be affected by social settings.

6-2 Observation Techniques

Observation methods are techniques in which phenomena of interest involving people, objects, and/or activities are systematically observed and documented.

We begin our description of qualitative research techniques with **observation methods**, which are techniques in which phenomena of interest involving people, objects, and/or activities are systematically observed and documented. As we describe each observation technique, you will see that each is unique in how it obtains observations.

TYPES OF OBSERVATION

Four general ways of organizing observations are (1) direct versus indirect, (2) covert versus overt, (3) structured versus unstructured, and (4) in situ versus invented.

At first glance, it may seem that observation studies can occur without any structure; however, it is important to adhere to a plan so that the observations are consistent and comparisons or generalizations can be made without worrying about any conditions of the observation method that might confound the findings. There are four general ways of making observations: (1) direct versus indirect, (2) overt versus covert, (3) structured versus unstructured, and (4) in situ versus invented.

Observing behavior as it occurs is called direct observation.

Direct Versus Indirect Observation methods might be classified as direct versus indirect according to whether or not the phenomena is being observed in real time. Observing behavior as it occurs is called **direct observation**.[6] For example, if we are interested in finding out how much shoppers squeeze tomatoes to assess their freshness, we can observe people actually picking up the tomatoes. Direct observation has been used by Kellogg's to understand breakfast rituals, by a Swiss chocolate maker to study the behavior of "chocoholics," and by the U.S. Post Office's advertising agency to come up with the advertising slogan "We Deliver."[7] It has also been used by General Mills to understand how children eat breakfast, leading to the launch of Go-Gurt, a midmorning snack for schoolchildren.[8]

With indirect observation, the researcher observes the effects or results of the behavior rather than the behavior itself. Types of indirect observations include archives and physical traces.

Some behaviors, such as past actions, cannot be directly observed. In those cases, we must rely on **indirect observation**, which involves observing the effects or results of the behavior rather than the behavior itself. Types of indirect observations include archives and physical traces.

Archives are secondary sources, such as historical records, that can be applied to the present problem. These sources contain a wealth of information and should not be overlooked or underestimated. Many types of archives exist. For example, records of sales calls may be inspected to determine how often salespeople make cold calls. **Physical traces** are tangible evidence of some past event. For example, we might turn to "garbology" (observing the trash of subjects being studied) as a way of finding out how much recycling of plastic milk bottles occurs. A soft drink company might do a litter audit to assess how much impact its aluminum cans have on the countryside. A fast-food company such as Wendy's might measure the amount of graffiti on buildings located adjacent to prospective location sites as a means of estimating the crime potential for each site.[9]

Covert Versus Overt Covert versus overt observation refers to the degree with which subjects are aware that their behavior is being observed. With **covert observation**, the subject is unaware that he or she is being observed. An example is a "mystery shopper" who is hired by a retail store chain to record and report on sales clerks' assistance and courtesy. One-way mirrors and hidden cameras are a few of the other ways used to prevent subjects from becoming aware that they are being observed. The aim of this approach is to observe typical behaviors; if the subjects were aware they were being watched, they might change their behavior, resulting in observations of atypical behavior. If you were a store clerk, how would you act if the department manager told you he would be watching you for the next hour? You would probably be on your best behavior for those 60 minutes. Covert observation has proved illuminating in studies of parents and children shopping together in supermarkets.[10] With direct questions, parents might feel compelled to say that their children are always on their best behavior while shopping.

> With covert observation, the subject is unaware that he or she is being observed.

Sometimes it is impossible for the respondent to be unaware that someone is watching. Examples of **overt observation**, all of which require the subjects' knowledge, include laboratory settings, recordings of sales calls, People Meters (Nielsen Media Research's device that is attached to a television set to record when and to what station a set is tuned), and Nielsen Audio's Personal Portable Meter. Because people might be influenced by knowing they are being observed, it is wise to always minimize the presence of the observer to the maximum extent possible.

> When the respondent knows he or she is being observed, this form of research is known as overt observation.

Structured Versus Unstructured Structured versus unstructured observation refers to the degree to which the phenomena to be observed are predetermined. When using **structured observation** techniques, the researcher identifies beforehand exactly which behaviors are to be observed and recorded. All other behaviors are "ignored." Often a checklist or a standardized observation form is used to isolate the observer's attention to specific factors. These highly structured observations typically require a minimum of effort on the part of the observer.

> The researcher identifies beforehand which behaviors are to be observed and recorded in structured observation.

Unstructured observation places no restriction on what the observer notes. All behavior in the episode under study is monitored. The observer watches the situation and records what he or she deems interesting or relevant. Of course, the observer is thoroughly briefed on the area of general concern. This type of observation is often used in exploratory research. For example, Black & Decker might send someone to observe carpenters working at various job sites as a means of better understanding how the tools are used and to help generate ideas as to how to design the tools for increased safety.

> In using unstructured observation, there are no predetermined restrictions on what the observer records.

In Situ Versus Invented In situ versus invented observation refers to the extent that behavior is observed in its natural environment versus in an artificial, or invented, environment. With **in situ observation**, the researcher observes the behavior exactly as it happens in a natural environment. For instance, a motion-sensitive camera might be placed in people's kitchens to observe the behavior of family members as they inspect the contents of their refrigerator, prepare breakfast, unpack groceries, and conduct the many other routine activities that occur in kitchens. Mystery shopping is done in situ. Midas improved its service quality by having customers make videos of themselves as they made car service appointments.[11]

> With in situ observation, the researcher observes the behavior exactly as it happens in a natural environment.

Invented observation occurs when the researcher creates a simulated environment in order to improve understanding of a phenomenon. For example, a researcher might ask people to make a video as they try out a new toilet bowl cleaner. Whirlpool has test kitchens at its headquarters, in which researchers observe volunteers conducting kitchen-related tasks as a means to improve the performance of Whirlpool appliances.[12]

> Invented observation occurs when the researcher creates a simulated environment in order to improve understanding of a phenomenon.

APPROPRIATE CONDITIONS FOR THE USE OF OBSERVATION

Certain conditions must be met before a researcher can successfully use observation as a marketing research tool. First, the event must occur during a relatively short time interval, and the observed behavior must occur in a public setting. In addition, observation is typically used when the possibility of faulty recall rules out collecting information by asking the subject.

Short time interval means that the event must begin and end within a reasonably short time span. Examples include a shopping trip in a supermarket, waiting in a teller line at a bank, purchasing a clothing item, or observing children as they watch a television program. Some decision-making processes can take a long time (for example, buying a home), and it would be unrealistic to observe the entire process. As a result, observational research is usually limited to scrutinizing activities that can be completed in a relatively short time or to observing certain phases of those activities with a longer time span.

Public behavior refers to behavior that occurs in a setting the researcher can readily observe. Actions such as personal hygiene procedures or private worship are not public activities and therefore are not suitable for observational studies such as those described here.

Faulty recall occurs when actions or activities are so repetitive or automatic that the observed person cannot recall specifics about the behavior under question. For example, people cannot recall accurately how many times they looked at their wristwatch while waiting in a long line to buy a ticket to a best-selling movie or which brands of cookies they looked at while grocery shopping. Observation is necessary under circumstances of faulty recall to fully understand the behavior at hand. Faulty recall is one of the reasons that companies have experimented for many years with mechanical devices to observe these behaviors.[13]

ADVANTAGES OF OBSERVATIONAL DATA

Observational research has the advantage of seeing what consumers actually do instead of relying on their self-report of what they think they do.

Observation of humans in their natural context is the approach that has been used by anthropologists for more than 100 years and is an accepted method of conducting marketing research.[14] Typically, the subjects of observational research are unaware they are being studied. Because of this, they react in a natural manner, giving the researcher insight into actual, not reported, behaviors. As previously noted, observational research methods also mean that there is no chance for recall error. The subjects are not asked what they remember about a certain action. Instead, they are observed while engaged in the act. In some cases, observation may be the only way to obtain accurate information. For instance, children who cannot yet verbally express their opinion of a new toy will do so by simply playing or not playing with the toy. Retail marketers commonly gather marketing intelligence about competitors and about their own employees' behaviors by hiring the services of mystery shoppers who pose as customers but who are actually trained observers.[15] Of course, mystery shopping should be conducted in an ethical manner, as described in the MRA code of ethics excerpt in Marketing Research Insight 6.2. In some situations, data can be obtained with better accuracy and less cost by using observational methods as opposed to other means. For example, counts of in-store traffic can often be made by means of observational techniques more accurately and less expensively than by using survey techniques. Also, mixed methods researchers will use observation techniques to supplement and complement other techniques.[16]

LIMITATIONS OF OBSERVATIONAL DATA

The major disadvantages of observational research are the generally small sample size, which may not be representative of the population, and the inability to determine consumers' motives, attitudes, and intentions.

The limitations of observation reflect the limitations of qualitative research in general. With direct observation, typically only small numbers of subjects are studied and usually under special circumstances, so their representativeness is a concern.[17] This factor, plus the subjective interpretation required to explain the observed behavior, usually forces the researcher to consider his or her conclusions to be tentative. Certainly, the greatest drawback of all observational methods is the researcher's inability to pry beneath the behavior observed and to interrogate the person on motives, attitudes, and all of the other unseen aspects of why what was observed took place.

Only when these feelings are relatively unimportant or are readily inferred from the behavior is it appropriate to use observational research methods. For example, facial expression

MARKETING RESEARCH INSIGHT 6.2 *Ethical Consideration*

Marketing Research Association Code of Ethics

Mystery Shopping

Mystery shopping is a long-established research technique used by a wide variety of commercial, governmental, and other organizations. Its purpose is to help such groups to assess and improve the standards of service they provide to their customers by comparing their achieved performance against their own targets and against the standards provided by competitors and other organizations. The approach involves the use of evaluators who are specially trained to observe and measure the nature and quality of the services being offered to customers. These mystery shoppers pose as consumers and chronicle detailed information about their mystery shopping experience using questionnaires or narrative reports.

The MRA considers mystery shopping a legitimate form of marketing research when it is employed for customer satisfaction purposes—that is, to determine likely customer perceptions and needs. It is not considered marketing research when it is used for nonresearch purposes such as identifying individuals for disciplinary actions, falsely elevating sales by creating a

Mystery shopping involves the use of evaluators who are specially trained to observe and measure the nature and quality of the services being offered to customers.

demand for products or services that does not really exist in the current marketplace, or obtaining personal information for non-research purposes.

Source: Marketing Research Association, Inc. THE CODE OF MARKETING RESEARCH STANDARDS Ratified March, 2007, p. 37. Used courtesy of the Marketing Research Association, Inc.

---

might be used as an indicator of a child's attitudes or preferences for various types of fruit drink flavors because children often react with conspicuous physical expressions. But adults and even children usually conceal their reasons and true reactions in public, and this fact necessitates a direct questioning approach because observation alone cannot give a complete picture of why and how people act the way they do.

6-3 Focus Groups

A frequently used qualitative research technique is **focus groups**, which are small groups of people brought together and guided by a moderator through an unstructured, spontaneous discussion for the purpose of gaining information relevant to the research problem.[18] Although focus groups should encourage openness on the part of the participants, the approach ensures that discussion is "focused" on some general area of interest. For example, Verizon conducted a series of focus groups with teenagers and adults under the age of 34 to "focus" on how younger consumers watch video. The focus groups, combined with results from observation studies, supported Verizon's conjecture that this age group watched and shared videos mainly on smartphones. The result of this study was the launch of go90, an ios and android mobile service, targeted to teenagers and young adults.[19]

Focus groups represent a useful technique for gathering information from a limited sample of respondents. The information can be used to generate ideas, to learn the respondents' "vocabulary" when relating to a certain type of product, or to gain some insights into basic needs and attitudes.[20] In a 2015 survey of marketing professionals, 91% of respondents agreed that focus groups were effective or very effective at delivering actionable insights.[21] They have become so popular in marketing research that many large cities throughout the world

Focus groups are small groups of people brought together and guided through an unstructured, spontaneous discussion for the purpose of gaining information relevant to the research problem.

Information from focus groups can be used to generate ideas, to learn the respondents' "vocabulary" when relating to a certain type of product, or to gain some insights into basic needs and attitudes.

have companies that specialize in performing focus group research. You will most certainly encounter focus group research if you become a practicing marketing manager. Focus groups are an invaluable means of regaining contact with customers when marketers have lost touch, and they are helpful in learning about new customer groups.

HOW FOCUS GROUPS WORK

Focus group participants' comments are encouraged and guided by moderators.

In a traditional focus group, a small group of people (about 6 to 12 persons) are brought together in a dedicated room, with a one-way mirror for client viewing, for about two hours. Focus group participants are guided by **moderators**. The training and background of the moderator are extremely important for the success of the focus group.[22] Focus group moderators are responsible for creating an atmosphere that is conducive to openness, yet they must make certain the participants do not stray too far from the central focus of the study. Good moderators have excellent observation, interpersonal, and communication skills to recognize and overcome threats to a productive group discussion. They must be able to tactfully encourage quieter participants to open up and give their opinions, while making sure that no one participant dominates the group. They are prepared, experienced, and armed with a detailed list of topics to be discussed.[23] It is also helpful if focus group moderators can eliminate any preconceptions on discussion topics from their minds. The best moderators are experienced, enthusiastic, prepared, involved, energetic, and open-minded.[24] With an incompetent moderator, the focus group can become a disaster.

Focus group company principals are sometimes referred to as qualitative research consultants (QRCs). The QRC prepares a **focus group report** that summarizes the information provided by the focus group participants relative to the research questions. Two factors are crucial when analyzing the data. First, some sense must be made by translating the statements of participants into categories or themes and then reporting the degree of consensus apparent in the focus groups.[25] Second, the demographic and buyer behavior characteristics of focus group participants should be judged against the target market profile to assess to what degree the groups represent the target market.

The focus group report reflects the qualitative aspect of this research method. It lists all themes that have become apparent, and it notes any diversity of opinions or thoughts expressed by the participants. It will also have numerous verbatim excerpts provided as evidence.[26] In fact, some reports include complete transcripts or video recordings of the focus group

 Active Learning

Learn More About Qualitative Research

Go to the Qualitative Research Consultants Association website (www.qrca.org). Click on "About Qual Research" to access the "When to Use Qualitative Research" page. Now let's consider the example of recommendations made by a university's faculty senate to the administration. For each of these recommendations, indicate whether qualitative research should be used to evaluate students' opinions. What are the pros and cons of using this form of research in each case?

1. Require all students to park at a central parking lot two miles from campus and take shuttle buses to campus.
2. Increase tuition by 10%.
3. Schedule classes on Monday/Wednesday or Tuesday/Thursday, leaving Friday for student organization meetings and group project work.
4. Require students to take at least 18 hours of course work during summer school.
5. Require every student to purchase and bring an iPad to class.

discussion. This information is then used as the basis for further research studies or even for more focus groups. If the information is used for subsequent focus groups, the client uses the first group as a learning experience, making any adjustments to the discussion topics as needed to improve the research objectives. Although focus groups may be the only type of research used to tackle a marketing problem or question, they are also used as a beginning point for quantitative research efforts; that is, a focus group phase may be used to gain a feel for a specific survey that will ultimately generate standardized information from a representative sample.

ONLINE FOCUS GROUPS

The **online focus group** is a contemporary focus group in which respondents communicate via an Internet forum, which clients can observe. Typically, online focus groups allow the participants the convenience of being seated at their own computers, while the moderator operates out of his or her office. The online focus group is "virtual" in that it communicates electronically and does not have face-to-face contact. For example, FocusVision Worldwide (http://www.focusvision.com) has an online focus group system using webcams and voice communication that connect the moderator and focus group members in real time while clients can observe and send chat messages to the moderator during the discussion if they wish. Online focus groups have the following advantages over traditional focus groups: (1) no physical setup is necessary, (2) transcripts are captured on file in real time, (3) participants can be in widely separated geographic locations, (4) participants are comfortable in their home or office environments, and (5) the moderator can exchange private messages with individual participants. Innovative approaches are possible, as some researchers combine online with telephone communications for maximum effectiveness.[27] Nonetheless, there are some disadvantages to online focus groups: (1) observation of participants' body language is not possible, (2) participants cannot physically inspect products or taste food items, and (3) participants can lose interest or become distracted.[28]

Online focus group participants are in relaxed surroundings, but they can become bored or distracted.

Respondents to an online focus group communicate via the Internet, and clients may observe the virtual chat.

A variation of the online focus group is conducted in a traditional setting, but the client watches online. For example, Focus Pointe Global (http://www.focuspointeglobal.com), which operates facilities in 18 cities in the United States, offers clients the ability to view focus groups online using streaming video. The focus group is conducted at a traditional focus group facility with the participants seated with the moderator. This type of online focus group allows several members of the client firm to observe the focus group at their own location. This saves the client firm travel expense and time. While they will not replace traditional focus groups, online focus groups offer a viable research method.[29]

ADVANTAGES OF FOCUS GROUPS

The four major advantages of focus groups are that (1) they generate fresh ideas; (2) they allow clients to observe their participants; (3) they may be directed at understanding a wide variety of issues, such as reactions to a new food product, brand logo, or television ad; and (4) they allow fairly easy access to special respondent groups, such as lawyers or doctors (whereas it may be very difficult to find a representative sample of these groups).

DISADVANTAGES OF FOCUS GROUPS

There are three major disadvantages to focus groups: (1) They do not constitute representative samples; therefore, caution must be exercised in generalizing findings; (2) success is greatly dependent on the ability of the moderator; and (3) it is sometimes difficult to interpret the results of focus groups (the moderator's report is based on a subjective evaluation of participants' statements and interactions).

WHEN SHOULD FOCUS GROUPS BE USED?

When the research objective is to explore or describe rather than predict, focus groups may be an alternative. They work well for the following situations: A company wants to know "how to speak" to its market; what language and terms do its customers use? What are some new ideas for an ad campaign? Will a new service we are developing have appeal to customers, and how can we improve it? How can we better package our product?[30] In all these cases, focus groups can describe the terms customers use; their reactions and ideas for ads; the reasons why service, product, or package features are appealing; and suggestions for improving the company's delivery of benefits. Refer to the following section, "Some Objectives of Focus Groups," for elaboration on when focus groups are particularly useful.

WHEN SHOULD FOCUS GROUPS NOT BE USED?

Because focus groups are based on a small number of persons who are not representative of some larger population, care must be exercised in using focus groups. If the research objective is to predict, focus groups should not be used. For example, if we show 12 persons in a focus group a new product prototype and 6 say they will buy it, it is not defensible to predict that 50% of the population will buy it. Likewise, if the research will dictate a major, expensive decision, the company should not rely solely on the use of focus groups. If a high-stakes decision is at hand, research that is representative of some population and that has some known margin of error (quantitative research) should be used.

SOME OBJECTIVES OF FOCUS GROUPS

There are four main objectives of focus groups: (1) to generate ideas; (2) to understand consumer vocabulary; (3) to reveal consumer needs, motives, perceptions, and attitudes about products or services; and (4) to understand findings from quantitative studies.

Focus groups *generate ideas* for managers to consider. Krispy Kreme has conducted focus groups to help design new product choices and stores. If managers consistently hear that their customers prefer their doughnuts but go elsewhere for gourmet coffees, this gives Krispy Kreme management ideas for changing their product mix to include gourmet coffee. Mothers talking about the difficulties of strapping children in car restraint seats give designers of these products ideas. Consumers discussing the difficulties of moving furniture give rise to innovations in furniture designed for portability.

To *understand consumer vocabulary* entails using a focus group to stay abreast of the words and phrases consumers use when describing products to improve communications about those products or services. Such information may help in advertising copy design or in the preparation of an instruction pamphlet. This knowledge refines research problem definitions and also helps structure questions for use in later quantitative research.

The third objective—to *reveal consumer needs, motives, perceptions, and attitudes* about products or services—involves using a focus group to refresh the marketing team's understanding of what customers really feel or think about a product or service. Alternatively, managers may need early customer reactions to changes being considered in products or services.[31] Focus groups are commonly used during the exploratory phase of research.[32] This application is useful in generating objectives to be addressed by subsequent research.

Finally, to *understand findings from quantitative studies* requires using focus groups to better comprehend data gathered from other surveys. Sometimes a focus group can reveal why the findings came out a particular way. For example, a bank image survey showed that a particular branch consistently received lower scores on "employee friendliness." Focus group research identified the problem as being several frontline employees who were so concerned with efficiency that they appeared to be unfriendly. The bank revised its training program to remedy the problem.

Warner-Lambert is one company that has successfully used focus groups to accomplish all four of these objectives. Its consumer health products group, which markets over-the-counter health and beauty products as well as nonprescription drugs, uses focus groups extensively.[33] In fact, Warner-Lambert uses a combination of qualitative research techniques to gain background information, to reveal needs and attitudes related to health and beauty products, and to stimulate brainstorming new ideas. Focus groups have been useful in understanding basic shifts in consumer lifestyles, values, and purchase patterns.

OPERATIONAL ASPECTS OF TRADITIONAL FOCUS GROUPS

Before a traditional focus group is conducted, certain operational questions should be addressed. It is important to decide how many people should take part in a focus group, who they should be, how they will be selected and recruited, and where they should meet. General guidelines exist for answering these questions. A discussion of each follows.

How Many People Should Be in a Focus Group? According to standard industry practice, the optimal size of a traditional focus group is 6 to 12 people. A small group (fewer than six participants) is not likely to generate the energy and group dynamics necessary for a truly beneficial focus group session. A small group will often result in awkward silences and force the moderator to take too active a role in the discussion just to keep the discussion alive. Similarly, a group with more than a dozen participants may prove too large to be conducive to a natural discussion. As a focus group becomes larger in size, it tends to become fragmented. Those participating may become frustrated by the inherent digressions and side comments. Conversations may break out among two or three participants while another is talking. This situation places the moderator in the role of disciplinarian, in which he or she is constantly calling for quiet or order rather than focusing the discussion on the issues at hand.

> The optimal size of a focus group is 6 to 12 people.

Unfortunately, it is often difficult to predict the exact number of people who will attend the focus group interview. Ten may agree to participate, and only 4 may show up; 14 may be invited in hopes that 8 will show up, and all 14 may arrive. Of course, if this occurs, the researcher faces a judgment call as to whether or not to send some home. There is no guaranteed method to ensure a successful participation ratio. Incentives (which will be discussed later) are helpful but definitely not a certain way of gaining acceptance. Although 6 to 12 is the ideal focus group size, because of the uncertainty of participation, focus groups with fewer than 6 or more than 12 do take place.

Who Should Be in the Focus Group? It is generally believed that the best focus groups are composed of participants who share homogeneous characteristics. This requirement is sometimes automatically satisfied by the researcher's need to have particular types of people in the focus group. For instance, the focus group may be comprised of executives who use satellite phones, building contractors who specialize in building homes over $500,000 in value, or salespeople who are experiencing some common customer service difficulty. With consumer products, the focus group's common trait may just be that everyone buys salsa.

> Ideally, focus group members should be homogeneous.

The need for similar demographic or other relevant characteristics in focus group members is accentuated by the fact that participants are typically strangers. In most cases, they are not friends or even casual acquaintances, and many people feel intimidated or at least hesitant to voice their opinions and suggestions to a group of strangers. But participants typically feel more comfortable once they realize they have similarities such as their age (they may all be in their early 30s), job situations (they may all be junior executives), family composition (they may all have preschool children), purchase experiences (they may all have bought a new car in the past year), or even leisure pursuits (they may all play tennis). Furthermore, by conducting a group that is as homogeneous as possible with respect to demographics and other characteristics, the researcher is assured that differences in these variables will be less likely to confuse the issue being discussed.

More than one focus group should always be conducted.

How Many Focus Groups Should Be Conducted? The answer to how many focus groups should be conducted is always "more than one." Because each focus group tends to have its own personality, findings should never be based off a single focus group. Technically speaking, the rule is to hold as many focus groups as it takes to reach a saturation point in terms of gaining new information. In reality, however, focus groups take a great deal of planning, and it is hard to know in advance exactly how many to conduct. Generally speaking, three to four focus groups are conducted for small projects, and nine to twelve focus groups are conducted for large projects. For example, if Kraft Cracker Barrel Cheese was testing ideas for a new advertising campaign via focus groups, the Cracker Barrel brand team might conduct a total of nine focus groups: three each involving heavy users, light users, and non-users of Cracker Barrel cheese in the cities of Boston, Chicago, and San Diego.

Selection of focus group members is determined by the purpose of the focus group.

How Should Focus Group Participants Be Recruited and Selected? As you can guess, the selection of focus group participants is determined largely by the purpose of the focus group. For instance, if the purpose is to generate new ideas on GPS system improvements, the participants must be consumers who own a GPS system. If the focus group is intended to elicit building contractors' reactions to a new type of central air-conditioning unit, it will be necessary to recruit building contractors. It is not unusual for companies to provide customer lists or for focus group recruiters to work from secured lists of potential participants. For instance, with building contractors, the list might come from the local Yellow Pages or a building contractor trade association membership roster. In any case, it is necessary to initially contact prospective participants by telephone to qualify them and then to solicit their cooperation in the focus group. Occasionally, a focus group company may recruit by requesting shoppers in a mall to participate, but this approach is rare.

As we noted earlier, "no-shows" are a problem with focus groups, and researchers have at least two strategies to entice prospective participants. Incentives are used to encourage recruits to participate in focus groups. These incentives range from monetary compensation for the participant's time to free products or gift certificates. Many focus group companies use callbacks, email, or text messages during the day immediately prior to the focus group to remind prospective participants they have agreed to take part. If one prospective participant indicates that some conflict has arisen and he or she cannot be there, it is then possible to recruit a replacement. Neither approach works perfectly, as we indicated earlier, and anticipating how many participants will show up is always a concern. Some focus group companies have a policy of overrecruiting, and others have lists of people they can rely on to participate, given that they fit the qualifications.

Where Should a Focus Group Meet? Since the focus group discussion will generally last 90 minutes to two hours, it is important that the physical arrangement of the group be comfortable and conducive to group discussion. Focus groups ideally are conducted in large rooms set up in a format suitable given the research objective. In some cases, in which it is important to have face-to-face interaction, a round table format would be ideal. Other formats are more suitable for tasting foods or beverages or for viewing video. The overriding consideration is that the moderator has good eye contact with every participant.[34]

Focus groups are held in a variety of settings. An advertising company conference room, a moderator's home, a respondent's home, the client's office, hotels, and meeting rooms at churches are all locations in which focus groups can be held. Aside from a seating arrangement in which participants can all see one another, the second critical requirement in selecting a meeting place is to find one quiet enough to permit an intelligible audiotaping of the sessions. Marketing research firms with focus group facilities similar to those we described at the beginning of this section offer ideal settings for focus groups since they are specifically set up for focused discussions, with recording equipment that is ready to be used and one-way mirrors through which brand teams can observe focus groups in progress.

When Should the Moderator Become Involved in the Research Project? Moderators should not be viewed as robots needed to lead a discussion who may be hired at the last minute to run the focus groups. The focus group's success depends on the participants'

Focus group facilities often have one-way mirrors through which a brand team can observe focus groups in progress.

involvement in the discussion and in their understanding of what is being asked of them. Productive involvement is largely a result of the moderator's effectiveness, which in turn is dependent on his or her understanding of the purpose and objectives of the interview. Unless the moderator understands what information the researcher is after and why, he or she will not be able to phrase questions effectively. It is good policy to have the moderator contribute to the development of the project's goals to guide the discussion topics. By aiding in the formation of the topics (questions), he or she will be familiar with them and will be better prepared to conduct the group. It is important when formulating questions that they be organized into a logical sequence and that the moderator follow this sequence to the furthest extent possible. The moderator's introductory remarks are influential; they set the tone for the session. All subsequent questions should be prefaced with a clear explanation of how the participants should respond, for example, how they really feel personally, not how they think they should feel. This allows the moderator to establish a rapport with participants and to lay the groundwork for the interview's structure.

How Are Focus Group Results Reported and Used? As we noted earlier, focus groups report some of the subtle and obscure features of the relationships among consumers and products, advertising, and sales efforts. They furnish qualitative data on matters such as consumer language; emotional and behavioral reactions to advertising; lifestyle; relationships; the product category and specific brand; and unconscious consumer motivations relative to product design, packaging, promotion, or any other facet of the marketing program under study. However, focus group results are qualitative and not perfectly representative of the general population.

Marketing Research on YouTube™ To learn how NOT to conduct focus groups, go to **www. youtube.com** and search for "The #1 Focus Group Moderator in the World."

What Other Benefits Do Focus Groups Offer? The focus group approach is firmly entrenched in the marketing research world as a mainstay technique. Because they are of reasonable total cost when compared with large-scale quantitative surveys involving a thousand or more respondents, adaptable to managers' concerns, and capable of yielding immediate results, focus groups are an appealing qualitative research method. Moreover, face-to-face focus groups are becoming common worldwide, and online focus groups are boosting the popularity of focus groups with new capabilities.[35] They are a unique research method because they permit marketing managers to see and hear the market. Managers become so engrossed in their everyday problems and crises that they find it refreshing to see their customers in person. It is common for marketing managers to come away from a focus group session observation stimulated and energized to respond to the market's desires.

6-4   Ethnographic Research

Ethnographic research is a term borrowed from anthropology to describe a detailed, descriptive study of a group and its behavior, characteristics, culture, and so on.

Ethnographic research, an approach borrowed from anthropology, is defined as a detailed, descriptive study of a group and its behavior, characteristics, and culture.[36] *Ethno* refers to people, and *graphy* refers to a field of study. Ethnographic research is used in marketing to gain a deeper and more comprehensive understanding of the consumer and consumer behavior by studying the behavior where it occurs for prolonged periods. Ethnography is particularly effective for studying trends, personal habits, lifestyle factors, and the effect of social and cultural context on consumption behavior. Ethnography uses several different types of research, including immersion, participant observation, and informal and ongoing in-depth interviewing. Ethnographers pay close attention to words, metaphors, symbols, and stories people use to explain their lives and communicate with one another.[37]

Marketers increasingly use ethnography to study consumer behavior, such as how people act when buying cars or in restaurants, or how people change when they become parents.[38] Kellogg's regularly uses ethnographic techniques to study breakfast and snacking behavior, particularly in developing nations, such as South Africa, India, and Mexico. According to Mike Mickunas, vice president of global insights and planning at Kellogg's, the company gets its top leaders involved in the ethnographic studies. Mickunas states, "It's something when your CEO comes into your business meeting in Mumbai and is looking at a portfolio plan and can ask questions based on his direct experience of sitting across the table from a mom over breakfast."[39] Many marketing research companies and client-side marketing research departments regularly hire employees trained in ethnography. Some marketing research companies, such as Context-Based Research Group and Housecalls, Inc., specialize in ethnography.

One popular form of ethnographic research is called the *shopalong*. Just as it sounds, **shopalongs** are a type of research in which a researcher accompanies a shopper (with permission) on a shopping trip and observes and records the shopper's activities. The researcher generally audiotapes, videotapes, or takes photos of the shopper as he or she does the shopping. The participant is often interviewed prior to or after conducting the shopping activity.

Shopalongs are a type of research in which a researcher accompanies a shopper (with permission) on a shopping trip and observes and records the shopper's activities.

Here are other examples of ethnographic marketing research provided by the Qualitative Research Consultants Association:[40]

- Observing mothers at home making dinner for the household
- Observing what men eat at breakfast and why
- Walking with seniors in their walking groups and listening to them discuss their hopes, fears, worries, health, and family/friends
- Watching people use a product they have been given days ago to find out how it fit into their routine (test product or a competitive product)
- Observing the "before and after" of someone taking a medication and how it makes or does not make a difference in that person's life

Learn about ethnographic research by going to www.youtube.com and searching for "Sports Fan Ethnography."

MOBILE ETHNOGRAPHY

A type of ethnography that has emerged as smartphone ownership has risen is *mobile ethnography*. **Mobile ethnography** is a type of marketing research in which respondents document their own experiences through their mobile phones. Mobile ethnography is sometimes called mobile qualitative, or simply mobile qual. With mobile ethnography, researchers recruit respondents to record their own activities and emotions, using their phones to take photos and videos accompanied by audio explanations. For example, respondents might be asked to document their own participation in milestone events, such as celebrations or funerals, or in more mundane activities such as making breakfast or taking the dog for a walk. Mobile ethnography can be especially useful for documenting private behavior, such as waking up in the morning or administrating medical treatments.

Mobile ethnography is a type of marketing research in which respondents document their own experiences through their mobile phones.

MARKETING RESEARCH INSIGHT 6.3   *Digital Marketing Research*

Applications of Mobile Ethnography

As smartphone ownership has risen, mobile ethnography has become an increasingly prevalent form of marketing research. Following are three examples of studies using mobile ethnography.

Entertaining at Home

Kraft Foods paired with the marketing research company BrainJuicer to explore consumers' emotional relationship with food. BrainJuicer recruited a diverse group of 150 U.S. participants who agreed to host and document a self-catered event. Respondents were asked to use their smartphones to tell the story of their event, including shopping, planning, prepping, holding the actual event, and cleaning up. The research team felt that allowing the respondents to document their own event brought to life both the stress and reward that accompany entertaining. Based on the videos, pictures, and texts that resulted from this project, Kraft uncovered 16 themes related to entertaining, leading to new ideas for product innovation.

Mobile ethnography can uncover authentic behavior and feelings that a researcher might miss, with the participants viewed as the experts of their own lives.

Touring Museums

A team of tourism researchers wished to understand the experience of Generation Y consumers in museums. Using an app designed for mobile ethnography, MyServiceFellow, participants were asked to rate and provide comments on their experiences as they toured the National Museum of Australia in Canberra. The participants reflected on a number of experiences in their tour, from parking, to interactions with the staff, to their overall museum experience. The findings highlighted problems, such as confusing signs in the parking area, and positive elements, which included the helpfulness of the museum staff.

Caring for Hair

Procter & Gamble teamed up with the research company Revelation to examine hair care among U.S. Latinos. Revelation recruited 20 Latinos to perform a series of exercises over a three-day period, using their smartphones to provide text and images. The activities were designed to increase knowledge of the respondents' ideas of health and beauty. The results allowed P&G to gain a richer understanding of the definition of healthy hair, providing insights for its product development department.

Sources: Appleton, E. (2014, April 3). Mobile qualitative—How does it fit in the research toolkit? *GreenBook.* Retrieved from http://www.greenbookblog.org/2014/04/03/mobile-qualitative-how-does-it-fit-in-the-research-toolkit/; Hunt, A. (2014, December). Mobile ethnography let Kraft capture the highs and lows of party planning and hosting. *Quirk's Marketing Research Review, 28*(12), 30–33; Muskat, M., Muskat, B., Zehrer, A., & Johns, R. (2013, September). Generation Y: Evaluating services experiences through mobile ethnography. *Tourism Review, 68*(3), 55–71.

The advantage of mobile ethnography is that it can uncover authentic behavior and feelings that a researcher might miss, with respondents viewed as the experts of their own lives. A limitation is that respondents are often not aware of their own habitual or unconscious behavior as they interact with products and services. As a result, they might miss important insights that a trained researcher would notice. This has led some researchers to say that, while mobile methods are valuable, they cannot legitimately be called ethnography.[41] A number of mobile apps—some free and some for a price—have been developed that provide tools to assist with mobile ethnography, including MyServiceFellow, QualBoard, Field Notes, and MyInsights. Marketing Research Insight 6.3 provides some examples of how mobile ethnography is used.

NETNOGRAPHY

Netnography (InterNET plus ethNOGRAPHY) is the name for the ethnographic study of online activities. Coined by Robert Kozinets, netnography is used to examine the online interactions of individuals and communities on the Internet, as well as the relationships between

Netnography is the name for the ethnographic study of online activities.

people and electronics.[42] Netnography can be applied to the study of user-generated content on social media (see Chapter 5). Netnographic studies have been used to examine how consumers share style ideas on a Swedish fashion blog[43] and how individuals get support for health-related goals through social media sites.[44]

6-5 Marketing Research Online Communities

Marketing research online communities (MROCs) are groups of people that are brought together online to interact, provide ideas and opinions, and complete tasks.

A popular and growing trend in marketing research is the use of *marketing research online communities* to gain insights, with about half of marketing research professionals in a 2014 survey claiming that their firm has used this research technique.[45] **Marketing research online communities** (MROCs), also called online panels, are groups of respondents that are brought together online to interact, provide opinions and ideas, and complete tasks. Online communities are inexpensive and flexible, allowing a wide variety of data to be collected, including posts, photos, and videos. Online communities can complete a number of tasks, including responding to open-ended questions, providing product and advertising feedback, keeping journals, and taking mini-polls using computers, tablets, or mobile phones. Creative tasks can be assigned to online communities, such as asking members for ideas for a name for a product or requesting recipes that incorporate a food product as an ingredient. Participants are often asked to share photos or videos of themselves interacting with products or services. Online communities are particularly effective for gaining insights from millennials and Generation Z, since younger consumers are the most avid users of social media.[46] An example is the online community maintained by MTV to gain insights into the views of teenagers and young adults, as described by Alison Hillhouse in the introduction to this chapter.

Participants in marketing research online communities are selected according to their demographics or interests. Project communities are recruited for a short-term project, while ongoing communities can remain intact for months or even years. Communities should be small enough to encourage interactivity among members but large enough that sufficient feedback is produced. Community sizes vary greatly, but communities often have between 50 and 300 members.

Like focus groups, marketing research online communities have moderators to manage the conversations. Moderators strive to get truthful, authentic responses from members while maintaining a positive environment. Since the strength of online communities comes from collaboration among members, moderators attempt to generate peer-to-peer interactions in the communities.

Some online communities are focused on a single brand, while others discuss a variety of brands. Among the many brands that have used online communities to help shape their message are Dannon Activia yogurt and National Car Rental. Some companies, such as MTV, create their own brand-centered communities. More commonly, companies contract with marketing research suppliers to host the communities. Among the many marketing research companies that host online communities are CSpace, MarketVision, and C+R Research. Some marketing research companies have apps to support activities of their online communities and allow community members to post material easily to their mobile devices. For example, Gongos Research has an app called iCommunities for its members to use.

In one example of the use of online communities, the marketing research firm Communispace collaborated with the Advertising Research Foundation to examine consumers' unconscious shopping behavior. Among other activities, community members were asked to participate in a mobile ethnography activity, in which they were instructed to document anything they saw or experienced that might affect their perceptions of three types of products: grocery products, automobiles, and mobile devices. The community members uploaded photos and videos that were also automatically tagged geographically by the app. Insights gained by this research project were that consumers continue to be heavily influenced by advertising and that having firsthand experience with a product is invaluable for getting consumers to ultimately purchase the product.[47]

The advantages of marketing research online communities are that they are relatively inexpensive and can be assembled quickly. They can accommodate multimedia responses, including images, audio recordings, and video recordings. They allow unique perspectives of consumers' lives by providing live examples of how social influences work and allowing researchers a greater

TABLE 6.1 **Comparisons of Traditional Focus Groups, Online Focus Groups, and Marketing Research Online Communities (MROCs)[48]**

	In-Person Focus Groups	Online Focus Groups	MROCs
Interactivity among participants	√	√	√
Real-time client viewing	√	√	√
High-quality viewing experience	√		
Full view of body language/facial expressions	√		
High-quality audio-video recording	√		
Video accessibility (e.g., archiving, clipping, replay)	√		
Reduced travel for clients		√	√
Reduced travel for moderators		√	√
Regional diversity of participants		√	√
Communication through computer, tablet, or smartphone		√	√
Longitudinal perspective allowed			√
Opinion and insights shared anywhere			√
Multiple segments can be represented simultaneously and compared			√
Flexible timing			√

understanding of community dynamics. They are convenient for the participants, since they can participate in the online activities when they have time and where they are comfortable. Online communities can provide longitudinal data through long-standing community members. Alternatively, online communities can be convened for a few weeks to participate in a focused project.

Online communities are only appropriate for populations that are online constantly, since the best members respond to queries promptly. Because of this there is a real danger that community members do not represent the population of interest well. In addition, it is difficult to keep community members motivated over extended periods of time and members drop out frequently. In contrast to focus groups, moderators cannot ensure that every community member participates. In addition, due to the anonymity provided by online communities, there is no way that moderators can ascertain if community members are being honest. Another disadvantage of online communities is the large amount of data that they generate. It is often difficult for managers to keep up on a regular basis with the posts.[49] The data produced by online communities should be organized and reported on a regular basis—else, why bother?

To summarize important differences in the three methods, Table 6.1 compares traditional focus groups, online focus groups, and marketing research online communities on a number of factors.

6-6 Other Qualitative Research Techniques

Along with observation techniques, focus groups, ethnographic techniques, and online communities, there are many other qualitative research techniques available to marketing researchers. Other such methods include in-depth interviews, protocol analysis, various projective techniques, and neuromarketing.

IN-DEPTH INTERVIEWS

An **in-depth interview**, commonly referred to as an IDI, is defined as a set of probing questions posed one-on-one to a subject by a trained interviewer to gain an idea of what the respondent thinks about something or why he or she behaves in a certain way. It is sometimes conducted

An in-depth interview, commonly referred to as an IDI, is defined as a set of probing questions posed one-on-one to a respondent by a trained interviewer to gain an idea of what the respondent thinks about something or why he or she behaves in a certain way.

in the respondent's home or possibly at a central interviewing location, such as a mall-intercept facility, where several respondents can be interviewed in depth in a relatively short time.

The objective of in-depth interviews is to obtain unrestricted comments or opinions and to ask questions that will help the marketing researcher better understand the various dimensions of these opinions as well as the reasons for them. Of primary importance is the compilation of the data into a summary report to identify common themes. New concepts, designs, advertising, and promotional messages can arise from this method.[50] Compared to focus groups, IDIs are better at investigating complex interrelationships, needs, and motivations for purchasing behaviors.[51] When IDIs are conducted over the telephone, they are referred to as *tele-depth interviews (TDIs)*. Some companies use the Internet as a way to display visuals, in which case the approach is referred to as *Web-TDI*.[52]

There are advantages and disadvantages to in-depth interviewing. Interviewers have the ability to probe by asking many additional questions based on a participant's responses. This enables the research technique to generate rich, deep responses. In-depth responses may be more revealing in some research situations than responses to predetermined, yes–no questions typical of a structured survey. If used properly, IDIs can offer great insight into consumer behavior.[53,54] However, this advantage also leads to the major disadvantage of in-depth interviewing, which is the lack of structure in the process. Unless interviewers are well trained, the results may be too varied to give sufficient insight into the problem. IDIs are especially useful when the researcher wants to understand decision making on the individual level, details about how products are used, or the emotional and sometimes private aspects of consumers' lives.[55,56]

In-depth interviews should be conducted by a trained fieldworker who is equipped with a list of topics or open-ended questions. The interviewee is not provided a list of set responses and then instructed to select one from the list. Rather, the interviewee is encouraged to respond in his or her own words, and the interviewer is trained in asking probing questions such as "Why is that so?" "Can you elaborate on your point?" and "Would you give me some specific reasons?" These questions are not intended to tap subconscious motivations; rather, they simply ask about conscious reasons to help the researcher form a better picture of the respondent's thoughts. The interviewer may record responses or take detailed notes. Although it is typical to conduct face-to-face IDIs, they can be done over the telephone when interviewees are geographically dispersed.[57] In-depth interviews are versatile, but they require careful planning, training, and preparation.[58]

Laddering is a technique used in in-depth interviews in an attempt to discover how product attributes are associated with desired consumer values.

Laddering is a technique used in in-depth interviews in an attempt to discover how product attributes are associated with desired consumer values. Essentially, values that are important to consumers are determined, such as "good health." Next, researchers determine which routes consumers take to achieve their values, such as exercising, eating certain foods, reducing stress, and so on. Finally, researchers attempt to determine which specific product attributes are used as a means of achieving the end result that is the desired value. Through in-depth interviews researchers may learn that low-sodium foods or "white meats" are instrumental in achieving "good health."[59] The term *laddering* comes from the notion that the researcher is trying to establish the linkages, or steps, leading from product attributes to values.

The summary report for the in-depth interview will look very similar to one written for a focus group study; that is, the analyst looks for common themes across several in-depth interview transcripts, and these are noted in the report. Verbatim responses are included in the report to support the analyst's conclusions, and any significant differences of opinion that are found in the respondents' comments are noted as well. Again, it is vital to use an analyst who is trained and experienced in interpreting the qualitative data gathered during in-depth interviews.

PROTOCOL ANALYSIS

Protocol analysis places people in a decision-making situation and asks them to verbalize everything they considered.

Protocol analysis involves placing a person in a decision-making situation and asking him or her to verbalize everything he or she considers when making a decision. This special-purpose qualitative research technique has been developed to peek into the consumer's decision-making processes. Often an audio recorder is used to maintain a permanent record of the person's thinking. After several people have provided protocols, the researcher reviews them and looks for commonalities, such as evaluative criteria used, number of brands considered, types and sources of information used, and so forth.

PROJECTIVE TECHNIQUES

Projective techniques involve situations in which participants are placed in (projected into) simulated activities in the hopes that they will divulge things about themselves that they might not reveal under direct questioning. Projective techniques are appropriate in situations in which the researcher is convinced that respondents will be unable or unwilling to relate their true opinions. Such situations may include socially undesirable behaviors such as smoking or road rage, illegal practices such as betting on football games, or sensitive behavior such as using deodorant or dieting.

Five common projective techniques are used by marketers: the word-association test, the sentence completion test, the picture test, the cartoon or balloon test, and role-playing activity. A discussion of each follows.

Projective techniques involve situations in which participants are placed in (projected into) simulated activities in the hopes that they will divulge things about themselves that they might not reveal under direct questioning.

Word-Association Test A **word-association test** involves reading words to a respondent who then answers with the first word that comes to mind. These tests may contain over 100 words and usually combine neutral words with words being tested in ads or words involving product names or services. The researcher then looks for hidden meanings or associations between responses and the words being tested on the original list. This approach is used to uncover people's real feelings about these products or services, brand names, or ad copy. The time taken to respond, called "response latency," and/or the respondents' physical reactions may be measured and used to make inferences. For example, if the response latency to the word "duo" is long, it may mean that people do not have an immediate association with the word.

A word-association test involves reading words to a respondent who then answers with the first word that comes to mind.

Decision Analyst, Inc., uses word-association tests in its battery of qualitative online research services. Anywhere from 50 to 75 words are given to online respondents as stimuli. Respondents then type the first word, association, or image that comes to mind. Sample sizes are typically 100 to 200 persons, and the entire process lasts about 30 minutes. Decision Analyst states that this projective technique is helpful in determining awareness or exploring the imagery or other associations that are linked to brands.[60]

Sentence-Completion Test With a **sentence-completion test**, respondents are given incomplete sentences and asked to complete them in their own words. The researcher then inspects these sentences to identify themes or concepts. The notion here is that respondents will reveal something about themselves in their responses. For example, suppose that Lipton is interested in expanding its hot bagged tea market to teenagers. A researcher might recruit high school students and instruct them to complete the following sentences:

With a sentence-completion test, respondents are given incomplete sentences and asked to complete them in their own words. The researcher then inspects these sentences to identify themes or concepts.

Someone who drinks hot tea is _____.

Hot tea is good to drink when _____.

Making hot tea is _____.

My friends think tea is _____.

The researcher examines the written responses and attempts to identify central themes. For instance, the theme identified for the first sentence might be "healthy," which would signify that hot tea is perceived as a beverage for those who are health conscious. The theme for the second sentence might be "it's cold outside," indicating that tea is perceived as a cold-weather drink, whereas the theme for the third sentence may turn out to be "messy," denoting the students' reaction to using a tea bag. Finally, the last sentence theme might be "okay," suggesting there are no peer pressures working to cause high school students to avoid drinking tea. Given this information, Lipton might deduce that there is room to capitalize on the hot-tea market with teens.

Picture Test With a **picture test**, sometimes called a "thematic apperception test," a picture is provided to participants, who are instructed to describe their reactions by writing a short story about the picture. The researcher analyzes the content of these stories to ascertain feelings, reactions, or concerns generated by the picture. Such tests are useful when testing pictures being considered for use in brochures and print advertisements and on product packaging. For example, a test advertisement might depict a man holding a baby, and the ad headline might say, "Ford includes driver and passenger air bags as standard equipment because you love your family." A picture test may well divulge something about the picture that is especially negative or distasteful. Perhaps unmarried male respondents cannot relate to the ad because they do not have children and have not experienced strong feelings for children. On the other hand, it may turn out that the picture has a much more neutral tone than Ford's advertising agency intended. It may be that the picture does not generate feelings of concern and safety for the family in married respondents with young children. In any case, without the use of a picture test, it would be difficult to determine the audience's reactions.

With a picture test, a picture is provided to participants who are instructed to describe their reactions by writing a short story about the picture.

Cartoon or Balloon Test With a **balloon test**, a line drawing with an empty "balloon" above the head of one of the actors is provided to subjects who are instructed to write in the balloon what the actor is saying or thinking. The researcher then inspects these thoughts to find out how subjects feel about the situation described in the cartoon. For example, when shown a line drawing of a situation in which one of the characters is making the statement, "Ford Explorers are on sale with a discount of $4,000 and 0% interest for 48 months," the participant is asked how the other character in the drawing would respond. Feelings and reactions of the respondents are judged based on their answers.

With a balloon test, a line drawing with an empty "balloon" above the head of one of the actors is provided to respondents, who are instructed to write in the balloon what the actor is saying or thinking.

Role-Playing Activity With **role playing**, participants are asked to pretend they are a "third person," such as a friend or neighbor, and to describe how they would act in a certain situation or to a specific statement. By reviewing their comments, the researcher can spot latent reactions, positive or negative, conjured up by the situation. It is believed that some of the respondents' true feelings and beliefs will be revealed by this method because they can pretend to be another individual. For example, if Ray-Ban is developing a new "Astronaut" sunglasses model with superior ultraviolet-light filtration, space-age styling, and a cost of about $200, role playing might be used to fathom consumers' initial reactions. In this use of role playing, respondents could be asked to assume the role of a friend or close workmate and to indicate what they would say to a third person when they learned that their friend had purchased a pair of Astronaut sunglasses. If consumers felt the Astronaut model was overpriced, this feeling would quickly surface. On the other hand, if the space-age construction and styling were consistent with these consumers' lifestyles and product desires, this fact would be divulged in the role-playing comments.

With role playing, participants are asked to pretend they are a "third person," such as a friend or neighbor, and to describe how they would act in a certain situation or to a specific statement.

These projective techniques were adapted from psychology by marketing researchers many years ago. They remain in use today, although some marketing researchers have developed new projective techniques, many of which are proprietary. Table 6.2 provides information on five such projective techniques that were developed and are used by Talking Business (http://www.TalkingBusiness.net), a qualitative research firm that specializes in innovative research and strategic brand development.

As with in-depth interviews, all of these projective techniques require highly qualified professionals to interpret the results. This increases the cost per respondent compared with other survey methods. Projective techniques can be used in combination with focus groups or in-depth interviews. In one study, researchers wanted to know how young people aged 18 to 24 in the United Kingdom felt about the UK Conservative Party. The researchers conducted eight focus groups with young adults from three places in the United Kingdom, combining focus group discussions with projective techniques that included picture associations and

TABLE 6.2 Projective Techniques That Can Be Used with Focus Groups[61]

Technique Name	Description	Application
Sort Me Up	Respondents are given products (or cards with product names) and asked to sort them into groups and then to provide a descriptive name for each group	Reveals competitive sets of products and brands Offers segmentation implications Shows how consumers perceive products and brands
Sort Me Straight	For each attribute, respondents rank cards with brand names from most to least	Identifies how the target brand performs on specific attributes with respect to competing brands
Picture This, Picture That	Respondents are given several pictures that represent a wide range of emotions and asked to select pictures that represent specific brand/category/situations	Reveals images and emotions that are associated with specific brand/category/situations
Color My World	Respondents are given several color swatches (paint chips) and asked to select color(s) that represent specific brand/category/situations	Offers insight into positive and negative imagery and associations for specific brand/category/situations
Dot, Dot, Dot	Respondents are given 10 dot-shaped stickers or tokens and asked to allocate them across flavors, brands, advertisements, etc.	Provides a relative ranking for each of the alternatives; follow-up probing reveals why certain alternatives are favored

sentence-completion techniques. Adding the projective techniques to the focus groups gave the researchers insight into the deep-seated feeling of the young adults.[62]

NEUROMARKETING

Neuromarketing, also called physiological measurement or consumer neuroscience, involves the study of an individual's involuntary responses to marketing stimuli, including eye movement, heart rate, skin conductance, breathing, brain activity (using functional magnetic resonance imaging [fMRI]), and brain waves (electroencephalography [EEG]). The notion behind neuromarketing research is that physiological reactions cannot be consciously controlled, so they possibly reveal reactions that the individual is unaware of or unwilling to divulge. Practitioners claim that these methods can reveal people's emotions and intensity of opinions in ways that would not be possible with other types of research methods.

> Neuromarketing is the study of an individual's involuntary responses to marketing stimuli, including eye movement, heart rate, skin conductance, breathing, and brain activity.

A number of marketing research companies specialize in neuromarketing, such as Neurosense and BrainJuicer. Many of the largest full-service marketing research companies, including Nielsen, Kantar, and Ipsos, have neuromarketing research among their specialties. Some of the many client companies that have used neuromarketing to measure consumers' emotions are Campbell Soup, Procter & Gamble, Google, Disney, and Frito-Lay.[63,64] We will briefly discuss three techniques that are used in neuromarketing research: neuroimaging, eye tracking, and facial analysis.

Neuroimaging **Neuroimaging**, or viewing brain activity, may aid marketing researchers to better understand consumers' unconscious emotions. By using neuroimaging and understanding the neuroscience behind it, marketing researchers hope to more accurately posit what consumers really want (which can be different from what they say they want), what appeals to them, and what drives them to buy. For example, one neuroimaging experiment using fMRI found that when participants were made to feel rejected in a computer game they experienced greater activation in the same brain region associated with physical pain.[65]

> Neuroimaging is viewing activity in the brain to better understand consumers' unconscious emotions.

Electroencephalography (EEG), or the measure of electrical activity in the brain, is also used to measure consumers' responses to products and advertising. The development of inexpensive, portable, easy-to-use technology has made EEG more accessible for marketing research. In one example, the Canadian public communications and media company Rogers Communication collaborated with the company Brainsights to examine how consumers respond to its hockey programming. Rogers recruited and paid volunteers to wear headgear that measured their brain activity as they watched hockey in bars.

Eye Tracking **Eye tracking** is a technique for measuring eye positions and eye movement. Which part of an ad "catches the consumer's eye?" Where do shoppers look first when they walk into a supermarket aisle? Eye tracking is helpful for measuring usage of computer games, interactive television, software, and mobile devices. For example, AT&T has begun to use eye tracking coupled with in-depth interviewing to understand how customers interact with its customer service website.[66] Eye tracking is also useful in analyzing how consumers process advertisements.[67] In addition, eye tracking is often paired with virtual stores for researchers to examine the most effective ways to display products. Mobile eye tracking (using eye-tracking glasses) is used to measure eye movement in natural environments such as in stores or at home.

> Eye tracking is a technique for measuring eye positions and eye movement.

Facial Coding **Facial coding** is a system that is used to measure universal expressions of emotions, such as happiness, sadness, fear, and surprise, by their appearance on people's faces. Trained "coders" follow a procedure in which they code multiple facial muscles of consumers, based on video recordings of the consumers observing predetermined material. The equipment used in facial coding is inexpensive, since only a computer on which participants can watch content and an internal or external video camera to record the participants are needed. Facial coding is most frequently used to measure responses to products and to advertising. In one experiment, facial coding was used to measure the facial expressions of college students as they observed 13 Super Bowl television advertisements involving automobiles. The results indicated that facial expressions can be a stronger indicator of future sales than survey responses.[68]

> Facial coding is a system that is used to measure universal expressions of emotions, such as happiness, sadness, fear, and surprise, by their appearance on people's faces.

The Controversy The use of neuromarketing can be controversial. Political campaigns have come under criticism for using neuromarketing techniques to shape their promotions. Nevertheless, according to the *New York Times*, neuromarketing methods have been used in political campaigns in a number of countries on at least three continents. For example, during his 2012 campaign, Mexican president Enrique Peña Nieto used a number of neuromarketing experiments to develop his message. The use of neuromarketing in political campaigns in the United States remains more limited, perhaps because of the stigma attached to these methods.[69]

The two main criticisms of neuromarketing are somewhat contradictory. The first is that the methods are used to manipulate consumers, while the second is that neuromarketing is "pseudoscience" and is not actually effective. Neuromarketing techniques are evolving rapidly and, for the most part, best practices have yet to be established for their use. While some researchers remain skeptical that neuromarketing methods are superior to less expensive and invasive methods of research, a limited amount of recent research has demonstrated that neuromarketing can be superior to traditional methods for some purposes.[70] Wearable technology, such as Google Glass and Apple Watch, may add to the credibility of neuromarketing by measuring consumers' responses to marketing stimuli under more natural conditions. The company Innerscope Research, owned by Nielsen, has developed a wearable belt that can measure emotional responses as consumers take part in their everyday activities. With the price of some of the technology used in neuromarketing decreasing rapidly, it has been predicted that testing advertising using these techniques could become standard for some larger companies in the future.[71] Altogether, the field of neuromarketing is changing quickly and merits watching.

STILL MORE QUALITATIVE TECHNIQUES

While this chapter highlights the most commonly used types of qualitative methods in the marketing research industry, a number of additional qualitative techniques can be used. An international nonprofit organization, Qualitative Research Consultants Association (QRCA), was created in 1983 to promote and advance excellence in qualitative research. Information about traditional and leading-edge qualitative techniques can be found on QRCA's website (http://www.qrca.org). More information about QRCA can be found in Marketing Research Insight 6.4.

MARKETING RESEARCH INSIGHT 6.4 — *Practical Application*

Qualitative Research Consultants Association (QRCA) Cultivates Excellence in Qualitative Research

Shannon Thompson, Executive Director, QRCA.

Since 1983, the Qualitative Research Consultants Association (QRCA) has cultivated excellence in qualitative research. For everyone involved in the practice and use of qualitative research, QRCA keeps qualitative at peak performance for today and tomorrow. QRCA brings together the best people and resources in qualitative, at the leading edge of both traditional and new methodologies, with the following features:

- The strongest qualitative resources
- Access to the latest methods, ideas, and expert innovators
- Leading-edge wisdom and experience
- A unique, warm culture of open learning, shared knowledge, and welcoming access

QRCA members are those involved in the design, implementation, and analysis of qualitative research around the globe. Qualitative research is changing dramatically and quickly with new tools, platforms, and technology. QRCA helps member practitioners understand and integrate new ideas into their practice, makes sure their skills are powerful and current, and provides the expertise and fresh thinking their clients seek. QRCA members share leading-edge wisdom and experience via conferences, local programs at nearly 20 chapters across North America plus innovative virtual programs for our international members, Qcast webinars, special-interest groups (including Ethnography, Online Qualitative, Pharma/Health Care, Social Media Research, Latino Research, Creativity + Innovation, and Young Professionals), the member-only forum, and publications.

Find out more about QRCA at http://www. qrca.org.

For those who are just entering the world of qualitative research, QRCA offers Young Professional Grants and Global Scholarships to encourage enthusiastic new qualitative research consultants to join the association. For those who use and purchase qualitative research services, QRCA and its members are the best resource in qualitative, keeping them at the leading edge of both traditional and new methodologies. Because they rely on research partners' expertise and fresh thinking to advise them on the best way to utilize research, research users can feel confident they are getting the best when they work with QRCA and its members—benefiting from the strongest resources and access to the latest methods, ideas, and expert innovators. QRCA members' leading-edge wisdom and experience are available to research users and buyers via select presentations, webinars, and publications and demonstrated in the work they do for their clients.

Source: Courtesy Shannon Thompson, QRCA

Synthesize Your Learning

This exercise will require you to take into consideration concepts and material from the following chapters:

Chapter 5	Secondary Data and Packaged Information
Chapter 6	Qualitative Research Techniques

Lucy Betcher had worked as a consultant for the Small Business Administration for a number of years. Her old high school classmates and their spouses gather at least once a year to renew friendships. Judy Doyle, Mike Fuller, Adele Smith, Nancy Egolf, Joy Greer, and Jackie Reynolds had different careers and several were retiring. At their last reunion, Jackie mentioned to Lucy that she was interested in doing something else after retiring from teaching. Adele overheard this conversation and said she was interested in trying something new as well. Could Lucy, with all her years of helping others get started in business, assist her friends?

The next morning, while sitting on Todd and Joy's comfortable balcony overlooking boats in a canal, Lucy asked the entire group: "Jackie and Adele are interested in getting into some sort of business opportunity. Do any of you have any thoughts on this?"

Having spent a successful career in pharmaceutical sales, Mike said, "There are opportunities for services for senior citizens in terms of prescription drug management and administration."

Mike noted that many older people still in their homes or living in retirement centers had difficulty keeping track of getting their prescriptions filled and taking their medications on schedule.

"It's a real problem when people get to be 85 and over," Mike said. "I see a growing need for a personal service that would provide this type of care."

Nancy and Judy talked about a unique coffee shop they had patronized. Not only was the staff knowledgeable about different types of coffees and helpful in guiding customers to sample different flavors, but the shop also sold a variety of coffee makers and tea makers and books on coffee and teas. However, what they really liked was the atmosphere. Instead of the placid and contemplative ambience that most coffee shops offer, this shop featured different "learning" exhibits where you could interact and discover something new. The topics changed weekly—local history, coffee making, art, music, and readings by authors.

The two women were fascinated with the shop and had talked to the owner about franchising the concept so they could each start one in their hometowns in Pennsylvania and New York. The owner told them he had several successful franchises operating. The biggest challenge the prospective coffee shop owners would face initially would be in finding a location that would attract the clientele who would embrace the product and atmosphere and return regularly. The owner obviously couldn't help them make those decisions in their hometowns, so they would need help finding the best locations there.

1. Looking back at Chapter 5, what secondary data could identify the number of persons in different age groups in each CBSA?

2. Based on what you learned in Chapter 5, identify a packaged services firm that would be helpful in locating a successful coffee shop in different locales. Assume that since the coffee shop owner has several successful coffee shops, the owner has a database of current customer information.

3. In considering either the prescription service or the coffee shop venture, what qualitative research techniques would you now recommend that the prospective business owners use? Why would you recommend these qualitative techniques?

Summary

This chapter described the various qualitative research techniques used by marketing researchers. Quantitative research uses predetermined structured questions with predetermined structured response options. It is also normally characterized by the use of large samples. Qualitative research is much less structured than quantitative approaches. Qualitative research involves collecting, analyzing, and interpreting data by observing what people do or say. The observations and statements are in an unstructured, nonstandardized form. The advantage of qualitative research is that it allows researchers to gather deeper, richer information from respondents. Mixed methods research involves using both qualitative and quantitative research methods.

Observation is a qualitative research technique in which researchers observe what consumers do rather than communicate with them. Observational techniques can be direct or indirect, covert or overt, structured or unstructured, and in situ or invented. Circumstances most suited to observational studies involve a (1) short time interval, (2) public behavior, and (3) the likelihood of faulty recall if respondents are asked about previous experiences. The primary advantage of observation is that researchers record what respondents actually do instead of relying on their recall of what they think they do. The limitations of observation studies are that they often rely on small samples, so representativeness is a concern. Another disadvantage is the subjective interpretation required to explain the behavior observed. Researchers do not know consumers' motives, attitudes, or intentions.

Focus groups, or moderated small-group discussions, are a popular form of qualitative research. The major task of the moderator is to ensure freewheeling and open communication that stays focused on the research topic. Traditional focus groups use about 6 to 12 persons in a dedicated room, with a one-way mirror for client viewing. Recent innovations in contemporary focus groups include online focus groups in which clients may observe from a distant location via video streaming over the Internet. Another form of online focus group allows people to participate from their homes or any remote location where they observe and respond to other participants via chat rooms. Focus groups have the following advantages: (1) They generate fresh ideas; (2) they allow clients to observe their participants; and (3) they may be directed at understanding a wide variety of issues. Disadvantages include lack of representativeness, subjective evaluation of the meaning of the discussions, and high costs per participant. Focus groups should be used when there is a need to describe marketing phenomena. They should not be used when there is a need to predict a phenomenon such as projecting sales for a new product evaluated by a focus group. Four main objectives of focus groups are to generate ideas; to understand consumer vocabulary; to reveal consumer needs, motives, perceptions, and attitudes on products or services; and to better understand findings from quantitative studies.

To convene a focus group, marketing researchers should have 6 to 12 participants sharing similar characteristics and should come up with a plan for potential "no shows." Focus group facilities exist in most major cities, but any large room with a central table can be used. The moderator's role is key to a successful focus group, and he or she should become involved early on in the research project.

Ethnographic research, an approach borrowed from anthropology, is defined as a detailed, descriptive study of a group and its behavior, characteristics, and culture.

Ethnographic research involves observing consumers in near-natural settings to monitor their behaviors, relations with others, and emotions. Smartphone ownership has led to mobile ethnography, a type of marketing research in which respondents document their own experiences through their own mobile phones. Another variation of ethnography is netnography, in which online activities are studied.

In recent years, marketing research online communities have become a popular form of research, in which groups of targeted populations are brought together online to interact, provide opinions and ideas, and complete tasks. Online communities are inexpensive and flexible, allowing a wide variety of data to be collected, including posts, photos, and videos.

Another qualitative technique involves in-depth interviews (IDIs) to examine consumer motivations and hidden concerns. Protocol analysis induces participants to "think aloud" so the researcher can map the decision-making process a consumer uses in making a purchase decision. Projective techniques, such as word association, sentence completion, or role playing, are also useful in unearthing motivations, beliefs, and attitudes that subjects may not be able to express well verbally.

Neuromarketing is the study of an individual's involuntary responses to marketing stimuli. Types of neuromarketing include neuroimaging, eye tracking, and facial coding. Neuromarketing is an emerging field that may offer additional qualitative insights into consumer behavior.

Key Terms

Quantitative research (p. 143)
Qualitative research (p. 144)
Mixed methods research (p. 144)
Observation methods (p. 146)
Direct observation (p. 146)
Indirect observation (p. 146)
Archives (p. 146)
Physical traces (p. 146)
Covert observation (p. 147)
Overt observation (p. 147)
Structured observation (p. 147)
Unstructured observation (p. 147)
In situ observation (p. 147)

Invented observation (p. 147)
Focus groups (p. 149)
Moderators (p. 150)
Focus group report (p. 150)
Online focus group (p. 151)
Ethnographic research (p. 156)
Shopalong (p. 156)
Mobile ethnography (p. 156)
Netnography (p. 157)
Marketing research online
    communities (p. 158)
In-depth interview (p. 159)
Laddering (p. 160)

Protocol analysis (p. 160)
Projective techniques (p. 161)
Word-association test (p. 161)
Sentence-completion test (p. 161)
Picture test (p. 162)
Balloon test (p. 162)
Role playing (p. 162)
Neuromarketing (p. 163)
Neuroimaging (p. 163)
Eye tracking (p. 164)
Facial coding (p. 164)

Review Questions/Applications

6-1. Define quantitative research. Define qualitative research. List the differences between these two research methods. What is mixed methods research?

6-2. What is meant by an "observation technique"? What is observed, and why is it recorded?

6-3. Indicate why covert observation would be appropriate for a study on how parents discipline their children when dining out.

6-4. Describe a traditional focus group.

6-5. Describe two formats of online focus groups.

6-6. Describe at least three different uses of focus groups.

6-7. How are focus group participants recruited, and what is a common problem associated with this recruitment?

6-8. Should the members of a focus group be similar or dissimilar? Why?

6-9. Describe what a focus group setting looks like and how a focus group would take place in such a setting.

6-10. What are the qualities that are essential in order to effectively moderate a focus group discussion? Why are these qualities important?

6-11. Indicate how a focus group moderator should handle each of the following cases: (a) A participant is loud and dominates the conversation; (b) a participant is obviously suffering from a cold and goes into coughing fits every few minutes; (c) two participants who, it turns out, are acquaintances persist in a private conversation about their children; and (d) the only minority representative participant in the focus group looks uncomfortable with the group and fails to make any comments.

6-12. What should be included in a report that summarizes the findings of a focus group?

6-13. Indicate the advantages and disadvantages of client interaction in the design and execution of a focus group study.

6-14. What is ethnographic research? Discuss how a marketing researcher could get into an ethically sensitive situation using the technique.

6-15. How is neuromarketing helpful in market research studies?

6-16. How does laddering as a technique help in qualitative research?

6-17. Why are projective techniques used? Name any three commonly used projective techniques.

6-18. Describe (a) sentence-completion, (b) word-association, and (c) balloon test. Create one of each of these that might be used to test the reactions of parents whose children are bed wetters to absorbent underpants that their children would wear under their nightclothes.

6-19. What is *facial coding*? How would you present to a potential client the advantages of this technique?

6-20. Associated Grocery Stores (AGS) has always used paper bags for sacking groceries in its chain of retail supermarkets. Management has noticed that some competitors are offering reusable bags to their customers. AGS management isn't certain just how strongly consumers in its markets feel about having to bring the reusable bags every time they visit the supermarket. Select two projective techniques. First, defend your use of a projective technique. Second, describe in detail how your two chosen techniques would be applied to this research problem.

6-21. Your university is considering letting an apartment management company build an apartment complex on campus. To save money, the company proposes to build a common cooking area for every four apartments. This area would be equipped with an oven, stove-top burners, microwave oven, sink, food preparation area, garbage disposal, and individual mini-refrigerators with locks on them for each apartment. Two students would live in each apartment, so eight students would use the common cooking area. You volunteer to conduct focus groups with students to determine their reactions to this concept and to brainstorm suggestions for improvements. Prepare the topics list you would have as a guide in your role as moderator.

CASE 6.1

The College Experience

This case was provided by Professor Daniel Purdy, Lecturer, and Professor Wendy Wilhelm, Professor of Marketing, both of Western Washington University.

The College of Business at Western Washington University is a full-service business school at a midsized regional university. The College of Business specializes in undergraduate business education with selected graduate programs. While the college emphasizes mostly professional education, it does so within a liberal arts context. Business majors range from standards such as accounting, marketing, and finance to more unique offerings, such as the highly successful manufacturing and supply chain management degree.

The college is committed to a student-centered style of education that emphasizes the students not as customers but as equal stakeholders in the process of education. As part of its commitment to involving the students as true partners, the college has recently begun the process of conducting focus groups of undergraduate and graduate students. The objective of these focus groups is to identify negative and positive attitudes about the college and develop new ideas to improve the college.

The following is an excerpt from the transcript of the first undergraduate focus group. This group included 14 students with the following makeup: 50% male and 50% female; 93% work part time or more, and 7% do not work;

and 29% management majors, and other majors no more than 15% each.

Moderator: So what do you guys think are some ways that the college (not the university) can be improved?

Jeff: I really like the fact that professors are accessible and willing to help, and a lot of them let us call them by their first name. Something that I think could be better is that we don't spend enough time learning how to do things but instead professors spend too much time talking about theory.

Sarah: Yeah, I agree totally. It seems like most of the time we aren't learning practical skills but just talking about what we "should" do, not really learning how to do it.

Moderator: Interesting points. How would you suggest the college try to increase the amount of practical learning?

Todd: It would really be cool if we could do more real-life professional work in our classes. Things like skill-based projects that focus on doing what we would really do in our profession.

Tim: I think we should all have to do a mandatory internship as part of our major. Right now, some majors let you do it as an elective, but they are really hard to find and get.

Moderator: Good ideas. Are there other things you think we could improve?

Rhonda: I agree that the professors try really hard to be open to students, but the advising is really not very good. I don't know how to fix it, but I know my advisor is pretty much useless.

Ariel: I know, I know. It is so frustrating sometimes. I go to my advisor and she tells me to just fill in my degree planning sheet and she'll sign it. It's like they don't even know what I should be taking or why.

Jon: My advisor is kind of funny. He just tells me that he doesn't really know that much about classes he doesn't teach and my guess is as good as his. At least he's honest anyway.

Moderator: Ok, so the advising you are getting from the faculty leaves a little to be desired. What do you guys do to figure out how to plan your degrees if your advisors aren't helping much?

Sarah: I just ask my friends who are further along in the major than I am.

Mark: Yeah, me too. In the Student Marketing Association we all give each other advice on what professors are good, what classes go good together, which have prerequisites and stuff like that. It would be cool if we could have something like that for the whole college.

Moderator: Do you think the college could be improved if we developed some sort of peer-advising program?

Using these excerpts as representative of the entire focus group transcript, answer the following questions:

1. Do you think focus groups were the appropriate research method in this case, given the research objectives? What other type(s) of research might provide useful data?
2. Evaluate the questions posed by the moderator in light of the research objectives/question: (a) Are any of them leading or biased in any way? (b) Can you think of any additional questions that could or should be included?
3. Examine the findings. How is the college perceived? What are its apparent strengths and weaknesses?
4. Can we generalize these findings to all of the college's students? Why or why not?

Text: By permission, Mr. Daniel Purdy and Dr. Wendy Wilhelm, Western Washington University.

CASE 6.2 INTEGRATED CASE

Auto Concepts

Nick Thomas, CEO of Auto Concepts, has begun formulating some concepts in terms of the types of car models to pursue to bring his parent company product line back to life. He has been using a cross-functional approach to new product development involving finance, production, R&D, marketing, and advertising in his planning. Ashley Roberts, from advertising, is discussing some of the general plans for the new car models with Nick. He tells Ashley that Auto Concepts needs more marketing research information about customer preferences for different types of cars. One model being considered is a small, almost scooter-like car. Other models are larger but still much smaller than "traditional" cars to obtain suitable mpg ratings. Ashley knows this information is crucial for effective advertising strategy and

tactics. She wonders if the customers who prefer the new, smaller models possess different sets of salient values. Perhaps those who prefer the scooter-like model would value excitement and entertainment in their lives while those expressing a preference for the larger-sized, high-mpg models would place a higher priority on social recognition versus harmony with the environment or some other value. If differences are found, the ad strategy can alter the values emphasized in the ad's visuals and copy to suit the model of the car being promoted (e.g., depicting an exciting life, thrill of the drive, or sense of accomplishment or recognition of contributing to environmental problems, and so on).

What technique identified in this chapter would help Ashley Roberts with this advertising task? Why?

7 Evaluating Survey Data Collection Methods

Schlesinger Associates

Steve Schlesinger, CEO, Schlesinger Associates

Schlesinger Associates is a leading international data collection company that prides itself on providing high-quality recruitment and project management services for any qualitative or quantitative marketing research methodology. Schlesinger has an ongoing commitment to providing a broad range of research solutions to meet developing needs and to explore new solutions to support better research insights for its clients in rapidly changing marketplaces. Key methodologies the company provides include focus groups, in-depth interviews, ethnographic studies, online and mobile surveys, and online qualitative solutions, such as webcam-enabled focus groups, discussion boards, and online communities. In addition, Schlesinger offers leading-edge research labs that can harness behavioral and emotional measures technology to add value to research. These labs include usability labs, facial coding labs, eye-tracking labs, EEG neuromarketing labs, and biometric labs. Specializing in health care, consumer, business-to-business, and IT research services, Schlesinger's extensive, profiled, and stringently verified panel, together with varied recruitment methods, allows for highly engaged pools of research participants across a variety of target audiences, be they geographic, demographic, psychographic, or behavioral. Schlesinger Associates has offices in key U.S. markets that host high-specification focus group facilities, top rated in the world by the Impulse Survey of Focus Group Facilities.

Over the last decade, Schlesinger has successfully acquired leading data collection companies in Europe: The Research House in London, ConsuMed Research & Passerelles in Paris, and Schmiedl Marktforschung in Berlin, Frankfurt, and Munich. The company's Global Solutions team, together with strategic global partnerships, allows researchers to take the pulse of markets worldwide. Advisors by Schlesinger is Schlesinger's most recent initiative. This service connects knowledge seekers with vetted world-class thought leaders and then facilitates one-on-one consultations and advisory boards. Scientists, clinicians, managed care executives, health care payers, and administrators are just some of the types of

Schlesinger Associates

Quality Without Compromise

Visit Schlesinger Associates at www.SchlesingerAssociates .com

experts available to clients including consulting firms, market research firms, and financial service firms. Schlesinger also provides complementary services, such as transcription, translation, interpretation, and note-taking, to complete its turnkey data collection solution. In 2016 Schlesinger Associates marked 50 years of passion, partnership, and innovation. The company has grown rapidly from a turnover of $100,000 in 1966 to over $100 million today.

CEO Steve Schlesinger attributes the success of the company to a very powerful business and leadership relationship with his partner and joint owner Mike Sullivan, president of the company, and the support of a talented and dynamic senior leadership group. The leadership believes deeply in its core values of quality, service excellence, and partnership set out by the company's founder Sarah Schlesinger. These remain the guiding principles for all employees, underpinning the company's mission and vision equally for its client services as for its corporate and social responsibilities. Steve Schlesinger commented, "The daily driving force of our company vision is '**People Passion & Purpose**': recruiting, developing, and communicating with our **People** for success. Feeling real **Passion** for our relationships and what we do. Having clear **Purpose** through management by objectives at all levels, disciplined performance measures, calculated risk taking, dusted with a strong belief in the 'art of possibility.'" Schlesinger Associates has strong marketing research industry links with a long history of its people being committed to and being honored for volunteer work for associations and other initiatives that improve market research today and shape tomorrow. Schlesinger's marketing and client development strategy is focused on in-person industry events and in-person client relationships. Sponsorship of education and event attendance programs enables young researchers to be immersed in industry activity and to learn to develop a voice early in their careers.

Source: Text and photos courtesy of Steve Schlesinger and SchlesingerAssociates.

As you are learning in this course and as apparent in our Schlesinger Associates opening vignette, there are many different ways of conducting marketing research studies. In previous chapters, we discussed different forms of research, such as focus groups, experiments, and surveys. There are many ways of gathering information among these various types of studies. In this chapter, our attention is on surveys. A **survey** involves interviews with a large number of respondents using a predesigned questionnaire.[1] Communication is necessary to learn what respondents are thinking—their opinions, preferences, or planned intentions. Large numbers of respondents may be required to collect a large enough sample of important subgroups or to ensure that the study accurately

Surveys involve interviews with a large number of respondents using a predesigned questionnaire.

represents some larger population. In this chapter we focus on the various methods used to collect data for surveys.

Historically, survey data collection has been largely driven by technology. The earliest technology was paper based in the form of personal interviews or mail surveys using printed questionnaires. This mode of data collection was displaced when nationwide calling became affordable, which occurred when competition was introduced into the telecommunications networks and drove long-distance rates down. Telephone-based data collection, in turn, provided impetus to automated dialers and the emergence of computers, which created CATI (computer-assisted telephone interviewing). CATI systems greatly improved the productivity of telephone interviewers through automated dialing, tracking performance statistics that could be reported back to management, and enabling the programming of skip patterns and other logic. Telephone surveys have been largely supplanted by Internet-based or online surveys that afford a host of efficiencies. The newest and currently most popular form of data collection is the use of panels, which are immense groups of potential respondents who are recruited and compensated by companies that provide access to them for a fee. Such panel companies, normally online, guarantee researchers access to practically any identified population with maximum speed and minimal data collection errors.

This chapter begins with a short discussion on why surveys are popular and advantageous. Next, it describes basic survey modes: (1) person-administered surveys, (2) computer-assisted surveys, (3) computer-administered surveys, (4) self-administered surveys, and (5) mixed-mode, sometimes called "hybrid," surveys. While online surveys are extremely popular, it is important that you understand the uses and nuances of alternative data collection methods because each survey is unique and online data collection may not always be the best method.

Accordingly, we discuss the advantages and disadvantages of each of these modes and present the various alternative methods of collecting data within each of three basic data collection modes. For example, person-administered surveys may be conducted through mall intercepts or by telephone. Finally, we discuss factors a market researcher should consider when deciding which data collection method to use.

7-1   Advantages of Surveys

Key advantages of surveys include standardization, ease of administration, ability to tap the "unseen," suitability to tabulation and statistical analysis, and sensitivity to subgroup differences.

Compared to observation or other qualitative methods, survey methods allow the collection of significant amounts of data in a systematic, economical, and efficient manner, and they typically involve large sample sizes. There are five advantages of using survey methods: (1) standardization, (2) ease of administration, (3) ability to tap the "unseen," (4) suitability to tabulation and statistical analysis, and (5) sensitivity to subgroup differences (see Table 7.1).

TABLE 7.1   Five Advantages of Surveys

Advantage	Description
Provides standardization	All respondents react to questions worded identically and presented in the same order. Response options (scales) are the same, too.
Is easy to administer	Interviewers read questions to respondents and record their answers quickly and easily. In many cases, the respondents read and respond to the questionnaires themselves.
Gets "beneath the surface"	While not as detailed as in-depth interviews or focus groups, it is common to ask questions about motives, circumstances, sequences of events, or mental deliberations, none of which are available in observation studies.
Is easy to analyze	Standardization and computer processing allow for quick tallies, cross tabulations, and other statistical analyses despite large sample sizes.
Reveals subgroup differences	Respondents can be divided into segments or subgroups (e.g., users vs. nonusers or age-groups) for comparisons in the search for meaningful differences.

 **Active Learning**

Experience the Advantages of Surveys

To experience the advantages of surveys firsthand, administer the following survey to four friends, two males and two females. You can either (1) copy the questions on paper and hand them to each friend or (2) read each question and record the answers of each friend separately. However, in the second option, you should keep each friend's answers separate from the others.

1. Did you watch television last night?
_____Yes _____No

2. (If yes) For about how many hours did you watch television last night?
_____ Less than 1
_____ Between 1 and 2
_____ Between 2 and 4
_____ More than 4

3. Why do you usually watch television? (Select only one.)
_____ Entertainment (variety, humor, sports, talk)
_____ Education (science, news, documentary, cooking)
_____ Escape (science fiction, reality, fantasy)
_____ Excitement (action, drama, travel)

4. What is your gender?
_____ Male
_____ Female

Now that you have administered the survey, let's consider each advantage.

Standardization. How have the response options for questions 2 and 3 standardized the survey? In other words, what answers might have come about if you did not give your respondents these specific response categories from which to pick?

Ease of Analysis. What percent of your friends who took part in the survey watched television last night? What percent of them watched TV for four or more hours? To answer these questions, how long did it take for you to tabulate the findings? Also, since the respondents checked off or voiced the answers, how did this make your analysis task easy?

Ease of Administration. How difficult was it for you to administer the survey? One way to answer this is to estimate how long it took for each respondent, on average, to complete the survey.

Get Beneath the Surface. Do your friends watch television mostly for entertainment, education, escape, or excitement? Tabulate the answers to question 3 to find out. Notice that with a single question you have discovered the reasons, or motivations, for your friends' television viewing.

Subgroup Differences. Do the two males differ from the two females? Do separate percentage tabulations for each gender and compare the percentages. In a matter of a few minutes, you can spot whether or not differences exist in the subgroups and what the differences are.

7-2 Modes of Data Collection

DATA COLLECTION AND IMPACT OF TECHNOLOGY

As we noted at the beginning of this chapter, the data collection step in the marketing research process has undergone great changes due to technology. Actually, there are two reasons for the most recent change. First, in the past two decades, there has been a dramatic decline in the willingness of the general public to take part in surveys and, second, computer and telecommunications technology has advanced significantly and opened new, efficient ways for marketing researchers to collect data. With respect to declining survey response rates, Roger Tourangeau[2] has identified the major reasons for this trend. The factors underlying a growing unwillingness in the U.S. public to take part in surveys are the common use of "gatekeepers," such as answering machines, caller ID, and call blocking; reduced amounts of free time; decline in the public's engagement with important issues; rising percentage of foreign-born Americans who are not fluent in English; and increases in the number of elderly who have comprehension and expression difficulties. There is also a growing desire for privacy among Americans. Indeed, the declining cooperation rates are being experienced worldwide, not just in the United States. These rising nonresponse rates have caused marketing researchers to rethink the use of traditional data collection methods.

Coincidentally, technology has opened doors to new data collection methods, although it has not solved the nonresponse problem. Two primary reasons for the technology push are the rising costs of traditional data collection such as CATI and consumers' adoption of new communication systems.[3] The cost of doing research has increased along with the rising prices of energy, personnel, and support functions. To remain competitive and, in some cases, to remain in business, marketing research companies have sought out data collection cost-saving alternatives of many types. At the same time, consumers have integrated personal, tablet, and other mobile computers into their lives, and large segments of the population have adopted mobile communication systems. To stay relevant, marketing research companies have necessarily adapted to these new communication systems.

The rise of technology and the rapid adoption of sophisticated personal communication systems by consumers underlie a troublesome data collection dilemma faced by marketing researchers all over the globe. As you will soon learn, changes due to technological advances are making the data collection process faster, simpler, more secure, and even less expensive. Nonetheless, the response rate—the percentage of the individuals who are asked to participate in a survey who actually take part in that survey—is low and declining yearly.[4] At the same time, a "squeeze" is apparent in the rising percentage of noncontacts, or the percentage of those individuals who researchers attempt to contact to ask to take part in a survey who cannot be reached. The problem is especially significant with telephone interviewing, as telephone users have effectively blocked marketing researchers with caller ID, answering devices, and the like. Online participants have comparable means of avoiding surveys.

Data collection method trends are readily seen in Figure 7.1, which presents recent levels of use of online, CATI (telephone), paper-and-pencil, and computer-assisted personal interviewing. The figure presents the findings of surveys of the marketing research industry worldwide conducted annually for the past several years.[5] The figure shows the dramatic rise in online surveys and the concurrent decline in CATI (telephone) and paper-and-pencil

Computer technology has dramatically changed data collection in recent years.

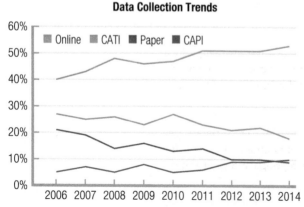

FIGURE 7.1 Recent Data Collection Trends

TABLE 7.2 **Data Collection and Computer Technology**

	No Computer	Computer
Interviewer	**Person administered** Interviewer reads questions and records the answers on paper.	**Computer assisted** Interviewer reads the questions and uses computer technology to record the answers and/or otherwise assist in the interview.
No interviewer	**Self-administered** Respondent reads the questions on a page and responds by writing on the questionnaire.	**Computer administered** Computer communicates the questions and records the respondent's answers.

surveys along with a modest increase in computer-assisted personal interviews. Thus, the impact of computer technology is readily apparent in Figure 7.1.

Despite the impression of Figure 7.1 that online surveys are eclipsing all other methods, data collection is currently a blend of traditional, or low-technology, methods and contemporary, or high-technology, approaches. As noted in Table 7.2, the four possible types of data collection are characterized by (1) whether an interviewer is used and (2) whether computer technology is employed. Thus, data collection can be person administered, computer assisted, computer administered, or self-administered. We will describe each form of administration in detail. Each data collection mode has special advantages and disadvantages that we describe in general before discussing the various types of surveys found within each category. Plus, each form is evolving and being reinvented with technology.[6] Specific advantages and disadvantages on these various types are discussed later in the chapter.

PERSON-ADMINISTERED SURVEYS

In a **person-administered survey**, an interviewer reads questions, either face-to-face or over the telephone, to the respondent and records his or her answers without the use of a computer. This was the primary administration mode for many years. However, its popularity fell off as costs increased and as computer technology advanced. Nevertheless, person-administered surveys are still used, and we describe the advantages and disadvantages associated with these surveys next.

In a person-administered survey, an interviewer reads questions, either face-to-face or over the telephone, to the respondent and records his or her answers without the use of a computer.

Advantages of Person-Administered Surveys Person-administered surveys have four unique advantages: They offer feedback, rapport, quality control, and adaptability.[7] The presence of an interviewer allows for on-the-spot instructions and helps respondents to stay on task.

1. Feedback Interviewers often respond to direct questions from respondents during an interview. Sometimes respondents do not understand the instructions, they may not hear the question clearly, or they might become distracted during the interview. A human interviewer may be allowed to adjust his or her questions according to verbal or nonverbal cues. When a respondent begins to fidget or look bored, the interviewer can say, "I have only a few more questions." Or if a respondent makes a comment, the interviewer may jot it down as a side note to the researcher.

2. Rapport Some people distrust surveys in general, or they may have some suspicions about the survey at hand. It is often helpful to have another human being present to develop some rapport with the respondent early on in the questioning process. A person can create trust and understanding that nonpersonal forms of data collection cannot achieve.

Personal interviewers can build rapport with respondents who are initially distrustful or suspicious.

© Rineca/Shutterstock

Without a personal interviewer, a respondent may fail to understand survey questions.

3. Quality Control An interviewer sometimes must select certain types of respondents based on gender, age, or some other distinguishing characteristic. Personal interviewers may be used to ensure that respondents are selected correctly. Using a personal interviewer ensures that every question will be asked of the respondent. Additionally, some researchers feel that respondents are more likely to be truthful when they respond face-to-face.

4. Adaptability Personal interviewers can adapt to respondent differences. It is not unusual, for instance, to find an elderly person or a very young person who must be initially helped step-by-step through the answering process to understand how to respond to questions. Interviewers are trained to ensure that they do not alter the meaning of a question by interpreting the question to a respondent. In fact,

> Personal interviewers can adapt to differences in respondents, but they must be careful not to alter the meaning of a question.

interviewers should follow precise rules on how to adapt to different situations presented by respondents.

Disadvantages of Person-Administered Surveys The drawbacks to using human interviewers are human error, slowness, cost, and interview evaluation.

1. Humans Make Errors Human interviewers may ask questions out of sequence, or they may change the wording of a question, which may change the meaning of the question altogether. Humans can make mistakes recording the information provided by the respondent. Human interviewers may make any number of errors when they become fatigued or bored from repetition.

While not an "error" in the sense we are discussing, another danger of using personal interviewers is the potential for "cheating," such as trying to steer survey participants to certain responses or purposefully recording answers that do not reflect the participants' responses.

2. Slow Speed Collecting data using human interviewers is slower than other modes because of necessary sequential interviewing. Although pictures, videos, and graphics can be handled by personal interviewers, they cannot accommodate them as quickly as, say, computers. Sometimes personal interviewers simply record respondents' answers using pencil and paper, which necessitates a separate data-input step to build a computer data file. For this reason, increasing numbers of data collection companies have shifted to the use of laptop computers that immediately add the responses to a data file.

> The disadvantages of person-administered surveys are human error, slow data collection, high cost, and interview evaluation apprehension among respondents.

3. High Cost Naturally, the use of a face-to-face interviewer is more expensive than, say, mailing the questionnaire to respondents. Typically, personal interviewers are highly trained and skilled, which explains the expense factor. Of course, a telephone personal interviewer is less expensive, but this method is still more costly than mail or online surveys.

> Interview evaluation occurs when the interviewer's presence creates anxieties in respondents that may cause them to alter their normal responses.

4. Fear of Interview Evaluation Another disadvantage of person-administered surveys is that the presence of another person may create apprehension,[8] called *interview evaluation*, among certain respondents. **Interview evaluation** may occur when another person is involved in the interviewing process and some respondents are apprehensive that they are answering "correctly." Even when responding to questions from a perfect stranger, some people become anxious about the possible reaction of the interviewer to their answers. They may be concerned as to how the interviewer evaluates their responses, especially on personal topics, such as personal hygiene, political opinions, financial matters, and age. The presence of a human interviewer may cause survey respondents to answer differently than they would in a nonpersonal data collection mode. Some respondents, for example, try to please the interviewer by saying what they think the interviewer wants to hear.

COMPUTER-ASSISTED SURVEYS

Computer technology represents an attractive, efficient, and flexible option with respect to survey mode, and new developments occur almost every day. While person-administered surveys were the industry mainstay, computer-assisted survey methods have grown to a dominant position in developed countries. In this mode, a telephone interviewer may read questions and record answers on a computer screen, or a personal interviewer may use a tablet computer as an aid in administering a survey. In a **computer-assisted survey**, the interviewer basically verbalizes the questions while relying to some degree on computer technology to facilitate the interview work. Here the computer accommodates the interview process by, for example, showing the questions to read, allowing storage of the answers, or, perhaps, even demonstrating some product feature with a video or pictures. Computer technology assists the interviewer by making the interview process more efficient and effective. As you would expect, computer-assisted surveys have many advantages and a few disadvantages.

Technology plays a support role in the interviewer's work in a computer-assisted survey.

Advantages of Computer-Assisted Surveys

There are variations of computer-assisted surveys. The interviewer may be calling on a phone or interacting with respondents face-to-face. The computer may provide and record all questions and answers, say on a pad or tablet, or it may be used to cryptically record answers. Regardless of which variation is considered, at least four advantages of computer-assisted surveys are evident: speed; relatively error-free interviews; use of pictures, audiovisuals, and graphics; and immediate capture of data. Of course, because a trained interviewer is present, computer-assisted data collection automatically garners the benefits of person-administered data collection.

1. Speed Perhaps the greatest single advantage of computer-assisted data collection is its ability to gather survey data very quickly. The computer-assisted approach is much faster than the purely human interview approach. A computer does not become fatigued or bored, and it does not make human errors. The speed factor translates into cost savings.

Computer-assisted surveys are fast, error free, capable of using pictures or graphics, able to capture data in real time.

2. Relatively Error-Free Interviews Properly programmed, the computer-assisted approach guarantees zero computer errors, although it cannot prevent interviewer errors, such as inadvertently skipping questions, asking inappropriate questions based on previous responses, misunderstanding how to pose questions, or recording the wrong answer.

3. Use of Pictures, Audiovisuals, and Graphics Computer graphics can be integrated into questions as they are viewed on a computer screen. Rather than having an interviewer pull out a picture of a new type of window air conditioner, for instance, computer graphics can show it from a 360-degree perspective. High-quality video may be programmed so that the respondent can see the product in use or can be shown a wide range of audiovisual displays.

4. Immediate Capture of Data Usually responses are captured at the same time they are entered into the computer. At the end of the interviewer's day, he or she typically transmits the respondents' data to the central office, or it may be done in real time via wireless communication. With computer-assisted telephone interviews, responses are stored immediately because a central computer system is used.

The immediate capture of data by computer-administered surveys is an important advantage of this data collection mode.

Disadvantages of Computer-Assisted Surveys

The primary disadvantages of computer-assisted surveys are that they require some level of technical skill and setup costs may be significant.

1. Technical Skills May Be Required A wide range of computer-assisted methods is available to marketing researchers. While the simplest options require minimal technical skills and even interviewers with low-level computer skills can master them quickly, more sophisticated versions (such as CATI, to be described later) require considerable programming skill to master the computer interfaces.

2. Setup Costs Can Be High While computer technology can result in increases in productivity, there can be high setup costs associated with getting some of these systems in place and operational. Computer-assisted systems, such as electronic notebooks or tablets, incur initial purchase costs. With the most sophisticated computer-assisted survey types, programming and debugging must take place with each survey. Depending on what type of computer-assisted survey is under consideration, these costs, including the associated time factor, can render computer-assisted delivery systems for surveys somewhat less attractive relative to other data collection options.

> Disadvantages of computer-assisted data collection are the requirement of technical skills and high setup costs.

SELF-ADMINISTERED SURVEYS

In a **self-administered survey**, the respondent completes the survey on his or her own with no agent—human or computer—administering the interview.[9] We are referring to the prototypical "paper-and-pencil" survey here where the respondent reads the questions and responds directly on the questionnaire. Normally, the respondent goes at his or her own pace, and often he or she selects the place and time to complete the survey. He or she also may decide when the questionnaire will be returned. In other words, responding to the questions is entirely under the control of the respondent.

> In a self-administered survey, the respondent completes the survey on his or her own; no human or computer agent administers the interview.

Advantages of Self-Administered Surveys
Self-administered surveys have three important advantages: reduced cost, respondent control, and reduced interview evaluation apprehension.

1. Reduced Cost Eliminating the need for an interviewer or an administering device such as a computer program can result in significant cost savings.

2. Respondent Control Respondents can control the pace at which they respond, so they may not feel rushed. Ideally, a respondent should be relaxed while responding, and a self-administered survey may effect this relaxed state.

3. Reduced Interview Evaluation Apprehension As we noted earlier, some respondents feel apprehensive when answering questions, or the topic may be sensitive, such as gambling,[10] smoking, or personal hygiene. The self-administered approach takes the administrator, whether human or computer, out of the picture, and respondents may feel more at ease.

> Self-administered surveys have three important advantages: reduced cost, respondent control, and no interview evaluation apprehension.

Disadvantages of Self-Administered Surveys
The disadvantages of self-administered surveys are respondent control, lack of monitoring, and high questionnaire requirements.

1. Respondent Control Because self-administration places control of the survey in the hands of the prospective respondent, this type of survey is subject to the possibilities that respondents will not complete the survey, will answer questions erroneously, will not respond in a timely manner, or will refuse to return the survey.

2. Lack of Monitoring With self-administered surveys, there is no opportunity for the researcher to monitor or interact with the respondent during the course of the interview. A monitor can offer explanations and encourage the respondent to continue. But with a self-administered survey, respondents who do not understand the meaning of a word or who are confused about how to answer a question may answer improperly or become frustrated and refuse to answer at all.

> The disadvantages of self-administered surveys are respondent control, lack of monitoring, and high questionnaire requirements.

3. High Questionnaire Requirements Because of the absence of the interviewer or an internal computer check system, the burden of respondent understanding falls on the questionnaire itself. Not only must it have perfectly clear instructions, examples, and reminders throughout, the questionnaire must also entice the respondents to participate and encourage them to continue answering until all questions are complete. Questionnaire design is important regardless of the data collection mode. However, with self-administered surveys, clearly the questionnaire must be thoroughly reviewed and accurate before data collection begins. You will learn more about designing questionnaires in Chapter 9.

With self-administered surveys, the questionnaire must be especially thorough and accurate to minimize respondent errors.

COMPUTER-ADMINISTERED SURVEYS

In a **computer-administered survey**, a computer plays an integral role in posing the questions and recording respondents' answers. The prototypical computer-administered survey is an online survey in which respondents are directed to a website that houses the questionnaire. Amazingly sophisticated web-based questionnaire design systems can easily qualify respondents, skip questions that should not be asked based on previous answers, include randomly administered stimuli, use quota systems for sample sizes, display a range of graphics and audiovisuals, and accomplish a large variety of tasks in place of a human interviewer. Computer-administered surveys are not bound to the Internet, as they can be adapted for telephone delivery, called "interactive voice response" (IVR) surveys that use prerecorded or computer voice and allow respondents to answer questions either verbally or with a phone keypad.

Advantages of Computer-Administered Surveys As just noted, computer-administered surveys provide a wide variety of user-friendly features; they can be relatively inexpensive, and most respondents are quite comfortable with most computer-administered survey topics.

1. Many User-Friendly Features A great many online questionnaire design systems are available, and the large majority of them are easy to program as long as the user has modest computer skills. So, for the researcher, many have built-in question libraries, simple skip logic, and copy-and-paste features. They easily accommodate graphics and video snippets of almost any type. Some have respondent-interactive features such as drag-and-drop, sliding scales, constant sum scales, graphic rating scales, and more. Most have annotated screen capture and/or video help systems. Many are linked to online panel companies so the researcher can access practically any typical respondent group almost immediately (for a price). They host the online questionnaires, collect the data, offer simple statistical and graphical analyses, and afford downloads of the data into multiple formats such as Excel or SPSS. On the respondent side, computer-administered surveys are easy, efficient, and sometimes fun.[11]

2. Relatively Inexpensive Many of these systems are designed for the DIY (do-it-yourself) marketing researcher, so they have free trial versions and graduated pricing systems that make them affordable. Of course, the most sophisticated systems are expensive, although not on a per-survey basis for marketing research companies that perform many surveys annually.

3. Reduction of Interview Evaluation Concern in Respondents Concerns among respondents that they should give the "right" or "desirable" answers tend to diminish when they interact with a computer.[12] In such cases, some researchers believe that respondents will provide more truthful answers to potentially sensitive topics. A related emerging advantage of online surveys is that when they are coupled with opt-in or "permission marketing," they have high response rates. That is, where a panel or database of a firm's customers has agreed to respond to online survey requests from a research firm or the company, studies have shown that respondents are more cooperative and more actively involved in the survey, and response inducements such as prenotifications and personalization are unnecessary.[13]

Computer-administered surveys are user friendly, inexpensive, and not threatening to respondents.

Disadvantage of Computer-Administered Surveys

Require Computer-Literate and Internet-Connected Respondents Whereas the first requirement is a low hurdle, there are instances where respondents do not qualify—for example, some children, senior citizens, or disadvantaged socioeconomic groups. Many foreign countries have low computer and Internet penetration levels that discourage the use of computer-administered surveys.

MIXED-MODE SURVEYS

Mixed-mode surveys, sometimes referred to as hybrid surveys, use multiple data collection modes.

Mixed-mode surveys, sometimes referred to as *hybrid surveys*, use multiple data collection modes. It has become increasingly popular to use mixed-mode surveys in recent years. Part of this popularity is due to the increasing use of online survey research. As more and more respondents have access to the Internet, online surveys, a form of computer-administered surveys, are often combined with some other method, such as telephone surveying, a form of person-administered surveying. Another reason for the popularity of mixed-mode surveys is the realization by marketing researchers that respondents should be treated like customers.[14] Basically, this realization translates into the need to match the data collection mode with respondent preferences insofar as possible to foster respondent goodwill[15] and maximize the quality of data collected.[16]

With a mixed-mode approach, a researcher may use two or more survey data collection modes to access a representative sample,[17] or modes may be used in tandem, such as use of the Internet to solicit respondents who agree to a face-to-face interview.[18] Some companies are experimenting with multiple mobile media modes to match up with mobile consumers who use social media.[19] Also, as in the case of eBay's use of hybrid research,[20] these surveys may facilitate the use of both quantitative and qualitative techniques to do "deep dives" into understanding the buyer–seller trust relationship.

Advantage of Mixed-Mode Surveys

The advantage of mixed-mode surveys is that researchers can take advantage of each of the various modes to achieve their data collection goals.

Multiple Avenues to Achieve Data Collection Goal The main benefit of mixed-mode surveys is that researchers can take advantage of each of the various modes to achieve their data collection goals. Generally, mixed-mode surveys afford better coverage of the population, result in somewhat higher response rates, sometimes shorten questionnaire lengths, and may lessen total survey costs.[21]

A disadvantage of the mixed-mode survey is that the researcher must assess the effects the mode may have on response data.

Disadvantages of Mixed-Mode Surveys
There are two primary disadvantages of using hybrid data collection modes.

1. The Survey Mode May Affect Response One reason for researchers' past reluctance to use mixed modes for gathering data is concern that the mode used may affect responses given by consumers.[22] Will consumers responding to an in-home interview with a personal interviewer respond differently than those responding to an impersonal, online survey? This disparity has been shown in comparing an online survey to a telephone survey[23] and for web versus mail surveys.[24] Studies have been conducted to assess differences between data collection methods in mixed-mode applications.[25] The results of studies addressing the question of survey mode effects on respondents are not entirely consistent, so our warning is that the researcher must assess differences in data collected to determine if the data collection mode explains any disparities.

Multiple modes add to the complexities of data collection such as differences in instructions and integration of data from different sources.

2. Additional Complexity Multiple modes add to the complexities of data collection.[26] For example, if you are conducting a survey online and by telephone, the wording of the instructions must be different to accommodate those reading instructions they themselves are to follow (for online respondents) versus a telephone interviewer reading the instructions to the respondent. Further, data from the two sources will need to be integrated into a single dataset, so much care must be taken to ensure data are compatible. Even within a particular data collection method, there can be a mixture of different types of information, which increases the complexity of marketing research.

7-3 Descriptions of Data Collection Methods

Now that you have an understanding of the pros and cons of person-administered, self-administered, computer-assisted, and computer-administered surveys, we can describe the various interviewing techniques used in each mode. Not including mixed-mode surveys, several data collection methods are used by marketing researchers (Table 7.3):

Person-administered/computer-assisted (when a computer is used to facilitate) surveys:

1. In-home survey
2. Mall-intercept survey
3. In-office survey
4. Telephone survey

Computer-administered surveys:

5. Fully automated survey
6. Online survey

Self-administered surveys:

7. Group self-administered survey
8. Drop-off survey
9. Mail survey

Before we describe the various ways of performing a survey, we want to inform you that the Marketing Research Association (MRA) Code of Ethics explicitly addresses ethical standards for all and specific forms of surveys. When you read the MRA Code excerpts included

TABLE 7.3 Various Ways to Gather Data

Data Collection Method	Description
In-home interview	The interviewer conducts the interview in the respondent's home. Appointments may be made ahead by telephone.
Mall-intercept interview	Shoppers in a mall are approached and asked to take part in the survey. Questions may be asked in the mall or in the mall-intercept company's facilities located in the mall.
In-office interview	The interviewer makes an appointment with business executives or managers to conduct the interview at the respondent's place of work.
Telephone interview	Interviewers work in a data collection company's office using cubicles or work areas for each interviewer, usually reading questions on a computer monitor. Often the supervisor has the ability to "listen in" to interviews and to check that they are being conducted correctly.
Fully automated interview	A computer is programmed to administer the questions. Respondents interact with the computer and enter in their own answers by using a keyboard, by touching the screen, or by using some other means.
Online survey	Respondents answer a questionnaire that resides on the Internet.
Group self-administered survey	Respondents take the survey in a group context. Each respondent works individually, but they meet as a group, which allows the researcher to economize.
Drop-off survey	Questionnaires are left with the respondent to fill out. The administrator may return at a later time to pick up the completed questionnaire, or it may be mailed in.
Mail survey	Questionnaires are mailed to prospective respondents, who are asked to fill them out and return them by mail.

MARKETING RESEARCH INSIGHT 7.1   *Ethical Consideration*

Marketing Research Association Code of Ethics: Respondent Participation

1. **Treat respondents with respect and in a professional manner.**

2. **Protect the rights of respondents, including the right to refuse to participate in part or all of the research process.**

   Researchers must respect the bounds of cooperation set by respondents, who control the parameters under which information is given. In practice, this means all of the following:

   - *Respondent agreement to participate in research must be obtained upfront, rather than after the fact.*
   - *Consent must be granted freely, without coercion.*
   - *Consent may be withdrawn by the respondent at any point during the contact.*
   - *Consent must be granted expressly for participation in any subsequent studies.*
   - *An explicit opt-out request for any future contact or participation at any point during the process will be honored.*
   - *All reasonable precautions are taken so that respondents are in no way adversely affected as a result of their participation in a marketing research project.*

25. **Provide detailed written or verbal study instructions to those engaged in the data collection process.**

    Accurate data can be obtained only when all parties to the research process are committed to quality. Principal investigators must ensure that staff involved in sampling, fieldwork, data processing, analysis and other facets of a study receive appropriate, detailed instructions so that operations are completed as planned. Documentation should be created

and preserved at every step of a project so that subsequent investigators can understand and replicate study findings.

5. **Proactively or upon request identify by name the research organization collecting data.**

16. **Take special care and adhere to applicable law when conducting research across state and national borders and with vulnerable populations, including but not limited to children.**

    Specific laws and regulations govern research among these groups, and it is incumbent upon marketing researchers to ensure compliance obligations for all vulnerable populations are met, regardless of any specific interviewing method or response technology in use.

    Research among children requires knowledge and adherence to unique precautions that apply to all respondents under the age of majority, i.e. minors.

    Other vulnerable groups include but are not limited to:

    - *Elderly/aged persons*
    - *Cognitively impaired persons*
    - *Prisoners*
    - *Patients or others with medical issues*

25. **Provide detailed written or verbal study instructions to those engaged in the data collection process.**

    Accurate data can be obtained only when all parties to the research process are committed to quality. Principal investigators must ensure that staff involved in sampling, fieldwork, data processing, analysis and other facets of a study receive appropriate, detailed instructions so that operations are completed as planned. Documentation should be created and preserved at every step of a project so that subsequent investigators can understand and replicate study findings.

Marketing Research on YouTube™ To learn more about conducting a survey, go to www.youtube.com and search for "Quantitative Surveying Methods."

In-home interviews are used when the survey requires respondents to see, read, touch, use, or interact with a product prototype and when the researcher believes the security and comfort of respondents' homes are important in affecting the quality of the data collected.

in Marketing Research Insight 7.1, you will see that the code has standards for the professional treatment of respondents, the requirement for detailed instructions of interviewers, the prohibition on using a respondent for multiple surveys at the same time, and the requirement to obey laws of various types regarding the recruitment of Internet respondents.

PERSON-ADMINISTERED/COMPUTER-ASSISTED INTERVIEWS

To recap, person-administered interviews use human interviewers who may rely on computer assistance in which case the interviewer is computer-assisted. The critical feature is that a human is conducting the interview. There are four common variations of person-administered/computer-assisted interviews, and their differences are based largely on the location of the interview. These methods include the in-home interview, the mall-intercept interview, the in-office interview, and the telephone interview.

In-Home Surveys As the name implies, an **in-home survey** is conducted by an interviewer who enters the home of the respondent. In-home interviews take longer to recruit participants, and researchers must travel to and from respondents' homes. Therefore, the cost per interview is relatively high. Two factors justify the high cost of in-home interviews. First, the marketing researcher must believe that personal contact is essential to the success of the interview. Second, the researcher must be convinced that the in-home environment is conducive to the questioning process. In-home interviews are useful when the research objective requires a respondent's physical presence to see, read, touch, use, or interact with the research object, such as a product prototype. In addition, the researcher may believe that the security and comfort of respondents' homes are important elements affecting the quality of the data collected. For example, the Yankelovich Youth MONITOR conducts in-home interviews of children who are age 6 and older so that both parents and children are comfortable with the interviewing process.[27] Computer-assisted personal interviews afford efficiencies and benefits.[28] However, programming and testing are necessary for success.[29]

In-home interviews facilitate interviewer–interviewee rapport.

Some research objectives require the respondents' physical presence to interact with the research object. A company develops a new type of countertop toaster oven that is designed to remain perfectly clean. However, to get the benefit of clean cooking, it must be set up according to different cooking applications (pizza versus bacon, for example), and the throwaway "grease-catch foil" must be placed correctly at the bottom of the unit to work properly. Will consumers be able to follow the setup instructions? This is an example of a study that would require researchers to conduct surveys in respondents' home kitchens. Researchers would observe as respondents open the box, unwrap and assemble the device, read the directions, and cook a meal. All of this may take an hour or more. Again, respondents may not be willing to travel somewhere and spend an hour on a research project. They may be more likely to do this in their own home.

Mall-Intercept Surveys Although the in-home interview has important advantages, it has the significant disadvantage of cost. The expense of in-home interviewer travel is high, even for local surveys. Patterned after "man-on-the-street" interviews pioneered by opinion-polling companies and other high-traffic surveys conducted in settings where crowds of pedestrians pass by, the **mall-intercept survey** is one in which the respondent is encountered and questioned while he or she is visiting a shopping mall. A mall-intercept company generally has offices in a large shopping mall, usually one that draws from a regional rather than a local market area. Typically, the interview company negotiates exclusive rights to do interviews in the mall and, thus, forces all marketing research companies that wish to do mall intercepts in that area to use that interview company's services. In any case, the travel costs are eliminated

Mall-intercept interviews are conducted in large shopping malls, and they are less expensive per interview than are in-home interviews.

because respondents incur the costs themselves by traveling to the mall. Mall-intercept interviewing has acquired a major role as a survey method because of its ease of implementation[30] and is available in many countries.[31] Shoppers are intercepted in the pedestrian traffic areas of shopping malls and either interviewed on the spot or asked to move to a permanent interviewing facility located in the mall office. Although some malls do not allow marketing research interviewing because they view it as a nuisance to shoppers, many permit mall-intercept interviews and may rely on these data themselves to fine-tune their own marketing programs. Mall-intercept companies are adopting high-tech approaches, such as iPads and other mobile devices, and they are experimenting with kiosks to attract respondents.[32]

In addition to low cost, mall interviews have many of the benefits associated with in-home interviewing. As we noted earlier, the most important advantage is the presence of an interviewer who can interact with the respondent.[33] However, a few

© Syda Productions/123RF

The representativeness of mall interview samples is always an issue.

drawbacks are specifically associated with mall interviewing. First, sample representativeness is an issue, for most malls draw from a relatively small area in close proximity to their location. If researchers are looking for a representative sample of some larger area, such as the county or MSA, they should be wary of using the mall intercept. Some people shop at malls more frequently than others and therefore have a greater chance of being interviewed.[34] Recent growth of nonmall retailing concepts, such as catalogs and stand-alone discounters such as Walmart and, of course, online vendors such as Amazon, mean that more mall visitors are recreational shoppers rather than convenience-oriented shoppers, resulting in the need to scrutinize mall-intercept samples as to what consumer groups they actually represent. Also, many shoppers refuse to take part in mall interviews for various reasons. Nevertheless, special selection procedures called *quotas*, which are described in Chapter 9, may be used to counter the problem of nonrepresentativeness.

A second shortcoming of mall-intercept interviewing is that a shopping mall does not have a comfortable home environment that is conducive to rapport and close attention to details. The respondents may feel uncomfortable because passersby stare at them; they may be pressed for time or otherwise preoccupied by various distractions outside the researcher's control. These factors may adversely affect the quality of the interview. Some interview companies attempt to counter this problem by taking respondents to special interview rooms located in the interview company's mall offices. This procedure minimizes distractions and encourages respondents to be more relaxed. Some mall interviewing facilities have kitchens and rooms with one-way mirrors.

In-Office Surveys   Although the in-home and mall-intercept interview methods are appropriate for a wide variety of consumer goods, marketing research conducted in the B2B or organizational market typically requires interviews with business executives, purchasing agents, engineers, or other managers. Normally, **in-office surveys** take place in person while the respondent is in his or her office or perhaps in a company lounge area. Interviewing businesspeople face-to-face has essentially the same advantages and drawbacks as in-home consumer interviewing. For example, if Knoll, Inc., wants information regarding user preferences for different adjustment features that might be offered in an ergonomic office chair designed for business executives, it would make sense to interview prospective users or purchasers of these chairs. It would also be logical that these people would be interviewed at their places of business.

> In-office interviews are conducted at executives' or managers' places of work because they are the most suitable locations.

As you might imagine, in-office personal interviews incur relatively high costs. Those executives qualified to give opinions on a specific topic or individuals who would be involved in product purchase decisions must first be located. Sometimes names can be obtained from sources such as industry directories or trade association membership lists. More frequently, screening must be conducted over the telephone by calling a particular company that is believed to have executives of the type needed. However, locating those people within a large organization may be time consuming. Once a qualified person is located, the next step is to persuade that person to agree to an interview and then set up a time for the interview. This may require a sizable incentive. Finally, an interviewer must go to the particular place at the appointed time. Even with appointments, long waits are sometimes encountered, and cancellations are not uncommon because businesspersons' schedules sometimes shift unexpectedly. Added to these cost factors is the fact that interviewers who specialize in businesspeople interviews are more costly in general because of their specialized knowledge and abilities. They have to navigate around gatekeepers such as secretaries, learn technical jargon, and be conversant on product features when the respondent asks pointed questions or even criticizes questions as they are posed to him or her. Technology, naturally, is impacting personal interviewing with the emergence of web interviewing systems or Internet conversation systems such as Skype that eliminate most of the logistical aspects of personal interviews at home, in the office, or even with groups.

> In-office personal interviews incur costs because of difficulties in accessing qualified respondents.

Telephone Surveys   As we have mentioned previously, the need for a face-to-face interview is often predicated on the necessity of the respondent's physical inspection of a product, advertisement, or packaging sample. On the other hand, it may be vital that the interviewer watch the respondent to ensure that correct procedures are followed or otherwise to verify something about the respondent or his or her reactions. However, if physical contact is not necessary, telephone interviewing is an attractive option. There are a number of advantages as well as disadvantages associated with telephone interviewing.[35]

The advantages of telephone interviewing are many, and they explain why phone surveys are common in marketing surveys. First, the telephone is a relatively inexpensive way to collect survey data. Telephone charges are much lower than the cost of a face-to-face interview. A second advantage of the telephone interview is that it has the potential to yield a high-quality sample. If the researcher employs random dialing procedures and proper callback measures, the telephone approach may produce a better sample than any other survey procedure. A third important advantage is that telephone surveys have quick turnaround times. Most telephone interviews are of short duration anyway, but a good interviewer may complete several interviews per hour. Conceivably, a study could have the data collection phase executed in a few days with telephone interviews. In fact, in the political polling industry in which real-time information on voter opinions is essential, it is not unusual to have national telephone polls completed in a single night. However, a significant percentage of households are dropping wire-line phone service in favor of mobile phones. This trend is more prevalent in younger populations, so researchers are gravitating to mobile device administration of surveys.

> Advantages of telephone interviews are cost, quality, and speed.

Unfortunately, the telephone survey approach has several shortcomings. First, the respondent cannot be shown anything or physically interact with the research object. This shortcoming ordinarily eliminates the telephone survey as an alternative in situations requiring that the respondent view product prototypes, advertisements, packages, or anything else. A second disadvantage is that the telephone interview does not permit the interviewer to make the various judgments and evaluations that can be made by the in-person interviewer. For example, judgments regarding respondent income based on a respondent's home and other outward signs of economic status cannot be made. Similarly, the telephone does not allow for the observation of body language and facial expressions, nor does it permit eye contact. On the other hand, some may argue that the lack of face-to-face contact is helpful. Self-disclosure studies have indicated that respondents provide more information in personal interviews, except when the topics are threatening or potentially embarrassing. Questions on alcohol consumption, contraceptive methods, racial issues, or income tax reporting will probably generate more valid responses when asked in the relative anonymity of the telephone than when administered face-to-face. A review article concluded that, compared to face-to-face interviews, telephone interviews elicit more suspicion and less cooperation, generate more "no opinions" and socially desirable answers, and foster more dissatisfaction with long interviews.[36]

A third disadvantage of the telephone interview is that marketing researchers are more limited in the quantity and types of information they can obtain. Very long interviews are inappropriate for the telephone, as are questions with lengthy lists of response options that respondents will have difficulty remembering when they are read over the telephone. Respondents short on patience may hang up during interviews, or they may utter short and convenient responses just to speed up the interview. Obviously, the telephone is a poor choice for conducting an interview with many open-ended questions where respondents make comments or give statements, as the interviewer will have great difficulty recording these remarks.

> The telephone is a poor choice for conducting a survey with many open-ended questions.

The final—and perhaps and most significant—problem with telephone surveys is the growing threat to its existence as a result of increased noncooperation by the public. This situation is compounded by consumers' use of answering machines, caller recognition, and call-blocking devices. Another difficulty is that legitimate telephone interviewers must contend with the negative impression people have of telemarketers.

> Telephone interviewers must contend with the negative impression people have of telemarketers.

Despite their shortcomings and declining response rates, telephone surveys remain somewhat popular. In fact, when monetary incentives, assurance that it is not a sales call, and a promise of a short survey are involved, response rates are quite good, according to one study conducted in New Zealand.[37]

Central location telephone surveying involves a field data collection company housing a multitude of telephone lines at one location from which interviewers make calls. Usually, interviewers have separate enclosed work spaces and lightweight headsets that free both hands so they can record responses. Everything is done from this central location. Obviously, there are many advantages to operating from a central location. For example, resources are pooled, and interviewers can handle multiple surveys, such as calling plant managers in the afternoon and households in the evening hours. The reasons accounting for the prominence of the central location phone interview are efficiency and control. Efficiency is gained when everything is performed at a single location and further acquired by the benefit that multiple telephone surveys can be conducted simultaneously.

> Central location interviewing is the current telephone survey standard because it affords efficient control of interviewers.

Perhaps the most important advantage of central location interviewing is quality control. Recruitment and training are performed uniformly at this location. Interviewers can be oriented to the equipment, study the questionnaire and its instructions, and practice the interview among themselves over their phone lines. Also, the actual interviewing process can be monitored. Most telephone interviewing facilities have monitoring equipment that permits a supervisor to listen in on an interview as it is being conducted. Interviewers who are not doing the interview properly can be spotted and the necessary corrective action taken. Ordinarily, each interviewer will be monitored at least once per shift,[38] but the supervisor may focus attention on newly hired interviewers to ensure they are doing their work correctly. The fact that interviewers never know when the supervisor will listen in tends to ensure more diligence. Also, completed questionnaires are checked on the spot as a further quality control check. Interviewers can be immediately informed of any deficiencies in filling out the questionnaire. Finally, there is control over interviewers' schedules. That is, interviewers report in and out and work regular hours, even if they are evening hours, and make calls during the time periods stipulated by the researcher as appropriate interviewing times.

The most advanced central location telephone interview companies operate with **computer-assisted telephone interviews (CATI).** Although each system is unique and new developments occur regularly, we can describe a typical setup. Each interviewer is equipped with a hands-free headset and is seated in front of a computer screen that is driven by the company's computer system. Often the computer dials the prospective respondent's telephone automatically, and the computer screen provides the interviewer with the introductory comments. As the interview progresses, the interviewer moves through the questions by pressing a key or a series of keys on the keyboard. Some systems use light pens or pressure-sensitive screens.

> With CATI, the interviewer reads the questions on a computer screen and enters respondents' answers directly into the computer program.

The questions and possible responses appear on the screen one at a time. The interviewer reads the questions to the respondent and enters the response codes, and the computer moves on to the next appropriate question. For example, an interviewer might ask if the respondent owns a dog. If the answer is "yes," there could appear a series of questions regarding what type of dog food the dog owner buys. If the answer is "no," these questions would be inappropriate. Instead, the computer program skips to the next appropriate question, which might be "Do you own a cat?" In other words, the computer eliminates the human error potential that would exist if this survey were done in non-CATI interviewing. The human interviewer is just the "voice" of the computer, but because telephone communication is used, the respondent usually does not have any clue that a computer is involved.

> With CATI, the interviewer is the "voice" of the computer.

With CATI, the computer can be used to customize questions. For example, in the early part of a long interview, the interviewer might ask a respondent the years, makes, and models of all cars he or she owns. Later interview questions might focus on each vehicle. The question might come up on the interviewer's screen as follows: "You said you own a Lexus. Who in your family drives this car most often?" Other questions about this car and others owned would appear in similar fashion. Similarly, most CATI systems do not permit users to enter an "impossible" answer. For example, if a question has three possible answers with codes A, B, and C and the interviewer enters a D by mistake, the computer will refuse the answer until an acceptable

> Most CATI systems are programmed to reject wrong answers.

code is entered. If a combination or pattern of answers is impossible, the computer will not accept an answer, or it may alert the interviewer to the inconsistency and move to a series of questions that will resolve the discrepancy. Finally, data are entered directly into a computer file as the interviewing is completed, so tabulations may be run at any point in the study. The many advantages and quick turnaround of CATI and CAPI (computer-assisted personal interviewing) make them mainstay data collection methods for many syndicated omnibus survey services.[39, 40]

As you are learning, computer-assisted interviews vary by the method of delivery, meaning with or without an interviewer and, if an interviewer is present, by face-to-face or telephone administration. Read Marketing Research Insight 7.2 to find out how CASI, CAPI, and CATI differ in response quality.

MARKETING RESEARCH INSIGHT 7.2   *Digital Marketing Research*

Which Computer-Assisted Interview Is Best: CASI, CAPI, or CATI?

As has been pointed out repeatedly in this chapter on data collection, computer technology has become the marketing researcher's best friend and is heavily relied upon. There are, however, various flavors or varieties of computer integration or support for interviews. There are three popular options:

- Computer-Assisted Self Interviewing (CASI)—the respondent answers questions without any human interviewer or assistance such as an online survey.
- Computer-Assisted Personal Interviewing (CAPI)—an interviewer administers the questions and records the respondent's verbal responses in a face-to face context with the aid of a computer, such as a laptop or tablet that takes the place of "hard copy" and receives and stores the respondent's answers.
- Computer-Assisted Telephone Interviewing (CATI)—an interviewer administers the questions and records the respondent's verbal responses over the telephone with the aid of a computer, such as a laptop or tablet that takes the place of "hard copy" and receives and stores the respondent's answers.

Although these three computer-assisted data collection methods are similar, there are some intuitive differences among them. For example, CASI facilitates privacy and anonymity because there is no human present or on the telephone line. Thus, one would expect CASI respondents to be more honest and open. Stated differently, the presence of someone to hear and record the respondent's answers may cause some respondents to underreport or downplay their answers to questions that touch on personal or emotional topics, such as sexual behaviors, use of drugs, alcohol consumption, risky behaviors, and the like. Answering questions about even less personal and emotional issues can also be affected, such as attending religious services, reading newspapers daily, watching certain television shows, making efforts to conserve resources, and purchasing premium or luxury brands. Moreover, because respondents move through the survey at their own pace, they may feel less pressured to respond quickly, particularly with open-ended questions where they compose a written comment or response. If there are graphics or visuals, respondents do not feel compelled to give an answer quickly to an interviewer who is waiting for it, so they may take more time to study, absorb, or process these visuals.

Researchers[41] investigated how CASI, CAPI, and CATI influenced survey responses. They created three data collection situations, one for each type of computer-assisted interviewing, and administered each one to matched samples of respondents. Although the study compared a number of difference measures of response behavior, it was found that for CAPI and CATI, both requiring the face-to-face or voice presence, respectively, of an interviewer, CAPI obtained better responses than did CATI some of the time. CASI, with no interviewer present, generally performed better than CAPI or CATI in obtaining "better" responses most of the time.

The findings of this study suggest that in general CASI is a better choice than CAPI or CATI, and CAPI is probably better than CATI, when any or a combination of the following topics is being researched:

- Socially undesirable personal behavior such as sexual activity, drug use, or driving violations
- Socially desirable behaviors such as not watching soap operas, watching news reports daily, managing finances
- Obtaining truthful extreme answers or obtaining fewer "no opinion" responses
- Obtaining truthful "don't know" answers
- Reading or studying visuals such as advertisements or the like
- Obtaining truthful opinions on politically charged topics

Is CASI always better? Consider that this study used respondents who were provided by a panel company. In other words, these were "seasoned" respondents who had experiences with online and other surveys, so they all probably had very high comfort levels with surveys in general. Less experienced respondents, meaning the general public, who have lower comfort levels with surveys will probably exhibit more interview apprehension when interviewers are present.

 Active Learning

Setting Up Controls for a Telephone Interview

For this Active Learning exercise, assume your marketing research course requires team projects and your team decides to research why students at your university chose to attend it. Your five-member team will conduct telephone interviews of 200 students selected at random from your university's student directory, with each team member responsible for completing 40 interviews by calling from his or her apartment or dorm room. You have volunteered to supervise the telephone interviewing. You have read about the tight controls in effect with central telephone interview companies, and you realize that quality assurance procedures should be in place with your student team member telephone interviewers. To satisfy each of the following telephone quality issues, what procedure would you propose to use?

Quality Assurance Procedure	Write Your Proposed Procedures Here
The student team member interviewers should call the right students at the proper times of the day.	
They must conduct the interviews correctly by reading the instructions and "skipping" questions as required by the respondent's answers.	
The 40 interviews should be conducted on schedule.	
Interviewers should be instructed on how to handle "no answers" and answering machines.	
A mechanism should be in place to detect bogus interview data in case some interviewers decide to submit false results.	

You may want to review the descriptions of how central location telephone surveys are conducted to see if your answers to these questions about your team research project are consistent with standard practices in marketing research described in this chapter. After you complete this exercise, write about how control of telephone interviews would be easier if done in a central location telephone facility.

COMPUTER-ADMINISTERED INTERVIEWS

As we have pointed out, computer technology has had a very significant impact on survey data collection. While new forms are constantly evolving, we will describe two variations of computer-administered interview systems. In one, a "synthetic" human interviewer is used, meaning that the questions are prerecorded or a computer "voice" is generated. Thus, it may sound as if a human interviewer is doing the questioning, but it is really a machine. Second, as you saw in Figure 7.1, the Internet-based interview has charged to the forefront of survey techniques, and we describe online surveys in this section as well.

Fully Automated Survey Some companies have developed **fully automated surveys**, in which the survey is administered by a computer but not online. With one such system, a computer dials a phone number, and a recording is used to introduce the survey. The respondent then uses the push buttons on his or her telephone to make responses, thereby interacting directly with the computer. In the research industry, this approach is known as **completely automated telephone survey (CATS)**. CATS has been successfully employed for customer satisfaction studies, service quality monitoring, Election Day polls, product/warranty registration, and even in-home product tests with consumers who have been given a prototype of a new product.[42] When CATS is used with telephone communication, and the respondent verbalizes responses that are interpreted by the computer, the method is sometimes called IVR, for interactive voice response.

Marketing Research on YouTube™ To see how to set up a completely automated telephone system, go to **www.youtube.com** and search for "Learn About PrecisionPolling.com."

In another system, the respondent sits or stands in front of the computer unit and reads the instructions from the screen. Each question and its various response options appear on the screen, and the respondent answers by pressing a key or touching the screen. For example, the respondent may be asked to rate how satisfied, on a scale of 1 to 10 (where 1 is very unsatisfied and 10 is very satisfied), he or she was the last time he or she used a travel agency to plan a family vacation. The instructions would instruct the respondent to press the key with the number appropriate to his or her degree of satisfaction. The respondent might press a 2 or a 7, depending on his or her experience and expectations. However, if the respondent presses 0 or a letter key, the computer could be programmed to beep, indicating that the response was inappropriate, and instruct the respondent to make another entry.

All of the advantages of computer-driven interviewing are found in this approach. In addition, the interviewer expense or extra cost of human voice communication capability for the computer is eliminated. Because respondents' answers are saved in a file during the interview itself, tabulation can take place on a daily basis, and it is a simple matter for the researcher to access the survey's data at practically any time.[43]

Online Surveys The **Internet-based questionnaire** in which the respondent answers questions online has become the industry standard for surveys in virtually all high-Internet-penetration countries. Internet-based online surveys are fast, easy, and inexpensive.[44] The questionnaires accommodate all of the standard question formats, and they are very flexible, including the ability to present pictures, diagrams, or displays to respondents. Smartphone versions of online surveys are evolving.[45] Internet-based or web surveys have earned varying levels of popularity around the world, but online surveys do require some technical skills and have unique practical challenges such as scrolling pages and appearance.[46]

Read Marketing Research Insight 7.3 to learn how researchers investigated how the "cool" aspects of fashions are motivators for college students who purchase trendy clothes by using an online data collection method.

Online data collection has profoundly changed the marketing research landscape,[47] particularly in the case of online panels.[48] For instance, using such a panel, a company could conduct "episodic" research of customer satisfaction instead of one large study per year, facilitating "continuous market intelligence" through a survey posted permanently on the web and modified as the company's strategies are implemented. Company managers can click up tabulated customer reactions on a daily basis.[49] Some researchers refer to this advantage of online surveys as *real-time research.*[50] Regardless, the speed, convenience, and flexibility of online surveys make them very attractive in all cases.[51] One serendipitous aspect of online surveys is that because the researcher can monitor survey response progress on a continual basis, it is possible to spot problems with the survey and to make adjustments to correct these problems.

Returning to the topic at hand, the online survey is no cure-all for a marketing researcher's data collection woes, as the marketing research industry quickly learned that its honeymoon with Internet surveys was short. Their novelty soon wore off, and Internet surveys quickly began exhibiting symptoms of low cooperation rates that diminish the quality of telephone and mail surveys. Marketing researchers were quick to realize that online surveys presented design challenges and opportunities related to fostering cooperation in potential respondents.

If you want to learn how to do an online survey using Google Docs, go to **www.youtube.com** and search for "Create a Free Online Survey Using Google Docs (Free Online Survey Tool)."

Online surveys have important advantages of speed and low cost plus real-time access of data; however, there are drawbacks of sample representativeness, respondent validation, and difficulty in asking probing types of questions.

Online surveys allow respondents to participate while in relaxed and comfortable surroundings.

MARKETING RESEARCH INSIGHT 7.3   *Practical Application*

Web Survey Reveals College Students' Motivations for "Cool" Clothing

College students, often referred to as Generation Yers, are very different consumers as compared to their parents or other demographic consumer segments. In particular, Gen Yers have substantially greater purchasing power, which they spend on purchases such as music, movies, food, and television. They are also "into" clothing and strong brands. Consequently, Gen Yers patronize high-end department stores and specialty clothing stores. They think nothing of paying premium prices for fashion items that are "cool."

Marketing researchers[52] studying the fashion adoption of Gen Yers identified the following five different types of "coolness" that motivate their purchases of innovative clothing.

- Singular cool—unique, novel, and exclusive
- Personal cool—expression of individuality and identity
- Aesthetic cool—flattering color, cut, and/or style
- Functional cool—affordable and/or comfortable
- Quality cool—good construction and longevity

These researchers constructed a long questionnaire dealing with measures of these five kinds of coolness, demographic factors, and fashion adoption. They specifically wanted to survey college students because of their fashion consciousness and open-mindedness toward innovative products. They mulled over the data collection method alternatives and realized that in-home personal interviews were not feasible because they would need to send interviewers to dorm rooms, apartments, sororities, and fraternity houses. Telephone interviews were impractical because of the long survey, and mail surveying was definitely out of the question. So, in order to fit in with the high-technology comfort zones of college students, they created an online survey. Instructors of 11 different courses at a major U.S. university notified their students of the survey and provided access details. A sizeable sample of college students completed the survey in a matter of a few days, and the sample's demographic profile (age, gender, ethnic group, etc.) approximated that of the university as a whole.

Of course, the researchers were aware that fashion adoption is not uniform across all college students, so they separated the sample into high- and low-income groups. It was discovered that the clothing fashion adoption of low-income college students is driven by three types of coolness: the perceived high quality of the item, the uniqueness of the item, and the color, cut, or style. High-income college students have somewhat different motivations, as it was discovered that they also purchase new fashion due to uniqueness and color, cut, or style; however, they are motivated as well by expression of their personality or individuality. An interesting difference is that high-income college students are negatively motivated by functionality, meaning that they adopt new fashions even if they are high priced, uncomfortable, and not totally functional.

 Active Learning

Learn About Online Marketing Research Software Systems

Several companies have developed online questionnaire design and hosting systems. A quick search using Google will likely turn up 20 or more competitors. Practically all of these companies allow you to use their systems on a trial basis. Select one and download or otherwise gain access to the online survey system. Now answer each of the following questions:

1. How do you create the following question and answers on this system: *Have you purchased something at a Best Buy store in the past month?*
   Yes   No
2. What is skip logic, and how does it work on this system if you want the respondents who did purchase something at Best Buy to indicate whether they bought a 3-D HDTV?
3. Is the system user friendly? Why or why not?
4. What feature best demonstrates that this system is using sophisticated computer and/or Internet technology?

SELF-ADMINISTERED SURVEYS

Recall that a self-administered survey is one in which the respondent is in control, often deciding when to take the survey, where to take it, and how much time and attention to devote to it. With a self-administered survey, the respondent always decides what questions he or she will or will not answer. That is, the respondent fills in answers to a static copy of the questionnaire, which is what we have referred to as a paper-and-pencil questionnaire in previous descriptions. Probably the most popular type of self-administered survey is the mail survey; however, researchers may consider two other variations from time to time: the group self-administered survey and the drop-off survey.

Before continuing, let's address why Internet-based interviews are not categorized as self-administered. They do not fall into this category because the sophistication of Internet-based questionnaire design software does not allow respondents to avoid answering key questions. For example, the program may be set up to remind a respondent that a certain question was not answered. This prompt continues until the respondent answers the question. In addition, online questionnaire systems usually have skip logic, meaning that questions that are not appropriate to ask based on previous answers (e.g., Do you own a car? If no, do not ask questions about the car; if yes, do ask questions about the car) are not seen by the respondent. Some online questionnaire systems have display logic meaning that certain questions are asked, or displayed, only if answers to prior questions trigger them. For example, "yes" answers to "Have you ordered take-out in the past 30 days?" and "Did you pick it up at a drive-through window?" would trigger the display of questions about satisfaction with take-out and drive-through window service. Because we consider the ability of Internet surveys to stop respondents from "opting out" of questions and skip and display logic to be significant quality control features, we have not included Internet-based interviews in the self-administered group.

Group Self-Administered Survey Basically, a **group self-administered survey** entails administering a questionnaire to respondents in groups rather than individually for convenience and to gain economies of scale. For example, 20 or 30 people might be recruited to view a TV program sprinkled with test commercials. All respondents would be seated in a viewing room facility, and a video would run on a large television projection screen. Then they would be given a questionnaire to fill out regarding their recall of test ads, their reactions to the ads, and so on. As you would suspect, it is handled in a group context primarily to reduce costs and to provide the ability to interview a large number of people in a short time.

> Group self-administered surveys economize in time and money because a group of respondents participates simultaneously.

Variations for group self-administered surveys are limitless. Students can be administered surveys in their classes; church groups can be administered surveys during meetings; and social clubs and organizations, company employees, movie theater patrons, and other groups can be administered surveys during meetings, work, or leisure time. Often the researcher will compensate the group with a monetary payment as a means of recruiting the support of the group's leaders. In all of these cases, each respondent works through the questionnaire at his or her own pace. Granted, a survey administrator may be present, so there is some opportunity for interaction concerning instructions or how to respond, but the group context often discourages the respondents from asking all but the most pressing questions.

Drop-Off Survey Another variation of the self-administered survey is the **drop-off survey**, sometimes called "drop and collect," in which the survey representative approaches a prospective respondent, introduces the general purpose of the survey to the prospect, and leaves it with the respondent to fill out on his or her own. Essentially, the objective is to gain the prospective respondent's cooperation. The respondent is told that the questionnaire is self-explanatory and that it will be left with him or her to fill out at leisure. Perhaps the representative will return to pick up the questionnaire at a certain time, or the respondent may be

> Drop-off surveys must be self-explanatory because they are left with the respondents, who fill them out without assistance.

instructed to complete and return it by prepaid mail. Normally, the representative will return on the same day or the next day to pick up the completed questionnaire. In this way, a representative can cover a number of residential areas or business locations in a single day with an initial drop-off pass and a later pick-up pass. Drop-off surveys are especially appropriate for local market research undertakings in which travel is necessary but limited. They have been reported to have quick turnaround, high response rates, minimal interviewer influence on answers, and good control over how respondents are selected; plus, they are inexpensive.[53] Studies have shown the drop-off survey improves response rates with business or organizational respondents.[54]

Variations of the drop-off method include handing out the surveys to people at their places of work, asking them to fill them out at home, and then to return them the next day. Some hotel chains have questionnaires in their rooms with an invitation to fill them out and turn them in at the desk on checkout. Restaurants sometimes ask customers to fill out short questionnaires before they leave. Stores sometimes have short surveys on customer demographics, media habits, purchase intentions, or other information that customers are asked to fill out at home and return on their next shopping trip. A gift certificate drawing may even be used as an incentive to participate. As you can see, the term *drop-off* can be stretched to cover any situation in which the prospective respondent encounters the survey as though it were "dropped off" by a research representative.

Mail Survey A **mail survey** is one in which the questions are mailed to prospective respondents who are asked to fill them out and return them to the researcher by mail.[55] Part of its attractiveness stems from its self-administered aspect: There are no interviewers to recruit, train, monitor, and compensate. Similarly, mailing lists are readily available from companies that specialize in this business, and it is possible to access specific groups of target respondents. For example, it is possible to obtain a list of physicians specializing in family practice who operate clinics in cities larger than 500,000 people. Also, one may opt to purchase computer files, printed labels, or even labeled envelopes from these companies. In fact, some list companies will even provide insertion and mailing services. A number of companies sell mailing lists, and most, if not all, have online purchase options. On a per-mailed respondent basis, mail surveys are inexpensive. But mail surveys incur all of the problems associated with not having an interviewer present that were discussed earlier in this chapter.

Mail surveys suffer from nonresponse and self-selection bias.

Self-selection bias means respondents who return surveys by mail may differ from the original sample.

Despite the fact that the mail survey was once described as "powerful, effective, and efficient"[56] by the American Statistical Association, this research vehicle is plagued by two major problems. The first is **nonresponse**, which refers to questionnaires that are not returned. The second is **self-selection bias**, which means that those who do respond are probably different from those who do not fill out the questionnaire and return it; therefore, the sample gained through this method is nonrepresentative of the general population. Research shows that self-selected respondents can be more interested and involved in the study topic.[57] To be sure, the mail survey is not the only survey method that suffers from nonresponse and self-selection bias.[58] Failure to respond is found in all types of surveys, and marketing researchers must be constantly alert to the possibilities that their final samples are somehow different from the original set of potential respondents because of some systematic tendency or latent pattern of response. Whatever the survey mode used, those who respond may be more involved with the product, they may have more education, they may be more or less dissatisfied, or they may even be more opinionated in general than the target population of concern.[59] Mail survey researchers have tried a wide range of tactics and incentives to increase the response rate, but no huge increases have occurred.

Marketing Research Insight 7.4 describes how a mail delivery and return method was used to survey a very special target population, namely, South African safari hunters. Under the circumstances of the project, a mail approach did result in a successful survey.

MARKETING RESEARCH INSIGHT 7.4   *Global Application*

How to Survey South African Safari Hunters

Sometimes a marketing researcher is asked to study unusual topics, as was the case with a recent survey conducted in South Africa. Actually, the survey did not take place in South Africa, but it concerned individuals who had visited that country in the past few years for the specific purpose of big game hunting. The following is a description[60] of the phenomenon under investigation.

> Even though the hunting safari occurs mainly on privately owned game ranches, it is regulated by a well-organized game ranching and professional hunting industry. A hunting outfitter typically provides all the services required by the visiting hunter. These include the arrangement of the hunt, obtaining the necessary hunting permits, dealing with landowners, and seeing to written agreements regarding trophy fees, daily rates, and the species and sex of game offered. Other services relate to ground transportation, accommodation, domestic air charters, actual hunting, and preparation, packaging, and shipping of trophies. The outfitter is assisted by trained professional hunters (individuals who have attended a registered professional hunting school, passed the theoretical and practical examinations set by the relevant Provincial Nature Conservation Authorities, and possess the specified knowledge, abilities, skills, and experience. The latter includes at least sixty days experience hunting dangerous game). Hunters can choose a package from a selection of safaris. The final cost of the safari is negotiated and depends on the availability of the hunting area, dates and species, the status of the booking sheet, and the reputation of the outfitter and/or professional hunter. These negotiations can take up to 18 months, with the typical big-game hunter paying over US$100,000 for a 21-day hunting experience. This figure excludes costs for additional guests, such as observers or family members, who accompany the hunter.

As one would imagine, safari hunters are a very unusual set of individuals, and conducting a survey with this population poses challenges not found with most other populations. For one, these individuals can live practically in anywhere in the world. Personal interviews are not feasible for this reason. Mall-intercept surveys and group-based data collection are likewise impractical. Safari hunters are obviously very wealthy, and they undoubtedly guard their personal privacy tenaciously. They are very unlikely to take part in any survey regardless of the data collection method employed.

However, as can be seen in the preceding description, several forms of paperwork, such as permits, contracts, and agreements, identify and include contact information for safari hunters. Unfortunately, the country of South Africa and the professional hunting industry maintain strict confidentiality of all such information. To access this population, the researchers turned to a "professional facilitator" who agreed to act as an intermediary for the survey. The facilitator agreed to distribute about 2,000 survey packages to hunters who had participated in a South African safari in past years. The researchers then designed a paper-and-pencil questionnaire with a postage-paid reply envelope and necessarily used a mail survey for the data collection. The response rate was about 13%, which is typical of mail surveys, but 19% of the returned questionnaires were found to have a substantial number of unanswered questions, which is also a typical and unfortunate characteristic of mail surveys that are self-administered. Nonetheless, the researchers considered the survey to be a success. Most likely, the professional facilitator's solicitation caught the attention of the respondents and convinced them of the importance and seriousness of the survey, plus the overall positive experience of the safari certainly caused some of the professional hunters to complete the survey.

The typical South African safari hunter is from the United States (76%), male (98%), between 40 and 69 years old (83%), highly educated with high income, and an experienced hunter. Safari hunting is closely related to the hunter's personal values of conservation, understanding nature, escape, and heritage. It is also somewhat related to gaining the admiration of others for hunting trophies, and it is closely related to the hunter's need for excitement, adventure, sport, and challenge. Finally, safari hunters enjoy the opportunities their safaris afford for learning about others, meeting other hunters, and meeting new people. The survey also revealed the uniqueness of South Africa as a hunting safari location, for the hunters agreed strongly that South Africa has abundant natural beauty with a wide variety of habitat and game species. They agreed that South Africa is a truly unique hunting experience and that hunting there was "a dream come true."

7-4 Working with a Panel Company

As we have noted numerous times, the marketing research industry is plagued with almost universal reluctance in the population to take part in surveys. This situation means that no matter what data collection method is used, sample size targets and sample composition requirements are exceedingly difficult to attain. For instance, if 5,000 random telephone calls are made, perhaps only 5% will result in completed surveys, or if a like number of email invitations are sent to a company's customers who agree to receive them, a large percentage of those who take part in the survey may be exceptionally loyal customers but the survey may be testing tactics to solidify the patronage of new customers. Similarly, in either case, there may evidence of respondents speeding through the survey, skipping questions, or providing suspicious answers to key questions. The resulting poor data quality of such "cold call" or even "respondent friendly" surveys is an unfortunate reality and, as will be described in the next section of this chapter, good data quality is a prime objective of every survey.

Rising to the forefront of data collection is a special kind of marketing research institution known as a panel company. A **panel company** recruits large numbers of potential respondents who agree to take part in surveys for compensation. "Large" is an understatement, because some panel companies claim to have hundreds of thousands of members worldwide, and a few claim 1 or 2 million. These respondents agree to reply to any survey quickly and provide complete and truthful answers. Normally, the panel members are motivated by points or a similar awards system that accumulates as they take part in surveys, which they can redeem for products and/or services.

ADVANTAGES OF USING A PANEL COMPANY

The popularity of panel companies should be readily understandable by reviewing the following advantages they represent.

1. **Fast Turnaround** Most panel companies are online, meaning that their panelist members can be contacted almost immediately by email or text, and they complete online surveys in a day or two after being contacted.
2. **High Quality** Panelists agree to careful completion of surveys, and the best panel companies have internal checks as to timely turnaround, diligence in responding to survey questions, and accuracy.
3. **Database Information** Panelists often provide large amounts of demographic, lifestyle, purchase behavior, and other descriptive information as part of the sign-up process. Thus, there is a wealth of information for each panelist in the panel company's database storage. This information may be purchased for each panelist respondent, which subsequently reduces the length of the questionnaire for a survey. Normally, the panel company charges by the number of questions on the survey, so this affords some savings.
4. **Access to Targeted Respondents** Since panelists are known in the database with respect to demographics, health profile, possessions, experiences, and the like, it is very easy for the panel company to customize the alerts to only panelists who qualify or are consistent with the parameters of the client's sample characteristics. For instance, an automobile manufacturer may want to survey SUV owners who have two or more children under 13 years of age, or a home environmental controls company like Nest may require a sample of homeowners of two-story houses located in Snowbelt states. The fact that panel companies have hundreds of thousands of panel members allows them to deliver sizeable samples with special qualifications.
5. **Integrated Features** The leading panel companies usually have several survey services for customers. For example, not only do they provide efficient data collection, but also they often have questionnaire design capabilities, data analysis and dashboards, preset survey schedules, tracking studies, and qualitative research capabilities such as online focus groups, in-home usage tests, and more. In fact, some operate as full-service, custom-designed marketing research organizations if the client desires.

DISADVANTAGES OF USING A PANEL COMPANY

The rapid growth and very significant adoption of panel companies by marketing researchers suggest that they are a panacea to the world's refusal to take part in surveys, and in some ways, they most certainly are, but there are some downsides to their use. In truth, the most conscientious panel companies take great pains to minimize these disadvantages.

1. **Not random samples** As you will learn in a subsequent chapter, the statistically correct survey garners a sample that accurately represents all members of its population. Obviously, some people are reticent to join a panel or they may have technology constraints that disallow joining, so despite the thousands and thousands of potential respondents in a panel, some general population members are not included. On the other hand, there is evidence that panel members are substantially heavier online users than the general population.[61] A study of the panels maintained by Nielsen and Information Resources, Inc., major players in the panel industry, found overrepresentation of younger and female members compared to the U.S. Census.[62] A panel company can deliver a targeted sample, meaning it will match up with the marketing researcher's demographic and other parameters, but not a random sample.

2. **Overused respondents** Depending on size and usage, the panel pool may be tapped multiple times in a short time period. Some panelists may become overtaxed or jaded as a result. Certainly, not all panel companies overtax their panel members, but an investigation into several of the most notable panel companies found some instances where panelists were bombarded with multiple invitations weekly, and some even experience more than one survey invitation daily.[63]

3. **Cost** As you can imagine, creating, maintaining, and operating a panel, often across several countries and multiple languages, is costly. Panel companies, of course, spread this cost across their numerous clients who desire all attendant advantages so the price is not staggering for any single client. Nevertheless, clients of panel companies are well aware that their desire for high data quality, access to special types of respondents, fast data collection, and other advantageous aspects of panel companies result in considerably more expense than do-it-yourself research.

TOP PANEL COMPANIES

There is no agreed-upon measuring stick for panel companies, as they are complex in scope, size, services, and special features. However, at least one industry expert has organized a list of the top online panel companies,[64] and we have provided the top 10 from this list in Table 7.4. Panel companies, and in particular online panel

TABLE 7.4 Top 10 Online Panel Companies

Company Name	Factoid(s)	Website Address
Survey Sampling, Inc.	One of the biggest; 30 offices in 72 countries	http://www.surveysampling.com
Toluna	750 data points in database for each member	http://www.toluna-group.com
Research Now	More than 6 million panelists in 37 countries	http://www.researchnow.com
Cint	One of the most advanced technologically	http://www.cint.com
All Global	Specializes in health care research in Europe, North America, South America, and Asia	http://www.allglobal.com
Lightspeed GMI	Data quality leader; best practices prototype	http://www.lightspeedresearch.com
Vision Critical	Specializes in building customized panel communities	http://www.visioncritical.com
KL Communications	Innovative "crowdweaving" service	http://www.klcommunications.com
Authentic Response (criticalmix)	Exceptionally high service quality rating	http://www.authenticresponse.com
Schlesinger Associates	Reliable and robust (many sources) data collection	http://www.schlesingerassociates.com

companies, will continue to grow and dominate the data collection landscape. Leading companies improve, challengers enter with innovative approaches, and mergers happen every year. The companies in Table 7.4 or others that assume leadership in this industry in the coming years will be the mainstays of data collection for the foreseeable future.

7-5 Choice of the Survey Method

How does a marketing researcher decide what survey method to use? Since you have read our descriptions, you now know that each data collection method has unique advantages, disadvantages, and special features. In its annual survey of marketing research company practices, Greenbook typically asks about the importance of various considerations when selecting a data collection method. Both research companies and their clients agree that three considerations are paramount: speed, cost, and data quality.[65] Accordingly, we have developed Table 7.5, which lists how each of the nine different data collection methods we have described stacks up on each consideration. As you can see by reviewing this table, there is no "perfect" data collection method. The marketing researcher is faced with the problem of selecting the one survey mode that is most suitable in a given situation. We hasten to warn you that our table includes generalizations and that each data collection situation is unique.

In selecting a data collection mode, the researcher balances quality against cost, time, and other considerations.

How does a researcher decide the best survey mode for a particular research project? When answering this question, the researcher should always have the overall quality of the data collected as a foremost concern. Even the most sophisticated techniques of analysis cannot make up for poor data. The researcher must strive to choose a survey method that achieves the highest quality of data allowable with the time, cost, and other special considerations[66] involved with the research project at hand. We wish we could provide a set of questions about these considerations that, when answered, would point to the single most appropriate data collection method. However, this is not possible because situations are unique and researchers have to apply good judgment to narrow down the many candidate data collection methods to one that best fits the circumstances. In some cases, these judgments are quite obvious, but in others, they require some careful thinking. Also, as we have indicated in our descriptions, new data collection methods have emerged and

TABLE 7.5 **Relative Speed, Cost, and Data Quality of Common Data Collection Methods***

Method	Speed	Cost	Data Quality
In-home interview	Slow	High	High
Mall-intercept interview	Fast	Medium	Medium
In-office interview	Slow	High	High
Telephone interview	Fast	Low	Low
Fully automated interview	Fast	Medium	Medium
Online survey	Fast	Medium	Medium
Group self-administered survey	Medium	Low	Low
Drop-off survey	Fast	Low	Low
Mail survey	Slow	Low	Low

*These judgments are generalizations; the special circumstances and considerations of each survey must be taken into account in the final determination of best data collection method.

When selecting a survey method, a researcher uses several considerations.

improvements in existing methods have come about, so the researcher must constantly update his or her knowledge of these data collection methods. Nonetheless, data quality, time, cost, and special circumstances are prime considerations in the data collection method decision.

HOW FAST IS THE DATA COLLECTION?

Sometimes data must be collected quickly. There are many reasons for tight deadlines. A national campaign is set to kick off in four weeks, and one component needs testing. A trademark infringement trial, set to begin in four weeks, needs a survey of the awareness of the company's trademark. An application for a radio license with the FCC is due in six weeks, and a listenership study of other stations in the area must be conducted. These are just a few time constraints in data collection. The traditional choice in projects with a short time horizon is a telephone survey. Today, online surveys are exceptionally fast data collection alternatives. Magazine ads, logos, and other marketing stimuli may be evaluated in online surveys. Poor choices under the condition of a short time horizon would be in-home interviews or mail surveys because their logistics require long time periods.

A short deadline may dictate which data collection method to use.

HOW MUCH DOES THE DATA COLLECTION COST?

With a generous budget, any appropriate data collection method can be considered, but with a tight budget, the more costly data collection methods must be eliminated from consideration. With technology costs dropping and Internet access becoming more and more common, online survey research options have become attractive even when the data collection budget is austere. For example, some online survey companies allow their clients to design the questionnaire and select the target sample type and number from their panels. Here, surveys can be completed for a few hundred or a few thousand dollars, which, most researchers would agree, is a small data collection budget. Of course, the researcher must be convinced that the panel members are those he or she desires to survey.

HOW GOOD IS THE DATA QUALITY?

In our descriptions of the nine common data collection methods, disadvantages such as lack of monitoring, difficulties in allowing respondents to examine or try out prototypes, access of certain population segments, and even acceptable respondent time-on-task diminish the quality of the data collected in any given survey. Ideally, survey data should be deep, broad, and truthful, that is, of the highest quality, but data collection method constraints and realities tend to diminish data quality. Sometimes, required data quality drives the survey method: There might be a requirement that the respondent inspect an advertisement, package design, or logo. Or the researcher may want respondents to handle a prototype product, taste formulations, or watch a video. At other times practical considerations, such as a short deadline or limited funds, force the researcher to be less adamant for the highest data quality possible. Typically, when requirements such as these are built into the survey, the researcher has discussed data collection issues early on with the client and agreed on a data collection mode that accommodates the client's time, cost, and other requirements.

If respondents need to see, handle, or experience something, the data collection mode must accommodate these requirements.

For example, if the respondent needs to view photos of a logo or magazine ad, mail surveys or online surveys may be considered. If the respondent needs to observe a short video or moving graphic, online surveys may be considered. If the respondent needs to watch a 20-minute infomercial, mailed videos, mall intercepts, or special online systems can be considered. If the respondent is required to handle, touch, feel, or taste a product, mall-intercept company services are reasonable. If a respondent is required to actually use a product in a realistic setting, in-home interviews may be the only data collection method that will work.

OTHER CONSIDERATIONS

It is not possible to list all other considerations because every survey is unique, but we will note two considerations that are almost always part of the survey method decision. One is the incidence rate, while the other is situational factors that have a bearing on the selection of the data collection method. By **incidence rate** we are referring to the percentage of the population that possesses some characteristic necessary to be included in the survey. Rarely are research projects targeted to "everyone." In most cases, there are qualifiers for being included in a study. Examples are registered voters, persons owning and driving their own automobile, and persons age 18 and older. Sometimes the incidence rate is very low. A drug company may want to interview only men above 50 with medicated cholesterol above the 250 level. A cosmetics firm may only want to interview women who were planning facial cosmetic surgery within the next six months. In low-incidence situations such as these, certain precautions must be taken in selecting the data collection method. In the examples of people with a specific medical condition or interest in cosmetic surgery, it would be foolishly time consuming and expensive to send out interviewers door-to-door looking for members who have the qualifications to participate in the study. A data collection method that can screen respondents easily and inexpensively, such as with telephone or Internet modes, is desirable with a low-incidence-rate situation because a great many potential respondents must be contacted but a large percentage of these would not qualify to take the survey. Of course, the marketing research industry has worked with low-incidence populations for a long time, and online panels that are maintained by research providers are often touted as affordable ways for researchers to access the low-incidence panel members who have been previously identified.[67]

The incidence rate, the percentage of the population that possesses some characteristic necessary to be included in the survey, affects the decision about data collection mode.

Finally, on occasion, data collection method choice is shaped by situational factors such as cultural norms and/or communication or other systems that are in place. These considerations have become more of an issue as more and more marketing research companies operate around the globe. For example face-to-face is the preferred mode for Spaniards. However, in Scandinavia, residents are uncomfortable allowing strangers in their homes. Therefore, telephone and online surveying is more popular than door-to-door interviewing.

Cultural norms and/ or limitations of communications systems may limit the data collection mode choice.

On the other hand, in India, less than 10% of residents have a telephone, and online access is very low; as a result, door-to-door interviewing is used often.[68] In Canada, where incentives are typically not offered to prospective respondents, there is heavy use of telephone surveys.

Summary

We began the chapter noting that surveys are interviews of large numbers of respondents using a predesigned questionnaire and that surveys have the following advantages: standardization, easy administration, can get "beneath the surface" of actions, easy analysis, and ability to study subgroups. Surveys involve data collection that can occur with or without an interviewer present and with or without the use of a computer. Technology has very greatly impacted data collection. The data collection step in the marketing research process is accomplished via five basic survey modes: (1) person-administered surveys, (2) computer-assisted surveys, (3) computer-administered surveys, (4) self-administered surveys, and (5) mixed-mode, sometimes called *hybrid*, surveys. Person-administered survey modes are advantageous because they allow feedback, permit rapport building, facilitate certain quality controls, and capitalize on the adaptability of a human interviewer. However, they are slow, prone to human error, and costly, and they sometimes produce respondent apprehension known as *interview evaluation*. Computer-assisted interviews have all the person-administered survey advantages and disadvantages, with added advantages of less error, more efficiency, and use of computer media.

Computer-administered interviews, on the other hand, are faster and error free; they may include pictures or graphics capabilities, allow for real-time capture of data, and make respondents feel more at ease because another person is not listening to their answers. Disadvantages are that technical skills are sometimes required, and high set-up costs may be required if users are not computer literate. Self-administered survey modes have the advantages of reduced cost, respondent control, and no interview evaluation apprehension. The disadvantages are that respondents may not complete the task or complete the task in error, there is no monitor to guide respondents, and the questionnaire must be "perfect" to facilitate self-administration.

Finally, mixed-mode or hybrid surveys use multiple data collection methods. The advantage of mixed-mode surveys is that researchers can take the advantages of each of the various modes to achieve their data collection goals.

Disadvantages are that different modes may produce different responses to the same research question, and researchers must evaluate these differences. In addition, multimode methods result in greater complexities, as researchers must design different questionnaires and be certain that data from different sources all come together in a common database for analysis.

At least nine alternative survey data collection methods may be used: (1) in-home interviews, which are conducted in respondents' homes; (2) mall-intercept interviews, conducted by approaching shoppers in a mall; (3) in-office interviews, conducted with executives or managers in their places of work; (4) telephone interviews, either from central location telephone interviews conducted by workers in a telephone interview company's facilities or using a CATI system; (5) computerized, fully automated surveys; (6) online surveys; (7) group self-administered surveys, in which the questionnaire is handed out to a group for individual responses; (8) drop-off surveys, in which the questionnaire is left with the respondent to be completed and picked up or returned at a later time; and (9) mail surveys, in which questionnaires are mailed to prospective respondents who are requested to fill them out and mail them back. The specific advantages and disadvantages of each data collection method were discussed.

Because there is reluctance worldwide to take part in surveys and in combination with technological advances, panel companies have become a viable and popular means of data collection. A panel company recruits large numbers of potential respondents who agree to take part in surveys for compensation. These companies can deliver fast turnaround, high-quality database information, access to targeted respondents, and integrated services. Even though they do not deliver random samples, their panels are sometimes overworked, and they are not cheap, panel companies dominate the data collection landscape.

Researchers must take into account several considerations when deciding on a survey data collection mode: (1) speed of data collection, (2) cost of data collection, (3) the resulting data quality, and (4) other considerations such as incidence rate or special circumstances of the survey. All should be considered, but one or more factors may be paramount because each data collection situation is unique. Ultimately, the researcher will select a data collection mode with which he or she feels comfortable and one that will result in the desired quality and quantity of information without exceeding time or budget constraints.

Key Terms

Survey (p. 171)
Person-administered survey (p. 175)
Interview evaluation (p. 176)
Computer-assisted survey (p. 177)
Self-administered survey (p. 178)
Computer-administered survey (p. 179)
Mixed-mode survey (p. 180)
In-home survey (p. 182)

Mall-intercept survey (p. 183)
In-office survey (p. 184)
Central location telephone survey (p. 186)
Computer-assisted telephone interviews (CATI) (p. 186)
Fully automated survey (p. 188)
Completely automated telephone survey (CATS) (p. 188)

Internet-based questionnaire (p. 189)
Group self-administered survey (p. 191)
Drop-off survey (p. 191)
Mail survey (p. 192)
Nonresponse (p. 192)
Self-selection bias (p. 192)
Panel company (p. 194)
Incidence rate (p. 198)

Review Questions/Applications

7-1. List the major advantages of survey research methods over qualitative methods. Can you think of any drawbacks; if so, what are they?

7-2. How and why has technology impacted data collection from the recent past through the present?

7-3. What aspects of person-administered surveys make them attractive to marketing researchers? What aspects make them unattractive?

7-4. What aspects of computer-assisted surveys make them attractive to marketing researchers?

7-5. What are the advantages of person-administered over self-administered surveys, and vice versa?

7-6. What would be the motivation for a researcher to consider a mixed-mode survey?

7-7. Indicate the differences between (a) in-home surveys, (b) mall-intercept surveys, and (c) in-office surveys. What do they share in common?

7-8. Why were telephone surveys popular before widespread Internet access?

7-9. Indicate the pros and cons of self-administered surveys.

7-10. What advantages do online surveys have over various types of self-administered surveys?

7-11. What are the major disadvantages of a mail survey?

7-12. How does a drop-off survey differ from a regular mail survey?

7-13. What is a panel company and why are such companies dominating survey data collection today?

7-14. How does the incidence rate affect the choice of a data collection mode?

7-15. Is a telephone interview inappropriate for a survey that has as one of its objectives a complete listing of all possible advertising media a person was exposed to in the last week? Why or why not?

7-16. NAPA Auto Parts is a retail chain specializing in stocking and selling both domestic and foreign automobile parts. To learn about the company's customers, the marketing director sends instructions to all 2,000 store managers telling them that whenever a customer makes a purchase of $150 or more, they are to write down a description of the customer who made that purchase. They are to do this just for the second week in October, writing each description on a separate sheet of paper. At the end of the week, they are to send all sheets to the marketing director. Comment on this data collection method.

7-17. Recommend and justify the type of survey mode for the following cases:

a. Super-Juice would like to test a fruit-based smoothie and a dairy-based smoothie.

b. Super-Connection, a telecommunications company, requires information on the degree to which its post-paid customers are satisfied with the services provided.

c. Clean-Pro is considering a vacuum cleaner with new mopping functions and wants to know people's reaction to it.

d. The Residents' Committees (RCs) has received numerous complaints about irresponsible security guards and noisy neighbors and wants to know how to resolve these problems.

7-18. Nonresponse is a growing problem for marketing researchers. The problem is more prevalent in mail surveys, in which respondents are asked to fill out a questionnaire and return it by mail. The reasons for nonresponse could be that the respondents are unavailable, are not willing to participate, or are unable to answer the survey questions. However, many organizations may still consider using this survey mode because it is self-administered and inexpensive. Suggest ways to increase the response rate.

7-19. Compu-Ask Corporation has developed a stand-alone computerized interview system that can be adapted to almost any type of survey. It can fit on a handheld tablet computer, and the respondent directly answers questions using a stylus once the interviewer has turned on the tablet and started up the program. Indicate the appropriateness of this interviewing system in each of the following cases:

a. A survey of plant managers concerning a new type of hazardous waste disposal system

b. A survey of high school teachers to see if they are interested in a company's videos of educational public broadcast television programs

c. A survey of consumers to determine their reactions to a nonrefrigerated variety of yogurt

7-20. Pet-Pro is a company that imports and markets pet food feeders to customers in Malaysia. The food feeder, which is called "Smart Feeder," allows pet owners to feed pre-determined quantities of food at pre-set times to their pets. The system has built-in webcam and Wi-Fi technology, allowing the pet owners to watch their pets from anywhere and at any time. It also has a voice recording system that allows the pet owners to record their voice. The manager of Pet-Pro would like to find out pet lovers' perceived value of such a product and the likelihood of their buying it. The manager of Pet-Pro wants to understand the advantages and disadvantages of using the following survey modes: (a) in-home interview, (b) mall intercept, (c) online survey, (d) drop-off survey, and (e) CATI survey.

CASE 7.1

Machu Picchu National Park Survey

In Peru, there are many ruins of the temples and palaces of the Inca Indians, who attained what some historians consider to be the highest accomplishments in the Americas for agriculture, engineering, monument building, and craftsmanship. Unfortunately, the Incas were no match for the Spanish explorers, who, with firearms and horses, defeated the entire Incan Empire in a matter of a few years in the 1560s.

In 1913, Hiram Bingham discovered the Incan complex called Machu Picchu, which was not plundered by the Spanish Conquistadors. It is the best-preserved Incan ruin of its type, and it is on the World Heritage List of UNESCO (http://whc.unesco.org/en/list/274). Located at 8,000 feet above sea level on a mountain at the border of the Andes Mountains and the Peruvian jungle, Machu Picchu is still very difficult to access, as it requires a three-hour mountain train ride to reach from Cusco, Peru, the closest city. Normally, tourists board the train very early in the morning in Cusco and arrive at the Machu Picchu village train station around 10 a.m. They then board buses that take 30 minutes to climb up the 6-mile switchback dirt road to the entrance of Machu Picchu. With guides or on their own, tourists wander the expansive Machu Picchu ruins, have lunch at the Machu Picchu lodge located at the top of the mountain, and hurry to catch the bus down the mountain so they will not miss the one train that leaves around 3 p.m. to return to Cusco. Some tourists stay overnight at the Machu Picchu Lodge or in one of the six hotels located at the base in Machu Picchu village. At peak season, approximately 1,000 tourists visit Machu Picchu daily.

Machu Picchu is a Peruvian national park, and since it is one of the top tourist attractions in the world, the national park department wishes to conduct a survey to research the satisfaction of tourists with the park's many features and with their total experience on their visit to Peru. With the help of a marketing researcher who specializes in tourism research, the park department officials have created a self-administered questionnaire for its survey. Now they must choose from several alternatives for gathering the data. Using concepts in this chapter and your knowledge of data collection methods and issues, answer the following questions.

1. If the questionnaire is an online survey, would it be successful? Why or why not?
2. If the park department uses a mail survey, what issues must be resolved? Would it be successful? Why or why not?
3. If the seven hotels in the Machu Picchu area each desired to know how its customers felt about the hotel's services, prices, and accommodations, how might both the park department and the hotels work together on data collection to effect a mutually beneficial survey?
4. Using the knowledge that the Peruvian national park department has meager resources for marketing research, suggest a different method (not online, not mail, and not partnering with the local hotels) with the potential of effecting a high response rate and high-quality responses.

CASE 7.2

Advantage Research, Inc.

Joe Spivey is president of Advantage Research, Inc. The firm specializes in customized research for clients in a variety of industries by conducting computer-assisted mall interviews in five of the largest malls in the United States. It operates a computer-assisted telephone interview (CATI) facility with 100 calling stations. Housed in this facility is an interactive voice response (IVR) capability. Its Advantage Online division specializes in online surveys and has recruited over 200,000 panel members residing in North America. There is a database with over 250 bits of information (demographic, lifestyle, possessions, etc.) gathered and stored for every Advantage Online panel member. If necessary, Joe will subcontract the services of other research firms in order to provide his client with the most appropriate data collection method. In a daily meeting with his project directors, Joe discusses each client's special situation. Here is a summary of the major aspects of today's three client discussions.

Client 1: A small tools manufacturer has created a new device for sharpening high-precision drill bits. High-precision drill bits are used to drill near-perfect holes in devices such as engine blocks. Such applications have demanding specifications, and drill bits may be used only a few times before being discarded. However, the new sharpening device takes the bits back to original specifications, and the bits can be resharpened and used in as many as a dozen applications. After testing the device and conducting several focus groups in order to get modification suggestions, the client is now ready for more information on sales presentation methods. The project director and the client have developed several different sales presentation formats. The client wishes to have some market evaluation of these presentations before launching a nationwide training program of the company's 125-person sales force.

Client 2: A regional bakery markets several brands of cookies and crackers to supermarkets throughout California, Nevada, Arizona, and New Mexico. The product category is very competitive and competitors use a great deal of newspaper and television advertising, with the most progressive competitors moving into social media advertising. The bakery's vice president of marketing desires more analytics in making the promotional decisions for the firm. She has lamented that while she spends several million dollars a year on promotions in the four states, she has no measure with which to evaluate the effectiveness of the expenditures. Advantage Research's project director has recommended a study that will establish baseline measures of top-of-mind brand awareness (called TOMA, this measure of awareness is achieved by asking respondents to name the first three brands that come to mind when thinking of a product or service category, such as "cookies"), attitudes, and preferences.

Client 3: An inventor has developed a new device that sanitizes a toothbrush each time the brush is used and replaced in the device. The device uses steam to sanitize the brush, and lab tests have shown the mechanism to be very effective at killing virtually all germs and viruses. There is an app that communicates with the toothbrush sanitizer, tracking its use and effectiveness, and notifies the user when to replace the cleaning filters and fluids. The inventor has approached a large manufacturer that is interested in buying the rights to the device. But the manufacturer wants to know if people have any concerns with toothbrush sanitization and whether or not they would be willing to purchase a countertop, plug-in device with app to keep their tooth-brush sterile. The project director states that the manufac-turer is interested in a survey that covers the United States and Canada using a sample size of 3,000 representative people. The inventor is anxious to supply this information very quickly before the manufacturer loses interest in the idea.

1. For each client's survey, take each of the nine data col-lection methods identified in this chapter and specify what you think are the strongest and weakest aspects of using that data collection method for the client's survey situation.

2. Based on your analysis from the preceding ques-tion and taking into consideration any other relevant aspects, decide which is the best data collection method for each client's survey. Defend your choice in each case.

3. Assume that you are the project director recommend-ing the data collection method you have chosen for each client's survey in the preceding question, but during the next daily meeting, Joe and the other proj-ect directors vote your recommendations down. What is the next best data collection method in your mind for each client's survey? Defend your choice in each case.

8 Understanding Measurement, Developing Questions, and Designing the Questionnaire

MARC USA: Using Behavioral Economics to Understand Consumer Choice

Jim McConnell, group director, Consumer Insights

We've all been there. You think you're going to do one thing and end up doing something entirely different. Maybe you spend more than you planned or buy something you said you never would. Worst case, you make a decision that is not in your best interest. It's as if your decision-making ability has a mind of its own. The fact is up to 95% of decision making starts in the emotional, mostly unconscious, parts of the brain. It's where our real reasons for the choices we make lie. This knowledge, along with the desire to understand and influence choice, has fueled recent research advances in behavioral economics. And marketers, whose role is to understand and influence behaviors, are paying attention. At MARC USA, we're leveraging brain science and behavioral economics to help us better understand how decisions are made so we can create communications that change behavior—whether it's about a purchase choice or an important health issue.

Our tool box includes dozens of foundational behavioral economic principles, with labels like Framing, Loss Aversion, Default Bias, Relativity, Herding, Power of Free, Fear of Regret, Anchoring, Chunking, Paradox of Choice, Social Proof, and more. As an example, let's see how Social Proof comes into play in changing what people do at the onset of heart attack symptoms. Social Proof assumes that something is good (or bad) based on the behavior of family, friends, and even strangers, and people will often copy another's behavior and avoid behaviors that others avoid. We worked with the American Heart Association (AHA) to change behavior of calling 9-1-1 at the first sign of a heart attack. For years, the AHA approach was to remind people of heart attack symptoms, often by a victim or medical professional. If people simply knew they had life-threatening symptoms, they would call, right? Wrong. The percentage of people calling 9-1-1 didn't change. People wait and wait. When the symptoms can't be overlooked any longer, more often than not, they drive themselves or their loved one to the hospital. So why don't people make the right decision, even when they know they are experiencing the very symptoms that could kill them? Our research showed that people often don't call 9-1-1 because they are embarrassed and don't want to make a fuss, especially if it might be a false alarm. To many, the fear of doing something out of the norm was greater than their fear of dying—Social Proof in action!

A new intervention was clearly needed. With this insight, MARC USA designed a communications campaign to create a new social norm—making it socially unacceptable *not* to call 9-1-1. The idea came to life in a TV spot plus print and outdoor executions in which a violent heart—complete with arms and legs—attacks a man sitting on a park bench as bystanders watch and do nothing. We made it appear ridiculous to watch a heart attack and not act. We asked, "Why wouldn't you call 9-1-1 at the first sign of a heart attack?" The unexpected, edgy ads produced staggering results. Within three months of launch, the number of heart attack patients or those around them calling 9-1-1 in the test market rose from 58% to 76% and continued to rise, reaching 80% six months later. Yes, a marketing campaign can produce behavior change—and tapping into behavioral economics to understand and confront the real reasons behind behaviors was the catalyst.

Source: Text and photos courtesy of Jim McConnell and MARC USA.

Visit MARC USA at
marcusa.com

8-1 Basic Measurement Concepts

As this chapter's opening remarks by Mr. McConnell reveal, marketing research relies heavily on **measurement**, which is defined as determining a description or the amount of some property of an object that is of interest to the researcher. For instance, a marketing manager may want to determine what brand a person typically purchases or how much of the product he or she uses in a certain time period. This information, once compiled, can help answer specific research objectives such as determining product opinions and usage.

But what are we really measuring? We are measuring properties—sometimes called characteristics, attributes, or qualities—of objects. Objects include consumers, brands, stores, advertisements, or whatever construct is of interest to the researcher working with a particular manager. **Properties** are the specific features or characteristics of an object that can be used to distinguish it from another object. For example, assume the object we want to research is a consumer. As depicted in Figure 8.1, the properties of interest to a manager who is trying to define who buys a specific product are a combination of demographics, such as age and gender, and buyer behavior, which includes such things as the buyer's preferred brand and perceptions of various brands. Once the object's designation on a property has been determined, we say that the object has been measured on that property. Measurement underlies

Measurement is determining a description or amount of some property of an object that is of interest to the researcher.

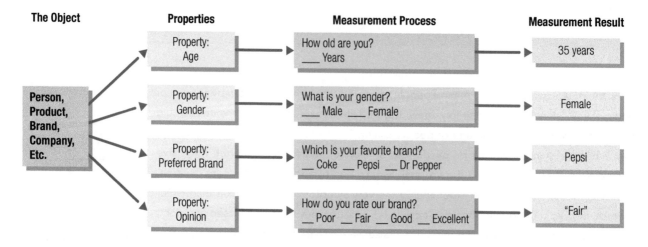

FIGURE 8.1 How Measurement Works in Marketing Research

marketing research to a great extent because researchers are keenly interested in describing marketing phenomena. Furthermore, researchers are often given the task of finding relevant differences in the profiles of various customer types, and measurement is a necessary first step in this task.

Measurement is a simple process as long as we are measuring **objective properties**, which are physically verifiable characteristics such as age, income, number of bottles purchased, store last visited, and so on. They are observable and tangible. Typically, objective properties such as gender are preset as to appropriate response options, such as "male" or "female." However, marketing researchers often desire to measure **subjective properties**, which cannot be directly observed because they are mental constructs such as a person's attitude or intentions. Subjective properties are unobservable and intangible. In this case, the marketing researcher must ask a respondent to translate his or her feelings or opinions onto a measurement continuum, which is not an easy task. To do this, the marketing researcher must adapt or develop rating scale formats that are very clear and used identically by respondents. This process is known as **scale development**, which is designing questions and response formats to measure the subjective properties of an object.[1] Our exploration of this process begins with introducing some basic measurement concepts.

> Objective properties are observable and tangible. Subjective properties are unobservable and intangible, and they must be translated onto a rating scale through the process of scale development.

8-2 Types of Measures

Marketing researchers describe measures in several different ways. In this section we describe the three measures used by SPSS: nominal, ordinal, and scale. This approach will facilitate your future use of SPSS because it will link your questionnaire design knowledge with the concepts used in SPSS.

NOMINAL MEASURES

Nominal measures are defined as those that use only labels; that is, they possess only the characteristic of description. Examples include designations as to race, religion, type of dwelling, gender, brand last purchased, and buyer/nonbuyer. Answers involve yes–no, agree–disagree, or any other instance in which the descriptors cannot be differentiated except qualitatively. If you describe respondents in a survey according to their occupation—financial analyst, firefighter, computer programmer—you have used a nominal scale. Note that these examples of a nominal scale only categorize the consumers. They do not provide other information such as "greater than," "twice as large," and so forth. Examples of nominally scaled questions are found in Table 8.1A.

> Nominal scales label objects.

ORDINAL MEASURES

Ordinal measures permit the researcher to rank order the respondents or their responses. For instance, if the respondent is asked to indicate his or her first, second, third, and fourth choices of brands, the results are ordinally scaled. Similarly, if one respondent checks the category "Commute regularly" on a travel-frequency scale and another checks the category "Commute infrequently," the result is an ordinal measurement because we know that the first respondent commutes more than the second one, but not by how much. Ordinal scales indicate only relative size differences among objects: greater than, less than, or equal to. The natural order of the objects (first, second, etc.) is known, but the exact differences between objects are unknown. See some examples of ordinal measures in Table 8.1B.

Ordinal measures rank objects, but their exact differences are unknown.

SCALE MEASURES

Scale measures are those in which the distance between each level is known. There are two types of scale measures. **Ratio scale** measures are ones in which a true zero origin exists—such as an actual number of purchases in a certain time period, dollars spent, miles traveled, number of children in the household, or years of college education. As you can see, ratio scales are easy for respondents to understand as they are in dollars, miles, years, or some other familiar denomination. The ratio characteristic allows us to construct ratios when comparing results of the measurement. One person may spend twice as much or travel one-third as far as another. Refer to Table 8.1D for examples.

Ordinal scales indicate only relative size differences between objects.

Ratio scales have a true zero point.

Interval scale measures are rating scales for subjective properties where, for adjacent levels, the distance is normally defined as one scale unit. For example, a coffee brand rated 3 in taste is one unit away from one rated 4. Implicitly, equal intervals exist between the adjacent level descriptors. That is, if you are asked to evaluate a store's salespeople by selecting a single designation from a list of "extremely friendly," "very friendly," "somewhat friendly," "somewhat unfriendly," "very unfriendly," or "extremely unfriendly," the researcher assumes that each designation is one unit away from the preceding or succeeding one. In these cases, we say that the scale is an *assumed interval*. Interval scales, such as those in Table 8.1C, may be intuitive for respondents, but they always measure subjective properties, and as you will soon learn, they require careful judgment on the part of the marketing researcher when used.

Interval scales are used to measure unobservable constructs.

Learn about basic scales used in marketing research by going to **www.youtube. com** and search for "Variable measurement scales."

Because most subjective, or psychological, properties exist on a continuum ranging from one extreme to another in the mind of the respondent, it is common practice to use interval scale questions to measure them. Sometimes numbers are used to indicate a single unit of distance between each position on the scale. Usually, but not always, the scale ranges from an extreme negative through a neutral to an extreme positive designation. As you will soon learn, the neutral point is not considered zero, or an origin; instead, it is considered a point along the continuum. In the examples in Table 8.2, you will see that all of them span a continuum ranging from extremely negative to extremely positive, usually with a "no opinion" position in the middle of the scale.[2] As shown in Tables 8.1C and 8.2, these descriptors are evenly spaced on a questionnaire; as such, the labels connote a continuum and the check lines are equal distances apart. By wording or spacing the response options on a scale so they appear to have equal intervals between them, the researcher achieves a higher level of measurement than on ordinal and nominal scales, thereby allowing the researcher to see finer distinctions among respondents' properties.

TABLE 8.1   Examples of the Use of Different Types of Measures

A. Nominal Measure Questions

1. Please indicate your gender.

    _____ Male _____ Female

2. Are you planning on purchasing a new automobile in the next six months?

    _____ Yes _____ No _____ Unsure

3. Do you recall seeing a Delta Airlines advertisement for "carefree vacations" in the past week?

    _____ Yes _____ No

B. Ordinal Measure Questions

1. Please rank each brand in terms of your preference. Place a "1" by your first choice, a "2" by your second choice, and so on.

    _____ 3 Musketeers

    _____ Baby Ruth

    _____ Milky Way

2. In your opinion, the prices at Walmart are

    _____ Higher than Sears

    _____ About the same as Sears

    _____ Lower than Sears

C. Interval Scale Measure Questions

1. Please rate each of the following television shows in terms of your overall enjoyment.

	Rating (Circle One)									
Show	Not Enjoyable									Very Enjoyable
America's Got Talent	1	2	3	4	5	6	7	8	9	10
American Idol	1	2	3	4	5	6	7	8	9	10
Dancing with the Stars	1	2	3	4	5	6	7	8	9	10

2. Indicate your degree of agreement with the following statements by circling the appropriate number.

	Strongly Disagree				Strongly Agree
a. I always look for bargains.	1	2	3	4	5
b. I enjoy being outdoors.	1	2	3	4	5
c. I love to cook.	1	2	3	4	5

3. Please rate the Chevrolet Camaro by checking the line that best corresponds to your evaluation of each item listed.

    Slow pickup _____ _____ _____ _____ _____ _____ _____ Fast pickup

    Good design _____ _____ _____ _____ _____ _____ _____ Bad design

    Low price   _____ _____ _____ _____ _____ _____ _____ High price

D. Ratio Scale Measure Questions

1. Please indicate your age.

    _____Years

2. Approximately how many times in the last month have you purchased something over $10 in price at a 7-Eleven store?

    0 1 2 3 4 5 More (specify:_____)

3. How much do you think a typical purchaser of a $250,000 term life insurance policy pays per year for that policy?

    $_____

TABLE 8.2   The Intensity Continuum Underlying Scaled-Response Question Forms

Extremely Negative			Neutral			Extremely Positive
Strongly Disagree	Disagree	Somewhat Disagree	Neither Agree nor Disagree	Somewhat Agree	Agree	Strongly Agree
1	2	3	4	5	6	7
Extremely Dissatisfied	Very Dissatisfied	Somewhat Dissatisfied	No Opinion	Somewhat Satisfied	Very Satisfied	Extremely Satisfied
1	2	3	4	5	6	7
Extremely Unfavorable	Very Unfavorable	Somewhat Unfavorable	No Opinion	Somewhat Favorable	Very Favorable	Extremely Favorable
1	2	3	4	5	6	7

8-3   Interval Scales Commonly Used in Marketing Research

It is not good practice to invent a novel scale format with every questionnaire. Instead, marketing researchers often fall back on standard types used by the industry. By now you know that marketing researchers often measure subjective properties of consumers. There are various terms and labels given to these constructs, including attitudes, opinions, evaluations, beliefs, impressions, perceptions, feelings, and intentions. Because these constructs are subjective, the marketing researcher must develop some means of allowing respondents to express the direction and intensity of their impressions in a convenient and understandable manner. To do this, the marketing researcher uses interval scales. In this section, we will describe the basic interval scale formats that are most common in marketing research practice. You will find these scale formats time and again on questionnaires; hence, we refer to them as **workhorse scales** because they do the bulk of the measurement work in marketing research.

Marketing researchers often rely on the standard measures known as *workhorse scales*.

© Becky Swora/Shutterstock

Marketing researchers use standard scales rather than inventing new ones for each research project.

THE LIKERT SCALE

An interval scale commonly used by marketing researchers[3] is the **Likert scale**, in which respondents are asked to indicate their degree of agreement or disagreement on a symmetric agree–disagree scale for each of a series of statements.[4] That is, the scale captures the intensity of their feelings toward the statement's claim or assertion because respondents are asked how much they agree or disagree with the statement. With this scale, it is best to use "flat" or plain statements and let the respondent indicate the intensity of his or her feelings by using the agree–disagree response continuum position. Table 8.3 presents an example of its use in an online survey.

The Likert type of response format, borrowed from a formal scale development approach introduced by Rensis Likert, has been extensively modified and adapted by marketing researchers;[5] so much, in fact, that its definition varies from researcher to researcher. Some assume that any intensity scale using descriptors such as "strongly," "somewhat," and "slightly" is a Likert variation. Others use the term only for questions with agree–disagree

The Likert scale format measures intensity of agreement or disagreement.

TABLE 8.3 **Example of a Likert Scale**

Indicate the degree to which you agree or disagree with each of the following statements.

Statement	Strongly Agree	Agree	Neutral	Disagree	Strongly Disagree
Levi's 501 jeans are good looking.	◉	◉	◉	◉	◉
Levi's 501 jeans are reasonably priced.	◉	◉	◉	◉	◉
Your next pair of jeans will be Levi's 501 jeans.	◉	◉	◉	◉	◉
Levi's 501 jeans are easy to identify on someone.	◉	◉	◉	◉	◉
Levi's 501 jeans make you feel good.	◉	◉	◉	◉	◉

response options. We tend to agree with the second opinion and prefer to refer to any scaled measurement other than an agree–disagree dimension as a "sensitivity" or "intensity" scale. But this convention is only our preference, and you should be aware that different researchers embrace other designations.

A special application of the Likert question form called the **lifestyle inventory** takes into account the values and personality traits of people as reflected in their unique activities, interests, and opinions (AIOs) toward their work, leisure time, and purchases. Examples of lifestyle statements are "I shop a lot for specials," "I prefer to pay for purchases with my debit card," or "My children are an important part of my life." Lifestyle questions measure consumers' unique ways of living. These questions can be used to distinguish among types of purchasers such as heavy versus light users of a product, store patrons versus nonpatrons, or other customer types. They can assess the degree to which a person is, for example, price-conscious, fashion-conscious, an opinion giver, a sports enthusiast, child oriented, home centered, or financially optimistic. The technique was originated by advertising strategists who wanted to obtain descriptions of groups of consumers as a means of establishing more effective advertising. The underlying belief is that knowledge of consumers' lifestyles, as opposed to just demographics, offers direction for marketing decisions. Many companies use psychographics as a market targeting tool.[6]

The Likert 5-point scale is flexible when it comes to measuring constructs or concepts. It is also amenable to sophisticated statistical analysis that has the potential to reveal important relationships or associations among constructs.

THE SEMANTIC DIFFERENTIAL SCALE

A specialized interval scale format that has sprung directly from the problem of translating a person's qualitative judgments into metric estimates is the **semantic differential scale**. Like the Likert scale, this one has been borrowed from another area of research, namely, semantics. The semantic differential scale contains a series of bipolar adjectives for the various properties of the object under study, and respondents indicate their impressions of each property by indicating locations along its continuum. The focus of the semantic differential is on the measurement of the meaning of an object, concept, person, or experience.[7] Because many marketing stimuli have meanings, mental associations, or connotations, this type of synthetic scale works well when the marketing researcher is attempting to determine brand, store, or other images.[8]

The construction of a semantic differential scale begins with the determination of a concept or object to be rated, usually a brand or company. The researcher then selects bipolar pairs of words or phrases that could be used to describe the object's salient properties.

A lifestyle inventory measures a person's activities, interests, and opinions with a Likert scale.

Marketing Research on YouTube™ To see a "cute" presentation on the Likert scale, launch **www.youtube.com**, and search for "Using the Likert Scale to evaluate a kid's Halloween party."

The semantic differential scale is a good way to measure a brand, company, or store image.

 **Active Learning**

Construct a College Student Lifestyle Inventory

As a college student yourself, you can easily relate to the dimensions of college student lifestyle. In this Active Learning exercise, take each of the following college student activities and write the Likert scale statement that could appear on a college student lifestyle inventory questionnaire. Be sure to model your statements as recommended in our descriptions of the Likert scale workhorse scale format.

College Lifestyle Dimension	Write Your Statement Below	Strongly Disagree	Disagree	Neither Disagree nor Agree	Agree	Strongly Agree
Studying		1	2	3	4	5
Going out		1	2	3	4	5
Working		1	2	3	4	5
Exercising		1	2	3	4	5
Shopping		1	2	3	4	5
Dating		1	2	3	4	5
Spending money		1	2	3	4	5

Depending on the object, some examples might be "friendly–unfriendly," "hot–cold," "convenient–inconvenient," "high quality–low quality," and "dependable–undependable." The opposites are positioned at the endpoints of a continuum of intensity, and it is customary to use five or seven separators between each point. The respondent then indicates his or her evaluation of the performance of the object, say, a brand, by checking the appropriate line. The closer the respondent checks to an endpoint on a line, the more intense is his or her evaluation of the object being measured.

Table 8.4 shows a semantic differential scale for a survey for Chipotle Mexican Grill. The respondents also rated Jose's Macho Taco Restaurant on the same survey. You can see that each respondent has been instructed to indicate his or her impression of various restaurants such as Chipotle by checking the appropriate circle between the several bipolar adjective phrases. As you look at the phrases, you should note that they have been randomly flipped to avoid having all of the "good" ones on one side. This flipping procedure is used to avoid the **halo effect**,[9] which is a general feeling about a store or brand that can bias a respondent's impressions on its specific properties.[10] For instance, let's say respondents who are big fans of Chipotle complete a survey with all the positive items on the right-hand side and all the negative on the left-hand side; they might check the answers on the right-hand side without reading each characteristic carefully. But it is entirely possible that some specific aspects of the Chipotle dining experience might not be as good as others. Perhaps the restaurant is not located in a convenient place, or the menu is not as broad as some might like. Randomly flipping favorable and negative ends of the descriptors in a semantic differential scale minimizes the halo effect.[11] Also, there is some evidence that when respondents are ambivalent about the survey topic, it is best to use a balanced set of negatively and positively worded questions.[12]

When using a semantic differential scale, you should control for the halo effect.

One of the most appealing aspects of the semantic differential scale is the ability of the researcher to compute averages and then to plot a "profile" of the brand or company image. Each check line is assigned a number for coding. Usually, the numbers 1, 2, 3, and so on, beginning from the left side, are customary. Then, because a metric scale is used, an average may be computed for each bipolar pair. The averages are plotted as you see them, and marketing researchers have a nice graphical communication vehicle with which to report the findings to their clients.

With a semantic differential scale, a researcher can plot the average evaluation on each set of bipolar descriptors.

TABLE 8.4   Example of a Semantic Differential Scale

Indicate your impression of *Chipotle* restaurant by checking the bubble corresponding to your opinion for each pair of descriptors.

High prices	○	○	○	○	○	○	○	Low prices
Inconvenient location	○	○	○	○	○	○	○	Convenient location
For me	○	○	○	○	○	○	○	Not for me
Warm atmosphere	○	○	○	○	○	○	○	Cold atmosphere
Limited menu	○	○	○	○	○	○	○	Wide menu
Fast service	○	○	○	○	○	○	○	Slow service
Low-quality food	○	○	○	○	○	○	○	High-quality food
A special place	○	○	○	○	○	○	○	An everyday place

Presentation of the Results

High prices								Low prices
Inconvenient location								Convenient location
Not for me								For me
Cold atmosphere								Warm atmosphere
Limited menu								Wide menu
Slow service								Fast service
Low-quality food								High-quality food
An everyday place								A special place

●────● Chipotle Mexican Grill
●·········● Jose's Macho Taco Restaurant

THE STAPEL SCALE

A Stapel scale is easily recognized, as it has numbers that range from a minus end to a corresponding plus end, with or without a zero as the midpoint.

A **Stapel scale** relies not on bipolar terms but on positive and negative numbers, typically ranging from +5 to –5. The scale may or may not have a neutral zero. The Stapel scale is easier to construct than a semantic differential scale because the researcher does not need to come up with bipolar adjectives for each attribute. It is also flexible to administer, as respondents do not need to "see" the scale the way they do when responding to a semantic differential scale. However, to use a Stapel scale properly, respondents must feel comfortable with the use of negative numbers.

Before we leave this section on the most commonly used scales by marketing researchers, it is important that we note that visual scales of various types are easily created with the questionnaire design software options (to be described later) that are available. Read Marketing Research Insight 8.1 to learn about some of these visual scales that no doubt will gain popularity in the near future.

MARKETING RESEARCH INSIGHT 8.1   *Digital Marketing Research*

Visual Scales

Online questionnaire design companies have evolved question response formats from check boxes and radio buttons into interactive graphical scales with many variations. With user-friendly point-and-click features, questionnaire designers can choose from a large number of these scales that are engaging and entertaining for respondents to use while taking surveys. Here are some examples of the basic types.

Sliders allow the respondent to drag an indicator on a bar or to drag the end of a bar to indicate the amount of intensity.

64

50

Stars let respondents indicate a star rating including half-stars if desired.

3.5

Graphic sliders incorporate clip art of various objects and sliders.

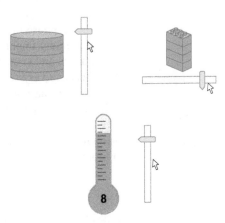

As can be imagined, there are many options as to layout, orientation, images, and so on. It is too early to assess the degree to which these visual scales offer more advantages than traditional static scale formats with respect to data quality, but questionnaire developers now have some tools to counter the monotony and boredom often suffered by respondents as they see page after page of matrix-type scales. Proponents of visual scales believe that they are more engrossing, meaning that respondents take more time and effort to use them, and make taking surveys more enjoyable.

TWO ISSUES WITH INTERVAL SCALES USED IN MARKETING RESEARCH

Our three workhorse scales—Likert, semantic differential, and Stapel—simply introduce you to the basic formats possible for interval scales. Many varieties exist and are easily constructed with questionnaire design software that will be described soon. But, regardless of form or format, we must describe two issues in the use of interval scales. The first issue is whether to include the middle, neutral response option. Our Likert scale, lifestyle, and semantic differential examples all have a neutral point, but some researchers prefer to leave out the neutral option on their scales. Valid arguments exist for both options.[13] Those arguing for the inclusion of a neutral option believe that some respondents do not have opinions formed on that item, and they must be given the opportunity to indicate their ambivalence. Proponents of not including a neutral position, however, believe that respondents may use the neutral option as a dodge or a method of hiding their opinions.[14] Eliminating the neutral position forces these respondents to indicate their opinions or feelings.

The second issue concerns whether to use a symmetric or a nonsymmetric scale. A **symmetric interval scale** is "balanced," as it has equal amounts of positive and negative positions, and typically it has "no opinion" or "neutral" separating the negative and positive

Use a neutral response option when you think respondents have a valid "no opinion" response.

sides, as is the case in our examples in Table 8.2. But not all constructs have counter opposing ends. That is, a **nonsymmetric interval scale**, which has mainly degrees of positive positions, would be more appropriate because most people do not think in degrees of negative response.

Sometimes, common sense causes the researcher to conclude that only the positive side is appropriate.[15] For example, suppose you were asked to indicate how important having jail bail bond protection was for you as a feature when you purchased automobile insurance. It is doubtful that you would differentiate between "extremely unimportant," "very unimportant," or "somewhat unimportant," but you could indicate how important it was to you with the response options of "not important" to "somewhat important," "very important," and "extremely important." In fact, for many constructs, symmetric scales are awkward or nonintuitive and should not be used.[16] Consequently, some scales contain only the positive side, because very few respondents would make use of the negative side. When in doubt, a researcher can pretest both complete and one-sided versions to see whether respondents will use the negative side. As a general rule, it is best to pretest a sensitivity scale to make sure it is being used in its entirety. Some individuals, such as Hispanics, have tendencies to use only one end of a scale,[17] and pretests should be used to find a scale that will be used appropriately.

Use common sense in deciding whether to have a completely symmetric scale.

THE SCALE SHOULD FIT THE CONSTRUCT

It has been our experience that when you study each workhorse scale and the other scaled-response question formats described in this chapter, each one makes sense. However, when faced with the actual decision as to what scale to recommend in a given situation, it is difficult for neophyte marketing researchers to sort these scales out. As we indicated in Chapter 3, the mind-set of marketing researchers is geared toward the actual survey steps, and questionnaire design is a vital step that they must think about when formulating marketing research proposals. In those situations, researchers rely on "constructs," or standard marketing concepts, and develop a mental vision of how each construct will be measured. This mental vision, which we defined in Chapter 3, is called an *operational definition*.

Table 8.5 offers a quick reference to appropriate scales pertaining to the constructs most often measured by marketing researchers. You will notice that the scales in this table are interval scaled because most of the constructs are attitudinal or intensity scales, and the general recommendation is to use the highest-level scale possible.[18] Of course, while this is not a complete list of marketing constructs, the constructs in Table 8.5 are often involved in marketing research undertakings.

Researchers tend to rely on "tried-and-true" scale formats.

A great many variations of interval scales are used in marketing research. If you choose a career in the marketing research business, you will come to realize that each marketing research company or marketing research department tends to rely on "tried-and-true" formats that they apply from study to study. There are good reasons for this practice of adopting a preferred question format. First, it expedites the questionnaire design process. That is, by selecting a standardized scaled-response form that has been used in several studies, there is no need to be creative and invent a new form. This saves both time and costs.[19] Second, testing a standardized scaled-response format across several studies offers the opportunity to assess its reliability as well as its validity. Both of these topics are discussed in detail in the next sections of this chapter, which introduce the basic concepts involved with reliability and validity of measurements and illustrate the methods used to assess reliability and validity.

© Ana Blazic Pavlovic/Shutterstock

Figuring out what scale to use and when is challenging for a neophyte marketing researcher.

TABLE 8.5 **Commonly Used Interval Scales for Selected Constructs**

Construct	Response Scale
Brand/store image	Semantic differential (with 5 or 7 scale points) using a set of bipolar adjectives Example: *Refer to example on page 211.*
Frequency of use	Labeled (Never, Rarely, Sometimes, Often, Quite often, Very often) OR number of times per relevant time period (e.g., month) Example: *How often do you buy takeout Chinese dinners?*
Importance	Labeled (Unimportant, Slightly important, Important, Quite important, Very important) OR numbered rating using 5 scale points Example: *How important is it to you that your dry-cleaning service has same-day service?*
Intention to purchase	Labeled (Very unlikely, Unlikely, Somewhat unlikely, Undecided, Somewhat likely, Likely, Very likely) OR 100% probability Example: *The next time you buy cookies, how likely are you to buy a fat-free brand?*
Lifestyle/opinion	Likert (Strongly disagree–Strongly agree with 5 scale points) using a series of lifestyle statements Example: *Indicate how much you agree or disagree with each of the following statements.* 1. *I have a busy schedule.* 2. *I work a great deal.*
Performance or attitude	Labeled (Poor, Fair, Good, Very good, Excellent) OR numbered rating scale using 5 scale points OR Stapel scale using –3 to +3 Example: *Indicate how well you think Arby's performs on each of the following features.* 1. *Variety of items on the menu* 2. *Reasonable price* 3. *Location convenient to your home*
Satisfaction	Labeled (Very satisfied, Satisfied, Somewhat satisfied, Neutral, Somewhat unsatisfied, Unsatisfied, Very unsatisfied) OR 10-point satisfaction scale where 1 = "Not at all satisfied" and 10 = "Completely satisfied" Example: *Based on your experience with Federal Express, how satisfied have you been with its overnight delivery service?*

8-4 Reliability and Validity of Measurements

Ideally, a measurement used by a marketing researcher should be reliable and valid. With a **reliable measure**, a respondent responds in the same or very similar manner to an identical or near-identical question. Obviously, if a question elicits wildly different answers from the same person and you know the person is unchanged between administrations of the question, something is very wrong with the question. It is unreliable.[20]

Validity, on the other hand, refers to the accuracy of the measurement: It is an assessment of the exactness of the measurement relative to what actually exists. A **valid measure** is truthful. To illustrate this concept and its difference from reliability, think of a respondent who is embarrassed by a question about his income. This person makes under $40,000 per year, but he does not want to share that with the interviewer. Consequently, he responds with the highest category, "Over $100,000." In a retest of the questions, the respondent persists in his lie by stipulating the highest income level again. Here, the respondent has been perfectly consistent (that is, reliable), but he has also been completely untruthful (that is, invalid). Of course, lying is not the only reason for invalidity. The respondent may have a faulty memory, may have a misconception, or may even be a bad guesser, which causes his responses to not conform to reality.[21] Technical procedures exist for assessment of reliability and validity, although they are beyond the scope of this textbook.

Reliable measures obtain identical or very similar responses from the same respondent.

8-5   Designing a Questionnaire

A **questionnaire** is the vehicle used to present the questions the researcher desires respondents to answer. A questionnaire serves six key functions: (1) It translates the research objectives into specific questions asked of respondents. (2) It standardizes those questions and the response categories so that every participant responds to identical stimuli. (3) By its wording, question flow, and appearance, it fosters cooperation and keeps respondents motivated throughout the interview. (4) It serves as an enduring record of the research. (5) Depending on the data collection mode used, such as online, a questionnaire can speed up the process of data analysis. (6) Finally, it contains the information on which reliability and validity assessments may be made. In other words, questionnaires are used by researchers for quality control.

> A questionnaire presents the survey questions to respondents.

Given that it serves all of these functions, the questionnaire is at the center of the research process. In fact, studies have shown that questionnaire design directly affects the quality of the data collected. Even experienced interviewers cannot compensate for questionnaire defects.[22] The time and effort invested in developing a good questionnaire are well spent.[23] Designing a questionnaire requires the researcher to go through a series of interrelated steps.

THE QUESTIONNAIRE DESIGN PROCESS

Questionnaire design is a systematic process in which the researcher contemplates various question formats, considers a number of factors characterizing the survey at hand, words the various questions carefully, organizes the questionnaire's layout, and ultimately launches the survey.

> Questionnaire design is a systematic process that requires the researcher to go through a series of considerations.

Figure 8.2 offers a flowchart of the various phases in a typical questionnaire design process. Beginning with the research objectives, the researcher identifies the properties of constructs of interest and decides what type of measure to use for each one. Next, the wording of each question is addressed, after which the researcher decides on the flow or order of the questions on the questionnaire. Finally, the client is briefed, final testing takes place, coding is checked, and the questionnaire is then launched for data collection.

> **Marketing**
> **Research**
> **on YouTube™**
> To watch a presentation on effective online questionnaire design, launch **www.youtube.com**, and search for "How to Create a Free Online Survey with Google Docs."

As you can see, a significant part of questionnaire design involves the development of individual questions in the survey, identified as "Decide on Wording" in the figure. As you can imagine, a question will ordinarily go through a series of drafts before it is in acceptable final form. In fact, even before the question is constructed, the researcher mentally reviews alternative question response scale formats to decide which ones are best suited to the survey's respondents and circumstances. As the question begins to take shape, the researcher continually evaluates the question and its response options. Changes are made, and the question's wording is reevaluated to make sure that it is asking what the researcher intends. Also, the researcher strives to minimize **question bias**, defined as the ability of a question's wording or format to influence respondents' answers.[24] Question development takes place for every question pertaining to each research objective. We elaborate on question development and the minimization of question bias in the following sections.

> Question bias occurs when the question's wording or format influences the respondent's answer.

With a custom-designed research study, the questions on the questionnaire, along with its instructions, introduction, and general layout, are all systematically evaluated for potential error and revised accordingly. Generally, this evaluation takes place at the researcher's end, and the client will not be involved until after the questionnaire has undergone considerable development and evaluation by the researcher. The client is given the opportunity to comment on the questionnaire during the client approval

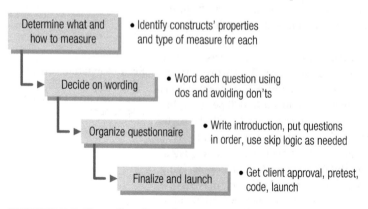

FIGURE 8.2 Question Development and Questionnaire Design Process

step, in which the client reviews the questionnaire and agrees that it covers all appropriate issues. This step is essential, and some research companies require the client to sign or initial a copy of the questionnaire as verification of approval. Granted, the client may not appreciate all the technical aspects of questionnaire design, but he or she is vitally concerned with the research objectives and can comment on the degree to which the questions on the questionnaire appear to address these objectives. Prior to client approval, the questionnaire normally undergoes a pretest, which is an actual field test using a limited sample to reveal any difficulties that might still lurk in wording, instructions, administration, and so on. We describe pretesting more fully later in this chapter.[25] Response codes, to be described later as well, are decided, and the questionnaire is finalized.

You will soon learn several guidelines to good questionnaire design, but as a preview to your learning, we have prepared Marketing Research Insight 8.2, which lists several best practices in questionnaire design.

MARKETING RESEARCH INSIGHT 8.2   *Practical Application*

Questionnaire Design Best Practices

While some may consider questionnaire design—including question wording, choice of response scales, question flow, and so on—an art rather than a science, there has been a fair amount of research and writing on what works best. Recently, a comprehensive review was conducted of research on questionnaire design, and the author[26] of that article issued recommendations for various aspects of the questionnaire design process. We have recast his recommendations into the following 11 best practices for designing a questionnaire.

1. Questions should be as clear, simple, specific, and relevant for the study's research aims as possible.
2. Questions should focus on current attitudes and very recent behavior.
3. More general questions should precede more specific questions.
4. Vague words should be avoided. Carefully pretest response options that seem ambiguous.
5. Likert-type response scales should range from five to eight response options.
6. When appropriate, include a neutral or no opinion middle option in a scale to increase validity and reliability.
7. All numeric labels should be shown to respondents.
8. Numeric and verbal scale endpoints should be explicit.
9. "Disagree" options should have lower numeric values attached to them than "Agree" options.
10. Use a "Don't know" response option when respondents may hesitate due to unfamiliarity, lack of information, or reluctance.
11. Demographic questions should be put at the end of the questionnaire.

8-6 Developing Questions

Question development is the practice of selecting appropriate response formats and wording questions that are understandable, unambiguous, and unbiased. Marketing researchers take great care in developing research questions that measure (1) attitudes, (2) beliefs, (3) behaviors, and (4) demographics[27] because they desire reliable and valid responses. Question development is absolutely vital to the success of the survey. Here is a corny example to make our point that question wording is crucial. How would you respond to the following question that might appear on a questionnaire?

> *Question development is the practice of selecting appropriate response formats and wording questions that are understandable, unambiguous, and unbiased.*

>   *Are you trying to control your compulsive gambling?*
>   _____ *Yes* _____ *No*

If you answer "Yes" or "No," you are admitting to a gambling addiction. Either way, the conclusion is that everyone who took part in the survey gambles compulsively. But we all know that everyone is not a compulsive gambler, so the question wording must be flawed, and it surely is.[28]

A single word can make a difference in how study participants respond to a question, and there is considerable research to illustrate this point. For example, researchers in one study let subjects view a picture of an automobile for a few seconds. Then they asked a single question, but they changed one word. They asked, "Did you see the broken headlight?" to one group of participants and asked, "Did you see a broken headlight?" to another group. Only the "a" and the "the" were different, yet the question containing the "the" produced more "Don't know" and "Yes" answers than did the "a" question.[29] Our point is that as little as one word in a question can result in question bias that will distort the survey findings. Unfortunately, words that we use commonly in speaking to one another sometimes encourage biased answers when they appear on a questionnaire because their literal interpretations are impossible to answer. For example, "Did you ever use a Laundromat?" means anytime in your lifetime; "Did you have any concerns about your cell phone's reception?" means absolutely even the tiniest concern; and "Do you always buy Bose products?" means every time without fail. These commonly used words are *extreme absolutes*, meaning that they place respondents in a situation where they must either agree fully or they must completely disagree with the extreme position in the question.

Some words, when taken literally, introduce question bias.

FOUR DOS OF QUESTION WORDING

Question evaluation amounts to scrutinizing the wording of a question to ensure that question bias is minimized and that the question is worded so that respondents understand it and can respond to it with relative ease. As we noted earlier, question bias occurs when the phrasing of a question influences a respondent to answer wrongly or with other than perfect accuracy. Ideally, every question should be examined and tested according to a number of crucial factors known to be related to question bias. To be sure, question evaluation is a judgment process, but we can offer four simple guidelines, or "dos," for question wording.[30] We strongly advise ensuring that the question is (1) focused, (2) simple, (3) brief, and (4) crystal clear. A discussion of these four guidelines follows.

The researcher uses question evaluation to scrutinize a possible question for question bias.

The Question Should Be Focused on a Single Issue or Topic To the greatest extent possible, the question must be focused on the specific issue or topic.[31] Questions that violate this guideline are vague and prone to inconsistent interpretation. For example, take the question "What type of hotel do you usually stay in when on a trip?" The focus of this question is vague because it does not narrow down the type of trip or when the hotel is being used. For example, is it a business or a pleasure trip? Is the hotel at a place en route or at the final destination? A more focused version is "When you are on a family vacation, what type of destination hotel do you typically use?" As a second example, consider how "unfocused" the following question is: "When do you typically go to work?" Does this mean when do you leave home for work or when do you actually begin work once at your workplace? A better question would be "At what time do you ordinarily leave home for work?"

A question should be focused.

The Question Should Be Brief Unnecessary and redundant words should always be eliminated. This requirement is especially important when designing questions that will be administered verbally, such as over the telephone. Brevity will help the respondent comprehend the central question and reduce the distraction of wordiness. Here is a question that suffers from a lack of brevity: "What are the considerations that would come to your mind while you are confronted with the decision to have some type of repair done on the automatic icemaker in your refrigerator assuming that you noticed it was not making ice cubes as well as it did when you first bought it?" A better, brief form would be "If your icemaker was not working right, how would you correct the problem?" One source recommends that a question should be no more than 20 words long.[32]

A question should be brief.

The Question Should Be Grammatically Simple A simple sentence is preferred because it has only a single subject and predicate, whereas compound and complex sentences are busy with multiple subjects, predicates, objects, and complements. The more complex the sentence, the greater the potential for respondent error. With more conditions to remember, the respondent's attention may wane, or he or she may concentrate on only one part of the question. To avoid these problems, the researcher should strive to use only simple sentence structure[33]—even if two separate sentences are necessary to communicate the essence of the question. Take the question "If you were looking for an automobile that would be used by the head of your household who is primarily responsible for driving your children to and from school, music lessons, and friends' houses, how much would you and your spouse discuss the safety features of one of the cars you took for a test drive?" A simple approach is "Would you and your spouse discuss the safety features of a new family car?" followed by (if yes) "Would you discuss safety 'very little,' 'some,' 'a good deal,' or 'to a great extent'?"

A question should be grammatically simple.

The Question Should Be Crystal Clear[34,35] It is essential that all respondents "see" the question identically. Crystal clear means extremely obvious and easy to understand. It is best to avoid words that are imprecise or open to misinterpretations. For example, the question "How many children do you have?" is unclear because it can be interpreted in various ways. One respondent might think of only those children living at home, whereas another might include children from a previous marriage. A better question is "How many children under the age of 18 live with you in your home?" To develop a crystal clear question, the researcher may be forced to slightly abuse the previous guideline of simplicity, but with a bit of effort, question clarity can be obtained with an economical number of words.[36] One author has nicely summarized this guideline: "The question should be simple, intelligible, and clear."[37]

A question should be crystal clear.

Do not use leading questions that have strong cues on how to answer.

FOUR DO NOT'S OF QUESTION WORDING

In four "do not" situations question bias is practically assured. An awareness of these problem areas can help avoid them or spot them when you are reviewing a questionnaire draft. Specifically, the question should not be (1) leading, (2) loaded, (3) double-barreled, or (4) overstated. Before we describe each instance of a poorly worded question, we wish to point out that if any one of them is used intentionally by a researcher, it is a violation of the Marketing Research Association's Code of Ethics. Marketing Research Insight 8.3 states simply that any "framing," or wording of questions that influences a respondent's answer, is wrong.

Do Not "Lead" the Respondent to a Particular Answer A **leading question** gives a strong cue or expectation as to what answer to provide.[38] Therefore, it biases responses. Consider this question: "Don't you

© Bikeriderlondon/Shutterstock

"Don't you think children eat too much junk food?" is a leading question.

worry when using your credit card for online purchases?" The respondent is being led because the question wording insinuates that one should worry. Therefore, the question "leads" respondents to the conclusion that there must be some worries and, therefore, they will likely agree with the question, particularly respondents who have no opinion. Rephrasing the question as "Do you have concerns when using your credit card for online purchases?" is a much more objective request of the respondent. Here the respondent is free—that is, not led—to respond "yes" or "no." Examine the following questions for other forms of leading questions:

As a Cadillac owner, you are satisfied with your car, aren't you?	This is a leading question because the wording presupposes that all Cadillac owners are satisfied. It places the respondent in a situation where disagreement is uncomfortable and singles him or her out as an outlier.
Have you heard about the satellite Internet service that everyone is talking about?	This is a leading question because it conditions the respondent in terms of answering in a socially desirable manner. In other words, few people would want to admit they are clueless about something "everybody is talking about."[39]

Do Not Use "Loaded" Wording or Phrasing Whereas leading questions are typically obvious, loaded questions are stealthy. That is, a **loaded question** has buried in its wording elements a sneaky presupposition, or it might make reference to universal beliefs or rules of behavior. It may even apply emotionalism or touch on a person's inner fears. Our compulsive gambling question was loaded because it presupposes that respondents have a gambling problem. Some researchers refer to a loaded question simply as a "biased question."[40] Identifying bias in a question requires thoughtful judgment. For example, a company marketing mace for personal use may use the question, "Should people be allowed to protect themselves from harm by using a Taser in self-defense?" Obviously, most respondents will agree with the need to protect oneself from harm, and self-defense is acceptable, but these are loaded concepts because no one wants to be harmed and self-defense is only legal if one is attacked. Eliminating the loaded aspect of this question would result in the question, "Do you think carrying a Taser for personal safety is acceptable?" As you can see, the phrasing of each question should be examined thoroughly to guard against the various sources of question bias error. With the new wording of the question in our example, we do not load it by mentioning harm or self-defense.

Do not use loaded questions that have unjustified assumptions.

Do Not Use a "Double-Barreled" Question A **double-barreled question** is really two different questions posed in one question.[41] With two questions posed together, it is difficult for a respondent to answer either one directly.[42] Consider a question asked of patrons at a restaurant, "Were you satisfied with the restaurant's food and service?" How do respondents answer? If they say "yes," does it mean they were satisfied with the food? The service? Both? The survey would be much improved by asking two questions: one about the food and another about service. In general, any question with more than one subject or more than one predicate is double-barreled.

Do not use double-barreled questions that ask two questions at the same time.

Do Not Use Words That Overstate the Case An **overstated question** places undue emphasis on some aspect of the topic. It uses what might be considered "dramatics" to describe the topic. Here is an example that might be found in a survey conducted for Ray-Ban sunglasses: "How much do you think you would pay for a pair of sunglasses that will protect your eyes from the sun's harmful ultraviolet rays, which are known to cause blindness?" As you can see, the overstatement concerns the effects of ultraviolet rays, and because of this overstatement, respondents may be compelled to think about how much they would pay for something that can prevent blindness and not about how much they would really pay

Do not use overstated questions with wording that overemphasizes the case.

for sunglasses. A more toned-down and acceptable question wording would be, "How much would you pay for sunglasses that will protect your eyes from the sun's glare?" Avoid using words that overstate conditions. It is better to present the question in a neutral tone rather than in a strongly positive or negative tone.

To be sure, there are other question wording pitfalls.[43] For example, it is nonsensical to ask respondents about details they don't recall ("How many and what brands of aspirin did you see last time you bought some?"), to pose questions that invite guesses ("What is the price per gallon of premium gasoline at the Exxon station on the corner?"), or to ask respondents to predict their actions in circumstances they cannot fathom ("How often would you frequent this new, upscale restaurant that will be built 10 miles from your home?"). Using common sense in developing questions for your questionnaire will help to avoid most sources of question wording bias.

 Marketing Research on YouTube™ For tips on developing good survey questions, launch **www.youtube.com**, and search for "7 Tips for Good Survey Questions."

 Active Learning

Identify and Reword 'Bad' Questions

Can you identify what is "bad" about a question and correct it? Here are some questions that might appear on a questionnaire. Each violates at least one of the dos-and-don'ts question wording presented in this chapter. For each question, write a short description about what makes it problematic, identify the "do" or "don't" it violates, and suggest a better version.

Question	What's the Problem?	What's a Better Question?
How do you feel about car seats for infants?		
When your toddler wants to ride in the car with you when you run errands or pick up your older children at school, practice, or a friend's home, do you use an infant car seat?		
If using an infant car seat is not convenient for you to use, or when you are in a hurry and your toddler is crying, do you still go ahead and use the infant car seat?		
How much do you think you should have to pay for an infant seat that restrains and protects your toddler in case someone runs into your car or you lose control of your car and run into a light post or some other object?		
Shouldn't concerned parents of toddlers use infant car seats?		
Since infant car seats are proven to be exceptionally valuable, do you agree that infant car seats be used for your loved ones?		
Do you think parents who are responsible citizens and who are aware of driving dangers use infant car seats?		
If you had an accident with your toddler on board, do you believe an infant car seat could protect your child from being maimed?		

TABLE 8.6   **Examples of Dos and Don'ts for Question Wording**

Do-or-Don't Guideline	Problematic Question	Improved Question
Do: Be focused	How do you feel about your automobile's navigation system?	Please rate your automobile's navigation system for each of the following features. (Features are listed.)
Do: Be brief	When traffic conditions are bad, do you or do you not rely on your automobile's navigation system to find the fastest way to work?	Does your automobile navigation system help you arrive at work on time?
Do: Be grammatically simple	If you needed to find your child's best friend's house that was over 10 miles from your house for your child to attend a birthday party, would you rely on your automobile navigation system to get you there?	To what extent would you rely on your automobile navigation system to find a friend's house?
Do: Be crystal clear	Is your automobile navigation system useful?	How useful is your automobile navigation system for each of the following occasions? (Occasions are listed.)
Don't: Lead	Shouldn't everyone have a navigation system in their automobile?	In your opinion, how helpful is an automobile navigation system?
Don't: Load	If navigation systems were shown to help us decrease our depletion of world oil reserves, would you purchase one?	How much do you think an automobile navigation system might save you on gasoline?
Don't: Double-barrel	Would you consider purchasing an automobile navigation system if it saved you time, money, and worry?	Would you consider buying an automobile navigation system if you believed it would reduce your commuting time by 10%? (Separate questions for money and worry savings.)
Don't: Overstate	Do you think an automobile navigation system can help you avoid traffic jams that may last for hours?	To what extent do you believe an automobile navigation system will help you avoid traffic congestion?

Table 8.6 summarizes guidelines for question wording and applies the dos and don'ts discussed thus far to a survey on automobile navigation systems. This table provides examples of problematic questions that violate the associated question wording recommendation along with improved examples that abide by the recommendations. Use Table 8.6 as a handy study guide and a reference to keep our question wording recommendations foremost in your mind when you are involved in question development.

Adhering to these guidelines is standard operating procedure for seasoned researchers, but slips do occur occasionally even for the most experienced professionals. This potential for mistakes explains why many researchers use "experts" to review drafts of their questionnaires. For example, it is common for the questionnaire to be designed by one employee of the research company and then given to a colleague who understands questionnaire design for a thorough inspection for question bias as well as **face validity**—that is, if the questions "look right."

8-7 Questionnaire Organization

Now that you have learned about question development, we can turn to the organization of the questionnaire. Normally, the researcher creates questions by starting with each research objective in turn and developing the questions that relate to each objective. In other words, the questions are developed but not arranged on the questionnaire. **Questionnaire organization** is the sequence or "flow" of statements and questions that make up a questionnaire. Questionnaire organization is a critical concern because the questionnaire's arrangement and the

Questionnaire organization pertains to the introduction and actual flow of questions on the questionnaire.

ease with which respondents complete the questions have potential to affect the quality of the information that is gathered. Well-organized questionnaires motivate respondents to be conscientious and complete, while poorly organized surveys discourage and frustrate respondents and may even cause them to stop answering questions in the middle of the survey. We will describe two critical aspects of questionnaire organization: the introduction and the actual flow of questions in the questionnaire body.

THE INTRODUCTION

The introduction is crucial in questionnaire design.[44] The **introduction** sets the stage; it is what a potential respondent reads or hears before he or she begins answering survey questions. Of course, each survey and its target respondent group are unique, so a researcher cannot use a standardized introduction. In this section, we discuss five functions that are accomplished by the introduction.

Who is Doing the Survey? First, it is common courtesy for the interviewer to introduce himself or herself at the beginning of a survey. Additionally, the sponsor of the survey may be identified. There are two options with respect to sponsor identity. With an **undisguised survey**, the sponsoring company is identified, but with a **disguised survey**, the sponsor's name is not divulged to respondents. The choice of which approach to take rests with the survey's objectives or with the researcher and client who agree whether disclosure of the sponsor's name or true intent can in some way influence respondents' answers. Another reason for disguise is to prevent alerting competitors to the survey.

The decision about whether to use a disguised survey depends on the survey's objectives, possible undue influence with knowledge of the client, or desire not to alert competitors of the survey.

What is the Survey About? Second, the general purpose of the survey should be described clearly and simply. By simply, we mean that the purpose may be expressed generically in one or two sentences. Typically, respondents are not informed of the several specific purposes of the survey, as it would be boring and perhaps intimidating to list all the research objectives. Consider a bank hiring a marketing research firm to conduct a survey. The actual purpose of the survey is to determine the bank's image relative to that of its competitors. However, researchers conducting the survey need only say, "We are conducting a survey on customers' perceptions of financial institutions in this area." This satisfies the respondent's curiosity and does not divulge the name of the bank.

How did You Pick Me? Third, prospective respondents must be made aware of how and why they were selected. Just a short sentence to answer the respondent's mental question of "Why me?" will suffice. Telling respondents that they were "selected at random" usually is sufficient. Of course, you should be ethical and tell them the actual method that was used. If their selection wasn't random, you should inform them as to which method was used but in a nontechnical manner.

The introduction should indicate to respondents how they were selected.

Motivate Me to Participate Fourth, prospective respondents must be asked for their participation in the survey. If you are conducting a personal interview or a telephone interview, you might say something like "I would now like to ask you a few questions about your experiences with automotive repair shops. OK?" You should be as brief as possible, yet let the respondent know you are getting ready for him or her to participate by answering questions. This is also the appropriate time to offer an incentive to participate. **Incentives** are offers to do something for the respondent to increase the probability that the respondent will participate in the survey. Researchers may use various incentives to encourage participation. As consumers have become more resistant to telemarketers and marketing researchers' pleas for information, researchers are reporting they must offer increased incentives. Offering a monetary incentive, providing a product sample, and giving a copy of study results are examples. Other incentives encourage respondent participation by letting them know the importance of their participation: "You are one of a select few, randomly chosen, to express your views on a new type of automobile tire." Or the topic itself can be highlighted for importance: "It is important that consumers let companies know whether they are satisfied."

Other forms of incentives address respondent anxieties concerning privacy. Two methods tend to reduce these anxieties and, therefore, increase participation. The first is ensuring **anonymity**, in which the respondent is not known and therefore is assured that neither the respondent's name nor any identifying designation will be associated with his or her responses. The second method is **confidentiality**,[45] which means the respondent's name is known by the researcher but is not divulged to a third party, namely, the client. Anonymous surveys are most appropriate in data collection modes where the respondent responds directly on the questionnaire. Any self-administered survey qualifies for anonymity as long as the respondent does not indicate his or her identity and provided the questionnaire does not have any covert identification tracing mechanism. However, when an interviewer is used, appointments and/or callbacks are usually necessary, so there typically is an explicit designation of the respondent's name, address, telephone number, and so forth associated with the responses. In this case, confidentiality may be required.

Am I Qualified to Take Part? A fifth and final function of the introduction is to qualify prospective respondents if they are to be screened for their appropriateness to take part in the survey. **Screening questions** are used to ferret out respondents who do not meet the qualifications necessary to take part in the research study.[46] Whether you screen respondents depends on the research objectives. If the survey's objective is to determine the factors used by consumers to select an automobile dealer for the purpose of purchasing a new car, you may want to screen out those who have never purchased a new car or those who have not purchased a new car within the last, say, two years. For those who answer "no" to the question "Have you purchased a new car within the last two years?" the survey is terminated with a polite "Thank you for your time." Some would argue that you should put the screening question early on so as to not waste the time of the researcher or the respondent. This should be considered with each survey. We place screening questions last in the introduction because we have found it awkward to begin a conversation with a prospective respondent without first taking care of the four items we just discussed.

The creation of the introduction should entail just as much care and effort as the development of the questions on the questionnaire. The first words heard or read by prospective respondents will largely determine whether they will take part in the survey. It makes sense, therefore, for the researcher to labor over an invitation or opening until it has a maximum chance of eliciting the respondents' cooperation to take part in the survey.[47] If the researcher is unsuccessful in persuading prospective respondents to take part in the survey, all of his or her work on the questionnaire will have been in vain.[48]

QUESTION FLOW

Question flow pertains to the sequencing of questions or blocks of questions, including any instructions, on the questionnaire. Each research objective gives rise to a question or a set of questions. As a result, as indicated in Figure 8.2, questions are usually developed on an objective-by-objective basis. However, to facilitate respondents' ease in answering questions, the organization of these sets of questions should follow some understandable logic as much as possible. A commonly used sequence of questions is presented in Table 8.7. Questions should be organized in a logical or commonsense progression.[49] Of course, it should be obvious that an objective is to keep the questionnaire as short as possible, as long questionnaires have a negative effect on the response rate.[50] If necessary, the first few questions are normally screening questions, which will determine whether the potential respondent qualifies to participate in the survey based on certain selection criteria the researcher has deemed essential.

Once the individual qualifies to take the survey, the next questions may serve a "warm-up" function. **Warm-up questions** are simple and easy-to-answer questions that are used

Anonymity means the respondent is not known and, therefore, may not be identified, while confidentiality means the respondent's identity is not to be divulged to a client or any other third party.

Screening questions are used to identify respondents who do not meet the qualifications necessary to take part in the research study.

Warm-up questions are used near the beginning of the survey to get the respondent's interest and demonstrate the ease of responding to the research request.

TABLE 8.7 **Logical Sequence of Survey Questions**

Question Type	Order	Examples	Rationale
Screens	First questions asked	"Have you shopped at Old Navy in the past month?" "Is this your first visit to this store?"	Used to select the respondent types desired by the researcher to be in the survey
Warm-ups	Immediately after any screens	"How often do you go shopping for casual clothes?" "On what days of the week do you usually shop for casual clothes?"	Easy to answer; shows respondent that survey is easy to complete; generates interest
Transitions (statements and questions)	Prior to major sections of questions or changes in question format	"Now, for the next few questions, I want to ask about your family's TV viewing habits." "Next, I am going to read several statements and, after each, I want you to tell me if you agree or disagree with this statement."	Notifies respondent that the subject or format of the following questions will change
Complicated and difficult-to-answer questions	Middle of the questionnaire; close to the end	"Rate each of the following 10 stores on the friendliness of their salespeople on a scale of 1 to 7." "How likely are you to purchase each of the following items in the next three months?"	Respondent has committed himself or herself to completing the questionnaire; can see (or is told) that there are not many questions left
Classification and demographic questions	Last section	"What is the highest level of education you have attained?"	Questions that are "personal" and possibly offensive are placed at the end of the questionnaire

to get the respondents' interest[51] and to demonstrate the ease of responding to the research request. Ideally, warm-up questions pertain to the research objectives, but the researcher may opt for a few quick and easy superfluous questions to heighten the respondent's interest so that he or she will be more inclined to deal with the harder questions that follow.

Transitions are statements or questions used to let the respondent know that changes in question topic or format are about to happen. A statement such as "Now, I would like to ask you a few questions about your TV viewing habits" is an example of a transition statement. Such statements aid in making certain that the respondent understands the line of questioning. Transitions include "skip" questions. The response to a **skip question** affects which question will be answered next. An example is the question "When you buy groceries, do you usually use coupons?" If the person responds in the negative, questions asking the details of coupon usage are not appropriate, and the questionnaire will instruct the respondent (or the interviewer, if one is being used) to skip over or to bypass those questions. If the researcher has a great number of transitions and skip questions, he or she may consider making a flowchart of the questions to ensure there are no errors in the instructions.[52]

As Table 8.7 reveals, it is good practice to "bury" complicated and difficult-to-answer questions deep in the questionnaire. Scaled-response questions, such as semantic differential scales, Likert-type response scales, or other questions that require some degree of mental activity, such as evaluating choices, voicing opinions, recalling past experiences, indicating intentions, or responding to "what if" questions, are found here. There are two main reasons for this placement. First, by the time the respondent has arrived at these questions, he or she has answered several relatively easy questions and is now caught up in a responding mode in which he or she feels some sort of commitment. Thus, even though the questions in this section require more mental effort, the respondent will feel more compelled to complete the questionnaire than to break it off. Second, if the questionnaire is self-administered, the respondent

Transitions are statements made to let the respondent know that changes in question topic or format are forthcoming.

The more complicated and difficult-to-answer questions are placed deep in the questionnaire.

Attention should be given to placing the questions developed into a logical sequence to ease respondent participation.

will see that only a few sections of questions remain to be answered. The end is in sight, so to speak. If the survey is being administered by an interviewer, the questionnaire will typically have prompts included for the interviewer to notify the respondent that the interview is in its final stages. Also, experienced interviewers can sense when respondents' interest levels sag, and they may voice their own prompts, if permitted, to keep respondents on task. Online surveys often have a "% complete" bar or indication that the survey is close to completion.

The final section of a questionnaire is traditionally reserved for classification questions. **Classification questions**, which almost always include demographic questions, are used to

 Active Learning

Decide on Questionnaire Order in a Questionnaire

For a survey to determine the attractiveness of a possible new restaurant, the following table identifies each of the research objectives as well as a possible measurement scale to be used with each research objective. Using your newly acquired knowledge of question flow and questionnaire organization, for each objective, indicate where on the questionnaire you recommend placing the question(s) pertaining to that research objective. Jot down your reasoning for your recommendation on question order as well.

Research Objective and Description	How to Measure?	Order in the Questionnaire and Reason(s) for This Order
Will the restaurant be successful? Will a sufficient number of people patronize the restaurant?	Describe the restaurant concept and ask intentions to purchase there on a scale.	
How should the restaurant be designed? What about décor, atmosphere, specialty entrées and desserts, wait staff uniforms, reservations, special seating, and so on?	Determine respondents' preferences for each of the several possible design features on a preference scale.	
What should be the average price of entrées? How much are potential patrons willing to pay for the entrées as well as for the house specials?	Describe standard entrées and possible house specials and identify how much respondents are willing to pay using price ranges.	
What is the optimal location? How far from patrons' homes are patrons willing to drive, and are there any special location features (such as waterfront deck seating, free valet parking, no reservations, etc.) to take into consideration?	Determine furthest driving distance respondents are willing to drive to the new restaurant for each location feature.	
What is the profile of the target market?	Ask for demographics of the respondents.	
What are the best promotional media? What advertising media should be used to best reach the target market?	Determine normal use of various local media, such as newspaper, radio, and television, and identify specifics, such as what newspaper sections are read, what radio programming respondents prefer, and what local television news times are watched.	

classify respondents into various groups for purposes of analysis. For instance, the researcher may want to classify respondents into categories based on age, gender, and income level. The placement of classification questions such as these at the end of the questionnaire is useful because some respondents will consider certain demographic questions "personal," and they may refuse to give answers to questions about the highest level of education they attained, their age, their income level, or marital status.[53] In these cases, if a respondent refuses to answer, the refusal comes at the very end of the questioning process. If it occurred at the beginning, the interview would begin with a negative tone, perhaps causing the person to think that the survey will be asking any number of personal questions, and the respondent may very well object to taking part in the survey at that point.[54]

Demographics questions, sometimes called classification questions, *are used to classify respondents into various groups for purposes of analysis.*

8-8   Computer-Assisted Questionnaire Design

Computer-assisted questionnaire design refers to software that allows users to use computer technology to develop and disseminate questionnaires and to retrieve and analyze data gathered by the questionnaire. A quick Google or Bing or other search will reveal a considerable number of companies that have online questionnaire design systems including Qualtrics®, SurveyMonkey®, SnapSurveys®, SmartSurvey®, KeySurvey®, and others. Just about all of these companies have free trial versions and/or extensive demonstrations of their capabilities. Most are web-based systems, so there is practically no installation, and users need only to have Internet access to use them.

Computer-assisted questionnaire design is easy, fast, friendly, and flexible.

The trial versions typically have limitations such as a short expiration date or allowing only a small number of responses. Most have short-term subscriptions that are reasonable and longer enterprise licenses that are bargains for researchers who do many such surveys in a year. Computer-assisted questionnaire design software packages offer several advantages: Compared to using a word processor, they are easier, faster, friendlier, and provide significant functionality.[55] Users simply point and click to access a large array of questionnaire design features, and extensive documentation, examples, templates, and helpful hints are normally included. In this section, we discuss the functionality of computer-assisted questionnaire design programs.

Computer-assisted questionnaire design programs have question types, question libraries, real-time data capture, and downloadable datasets.

Marketing Research on YouTube™ To learn about one company's survey software, launch **www.youtube.com** and search for "Survey Software: What Is Snap Survey Software?"

QUESTION CREATION

The typical questionnaire design program will query the user on, for example, what type of question to use, how many response categories to include, whether multiple responses are permitted, and how response options will appear on the questionnaire. Usually, the program offers a selection list of question types such as closed-ended, open-ended, numeric, or scaled-response questions. Visual scales with sliders, graphics of all kinds, and interactive features are commonplace. The program may even have a question library[56] feature that provides "standard" questions on constructs that researchers often measure, such as demographics, importance, satisfaction, performance, or usage. Plus, the researcher can upload graphics files of various types if these are part of the research objectives. Most computer-assisted questionnaire design programs are quite flexible and allow the user to modify question formats, build blocks or matrices of questions with the identical response format, include an introduction and instructions to specific questions, and move the location of questions with great ease. Often the appearance can be modified to the designer's preferences for font, background, color, and more, including mobile device layouts.

Most computer-assisted questionnaire design systems provide for mobile device layout and administration.

© Bloomua/Shutterstock

SKIP AND DISPLAY LOGIC

Skip logic lets the questionnaire designer direct the online survey to skip questions based on answers given to previous questions. For instance, if the answer is "Yes" to the question, "Did you order a Papa John's Pizza delivery for your family in the past month?" the respondent will be directed to several questions about Papa John's Pizza, but if the answer is "No," these questions will be skipped. That is, the "No" respondent will not see these questions. **Display logic** is similar to skip logic, and the survey displays or asks questions that are appropriate based on the respondent's prior answers. With display logic, there can be a list of companies with a question, such as "Check all the pizza delivery companies you have used in the past month." Then the program asks, or displays, only those questions pertaining to the company or companies indicated.

DATA COLLECTION AND CREATION OF DATA FILES

Computer-assisted questionnaire design programs create online survey questionnaries. Once online, the survey is ready for respondents who are alerted to the online survey with whatever communication methods the researcher wishes to use. Normally, a data file is built as respondents take part—that is, in real time. To elaborate, each respondent accesses the online questionnaire, registers responses to the questions, and typically clicks on a "Submit" button at the end of the questionnaire. The submit signal prompts the program to write the respondent's answers into a data file, so the data file grows in direct proportion to and at the same rate as respondents submit their surveys. Features such as requesting an email address are often available to block multiple submissions by the same respondent. The data file can be downloaded at the researcher's discretion, and several different formats, including SPSS-readable files, are usually available.

READY-MADE RESPONDENTS

Questionnaire design companies are cognizant of the public's reluctance to take part in surveys, so many partner with a panel company and integrate panel sample access into their questionnaire design websites so users can seamlessly gain access to the panel company's respondents. Sometimes the panel company being used is apparent, while at other times it is less obvious. Regardless, the user purchases access to respondents according to the pricing system negotiated in the partnership. If the user does not want to use panel access, he or she can simply launch the survey and provide the web address of the online questionnaire to prospective respondents.

DATA ANALYSIS, GRAPHS, AND DOWNLOADING DATA

Many of the software programs for questionnaire design have provisions for data analysis, graphic presentation, and report formats of results. Some packages offer only simplified graphing capabilities, whereas others offer different statistical analysis options. It is useful to researchers to monitor the survey's progress with these features. The graph features vary, and some of these programs enable users to create professional-quality graphs that can be saved and/or embedded in word processor report files. Of course, all provide for downloading the survey data in a variety of formats such as Excel (csv), text, and even SPSS, as most marketing researchers prefer to use more powerful analysis and data visualization tools than are typically available with the questionnaire design systems.

We have highlighted only some of the major features of questionnaire design systems. One feature that resonates with the way some respondents prefer to take surveys is the mobile device format. However, the mobile device option has obvious constraints that must be taken into consideration. It is unwise to take a questionnaire designed for online administration and simply let the questionnaire design system present it in mobile device format. Marketing Research Insight 8.4 lists some tips issued by the president of a marketing research company with deep expertise in mobile administration.

MARKETING RESEARCH INSIGHT 8.4   *Practical Application*

Tips for Effective Mobile Marketing Research

Mobile marketing research is the fastest-growing form of data collection, and it means that respondents are increasingly being asked to respond to questions on their mobile devices or smartphones. This trend has significant implications for questionnaire design, as the viewing area on a smartphone is much smaller than on desktop PCs, laptops, and even tablets. The president of CatalystMR®, a company with deep experience and recognized expertise in mobile surveys, recently gave several tips for companies that wish to succeed in this data collection arena. Here are some bullets from his article.[63]

- Keep the survey length from 10 to 15 minutes or less.
- Limit scales to 5 points (maximum 7 points).
- Limit the amount of text for each question.
- Avoid ranking questions and others that require scrolling.
- Program one question per screen.
- Use skip logic, as it works well with mobile devices.
- Pay careful attention to the survey introduction.
  - Keep it engaging.
  - Keep it short, clear, and compelling.
  - Make it clear that the invitation is being sent only to a select group (if true).

8-9 Finalize the Questionnaire

Regardless of whether or not the questionnaire is designed for online administration, there are two steps remaining: precoding and pretesting.

CODING THE QUESTIONNAIRE

An important task in questionnaire design is **coding**, or using numbers associated with question response options to facilitate data analysis after the survey has been conducted. Online questionnaires typically do coding automatically. The logic of coding is simple once you know the ground rules. The primary objective of coding is to represent each possible response with a unique number because numbers are easier and faster to use in computer tabulation programs, such as SPSS, which you learn how to use and interpret in subsequent chapters.

Here are the basic rules for questionnaire coding:

Codes are numbers associated with question responses to facilitate data entry and analysis.

- Every closed-ended question should have a code number associated with every possible response.
- Use single-digit code numbers, beginning with "1," incrementing them by 1 and using the logical direction of the response scale.
- Use the same coding system for questions with identical response options regardless of where these questions are positioned in the questionnaire.
- Remember that a "check all that apply" question is just a special case of a "yes" or "no" question, so use a 1 (= yes) and 0 (= no) coding system for each response option.
- Whenever possible, set up the coding system before the questionnaire is finalized.

For a hard-copy questionnaire, codes are normally placed in parentheses beside the answers. In an online questionnaire, the codes are set up internally and not displayed. For labeled scales, it is recommended that the numbers match the direction of the scale. For example, the codes 1–5 would match a Poor-Fair-Good-Very good-Excellent scale. If we happened to have a 5-point Likert scale with Strongly disagree to Strongly agree response options in our questionnaire, the codes would be 1–5. For any interval scale questions in which numbers are used as the response categories, the numbers are already on the questionnaire, so there is no need to use codes for these questions.

Finally, occasionally a researcher uses an **"all that apply" question** that asks respondents to select more than one item from a list of possible responses.[57] With "all that apply" questions, the standard approach is to have each response category option coded with a 0 or a 1. The designation 0 will be used if the category is not checked, whereas a 1 is used if it is checked by a respondent. It is as though the researcher asked each item in the list with a yes/no response.

The codes for an "all that apply" question are set up as though each possible response was answered with "yes" or "no."

PRETESTING THE QUESTIONNAIRE

A pretest is a dry run of a questionnaire to find and repair difficulties that respondents encounter while taking the survey.

Refer back to Figure 8.2, and you will find that as part of the questionnaire finalization process, a pretest should be made of the entire questionnaire.[58] A **pretest** involves conducting a dry run of the survey on a small, representative set of respondents to reveal questionnaire errors before the survey is launched.[59] Pretest participants should be representative of the target population under study. Before the questions are administered, participants are informed of the pretest, and their cooperation is requested in spotting words, phrases, instructions, question flow, or other aspects of the questionnaire that appear confusing, difficult to understand, or otherwise problematic. Normally, from 5 to 10 respondents are involved in a pretest, and the researcher looks for common problem themes across this group.[60] For example, if only one pretest respondent indicates some concern about a question, the researcher probably would not attempt modification of its wording, but if three mention the same concern, the researcher would be alerted to the need to undertake a revision. Ideally, when making revisions, researchers ask the following questions from a respondent's point of view: Is the meaning of the question clear? Are the instructions understandable? Are the terms precise? Are there any loaded or charged words?[61] Because researchers can never completely replicate the respondent's perspective, a pretest is extremely valuable.[62]

 Synthesize Your Learning

This exercise will require you to take into consideration concepts and material from these two chapters.

Chapter 7	Evaluating Survey Data Collection Methods
Chapter 8	Understanding Measurement, Developing Questions, and Designing the Questionnaire

Moe's Tortilla Wraps

Moe's sandwich shop sells wraps that are made with tortillas rather than sandwich bread. Seven Moe's units are located in the greater San Diego, California, area, and Moe is thinking about setting up a franchise system to go "big time" with statewide coverage. Moe hires a marketing strategy consultant, who recommends that he conduct a baseline survey of his seven San Diego units to better understand his customers and to spot strengths and weaknesses he might not be aware of. The consultant recommends that Moe also do a survey of consumers in the San Diego area who are not Moe's Tortilla Wraps customers or who are infrequent customers to see if there are weaknesses or factors that are preventing them from being loyal customers. Finally, the consultant recommends that surveys be done in three of the possible expansion metropolitan areas of San Francisco, Sacramento, and Los Angeles to ascertain the attractiveness of and market potential for Moe's Tortilla Wraps to sandwich shop users in these cities. The consultant mentions that, ideally, the three surveys would have some equivalent or highly similar questions to facilitate comparisons of the findings among the surveys.

Together Moe and the consultant agree on the following research objectives.

Research Objectives for Users of Moe's Tortilla Wraps Survey in San Diego, California

1. How often do users purchase a sandwich at Moe's?

2. Overall, how satisfied are users with Moe's Tortilla Wraps?

3. How do they rate the performance of Moe's Tortilla Wraps on the following aspects?

   a. Competitive price
   b. Convenience of locations
   c. Variety of sandwiches
   d. Freshness of sandwich fillings
   e. Speed of service

    f. Taste of wraps

    g. Uniqueness of sandwiches

  4. Obtain a demographic profile of the sample.

Research Objectives for Nonusers of Moe's Tortilla Wraps Survey in San Diego, California

1. How often do people purchase sandwiches from sandwich shops?

2. Overall, how satisfied are they with the sandwich shop they use most often?

3. Have they heard of Moe's Tortilla Wraps?

4. If so, have they used Moe's in the past six months?

5. If so, how do they rate Moe's Tortilla Wraps performance on the following various aspects?

    a. Competitive price

    b. Convenience of locations

    c. Variety of sandwiches

    d. Freshness of sandwich fillings

    e. Speed of service

    f. Taste of wraps

    g. Uniqueness of sandwiches

6. Obtain a demographic profile of the sample.

Research Objectives for Potential Users of Moe's Tortilla Wraps Survey in San Francisco, Sacramento, and Los Angeles, California

1. How often do people purchase sandwiches from sandwich shops?

2. How do they rate the sandwich shop they use most often on the following various aspects?

    a. Competitive price

    b. Convenience of locations

    c. Variety of sandwiches

    d. Freshness of sandwich fillings

    e. Speed of service

    f. Taste of sandwiches

    g. Uniqueness of sandwiches

3. Given the following description ...

A sandwich shop that uses tortillas rather than bread for its sandwiches. It specializes in Southwest-flavored beef, chicken, ham, or processed-meat sandwiches dressed with cheese, chopped lettuce, tomato, onions, and/or peppers and topped with salsa or a spicy chipotle dressing, all priced at about the same you would pay for a sandwich at Jack in the Box.

What is their reaction to the use of tortilla in place of bread in a sandwich?

4. How likely are they to use this sandwich shop if it was at a convenient location in their city?

5. Obtain a demographic profile of the sample.

For each set of objectives associated with each target group of consumers, decide on and justify a data collection method. Given your chosen data collection method, design the full questionnaire, including selecting measurement scales, developing questions, and finalizing the appearance of the questionnaire for each of the three Moe's Tortilla Wraps surveys. In your deliberations, keep in mind that cost is a concern, as Moe does not have deep pockets to finance this research. However, his expansion plans are not on a fast timetable, so the completion time of the surveys is not especially critical. Of course, it is important to have survey findings that are representative of the respective target consumers for each survey.

Summary

This chapter discussed the concepts involved in measurement of the subjective properties of marketing phenomena. The three types of measures used in marketing research are (1) nominal or simple classifications, (2) ordinal or rank order, and (3) scale measures that include ratio scales using real numbers with a true zero and interval scales using equal-appearing spaced gradations. Marketing researchers commonly use interval scales to measure subjective properties of objects. First, the Likert scale appears as an agree–disagree continuum with five to seven positions. Lifestyle questions use a Likert approach to measure people's attitudes, interests, and opinions. Second, the semantic differential scale uses bipolar adjectives to measure the image of a brand or a store. Third, the Stapel scale uses a symmetric + and – number system. Some constructs are measured with a symmetric interval scale, whereas others that do not have gradations of negativity are commonly measured with a nonsymmetric interval scale.

Finally, reliability and validity of measurement were described. Reliability is the degree to which a respondent is consistent in his or her answers. Validity, on the other hand, is the accuracy of responses. It is possible to have reliable measures that are inaccurate and, therefore, not valid.

The questionnaire design process involves question development to ensure unbiased questions and question organization, or sequencing, on the questionnaire. We advocate that the designer follow a step-by-step development process that begins with determining what constructs and properties to measure, deciding the precise wording of questions by using dos-and-don'ts guidelines, organizing the questionnaire components with the appropriate question flow, and finalizing it into launch mode. The objective of question development is to create questions that minimize question bias and to ensure that questions are focused, simple, brief, and crystal clear. Question bias is most likely to occur when the question wording is leading, loaded, double-barreled, or overstated.

The organization of questions on the questionnaire is critical, including the first statements or introduction to the survey. The introduction should identify the sponsor of the survey, relate its purpose, explain how the respondent was selected, solicit the individual's cooperation to take part, and, if appropriate, qualify him or her to take part in the survey. The order and flow of questions on the questionnaire relate to the roles of screens, warm-ups, transitions, "difficult" questions, and classification questions.

Survey questions are typically coded with numbers corresponding to all possible responses to facilitate analysis. Marketing researchers typically use web-based software systems that perform online questionnaire design; we briefly described the several advantageous features of these programs. This chapter concluded with a discussion of the function of and details for pretesting a questionnaire.

Key Terms

Measurement (p. 205)
Properties (p. 205)
Objective properties (p. 206)
Subjective properties (p. 206)
Scale development (p. 206)
Nominal measures (p. 206)
Ordinal measures (p. 207)
Scale measures (p. 207)
Ratio scale (p. 207)
Interval scale (p. 207)
Workhorse scales (p. 209)
Likert scale (p. 209)
Lifestyle inventory (p. 210)
Semantic differential scale
  (p. 210)
Halo effect (p. 211)
Stapel scale (p. 212)
Symmetric interval scale (p. 213)

Nonsymmetric interval scale
  (p. 214)
Reliable measure (p. 215)
Valid measure (p. 215)
Questionnaire (p. 216)
Questionnaire design (p. 216)
Question bias (p. 216)
Question development (p. 217)
Question evaluation (p. 218)
Leading question (p. 219)
Loaded question (p. 220)
Double-barreled question (p. 220)
Overstated question (p. 220)
Face validity (p. 222)
Questionnaire organization
  (p. 222)
Introduction (p. 223)
Undisguised survey (p. 223)

Disguised survey (p. 223)
Incentives (p. 223)
Anonymity (p. 224)
Confidentiality (p. 224)
Screening questions (p. 224)
Question flow (p. 224)
Warm-up questions (p. 224)
Transitions (p. 225)
Skip question (p. 225)
Classification questions (p. 226)
Computer-assisted questionnaire
  design (p. 227)
Skip logic (p. 228)
Display logic (p. 228)
Coding (p. 229)
"All that apply" question
  (p. 229)
Pretest (p. 230)

Review Questions/Applications

8-1. What is measurement? In your answer, differentiate an object from its properties, both objective and subjective.

8-2. Distinguish the three measures used in marketing research.

8-3. How does an interval scale differ from a ratio scale?

8-4. Explain what is meant by a continuum along which subjective properties of an object can be measured.

8-5. What are the arguments for and against the inclusion of a neutral response position in a symmetric scale?

8-6. Distinguish among a Likert scale, a lifestyle scale, and a semantic differential scale.

8-7. What is the halo effect, and how does a researcher control for it?

8-8. Provide questions to measure each of the constructs that follow. Before you construct the measure, consult a source book to find a concise definition of the construct. Relate the definition and then provide the question.
  a. Brand loyalty
  b. Intentions to purchase
  c. Importance of "value for the price"
  d. Attitude toward a brand
  e. Recall of an advertisement
  f. Past purchases

8-9. How does reliability differ from validity? In your answer, define each term.

8-10. What is a questionnaire, and what functions does it serve?

8-11. What is meant by the statement that questionnaire design is a systematic process?

8-12. What are the four guidelines or "dos" for question wording?

8-13. What are the four "don'ts" for question wording? Describe each.

8-14. What is the purpose of a questionnaire introduction, and what should it accomplish?

8-15. Indicate the functions of (a) screening questions, (b) warm-ups, (c) transitions, (d) "skip" questions, and (e) classification questions.

8-16. What is coding and why is it used? Relate the special coding requirement with "all that apply" questions.

8-17. Koharu Café, popular in the Kuala Lumpur city center, has been seeing a decline in the number of customers over the last three months. The manager understands that it is important to retain customers in order for the café to enjoy long-term customer loyalty. He suspects that the decline in the number of customers is due to deterioration in the quality of customer service at the café. He commissions you as a consultant to help gauge customers' satisfaction with the quality of service at the café. Your findings will help the café to make better operational decisions. You are charged with the responsibility of developing a suitable research instrument that will help the café achieve its objective.

8-18. Each of the following examples involves a market researcher's need to measure some construct. Devise an appropriate scale for each one. In working out the scale, you are required to clearly indicate its scaling assumptions, the number of response categories, use or nonuse of a "no opinion" or neutral response category, and face validity.
  a. A private hospital would like to know the effectiveness of a new painkiller that its pediatrics department is prescribing to children who are suffering chronic pain.
  b. Wholesome Ingredients House (WIH) would like to launch a new type of cheese. WIH would like to find out consumers' opinions on the texture of the new cheese.
  c. ProVehicle, a car manufacturer in a developing country, will be launching an economical version of a hybrid car in two years. A major concern for ProVehicle is whether its consumers are convinced of the reliability of this car. ProVehicle would like to find out consumers' purchase intention for its new model.

8-19. Marks & Spencer (M&S) is a well-known multinational retailer that sells high-quality products in the clothing, food, and home-products categories. They have set up retail outlets in few prime locations in West Malaysia and are now planning to start a chain of M&S-branded cafés. However, before launching the project, the management team at M&S would like to gauge (a) consumers' perception of M&S and (b) consumers' acceptance of the chain of cafés that M&S plans to set up. Design a Likert measurement scale that can be used in a telephone study to help find out consumers' views on these two points.

8-20. Listed here are five different aspects of a questionnaire to be designed for the crafts guild of Maui, Hawaii. It is to be administered by personal interviewers who will intercept tourists as they are waiting at the Maui Airport in the seating areas of their departing flight gates. Indicate a logical question flow on the questionnaire using the guidelines in Table 8.3.
  a. Determine how they selected Maui as a destination.
  b. Discover what places they visited in Maui and how much they liked each one.
  c. Describe what crafts they purchased, where they purchased them, when they bought them, how

much they paid, who made the selection, and why they bought those particular items.

d. Specify how long they stayed and where they stayed while on Maui.

e. Provide a demographic profile of each tourist interviewed.

8-21. Using an Internet search engine of your choice, choose a computer-assisted questionnaire design platform such as SurveyMonkey® or SmartSurvey®. Sign up for their free trial plan, and familiarize yourself with the platform and its capabilities. With each of the following possible features of computer-assisted questionnaire design platforms, briefly relate the specifics on how the platform you have chosen provides the feature. Mention how these features can help in designing surveys which use web interviews.

a. Question-type options (including those using audio and visual media)

b. Web interviews in multiple languages

c. Survey distribution and data collection

d. Reporting and results analysis

e. Integration of the survey platform with popular social media networks

f. Customization of their services and platform features

8-22. Comfort Vision (CV) has developed new weekly-disposable contact lenses that can focus automatically, that enable clear vision at any time of the day or night and aid nearsightedness or farsightedness. This variety of lenses is targeted at individuals who are above 38 years of age and have poor eyesight at close or large distances. CV has enlisted the help of some optometrists to look for respondents to try the lenses for two weeks. The respondents would need to be above 38 years of age and could be nearsighted or farsighted. They would need to provide feedback on the ability of the lenses to focus automatically, their clarity of vision at night, their sharpness of vision, and their overall comfort when wearing the lenses. Respondents would be given two pairs of two-week contact lenses, after which they would have to answer some interviewer-administered survey questions related to the new pair of contact lenses. In addition to that, each subject will be gifted a pair of sunglasses worth $200 after completing the survey. Draft a script to use when approaching the subject and inviting the subject to take part in the survey.

CASE 8.1

Extreme Exposure Rock Climbing Center Faces The Krag

For the past five years, Extreme Exposure Rock Climbing Center has enjoyed a monopoly. Located in Sacramento, California, Extreme Exposure is the dream of Kyle Anderson, a former extreme sports participant who had to "retire" due to repeated injuries resulting from this activity. Kyle has worked hard to make Extreme Exposure the best rock-climbing facility in the northwestern United States.

Kyle's rock-climbing center has over 6,500 square feet of simulated rock walls to climb with about 100 different routes up to a maximum of 50 vertical feet. Extreme Exposure's design permits the four major climbing types: top-roping, where the climber climbs up with a rope anchored at the top; lead-climbing, where the climber tows the rope that he or she fixes to clips in the wall while ascending; bouldering, where the climber has no rope but stays near the ground; and rappelling, where the person descends quickly by sliding down a rope. Climbers can buy daily or monthly passes or annual memberships. Rental cost for shoes and harnesses is inexpensive, and helmets are available free of charge as all climbers must wear protective helmets. In addition to individual and group climbing classes, Extreme Exposure has several group programs, including birthday parties, a kids' summer camp, and corporate team-building classes.

Kyle notices a newspaper article about another rock-climbing center called The Krag, which will be built in Sacramento in the next six months. He notes the following items about The Krag that are different from Extreme Exposure: (1) The Krag will have climbs up to a maximum of 60 vertical feet, (2) it will have a climber certification program, (3) there will be day trips to outdoor rock-climbing areas, (4) there will be group overnight and extended-stay rock-climbing trips to the Canadian Rockies, and (5) The Krag's annual membership fee will be about 20% lower than Extreme Exposure's fee.

Kyle chats with Dianne, one of his Extreme Exposure members who is in marketing, during a break in one of her climbing visits. Dianne summarizes what she believes Kyle needs to find out about his current members:

1. What is the demographic and rock-climbing profile of Extreme Exposure's members?

2. How satisfied are members with Extreme Exposure's climbing facilities?

3. How interested are its members in (a) day trips to outdoor rock-climbing areas, (b) group overnight and/or extended-stay rock-climbing trips to the Canadian Rockies, (c) single (one person), couple, and/or family rock-climbing adventures with a personal rock-climbing guide, and (d) a rock climber certification program that would require at least five outside climbing sessions?

4. What are members' opinions of the annual membership fee charged by Extreme Exposure?
5. Will members consider leaving Extreme Exposure to join a new rock-climbing center with climbs that are 10 feet higher than the maximum climb at Extreme Exposure?
6. Will members consider leaving Extreme Exposure to join a new rock-climbing center with higher climbs and a lower annual membership fee?

For each of Dianne's questions, identify the relevant construct and indicate how it should be measured.

CASE 8.2 INTEGRATED CASE

Auto Concepts

Nick Thomas, CEO of Auto Concepts, has hired CMG Research to perform a survey. Cory Rogers, vice president of CMG Research, now feels he has a good grasp of the research objectives needed to conduct the research study. Furthermore, he has taken some time to write operational definitions of the constructs, so he has done most of the preliminary work on the questionnaire. The next step is questionnaire design. Cory and Nick have decided that the most reasonable approach to the survey is to use an online panel. This alternative, while somewhat expensive, will guarantee that the final sample is representative of the market. That is, companies that operate such panels assure buyers of their services that the sample will represent any general target market that a buyer may desire to have represented. In the case of Auto Concepts, the market of interest is "all automobile owners," meaning that practically all adults qualify.

Consequently, it is time to design a questionnaire suitable for administration to an online panel of adult consumers. The survey objectives relevant to questionnaire design for this phase of the research project include the following:

1. What are automobile buyers' attitudes toward
   a. Gasoline use contribution to global warming
   b. Global warming
2. Do attitudes related to global warming vary by market segment? Market segments are defined by the following demographics:
   a. Age
   b. Income
   c. Education
   d. Gender
   e. Family size
   f. Hometown size
   g. Dwelling type
3. What are consumer preferences and intentions for various types of fuel-efficient automobiles?
   a. Super cycle, one-seat all electric
   b. Runabout sport, two-seat all electric
   c. Runabout hatchback, two-seat gasoline hybrid
   d. Economy hybrid, four-seat diesel hybrid
   e. Economy standard, five-seat standard gasoline
4. What are the media habits of those who prefer the new automobile types?
   a. Reading the local newspaper (local news, state news, national, sports, etc.)
   b. Watching TV (comedy, drama, sports, reality, documentary, etc.)
   c. Listening to FM radio (easy listening, country, top 40, oldies, jazz, etc.)
   d. Reading magazines (general interest, business, science, sports, cooking, parenting, etc.)
5. What are the social media usage profiles of these consumers with respect to how often they engage in the following?
   a. Online blogging
   b. Content communities
   c. Social network sites
   d. Online games
   e. Virtual worlds

If necessary, go over the needed integrated case facts and information imparted to you in previous chapters, and design an online survey questionnaire for Auto Concepts. Aim for proper construct measurement, clear question wording, appropriate question flow, and all other principles of good questionnaire design. (Note: Your instructor may require you to use a specific online questionnaire design company for this assignment. If not, inquire as to your options for the construction of the questionnaire.)

Selecting the Sample

"WHERE WE ARE"

1 Establish the need for marketing research.

2 Define the problem.

3 Establish research objectives.

4 Determine research design.

5 Identify information types and sources.

6 Determine methods of accessing data.

7 Design data collection forms.

8 Determine the sample plan and size.

9 Collect data.

10 Analyze data.

11 Prepare and present the final research report.

InSites Consulting

Kristof De Wulf, CEO, InSites Consulting

INNOVATION IS OUR LIFE-BLOOD. From the start of InSites Consulting in 1997 until today, there has been only one constant: we are continuously pushing the boundaries of marketing research for deeper engagement, more inspiration, and longer-lasting impact. Listed as one of the top 5 most innovative marketing research agencies in the world (GRIT) and having been cheered by the industry with more than 25 international awards, we bring our clients to the future first. Today, we are proud to shape the future of more than one third of the world's global brands all across the globe.

COLLABORATION IS OUR BELIEF. We believe in the power of collaboration. Over the last 10 years, companies applying a collaborative mindset have grown no less than 3 times faster compared to 'Good to Great' companies. Times have changed since the famous quote of Henry Ford: "If I had asked people what they wanted, they would have said faster horses." Power shifted from organizations to individual consumers and employees, composing a world full of problem solvers who are creating billions of dollars' worth in value. Lifting on the virtues of today's collaborative economy, we outpace old and tried solutions and respond to today's business needs for more efficient, agile and impactful decision making.

CONSUMER INSIGHTS ARE OUR CURRENCY. We empower people with consumer insights to make companies better and more future proof. Our unique consumer insight ecosystem helps companies to put consumer insights at the heart of everything they do. We bring the voice of the consumer all the way up to the company boardroom in 3 different unique ways:

1. Consumer Consulting Boards to generate fresh and relevant consumer insights and to embed the voice of consumers in your organization. A Consumer Consulting Board is a closed, moderated online and mobile community of interesting and interested consumers collaborating with an organization or brand over time.

2. Consumer Activation Studios to share consumer insights faster throughout your organization, to sharpen consumer insights with a broader group of employees and to have employees act upon consumer insights. The Consumer Activation Studio is a SaaS (Software as a Service) corporate solution to unite and activate employees around consumer insights.

3. Insight Impact Surveys to validate the impact of (possible) marketing decisions and to measure the return on consumer insights.

InSites Consulting

Visit InSites Consulting at insites-consulting.com

MAXIMIZING RETURN ON INSIGHTS IS OUR PROMISE. We help our clients to maximize the return on their consumer insights, distinguishing ourselves in the following ways:

1. Deeper insights: we are experts in empowering, engaging, connecting and activating a diverse group of interesting and interested people as the basis for deep and meaningful collaboration

2. Better insights: we master the art of generating, activating and validating consumer insights that have the power to cause a big or a small transformation in your business

3. Longitudinal insights: we build, grow and protect a structural organizational capability to tap into the collaborative powers of both consumers and employees, allowing iterative and consecutive learning

4. Broader insights: we focus on driving organization-wide impact, translating consumer insights into measurable results focusing on agility, efficiency and market impact

5. Global insights: we have a global network of experienced, trained and certified moderators in over 50 countries around the world, efficiently driving collaboration on a global scale

Source: Text and photos courtesy of Kristof De Wulf and InSites Consulting.

International markets are measured in hundreds of millions of people, national markets comprise millions of individuals, and even local markets may constitute hundreds of thousands of households. To obtain information from every single person in a market is usually impossible and obviously impractical. For these reasons, marketing researchers make use of a sample. This chapter describes how researchers go about taking samples. As can be seen in our InSites Consulting vignette, both technology and globalization have combined to make taking a sample a complicated process. We begin with definitions of basic concepts, such as population, sample, and census. Then we discuss the reasons for taking samples. From

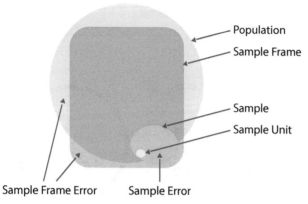

Population

Sample Frame

Sample

Sample Unit

Sample Frame Error   Sample Error

FIGURE 9.1 Basic Sampling Concepts

here, we distinguish the four types of probability sampling methods from the four types of nonprobability sampling methods. Because online surveys are popular, we discuss sampling aspects of these surveys. Finally, we present a step-by-step procedure for taking a sample, regardless of the sampling method used.

9-1 Basic Concepts in Samples and Sampling

Sampling has its own basic terminology: population, census, sample, sample unit, sample frame, sample frame error, and sample error. As we describe these concepts, it will be useful to refer to Figure 9.1, which depicts them in a way that conveys how they relate to one another.

POPULATION

> The population is the entire group under study as defined by research objectives.

A **population** is defined as the entire group under study as specified by the objectives of the research project. As can be seen in Figure 9.1, the population shape is the largest and most encompassing entity. Managers tend to have a less specific definition of the population than do researchers. This is because the researcher must use the description of the population precisely, whereas the manager uses it in a more general way.

For instance, let us examine this difference for a research project performed for Terminix Pest Control. If Terminix were interested in determining how prospective customers were combating roaches, ants, spiders, and other insects in their homes, the Terminix manager would probably define the population as "everybody who might use our services." However, the researcher in charge of sample design would use a definition such as "heads of households in those metropolitan areas served by Terminix who are responsible for insect pest control." Notice that the researcher has converted "everybody" to "households who are responsible for insect pest control" and has indicated more precisely who the respondents will be in the form of "heads of households." The definition is also made more specific by the requirement that the household be in a metropolitan Terminix service area. Just as problem definition error can be devastating to a survey, so can population definition error, because a survey's findings are applicable only to the population from which the survey sample is drawn. For example, if the Terminix population is "everybody who might use our services," it would include industrial, institutional, and business users as well as households. If a large national chain such as Hilton Hotels or Olive Garden Restaurants were included in the survey, then the findings could not be representative of households alone.

CENSUS

> A census requires information from everyone in the population.

A **census** is defined as an accounting of the complete population. In other words, if you wanted to know the average age of members of a population, you would have to ask each and every population unit his or her age and compute the average. Surely, you can see the impracticalities associated with a census, particularly when you think about target markets encompassing millions of consumers.

Perhaps the best example of a census is the U.S. census taken every 10 years by the U.S. Census Bureau (www.census.gov). The target population in the case of the U.S. census is all households in the United States. In truth, this definition of the population constitutes an "ideal" census, for it is virtually impossible to obtain information from every single U.S. household. At best, the Census Bureau can reach only a certain percentage of households, obtaining a census that provides information within the time period of the census-taking activity. Even with a public awareness promotional campaign budget of several hundred thousand dollars that covered all of the major advertising media forms, such as television, newspaper, and radio, and an elaborate follow-up procedure, the Census Bureau admits that its numbers are not 100% accurate.[1]

The difficulties encountered by U.S. census takers are identical to those encountered in marketing research. For example, there are instances of individuals who are in transition between residences, without places of residence, illiterate, incapacitated, illegally residing in the United States, or unwilling to participate. Marketing researchers undertaking survey research face all of these problems and a host of others. In fact, researchers long ago realized the impracticality and outright impossibility of taking a census of a population. Consequently, they turned to the use of subsets, or samples, which were chosen to represent the target population.

The population is the entire group under study.

SAMPLE AND SAMPLE UNIT

Both a sample and a sample unit are depicted in Figure 9.1. A **sample** is a subset of the population that suitably represents that entire group.[2] Once again, there are differences in how the manager and the researcher use this term. The manager will often overlook the "suitably" aspect of this definition and assume that any sample is a representative sample. However, the researcher is trained in detecting sample errors and is careful in assessing the degree of representativeness of the subgroup selected to be the sample.

The sample is a subset of the population, and the sample unit pertains to the basic level of investigation.

A **sample unit** is the basic level of investigation. That is, in the Terminix example, the unit is a household. For a WeightWatchers survey, the unit would be one person, but for a survey of hospital purchases of laser surgery equipment, the sample unit would be hospital purchasing agents because hospital purchases are being researched.

SAMPLE FRAME AND SAMPLE FRAME ERROR

You should notice in Figure 9.1 that the sample and sample unit exist within the area called the *sample frame*. A **sample frame** is a master source of sample units in the population. You can see in Figure 9.1 that the sample frame shape does not take in all of the population shape; further, it takes in some area that is outside the population's boundary. In other words, the sample frame does not always correspond perfectly to the population.

A sample frame is a master source of sample units in the population.

For instance, if a researcher has defined a population to be all automobile dealers in the state of Wyoming, she would need a master listing of these establishments as a frame from which to sample. Similarly, if the population being researched were certified public accountants (CPAs), a sample frame for this group would be needed. In the case of automobile dealers, a list service such as American Business Lists of Turnersville, New Jersey, which has compiled its list of automobile dealers' Yellow Pages listings, might be used. For CPAs, the researcher could use the list of members of the American Institute of Certified Public Accountants, located in New York City, which contains a listing of all accountants who have passed the CPA exam. Sometimes the researcher cannot find a list, and the sample frame becomes a matter of whatever access to the population the researcher can conceive, such as "all shoppers who purchased at least $50 worth of merchandise at a Radio Shack store in March."

A sample frame invariably contains **sample frame error**, which is the degree to which the sample frame fails to account for all of the population. From the figure, you can see that a sample frame may be incomplete, meaning it might omit some units, or it might be inaccurate,

MARKETING RESEARCH INSIGHT 9.1			*Digital Marketing Research*

Landline Versus Mobile Phone Sample Frames

Although not as popular as it once was, the telephone survey is still alive and well as a data collection method. However, as with many aspects of marketing research, technology has had a significant impact on telephone surveys. One such impact is the widespread adoption of CATI, computer-assisted telephone interviewing, which greatly facilitates random digit dialing (RDD). Thus, marketing researchers have become more efficient and effective in conducting telephone surveys. On the respondent side, technology has had a significant influence with the widespread adoption of mobile telephones, as many consumers have dropped their landlines for mobile phones. Researchers recently demonstrated the sample representation consequences of using a landline sample frame versus using a mobile phone sample frame for a telephone survey.[3] The following table highlights very significant differences in the resulting samples.

The differences clearly exhibit that landline samples draw from a population that is older, somewhat less urban, more female, less mobile, less educated, and of lower income.

Characteristic	Landline Frame	Mobile Phone Frame	Difference
Response rate	*22%*	*13%*	*9%*
Metropolitan resident	*60%*	*68%*	*8%*
Age (mean)	*53*	*39*	*14 years*
Male/female	*40%/60%*	*57%/43%*	*17%*
5 years or less at current residence	*23%*	*52%*	*29%*
High school graduate	*65%*	*77%*	*12%*
Income of $60,000 or more	*48%*	*57%*	*9%*

A listing of the population may be incomplete and/or inaccurate and thus contain sample frame error.

Learn about sample frames in marketing research by going to **www.youtube.com** and search for "Sample source and sampling frames."

meaning it may have units that are not actually in the population. A way to envision sample frame error is by comparing the list with the population and seeing to what degree the list adequately matches the targeted population. What do you think is the sample frame error in our sample of Wyoming automobile dealers? The primary error involved lies in using only Yellow Pages listings. Not all shops are listed in the Yellow Pages, as some have gone out of business, some have come into existence since the publication of the Yellow Pages, and some may not be listed at all. The same type of error exists for CPAs, and the researcher would have to determine how current the list is that he or she is using.[4]

To illustrate the impact of the sample frame on survey results, we have prepared Marketing Research Insight 9.1, which clearly illustrates how a landline sample frame differs from a mobile phone sample frame in the case of a telephone survey.

SAMPLING ERROR

Sampling error is any error in a survey that occurs because a sample is used.[5] Sampling error is caused by two factors. First, there is the method of sample selection, which, as you will learn later in this chapter, includes sample frame error. In Figure 9.1, the sample shape is inside the sample frame shape, but it includes some area outside the population shape. This type of sample error results when the sample frame is not completely faithful to the population definition. You will learn in this chapter that some sampling methods minimize this error factor, whereas others do not control it adequately. The second factor is the size of the sample. We discuss the relationship between sample size and sampling error in the following chapter, Chapter 10.

Whenever a sample is taken, the survey will reflect sampling error.

9-2   Reasons for Taking a Sample

By now you may have surmised at least two general reasons why a sample is almost always more desirable than a census. First, there are practical considerations, such as cost and population size, that make a sample more desirable than a census. Taking a census is expensive, as consumer populations may number in the millions. Even if the population is restricted to a medium-sized metropolitan area, hundreds of thousands of individuals can be involved.

Second, typical research firms or the typical researcher cannot analyze the huge amounts of data generated by a census. Although computer statistical programs can handle thousands of observations with ease, they slow down appreciably with hundreds of thousands, and most are unable to accommodate millions of observations. In fact, even before researchers consider the size of the computer or tabulation equipment to be used, they must consider the various data preparation procedures involved in just handling the questionnaires or responses and transferring these responses into computer files. If "hard-copy" questionnaires are to be used, the sheer physical volume can easily overwhelm the researcher's capabilities.

Defending the use of samples from a different tack, we can turn to an informal cost–benefit analysis to defend the use of samples. If the project director of our Terminix household survey had chosen a sample of 500 households at a cost of $10,000 and had determined that 20% of those surveyed "would consider" switching to Terminix from their current pest control provider, what would be the result if a completely different sample of the same size were selected in identical fashion to determine the same characteristic? For example, suppose the second sample resulted in an estimate of 22%. The project would cost $10,000 more, but what has been gained with the second sample? Common sense suggests very little additional information has been gained, for if the project director combined the two samples, he would come up with an estimate of 21%. In effect, $10,000 more has been spent to gain 1% more of information. It is extremely doubtful that this additional precision offsets the additional cost. We will develop this notion in more detail in the following chapter on sample size determination, where you will learn that perfectly acceptable precision or accuracy can be obtained with surprisingly small samples.

> Taking a sample is less expensive than taking a census.

9-3 Probability Versus Nonprobability Sampling Methods

All sample designs fall into one of two categories: probability or nonprobability. **Probability samples** are samples in which members of the population have a known chance (probability) of being selected into the sample. **Nonprobability samples**, on the other hand, are samples where the chances (probability) of selecting members from the population into the sample are unknown. Unfortunately, the terms *known* and *unknown* are misleading; to calculate a precise probability, one would need to know the exact size of the population, and it is impossible to know the exact size of the population in most marketing research studies. If we were targeting, for example, Uber users, the exact size of the population changes from week to week as a result of new adopters, old users dropping the service, and fluctuations in sales as a function of traffic dynamics, weather, and so forth. In fact, it is hard to think of cases in which the population size is known and stable enough to be associated with an exact number.

> With probability sampling, the chances of selection are known; with nonprobability sampling, they are not known.

The essence of a "known" probability rests in the sampling method rather than in knowing the exact size of the population. Probability sampling methods are those that ensure that, if the exact size of the population were known for the moment in time that sampling took place, the probability of any member of the population being selected into the sample could be calculated. In other words, this probability value is really never calculated in actuality, but we are assured by the sample method that the chances of any one population member being selected into the sample could be computed. This is an important theoretical notion underlying probability sampling.

> With probability sampling, the method determines the chances of a sample unit being selected into the sample.

With nonprobability methods there is no way to determine the probability even if the population size is known because the selection technique is subjective. As one author has described the difference, nonprobability sampling uses human intervention, whereas probability sampling does not.[6] Nonprobability sampling is sometimes called "haphazard sampling" because it is prone to human error and even subconscious biases.[7] The following descriptions underscore that the sampling method determines probability or nonprobability sampling.

9-4   Probability Sampling Methods

There are four probability sampling methods: simple random sampling, systematic sampling, cluster sampling, and stratified sampling. Table 9.1 introduces each of these methods.

Simple Random Sampling With **simple random sampling**, the probability of being selected into the sample is equal for all members of the population. This probability is expressed by the following formula:

Formula for simple random sample probability

$$\text{Probability of selection} = \text{sample size/population size}$$

With simple random sampling, if the researcher is surveying a population of 100,000 recent Apple Watch buyers with a sample size of 1,000 respondents, the probability of selection of any single population member into this sample would be 1,000 divided by 100,000, or 1 out of 100, calculated to be 1%.

Examples of simple random sampling include the random device method and the random numbers method.

The Random Device Method The **random device method** involves using an apparatus or a procedure to ensure that every member of the population has the same chance of being selected into the sample. Familiar examples of the random device method include the flipping of a coin to decide heads or tails, lottery numbers selected by numbered balls, a roulette wheel in a casino, and a hand dealt in a poker game. In every case, every member of the population has the same probability of being selected as every other member of that population: 1/2 for the coin toss, 5/69 Powerball lottery balls, 1/37 roulette numbers, or 5/52 cards. Applied to

> With simple random sampling, the probability of selection into the sample is "known" for all members of the population.

> The "random device" is a form of simple random sampling.

TABLE 9.1   Four Different Probability Sampling Methods

Simple Random Sampling

The researcher uses random numbers from a computer, random digit dialing, or some other random selection procedure that guarantees each member of the population in the sample frame has an identical chance of being selected into the sample.

Systematic Sampling

Using a sample frame that lists members of the population, the researcher selects a random starting point for the first sample member. A constant *skip interval*, calculated by dividing the number of population members in the sample frame by the sample size, is then used to select every other sample member from the sample frame. This procedure accomplishes the same end as simple random sampling, and it is more efficient.

Cluster Sampling

The sample frame is divided into groups called clusters, each of which must be highly similar to the others. The researcher can then randomly select a few clusters and perform a census of each one (one stage). Alternatively, the researcher can randomly select more clusters and take samples from each one (two stage). This method is desirable when highly similar clusters can be easily identified, such as subdivisions spread across a wide geographic area.

Stratified Sampling

If the population is believed to have a skewed distribution for one or more of its distinguishing factors (e.g., income or product usage), the researcher identifies subpopulations in the sample frame called *strata*. A simple random sample is then taken of each stratum. Weighting procedures may be applied to estimate population values, such as the mean. This approach is better suited than other probability sampling methods for populations that are not distributed in a bell-shaped pattern (e.g., skewed).

sampling, you can create a device for randomly choosing participants by their names or some other unique designation. For example, suppose you wanted to determine the attitudes of students in your marketing research class toward a career in marketing research. Assume that the class you have chosen as your population has 30 students enrolled. To do a **blind draw**, you write the name of every student on a 3-by-5 index card and put all the cards inside a container. Next, you place a top on the container and shake it vigorously. This procedure ensures that the names are thoroughly mixed. You then ask some person to draw the sample. This individual is blindfolded so that he or she cannot see inside the container. You would instruct him or her to take out 10 cards as the sample. In this sample, every student in the class has an equal chance of being selected with a probability of 10/30 or 33%—a 1-in-3 chance of being selected into that sample.

 Active Learning

Are Random Numbers Really Random?

Some people do not believe that random numbers are actually random. These individuals sometimes point out that certain numbers seem to repeat more frequently than other numbers in lotteries, or they may claim to have a "favorite" or "lucky" number that wins for them when gambling or taking a chance of some sort. You can test the randomness of random numbers by creating an Excel spreadsheet and using its random number function. Use the following steps to perform this test.

1. First, open Excel and place numbers 1–100 in cells A2–A101 with 1 in A2, 2 in A3, 3 in A4, etc., up to 100 in A101.

2. Place numbers 1–100 in cells C1–CX1, respectively.

3. Next, in cells C2–CX101, enter the Excel function =RANDBETWEEN(1,100). (Note: you can enter this formula into cell C2, then copy it and paste the copy into cells C2–CX101. You should see numbers that are whole integers ranging from 1 to 100 in cells C3–CX101.)

4. Next, in cell B2, enter =COUNTIF(C2:CX2,A2). Copy this formula and paste it into cells B2–B101. You will now see integers such as 0, 1, 2, 3, etc., in column B2–B101.

5. Finally, in cell B102, enter in the formula =AVERAGE(B2:B101). Format Cell B102 to be a Number with 2 decimal places.

6. Cell B102 is the average number of times the number in column A2–A101 appears in the corresponding row, meaning row C2–CX2 for A2 or 1, C3–CX3, for A3 or 2, and so on.

What is in cell B102? It is the average number of times out of 100 times that each number from 1 to 100 appeared in its respective row. In other words, if the average in cell B102 is 1, then every number from 1 to 100 had an equal chance of being in its respective row. Stated differently, B102 is the number of chances out of 100 for any number from 1 to 100 to be selected by Excel's random number function.

You can "redraw" all 1,000 random numbers in Excel by simply entering in a blank-Return anywhere in the spreadsheet. Try this with cell A1 several times, and you will see that the average changes slightly, but it will tend to "hover" around 1.0.

You can test the "lucky number" theory by copying row 101 into rows 105–114 and placing the lucky number into cells A105–A114. Create an average of cells B105:B114 in cell B115. Then do several repetitions by entering in a blank-Return and keep track of the numbers that appear in cell B115. You will find that it is typically 1, meaning that the lucky number has no more chance of being drawn than any of the 99 other random numbers.

Games of chance such as bingo, lottery, or roulette are based on random selection, which underlies random sampling.

A random number embodies simple random sampling assumptions.

The Random Numbers Method All of our random device examples involve small populations that are easily accommodated by the physical aspects of the device. With large populations, random devices become cumbersome (just try shuffling a deck of 1,000 playing cards). A tractable and more sophisticated application of simple random sampling is to use computer-generated numbers based on the concept of **random numbers**, which are numbers whose chance nature is assured. Computer programs can be designed to generate numbers without any systematic sequence to the numbers whatsoever—that is, they are random. A computer easily handles datasets of hundreds of thousands of individuals; it can quickly label each one with a unique number or designation, generate a set of random numbers, and match the random numbers with the unique designations of the individuals in the dataset to select or "pull" the sample. Using random numbers, a computer system can draw a huge random sample from a gigantic population in a matter of minutes and guarantee that every population member in the computer's files has the same chance of being selected in the sample.

Marketing Research Insight 9.2 shows the steps involved in using random numbers generated by a spreadsheet program to select students from this 30-member population. Beginning with the first generated random number, you would progress through the set of random numbers to select members of the population into the sample. If you encounter the same number twice within the same sample draw, the number is skipped over because it is improper to collect information twice from the same person.

✓ MARKETING RESEARCH INSIGHT 9.2 *Practical Application*

How to Use Random Numbers to Select a Simple Random Sample

Step 1: Assign a unique number to each member of the population.

Name	Number
Adams, Bob	1
Baker, Carol	2
Brown, Fred	3
Chester, Harold	4
Downs, Jane	5
...	↓
Zimwitz, Roland	30

Step 2: Generate random numbers in the range of 1 to N (30 in this case) by using the random number function in a spreadsheet program such as Microsoft Excel.[8] With Excel, use the =RANDBETWEEN(1,N) function described in the Active Learning exercise on the previous page to generate random numbers

in the range of 1 to N. The following set of random numbers was generated this way.

23	12	8	4	22	17	6	23	14	2	13

Select the first random number and find the corresponding population member. In the example, number 23 is the first random number.

Step 3: Select the person corresponding to that number into the sample.
#23—Stepford, Ann

Step 4: Continue to the next random number and select that person into the sample.
#12—Fitzwilliam, Roland

Step 5: Continue on in the same manner until the full sample is selected. If you encounter a number selected earlier, such as the 23 that occurs as the eighth random number, simply skip over it because you have already selected that population member into the sample. (This explains why 11 numbers were drawn.)

Advantages and Disadvantages of Simple Random Sampling Simple random sampling is an appealing sampling method simply because it embodies the requirements necessary to obtain a probability sample and, therefore, to derive unbiased estimates of the population's characteristics. This sampling method guarantees that every member of the population has an equal chance of being selected into the sample; therefore, the resulting sample, no matter what the size, will be a valid representation of the population.

However, there are some slight disadvantages associated with simple random sampling. To use either the random device or the random numbers approach, it is necessary to uniquely identify and label each and every population member. In the blind draw example, each student's name was written on an index card, and in the random numbers example, every population member was assigned a unique label or number. In essence, simple random sampling necessarily begins with a complete listing of the population, and current and complete listings are sometimes difficult to obtain. Incomplete or inaccurate listings of populations, of course, contain sample frame error. If the sample frame does not exist as an electronic list, it can be cumbersome to manually provide unique designations for each population member.

Using random numbers to draw a simple random sample requires a complete accounting of the population.

Simple Random Sampling Used in Practice There are two practical applications in which simple random sample designs are employed quite successfully: random digit dialing and computer-based random samples. In fact, these two general cases constitute the bulk of the use of simple random sampling in marketing research.

One instance in which simple random sampling is commonly employed is through the use of random digit dialing. **Random digit dialing (RDD)** is used in telephone surveys to overcome the problems of unlisted and new telephone numbers. Of course, a current challenge to random digit dialing is cell phone ownership.[9]

In random digit dialing, telephone numbers are generated randomly with the aid of a computer. These numbers are called, and telephone interviewers administer the survey to the respondent once the person has been qualified.[10] Before random digit dialing became essentially universal, the **plus-one dialing procedure**, in which numbers are selected from a telephone directory and a digit, such as a "1," is added to each number to determine which telephone number is then dialed was sometimes used. Alternatively, the last digit can be substituted with a random number.[11]

While random digit dialing was the marketing research industry's first wholesale incorporation of random sampling, with current computer technology, it is feasible to use random sampling in a wide variety of situations. For example, often companies possess computer lists, company files, or commercial listing services that have been converted into databases. Practically every database software program has a random number selection feature, so simple random sampling is easy to achieve if the researcher has a computerized database of the population. The database programs can work with random numbers of as many digits as are necessary, so even Social Security numbers with nine digits are no problem. Companies with credit files, subscription lists, or marketing information systems have the greatest opportunity to use this approach, or a research company may turn to a specialized sampling company such as Survey Sampling, Inc., to have it draw a random sample of households or businesses in a certain geographic area using its extensive databases.

Random digit dialing overcomes problems of unlisted and new telephone numbers.

In our chapter on the marketing research industry, we made note of the many companies that maintain consumer and business panels of various types, and practically every one of these companies sells access to random samples of their panels. That is, their panels, which sometimes number in the tens of thousands of individuals, are really megasamples of various types of populations. These panels operate as sample frames from which the panel company draws smaller random samples according to the specifications of their clients.

Systematic Sampling Before computer databases were largely available, researchers used a physical telephone book or a directory as the sample frame, in which case the time, expense,

Systematic sampling is more efficient than simple random sampling.

and practical implementation challenges of simple random sampling were daunting. Fortunately, an economical alternative probability sampling method was available. **Systematic sampling**, which is a way to select a random sample from a directory or list, is much more efficient (uses less effort) than simple random sampling. So, in the special case of a physical listing of the population, such as a membership directory or a telephone book, systematic sampling is advantageous to simple random sampling primarily due to the economic efficiency it represents. In this instance, systematic sampling can be applied with less difficulty and accomplished in a shorter time than can simple random sampling. Furthermore, in these instances, systematic sampling has the potential to create a sample that is almost identical in quality to samples created from simple random sampling.

To use systematic sampling, it is necessary to have a complete listing of the population. As noted earlier, the most common listing is a directory of some sort, but it might be a database. The researcher decides on a **skip interval**, which is calculated by dividing the number of names on the list by the sample size, as can be seen in the following formula:

Formula for skip interval

$$\text{Skip interval} = \text{population list size/sample size}$$

One must calculate a "skip interval" to use systematic sampling.

Names are selected based on this skip interval. For example, if one calculated a skip interval of 250, every 250th name would be selected into the sample. The use of this skip interval formula ensures that the entire list will be covered. Marketing Research Insight 9.3 shows how to take a systematic sample.

Why Systematic Sampling Is "Fair" Systematic sampling is probability sampling because it employs a random starting point, which ensures there is sufficient randomness in the systematic sample to approximate an equal probability of any member of the population being selected into the sample. In essence, systematic sampling envisions the list as made up of the skip interval number of mutually exclusive samples, each one of which is representative of the listed population. The random starting point guarantees that the selected sample is selected randomly.

How does the random starting point take place? With a directory or physical list as the sample frame, the efficient approach is to first generate a random number between 1 and the

MARKETING RESEARCH INSIGHT 9.3 *Practical Application*

How to Take a Systematic Sample

Step 1: Identify a listing of the population that contains an acceptable level of sample frame error.
Example: the telephone book for your city

Step 2: Compute the skip interval by dividing the number of names on the list by the sample size.
Example: 25,000 names in the phone book, sample size of 500, so skip interval = every 50th name

Step 3: Using random number(s), determine a starting position for sampling the list.
Example: *Select:* random number for page number
Select: random number for the column on that page
Select: random number for name position in that column (say, Jones, William P.)

Step 4: Apply the skip interval to determine which names on the list will be in the sample.
Example: Jones, William P. (skip 50 names); Lathum, Ferdinand B.

Step 5: Treat the list as "circular." That is, the first name on the list is now the initial name you selected, and the last name is now the name just prior to the initially selected one.
Example: When you come to the end of the phone book names (Zs), just continue on through the beginning (As).

number of pages to determine the page on which you will start. Suppose page 53 is drawn. Another random number would be drawn between 1 and the number of columns on a page to decide the column on that page. Assume the third column is drawn. A final random number between 1 and the number of names in a column would be used to determine the actual starting position in that column. Let's say the 17th name is selected. From that beginning point, the skip interval would be employed. The skip interval would ensure that the entire list would be covered, and the final name selected would be approximately one skip interval before the starting point. It is convenient to think of the listing as circular, so that A follows Z if the list were alphabetized, and the random starting point determines where the list "begins." Of course, with an electronic database, the starting point will be a random number between 1 and the number of individuals in the database.

The essential difference between systematic sampling and simple random sampling is apparent in the use of the words *systematic* and *random*. The system used in systematic sampling is the skip interval, whereas the randomness in simple random sampling is determined through the use of successive random draws. Systematic sampling skips its way through the entire population list from random beginning point to end, whereas random sampling guarantees that the complete population will be covered by successive random draws. The efficiency in systematic sampling is gained by two features: (1) the skip interval aspect and (2) the need to use random number(s) only at the beginning.

> Systematic sampling is more efficient than simple random sampling because only one or a very few random numbers need to be drawn at the beginning.

As we have indicated, a systematic sample requires a listing of the population, and we have included Marketing Research Insight 9.4, which describes how researchers in China

---

MARKETING RESEARCH INSIGHT 9.4 *Global Application*

Systematic Sample of Chinese Hospitals Reveals Video-on-Web Strategies

Despite being the most populated country in the world in the midst of a very aggressive modernization phase costing the Chinese government and private companies countless billions of dollars, some sectors are lagging. In particular, the Chinese medical sector in the form of Chinese hospitals is struggling to deliver better health practices to Chinese citizens. No single culprit exists; instead a number of factors can be identified that collectively have stymied the advancement of "e-health" campaigns. Among these factors are traditional Chinese medical practices such as herbal medicines, acupuncture, massage, and special diets that are revered by older Chinese citizens; low Internet penetration in rural areas; lack of technical expertise on the part of Chinese hospital administrators; and lack of resources. Recently, Chinese researchers decided to investigate the use of online videos by Chinese hospitals.[12]

These researchers found statistics attesting that 6.27 billion patient visits to doctors occurred in a typical year at approximately 22,000 public and private Chinese hospitals. Further, these hospitals hold 3.7 million beds with an occupancy rate of just under 90%.

The researchers wanted to study the use of e-health videos by Chinese hospitals by directly observing the contents of hospital websites. Because visiting thousands of these websites was an impossible task, they had to select a sample. The sample frame became an immediate problem, for there is no official list

of Chinese hospitals. The Chinese Healthcare Ministry reported a total of 22,000 hospitals in China, but it did not have a publically available list. The researchers conducted an extensive search, and they found a list of 19,084 Chinese hospitals that had been compiled by a private company about a year earlier. Because this list was available online, it became the sample frame, and the researchers selected every eighth hospital on the list. That is, they used a systematic sample with a skip interval of 8 to select 2,385 hospitals. The researchers then sought to visit the website of each selected hospital and to conduct content analysis on the video content found on the website.

Thus, with the use of probability sampling in the form of a systematic sample, the researchers' findings accurately describe the entire population of Chinese hospitals as follows:

- 42% have a website
- 22% with a website have at least one video on it
- About 10% have only one video
- About 7% have 2 to 10 videos
- About 3% have 11 to 30 videos
- About 1% have more than 30 videos

The researchers concluded that Chinese hospitals were greatly underutilizing videos on their websites, which is appalling given that China is one of the largest video consumption markets in the world.

 **Active Learning**

Take a Systematic Sample Using an Electronic List

This Active Learning exercise will give you experience in taking a systematic sample from an electronic list, such as a class roster or membership roll. For this exercise, you will use the Internet to search for a membership list in Excel. You will then apply systematic sampling steps as though you were selecting a sample of 100 members. First, you must find a list. Use Google or Bing or some other search engine to find "membership list." It does not matter what organization or association you find as long as it allows you to download the complete membership list in Excel. For instance, the USA Fencing Association has such a list (www.usfencing.org) of over 19,000 current members.

To draw a systematic sample, use the following steps:

1. Estimate the total number of individuals on the list. Typically, each member occupies a unique row, so all you need to do is to determine the number of rows in the dataset less any row(s) used for headings.
   Number of members in the list: _____

2. Determine the skip interval by dividing the number of members on the list by the sample size, 100.
   Skip interval: _____

3. Now, using some sort of random number generator such as an Excel function or a table of random numbers (typically found in a statistics textbook), select a random starting point. Using the Excel random number function "RANDBETWEEN," you can select a random number between 1 and the total number of members in your sample frame (the list you downloaded).

4. The RANDBETWEEN number you have obtained is the starting point for your sample. Go to that row in the database, adjusting for any heading row(s) at the top of the spreadsheet.

5. Using your skip interval, you can now select the sample of 100 members.

6. The procedure you have used here assumes that every one of your 100 randomly selected members will participate in the survey (100% response rate); however, this assumption is unrealistic. Assume that you expect a 50% response rate. What adjustment to the skip interval calculation can you make to accommodate the fact that every other prospective respondent will refuse to take part in the survey when asked?

---

selected a sample of hospitals in a study of how Chinese hospitals are using videos on their websites.

Disadvantage of Systematic Sampling The greatest danger in the use of systematic sampling lies in the listing of the population (sample frame). Sample frame error is a major concern for telephone directories because of unlisted numbers. It is also a concern for lists that are not current. In both instances, because the sample frame will not include certain population members, these members have no chance of being selected into the sample.

Cluster Sampling Another form of probability sampling is known as **cluster sampling**, in which the population is divided into subgroups called "clusters," each of which could represent the entire population. Note that the basic concept behind cluster sampling is similar to the one described for systematic sampling, but the implementation differs. The procedure uses some convenient means that identifies clusters that are theoretically identical, such as the pages of listings in a hard-copy directory. Any one cluster or page, therefore, could be a

With systematic sampling, the small loss in sampling precision is counterbalanced by its economic savings.

A cluster sampling method divides the population into groups, any one of which can be considered a representative sample.

representation of the population. Cluster sampling can even be applied to an electronic database (e.g., the clusters can be everyone whose name begins with A, B, C, etc.). It is easy to administer, and cluster sampling goes a step further in striving to gain economic efficiency over systematic sampling by simplifying the sampling procedure used.[13] We illustrate cluster sampling by describing a type of cluster sample known as area sampling.

Area Sampling as a Form of Cluster Sampling In **area sampling**, the researcher subdivides the population to be surveyed into geographic areas, such as census tracts, cities, neighborhoods, or any other convenient and identifiable geographic designation. The researcher has two options at this point: a one-step approach or a two-step approach. In the **one-step area sample** approach, the researcher may believe the various geographic areas (clusters) to be sufficiently identical to allow concentrating his or her attention on just one area and then generalizing the results to the full population. But the researcher would need to select that one area randomly and perform a census of its members. Alternatively, he or she may employ a **two-step area sample** approach to the sampling process. That is, for the first step, the researcher could select a random sample of areas, and then for the second step, he or she could decide on a probability method to sample individuals within the chosen areas. The two-step area sample approach is preferable to the one-step approach because there is always the possibility that a single cluster may be less representative than the researcher believes. But the two-step method is more costly because more areas and time are involved. Marketing Research Insight 9.5 illustrates how to take an area sample using subdivisions as the clusters.[14]

> Area sampling employs either a one-step or two-step approach.

Area grid sampling is a variation of the area sampling method. To use it, the researcher imposes a grid over a map of the area to be surveyed. Each cell within the grid then becomes a cluster. The difference between area grid sampling and area sampling lies primarily in the use of a grid framework, which cuts across natural or artificial boundaries, such as streets, rivers, city limits, or other separations normally used in area sampling. Geodemography has been used to describe the demographic profiles of the various clusters.[15] Regardless of how the population is sliced up, the researcher has the option of a one-step or a two-step approach.[16]

Disadvantage of Cluster (Area) Sampling The greatest danger in cluster sampling is cluster specification error that occurs when the clusters are not homogeneous. For example, if a subdivision association used area sampling to survey its members using its streets as cluster identifiers, and one street circumnavigated a small lake in the back of the subdivision, the "Lake Street" homes might be more expensive and luxurious than most of the other homes

---

MARKETING RESEARCH INSIGHT 9.5 *Practical Application*

How to Take a Two-Step Area Sampling Using Subdivisions

Step 1: Determine the geographic area to be surveyed and identify its subdivisions. Each subdivision cluster should be highly similar to all others.
Example: 20 subdivisions within 5 miles of the proposed site for our new restaurant; assign each a number.

Step 2: Decide on the use of one-step or two-step cluster sampling.
Example: Use two-step cluster sampling.

Step 3: (assuming two-step): Using random numbers, select the subdivisions to be sampled.

Example: Select four subdivisions randomly, say, numbers 3, 15, 2, and 19.

Step 4: Using some probability method of sample selection, select the members of each chosen subdivision to be included in the sample.
Example: Identify a random starting point; instruct fieldworkers to drop off the survey at every fifth house (systematic sampling).

Our area sampling example uses subdivisions as clusters.

in the subdivision. If, by chance, Lake Street was selected as a cluster in the survey, it would most likely bias the results toward the opinions of the relatively few wealthy subdivision residents. In the case of one-step area sampling, this bias could be severe.

Stratified Sampling   All of the sampling methods we have described thus far implicitly assume that the population has a normal, or bell-shaped, distribution for its key properties. That is, every potential sample unit is assumed to have a fairly good representation of the population, and any that are extreme in one way are perfectly counterbalanced by others that are oppositely extreme potential sample units. Unfortunately, it is common to work with populations in marketing research that contain unique subgroupings; you might encounter a population that is not distributed symmetrically across a normal curve. With this situation, unless you make adjustments in your sample design, you will end up with a sample described as "statistically inefficient"—that is, inaccurate. One solution is **stratified sampling**, which separates the population into different subgroups and then samples all of these subgroups.

> With stratified sampling, the population is separated into different strata, and a sample is taken from each stratum.

> Stratified sampling is used when the researcher is working with a "skewed" population divided into strata and wishes to achieve high statistical efficiency.

Working with Skewed Populations   A **skewed population** has a long tail on one side and a short tail on the opposite end. As such, it deviates greatly from the bell-shaped distribution that is assumed to be the case in the use of simple random, systematic, or cluster sampling. If any of these methods is used to draw the sample from a skewed distribution, it most certainly would be inaccurate.

For example, let's take the case of a college that is attempting to assess how its students perceive the quality of its educational programs. A researcher has formulated the question "To what extent do you value your college degree?" The response options are along a 5-point scale where 1 equals "Not valued at all" and 5 equals "Very highly valued." The population of students is stratified or divided by year: freshman, sophomore, junior, and senior. That is, the researcher identifies four strata that comprise the complete population of the college's students. We would expect the response to differ by stratum (the respondent's year classification) because seniors probably value a degree more than do juniors, who value a degree more than do sophomores, and so on. At the same time, you would expect that seniors would be more in agreement (have less variability) than would underclass students. This belief is due to the fact that freshmen are students who are trying out college, some of whom are not serious about completing it and do not value it highly but some of whom are intending to become doctors, lawyers, or professionals whose training will include graduate degree work as well as their present college studies. The serious freshmen students would value a college degree highly, whereas their less serious peers would not. Thus, we would expect much variability in the freshmen students, less in sophomores, still less in juniors, and the least with seniors. The situation might be something similar to the distributions illustrated in Figure 9.2. Note that this figure portrays the four class strata distributions as normal curves, whereas the entire college population of all four classes is a skewed curve.

With stratified random sampling, one takes a skewed population and identifies the sub-groups, or **strata**, contained within it. Simple random sampling, systematic sampling, or some other type of probability sampling procedure is then applied to draw a sample from each stratum because we typically believe that the individual strata have bell-shaped distributions. In other words, it is a "divide and conquer" approach to sampling.

Accuracy of Stratified Sampling How does stratified sampling result in a more accurate overall sample? This accuracy is achieved in two ways. First, stratified sampling allows for explicit analysis of each stratum. Our college degree example (Figure 9.2) illustrates why a researcher would want to know about the distinguishing differences between the strata to assess the true picture. Each stratum represents a different response profile, and by recognizing this, stratified sampling is a more accurate sample design.

Second, there is a procedure that allows the estimation of the overall sample mean by use of a **weighted mean**, whose formula takes into consideration the sizes of the strata relative to the total population size and applies those proportions to the strata's means. The population mean is calculated by multiplying each stratum by its proportion and summing the weighted

FIGURE 9.2
Four Strata in the Population of a College's Students

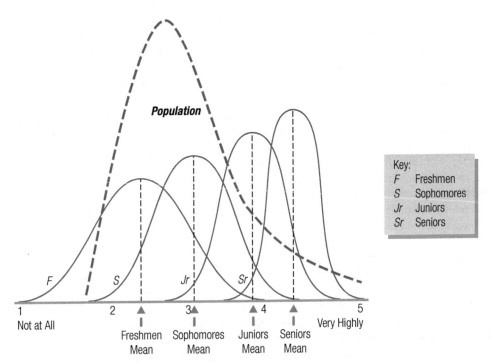

"To what extent do you value a college degree?"

A stratified sample may require the calculation of a weighted mean to achieve accuracy.

stratum means. This formula results in an estimate that is consistent with the true distribution of the population. This formula is used for two strata:

Formula for weighted mean

$$\text{Mean}_{\text{population}} = (\text{mean}_A)(\text{proportion}_A) + (\text{mean}_B)(\text{proportion}_B)$$

where A signifies stratum A, and B signifies stratum B.

Here is an example of the use of a weighted mean. A researcher separates a population of households that rent movies on a regular basis into two strata. Stratum A is families without young children, and stratum B is families with young children. When asked to use a scale of 1 = Poor, 2 = Fair, 3 = Good, 4 = Very good, and 5 = Excellent to rate Netflix on its movie selection, the means were computed to be 2.0 (Fair) for the families with young children (stratum B) sample and 4.0 (Very good) for the families without young children (stratum A) sample. The researcher knows from census information that families without young children account for 70% of the population, whereas families with young children account for the remaining 30%. The weighted mean rating for Netflix's movie selection is then computed as $(.7)(2.0) + (.3)(4.0) = 2.6$ (between fair and good in this fictitious example).

Researchers should select a basis for stratification that reveals different responses across the strata.

How to Apply Stratified Sampling Marketing researchers find stratified sampling especially useful when they encounter skewed populations. Prior knowledge of populations under study, augmented by research objectives sensitive to subgroupings, sometimes reveals that the population is not normally distributed. Under these circumstances, it is advantageous to apply stratified sampling to preserve the diversity of the various subgroups. Usually, a **surrogate measure**, which is some observable or easily determined characteristic of each population member, is used to help partition or separate the population members into their various subgroupings. For example, in the instance of the college, the year classification of each student is a handy surrogate. Researchers may divide the population into as many relevant strata as necessary to capture different subpopulations. For instance, the college might want to further stratify on college of study or grade-point average (GPA) ranges. Perhaps professional school students value their degrees more than do liberal arts students or high GPA students more than average GPA or failing students. The key issue is that researchers should use some basis for dividing the population into strata that results in different responses across strata. Also, there should be some logic or usefulness to the stratification system.

If the strata sample sizes are faithful to their relative sizes in the population, the research design reflects a **proportionate stratified sample**. Here you do not need to use the weighted formula because each stratum's weight is automatically accounted for by its sample size. But think for a moment about proportionate sampling: It erroneously assumes that the variability of each stratum is related to its size. Larger strata have more variability than small ones, but a large stratum could be composed of homogeneous individuals, translating to a relatively small stratum sample size, while a small stratum could be composed of very different individuals, translating to a relatively large stratum sample size. As a result, some researchers opt to use the stratum relative variability rather than the relative size as a factor in deciding stratum sample size. That is, if a stratum has low variability, precise estimates of that stratum may be obtained with a small sample size, and the "extra" sample saved could be allocated to strata with high variance. This provides for **statistical efficiency**, meaning for the same sample size researchers may obtain equivalent precision among the strata. This approach is called **disproportionate stratified sampling**, and a weighted formula needs to be used because the strata sizes do not reflect their relative proportions in the population. We have provided a step-by-step description of stratified sampling in Marketing Research Insight 9.6.

MARKETING RESEARCH INSIGHT 9.6 *Practical Application*

How to Take a Stratified Sample

Step 1: Be certain that the population's distribution for some key factor is *not* bell-shaped and that separate subpopulations exist.

Example: Condominium owners differ from apartment dwellers in their homeowners' insurance needs, so stratify by condo ownership and apartment dwelling.

Step 2: Use this factor or some surrogate variable to divide the population into strata consistent with the separate subpopulations identified.

Example: Use a screening question on condo ownership/apartment dwelling. This may require a screening survey using random digit dialing to identify respondent pools for each stratum.

Step 3: Select a probability sample from each stratum.

Example: Use a computer to select simple random samples for each stratum.

Step 4: Examine each stratum for managerially relevant differences.

Example: Do condo owners differ from apartment dwellers in the value of the furniture they own (and needs to be covered by insurance)? Answer: Condo owners average $15,000 in owned furniture value; apartment dwellers average $5,000 in owned furniture value.

Step 5: If stratum sample sizes are not proportionate to the stratum sizes in the population, use the weighted mean formula to estimate the population value(s).

Example: If condo owners are 30% and apartment dwellers are 70% of the population, the estimate of the average is ($15,000)(.30) + ($5,000)(.70) = $8,000 owned furniture value.

9-5 Nonprobability Sampling Methods

All of the sampling methods we have described thus far embody probability sampling assumptions. In each case, the probability of any unit being selected from the population into the sample is known, even though it cannot be calculated precisely. The critical difference between probability and nonprobability sampling methods is the mechanics used in the sample design. With a nonprobability sampling method, selection is not based on chance or randomness. Instead, a nonprobability sample is based on an inherently biased selection process, typically to reduce the cost of sampling.[17] With a nonprobability sample, the researcher has some savings in cost and/or time but at the expense of using a sample that is not truly representative of the population.[18] There are four nonprobability sampling methods: convenience samples, purposive samples, referral samples, and quota samples (Table 9.2). A discussion of each method follows.

© Julia Morgan Photography

With nonprobability sampling, there is a good possibility that nonrepresentative sample units will be selected. (New Orleans Saints fan Scott McGowan, dressed as the Joker.)

Convenience Samples Samples drawn from groups to which the researcher has easy access are called **convenience samples**. Typically, the most convenient areas to a researcher in terms of reduced time and effort turn out to be high-traffic areas, such as shopping malls or busy pedestrian intersections. The selection of the place and, consequently, prospective respondents is subjective rather than objective. Certain members of the population are automatically eliminated from the sampling process.[19] For instance, people who may be infrequent visitors or even nonvisitors of the particular high-traffic area being used would not be included. In the absence of strict selection procedures, some members of the population may be omitted because of their physical appearance, general demeanor, or the fact that they are in a group rather than alone. One author states, "Convenience samples … can be seriously misleading."[20]

It should be obvious that mall-intercept companies use convenience sampling to recruit respondents. For example, shoppers are encountered at large shopping malls and quickly qualified with screening questions. For those satisfying the desired population characteristics, a questionnaire may be administered or a taste test performed. Alternatively, the respondent

With nonprobability sampling methods, some members of the population do not have any chance of being included in the sample.

TABLE 9.2 Four Types of Nonprobability Sampling Methods

Convenience Sampling

The researcher or interviewer uses a high-traffic location, such as a busy pedestrian area or a shopping mall, as the sample frame from which to intercept potential respondents. Sample frame error occurs in the form of members of the population who are infrequent users or nonusers of that location. Other error may result from any arbitrary way the interviewer selects respondents from the sample frame.

Purposive Sampling

The researcher uses his or her judgment or that of some other knowledgeable person to identify who will be in the sample. Subjectivity and convenience enter in here; consequently, certain members of the population will have a smaller chance of selection than will others.

Chain Referral Sampling

Respondents are asked for the names or identities of others like themselves who might qualify to take part in the survey. Members of the population who are less well known or disliked or whose opinions conflict with the selected respondents have a low probability of being selected.

Quota Sampling

The researcher identifies quota characteristics, such as demographic or product use factors, and uses these to set up quotas for each class of respondent. The sizes of the quotas are determined by the researcher's belief about the relative size of each class of respondent in the population. Often, quota sampling is used as a means of ensuring that convenience samples will have the desired proportion of different respondent classes.

Marketing Research on YouTube™ To learn about nonprobability sampling methods, launch **www.youtube.com** and search for "Sampling 06: Non-Probability Sampling."

Mall intercepts are convenience samples.

Convenience samples may misrepresent the population.

may be given a test product and asked if he or she would use it at home. A follow-up telephone call some days later solicits his or her reaction to the product's performance. In this case, the convenience extends beyond easy access of respondents into considerations of setup for taste tests, storage of products to be distributed, and control of the interviewer workforce. Additionally, large numbers of respondents can be recruited in a matter of days. The screening questions and geographic dispersion of malls may appear to reduce the subjectivity inherent

Active Learning

Assess the Representativeness of Various Convenience Samples

Suppose the Athletic Department at your university is disappointed about student attendance of its "minor" collegiate sports events such as wrestling, cross country, and softball. The athletic director wants to learn why students do not attend these events. Listed here are possible locations for a convenience sample. Indicate what types of students would be overrepresented in the sample and what types would be underrepresented versus the population of students at your university for each case.

Convenience sample location	What students would be overrepresented?	What students would be underrepresented?
The University Recreation Center		
The University Commons		
The Library		
Physics 401 (Advanced class for physics majors)		

in the sample design, but in fact the vast majority of the population was not there and could not be approached to take part. There are ways of reducing convenience sample selection error using a quota system, which we discuss shortly.

Purposive Samples Unlike convenience samples, **purposive samples** require a judgment or an "educated guess" as to who should represent the population. Often the researcher or some individual helping the researcher who has considerable knowledge about the population will choose the types of individuals whom he or she feels constitute the sample. This practice is sometimes called a *judgment sample* or an *exemplar sample*. It should be apparent that purposive samples are highly subjective and, therefore, prone to much error.

With a purposive sample, one "judges" the sample to be representative.

Focus group studies use purposive sampling rather than probability sampling. In a recent focus group concerning the likely demand for low-fat, nutritious snacks, 12 mothers of preschool children were selected as representative of the present and prospective market. Six of the women also had school-age children, while the other six had only preschoolers. That is, the researcher purposely included the two types of focus group participants because in his judgment, these 12 women represented the population adequately for the purposes of the research. It must be quickly pointed out, however, that the intent of this focus group was far different from the intent of a survey. Consequently, the use of a purposive sample was considered satisfactory for this particular phase in the research process for the snacks. The focus group findings served as the foundation for a large-scale regional survey conducted two months later that relied on a probability sampling method.

As you would expect, there are grave ethical considerations attached to sample method decisions in marketing research. The relevant sections in the Marketing Research Association (MRA) Code of Ethics that pertain to sample methods are presented in Marketing Research Insight 9.7. The MRA states that researchers must explain sample methods to clients and disclose sample information such as the sample frame, sample method used, sample size, and sample error. Sample size and sample error is treated in the next chapter of your textbook.

MARKETING RESEARCH INSIGHT 9.7 *Ethical Consideration*

Marketing Research Association Code of Ethics: Sampling Method

30. Offer guidance to clients as to the appropriateness of the methodology being employed and sample selected to the fullest extent possible on each project.

Laypersons often do not have the necessary knowledge or experience to conduct research or to properly interpret data and recommend courses of action based upon that interpretation. Members must educate clients and the public in the proper methods and execution of marketing research, and use of research findings. When researchers are made aware of instances in which clients are improperly interpreting or otherwise using research, a professional duty exists to advise the errant party in the proper understanding or application of the data.

39. Provide appropriate disclosure of methods for all research released for public or media consumption.

Disclosure of methods statements as appropriate to include:

- *The method of data collection used*
- *The date(s) of data collection*
- *The sampling frame*
- *The sampling method*
- *The sample size*
- *The calculated margin of sampling error*

Source: Used courtesy of the Marketing Research Association.

A chain referral sample asks respondents to provide the names of additional respondents.

Chain Referral Samples Sometimes called "snowball samples," **chain referral samples** require respondents to provide the names of prospective respondents. Such samples begin when the researcher compiles a short list of possible respondents that is smaller than the total sample he or she desires for the study. After each respondent is interviewed, he or she is queried about the names of other possible respondents.[21] In this manner, additional respondents are referred by previous respondents. Or, as the informal name implies, the sample grows just as a snowball grows when it is rolled downhill. Some researchers call these simply "referral samples."

Chain referral samples are most appropriate when there is a limited or disappointingly short sample frame and when respondents can provide the names of others who would qualify for the survey. The nonprobability aspects of referral sampling come from the selectivity used throughout. The initial list may also be special in some way, and the primary means of adding people to the sample is by tapping the memories of those on the original list. While they rely heavily on social networks,[22] referral samples are often useful in industrial marketing research situations.[23]

Quota samples rely on key characteristics to define the composition of the sample.

Quota Samples When a researcher specifies percentages of the total sample for various types of individuals to be interviewed and selects them via nonprobability sampling, it is termed a **quota sample**. In other words, the researcher identifies groups in the population and sets the number of respondents (percentage of the final sample) for each group. Respondents are selected with convenience, purposive, referral, or some other nonprobability sampling method. For example, a researcher may desire the sample to be 50% males and 50% females. As we indicated earlier, quota samples are commonly used by marketing researchers who rely on mall intercepts, a convenience sample method. The quotas are determined through application of the research objectives and are defined by key characteristics used to identify the population. In the application of quota sampling, a fieldworker is provided with screening criteria that will classify the potential respondent into a particular quota group. For example, if the interviewer is assigned to obtain a sample quota of 50 each for black females, black males, white females, and white males, the qualifying characteristics would be race and gender. If our fieldworkers were assigned mall intercepts, each would determine through visual inspection where the prospective respondent falls and work toward filling the quota in each of the four groups. When based on the actual proportions of the various groups in the population, a quota system may reduce some of the nonrepresentativeness inherent in nonprobability samples, but it does not ensure a random sample.

Quota samples are appropriate when researchers have a detailed demographic profile of the population on which to base the sample.

Quota samples are best used by companies that have a firm grasp on the features characterizing the individuals they wish to study in a particular marketing research project. A large bank, for instance, might stipulate that the final sample be one-half adult males and one-half adult females because in the bank's understanding of its market, the customer base is equally divided between males and females. When done conscientiously and with a firm understanding of the population's characteristics, quota sampling can rival probability sampling in the minds of researchers.

IBM **SPSS**

IBM SPSS Student Assistant
IBM SPSS Quick Tour: Part I

9-6 Online Sampling Techniques

Sampling for Internet surveys poses special opportunities and challenges, but most of these issues can be addressed in the context of our probability and nonprobability sampling concepts.[24] The trick is to understand how the online sampling method in question works and to interpret the sampling procedure correctly with respect to basic sampling concepts.[25] Unfortunately, these sampling procedures are often "behind the scenes" or not obvious until one delves into the mechanics of the sample selection process. Basically, three types of samples are used with online surveys: (1) online panels, (2) river samples, and (3) list samples.

ONLINE PANEL SAMPLES

Online panel samples, as we have described and alluded to in various places in this textbook, are comprised of individuals who have agreed to participate in online surveys. Normally, they have registered with a panel company and have agreed to participate in surveys with some sort of compensation, such as points that can be redeemed for products and services. Panel members have divulged large amounts of information about themselves to the panel company, so it is easy for the company to select panelists who satisfy population membership criteria specified by clients, such as age range, education level, and household size. Panel companies have hundreds of thousands of prospective respondents, and they select them based on any such criteria and/or sampling requirements specified by their clients. Panel companies are especially adept at delivering "targeted samples" because they have huge databases of information regarding demographics, possessions, lifestyle, medical ailments, and so on that can be used to select panel members to be survey respondents. Online panel samples are popular, but there are lingering concerns about the true representativeness of samples provided by panel companies because their sample frames are imperfect.

Online samples include online panel samples, river samples, and email list samples.

RIVER SAMPLES

A **river sample** is created via the use of banners, pop-ups, or other online devices that invite website visitors to take part in the survey. The "river" is the steady stream of website visitors, and these invitations figuratively dip respondents out of the Internet river. Of course, the online questionnaire may have screening questions so that only qualified prospects are allowed to take part in the survey. The sample frame of a river sample is the stream of visitors visiting the site issuing the invitation, and river samples are considered random samples of these sample frames as long as the invitations are not unusual in duration, appearance, or relevance.

EMAIL LIST SAMPLES

Email list samples are those purchased or otherwise procured from someone or some company that has compiled email addresses of opt-in members of the population of interest. The vendor company can pull random samples and may have the ability to satisfy selection criteria specified by the client company. The list company may sell the list, or it might issue email invitations to maintain the propriety of email addresses on the list. Obviously, the master source list is the sample frame, so if the list company has been diligent, the email list sample will be a good representation of the population. However, if the list company has not done due diligence, there will be sample frame error in the email list.

A sample plan lists all the steps necessary to draw a sample.

9-7   Developing a Sample Plan

Up to this point, we have discussed various aspects of sampling as though they were discrete and seemingly unrelated decisions. However, they are logically joined in a definite sequence of steps, called the **sample plan**, which the researcher goes through to draw and ultimately arrive at the final sample.[26] These steps are listed and described in Table 9.3.

IBM SPSS
IBM SPSS Student Assistant
IBM SPSS Quick Tour: Part II

Marketing | Learn about the sample **Research** plan by going to **www.** **on YouTube™** | **youtube.com** and searching for "Developing a Sampling Plan."

TABLE 9.3 Steps in a Sample Plan

Step	Action	Description
1	Define the population.	Create a precise description of the group under investigation using demographics, buyer behavior, or other relevant constructs.
2	Obtain a sample frame.	Gain access to some master source that uniquely identifies all the units in the population with minimal sample frame error.
3	Decide on the sample method.	Based on survey objectives and constraints, endeavor to select the best probability sample method, or alternatively, if appropriate, select the best nonprobability sample method.
4	Decide on the sample size.	If a probability sampling plan is selected, use a formula; to be covered in the following chapter.
5	Draw the sample.	Using the chosen sample method, apply the necessary steps to select potential respondents from the sample frame.
6	Validate the sample.	Inspect some relevant characteristics of the sample (such as distribution of males and females, age ranges, etc.) to judge how well it matches the known distribution of these characteristics in the population.

Summary

Sampling methods facilitate marketing research without requiring a census of an entire population. Marketing researchers aim to avoid sample frame error, which includes omissions and inaccuracies that will adversely affect the sample drawn from it.

A sample is taken because it is too costly to perform a census and there is sufficient information in a sample to allow it to represent the population. We described four probability sampling methods in which there is a known chance of a member of the population being selected into the sample. Simple random sampling uses devices or aids, such as random numbers, to ensure that every member of the population has the same chance of being selected into the sample. Systematic sampling uses a random starting point and "skips" through a list. Cluster sampling can be applied to areas such as subdivisions so that only a few areas are selected and canvassed or sampled. Stratified sampling is used when different strata are apparent in the population and each stratum is randomly sampled.

We also described four nonprobability sampling methods that contain bias because all members of the population do not have a fair chance of being selected into the sample. Convenience sampling uses high-traffic locations, such as shopping malls, to make it easy for an interviewer to intercept respondents. Purposive sampling rests on someone's subjective judgment as to who should be in the sample. Chain referral sampling relies on respondents to give up names of friends to be asked to take part in the survey, and quota sampling is convenience sampling with quotas or limits on the numbers of respondents with specific characteristics. With the popularity of online surveys, online samples provided by panel companies, river samples that tap into the stream of online visitors to a website, and email samples are common. With knowledge of the sample method specifics, a researcher can assess the degree to which an online sample embodies random sampling requirements.

Finally, we described six steps needed to develop a sample plan: (1) define the relevant population, (2) obtain a sample frame, (3) decide on the sample method, (4) decide on the sample size, (5) draw the sample, and (6) validate the sample.

Key Terms

Population (p. 238)
Census (p. 238)
Sample (p. 239)

Sample unit (p. 239)
Sample frame (p. 239)
Sample frame error (p. 239)

Sampling error (p. 240)
Probability samples (p. 241)
Nonprobability samples (p. 241)

Review Questions/Applications

9-1. Distinguish a nonprobability from a probability sampling method. Which one is the preferable method and why? Indicate the pros and cons associated with probability and nonprobability sampling methods.

9-2. Why is a sample more desirable than a census? What are some of the reasons for taking a sample?

9-3. Name and explain four popular types of probability sampling methods and describe the advantages of each of these methods.

9-4. Briefly describe the steps of a sample plan.

9-5. Why is probability sampling widely preferred? To what situations, if any, is non-probability sampling better suited?

9-6. Differentiate one-step from two-step area sampling and indicate when each one is preferred.

9-7. What is a *weighted mean*? How can it be used?

9-8. How can the challenges of sampling for Internet surveys be addressed?

9-9. What is the difference between a convenience sample and a purposive sample?

9-10. Why is quota sampling often used with a convenience sampling method such as mall intercepts?

9-11. Provide the marketing researcher's definitions for each of the following populations:

a. Nest Thermostat, a company that sells a home thermostat that runs on the Internet of Things, wants to determine interest in an entry camera that activates with motion anytime someone enters a dwelling via the front door.

b. The manager of your student union is interested in determining if students desire a "universal" debit ID card that will be accepted anywhere on campus and in many stores off campus.

c. Joy Manufacturing Company decides to conduct a survey to determine the sales potential of a new type of air compressor used by construction companies.

9-12. Here are four populations and a potential sample frame for each one. With each pair, identify (1) members of the population who are not in the sample frame and (2) sample frame items that are not part of the population. Also, for each one, would you judge the amount of sample frame error to be acceptable or unacceptable?

Population	Sample Frame
a. Buyers of Scope mouthwash	Mailing list of *Consumer Reports* subscribers
b. Subscribers to SiriusXM satellite radio	State registration records of new automobile buyers
c. Prospective buyers of a new client and prospective client's tracking software product	Members of Sales and Marketing Executives International (a national organization of sales managers)
d. Users of weatherproof decking materials (to build outdoor decks)	Individuals' names registered at a recent home and garden show

9-13. A market researcher is proposing a survey for the Big Tree Country Club, a private country club that is contemplating several changes in its layout to make the golf course more championship caliber. The researcher is considering three different sample designs as a way to draw a representative sample of the club's golfers. The three alternative designs include the following:

a. Station an interviewer at the first hole tee on one day chosen at random, with instructions to ask every 10th golfer to fill out a self-administered questionnaire.

b. Put a stack of questionnaires on the counter where golfers check in and pay for their golf carts with a sign above the questionnaires offering an incentive for a "free dinner in the clubhouse" for three players who fill out the questionnaire and whose names are selected by a lottery.

c. Use the city telephone directory to conduct a plus-one dialing procedure. With this procedure, a random page in the directory would be selected, and a name on that page would be selected, both using a table of random numbers. The plus-one system would be applied to that name and every name listed after it until 1,000 golfers are identified and interviewed by telephone.

Assess the representativeness and other issues associated with this sample problem. Be sure to identify the sample method being contemplated in each case. Which sample method do you recommend using and why?

9-14. A researcher has the task of estimating how many units of a revolutionary new high-speed office copier machine (it does not require ink cartridges and it is guaranteed not to jam) will be purchased among businesses in Cleveland, Ohio, for the coming annual sales forecast. Her plan is to ask the likelihood that they will purchase the new device, and for those who are "very likely" to purchase, she wants respondents to estimate how many machines their company will buy. She has data to divide the companies into small, medium, and large firms based on number of employees at the Cleveland office.
a. What sampling plan should be used?
b. Why?

9-15. Honda USA is interested in learning what its 550 U.S. dealers think about a new service program the carmaker provided to dealers at the beginning of last year. Honda USA wants to know if the dealers are using the program and, if so, their likes and dislikes about it. The carmaker does not want to survey all 550 dealers but hopes to ensure that the results are representative of all dealers.
a. What sampling plan should be used?
b. Why?

9-16. Applebee's Restaurants has spent several tens of thousands of dollars advertising the restaurant during the last two years. Marketing executives want to measure what effect the advertising has had, and they decide to measure top-of-mind awareness (TOMA). A TOMA score for such a restaurant is the ranking a firm has as a result of asking a representative sample of consumers in the service area to "name a non-fast-food restaurant." The restaurant that is named by the most persons has the top TOMA score. It is important that Applebee's management conduct the TOMA survey on a representative sample in the metropolitan area.
a. What sampling plan should be used?
b. Why?

9-17. Belk has a chain of department stores across the South. Top management requires that each store manager collect, maintain, and respond to customer complaints (emails, letters, calls, etc.). Each store manager is supposed to keep a list of complaints that have been received. Top management is considering establishing a more formalized method of monitoring and evaluating the responses managers give to the complaints. They want some information that will tell them whether they need to develop such a formalized program or whether they can leave well enough alone and allow managers to use their discretion in handling the complaints. They want to review a sample of these complaints and the responses to them.
a. What sampling plan should be used?
b. Why?

CASE 9.1

Peaceful Valley Subdivision: Trouble in Suburbia

Located on the outskirts of a large city, the suburb of Peaceful Valley comprises approximately 6,000 upscale homes. The subdivision came about 10 years ago when a developer built an earthen dam on Peaceful River and created Peaceful Lake, a meandering 20-acre body of water. The lake became the centerpiece of the development, and the first 1,000 half-acre lots were sold as lakefront property. Now Peaceful Valley is fully developed with 50 streets, all approximately the same length with about 120 houses on each street. Peaceful Valley's residents are primarily young, professional, dual-income families with one or two school-age children.

Peaceful Valley has not been living up to its name in recent months. The Suburb Steering Committee has recommended that the community build a swimming pool, tennis court, and meeting room facility on four adjoining vacant lots in the back of the subdivision. Construction cost estimates range from $2.5 million to $3 million, depending on the size of the facility. Currently, every Peaceful Valley homeowner is billed $250 annually for maintenance, security, and upkeep of the development. About 75% of residents pay this fee. To finance the proposed recreational facility, every Peaceful Valley household would be expected to pay a one-time fee of $1,500, and annual fees would increase to $500 based on facility maintenance cost estimates.

Objections to the recreational facility come from various quarters. For some, the one-time fee is unacceptable; for others, the notion of a recreational facility is not appealing. Some residents have their own swimming pools, belong to local tennis clubs, or otherwise have little use for a meeting room facility. Other Peaceful Valley homeowners see the recreational facility as a wonderful addition where their children could learn to swim, play tennis, or just hang out under supervision.

The president of the Peaceful Valley Suburb Association has decided to conduct a survey to poll the opinions and preferences of Peaceful Valley homeowners regarding the swimming pool, tennis court, and meeting room facility concept. Review the following possible sample methods. Indicate your reactions and answers to the questions associated with each possible method.

1. There is only one street into and out of the subdivision. The president is thinking of paying his teenage daughter to stand at the stop light at the entrance to Peaceful Valley next week between the hours of 7:00 and 8:30 a.m. to hand out questionnaires to exiting drivers while they wait for the red light to change. The handouts would include addressed, postage-paid envelopes for returns. Identify what sample method the president would be using, list its pros and cons, and indicate how representative a sample would result.

2. The chairperson of the Suburb Steering Committee thinks the 1,000 homeowners whose houses are on the waterfront properties of Peaceful Lake are the best ones to survey because they paid more for their lots, their houses are bigger, and they tend to have lived in Peaceful Valley longer than other residents. If these 1,000 homeowners are used for the sample, what sample method would be involved, what are its pros and cons, and how representative a sample would result?

3. Assume that the Steering Committee chairperson's point that the 1,000 waterfront owners are not the same as the other 5,000 Peaceful Valley Subdivision homeowners is true. How should this fact be used to draw a representative sample of the entire subdivision? Identify the probability sampling method that is most appropriate, and indicate, step by step, how it should be applied here.

4. How would you select a simple random sample of those Peaceful Valley homeowners who paid their subdivision association dues last year? What, if any, sample bias might result from this approach?

5. How could a two-step cluster sample be used here? Identify this sample method and describe how it could be used to select a representative sample of Peaceful Valley households.

CASE 9.2

Jet's Pets

Jetadiah Brown wants to establish a pet store called Jet's Pets. Jet thinks there is an opportunity on the north side of the city because he knows that many new subdivisions have been built, and many families have bought homes there. Plus, he knows there are no pet stores located on the north side. This growth in the number of families and the lack of competitors strongly suggest a marketing opportunity for Jet's Pets.

Jet wants to survey the approximately 10,000 families in two ZIP code areas. Of course, he cannot survey all of them, so he must use a sample. For each of the following possible ways of selecting a sample of the families living in several subdivisions in two ZIP code areas: (1) identify the type of sample method; (2) identify the sample frame; (3) indicate what, if any, sample frame error there is; and (4) indicate the degree to which the resulting sample will be representative of all families living in the two ZIP code areas.

1. Place questionnaires in veterinarian clinics located in the two ZIP code areas for pet owners to fill out while they are waiting for the doctor to examine their pet.

2. Select every 100th name in the city telephone book; call and interview only those who live in the two ZIP code areas.

3. Use a random number system to select a single subdivision located somewhere in the two ZIP code areas, and then place questionnaires in the mailboxes of every home in that selected subdivision.

4. Announce in the local newspaper a "Cutest Dog Contest" with contestants sending in a photo and address information. Use the contestants who live in the two ZIP code areas as the sample.

5. Go to the local animal shelter and get the addresses of the past pet adopters who live in the two ZIP code areas. Send a mail survey to the nearest neighbor's address for each of the addresses obtained from the animal shelter. For example, if the adopter lives at 1 Green Street, send the mail questionnaire to the occupants at 2 Green Street.

10

Determining the Size of a Sample

"WHERE WE ARE"

1 Establish the need for marketing research.

2 Define the problem.

3 Establish research objectives.

4 Determine research design.

5 Identify information types and sources.

6 Determine methods of accessing data.

7 Design data collection forms.

8 Determine the sample plan and size.

9 Collect data.

10 Analyze data.

11 Prepare and present the final research report.

Lucid

Patrick Comer, founder and CEO, Lucid

Patrick Comer (CEO) and Brett Schnittlich (CTO) first envisioned Lucid on a Las Feliz, California, porch in the mid-2000s. The buying and selling of surveys, or "sample," had not yet grown into the Internet age. The opportunity was ripe to develop an automated online exchange, similar to the programmatic exchanges that transformed the advertising industry. The shift to online exchange would bring the sample business off of telephones and onto the Internet, increasing quality and efficiency—what used to take weeks could be finished like magic, in hours, for a fraction of the cost.

In 2010, Comer founded Federated Sample. The company raised a modest amount of funds and utilized profits from Federated Sample's services team to build out its Fulcrum software. Fulcrum quickly grew into the vision of its founders: a highly scalable SaaS business and the industry's first programmatic exchange. By mid-2015, nearly 6 billion questions had been answered, over 125 million unique visitors had completed a survey, and over $200 million of sample had been sold on the platform. By early 2015, Federated Sample had outgrown its name. It had matured into a technology company more aptly described as "software" than sample. Massive amounts of unique visitors and completed surveys had created a gold mine of data to power ventures outside of sample's confines but within market research's standards.

On August 19, 2015, Federated Sample became Lucid. The rebranding was more than a name change—it reflected a paradigm shift for the company. Now no longer a start-up, Lucid is a diversifying technology company in the market research space that is bent on perpetuating the significant growth of its first five years. All Lucid's efforts center on the alchemy of extracting clarity from chaos, as did the Fulcrum platform that started it all. The revamped brand tells the company's whole story: Lucid's mission is to bring transparency, clarity, and a touch of magic to the market research industry.

Source: Text and photos courtesy of Patrick Comer and Lucid.

Visit Lucid at https://luc.id/

RIWI Corp.

RIWI CEO Neil Seeman thought outside the box to create an innovative solution to an existing and recurring problem in the world of market research. The technology he invented was initially applied at the University of Toronto for global pandemic research. The Web-based technology, known as RDIT™ (Random Domain Intercept Technology), allows organizations to engage online populations that do not usually if ever answer surveys. The technology accesses randomized and diverse local populations based on unintentional Internet navigation and data input errors. Since its development in 2009, it has reached millions of respondents all over the world on all mobile devices including smartphones and tablets.

Neil Seeman, founder and CEO, RIWI Corp.

Because the RDIT methodology collects no personal information, respondents can answer questions more freely and with less bias, particularly with sensitive topics (e.g., same-sex marriage, marijuana use). Respondents are asked to identify their age and gender along with a series of questions that may vary based on the topic of research and the client. RDIT is the only technology of its kind in the world. It has the ability to reach beyond paid panel respondents or social media users and is able to engage the previously unengaged—that is, people who do not typically answer surveys. RDIT has been used in all sectors of the market from large global consumer packaged goods companies to nongovernmental organizations to governments themselves from all over the world. More specifically, RIWI has researched public opinions on various topics ranging from health care to global conflicts to electronic purchases.

Visit RIWI at www.riwi.com

Visit RIWI at www.riwi.com

Source: Text and photos courtesy of Neil Seeman and RIWI Corp.

I n the previous chapter, you learned that the method of sample selection determines its representativeness. Unfortunately, many managers falsely believe that sample size and sample representativeness are related, but they are not. By studying this chapter, you will learn that the size of a sample directly affects its degree of accuracy or error, which is completely different from its representativeness. As you can see in our opening company vignettes, technology now allows for relatively easy access to thousands of randomly selected respondents; however, as you will learn in this chapter, sample accuracy may be satisfactory with appreciably smaller numbers of respondents.

Marketing managers typically confuse sample size with sample representativeness.

The accuracy of a sample is a measure of how closely it reports the true values of the population it represents.

Consider this example to demonstrate that there is no relationship between the size of a sample and its representativeness of the population from which it is drawn. Suppose we want to find out what percentage of the U.S. workforce dresses "business casual" most of the workweek. We take a convenience sample by standing on a corner of Wall Street in New York City, and we ask everyone who will talk to us about whether they come to work in business casual dress. At the end of one week, we have questioned more than 5,000 respondents in our survey. Are these people representative of the U.S. workforce population? No, of course they are not. In fact, they are not even representative of New York City workers because a nonprobability sampling method was used. What if we asked 10,000 New Yorkers with the same sample method? No matter what its size, the sample would still be unrepresentative for the same reason.

There are two important points. First, only a probability sample, typically referred to as a *random sample*, is truly representative of the population and, second, the size of that random sample determines the sample's accuracy of findings.[1] **Sample accuracy** refers to how close a random sample's statistic (for example, percent of yes answers to a particular question) is to the population's value (that is, the true percent of agreement in the population) it represents. Sample size has a direct bearing on how accurate the sample's findings are relative to the true values in the population. If a random sample has 5 respondents, it is more accurate than if it had only 1 respondent; 10 respondents are more accurate than 5 respondents and so forth. Common sense tells us that larger random samples are more accurate than smaller random samples. But, as you will learn in this chapter, 5 is not 5 times more accurate than 1, and 10 is not twice as accurate as 5. The important points to remember at this time are that (1) sample method determines a sample's representativeness, while (2) sample size determines a random sample's accuracy. Precisely how accuracy is affected by the size of the sample constitutes a major focus of this chapter.

The selection method, not the size of the sample, determines a sample's representativeness.

We are concerned with sample size because a significant cost savings occurs when the correct sample size is calculated and used. To counter the high refusal rate that marketing research companies encounter when they do surveys, many companies have created respondent panels, as described earlier in this textbook. Tens and hundreds of thousands of consumers have joined these panels with the agreement that they will respond to survey requests quickly, completely, and honestly. These panels are mini-populations that represent consumer markets of many types. The panel companies sell access to their panel members for a fee per respondent, typically based on the length of the survey. If a marketing research project director requests a sample size of 10,000 respondents and the panel company charges $5 per respondent, the sample cost is 10,000 times $5, or $50,000. A sample size of 1,000 respondents would cost 1,000 times $5, or $5,000. Thus, if 1,000 is the "correct" sample size, there would be a $45,000 savings in the marketing research project cost. When marketing research proposals are submitted, the cost or price is included. The 10,000 sample size bid would be significantly higher in price than would be the 1,000 sample size bid, and it would probably not be competitive for that reason.

Accordingly, this chapter is concerned with random sample size determination methods. To be sure, sample size determination can be a complicated process,[2,3,4] but our aim in this chapter is to simplify the process and make it more intuitive. To begin, we share some axioms about sample size. These statements serve as the basis for the confidence interval approach, which is the best sample size determination method to use; we describe its underlying notions of variability, allowable sample error, and level of confidence. These are combined into a simple formula to calculate sample size, and we give some examples of how the formula works. Next, we describe four other popular methods used to decide on a sample's size that have important limitations. Finally, we briefly review some practical considerations and special situations that affect the final sample size.

10-1 Sample Size Axioms

How to determine the number of respondents in a particular sample is actually one of the simplest decisions in the marketing research process,[5] but it may appear bewildering because formulas are used. A sample size decision is usually a compromise between what is theoretically perfect and what is practically feasible. This chapter presents the fundamental concepts that underlie sample size decisions.[6]

There are two good reasons a marketing researcher should have a basic understanding of sample size determination. First, many practitioners have a **large sample size bias**, which is a false belief that sample size determines a sample's representativeness. This bias is represented by a common question: "How large a sample should we have to be representative?" We have already established that there is no relationship between sample size and representativeness, so you already know one of the basics of sample size determination. Second, a marketing researcher should have a basic understanding of sample size determination because sample size is often a major cost factor, particularly for personal interviews but even with telephone and online surveys. Consequently, understanding how sample size is determined will enable researchers to help managers to better manage their resources.

Table 10.1, which lists eight axioms about sample size and accuracy, should help to contradict the large sample size bias among many marketing research clients. An axiom is a universal truth, meaning that the statement will always be correct. However, we must point out that these axioms pertain only to probability samples, so they are true only as long as a random sample is being used. Remember, no matter how astonishing one of our statements might seem, it will always be true when dealing with a random sample. As we describe the confidence interval method of sample size determination, we will refer to each axiom in turn and help you understand the axiom.

The size of a sample has nothing to do with its representativeness. Sample size affects the sample accuracy.

10-2 The Confidence Interval Method of Determining Sample Size

The most correct method of determining sample size is the **confidence interval approach**, which applies the concepts of accuracy (margin of sample error), variability, and confidence interval to create a "correct" sample size. This approach is used by national opinion polling

The confidence interval approach is the correct method by which to determine sample size.

TABLE 10.1 The Axioms of Random Sample Size and Sample Accuracy

1. The only perfectly accurate sample is a census.

2. A random sample will always have some inaccuracy, which is referred to as *margin of sample error* or simply *sample error*.

3. The larger a random sample is, the more accurate it is, meaning the less margin of sample error it has.

4. Margin of sample error can be calculated with a simple formula and expressed as a ±% number.

5. You can take any finding in the survey, replicate the survey with a random sample of the same size, and be "very likely" to find the same finding within the ±% range of the original sample's finding.

6. In almost all cases, the margin of sample error of a random sample is independent of the size of the population.

7. A random sample size can be a tiny percent of the population size and still have a small margin of sample error.

8. The size of a random sample depends on the client's desired accuracy (acceptable margin of sample error) balanced against the cost of data collection for that sample size.

companies and most marketing researchers. To describe the confidence interval approach to sample size determination, we first must describe the four underlying concepts.

SAMPLE SIZE AND ACCURACY

The first axiom, *"The only perfectly accurate sample is a census,"* is easy to understand. You should be aware that a survey has two types of error: nonsampling error and sampling error. **Nonsampling error** pertains to all sources of error other than the sample selection method and sample size, including problem specification mistakes, question bias, data recording errors, or incorrect analysis. Recall from Chapter 9 that sampling error involves both sample selection method and sample size.[7] With a census, every member of the population is selected, so there is no error in selection. Because a census accounts for every single individual, and if we assume there is no nonsampling error, it is perfectly accurate, meaning that it has no sampling error.

However, a census is almost always infeasible due to cost and practical reasons, so we must use some random sampling technique. This fact brings us to the second axiom, *"A random sample will always have some inaccuracy, which is referred to as 'margin of sample error' or simply 'sample error.'"* This axiom emphasizes that no random sample is a *perfect* representation of the population. However, it is important to remember that a random sample is nonetheless a *very good* representation of the population, even if it is not perfectly accurate.

The third axiom, *"The larger a random sample is, the more accurate it is, meaning the less margin of sample error it has,"* serves notice that there is a relationship between sample size and accuracy of the sample. This relationship is presented graphically in Figure 10.1. In this figure, margin of sample error is listed on the vertical axis, and sample size is noted on the horizontal axis. The graph shows the sample error levels for samples ranging in size from 50 to 2,000. The shape of the graph is consistent with the third axiom because margin of sample error decreases as sample size increases. However, you should immediately notice that the graph is not a straight line. In other words, doubling sample size does not result in halving the sample error. The relationship is an asymptotic curve that will never achieve 0% error.

There is another important property of the sample error graph. As you look at the graph, note that at a sample size of around 1,000, the margin of sample error is about ±3% (actually ±3.1%), and it decreases at a very slow rate with larger sample sizes. In other words, once a sample is greater than, say, 1,000, large gains in accuracy are not realized even with large increases in the size of the sample. In fact, if it is already ±3.1% in accuracy, little additional accuracy is possible.

With the lower end of the sample size axis, however, large gains in accuracy can be made with a relatively small sample size increase. You can see this vividly by looking at the sample errors associated with smaller sample sizes in Table 10.2. For example, with a sample size

The only perfectly accurate sample is a census.

The larger the size of the (probability) sample, the less is its margin of sample error.

FIGURE 10.1
The Relationship Between Sample Size and Sample Error

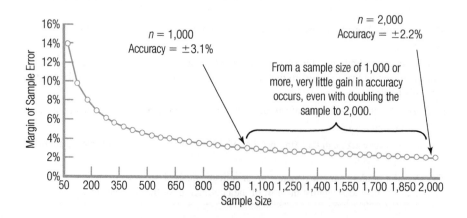

of 50, the **margin of sample error** is ±13.9%, whereas with a sample size of 200 it is ±6.9%, meaning that the accuracy of the 200 sample is roughly double that of the 50 sample. But as was just described, such huge gains in accuracy are not the case at the other end of the sample size scale because of the nature of the curved relationship. You will see this fact if you compare the sample error of a sample size of 2,000 (±2.2%) to that of a sample size of 10,000 (±1.0%): with 8,000 more in the sample, we have improved the accuracy only by 1.2%. So, while the accuracy surely does increase with greater and greater sample sizes, there is only a minute gain in accuracy when these sizes are more than 1,000 respondents.

The sample error values and the sample error graph were produced via the fourth axiom:[8] *"Margin of sample error can be calculated with a simple formula, and expressed as a ±% number."* The formula follows:

Margin of sample error formula

$$\text{Margin of Sample Error \%} = 1.96 \times \sqrt{\frac{p \times q}{n}}$$

Yes, this formula is simple; n is the sample size, and there is a constant, 1.96. But what are p and q?

p and q: THE CONCEPT OF VARIABILITY

Let's set the scene. We have a population, and we want to know what percent of the population responds "yes" to the question, "The next time you order a pizza, will you use Domino's?" We will use a random sample to estimate the population percent of "yes" answers. What are the possibilities? We might find 100% of respondents answering "yes" in the sample, we might find 0% of yes responses, or we might find something in between, say, 50% "yes" responses in the sample.

When we find a wide dispersion of responses—that is, when we do not find one response option accounting for a large number of respondents relative to the other items—we say that the results have much variability. **Variability** is defined as the amount of dissimilarity in respondents' answers to a particular question. If most respondents indicate the same answer on the response scale, the distribution has little variability because respondents are highly similar. On the other hand, if respondents are evenly spread across the question's response options, there is much variability because respondents are quite dissimilar. So, the 100% and the 0% agreement cases have little variability because everyone answers the same, while the 50% in-between case has a great deal of variability because with any two respondents, one answers "yes" while the other one answers "no."

The sample error formula pertains only to nominal data, or data in which the response items are categorical. We recommend that you always think of a yes/no question; the greater the similarity, meaning that the more you find people saying "yes" in the population, the less the variability in the responses. For example, we may find that the question "The next time you order a pizza, will you use Domino's?" yields a 90% to 10% distribution split between "yes" versus "no." In other words, most of the respondents give the same answer, meaning that there is much similarity in the responses and the variability is low. In contrast, if the question results in a 50/50 split, the overall response pattern is (maximally) dissimilar, and there is much variability. You can see the variability of responses in Figure 10.2. With the 90/10 split, the graph has one high side (90%) and one low side (10%), meaning almost everyone agrees on Domino's. In contrast, with disagreement or much variability in people's answers, both sides of the graph are near even (50%/50%).

TABLE 10.2 **Sample Sizes and Margin of Sample Error**

Sample Size (n)	Margin of Sample Error (Accuracy Level)
10	±31.0%
50	±13.9%
100	±9.8%
200	±6.9%
400	±4.9%
500	±4.4%
750	±3.6%
1,000	±3.1%
1,500	±2.5%
2,000	±2.2%
5,000	±1.4%
10,000	±1.0%

With a sample size of 1,000 or more, very little gain in accuracy occurs even with doubling or tripling the sample size.

Variability refers to how similar or dissimilar responses are to a given question.

© Nomad_Soul/Shutterstock

The less variability in the population, the smaller will be the sample size.

A 50/50 split in response signifies maximum variability (dissimilarity) in the population, whereas a 90/10 split signifies little variability.

The Domino's Pizza example relates to p and q in the following way:

$$p = \text{percent saying yes}$$
$$q = 100\% - p, \text{ or percent saying no}$$

In other words, p and q are complementary numbers that must always sum to 100%, as in the cases of 90% + 10% and 50% + 50%. The p represents the variable of interest in the population that we are trying to estimate.

In our sample error formula, p and q are multiplied. The largest possible product of p times q is 2,500, or 50% times 50%. You can verify this fact by multiplying other combinations of p and q, such as 90/10 (900), 80/20 (1,600), or 60/40 (2,400). Every combination will have a result smaller than 2,500; the most lopsided combination of 99/1 (99) yields the smallest product. If we assume the worst possible case of maximum variability, or 50/50 disagreement, the sample error formula becomes even simpler and can be given with two constants, 1.96 and 2,500, as follows:

Sample error formula with $p = 50\%$ and $q = 50\%$

$$\pm \text{ Margin of Sample Error } \% = 1.96 \times \sqrt{\frac{2,500}{n}}$$

This is the **maximum margin of sample error** formula we used to create the sample error graph in Figure 10.1 and the sample error percentages in Table 10.2. To determine how much sample error is associated with a random sample of a given size, all you need to do is to plug in the sample size in this formula.

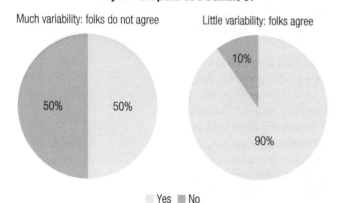

Will your next pizza be a Domino's?

Much variability: folks do not agree

50% / 50%

Little variability: folks agree

10% / 90%

Yes No

FIGURE 10.2 The amount of variability is reflected in the spread of the distribution.

THE CONCEPT OF A CONFIDENCE INTERVAL

The fifth sample size axiom states, *"You can take any finding in the survey, replicate the survey with a random sample of the same size, and be "very likely" to find the same finding within the ±% range of the original sample's finding."* This axiom is based on the concept of a confidence interval.

A **confidence interval** is a range whose endpoints define a certain percentage of the responses to a question. A confidence interval is based on the normal, or bell-shaped, curve commonly found in statistics. Figure 10.3 reveals that the properties of the normal curve are such that 1.96 multiplied by the standard deviation theoretically defines the endpoints for 95% of the distribution.

The theory called the **central limit theorem** underlies many statistical concepts, and this theory is the basis of the fifth axiom. A replication is a repeat of the original, so if we repeated our Domino's survey a great many times—perhaps 1,000—with a fresh random sample of the same size and we made a bar chart of all 1,000 percents of "yes" results, the central limit theorem holds that our bar chart would look like a normal curve. Figure 10.4 illustrates how the bar chart would look if 50% of our population members intended to use Domino's the next time they ordered a pizza.

Figure 10.4 reveals that 95% of the replications fall within ±1.96 multiplied by the sample error. In our example, 1,000 random samples, each with sample size (n) equal to 100, were taken; the percentage of yes answers was calculated for each sample and all of these were plotted in a line chart. The sample error for a sample size of 100 is calculated as follows:

Sample error formula with $p = 50\%$, $q = 50\%$, and $n = 100$

$$\pm \text{ Margin of Sample Error \%} = 1.96 \times \sqrt{\frac{2{,}500}{n}}$$

$$= 1.96 \times \sqrt{\frac{2{,}500}{100}}$$

$$= 1.96 \times \sqrt{25}$$

$$= 1.96 \times 5$$

$$= \pm 9.8$$

The result means that the limit of the 95% confidence interval in our example is 50% ± 9.8%, or 40.2% to 59.8%.

The confidence interval is calculated as follows:

Confidence interval formula

Confidence interval $= p \pm$ margin of sample error

How can a researcher use the confidence interval? This is a good time to leave the theoretical and move to the practical aspects of sample size. The confidence interval approach allows the researcher to predict what would be found if a survey were replicated many times. Of course, no client would agree to the cost of

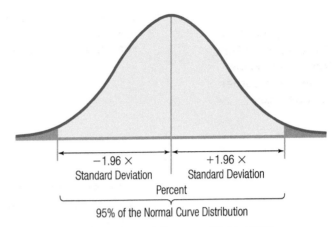

FIGURE 10.3 A Normal Curve with Its 95% Properties Identified

A confidence interval defines endpoints based on knowledge of the area under a bell-shaped curve.

Marketing Research on YouTube™ To learn about the central limit theorem, launch **www.youtube.com** and search for "The Central Limit Theorem … Kahn Academy."

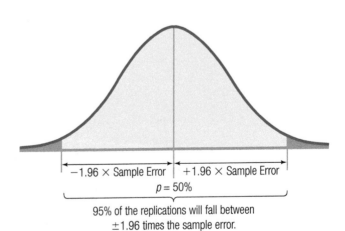

FIGURE 10.4 Plotting the Findings of 1,000 Replications of the Domino's Pizza Survey: Illustration of the Central Limit Theorem

FIGURE 10.5
Sampling Distributions Showing How the Sample Error Is Less with Larger Sample Sizes

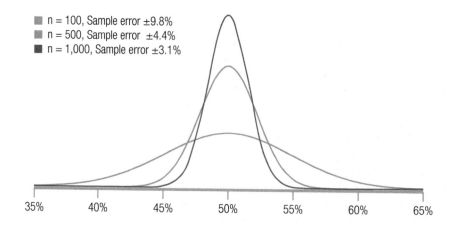

The confidence interval gives the range of findings if the survey were replicated many times with the identical sample size.

1,000 replications, but the researcher can say, "I found that 50% of the sample intends to order Domino's the next time. I am very confident that the true population percent is between 40.2% and 59.8%; in fact, I am confident that if I did this survey over 1,000 times, 95% of the findings will fall in this range." Notice that the researcher never does 1,000 replications; he or she just uses one random sample, uses this sample's accuracy information from p and q, and applies the central limit theorem assumptions to calculate the confidence intervals.

What if the confidence interval was too wide? That is, what if the client felt that a range from about 40% to 60% was not precise enough? Figure 10.5 shows how the sample size affects the shape of the theoretical sampling distribution and, more important, the confidence interval range. Notice in Figure 10.5 that the larger the sample, the smaller the range of the

 Active Learning

How Does the Level of Confidence Affect the Sample Accuracy Curve?

Thus far, the sample error formula has used a z value of 1.96, which corresponds to the 95% level of confidence. However, marketing researchers sometimes use another level of confidence—the 99% level of confidence with the corresponding z value of 2.58. For this Active Learning exercise, use the sample error formula with $p = 50\%$ and $q = 50\%$ but use a z value of 2.58 and calculate the sample error associated with the following sample sizes:

Sample Size (n)	Sample Error (e)
100	±_____%
500	±_____%
1,000	±_____%
2,000	±_____%

Plot your computed sample error ± numbers that correspond to 99% confidence level sample sizes of 100, 500, 1,000, and 2,000 in Figure 10.1. Connect your four plotted points with a curved line similar to the one already in the graph. Use the percentages in Table 10.2 to draw a similar line for the 95% confidence level sample sizes' sample error values. Using your computations and the drawing you have just made, write down two conclusions about the effect of a level of confidence different from 95% on the amount of sample error with samples in the range of the horizontal axis in Figure 10.3.

1. _____

2. _____

confidence interval. Why? Because larger sample sizes have less sample error, meaning that they are more accurate, and the range or width of the confidence interval is smaller with more accurate samples.

HOW POPULATION SIZE (N) AFFECTS SAMPLE SIZE

Perhaps you noticed an element that is absent in these discussions and calculations that is mentioned in the sixth sample size axiom, *"In almost all cases, the margin of sample error of a random sample is independent of the size of the population."* Our formulas do not include *N*, the size of the population! We have been calculating sample error and confidence intervals without taking the size of the population into account. Does this mean that a sample of 100 will have the same sample error and confidence interval of ±9.8% for a population of 20 million people who watched the last Super Bowl, 2 million Kleenex tissue buyers, and 200,000 Scottish terrier owners? Yes, it does. The only time the population size is a consideration in sample size determination[9] is in the case of a "small population," and this possibility is discussed in the final section in this chapter.

With few exceptions, the sample size and the size of the population are not related to each other.

Because the size of the sample is independent of the population size, the seventh sample size axiom, *"A random sample size can be a very tiny percent of the population size and still have a small margin of sample error,"* can now be understood. National opinion polls tend to use sample sizes ranging from 1,000 to 1,200 people, meaning that the sample error is around ±3%, or highly accurate. In Table 10.2, you will see that a sample size of 5,000 yields an error of ±1.4%, which is a very small error level, yet 5,000 is less than 1% of 1 million, and a great many consumer markets—cola drinkers, condominium owners, debit card users, allergy sufferers, home gardeners, Internet surfers, and so on—each comprise many millions of customers. Here is one more example to drive our point home: A sample of 500 is just as accurate for the entire population of China (1.3 billion people) as it is for the Montgomery, Alabama, area (375,000 people) as long as a random sample is taken in both cases. In both cases, the sample error is ±4.4%.

Marketing Research on YouTube™ | To learn about sample size, launch **www.youtube.com** and search for "How sample size is determined."

IBM SPSS
IBM SPSS Student Assistant
Milk Bone Biscuits: Setup Basics for Your IBM SPSS Dataset

10-3   The Sample Size Formula

You are now acquainted with the basic concepts essential to understanding sample size determination using the confidence interval approach. To calculate the proper sample size for a survey, only three items are required: (1) the variability believed to be in the population, (2) the acceptable margin of sample error, and (3) the level of confidence required in your estimates of the population values. This section will describe the formula used to compute sample size via the **confidence interval method**. As we describe the formula, we will present some of the concepts you learned earlier a bit more formally.

To compute sample size, only three items are required: variability, acceptable sample error, and confidence level.

DETERMINING SAMPLE SIZE VIA THE CONFIDENCE INTERVAL FORMULA

As you would expect, there is a formula that includes our three required items.[10] When considering a percentage, the formula is as follows:[11]

Standard sample size formula

$$n = \frac{z^2(pq)}{e^2}$$

where

    n = the sample size

    z = standard error associated with the chosen level of confidence (typically, 1.96)

    p = estimated percent in the population

    q = 100 − *p*

    e = acceptable margin of sample error

The standard sample size formula is applicable if you are concerned with the nominally scaled questions in the survey, such as yes or no questions.

Variability: $p \times q$ This sample size formula is used if we are focusing on some nominally measured question in the survey. For instance, when conducting our Domino's Pizza survey, our major concern might be the percentage of pizza buyers who intend to buy Domino's. If no one is uncertain, there are two possible answers: those who do and those who do not. Earlier we illustrated that if our pizza buyers' population has little variability—that is, if almost everyone, say, 90%, is a Domino's Pizza-holic—this belief will be reflected in the sample size formula calculation. With little variation in the population, we know that we can take smaller samples because this is accommodated in the formula by $p \times q$. The estimated percent in the population, p, is the mechanism that performs this translation along with q, which is always determined by p as $q = 100\% - p$.

Acceptable Margin of Sample Error: e The formula includes another factor—acceptable margin of sample error. **Acceptable margin of sample error** is the term e, which is the amount of sample error the researcher will permit to be associated with the survey. Notice that since we are calculating the sample size, n, the sample error is treated as a variable, meaning that the researcher (and client) will decide on some desirable or allowable level of sample error and then calculate the sample size that will guarantee that the acceptable sample error will be delivered. Recall that sample error is used to indicate how closely to the population percentage you want the many replications, if you were to take them. That is, if we performed any survey with a p value that was to be estimated—who intends to buy from Walmart, IBM, Shell, Allstate, or any other vendor versus any other vendor—the acceptable sample error notion would hold. Small acceptable sample error translates into a low percentage, such as ±3% or less, whereas high acceptable sample error translates into a large percentage, such as ±10% or higher.

Level of Confidence: z Finally, we need to decide on a level of confidence or, to relate to our previous section, the percentage of area under the normal curve described by our calculated confidence intervals. Thus far, we have used the constant 1.96 because 1.96 is the z value that pertains to 95% confidence intervals. Marketing researchers typically worry only about the 95% or 99% level of confidence. The 95% level of confidence is by far the most commonly used one, so we used 1.96 in the examples earlier and referred to it as a constant because it is the chosen z in most cases.

Actually, any level of confidence ranging from 1% to 100% is possible, but you would need to consult a z table to find the corresponding value. Market researchers almost never deviate from 95%, but if they do, 99% is the next likely level to be used. We have itemized the z values for the 99% and 95% levels of confidence in Table 10.3 for easy reference.

We are now finally ready to calculate sample size. Let us assume there is great expected variability ($p = 50\%$, $q = 50\%$) and we want ±10% acceptable sample error at the 95% level of confidence ($z = 1.96$). To determine the sample size needed, we calculate as follows:

Sample size computed with $p = 50\%$, $q = 50\%$, and $e = \pm 10\%$

© Andresr/Shutterstock

Managers sometimes find it unbelievable that a sample can be small yet highly accurate.

In marketing research, a 95% or 99% level of confidence is standard practice.

TABLE 10.3   Values of z for 95% and 99% Levels of Confidence

Level of Confidence	z
95%	1.96
99%	2.58

$$
\begin{aligned}
n &= \frac{1.96^2 \,(50 \times 50)}{10^2} \\
&= \frac{3.84\,(2{,}500)}{100} \\
&= \frac{9{,}600}{100} \\
&= 96
\end{aligned}
$$

For further validation of the use of the confidence interval approach, recall our previous comment that most national opinion polls use sample sizes of about 1,100 and claim about ±3% accuracy (allowable sample error). Using the 95% level of confidence, the computations would be:

Sample size computed with $p = 50\%$, $q = 50\%$, and $e = 3\%$

$$n = \frac{1.96^2 (50 \times 50)}{3^2}$$
$$= \frac{3.84 (2,500)}{9}$$
$$= \frac{9,600}{9}$$
$$= 1,067$$

Marketing Research on YouTube™ | To learn about sample size using proportions, launch **www.youtube.com** and search for "How to calculate sample size proportions."

In other words, if these national polls were to be ±3% accurate at the 95% confidence level, they would need to have sample sizes of 1,067 (or about 1,100 respondents). The next time you read in the news or see a report on a national opinion poll, check the sample size to see if there is a footnote or reference on the "margin of error." It is a good bet that you will find the error to be somewhere close to ±3% and the sample size to be in the 1,100 range.

What if the researcher wanted a 99% level of confidence in estimates? The computations would be as follows:

99% confidence interval sample size with $p = 50\%$, $q = 50\%$, and $e = 3\%$

$$n = \frac{2.58^2 (50 \times 50)}{3^2}$$
$$= \frac{6.66 (2,500)}{9}$$
$$= \frac{16,650}{9}$$
$$= 1,850$$

IBM **SPSS**
IBM SPSS Student Assistant
Milk Bone Biscuits: Modifying Variables and Values

 Active Learning

Sample Size Calculations Practice

While you can mentally follow the step-by-step sample size calculations examples we have just described, it is always more insightful for those just learning about sample size to perform the calculations themselves. In this Active Learning exercise, refer back to the standard sample size formula and use it to calculate the appropriate sample size for each of the following six cases. Each case represents a different question on a survey.

Case	Confidence Level	Value of p	Allowable Error	Sample Size (write your answer below)
Alpha	95%	65%	±3.5%	_____
Beta	99%	75%	±3.5%	_____
Gamma	95%	60%	±5%	_____
Delta	99%	70%	±5%	_____
Epsilon	95%	50%	±2%	_____
Zeta	99%	55%	±2%	_____

MARKETING RESEARCH INSIGHT 10.1   *Practical Application*

Determining Sample Size Using the Mean: An Example of Variability of a Scale

We have presented the standard sample size formula in this chapter, which assumes that the researcher is working with a case of percentages (*p* and *q*). However, there are instances when the reseacher is more concerned with the mean of a variable, in which case the percentage sample size formula does not fit. Instead, the researcher must use a different formula for sample size that includes the variability expressed as a standard deviation. That is, this situation calls for the use of the standard deviation, instead of *p* and *q*, to indicate the amount of variation. In this case, the sample size formula changes slightly to be the following:

Sample size formula for a mean

$$n = \frac{s^2 z^2}{e^2}$$

where

- *n* = the sample size
- *z* = standard error associated with the chosen level of confidence (typically, 1.96)
- *s* = variability indicated by an estimated standard deviation
- *e* = the amount of precision or allowable error in the sample estimate of the population

Although this formula looks different from the one for a percentage, it applies the same logic and key concepts.[12] As you can see, the formula determines sample size by multiplying the squares of the variability (*s*) and level of confidence values (*z*) and dividing that product by the square of the desired precision value (*e*).

First, let us look at how variability of the population is a part of the formula. It appears in the form of *s*, or the estimated standard deviation of the population. This means that, because we are estimating the population mean, we need to have some knowledge of or at least a good guess at how much variability there is in the population. We must use the standard deviation because it expresses this variation. Unfortunately, unlike our percentage sample size case, there is no "50% equals the most variation" counterpart, so we have to rely on some prior knowledge about the population for our estimate of the standard deviation. That prior knowledge could come from a previous study on the same population or a pilot study.

If information on the population variability is truly unknown and a pilot study is out of the question, a researcher can use a range estimate and knowledge that the range is approximated by the mean ±3 standard deviations (a total of 6).

On occasion, a market researcher finds he or she is working with metric scale data rather than nominal data. For instance, the researcher might have a 10-point importance scale or a 7-point satisfaction scale that is the critical variable with respect to determining sample size. Finally, we must express *e*, which is the acceptable error around the sample mean when we ultimately estimate the population mean for our survey. In the formula, *e* must be expressed in terms of the measurement units appropriate to the question. For example, on a 1–10 scale, *e* would be expressed as, say, a 0.25 scale unit.

Suppose, for example, that a critical question on the survey involved a scale in which respondents rated their satisfaction with the client company's products on a scale of 1 to 10. If respondents use this scale, the theoretical range would be 10, and 10 divided by 6 equals a standard deviation of 1.7, which would be the variability estimate. Note that this would be a conservative estimate, as respondents might not use the entire 1–10 scale, or the mean might not equal 5, the midpoint, meaning that 1.7 is the largest variability estimate possible in this case.[13]

Thus, if a survey were to have ±3% allowable sample error at the 99% level of confidence, it would need to have a sample size of 1,850, assuming the maximum variability (50%).

A researcher can calculate sample size using either a percentage or a mean. We have just described (and you have just used in the Active Learning exercise) the percentage approach to computing sample size. Marketing Research Insight 10.1 describes how to determine sample size using a mean. Although the formulas are different, the basic concepts involved are identical.

10-4   Practical Considerations in Sample Size Determination

Although we have discussed how variability, acceptable sample error, and confidence level are used to calculate sample size, we have not discussed the criteria used by the marketing manager and researcher to determine these factors. General guidelines follow.

HOW TO ESTIMATE VARIABILITY IN THE POPULATION

When applying the standard sample size formula using percentages, there are two alternatives: (1) expect the worst case or (2) guesstimate the actual variability. We have shown that with percentages the greatest or **worst-case variability** is 50%/50%. This assumption is the most conservative one, and it will result in the calculation of the largest possible sample size.

On the other hand, a researcher may want to use an educated guess about *p*, or the percentage, in order to lower the sample size. Remember that any *p/q* combination other than 50%/50% will result in a lower calculated sample size because *p* times *q* is in the numerator of the formula. A lower sample size means less effort, time, and cost, so there are good reasons for a researcher to try to estimate *p* rather than to take the worst case.

Surprisingly, information about the target population often exists in many forms. Researchers can estimate variance in a population by seeking prior studies on the population or by conducting a small pilot study. Census descriptions are available in the form of secondary data, and compilations and bits of information may be gained from groups such as chambers of commerce, local newspapers, state agencies, groups promoting commercial development, and a host of other similar organizations. Moreover, many populations under study by firms are known to them either formally through prior research studies or informally through business experiences. All of this information combines to help the research project director to grasp the variability in the population. If the project director has conflicting information or is worried about the timeliness or some other aspect of the information about the population's variability, he or she may conduct a pilot study to estimate *p* more confidently.[14,15]

> When estimating a standard deviation, researchers may rely on (a) prior knowledge of the population (previous study), (b) a pilot study, or (c) divide the range by 6.

> By estimating *p* to be other than 50%, the researcher can reduce the sample size and save money.

> Researchers can estimate variability by (a) assuming maximum variability ($p = 50\%$, $q = 50\%$), (b) seeking previous studies on the population, or (c) conducting a small pilot study.

HOW TO DETERMINE THE AMOUNT OF ACCEPTABLE SAMPLE ERROR

The marketing manager intuitively knows that small samples are less accurate, on average, than are large samples. But it is rare for a marketing manager to think in terms of sample error. It is up to the researcher to educate the manager on what might be acceptable or "standard" sample error.

Translated in terms of accuracy, the more accurate the marketing decision maker desires the estimate to be, the larger must be the sample size. It is the task of the marketing research director to extract from the marketing decision maker the acceptable range of allowable margin of error sufficient to make a decision. As you have learned, the acceptable sample error is specified as a plus or minus percent. That is, the researcher might say to the marketing decision maker, "I can deliver an estimate that is within ±10% of the actual figure." If the marketing manager is confused at this, the researcher can next say, "This means that if I find that 45% of the sample is thinking seriously about leaving your competitors and buying your brand, I will be telling you that I estimate that between 35% and 55% of your competitors' buyers are thinking about jumping over to be your customers." The conversation would continue until the marketing manager feels comfortable with the confidence interval range.

> Marketing researchers often must help decision makers understand the sample size implications of their requests for high precision, expressed as acceptable sample error.

HOW TO DECIDE ON THE LEVEL OF CONFIDENCE

All marketing decisions are made under a certain amount of risk, and it is mandatory to incorporate the estimate of risk, or at least some sort of a notion of uncertainty, into sample size determination. Because sample statistics are estimates of population values, the proper approach is to use the sample information to generate a range in which the population value is anticipated to fall. Because the sampling process is imperfect, it is appropriate to use an estimate of sampling error in the calculation of this range. Using proper statistical terminology, the range is what we have called the confidence interval. The researcher reports the range and the confidence he or she has that the range includes the population figure.

As we have indicated, the typical approach in marketing research is to use the standard confidence interval of 95%. This level translates to a *z* of 1.96. As you may recall from your statistics course, any level of confidence between 1% and 99.9% is possible, but the only other level of confidence that market researchers usually consider is 99%. With the 99% level

> Use of 95% or 99% level of confidence is standard in sample size determination.

of confidence, the corresponding z value is 2.58. The 99% level of confidence means that if the survey were replicated many times with the sample size determined by using 2.58 in the sample size formula, 99% of the sample p's would fall in the sample error range, or e.

However, since the z value is in the numerator of the sample size formula, an increase from 1.96 to 2.58 will increase the sample size. In fact, for any given sample error, the use of the 99% level of confidence will increase sample size by about 73%. In other words, using the 99% confidence level has profound effects on the calculated sample size. Are you surprised that most marketing researchers opt for a z of 1.96?

HOW TO BALANCE SAMPLE SIZE WITH THE COST OF DATA COLLECTION

The researcher must take cost into consideration when determining sample size.

Perhaps you thought we had forgotten the final sample size axiom, "***The size of a random sample depends on the client's desired accuracy (acceptable margin of sample error) balanced against the cost of data collection for that sample size.***" This is a crucial axiom, as it describes the reality of almost all sample size determination decisions. In a previous chapter, we commented on the cost of the research versus the value of the research and that there is always a need to make sure that the cost of the research does not exceed the value of the information expected from that research. In situations where data collection costs are significant, such as with personal interviews or in the case of buying access to online panel respondents, cost and value issues come into play vividly with sample size determination.[16] Because using the 99% level of confidence impacts sample size considerably, market researchers almost always use the 95% level of confidence.

To help you understand how to balance sample size and cost, let's consider the typical sample size determination case. First, a 95% level of confidence is used, so $z = 1.96$. Next, the $p = q = 50\%$ situation is customarily assumed, as it is the worst possible case of variability. Then the researcher and marketing manager decide on a *preliminary* acceptable sample error level. As an example, let's take the case of a researcher and a client initially agreeing to a ±3.5% sample error.

Using the sample size formula, the sample size, n, is calculated as follows.

Sample size computed with $p = 50\%$, $q = 50\%$, and $e = 3.5\%$

$$n = \frac{1.96^2 (50 \times 50)}{3.5^2}$$
$$= 3.84 (2{,}500)$$
$$= \frac{9{,}604}{12.25}$$
$$= 784 \ (rounded\ up)$$

A table that relates data collection cost and sample error is a useful tool when deciding on the survey sample size.

If the cost per completed interview averages around $20, then the cost of data collection for a sample size is 784 times $20, which equals $15,680. The client now knows the sample size necessary for a ±3.5% sample error and the cost for these interviews. If the client has issues with this cost, the researcher may create a table with alternative accuracy levels and their associated sample sizes based on knowing the standard sample size formula. The table could also include the data collection cost estimates so that the client can make an informed decision on the acceptable sample size. Although not every researcher creates a table such as this, the acceptable sample errors and the costs of various sample sizes are most certainly discussed when coming to an agreement on the survey's sample size. In most cases, the final agreed-to sample size is a trade-off between acceptable error and research cost. Marketing Research Insight 10.2 presents an example of how this trade-off occurs.

10-5 Other Methods of Sample Size Determination

In practice, a number of different methods are used to determine sample size, including some that are beyond the scope of this textbook.[17] The more common methods are described briefly in this section. As you will soon learn, most have limitations that make them undesirable, even

MARKETING RESEARCH INSIGHT 10.2   *Practical Application*

How Clients and Marketing Researchers Agree on Sample Size

In this fictitious example, we describe how sample size is determined for a survey for a water park owner who is thinking about adding an exciting new ride to be called "The Frantic Flume."

Larry, our marketing researcher, has worked with Dana, the water park owner, to develop the research objectives and basic research design for a survey to see if there is sufficient interest in the Frantic Flume ride. Yesterday, Dana indicated she wanted to have an accuracy level of ±3.5% because this was "just a little less accurate than your typical national opinion poll."

Larry did some calculations and created the following table, which he faxed to Dana.

The Frantic Flume Survey Sample Size, Sample Error, and Sample Data Collection Cost

Sample Size	Sample Error	Sample Cost*
784	±3.5%	$15,680
600	±4.0%	$12,000
474	±4.5%	$9,480
384	±5.0%	$7,680
317	±5.5%	$6,340
267	±6.0%	$5,340

*Estimated at $20 per completed interview

The following phone conversation now takes place.

LARRY: Did the fax come through okay?

DANA: Yes, but maybe I wish it didn't.

LARRY: What do you mean?

DANA: There is no way I am going to pay over $15,000 just for the data collection.

LARRY: Yes, I figured this when we talked yesterday, but we were talking about the accuracy of a national opinion poll then. Now we are talking about your water park survey. So I prepared a schedule with some alternative sample sizes, their accuracy levels, and their costs.

DANA: Gee, can you really get an accuracy level of ±6% with just 267 respondents? That seems like a very small sample.

LARRY: Small in numbers, but it is still somewhat hefty in price, as the data collection company will charge $20 per completed telephone interview. You can see that it will still amount to over $5,000.

DANA: Well, that's nowhere near $15,000! What about the 384 size? It will come to $7,680 according to your table, and the accuracy is ±5%. How does the accuracy thing work again?

LARRY: If I find that, say, 70% of the respondents in the random sample of your customers want the Frantic Flume at your water park, then you can be assured that between 65% and 75% of all of your customers want it.

DANA: And with $7,680 for data collection, the whole survey comes in under $15,000?

LARRY: I am sure it will. I can calculate a firm total cost using the 384 sample size.

DANA: Sounds like a winner to me. When can you get it to me?

LARRY: I'll have the proposal completed by Friday. You can study it over the weekend.

DANA: Great. I'll set up a tentative meeting with the investors for the middle of next week.

though you may find instances in which they are used and proponents who argue for their use. Since you are acquainted with the eight sample size axioms and you know how to calculate sample size using the confidence interval method formula, you should comprehend the limitations as we point out each one.

ARBITRARY "PERCENT RULE OF THUMB" SAMPLE SIZE

The **arbitrary approach** may take on the guise of a "percent rule of thumb" statement regarding sample size: "A sample should be at least 5% of the population in order to be accurate." In fact, it is not unusual for a marketing manager to respond to a marketing researcher's sample size recommendation by saying, "But that is less than 1% of the entire population!"

Arbitrary sample size approaches rely on erroneous rules of thumb.

You must agree that the arbitrary percentage rule of thumb approach certainly has some intuitive appeal in that it is very easy to remember, and it is simple to apply. Surely, you will not fall into the seductive trap of the percent rule of thumb, for you understand that sample size is not related to population size. Just to convince yourself, consider these sample sizes.

If you take 5% samples of populations with sizes 10,000, 1 million, and 10 million, the n's will be 500, 50,000, and 500,000, respectively. Now, think back to the sample accuracy graph (Figure 10.1). The highest sample size on that graph was 2,000, so obviously the percent rule of thumb method can yield sample sizes that are absurd with respect to accuracy. Further, you have also learned from the sample size axioms that a sample can be a very small percentage of the total population and have great accuracy.

Arbitrary sample sizes are simple and easy to apply, but they are neither efficient nor economical.

In sum, arbitrary sample sizes are simple and easy to apply, but they are neither efficient nor economical. With sampling, we wish to draw a subset of the population in a thrifty manner and to estimate the population values with some predetermined degree of accuracy. "Percent rule of thumb" methods lose sight of the accuracy aspect of sampling; they certainly violate some of the axioms about sample size and, as you just saw, they certainly are not cost-effective when the population under study is large.

CONVENTIONAL SAMPLE SIZE SPECIFICATION

Using conventional sample size can result in a sample that may be too small or too large.

The **conventional approach** follows some "convention" or number believed somehow to be the right sample size. Managers who are knowledgeable of national opinion polls may notice that they are often taken with sample sizes of between 1,000 and 1,200 respondents. They may question marketing researchers whose sample size recommendations vary from this convention. On the other hand, a survey may be one in a series of studies a company has undertaken on a particular market, and the same sample size may be applied each succeeding year simply because it was used last year. The convention might be an average of the sample sizes of similar studies, it might be the largest sample size of previous surveys, or it might be equal to the sample size of a competitor's survey the company somehow discovered.

Conventional sample sizes ignore the special circumstances of the survey at hand.

The basic difference between a percent rule of thumb and a conventional sample size determination is that the first approach has no defensible logic, whereas the conventional approach appears logical. However, the logic is faulty. We just illustrated how a percent rule of thumb approach such as a 5% rule of thumb explodes into huge sample sizes very quickly; conversely, the national opinion poll convention of 1,200 respondents would be constant regardless of the population size. Still, this characteristic is one of the conventional sample size determination method's weaknesses, for it assumes that (1) the manager wants an accuracy of around ±3% and (2) there is maximum variability in the population.

Adopting past sample sizes or taking those used by other companies can be criticized as well, for both approaches assume that whoever determined sample size in the previous studies did so correctly—that is, not with a flawed method. If a flawed method was used, you simply perpetuate the error by copying it, and if the sample size method used was not flawed, the circumstances and assumptions surrounding the predecessor's survey may be very different from those encompassing the present one. The conventional sample size approach ignores the circumstances surrounding the study at hand and may well prove to be much more costly than would be the case if the sample size were determined correctly.

The conventional approach mistakenly uses a "cookie cutter" that results in the same sample size for every survey.

STATISTICAL ANALYSIS REQUIREMENTS SAMPLE SIZE SPECIFICATION

On occasion, a sample's size will be determined using a **statistical analysis approach**, meaning that the researcher wishes to perform a particular type of data analysis that has sample size requirements.[18] In truth, the sample size formulas in this chapter are appropriate for the simplest data analyses.[19] We have not discussed statistical procedures as yet in this text, but we can assure you that some advanced techniques require certain minimum sample sizes to be reliable or to safeguard the validity of their statistical results.[20] Sample sizes based on statistical analysis criteria can be quite large.[21]

Sometimes a research objective is to perform subgroup analysis,[22] which is an investigation of subsegments within the population. As you would expect, the desire to gain knowledge about subgroups has direct implications for sample size.[23] It should be possible to look at each subgroup as a separate population and to determine sample size for each subgroup, along with the appropriate methodology and other specifics to gain knowledge about that subgroup. That is, if you were to use the standard sample size formula described in this chapter to determine the sample size and more than one subgroup was to be analyzed fully, this objective would require a total sample size equal to the number of subgroups multiplied by the standard sample size formula's computed sample size.[24] Once this is accomplished, all subgroups can be combined into a large group to obtain a complete population picture. If a researcher is using a statistical technique, he or she should have a sample size large enough to satisfy the assumptions of the technique. Still, a researcher needs to know if that minimum sample size is large enough to give the desired level of accuracy.

Sometimes the researcher's desire to use particular statistical techniques influences sample size.

COST BASIS OF SAMPLE SIZE SPECIFICATION

Sometimes termed the **"all you can afford" approach**, this method uses cost as an overriding basis for sample size. Returning to the eighth sample size axiom, managers and marketing research professionals are vitally concerned with the costs of data collection because they can mount up quickly, particularly for personal interviews, telephone surveys, and even mail surveys in which incentives are included in the envelopes. Thus, it is not surprising that cost sometimes becomes the only basis for sample size.

Exactly how the "all you can afford" approach is applied varies a great deal. In some instances, the marketing research project budget is determined in advance, and set amounts are specified for each phase. Here, the budget may have, for instance, $10,000 for interviewing, or it might specify $5,000 for data collection. A variation is for the entire year's marketing research budget amount to be set and to have each project carve out a slice of that total. With this approach, the marketing research project director is forced to stay within the total project budget, but he or she can allocate the money across the various cost elements, and the sample size ends up being whatever is affordable within the budget.

Using cost as the sole determinant of sample size may seem wise, but it is not.

Specifying sample size based on a predetermined budget is a case of the tail wagging the dog. That is, instead of establishing the value of the information to be gained from the survey as the primary consideration in determining sample size, the focus is on budget factors that usually ignore the value of the survey's results to management. In addition, this approach certainly does not consider sample accuracy at all. In fact, because many managers harbor a large sample size bias, it is possible that their marketing research project costs are overstated for data collection when smaller sample sizes could have sufficed quite well. As can be seen in our Marketing Research Insight 10.3, the Marketing Research Association Code of Ethics excerpt warns that marketing researchers should not misrepresent sample methodology; the code labels as unscrupulous taking advantage of any large sample size biases in clients as a means of charging a high price or inflating the importance of the findings.

Still, as the final sample size axiom advises, marketing researchers and their clients cannot decide on sample size without taking cost into consideration. The key is to remember *when* to consider cost. In the "all you can afford" examples we just described, cost drives the sample size determination completely. When we have $5,000 for interviewing and a data collection company tells us it charges $25 per completed interview, our sample is set at 200 respondents. However, the correct approach is to consider cost relative to the value of the research to the manager. If the manager requires extremely precise information, the researcher will surely suggest a large sample and then estimate the cost of obtaining the sample. The manager, in turn, should then consider this cost in relation to how much the information is actually worth. Using the cost schedule concept, the researcher and manager can then discuss alternative sample sizes, different data collection modes, costs, and other considerations. This is a healthier situation, for now the manager is assuming some ownership of the survey and

The appropriateness of using cost as a basis for sample size depends on when cost factors are considered.

Marketing Research Association Code of Ethics: Sample Considerations

Sample—All sample-based research (qualitative and quantitative) should state parameters of the sample design employed. These include information on:

- Population of interest
- Probability or non-probability design, with specifics on selection method, such as simple random, multistage, etc.
- Estimated population incidence of sample elements or segments
- Sampling frame and estimated degree of population coverage
- Sample size
- Cooperation and or response rates, as appropriate

Source: Used courtesy of the Marketing Research Association.

- Margin of error on the total sample and key segments of interest (for probability designs)

3. Influence no respondent's opinion or attitude through direct or indirect attempts, including the framing or order of questions.
During screening, prequalification or other qualification procedures and data collection, great care must be taken to source and collect information impartially so that research results accurately reflect reality.

Exceptions: Projects intending to determine how opinions can be manipulated such as message testing.

a partnership arrangement is being forged between the manager and the researcher. The net result will be a better understanding on the part of the manager as to how and why the final sample size was determined. This way cost will not be the only means of determining sample size, but it will be given the consideration it deserves.

10-6   Three Special Sample Size Determination Situations

In concluding our exploration of sample size, let's take up three special cases: sample size when sampling from small populations, sample size when using a nonprobability sampling method, and panel samples.

SAMPLING FROM SMALL POPULATIONS

Implicit to all sample size discussions thus far in this chapter is the assumption that the population is very large. This assumption is reasonable because there are multitudes of households in the United States, millions of registered drivers, millions of persons over the age of 65, and so forth. It is common, especially with consumer goods and services marketers, to draw samples from very large populations. Occasionally, however, the population is much smaller. This is not unusual in the case of B2B marketers. This case is addressed by the condition stipulated in our sixth sample size axiom, "In almost all cases, the accuracy (margin of sample error) of a random sample is independent of the size of the population."

> With small populations, you should use the finite multiplier to determine sample size.

As a general rule, a **small population** situation is one in which the sample exceeds 5% of the total population size. Notice that a small population is defined by the size of the sample under consideration. If the sample is less than 5% of the total population, you can consider the population to be of large size, and you can use the procedures described earlier in this chapter. On the other hand, if it is a small population, the sample size formula needs some adjustment with what is called a **finite multiplier**, which is an adjustment factor that is approximately equal to the square root of that proportion of the population not included in the sample. For instance, suppose our population size was considered to be 1,000 companies and we decided to take a sample of 500. That would result in a finite multiplier of about 0.71, or the square root of 0.5, which is ([1,000 − 500]/1,000). That is, we could use a sample of only 355 (or 0.71 × 500) companies, and it would be just as accurate as one of size 500 if we had a large population.

The formula for computation of a sample size using the finite multiplier is as follows:

Small population sample size formula

$$\text{Small Population Sample Size} = \text{sample size formula } n \times \sqrt{\frac{N - n}{N - 1}}$$

Here is an example using the 1,000 company population. Suppose we want to know the percentage of companies interested in a substance abuse counseling program for their employees offered by a local hospital. We are uncertain about the variability, so we use our 50/50 worst-case approach. We decide to use a 95% level of confidence, and the director of Counseling Services at Claremont Hospital would like the results to have an accuracy of ±5%. The computations are as follows:

Sample size computed with p = 50%, q = 50%, and e = 5%

$$
\begin{aligned}
n &= \frac{1.96^2 \, (pq)}{e^2} \\
&= \frac{1.96^2 \, (50 \times 50)}{5^2} \\
&= \frac{3.84 \, (2,500)}{25} \\
&= \frac{9,600}{25} \\
&= 384
\end{aligned}
$$

Now, since 384 is larger than 5% of the 1,000 company population, we apply the finite multiplier to adjust the sample size for a small population:

Example: Sample size formula to adjust for a small population size

$$
\begin{aligned}
\text{Small Size Population Sample} &= n\sqrt{\frac{N - n}{N - 1}} \\
&= 384\sqrt{\frac{1,000 - 384}{1,000 - 1}} \\
&= 384\sqrt{\frac{616}{999}} \\
&= 384\sqrt{.62} \\
&= 384 \times .79 \\
&= 303
\end{aligned}
$$

In other words, we need a sample size of 303, not 384, because we are working with a small population. By applying the finite multiplier, we can reduce the sample size by 81 respondents and achieve the same accuracy level. If this survey required personal interviews, we would gain a considerable cost savings.

> Appropriate use of the finite multiplier formula will reduce a calculated sample size and save money when performing research on small populations.

SAMPLE SIZE USING NONPROBABILITY SAMPLING

All sample size formulas and other statistical considerations treated in this chapter assume that some form of probability sampling method has been used. In other words, the sample must be random with regard to selection, and the only sampling error present is due to sample size. Remember, sample size determines the accuracy, not the representativeness, of the sample. The sampling method determines the representativeness. All sample size formulas assume that representativeness is guaranteed with use of a random sampling procedure.

> When using nonprobability sampling, sample size is unrelated to accuracy, so cost–benefit considerations must be used.

Synthesize Your Learning ───────────────────────

This exercise will require you to take into consideration concepts and material from these two chapters.

Chapter 9	Selecting the Sample
Chapter 10	Determining the Size of a Sample

Niagara Falls Tourism Association

One of the most popular tourist destinations in the United States is Niagara Falls, located on the U.S.–Canada border in northern New York. An estimated 12 million tourists visit Niagara Falls each year. However, while its attractiveness has not changed, environmental factors have recently threatened to significantly decrease these numbers. At least three factors are at work: (1) a sluggishly recovering national economy, (2) the substantial weakening of the global economy, and (3) increased competition by beefed-up marketing efforts of other tourist attractions that are experiencing declines due to the first two factors.

A large majority of Niagara Falls visitors are Americans who drive to the location, so family financial worries have the Niagara Falls Tourism Association especially concerned. The association represents all types of businesses in the greater Niagara area that rely on tourism. Among their members are 80 hotels that account for approximately 16,000 rooms. The hotels have anywhere from 20 to 600 rooms, with a large majority (about 80%, accounting for 30% of the rooms) being local and smaller, and the larger ones (the remaining 20%, accounting for 70% of the rooms) being national chains and larger. For all hotels in the area, occupancy at peak season (June 15–September 15) averages around 90%. The association wants to conduct a survey of current visitors to evaluate their overall satisfaction with their visit to the Niagara area and their intentions to tell friends, relatives, and coworkers to visit Niagara Falls. The association has designed a face-to-face interview questionnaire, and it has issued a request for proposals for sample design. It has received three bids, each of which is described here.

Bid 1. The Maid of the Mist union—employees of the company that operates the boats that take tourists on the Niagara River to view and experience the falls—proposes to do the interviews with tourists who are waiting for the Maid boats to return and load up. Union employees will conduct interviews with 1,000 adult American tourists (one per family group) during a one-week period in July at $3 per completed interview.

Bid 2. The Simpson Research Company, a local marketing research company, proposes to take a sample of the five largest association member hotels and conduct 200 interviews in the lobbies of these hotels with American tourists (one per family) during the months of July and August at a cost of $5 per completed interview.

Bid 3. The SUNY-Niagara Marketing Department, an academic unit in the local university, proposes to randomly select 20 hotels from all hotels in the area (not just those belonging to the Tourism Association) and to then select a proportional random sample of rooms, using room numbers, from each selected hotel based on hotel room capacities. It will interview 750 American tourists (one per family) in their rooms during the period of June 15–September 15 at a cost of $10 per completed interview.

Questions

1. What is the sample frame in each bid?
2. Identify the type of sample method and assess the representativeness of the sample with respect to American tourists visiting the Niagara Falls area.
3. Evaluate the accuracy (sample error) with each bid.
4. The Niagara Falls Tourism Association has budgeted $5,000 for data collection in this survey. Using information from your answers to questions 1 to 3 and further considering the total cost of data collection, which one of the proposals do you recommend that the Niagara Falls Tourist Association accept? Justify your recommendation.

The only reasonable way of determining sample size with nonprobability sampling is to weigh the benefit or value of the information obtained with that sample against the cost of gathering that information. Ultimately, this is a subjective exercise, as the manager may place significant value on the information for a number of reasons. For instance, the information may crystallize the problem, it may open the manager's eyes to vital additional considerations, or it might even make him or her aware of previously unknown market segments.[25] But because of the unknown bias introduced by a haphazard sample selection[26] process, it is inappropriate to apply sample size formulas. For nonprobability sampling, sample size is a judgment based almost exclusively on the value of the biased information to the manager, rather than desired precision, relative to cost. Many managers do select nonprobability sampling plans, knowing their limitations. In these cases, the sample size question is basically, "How many people will it take for me to feel comfortable in making a decision?"

IBM **SPSS**

IBM SPSS Student Assistant
Coca-Cola: Sorting, Searching, and Inserting Variables and Cases

SAMPLING FROM PANELS

As has been noted several times in this textbook, many prospective respondents refuse to take part in surveys, and this fact severely impacts the accuracy of the final sample. That is, sample size formulas assume 100% response rates: every person chosen takes part in the survey. Or, if anyone refuses, it is assumed that a perfectly identical person is drawn as a substitute. So, as also has been described earlier, panel companies recruit hundreds of thousands of panel members who take surveys for various types of compensation. Using a panel company is somewhat expensive, but it is expedient and guarantees delivery of the specified number of completed surveys. Most panel companies claim random selection of some sort, so there is the appearance of a random sample of the population. Consequently, it is common practice for marketing researchers, particularly the do-it-yourselfers, to consider a panel sample to be a random sample.

The truth is, however, that because panel members are volunteers who take part in surveys often, they are not truly representative of the general population. Panel samples are at best representative of the panel populations from which they are drawn. Often the panel population is a reasonable sample frame, and companies are content with the accuracy levels marketing researchers ascribe to their panel samples. Unfortunately, every panel is unique, and universal acceptance or condemnation of the integrity of a sample drawn from panel members is unacceptable. The marketing research industry is in the process of examining and generating guidelines for the assessment of the accuracy of panel samples.[27] For instance, recommendations have been put forth for diligent review of all responses to catch cheaters and speeders, for careful definition of sample parameters and selection criteria, for inspection to weed out respondents who take excessive amounts of surveys, and for scrutiny of IP addresses to ensure that international survey participants are located in countries they represent. At this time, panel sample integrity and accuracy are a work in progress that most probably will ultimately be incorporated in the Marketing Research Association Code of Ethics.

Summary

Many managers adhere to the "large sample size" bias. To counter this myth, eight sample size axioms relate the size of a random sample to its accuracy, or closeness of its findings to the true population value. These axioms are the basis for the confidence interval sample size determination method, which is the most correct method because it relies on sound logic based upon the statistical concepts of variability, confidence intervals, and margin of sample error.

When estimating a percentage, marketing researchers rely on a standard sample size formula that uses variability (p and q), level of confidence (z), and acceptable margin of sample error (e) to compute the sample size, n. Confidence levels of 95% or 99% are typically applied, equating to z values of 1.96 and 2.58, respectively. For variability with percentage estimates, the researcher can fall back on a 50%/50% split, which is the greatest variability case possible. When estimating a mean, another formula is used. The standard sample size formula is best considered a starting point for deciding the final sample size, for data collection costs must be taken into consideration. Normally, the researcher and manager will discuss the alternative sample error levels and their associated data collection costs to come to agreement on a final acceptable sample size.

Although they have limitations, there are other methods of determining sample size: (1) designating size arbitrarily, (2) using a "conventional" size, (3) basing size on the requirements of statistical procedures to be used, and (4) letting cost determine the size. Two sampling situations raise special considerations. With a small population, the finite multiplier should be used to adjust the sample size determination formula. With nonprobability sampling, a cost–benefit analysis should take place.

Key Terms

Sample accuracy (p. 264)
Large sample size bias (p. 265)
Confidence interval approach (p. 265)
Nonsampling error (p. 266)
Margin of sampling error (p. 267)
Variability (p. 267)
Maximum margin of sample error
  (p. 268)

Confidence interval (p. 269)
Central limit theorem (p. 269)
Confidence interval method
  (p. 271)
Acceptable margin of sample error
  (p. 272)
Worst-case variability (p. 275)
Arbitrary approach (p. 277)

Conventional approach (p. 278)
Statistical analysis approach
  (p. 278)
"All you can afford" approach
  (p. 279)
Small population (p. 280)
Finite multiplier (p. 280)

Review Questions/Applications

10-1. When determining sample size, what is the basic difference between a "percent rule of thumb" approach and a "conventional" approach?

10-2. What is the confidence interval formula for calculating sample size? Describe all the elements of the formula.

10-3. What are the disadvantages of using the "all you can afford" approach when determining sample size?

10-4. What are some of the methods that researchers could employ while estimating standard deviation?

10-5. Dabur wants to conduct a nationwide quantitative study to map the usage of almond oil. However, the variability is unknown to the manager, who wishes to calculate the sample size that she might need to conduct the research. She wants a confidence level of 95% with precision (allowable error) of ±5%. Determine the sample size using the formula in the text, and arrive at a figure that the manager could use in this case, where the variability is unknown.

10-6. How can sample size and the cost of data collection be balanced?

10-7. What is a *worst-case variability*?

10-8. What is a *small population*? What is a finite multiplier in the context of a small population?

10-9. A researcher knows from experience the average costs of various data collection alternatives:

Data Collection Method	Cost/Respondent
Personal interview	$50
Telephone interview	$25
Mail survey	$ 0.50 (per mail-out)

If $2,500 is allocated in the research budget for data collection, what are the levels of accuracy for the sample sizes allowable for each data collection method? Based on your findings, comment on the inappropriateness of using cost as the only means of determining sample size.

10-10. Hamdard Laboratories, a manufacturer of alternative medicines based in India, conducted a study last year and found that 30% of the public preferred alternative medicine over mainstream modern medicine for skin- and hair-related problems. This year, the company wants to have a nationwide telephone survey performed with random digit dialing. What sample size should be used in this year's study to achieve an accuracy level of ±2.5% at the 99% level of confidence? What about at the 95% level of confidence?

10-11. Allbookstores.com has a used textbook division. It buys its books in bulk from used book buyers who set up kiosks on college campuses during final exams, and it sells the used textbooks to students who log on to the allbookstores.com website via a secured credit card transaction. The used texts are then sent by United Parcel Service to the student. The company has conducted a survey of used book buying by college students each year for the past four years. In each survey, 1,000 randomly selected college students have been asked to indicate whether they bought a used textbook in the previous year. The results are as follows:

	Years Ago			
	1	2	3	4
Percent buying used text(s)	45%	50%	60%	70%

What are the sample size implications of these data?

10-12. American Ceramics, Inc. (ACI) has been developing a new form of ceramic that can withstand high temperatures and sustained use. Because of its improved properties, the project development engineer in charge of this project thinks the new ceramic will compete as a substitute for the ceramic currently used in spark plugs. She talks to ACI's marketing research director about conducting a survey of prospective buyers of the new ceramic material. During their phone conversation, the research director suggests a study using about 100 companies as a means of determining market demand. Later that day, the research director does some background work using the Thomas Register as a source of names of companies manufacturing spark plugs. A total of 312 companies located in the continental United States are found in the register. How should this finding impact the final sample size of the survey?

10-13. Here are some numbers you can use to sharpen your computational skills for sample size determination. Crest toothpaste is reviewing plans for its annual survey of toothpaste purchasers. With each case that follows, calculate the sample size pertaining to the key variable under consideration. Where information is missing, provide reasonable assumptions.

	Key Variable	Variability	Acceptable Error	Confidence Level
a	Market share of Crest toothpaste last year	23% share	4%	95%
b	Percent of people who brush their teeth per week	Unknown	5%	99%
c	How likely Crest buyers are to switch brands	30% switched last year	5%	95%
d	Percent of people who want tartar-control features in their toothpaste	20% two years ago; 40% one year ago	3.5%	95%
e	Willingness of people to adopt the toothpaste brand recommended by their family dentist	Unknown	6%	99%

10-14. Do managers really have a large sample size bias? Because you cannot survey managers easily, this exercise will use surrogates. Ask any five seniors majoring in business administration who have not taken a marketing research class the following questions. Indicate whether each of the following statements is true or false.

a. A random sample of 500 is large enough to represent all full-time college students in the United States.

b. A random sample of 1,000 is large enough to represent all full-time college students in the United States.

c. A random sample of 2,000 is large enough to represent all full-time college students in the United States.

d. A random sample of 5,000 is large enough to represent all full-time college students in the United States.

What have you found out about sample size bias?

10-15. The following items pertain to determining sample size when a mean is involved. Calculate the sample size for each case.

	Key Variable	Standard Deviation	Acceptable Error	Confidence Level
a	Number of car rentals per year for business trip usage	10	2	95%
b	Number of songs downloaded with iTunes per month	20	2	95%
c	Number of miles driven per year to commute to work	500	50	99%
d	Use of a 9-point scale measuring satisfaction with the brand	2	0.3	95%

10-16. The Andrew Jergens Company markets Wet Skin Moisturizers, which are applied to a woman's skin while she takes a shower. From previous research, Jergens management knows that 60% of all women use some form of skin moisturizer and 30% believe their skin is their most beautiful asset. There is some concern among management that women will associate the drying aspects of taking a shower while applying Wet Skin Moisturizer and not believe that it can provide a skin moisturizing benefit. Can these facts about use of moisturizers and concern for skin beauty be used in determining the size of the sample in the Wet Skin Moisturizers survey? If so, indicate how. If not, indicate why and how sample size can be determined.

10-17. Donald Heel is the Microwave Oven Division Manager of Sharp Products. Don proposes a $40 cash rebate program as a means of promoting Sharp's new crisp-broil-and-grill microwave oven. However, the Sharp president wants evidence that the program would increase sales by at least 25%, so Don applies some of his research budget to a survey. He uses the National Phone Systems Company to conduct a nationwide survey using random digit dialing. National Phone Systems is a fully integrated telephone polling company, and it has the capability of providing daily tabulations. Don decides to use this option, and instead of specifying a final sample size, he chooses to have National Phone Systems perform 50 completions each day. At the end of five days of fieldwork, the daily results are as follows:

Day	1	2	3	4	5
Total sample size	50	100	150	200	250
Percentage of respondents who would consider buying a Sharp microwave with a $40 rebate	50%	40%	35%	30%	33%

For how much longer should Don continue the survey? Indicate your rationale.

CASE 10.1

Target: Deciding on the Number of Telephone Numbers

Target is a major retail store chain specializing in good-quality merchandise and good values for its customers. Currently, Target operates about 1,700 stores, including more than 200 "Super Targets," in major metropolitan areas in 48 states. One of the core marketing strategies employed by Target is to ensure that shoppers have a special experience every time they shop at Target. This special shopping experience is enhanced by Target's "intuitive" department arrangements. For example, toys are next to sporting goods. Another shopping experience feature is the "racetrack" or extra wide center aisle that helps shoppers navigate the store easily and quickly. A third feature is the aesthetic appearance of its shelves, product displays, and seasonal specials. Naturally, Target continuously monitors the opinions and satisfaction levels of its customers because competitors are constantly trying to outperform Target and/or customer preferences change.

Target management has committed to an annual survey of 1,000 customers to determine these very issues and to provide for a constant tracking and forecasting system of customers' opinions. The survey will include customers of Target's competitors such as Walmart, Kmart, and Sears. In other words, the population under study is all consumers who shop in mass merchandise stores in Target's geographic markets. The marketing research project director has decided on the use of a telephone survey to be conducted by a national telephone survey data collection company, and he is currently working with Survey Sampling, Inc. (SSI), to purchase the telephone numbers of consumers residing in Target's metropolitan target markets. SSI personnel have informed him of the basic formula they use to determine the number of telephone numbers needed.

The formula is as follows:

Telephone numbers needed = completed interviews/ (working phone rate × incidence × completion rate)

where
  working phone rate = percent of telephone numbers that are "live"
  incidence = percentage of those reached that will take part in the survey
  completion rate = percentage of those willing to take part in the survey that will actually complete the survey

As a matter of convenience, Target identifies four different regions that are roughly equal in sales volume: North, South, East, and West.

1. With a desired final sample size of 250 for each region, what is the lowest total number of telephone numbers that should be purchased for each region?

2. With a desired final sample size of 250 for each region, what is the highest total number of telephone numbers that should be purchased for each region?

3. What is the lowest and highest total number of telephone numbers to be purchased for the entire survey?

Region	North		South		East		West	
	Low	High	Low	High	Low	High	Low	High
Working Rate	70%	75%	60%	65%	65%	75%	50%	60%
Incidence	65%	70%	70%	80%	65%	75%	40%	50%
Completion Rate	50%	70%	50%	60%	80%	90%	60%	70%

CASE 10.2

Scope Mouthwash

Scope, a Procter & Gamble (P&G) brand, competes with several other mouthwash brands. Listerine has been the market leader for the past several years while Scope, Crest, and Colgate have been market followers. In an attempt to make Scope more competitive, the Scope brand manager has decided to undertake an extensive market research investigation of the mouthwash market in the United States to discover unsatisfied latent needs in mouthwash users and to identify the strengths and weaknesses of the competitors. Hopefully, this research endeavor will generate some significant improvements for Scope that will ultimately result in appreciable market share. In particular, the decision has been made to purchase panel access, meaning that the online survey will be completed by individuals who have joined the ranks of the panel data company and agreed to periodically answer surveys online. Although these individuals are compensated by their panel companies, the companies claim that their panel members are highly representative of the general population. Also, because the panel members have provided extensive information about themselves such as demographics, lifestyles, and product ownership, which is all stored in the panel company database, a client can purchase these data without the necessity of asking these questions on its survey.

After doing some investigation, the Scope marketing team has concluded that several panel companies can provide a representative sample of U.S. households. Among these are Knowledge Networks, e-Rewards, and Survey Sampling International, and their costs and services seem comparable. For a "blended" online survey of about 25 questions, the cost is roughly $10 per completed response. "Blended" means a combination of stored database information and answers to online survey questions.

Thus, the costs of these panel company services are based on the number of respondents, and each company will bid on the work based on the nature and size of the sample.

The Scope brand manager is operating under two constraints. First, P&G top management has agreed to pay the total cost for all the research, and it is up to the Scope brand manager to spend this budget prudently. If a large portion of the budget is expended on a single activity, such as the cost of an online panel sample, there is less available for other research activities. Second, the Scope brand manager knows that P&G top management will expect this project to have a large sample size. Of course, from past experience, the brand manager realizes that large sample sizes are generally not required from a sample error standpoint, but he must be prepared to respond to questions, reservations, or objections from his P&G managers when the sample size is proposed. As preparation for the possible need to convince top management that his recommendation is the right decision for the sample size for the Scope survey, and with the help of his marketing research staff specialist, he decides to make a table that specifies sample error and cost of the sample.

For each of the following possible sample sizes listed here, calculate the associated expected cost of the panel sample and the sample error.

1. 20,000
2. 10,000
3. 5,000
4. 2,500
5. 1,000
6. 500

11

Dealing with Fieldwork and Data Quality Issues

"WHERE WE ARE"

1 Establish the need for marketing research.

2 Define the problem.

3 Establish research objectives.

4 Determine research design.

5 Identify information types and sources.

6 Determine methods of accessing data.

7 Design data collection forms.

8 Determine the sample plan and size.

9 Collect data.

10 Analyze data.

11 Prepare and present the final research report.

Discuss.io

Zach Simmons, founder, Discuss.io

Customer feedback is vital for successful product development. That type of feedback, however, can be more complex than most people anticipate. Quantitative market research, or the numerical evaluation of a market, is popular for charting overall efficacy. Qualitative methods such as focus groups and individual discussions, meanwhile, help us understand why products are appealing. Such methods also require a more interpersonal approach. Time-intensive recruiting and travel are common drawbacks of the method, as modern product development is far faster. Bringing qualitative research into the information age, Seattle-based Discuss.io makes possible remote market interviews in real time.

Online qualitative research platforms are simplifying the qualitative process significantly. Discuss.io, for instance, first is given a hypothesis or problem by a client. Then it formulates a discussion guide to help the brand filter key information from respondents. From there, its patent-pending Rapid Recruiter automatically matches brands with participants in their target demographics. Millions of participants volunteer from over 20 countries, and translators are available in 14 languages. Immediate access to respondents dramatically increases research agility and speed, dodging the usual months-long recruitment and review process. Further, it places far more voices and perspectives in the limelight. Researchers can make instant market segmentations across much of the world, radicalizing how brands develop and localize their goods.

Once impossible because of technological limitations, online interview services are now generating a resurgence in qualitative methods and theory. Bandwidth-efficient, HD video streams offer the same observational detail as real life. Qualitative market research analyzes the total communication picture, and body language plays a huge role. Lifelike detail is important in examining a participant's full set of reactions, as well as in facilitating productive conversation. With AV quality now up to par, online qualitative research matches the accuracy of its traditional, real-life counterpart.

Reducing project time condenses development cycles, particularly compared to traditional qualitative research. Discuss.io decreases expenses by up to 80%, as travel, facility rentals, accommodations, and the like are no longer needed. This opens new opportunities for brands that could not support the expense that past qualitative methods would have entailed. A huge enabler for organizations without large-scale budgets, Discuss.io helps level the playing field. Ideas once deemed too expensive or risky become worthwhile to investigate, spurring originality and innovation.

Online qualitative research's applicability is as vast as its potential. Unilever took an interest in Discuss.io's platform and unique approach in early 2014. Thirty pages of Unilever feedback and several platform revisions later, Discuss.io is now operating in 26 countries and serving dozens of clients. It has garnered numerous honors as well, having been named one of the Top 50 Most Innovative Research Firms in the 2015 GRIT Report and listed in Unilever's Foundry50. If the rising prominence of online qualitative research is any indication, Discuss.io and similar services will continue improving their technology and methods to enhance the opportunities available to organizations worldwide.

Source: Text and photos courtesy of Zach Simmons, CEO, Discuss.io

Visit Discuss.io at www.discuss.io

This chapter deals with data collection and data quality issues, an arena in which Discuss.io excels. There are two kinds of errors in survey research. The first is sampling error, which arises from the fact that we have taken a sample. Those sources of error were discussed in the previous chapter. Error may also arise from a respondent who does not listen carefully to the question or from an interviewer who is almost burned out from listening to answering machines or having prospective respondents hang up. This second type of error is called *nonsampling error*. This chapter discusses the sources of nonsampling errors and suggests how marketing researchers can minimize the negative effect of each type of error. We also address how to calculate the response rate to measure the amount of nonresponse error. We indicate what a researcher looks for in preliminary questionnaire screening after the survey has been completed to spot respondents whose answers may exhibit bias, such as always responding positively (or negatively) to questions.

11-1 Data Collection and Nonsampling Error

In the two previous chapters, you learned that the sample plan and sample size are important in predetermining the amount of sampling error you will experience. The significance of understanding sampling is that we can control sampling error.[1] The counterpart to sampling error is **nonsampling error**, which consists of all errors in a survey *except* those attributable to the sample plan and sample size. Nonsampling error includes (1) all types of nonresponse error, (2) data-gathering errors, (3) data-handling errors, (4) data analysis errors, and (5) interpretation errors. It also includes errors in problem definition and question wording—everything, as we have said, other than sampling error.

Nonsampling error consists of all errors in a survey except those due to the sample plan and sample size.

There is the potential for large nonsampling error to occur during the data collection stage in a survey.

Generally, there is great potential for large nonsampling error to occur during the data collection stage, so we discuss errors that can occur during this stage at some length. **Data collection** is the phase of the marketing research process during which respondents provide their answers or information in response to inquiries posed by the researcher. These inquiries may be direct questions asked by a live, face-to-face interviewer; they may be posed over the telephone; they may be administered by the respondent alone, as with an online survey; or they may take some other form of solicitation that the researcher has decided to use. Because nonsampling error cannot be measured by a formula as sampling error can, we describe the various controls that can be imposed on the data collection process to minimize the effects of nonsampling error.[2] Also, much marketing research utilizes panel companies that maintain very large numbers of respondents who are guaranteed to fill out surveys quickly and accurately. Therefore, we describe the safeguards that panel companies employ to ensure the quality of their data.

11-2 Possible Errors in Field Data Collection

Nonsampling errors are committed by fieldworkers and respondents.

A wide variety of nonsampling errors can occur during data collection. We divide these errors into two general types and further specify errors within each general type. The first general type is **fieldworker error**, defined as errors committed by the individuals who administer questionnaires, typically interviewers.[3] The quality of fieldworkers can vary dramatically depending on the researcher's resources and the circumstances of the survey, but it is important to keep in mind that fieldworker error can occur with professional data collection workers as well as with do-it-yourselfers. Of course, the potential for fieldworker error is less with professionals than with first-timers or part-timers. The other general type is **respondent error**, which consists of errors on the part of the respondent. These errors, of course, can occur regardless of the method of data collection, but some data collection methods have greater potential for respondent error than others. Within each general type, we identify two classes of error: intentional errors, or errors that are committed deliberately, and unintentional errors, or errors that occur without willful intent.[4] Table 11.1 lists the various errors/types of errors described in this section under each of the four headings. In the early sections of this chapter, we will describe these data collection errors; later, we will discuss the standard controls that marketing researchers employ to minimize these errors.

INTENTIONAL FIELDWORKER ERRORS

Intentional fieldworker errors occur whenever a data collector willfully violates the data collection requirements set forth by the researcher. We describe two variations of intentional fieldworker errors: interviewer cheating and leading the respondent. Both are constant concerns of all researchers.

Interviewer cheating occurs when the interviewer intentionally misrepresents respondents. You might think to yourself, "What would induce an interviewer to intentionally falsify

TABLE 11.1 Data Collection Errors Can Occur with Fieldworkers or Respondents

	Fieldworker Errors	Respondent Errors
Intentional Errors	• Cheating • Leading respondents	• Falsehoods • Nonresponse
Unintentional Errors	• Interviewer characteristics • Misunderstandings • Fatigue	• Misunderstanding • Guessing • Attention loss • Distractions • Fatigue

responses?" The cause is often found in the compensation system.[5] Interviewers may work by the hour, but another common practice is to reward them by completed interviews. That is, a telephone interviewer or a mall-intercept interviewer may be paid at a rate of $7.50 per completed interview. At the end of an interview day, he or she simply turns in the "completed" questionnaires (or data files, if the interviewer uses a laptop, tablet, or PDA system), and the number is credited to the interviewer. The opportunity to inflate the number of completed interviews is clear. Other interviewers may cheat by interviewing someone who is convenient to access instead of a person designated by the sampling plan. Again, the by-completed-interview compensation arrangement may provide an incentive for this type of cheating.[6] Further, most interviewers are not full-time employees,[7] and their integrity may be diminished as a result.

You might ask, "Wouldn't changing the compensation system for interviewers fix this problem?" There is some defensible logic for a paid-by-completion compensation system. Interviewers do not always work like production-line workers. With mall intercepts, for instance, there are periods of inactivity, depending on mall shopper flow and respondent qualification requirements. Telephone interviewers are often instructed to call only during a small number of "prime time" hours in the evening, or they may be waiting for periods of time to satisfy the policy on number of call-backs for a particular survey. Also, as you may already know, the compensation levels for fieldworkers are low, the hours are long, and the work is frustrating at times.[8] As a result, the temptation to turn in bogus completed questionnaires is certainly present, and some interviewers give in to this temptation.

The second error that we are categorizing as intentional on the part of the interviewer is **leading the respondent**, or attempting to influence the respondent's answers through wording, voice inflection, or body language. In the worst case, the interviewer may actually reword a question so that it does lead the respondent to answer in a certain way. For instance, consider the question: "Is conserving electricity a concern for you?" An interviewer can influence the respondent by changing the question to "Isn't conserving electricity a concern for you?"

Another area of subtle leading occurs in interviewers' cues. In personal interviews, for instance, interviewers might ever so slightly shake their heads "no" to questions they disagree with, and nod "yes" to those they agree with, while posing the question. Respondents may perceive these cues and begin responding in the manner signaled by interviewers' nonverbal cues. Over the telephone, interviewers might give verbal cues such as "unhuh" to responses they disagree with or "okay" to responses they agree with, and this continued reaction pattern may subtly influence respondents' answers. Again, we have categorized these examples as intentional errors because professional interviewers are trained to avoid them, so if they commit such errors, they are likely to be aware of their violations.

UNINTENTIONAL FIELDWORKER ERRORS

An **unintentional interviewer error** occurs whenever an interviewer commits an error while believing that he or she is performing correctly.[9] There are three general sources of unintentional interviewer errors: interviewer personal characteristics, interviewer misunderstandings, and interviewer fatigue. Unintentional interviewer error is found in the interviewer's personal characteristics such as accent, sex, and demeanor. It has been shown that under some circumstances, the interviewer's voice,[10] speech,[11] gender,[12] or lack of experience[13] can be a source of bias. The simple act of wearing a flower in the hair has been shown to increase compliance to survey requests by female interviewers.[14] In fact, the mere presence of an interviewer, regardless of personal characteristics, may be a source of bias.

Interviewer misunderstanding occurs when an interviewer believes he or she knows how to administer a survey but instead does it incorrectly.

Interviewer cheating is a concern, especially when compensation is calculated on a per-completed-interview basis.

Interviewers should not influence respondents' answers.

Unintentional interviewer errors include misunderstandings and fatigue.

© Warren Goldswain/Shutterstock

Personal characteristics such as appearance, dress, or accent may cause unintentional fieldworker errors.

 Active Learning

What Type of Cheater Are You?

Students who read about the cheating error we have just described are sometimes skeptical that such cheating goes on. However, if you are a "typical" college student, you probably have cheated to some degree in your academic experience. Surprised? Take the following test, and circle "Yes" or "No" under the "I have done this" heading for each statement.

Statement	I have done this.	
1. Allowed someone else to copy your homework/assignments	Yes	No
2. Collaborated on assignments you were supposed to do alone	Yes	No
3. Copied another student's homework/assignments	Yes	No
4. Told another student what was on an exam before he or she took it	Yes	No
5. Found out what was on an exam before taking it	Yes	No
6. Kept silent about other students who you know cheated	Yes	No
7. Split homework questions with another student and handed them in as your own work	Yes	No
8. Collaborated on take-home exams you were supposed to do alone	Yes	No
9. Lied about or exaggerated personal or family situations in order to get an assignment deadline extended	Yes	No
10. Lied about or exaggerated personal or family situations in order to delay taking an exam	Yes	No
11. Looked at or copied from someone else's exam during a test	Yes	No
12. Allowed someone else to copy from your exam during a test	Yes	No
13. Programmed extra help or information into a calculator to use on an exam	Yes	No
14. Brought in concealed information to use during an exam	Yes	No
15. Obtained a copy of an exam before it was officially available	Yes	No
16. Allowed someone else to do your work and turned it in as your own	Yes	No
17. Left the room during an exam to look up information or get help	Yes	No
18. Altered answers on a graded test or assignment and then submitted it for regrading	Yes	No
19. Removed tests from the classroom without an instructor's permission	Yes	No
20. Used a cell phone to transmit or receive information during an exam	Yes	No

Statements 1–10 are considered "trivial" cheating, and a majority of college students admit to them. Statements 11–20 are considered "serious" cheating, and perhaps up to 20% of college students are guilty of committing some of these actions. Thus, if you circled "Yes" for some of these cheating practices, you are consistent with most college students.[15] Now, if you and the majority of college students in general are cheating to some extent on examinations and assignments, don't you think that interviewers who may be in financially tight situations are tempted to "cheat" on their interviews?

As we have described, a questionnaire may include various types of instructions for the interviewer, a variety of response scales, directions on how to record responses, and other complicated guidelines to which the interviewer must adhere. As you can guess, there is often a considerable education gap between marketing researchers who design questionnaires and interviewers who administer them. Thus the instructions on the questionnaire are sometimes confusing to the interviewer. Interviewer experience cannot overcome poor questionnaire instructions.[16] When instructions are hard to understand, the interviewer will usually struggle to comply with the researcher's wishes but may fail to do so.[17]

The third type of unintentional interviewer error involves **fatigue-related mistakes**, which can occur when an interviewer becomes tired. You may be surprised that fatigue can enter into asking questions and recording answers, because these tasks are not physically demanding, but interviewing is labor-intensive[18] and can become tedious and monotonous. It is repetitious at best, and it is especially demanding when respondents are uncooperative. Toward the end of a long interviewing day, the interviewer may be less mentally alert than earlier in the day, and this condition can cause slip-ups and mistakes. The interviewer might fail to obey a skip pattern, might forget to make note of the respondent's reply to a question, might hurry through a section of the questionnaire, or might appear or sound weary to a potential respondent who refuses to take part in the survey as a result.

INTENTIONAL RESPONDENT ERRORS

Intentional respondent errors occur when respondents willfully misrepresent themselves in surveys. There are at least two major intentional respondent errors: falsehoods and refusals. **Falsehoods** occur when respondents fail to tell the truth in surveys. They may feel embarrassed, they may want to protect their privacy, or they may even suspect that the interviewer has a hidden agenda, such as turning the interview into a sales pitch.[19] Sensitive topics have greater potential for misrepresentation.[20] For instance, personal income level is a sensitive topic for many people, disclosure of marital status is a concern for women living alone, age is a delicate topic for some, and questions about personal hygiene may offend some respondents. Respondents may also become bored, deem the interview process burdensome, or find the interviewer irritating. For a variety of reasons, they may want to end the interview in a hurry. Falsehoods may be motivated by a desire on the part of the respondent to deceive, or they may be mindless responses uttered just to complete the interview as quickly as possible. Although their findings were inconclusive, one set of researchers claimed that falsehoods are more likely among females, younger respondents, and less educated respondents but less likely with experienced interviewers and among respondents with positive attitudes toward research and positive prior research experiences.[21] Marketing Research Insight 11.1 is related to the issue of respondents lying.

The second type of intentional respondent error is nonresponse, which we have referred to at various times in this text. **Nonresponse** includes failure on the part of a prospective respondent to take part in the survey, premature termination of the interview, and refusal to answer specific questions on the questionnaire. In fact, nonresponse of various types is probably the most common intentional respondent error that researchers encounter. Some observers believe that survey research is facing tough times ahead because of a growing distaste for survey participation, increasingly busy schedules, and a desire for privacy.[22] By one estimate, the refusal rate of U.S. consumers is almost 90%.[23] Most agree that declining cooperation rates present a major threat to the industry.[24] Nonresponse in general, and refusals in particular, are encountered in virtually every survey conducted. Business-to-business (B2B) marketing research is even more challenging, presenting additional hurdles that must be cleared (such as negotiating "gatekeepers") just to find the right person to take part in the survey. We devote an entire section to nonresponse error later in this chapter.

UNINTENTIONAL RESPONDENT ERRORS

An **unintentional respondent error** occurs whenever a respondent gives a response that is not valid but that he or she believes is the truth. There are five

Sometimes respondents do not tell the truth.

Nonresponse is defined as failure on the part of a prospective respondent to take part in a survey or to answer a question.

Marketing Research on YouTube™ To learn about nonresponse, launch **www.youtube.com** and search for "Nonresponse—AAPOR 2008: Robert Groves."

© Lasse Kristensen/Shutterstock

Guesses are a form of unintentional respondent error.

MARKETING RESEARCH INSIGHT 11.1   *Digital Marketing Research*

FTF versus ACASI: Do Respondents Lie When Looking an Interviewer in the Eye?

Technology has given rise to the "audio computer-assisted self-interview," or ACASI, in which a computer is used to "read" questions to respondents. There are many variations of this approach, but essentially a computer voice or a prerecorded voice is used rather than a living human interviewer (referred to as "face-to-face" or FTF interviewing). The ACASI version may be administered over the telephone or with the respondent sitting in front of a laptop or desktop computer monitor. The FTF mode requires that the interviewer and the respondent be physically present at the same time, and as a result, both the respondent and the interviewer can observe each other's facial and body movements. As shown in many studies, survey respondents are more likely to give socially acceptable answers to human interviewers than to computer interviewers. Stated differently, it is easier to tell the truth about undesirable behaviors to a computer than to a real person.

Four researchers recently investigated lying in respondents by comparing FTF with ACASI.[25] In the FTF condition they administered an actual face-to-face interview in which the interviewer and respondent faced each other, and the interviewer read questions aloud from a laptop computer to the respondent and recorded the respondent's verbal answers on the computer. In the ACASI condition, the respondent sat facing the laptop computer and wore headphones, listening to each question that was prerecorded and administered upon the respondent's click. He or she then clicked the answer on the computer screen, and a "next" button moved the computer to the following question. Based on the data provided by these researchers in

their article, the following figure illustrates that the FTF condition consistently resulted in more favorable answers to socially desirable issues such as drinking moderately, saving regularly, and keeping up with the news. In fact, the average difference across all such behaviors was 20%. In other words, assuming that the answers to the computer-administered questions are the "truth," a face-to-face interviewer appears to inspire respondents to answer with lies 20% more often to score better on socially desirable behaviors. When asked to estimate the number of their sex partners since their 18th birthday, the FTF respondents answered with a median of 16, and the ACASI respondents' median was 14, which suggests that for socially undesirable behaviors, respondents may lie by as much at 15% when in the presence of a human interviewer.

Respondents Lie to Look Better to Human Interviewers

Unintentional respondent errors may result from misunderstanding, guessing, attention loss, distractions, or fatigue.

Sometimes a respondent will answer without understanding the question.

Whenever a respondent guesses, error is likely.

types of unintentional respondent errors: misunderstanding, guessing, attention loss, distractions, and fatigue. First, **respondent misunderstanding** occurs when a respondent gives an answer without comprehending the question and/or the accompanying instructions. Potential respondent misunderstandings exist in all surveys. Such misunderstandings range from simple errors, such as checking two responses to a question when only one is called for, to complex errors, such as misunderstanding terminology.[26] For example, a respondent may think in terms of net income for the past year rather than income before taxes as desired by the researcher. Any number of misunderstandings such as these can plague a survey.

A second form of unintentional respondent error is **guessing**, in which a respondent gives an answer when he or she is uncertain of its accuracy. Occasionally, respondents are asked about topics about which they have little knowledge or recall, but they feel compelled to provide an answer to the questions being posed. Respondents might guess the answer, and all guesses are likely to contain errors. Here is an example of a question very likely to elicit guessing: If you were asked to estimate the amount of electricity, in kilowatt-hours, that you used last month, how many would you say you used?

A third unintentional respondent error, known as **attention loss**, occurs when a respondent's interest in the survey wanes. The typical respondent is not as excited about the survey as the researcher is, and some respondents find themselves less and less motivated to take part in the survey as they work their way through the questionnaire. With attention loss,

MARKETING RESEARCH INSIGHT 11.2   *Practical Marketing Research*

Do Cell Phones Make a Difference in Data Quality?

Despite the widespread popularity of online surveys, telephone surveys remain a significant form of data collection. Many years ago, the land line telephone survey was the "gold standard" of data collection; however, cell phones and mobile phones have eclipsed the land line telephone's prominence. Researchers have many valid worries about the differences in data quality between land lines and mobile phones. A recent article[27] enumerated the reasons for these worries and compared the data quality of land line telephone interviews with that of mobile phone interviews. Four conditions are necessary for an optimal telephone interview. Here are those conditions and the aspects of a mobile phone interview that have the potential to reduce the quality of an interviewee's responses.

Condition 1: Ability to hear clearly. The mobile phone sometimes suffers from poor reception quality and from a multitude of distractions in the environment where the user is responding to survey questions. Also, respondents differ in their aural reception of cell phone calls and in their comfort with cell phone usage.

Condition 2: Sufficient attention. The mobile phone environment can be highly distracting, especially if the user is in a public location, in a work situation, or not at home. Also, cell phones are commonly used while multitasking, so the respondent may be watching television, exercising, or surfing the web during the interview.

Condition 3: Sufficient effort. Answering survey questions, regardless of the mode of the interview, requires cognitive effort in the forms of memory (recall), evaluation, judgment, and expression of opinions. Compared to land line conversation, cell phone communication tends to be short and superficial and done without a lot of thought.

Condition 4: Willingness to answer. Survey questions may touch on personal or private topics, but cell phones are often used in public where friends or strangers can hear the respondent's answers. This situation may deter respondents from answering such questions or from answering them honestly.

Thus, it would appear that the mobile phone interview has several strikes against its data quality, and the researchers who wrote the article sought to compare the incidence of known errors such as don't knows, excessive agreements, extreme answers, middle-of-the-roads, and speeding (some of these will be described later in this chapter) that land line respondents and mobile phone respondents made to the same survey. Surprisingly, they found that mobile phone respondents did not exhibit many differences from land line respondents. The only differences of note were that mobile phone respondents demonstrate less social desirability bias and that properly designed mobile phone interviews are slightly longer than land line interviews. Thus mobile phone respondents may take a bit longer due to multitasking or distractions, but their answers are apparently of the same quality as those of land line respondents. And on personal issues, the mobile phone interviewee may be a tad more honest than the land line interviewee.

respondents do not attend carefully to questions, they provide superficial and perhaps mindless answers, and they may refuse to continue taking part in the survey.

Fourth, **distractions**, such as interruptions, may occur while the questionnaire is being administered. For example, during a mall-intercept interview, a respondent might be distracted when an acquaintance walks by and says hello. A parent answering questions on the telephone might have to attend to a fussy toddler, or an online survey respondent might be prompted that an email message has just arrived. A distraction may cause the respondent to get "off track" or otherwise not take the survey as seriously as the researcher desires.

Fifth, unintentional respondent error can take the form of **respondent fatigue**, in which the respondent gets tired of answering questions. Whenever a respondent tires of a survey, deliberation and reflection diminish. Exasperation will mount and cooperation will decrease. The respondent might even opt for the "no opinion" response category just as a means of finishing the survey quickly.

Sometimes the mode of the survey engenders either more or less respondent error. In fact, the almost universal replacement of land line telephones with mobile or cell phones in some populations might be a cause for worry. Read Marketing Research Insight 11.2 to learn why cell phone interviews differ from land line interviews in ways that may affect data quality.

IBM **SPSS**
IBM SPSS Student Assistant:
Red Lobster: Recoding and Computing Variables

Active Learning

What Type of Error Is It?

It is sometimes confusing to students when they first read about intentional and unintentional errors and the attribution of errors to interviewers or respondents. To help you learn and remember these various types of data collection errors, see if you can correctly identify the type for each of the following data collection situations. Place an "X" in the cell that corresponds to the type of error that appears in each situation.

Situation	Interviewer Error		Respondent Error	
	Intentional	Unintentional	Intentional	Unintentional
A respondent says, "No opinion" to every question asked.				
When a mall-intercept interviewer is suffering from a bad cold, few people want to take the survey.				
Because a telephone respondent has an incoming call, he asks his wife to take the phone and answer the rest of the interviewer's questions.				
A respondent grumbles about doing the survey, so an interviewer decides to skip the demographic questions.				
A respondent who lost her job gives her last year's income level rather than the much lower one she will earn for this year.				

11-3   Field Data Collection Quality Controls

Precautions and procedures can be implemented to minimize the effects of the various types of errors just described. Please note that we said "minimize" and not "eliminate" because the potential for error always exists. However, by instituting the following controls, a researcher can reduce the nonsampling error involved with data collection. The field data collection quality controls that we describe are listed in Table 11.2.

CONTROL OF INTENTIONAL FIELDWORKER ERROR

Intentional fieldworker error can be controlled with supervision and validation procedures.

Two general strategies—supervision and validation—can be employed to guard against the interviewer intentionally committing an error.[28] **Supervision** consists of administrators overseeing the work of field data collection workers.[29] Most centralized telephone interviewing companies have a "listening in" capability that the supervisor can use to tap into and monitor any interviewer's line during an interview. Even though they have been told that the interview "may be monitored for quality control," the respondent and the interviewer may be unaware of the monitoring, so the "listening in" samples a representative interview performed by that interviewer. The monitoring may be performed on a recording of the interview rather than in real time. If the interviewer is leading or unduly influencing respondents, this procedure will spot the violation, and the supervisor can take corrective action such as reprimanding that interviewer. With personal interviews, the supervisor

TABLE 11.2 **How to Control Data Collection Errors**

Error Types	Control Mechanisms
Intentional fieldworker errors	
Cheating	Supervision
Leading respondent	Validation
Unintentional fieldworker errors	
Interviewer characteristics	Selection and training of interviewers
Misunderstandings	Orientation sessions and role playing
Fatigue	Required breaks and alternative surveys
Intentional respondent errors	
Falsehoods	Ensuring anonymity and confidentiality
	Incentives
	Validation checks
	Third-person technique
Nonresponse	Ensuring anonymity and confidentiality
	Incentives
	Third-person technique
Unintentional respondent errors	
Misunderstandings	Well-drafted questionnaire
	Direct questions
Guessing	Well-drafted questionnaire
	Response options, such as "unsure"
Attention loss	Reversal of scale endpoints
Distractions	Prompters
Fatigue	

might accompany an interviewer to observe that interviewer administering a questionnaire in the field. Because "listening in" without the consent of the respondent could be considered a breach of privacy, many companies now inform respondents that all or part of the call may be monitored and/or recorded.

Validation verifies that the interviewer did the work. This strategy is aimed at the falsification/cheating problem. There are various ways to validate the work. One type of validation is for the supervisor to recontact respondents to find out whether they took part in the survey. An industry standard is to randomly select 10% of the completed surveys for purposes of making a call-back to validate that the interview was conducted. A few sample questions might even be readministered for comparison purposes. In the absence of call-back validation, a supervisor may inspect completed questionnaires and may, with a trained eye, spot patterns in an interviewer's completions that raise suspicion of falsification. Interviewers who turn in bogus completed questionnaires are not always careful about simulating actual respondents. The supervisor might find inconsistencies (such as very young respondents with large numbers of children) that raise doubts about a questionnaire's authenticity.

An industry standard is verification of 10% of the completed surveys.

CONTROL OF UNINTENTIONAL FIELDWORKER ERROR

As you would expect, supervision is instrumental in minimizing unintentional interviewer error. We describe four mechanisms commonly used by professional field data

Unintentional fieldworker errors can be reduced with supervised orientation sessions and role playing.

collection companies in this regard: selection and training, orientation sessions, role playing,[30] and methods to reduce fatigue. Interviewer personal characteristics that can cause unintentional errors are best taken care of by the careful selection of interviewers. Following selection, it is important to train them well to avoid any biases resulting from manner, appearance, and so forth. **Orientation sessions** are meetings in which the supervisor introduces the survey and questionnaire administration requirements to the fieldworkers.[31] The supervisor might highlight qualification or quota requirements, note skip patterns, or go over instructions to the interviewer that are embedded throughout the questionnaire to standardize the interview across interviewers.[32] Finally, often as a means of becoming familiar with a questionnaire's administration requirements, supervisors often conduct **role-playing sessions**, which are dry runs or dress rehearsals of administering the questionnaire, with the supervisor or some other interviewer playing the respondent's role. Successive role-playing sessions serve to familiarize interviewers with the questionnaire's special administration aspects. To control for interviewer fatigue, some researchers require interviewers to take frequent breaks and/or to use alternate surveys, if possible. In short, the more competent the field interviewer becomes through training, supervision, and development of personal skills, the lower the potential for interviewer error.[33]

CONTROL OF INTENTIONAL RESPONDENT ERROR

To control intentional respondent error, it is important to minimize falsehoods and non-response tendencies on the part of respondents. Tactics useful in minimizing intentional respondent error include anonymity, confidentiality, incentives, validation checks, and the third-person technique.[34] **Anonymity** occurs when the respondent is assured that his or her name will not be associated with his or her answers. **Confidentiality** occurs when the respondent is given assurances that his or her answers will remain private. Both assurances are believed to be helpful in forestalling falsehoods. The assumption is that when respondents are guaranteed that they will remain nameless, they will be more comfortable in self-disclosure and will refrain from lying or misrepresenting themselves.[35]

> Tactics useful in minimizing intentional respondent error include anonymity, confidentiality, validation checks, and third-person technique.

> Incentives sometimes compel respondents to be more truthful while also discouraging nonresponse.

Another tactic for reducing falsehoods and nonresponse error is the use of **incentives**, which are cash payments, gifts, or something of value promised to respondents in return for their participation.[36] For participating in a survey, respondents may be paid cash or provided with redemption coupons. They might be given a gift such as a ball-point pen or a T-shirt. In a sense, respondents are being induced to tell the truth by direct payment. Respondents may now feel morally obligated to tell the truth because they will receive compensation. Or they may feel guilty at receiving an incentive and then not answering truthfully. Unfortunately, practitioners and academic researchers are just beginning to understand how to entice prospective respondents to take part in a survey.[37] For instance, only recently has relevance of the subject matter been documented to increase response rates.[38]

A different approach for reducing falsehoods is the use of **validation checks**, in which information provided by a respondent is confirmed during the interview. For example, in an in-home survey on Leap Frog educational products for preschool children, the interviewer might ask to see the respondent's Leap Frog unit and modules as a verification or validation check. A more unobtrusive validation is to have the interviewer check for older-appearing

© Tyler Olson/Shutterstock

Confidentiality and/or anonymity may reduce refusals to take part in a survey.

respondents who say they are young, shabbily dressed respondents who say they are wealthy, and so on. A well-trained interviewer will make note of suspicious answers.[39]

Finally, there is a questionnaire design feature that a researcher can use to reduce intentional respondent errors. Sometimes the opportunity arises to use the **third-person technique**, in which, instead of directly quizzing the respondent about a subject that might be embarrassing, the interviewer couches the question in terms of a third person who is similar to the respondent. For instance, a middle-aged man might be asked, "Do you think a person such as yourself uses Viagra?" Here, the respondent will probably think in terms of his own circumstances, but, because the subject of the question is some unnamed third party, the question is not seen as personal. In other words, the respondent will not be divulging personal and private information by talking about this fictitious other person. The third-person technique may be used to reduce both falsehoods and nonresponse.

With an embarrassing question, the third-person technique may make the situation less personal.

CONTROL OF UNINTENTIONAL RESPONDENT ERROR

The control of unintentional respondent error takes various forms as well, including well-drafted questionnaire instructions and examples, reversals of scale endpoints, and use of prompters. Clear-cut **questionnaire instructions and examples** are commonly used as a way of avoiding respondent confusion. We described these in our chapter on questionnaire design. Also, researchers sometimes resort to direct questions to assess respondent understanding. For example, after describing a 5-point agree–disagree response scale in which 1 = Strongly agree, 2 = Agree, 3 = Neither agree nor disagree, 4 = Disagree, and 5 = Strongly disagree, the interviewer might be instructed to ask, "Are these instructions clear?" If the respondent answers in the negative, the instructions are repeated until the respondent understands them. Guessing may be reduced by alerting respondents to response options such as "no opinion," "do not recall," or "unsure."

A tactic we described when we discussed the semantic differential is **reversals of scale endpoints**, in which instead of putting all of the negative adjectives on one side and all the positive ones on the other side, a researcher will switch the positions of a few items. Such reversals are intended to warn respondents that they must respond to each bipolar pair individually. With agree–disagree statements, this tactic is accomplished by negatively wording a statement every now and then to induce respondents to attend to each statement individually. Both of these tactics are intended to heighten the respondent's attention.

Ways to combat unintentional respondent error include well-drafted questionnaire instructions and examples, reversals of scale endpoints, use of scale endpoints, and use of prompters.

Finally, long questionnaires often include **prompters**, such as "We are almost finished," "That was the most difficult section of questions to answer," or other statements strategically located to encourage the respondent to remain on track. Sometimes interviewers will sense an attention lag or fatigue on the part of the respondent and provide their own prompters or comments to maintain the respondent's full participation in the survey. Online surveys often have a "% completed" scale or other indication that informs respondents of their progress in the survey.

Prompters are used to keep respondents on task and alert.

FINAL COMMENT ON THE CONTROL OF DATA COLLECTION ERRORS

As you can see, a wide variety of nonsampling errors can occur on the parts of both interviewers and respondents during the data collection stage of the marketing research process. Similarly, a variety of precautions and controls are used to minimize nonsampling error. Each survey is unique, of course, so we cannot provide universally applicable guidelines. We will, however, stress the importance of good questionnaire design in reducing these errors. Also, professional field data collection companies whose existence depends on how well they can

MARKETING RESEARCH INSIGHT 11.3   *Ethical Consideration*

Marketing Research Association Code of Ethics: Respondent Participation

The Marketing Research Association Code of Ethics specifies that the marketing research interviewer

2. Protect the rights of respondents, including the right to refuse to participate in part or all of the research process.

Researchers must respect the bounds of cooperation set by respondents, who control the parameters under which information is given. In practice, this means all of the following:

- *Respondent agreement to participate in research must be obtained upfront, rather than after the fact.*
- *Consent must be granted freely, without coercion.*
- *Consent may be withdrawn by the respondent at any point during the contact.*

- *Consent must be granted expressly for participation in any subsequent studies.*
- *An explicit opt-out request for any future contact or participation at any point during the process will be honored.*
- *All reasonable precautions are taken so that respondents are in no way adversely affected as a result of their participation in a marketing research project.*

Respondent cooperation is strictly on a voluntary basis. Respondents are entitled to withdraw from a research project. Company policies and/or interviewer instructions should state that the interviewer must give respondents the opportunity not to participate for any reason.

control interviewer and respondent error are commonly relied on by researchers who understand the true value of these services.

11-4   Nonresponse Error

Nonresponse was briefly described in our discussion of mail surveys. We will now describe this issue more fully, including various types of nonresponse, how to assess the degree of this error, and some ways of adjusting or compensating for nonresponse in surveys. Nonresponse was defined earlier as a failure on the part of a prospective respondent to take part in the survey or to answer specific questions on the questionnaire. Nonresponse has been labeled the marketing research industry's biggest problem,[40,41] and it is multinational in scope.[42] Compounding the problem has been the increase in the numbers of surveys, which means that the likelihood of being asked to participate in a survey has increased. Some industry observers believe that nonresponse is caused by fears of invasion of privacy, skepticism of consumers regarding the benefits of participating in research, and the use of research as a guise for telemarketing. Of course, it is unethical to force or trick people to respond. The Marketing Research Association Code of Ethics—portions of which are presented in Marketing Research Insight 11.3—clearly states that respondents have the right to refuse to participate in a study or to withdraw from a study at any time.

> There are three types of nonresponse error: refusals to participate in the survey, break-offs during the interview, and refusals to answer specific questions (item omissions).

The identification, control, and adjustments necessary for nonresponse are critical to the success of a survey. There are at least three different types of potential nonresponse error lurking in any survey: refusals to participate in the survey, break-offs during the interview, and refusals to answer specific questions, or item omission. Table 11.3 briefly describes each type of nonresponse.

TABLE 11.3   The Three Types of Nonresponses with Surveys

Name	Description
Refusal	The prospective respondent declines to participate in the survey.
Break-off	After answering some questions in the survey, the respondent stops participating.
Item omission	The respondent does not answer a particular question but does answer other questions.

REFUSALS TO PARTICIPATE IN THE SURVEY

A **refusal** occurs when a potential respondent declines to take part in the survey. Authoritative sources[43] comment that "today experiencing three or more refusals for every one completed interview is commonplace." Refusal rates differ by area of the country as well as by demographic differences. The reasons for refusals are many and varied.[44] People may be busy or have no interest in the survey. They may be turned off by the interviewer's voice or approach. The survey topic may be overly sensitive.[45] Or refusal may just be a standard response for some people.[46] Refusals may result from negative previous survey participation experiences.[47] People may decline to participate because they do not want to take the time or because they regard surveys as an intrusion of their privacy. Refusals are a concern even with panels.[48]

Refusals to participate in surveys are common worldwide.

BREAK-OFFS DURING THE INTERVIEW

A **break-off** occurs when a respondent reaches a certain point and then decides not to answer any more questions in the survey. As you would expect, there are many reasons for break-offs. For instance, the interview may take longer than the respondent expected; the topic and specific questions may prove to be distasteful, too personal, or boring; the instructions may be confusing; the survey may be too complex;[49] or a sudden interruption may occur.

REFUSALS TO ANSWER SPECIFIC QUESTIONS (ITEM OMISSION)

Even if a refusal or break-off does not occur, a researcher will sometimes find that specific questions have lower response rates than others. In fact, if a marketing researcher suspects ahead of time that a particular question, such as the respondent's annual income for last year, will generate some refusals, it is appropriate to include a designation such as "prefer not to answer" as a response option for that question on the questionnaire. Of course, some believe it is

A break-off may occur at any time during a survey.

not wise to put these designations on self-administered questionnaires, because respondents may use this option simply as a cop-out, when they might have provided accurate answers if the designation had not been there. **Item omission** is the phrase sometimes used to identify the percentage of the sample that did not answer a particular question.[50] Research has shown that sensitive questions elicit more item omissions, whereas questions that require more mental effort garner more "don't know" responses.[51] Item omissions have been found to occur regardless of survey mode or question type.[52] It is useful for a researcher to offer the "don't know" option with questions that require mental effort in order to reduce item omissions.

If they are tired, confused, uninterested, or interrupted, respondents may "break off" in the middle of an interview.

Occasionally, a respondent will refuse to answer a particular question that he or she considers too personal or a private matter.

WHAT IS A COMPLETED INTERVIEW?

Almost all surveys have some item omissions, break-offs, and partially completed surveys. Nonetheless, these respondents did provide some information. At which point does a break-off still constitute a completed interview? At which level of item omission do we deem a survey to be incomplete? A researcher must define or specify the criteria for a "completed interview." Ultimately, it is a judgment call and will vary with each marketing research project. Only in rare cases will it be necessary that all respondents answer all of the questions. In most other cases, the researcher will adopt some decision rule that defines completed versus not completed interviews. For example, in most research studies, there are questions directed at the primary purpose of the study. Also, there are usually questions that are asked for the purpose of adding insight into how respondents answered the primary questions. Such secondary questions often include a list of demographics questions, which, being more personal in nature, are typically placed at the end of the questionnaire. Because these secondary questions are not the primary focus of the study, a **completed interview** may be defined as one in which all the primary questions have been answered. In this way, the marketing researcher has data for primary questions and most of the data for secondary questions. Interviewers can then be given a specific statement about what constitutes a completed survey, such as "If the respondent answers through question 18, you may count it as a completion." (The demographics begin with question 19.) Likewise, the researcher must adopt a decision rule for determining the extent of item omissions necessary to invalidate a survey or a particular question. The American Association for Public Opinion Research offers these guidelines: complete survey: 80%–100% of applicable questions answered, partial completion: 50%–80% answered, and break-off: less than 50% answered.[53]

Marketing researchers must define a "completed" interview.

MEASURING RESPONSE RATE IN SURVEYS

Most marketing research studies report their response rates, and the currently accepted method of calculating this figure is based on a 1982 Council of American Survey Research Organizations (CASRO) report that provides a uniform definition and method for calculating the response rate.[54] According to the CASRO report and the American Association for Public Opinion Research, response rate is defined as the ratio of the number of completed interviews to the number of eligible units in the sample.[55] Here, in its simplest form, is the **CASRO response rate formula**:

The marketing research industry has an accepted way to calculate a survey's response rate.

$$\text{Response rate} = \frac{\text{Number of completed interviews}}{\text{Number of eligible units in sample}}$$

In most surveys, eligible units are respondents determined by screening or qualifying questions. For example, if we were working with a department store that was specifically concerned with its kitchenware department, we would determine eligibility for the survey by asking prospective respondents the screening question "Do you shop at Acme Department Store regularly?" For those who answered affirmatively, we would then ask, "Have you shopped in the kitchenware department at any time during the last three months?" Those respondents who again answered "Yes" would be eligible to take part in the survey.

Completions are eligible people who take part in the survey.

Let's assume we have a survey of 1,000 shoppers, and the results of the survey are the following:

Completions = 400

Ineligible = 300

Refusals = 100

Not reached = 200

This information enables you to calculate the number of sample units that are (a) eligible, (b) ineligible, and (c) not ascertained because they were not reached. When calculating the response rate, we have the number of completions in the numerator, and in the denominator we have the number of completions plus the numbers of those who refused, whose lines were busy, and who were eligible but did not answer. Because we do not talk to those who refuse (before the screening question), don't answer, have busy signals, or are not at home, how do we determine what percentage of these people would have been eligible? We multiply their number by the percentage of those we *did* talk with who are eligible. This method assumes that the same percentage of eligibles exists in the population of those we did talk with (of the 700 we talked with, 57% were eligible) as exists in the population of those we did not get to talk with (because of refusals, no answers, or busy signals). The formula for calculating the response rate for this situation follows.

CASRO Response Rate Formula (Expanded Form)

$$\text{Response rate} = \frac{\text{Completions}}{\text{Completions} + \left(\dfrac{\text{Completions}}{\text{Completions} + \text{Ineligible}}\right) \times (\text{Refusals} + \text{Not reached})}$$

Here are the calculations:

Calculation of CASRO Response Rate (Expanded Form)

$$\text{Response rate} = \frac{400}{400 + \left(\dfrac{400}{400 + 300}\right)(100 + 200)}$$

$$= \frac{400}{400 + (0.57)(300)}$$

$$= 70\%$$

 **Active Learning**

How to Calculate a Response Rate Using the CASRO Formula

Whereas the CASRO formulas seem simple and straightforward, questions arise about exactly how to interpret them when dealing with individual research projects. We have created this Active Learning exercise so you can appreciate what goes into the proper calculation of a response rate.

Assume you are doing this survey as a class project, and you have been assigned the task of conducting telephone interviews. You are given a list of randomly selected telephone numbers and told to fill a quota of five completions. You are instructed to make at least three contact attempts before giving up on a telephone number. Also, you are given a call record sheet where you are to write in the result of each call attempt. As you call each number, you record one of the following outcomes in the column corresponding to the contact attempt that pertains to that particular call. The results you can record are as follows:

Disconnected (D)—message from phone company that number is no longer in service.
Wrong Target (WT)—(ineligible) number is a business phone, and you are interested only in residences.
Ineligible Respondent (IR)—no one in household has purchased an automobile within last year.
Refusal (R)—subject refuses to participate.
Terminate (T)—subject begins survey but stops before completing all questions.
Completed (C)—questionnaire is completed.
Busy (BSY)—phone line is busy; attempt call-back at later time unless this is your third attempt.
No Answer (NA)—no one answers or you encounter a telephone answering device. You may leave a message and state that you will call back later, unless this is your third attempt.
Call Back (CB)—Subject has instructed you to call back at more convenient time; record call-back time and date, and return call unless this is your third attempt.

Let's assume that your list of numbers and codes looks like the following:

Telephone Number	1st Attempt	2nd Attempt	3rd Attempt
474-2892	No answer	No answer	Completed
474-2668	Busy	Ineligible respondent	
488-3211	Disconnected		
488-2289	Completed		
672-8912	Wrong target		
263-6855	Busy	Busy	Busy
265-9799	Terminate		
234-7160	Refusal		
619-6019	Call back	Busy	Busy
619-8200	Ineligible respondent		
474-2716	Ineligible respondent		
774-7764	No answer	No answer	
474-2654	Disconnected		
488-4799	Wrong target		
619-0015	Busy	Completed	
265-4356	No answer	No answer	Completed
265-4480	Wrong target		
263-8898	No answer	No answer	No answer
774-2213	Completed		

You should note that you completed your quota of 5 completed interviews with 19 telephone numbers. Look at the last code you recorded for each telephone number, and count the number of times you used each code. Insert these numbers into the following response rate formula to determine your correctly computed response rate:

$$\text{Response rate} = \frac{C}{C + \left(\frac{C}{C + IR + WT}\right)(BSY + D + T + R + NA)}$$

$$= \underline{\hspace{2cm}}\%$$

Note how ineligibles are handled in the formula. Both IR and WT are counted as ineligibles. The logic is that the percentage of eligibles among those you talked with is the same as the percentage of eligibles among those you did not talk with (BSY, D, T, R, and NA).

11-5 How Panel Companies Control Error

Skyrocketing nonresponse rates and the popularity of online surveys have prompted a number of firms to use a **panel company**—a company that accommodates surveyors by recruiting and selling access to very large, diverse groups of consumers and businesses. Panel members are compensated for completing online surveys very quickly and completely. Moreover, panel companies normally collect a wealth of information (demographic, life style, possessions, etc.) on each panel member as part of the recruitment and registration process, and these data may be purchased along with the survey questions, thus eliminating the need to ask for this information in the survey. Panel companies claim to provide representative samples of diverse populations, including citizens of foreign countries, and they can provide samples of very specific consumer types by inviting only those panel members who qualify on specific criteria to participate in any given survey.

The widespread popularity of online panels has given rise to a great many panel companies, some of which have been criticized for lax data quality controls. Especially at risk are the many do-it-yourself (DIY) marketing researchers and others who are not aware of the shortcomings often found in the quality of data generated via panels. In fact, practically every research association has some sort of formalized recommendations, best practices, standards, or admonishments to guide researchers in identifying the highest-quality panel companies when considering their services. For example, ESOMAR makes publically available its *28 Questions to Help Research Buyers of Online Samples* (which, incidentally, is the basis for Case 11.2 at the end of this chapter). It is beyond the scope of this text to describe all the nuances of panel data quality control, but Table 11.4 summarizes a number of representative best practices for online panels advocated by the Marketing Research Association (MRA).

11-6   Dataset, Coding Data, and the Data Code Book

For the vast majority of surveys, respondents' answers are typically contained in an electronic **dataset**, which is a matrix arrangement of numbers (mainly) in rows and columns similar to a Microsoft Excel or other spreadsheet. Each row pertains to the answers that a single

A dataset is an arrangement of numbers (mainly) in rows and columns.

TABLE 11.4   Illustrative Best Practices for Online Panels Quality Assurance*

Best Practice	Explanation
Panel purpose. Ensure that the panel is used solely for marketing research.	Some panel companies have members who are recruited via third-party product registration rather than for "marketing research purposes."
Recruitment. Panel members should be ethically invited or otherwise accorded an "opt-in" relationship with the panel company to participate in bona fide marketing surveys.	Some panel companies use spambots, spiders, or other dubious and unethical methods of gaining respondents.
Privacy. There should be a formal, published privacy policy concerning anonymity, confidentiality, and privacy of personal data of panel members.	Researchers who ensure privacy must have a guarantee by the panel company that panel member data are undiscoverable.
Participation. Panel members should not participate in multitudes of surveys in short periods of time.	Participation limits eliminate "professional respondents" and otherwise limit overrepresentation of these panel members in surveys.
Panel replacement. There should be a health-based attrition and replacement of panelists each year.	The MRA states that natural attrition, sometimes called "churn rate," ranges between 25% and 30% per year because of members who lose interest or are otherwise delisted.
Panel profiling. There should be abundant, up-to-date classification information on panel members.	Clients often wish to sample very specific subpopulations.
Data quality. There should be validation procedures in place, as well as provisions to minimize data quality errors on the part of panelists.	Tangible assurance that the desired panelists participated is desirable, and provisions should be in place for identifying "straightlining," "speeding" (both described later in this chapter), unreliability, and other respondent errors.

*This table is based on information posted on the website of the Marketing Research Association (www.marketingresearch.org).

Data coding is the identification of code values associated with the possible responses for each question on the questionnaire.

Researchers use data coding when preparing and working with a computer data file.

IBM SPSS

IBM SPSS Student Assistant:
Noxzema Skin Cream: Selecting Cases

To learn about the data code book, launch **www.youtube. com** and search for "Code book—Lisa Dierker."

respondent provides to the questions on the questionnaire. Each column represents a question on the questionnaire. Of course, if a question has multiple parts to it, then it will take up multiple columns. Because the answers vary from respondent to respondent, data pertaining to the questions or question parts are sometimes referred to as *variables*. Normally, the first row of a data matrix where the researcher locates a label such as "Age," "Gender," or "Satisfaction" identifies the question or question part associated with each column in the data matrix; these designations are often called *variable labels* or *variable names*.

The dataset is generated by an operation called **data coding**, which is defined as the identification of code values that are associated with the possible responses for each question on the questionnaire. You learned about data coding in the chapter on questionnaire design, where we described this same operation as *precoding*. Typically, these codes are numerical because numbers are quick and easy to input, and computers work with numbers more efficiently than they do with letter or text codes. In large-scale projects, and especially in cases where the data entry is performed by a subcontractor, researchers use a **data code book** that identifies (1) the questions on the questionnaire, (2) the variable name or label that is associated with each question or question part, and (3) the code numbers associated with each possible response to each question. With a code book that describes the data file, any analyst can work on the dataset, regardless of whether that analyst was involved in the research project during its earlier stages. As you will soon learn, after an SPSS dataset is fully set up, the data code book is contained in the dataset.

Because precoded questionnaires have response codes associated with the various responses, it is a simple matter to create a code book. However, the researcher will no doubt encounter missing data where respondents have failed to answer a question. What code is used when a missing item is encountered? The easiest and most acceptable code for a missing response is to use a blank, meaning that nothing is entered for that respondent on the question that was not answered. Practically all statistical analysis programs treat a blank as "missing," so a blank or empty cell is the universal default code to signify missing data.

With online surveys, the data file "builds" or "grows" as respondents submit their completed online questionnaires. That is, the codes are programmed into the questionnaire file automatically by the online questionnaire software and/or by the person who designs the online questionnaire. These codes are invisible to respondents and are typically viewable only for the questionnaire designer when using question edit mode. In the case of web-based surveys, the code book is vital as the researcher's only map to decipher the numbers found in the data file and to connect them to the answers to the questions on the questionnaire.

When doing data analysis, it is far more convenient to have findings tables use the labels on the questionnaire, such as "male" or "female," rather than the code numbers, such as "1" and "2." Thus practically all statistical analysis programs have features that enable users to identify the number codes and the associated word labels. With SPSS, it is easy to obtain the coding after the dataset has been set up. Figure 11.1 illustrates how the SPSS *Variable View* feature can be used to reveal the coding for each variable in an SPSS dataset. In other words, when finalized, an SPSS dataset makes the complete data code book for that dataset available to any user.

11-7   Data Quality Issues

Datasets should be inspected for errors.

Nonresponses appear in practically every survey. At the same time, some respondents may provide answers that exhibit a suspicious pattern. Both of these occurrences necessitate a separate phase of the data preparation stage in the marketing research process that involves inspecting respondents' answers in the dataset. Data quality is a concern for marketing researchers.[56] Obviously, the researcher's goal is to work with a set of data with as few data quality problems as humanly possible. Consequently, the researcher must examine the responses for data quality problems prior to analysis.

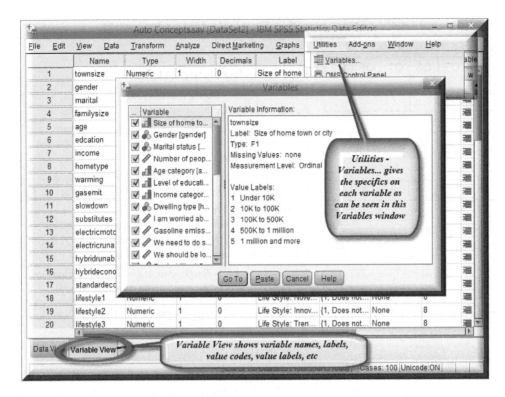

FIGURE 11.1 IBM **SPSS**

IBM SPSS Variable View and Variables Command Reveals a Dataset's Code Book

Source: Reprint Courtesy of International Business Machines Corporation, © International Business Machines Corporation.

WHAT TO LOOK FOR IN RAW DATA INSPECTION

The purpose of raw data inspection is to determine the presence of "bad" respondents and, as noted earlier, to throw out the ones with severe problems. Problem respondents fall into the following five categories: incomplete responses (break-offs), nonresponses to specific questions (item omissions), yea- or nay-saying patterns, and middle-of-the-road patterns. We describe each problem, and Table 11.5 provides an example of each one. In industry jargon, these are "exceptions," and they signal data quality errors to a researcher.

Incomplete Response An **incomplete response** is a break-off where the respondent stops answering in the middle of the questionnaire. Again, the reason why the survey was not completed may never be known. In Table 11.5, Respondent A stopped answering after Question 3.

Nonresponses to Specific Questions (Item Omissions) For whatever reason, a respondent sometimes leaves a question blank. In a telephone interview, he or she might decline to answer a question, and the interviewer might note this occurrence with the designation "ref" (refused) or some other code to indicate that the respondent failed to answer the question. In Table 11.5, Respondent B did not answer Questions 4 and 7.

Yea- or Nay-Saying Patterns Even when questions are answered, there can be signs of problems. A **yea-saying** pattern may be evident in the form of all "Yes" or "Strongly agree" answers.[57] An example is the "5" code for all Respondent C's answers to Questions 5–9 in Table 11.5. The yea-sayer has a persistent tendency to respond in the affirmative regardless of the question, and yea-saying implies invalid responses. The negative counterpart to yea-saying is **nay-saying**, which is identifiable as persistent responses in the negative, such as all the "1" codes for Respondent D's answers to Questions 4–9 in Table 11.5. Repeating the same answer on grid-type questions is a variation called "straightlining," which also signals a response quality problem.[58]

Raw data inspection determines the presence of "bad" respondents.

Some questionnaires may be only partially completed.

When a respondent does not answer a particular question, it is referred to as an *item omission*.

Yea-saying and nay-saying are seen as persistent tendencies on the part of some respondents to agree or disagree, respectively, with most of the questions asked.

To learn about data quality, launch **www. youtube.com** and search for "Data quality—lightspeedresearch."

TABLE 11.5 Identification of Data Quality Errors Found in Raw Data Matrix Inspection

Case	Q1	Q2	Q3	Q4	Q5	Q6	Q7	Q8	Q9	*Error Type*—Description of Error
	Data Matrix Column Labels									
A	1	2	3							*Break-off*—Questionnaire is incompletely filled out. No answers after Q3.
B	1	2	1		4	2		4	5	*Item omission*—The respondent refused to answer particular question(s) but answered others before and after it. Q4 and Q7 are not answered.
C	1	2	2	3	5	5	5	5	5	*Yea-saying*—Respondent exhibits persistence to respond favorably (yea) regardless of the questions. Q5–Q9 are all 5, the code for "Strongly agree."
D	2	1	3	1	1	1	1	1	1	*Nay-saying*—Respondent exhibits persistence to respond unfavorably (nay) regardless of the questions. Q5–Q9 are all 1, the code for "Strongly disagree."
E	2	1	3	1	3	3	3	3	3	*Middle-of-the-road*—Respondent indicates "no opinion" to most questions. Q5–Q9 are all 3, the code for "Neutral."

Code Book: Questions Q1–Q4 are 1 = Yes, 2 = No, 3 = No opinion; Questions Q5–Q9 are 1 = Strongly disagree, 2 = Disagree, 3 = Neutral, 4 = Agree, and 5 = Strongly agree

Some respondents hide their opinions by indicating "no opinion" throughout the survey.

Middle-of-the-Road Patterns The **middle-of-the-road pattern** is seen as a preponderance of "no opinion" responses, such as the "3" codes for Respondent E's Questions 5–9 in Table 11.5. No opinion is in essence no response, and prevalent no opinions on a questionnaire may signal low interest, lack of attention, or even objections to being involved in the survey. True, a respondent may not have an opinion on a topic, but if one gives many such answers, questions arise about how useful that respondent is to the survey. It should be noted that our yea-saying, nay-saying, and middle-of-the-road examples in Table 11.5 are extreme cases; sometimes these appear as tendencies such as almost all 4s and 5s for yea-saying, almost all 1s and 2s for nay-saying, and almost all "neutral" responses for middle-of-the-road errors. Online survey respondents who yea-say, nay-say, or give excessive "no opinion" answers are sometimes referred to as "speeders" because they are giving rapid-fire answers without reading the questions carefully. They are also called "straightliners" because they select the same answer time and again on a scale.[59] Unfortunately, response error tendencies are found worldwide. We have prepared Marketing Research Insight 11.4 to compare middle-of-the-road, yea-saying, and nay-saying response patterns across 15 countries.

Other Data Quality Problems Marketing researchers may encounter other bothersome problems during questionnaire screening. For example, respondents may check more than one response option when only one was supposed to be checked. They may have failed to look at the back of a questionnaire page and thus have missed all of the questions there. Or they may have ignored an agree–disagree scale and simply written in personal comments. Usually, detecting these errors requires physically examining the questionnaires. With online surveys, however, most such problems can usually be prevented by selecting options or requirements in the online questionnaire program that prevent the occurrence of such errors.

IBM **SPSS**

IBM SPSS Student Assistant:
Getting IBM SPSS Help

How to Handle Data Quality Issues When a researcher encounters data quality issues such as those just described, there are three options. First, if there are several egregious errors, the researcher is most likely to throw out the respondent's entire data row. Second, if the errors are minor and will not skew, or distort, the survey findings, the researcher will probably

MARKETING RESEARCH INSIGHT 11.4 *Global Application*

Data Quality Is a Global Concern

Marketing research is conducted on a global stage, and whenever a researcher deals with respondents who represent different cultures, different languages, and different social conventions, concerns about data quality arise. In a recent study, researchers investigated data quality and compared the degrees of middle-of-the-road responding, yea-saying, and nay-saying that they found.[60] Specifically, these researchers examined the responses of 5,569 respondents across 15 diverse countries and calculated the amounts of each of these three types of data quality problems. The following figures present standardized scores based on their findings of averages. With each graph, the 0 position on the vertical axis represents the average amount of the error found across all 15 countries. Points charted above 0 are greater than the "world" average, and points charted below 0 are lower than average. Thus, in the middle-of-the-road graph, this data quality problem is lowest in Brazil, South Korea, and France and greatest in Sweden, Singapore, and Germany. Average amounts are found in surveys of residents of the United States and the Netherlands. Yea-saying has a very different pattern, with low incidence of this error in surveys that take place in Germany, the Netherlands, and the United Kingdom, whereas high incidence is found in Brazil, South Korea, and India. "Average" yea-saying is found in surveys conducted in France, Japan, Canada, and the United States. One might expect yea-saying

and nay-saying to be negatively correlated—and they are, although not perfectly. In the nay-saying graph, the lowest incidences are found in Brazil, Singapore, and India, whereas the highest amounts of this error are found in the Netherlands, Japan, and South Korea. Average nay-saying tends to be exhibited in surveys administered in France, the United Kingdom, and the United States.

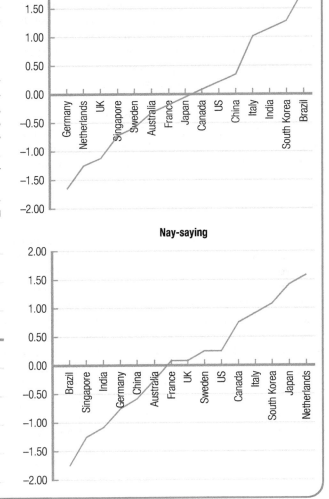

leave the respondent's entire data row in the dataset. Finally, if there is a combination of some obvious error-ridden responses and some valid responses, the researcher may opt to set the bad data items to blanks or missing data and to use only the good data items in subsequent analyses.

Summary

Total error in survey research is a combination of sampling error and nonsampling error. Sampling error may be controlled by the sample plan and the sample size. Researchers must know both the sources of nonsampling error and ways to minimize its effect on total error. The data collection phase of marketing research holds great potential for nonsampling errors. Intentional and unintentional errors on the parts of both interviewers and respondents must be regulated. Dishonesty, misunderstanding, and fatigue affect fieldworkers, whereas falsehoods, refusals, misunderstanding, and fatigue affect respondents. Several controls and procedures may be used to overcome these sources of error, such as supervision, validation, careful selection, and orientation sessions for interviewers. In addition, researchers use anonymity, confidentiality, incentives, validation checks, the third-person technique, well-drafted questionnaire instructions and examples, response options such as "unsure," reversals of scale endpoints, and prompters to minimize respondent errors.

Nonresponse errors of various types are encountered in the data collection phase; they include refusals to take part in the survey, break-offs during the survey, and item omission (not answering particular questions while answering all the others). Nonresponse error can be measured by calculating the response rate using the CASRO response rate formula.

Researchers are becoming increasingly dependent on panel companies, which maintain very large numbers of potential respondents who agree to answer surveys quickly and completely. Even though these companies hold nonresponse to a minimum and deliver seemingly representative samples, data quality is still an issue, and policies and procedures such as those listed in Table 11.5 should be strictly followed.

Responses to surveys are organized into a dataset, which consists of rows and columns of (mainly) numbers where each respondent is represented by a row and each question or question part is recorded in a column. Researchers use a data code book that indicates how the code numbers are related to the question responses on the questionnaire. Prior to data analysis, the dataset should be inspected for data quality issues such as incomplete responses, yea-saying, nay-saying, middle-of-the-road patterns, and other respondents whose answers are suspect. These respondents' answers should be removed from the dataset.

Key Terms

Nonsampling error (p. 289)
Data collection (p. 290)
Fieldworker error (p. 290)
Respondent error (p. 290)
Intentional fieldworker errors (p. 290)
Interviewer cheating (p. 290)
Leading the respondent (p. 291)
Unintentional interviewer errors (p. 291)
Interviewer misunderstanding (p. 291)
Fatigue-related mistakes (p. 293)
Intentional respondent errors (p. 293)
Falsehoods (p. 293)
Nonresponse (p. 293)
Unintentional respondent error (p. 293)

Respondent misunderstanding (p. 294)
Guessing (p. 294)
Attention loss (p. 294)
Distractions (p. 295)
Respondent fatigue (p. 295)
Supervision (p. 296)
Validation (p. 297)
Orientation sessions (p. 298)
Role-playing sessions (p. 298)
Anonymity (p. 298)
Confidentiality (p. 298)
Incentives (p. 298)
Validation checks (p. 298)
Third-person technique (p. 299)
Questionnaire instructions and examples (p. 299)

Reversals of scale endpoints (p. 299)
Prompters (p. 299)
Refusals (p. 301)
Break-offs (p. 301)
Item omission (p. 301)
Completed interview (p. 302)
CASRO response rate formula (p. 302)
Panel company (p. 304)
Dataset (p. 305)
Data coding (p. 306)
Data code book (p. 306)
Incomplete response (p. 307)
Yea-saying (p. 307)
Nay-saying (p. 307)
Middle-of-the-road pattern (p. 308)

Review Questions/Applications

11-1. Distinguish sampling error from nonsampling error.
11-2. How can sampling error be controlled?
11-3. Identify different types of intentional fieldworker errors and the controls used to minimize them.

Identify different types of unintentional fieldworker errors and the controls used to minimize them.

11-4. Identify different types of intentional respondent errors and the controls used to minimize them.

Identify different types of unintentional respondent errors and the controls used to minimize them.

11-5. Define *nonresponse*. List three types of nonresponse encountered in surveys.

11-6. Why is data quality a major concern for market researchers?

11-7. What is a *data code book*?

11-8. Why is data quality a concern for a researcher while working with a panel company?

11-9. Why is inspecting raw data important?

11-10. Your church is experiencing low attendance at its Wednesday evening Bible classes. You volunteer to design a telephone questionnaire aimed at finding out why church members are not attending these classes. Because the church has limited funds, members will be used as telephone interviewers. List the steps necessary to ensure high data quality in using this do-it-yourself option of field data collection.

11-11. Your business has started using a new market research company that charges roughly 30% lower than the more established company you were using in the past. The research results appear to be markedly different from previous surveys. When questioned, the market research company tells you to not worry and suspects that they are probably "unintentional respondent errors" caused by "fieldworker errors." What control mechanisms should have been used by the market research company?

11-12. Acme Refrigerant Reclamation Company performs large-scale reclamation of contaminated refrigerants as mandated by the U.S. Environmental Protection Agency. It wishes to determine what types of companies will make use of this service, so the marketing director designs a questionnaire intended for telephone administration. Respondents will be plant engineers, safety engineers, or directors of major companies throughout the United States. Should Acme use a professional field data collection company to gather the data? Why or why not?

11-13. You work part time for a telemarketing company. Your compensation is based on the number of credit card applicants you sign up. The company owner has noticed that the credit card solicitation business is slowing down, so she decides to take on some marketing research telephone interview business. When you start work on Monday, she assigns you to do telephone interviews and gives you a large stack of questionnaires to have completed. What intentional fieldworker errors are possible under the circumstances described here?

11-14. Indicate what specific intentional and unintentional respondent errors are likely with each of the following surveys.
   a. The Centers for Disease Control and Prevention sends out a mail questionnaire on attitudes and practices concerning the prevention of AIDS.
   b. Eyemasters has a mall-intercept survey performed to determine opinions and uses of contact lenses.
   c. Boy Scouts of America sponsors an online survey on Americans' views on humanitarian service agencies.

11-15. On your first day as a student marketing intern at the O-Tay Research Company, the supervisor hands you a list of yesterday's telephone interviewer records. She tells you to analyze them and to give her a report by 5 p.m. Well, get to it!

	Ronnie	Mary	Pam	Isabelle
Completed	20	30	15	19
Refused	10	2	8	9
Ineligible	15	4	14	15
Busy	20	10	21	23
Disconnected	0	1	3	2
Break-off	5	2	7	9
No answer	3	2	4	3

CASE 11.1

Skunk Juice

After brainstorming, two enterprising college students have come up with what they think is the perfect personal protection app. One of these entrepreneurs, an engineering major, has designed a cell phone case attachment with a spray nozzle. With the *Skunk Juice* app, the user can point the cell phone at an attacker and press "9," and it will shoot pepper spray at the attacker. Not only is the pepper spray

instantly debilitating if it touches any sensitive areas such as the eyes, but it also has a very obnoxious smell. Three successive presses of "9" auto-sends a 9-1-1 call, and the app notifies the 9-1-1 operator of the sender's location via GPS locator.

The second student, a marketing major, thinks the ideal target market for *Skunk Juice* is college women. He points out that on any given night on campus—and especially in the college's parking lots—female college students can be seen walking while using their cell phones or with their cell phones in their hands. The marketing student believes that college women who are worried about personal safety will be eager to buy the *Skunk Juice* app and cell phone cover attachment that holds the pepper spray feature as their cell phones are always in the "ready" state.

These two college students are, of course, working in a "bare bones" situation because they have tuition, living expenses, and all the other college student financial obligations to consider. However, their concept won the campus-wide "best budding idea" contest, and they have $1,000 to devote to marketing. The marketing major consults with his marketing research professor, who recommends that they conduct a survey of women enrolled in their college. Recognizing the meager budget, he suggests using the American Marketing Association (AMA) student chapter for personal interview data collection in a survey as a means of holding costs down. Personal interviews are necessary because the *Skunk Juice* app must be demonstrated and tested by respondents.

Although the enterprising entrepreneurs are excited about the survey, they are skeptical of the ability of students to execute this research. The professor offers to facilitate a meeting with them and the marketing research projects director of the student AMA chapter. He informs the AMA student chapter president of the opportunity and suggests that the marketing research projects director draft a list of the quality control safeguards that would be used in the *Skunk Juice* personal interview survey, utilizing 10 AMA student chapter interviewers (five teams) located at high-traffic locations on campus.

1. Take the role of the marketing research projects director. Draft all the interviewer controls you believe are necessary to ensure data collection comparable in quality to that gathered by a professional interviewing company.
2. The AMA student chapter president calls the marketing research projects director and says, "I'm concerned about the questionnaire's length. It will take over 20 minutes for the typical respondent to complete it. Isn't that length going to cause problems?" Again, take the role of the marketing research projects director. Indicate what nonresponse problems might result from the questionnaire's length and recommend ways to counter each of these problems.

CASE 11.2

Sony Televisions Ultra HD TV Survey

Located in Tokyo, Japan, Sony Mobile Communications is a prominent competitor in the worldwide electronics equipment market. Because of stagnant sales in its ultra HD TVs, that division has decided to use an online panel company as the data collection method for a survey on consumer attitudes and perceptions of Sony and its major competitors, such as Samsung and LG. Among the reasons for this decision are (1) use of an online questionnaire, (2) assurance of a random sample that represents U.S. households, (3) high response rate, (4) quick survey data collection, (5) low refusals to particular questions, (6) no need to ask about demographics, electronics ownership, and lifestyle, because these attributes of online panel members are known, and (7) reasonable total cost.

The Sony marketing research specialist heading up this survey has narrowed the choice to two online panel companies, based on inspections of their website descriptions, email and telephone communications, and other factors. The costs of using these companies are comparable, so no single provider is favored at this time. To assist in the selection process, the research team studies the set of questions published by the European Society for Opinion and Marketing Research (ESOMAR), *28 Questions to Help Research Buyers of Online Samples*.[61] The team selects five questions that are geared toward data quality. Each competing online panel company has prepared short responses to the five questions. Your task is to review the responses of Company A and Company B and to recommend which company to use. In your decision, remember that the assurance of highest data quality is the most important consideration.

Question 1. *What experience does your company have with providing online samples for market research?*

Company A: We have conducted market research since 1999. We are the only panel company to take advantage of computer technology and provide a truly nationally representative U.S. sample online.

Company B: We have supplied online U.S. samples since 1990 and European samples since 2000, and our Asian Panel went "live" in 2005. We have supplied approximately 5,000 online samples to our clients in the past 10 years.

Question 2. *Please describe and explain the type(s) of online sample sources from which you recruit respondents.*

Company A: Individuals volunteer for our online panel via our website, where they are informed that they will be compensated with redemption points based on the number of surveys in which they take part.

Company B: We recruit household members by asking them to join our panel, telling them they can have a say in the development of new products and services. They are rewarded with "credits" they can use to claim products.

Question 3. *What steps do you take to achieve a representative sample of the target population?*

Company A: Our master panel of over 100,000 individuals mirrors the population distribution of the U.S. Census with respect to 10 demographic factors such as gender, education, income, marital status, etc.

Company B: The client specifies the target market population using any one of 1,000 variables, including demographic, ownership, purchase behavior, and other variables. We invite panelists who meet the client's criteria to participate in the survey.

Question 4. *What profiling data are held on respondents? How is it done?*

Company A: We maintain extensive individual-level data in the form of about 1,000 variables, including demographics, household characteristics, financials, shopping and ownership, lifestyles, and more. All are updated every other year.

Company B: For each panelist, we have about 2,500 data points on demographics, assortment of goods and services owned, segmentation/lifestyle factors, health-related matters, political opinions, travel, financials, Internet usage, leisure activities, memberships, etc. Our updating is done annually.

Question 5. *Please describe your survey invitation process.*

Company A: Typically a survey invitation is sent via email and posted on every selected panel member's personal member page with a link to the online survey location: "Click here to start your survey." The email invitation is sent daily to selected panelists until the survey quota is filled.

Company B: Based on the client's sample requirements, we email selected panelists with a link to the online survey. After 48 hours, if the panelist has not participated, we send a reminder, and we do so again 48 hours after the first reminder.

12

Using Descriptive Analysis, Performing Population Estimates, and Testing Hypotheses

"WHERE WE ARE"

1 Establish the need for marketing research.
2 Define the problem.
3 Establish research objectives.
4 Determine research design.
5 Identify information types and sources.
6 Determine methods of accessing data.
7 Design data collection forms.
8 Determine the sample plan and size.
9 Collect data.
10 Analyze data.
11 Prepare and present the final research report.

Believe It or Not, You Already Know Basic Descriptive Statistics

What is the first question students ask their professor after the class takes a test?

© Wavebreakmedia/Shutterstock

When asked what is meant by basic descriptive statistics, most students start trying to recall some of the concepts they learned back in their basic statistics course. Of course, trying to recall these concepts is painful, as most students did not enjoy their required statistics course experience. Probably a few of you remember something about basic descriptive statistics, but it may come as a surprise to learn that *all* of you know what they are! That's correct. In fact, you use basic descriptive statistics frequently, even though you may not realize it, and we can prove it. What are the first few questions students ask their professors after they take a test? In our experience as professors, the questions go something like this…

First question: "What was the average score on the test?"

Let's suppose that your professor answers "85." Now, some of you were hoping to make much higher than a B and others of you may wonder, "Wow! I hope I made an 85 but I wonder how many scored below the average." So, the answer to the first question almost immediately gives rise to the second question.

Second question: "What was the grade distribution? How many As, Bs, Cs, and so on?"

These two "natural" questions that students ask about grades actually involve basic descriptive statistics. For a survey, basic descriptive statistics answer two fundamental questions: (1) How did the average person respond? and (2) How different are the others from this average? So, when your professor says the average grade was an 85, he or she is answering the first question. When your professor gives you the numbers, or percentages, of letter grades A, B, C, and so forth for the class, he or she is answering the second question. Note that it is important to know answers to both questions. Knowing only the first answer tells you the average performance of the class but not how different the other scores may be. While it is possible that everyone scored an 85, it is also possible that no one scored an 85; some may have scored very high and some may have scored very low! Note how these answers will cause the professor to make different interpretations of the average test score. In the first case, everyone is doing "average." In the second case, the class has some outstanding students and others who, for whatever reason, are not learning the material well at all. You can see why it is important to answer both these questions.

Let's think of a marketing research application of basic descriptive statistics. In our *Auto Concepts* case we have asked a sample of consumers many questions about their demographics, magazine readership, other media preferences, and the desirability of various fuel-efficient new automobile models that could be developed. After making certain that all the data have been correctly input into a computer program such as SPSS, the marketing researcher will run basic descriptive statistics. You will have the opportunity to work with this SPSS dataset as you read and do the Active Learning and Integrated Case exercises in this chapter. For now, simply read our example. We will look at the question: "How desirable is a five-seat economy gasoline automobile model?" The answers are measured on a 1–7 scale ranging from Very undesirable (1) to Very desirable (7). Now we are ready to answer our two questions: What was the average response to the question? Since we have an interval scale, "average" may be an arithmetic mean. As you will learn in this chapter, when you want to calculate an arithmetic mean, you run the SPSS command "Descriptives," which gives you the following output:

IBM **SPSS**

Descriptive Statistics					
	N	**Minimum**	**Maximum**	**Mean**	**Std. Deviation**
Desirability: 5-Seat Economy Gasoline	1,000	1	7	3.21	1.453
Valid N (listwise)	1,000				

We see our average as 3.21 on a 7-point scale. This is like knowing that our average test score is 85, which alone gives us some information. We know there is some preference for this auto; we don't have a really low score nor do we have an extremely high score. Now, what about our second question? How different are those who didn't have this "average" score? Statisticians use the term *variance* to describe the degree to which data vary. One measure of variance is the *standard deviation*, which is reported to us as 1.453. The higher this number, the more people differ from the average; the lower the number, the less they differ. Another measure of variance is the *range*. We see that some scored the minimum (1) and some scored the maximum (7). If we want to know how many scored in each of the seven different scale categories, we would run another SPSS command, "Frequencies." The output is shown here.

Desirability: 5-Seat Economy Gasoline				
	Frequency	**Percent**	**Valid Percent**	**Cumulative Percent**
Very undesirable	104	10.4	10.4	10.4
Undesirable	248	24.8	24.8	35.2
Somewhat undesirable	288	28.8	28.8	64.0
Neutral	141	14.1	14.1	78.1
Somewhat desirable	150	15.0	15.0	93.1
Desirable	51	5.1	5.1	98.2
Very desirable	18	1.8	1.8	100.0
Total	1,000	100.0	100.0	

With these two tables alone, the marketing researcher has provided the client with all the basic descriptive statistics the client needs to understand the responses to this question. In this chapter you will learn when and how to run "Descriptives" and "Frequencies" in SPSS. When you finish the chapter, you will be able to do more than just articulate what is meant by basic descriptive statistics. You will know how to use the powerful SPSS tool to generate them for you. You will also learn that basic descriptive statistics are the mainstay of most marketing research projects.

This chapter begins our discussion of the various statistical techniques available to the marketing researcher. As you will soon learn, these techniques are devices to convert formless data into valuable information, as illustrated in the vignette that opens this chapter. These techniques summarize and communicate patterns found in the datasets marketing researchers analyze. We preview five different types of statistical analyses commonly used by marketing researchers. Next, we define descriptive analysis and discuss descriptive measures such as the mode, median, and mean. We also discuss measures of variability, including the frequency distribution, range, and standard deviation. It is important to understand when each measure is appropriate, so this topic is also addressed. Finally, we show you how to obtain the various descriptive statistics available in SPSS.

We continue the chapter by noting that the term *statistic* applies to a number computed for a sample, whereas the term *parameter* pertains to the related population value. Next, we describe the concept of logical inference and show how it relates to statistical inference. There are two basic types of statistical inference, and we discuss both cases. The first is parameter estimation in which a value, such as the population mean, is estimated based on a sample's mean and its size. Second is hypothesis testing in which an assessment is made as to how much of a sample's findings support a manager's or researcher's a priori belief regarding the size of a population value. We provide formulas and numerical examples and also show examples of SPSS procedures and output using the Auto Concepts survey data.

12-1 Types of Statistical Analyses Used in Marketing Research

You learned in the previous chapter that a marketing researcher works with a dataset, which is an arrangement of numbers (mainly) in rows and columns. You also know that the columns represent answers to the various questions on the survey questionnaire, and the rows represent each respondent. The problem confronting the marketing researcher when faced with a dataset is **data analysis**, which is defined as the process of describing a dataset by computing a small number of statistics that characterize various aspects of the dataset. Data analysis distills the dataset while retaining enough information so the client can mentally envision its salient characteristics.[1]

There are five basic types of statistical analyses that can be used by marketing researchers to reduce a dataset: descriptive analysis, inference analysis, difference analysis, association analysis, and relationships analysis (Table 12.1). Each one has a unique role in the data analysis process; moreover, they are usually combined into a complete analysis of the information in order to satisfy the research objectives. These techniques are progressively more complex, but at the same time, they convert raw data into increasingly more useful information as they increase in complexity.

These introductory comments preview the subject matter that will be covered in this and other chapters. Because this is an introduction, we use the names of statistical procedures, but we do not define or describe them here. The specific techniques are all developed later in this textbook. It is important, however, that you understand each of the various categories of analysis available to the marketing researcher and comprehend generally what each is about.

DESCRIPTIVE ANALYSIS

Certain measures such as the mean, mode, standard deviation, and range are forms of **descriptive analysis** used by marketing researchers to describe the sample dataset in such a way as to portray the "typical" respondent and to reveal the general pattern of responses. Descriptive measures are typically used early in the analysis process and become foundations for subsequent analysis.[2]

Descriptive analysis is used to describe the variables (question responses) in a dataset (all respondents' answers).

TABLE 12.1 Five Types of Statistical Analyses Used by Marketing Researchers

Type	Description	Example	Statistical Concepts
Descriptive Analysis (Chapter 12)	Summarizes basic findings for the sample	Describes the typical respondent, describes how similar respondents are to the typical respondent	Mean, median, mode, frequency distribution, range, standard deviation
Inference Analysis (Chapter 12)	Determines population parameters, tests hypotheses	Estimates population values	Standard error, null hypothesis
Difference Analysis (Chapter 13)	Determines if differences exist	Evaluates the statistical significance of difference in the means of two groups in a sample	t test of differences, analysis of variance
Association Analysis (Chapter 14)	Determines connections	Determines if two variables are related in a systematic way	Correlation, cross-tabulation
Relationships Analysis (Chapter 15)	Finds complex relationships for the variables in the dataset	Determines how several independent variables are related to a key dependent variable	Multiple regression

INFERENCE ANALYSIS

Inference analysis is used to generate conclusions about the population's characteristics based on the sample data.

When statistical procedures are used by marketing researchers to generalize the results of the sample to the target population that it represents, the process is referred to as **inference analysis**. In other words, such statistical procedures allow a researcher to draw conclusions about the population based on information contained in the dataset provided by the sample.

Inferential statistics include hypothesis testing and estimating true population values using confidence intervals. We describe basic statistical inference in this chapter.

DIFFERENCE ANALYSIS

Occasionally, a marketing researcher needs to determine whether two groups are different. For example, the researcher may be investigating credit card usage and may want to see if high-income earners differ from moderate-income earners in how often they use American Express. The researcher may statistically compare the average annual dollar expenditures charged on American Express by high- versus moderate-income buyers. Important market segmentation information may come from this analysis. Or he or she may run an experiment to see which of several alternative advertising themes garners the most favorable impression. The researcher uses **difference analysis** to determine the degree to which real and generalizable differences exist in the population in order to help the manager make an enlightened decision on which advertising theme to use. Statistical differences analyses include the *t* test for significant differences between groups and analysis of variance. We define and describe them in Chapter 13.

© Paffy/Shutterstock

Differences analysis may reveal important distinctions among various types of credit card users.

Difference analysis is used to compare the mean of the responses of one group to that of another group, such as satisfaction ratings for "heavy" users versus "light" users.

Association analysis determines the strength and direction of relationships between two or more variables (questions in the survey).

ASSOCIATION ANALYSIS

Other statistical techniques are used by researchers to determine systematic relationships among variables. **Association analysis** investigates if and how two variables are related. For instance, are advertising recall scores positively associated with intentions to buy the advertised brand? Are expenditures on sales force training positively associated with sales force performance? Depending on the statistic used, the analysis may indicate the strength of the association and/or the direction of the association between two questions on a questionnaire in a given study. We devote Chapter 14 to descriptions of cross-tabulations and correlations that are basic association analysis methods used in marketing research.

RELATIONSHIPS ANALYSIS

Techniques are also available if the researcher is interested in determining more complex patterns of associations, but most of these procedures are beyond the scope of this textbook, with one exception. Statistical procedures and models are available to the marketing researcher to help make forecasts about future events; these fall under the category of **relationships analysis**. Regression analysis is commonly used by the marketing researcher to understand such complex connections. Because marketing managers are typically worried about several factors simultaneously, understanding connections among these factors is very desirable, as this understanding can provide very valuable insight of multiple relationships among the variables in a dataset. Regression analysis is described in depth in Chapter 15.

Relationships analysis allows insights into multiple relationships among variables.

It is not our intention to make you an expert in statistical analysis. Rather, the primary objective of our chapters on statistical analysis is to acquaint you with the basic concepts involved in each of the selected measures. You will certainly do basic statistical analysis throughout your marketing career, and it is very likely that you will encounter information summarized in statistical terms. So it is important for you to have a conceptual understanding of the commonly used statistical procedures. Our descriptions are intended to show you when and where each measure is appropriately used and to help you interpret the meaning of the statistical result once it is reported. We also rely heavily on computer statistical program output because you will surely encounter statistical program output in your company's marketing information system and/or summarized in a marketing research study report.

12-2 Understanding Descriptive Analysis

We now turn to the several tools in descriptive analysis available to the researcher to summarize the data obtained from a sample of respondents. In this chapter and in all other data analysis chapters, we are going to use the Auto Concepts survey dataset organized in an SPSS data file called **Auto Concepts.sav**. That way, you can reconstruct the data analysis on your own with SPSS using the dataset. To download this dataset, go to the following website http://www.pearsonglobaleditions.com/burns and find the dataset download area.

Two sets of measures are used extensively to describe the information obtained in a sample. The first set involves measures of central tendency or measures that describe the "typical" respondent or response. The second set involves measures of variability or measures that describe how similar (dissimilar) respondents or responses are to (from) "typical" respondents or responses. Other types of descriptive measures are available, but they do not enjoy the popularity of central tendency and variability. In fact, they are rarely reported to clients.

Commonly used descriptive analysis reveals central tendency (typical response) and variability (similarity of responses).

MEASURES OF CENTRAL TENDENCY: SUMMARIZING THE "TYPICAL" RESPONDENT

The basic data analysis goal involved in all **measures of central tendency** is to report a single piece of information that describes the most typical response to a question. The term *central tendency* applies to any statistical measure used that somehow reflects a typical or frequent response.[3] Three such measures of central tendency are commonly used as data analysis devices.[4] They are the mode, the median, and the mean. We describe each one in turn.

Three measures of central tendency are mode, median, and mean.

Mode The **mode** is a descriptive analysis measure defined as that value in a string of numbers that occurs most often. In other words, if you scanned a list of numbers constituting a field in a dataset, the mode would be that number that appeared more than any other.

You should note that the mode is a relative measure of central tendency, for it does not require that a majority of responses occurred for this value. Instead, it simply specifies the value that occurs most frequently, and there is *no* requirement that this occurrence is 50% or more. It can take on any value as long as it is the most frequently occurring number. If a tie for the mode occurs, the distribution is considered to be "bimodal." Or it might even be "trimodal" if there is a three-way tie.

With a set of numbers, the mode is that number appearing most often.

Median An alternative measure of central tendency is the **median**, which expresses that value whose occurrence lies in the middle of an ordered set of values. That is, it is the value such that one-half of all of the other values is greater than the median and one-half of the remaining values is less than the median. Thus, the median tells us the approximate halfway point in a set or string of numbers that are arranged in ascending or descending order while taking into account the frequency of each value. With an odd number of values, the median will always fall on one of the values, but with an even number of values, the median may fall between two adjacent values.

The median expresses the value whose occurrence lies in the middle of a set of ordered values.

To determine the median, the researcher creates a frequency or percentage distribution with the numbers in the string in either ascending or descending order. In addition to the raw percentages, he or she computes cumulative percentages and, by inspecting these, finds where the 50–50 break occurs. You should notice that the median supplies more information than does the mode, for a mode may occur anywhere in the string, but the median must be at the halfway point.

The mean is the arithmetic average of a set of numbers.

Marketing Research on YouTube™ | To learn about measures of central tendency, launch **www.youtube.com**, and search for "Measures of Central Tendency Rap."

Measures of variability reveal the typical difference between the values in a set of values.

Measures of variability include frequency distribution, range, and standard deviation.

A frequency (percentage) distribution reveals the number (percent) of occurrences of each number in a set of numbers.

Mean A third measure of central tendency is the **mean**, sometimes referred to as the average. It differs from the mode and the median in that a computation is necessary. The mean is computed through the use of the following formula:

Formula for a mean

$$\text{Mean } (\bar{x}) = \frac{\sum_{i=1}^{n} x_i}{n}$$

where

n = the number of cases

x_i = each individual value

$\sum$ signifies that all the x_i values are summed

As you can see, all of the members in the set of n numbers, each designated by x_i, are summed and that total is divided by the number of members in that set. The resulting number is the mean, a measure that indicates the central tendency of those values. It approximates the typical value in that set of values. Because the mean is determined by taking every member of the set of numbers into account through this formula, it is more informative than the median. The mean communicates a great deal of information, and it is a practically universally understood statistical concept.

MEASURES OF VARIABILITY: RELATING THE DIVERSITY OF RESPONDENTS

Although they are extremely useful, measures of central tendency are incomplete descriptors of the values in a particular set of numbers. That is, they do not indicate the variability of responses to a particular question or, alternatively, the diversity of respondents on some characteristic measured in our survey. To gain sensitivity for the diversity or variability of values, the marketing researcher must turn to measures of variability. All **measures of variability** are concerned with depicting the "typical" difference among the numbers in a set of values.

It is one matter to know the mode or some other measure of central tendency, but it is quite another matter to be aware of how close to that mean or measure of central tendency the rest of the values fall. Knowing the variability of the data could greatly impact a marketing decision based on the data because it expresses how similar the respondents are to one another on the topic under examination. Three measures of variability are frequency distribution, range, and standard deviation. Each measure provides its own unique version of information that helps to describe the diversity of responses.

Frequency and Percentage Distribution A **frequency distribution** is a tabulation of the number of times that each different value appears in a particular set of values. Frequencies themselves are raw counts, and normally these frequencies are converted into percentages for ease of comparison. The conversion is arrived at very simply through the division of the frequency for each value by the total number of observations for all of the values, resulting in a percent, called a **percentage distribution**. Of course, the sum of all these percent values is 100%.

To elaborate, a frequency distribution is an accounting of the occurrences of values in a set. It quickly communicates all the different values in the set, and it expresses how similar the values are. The percentage distribution is often used along with or in place of a frequency distribution because people can easily relate to percentages. Plus, percentage distributions are easily presented as

Variability indicates how different respondents are on a topic, such as what model of automobile is preferred.

pie or bar charts,[5] which are convenient graphical representations of these distributions that researchers find very helpful in communicating findings to clients or others.

Range The **range** identifies the distance between the lowest value (minimum) and the highest value (maximum) in an ordered set of values. Stated somewhat differently, the range specifies the difference between the endpoints in a set of values arranged in order. The range does not provide the same amount of information supplied by a frequency distribution; however, it identifies the interval in which the set of values occurs. The range also does not tell you how often the maximum and minimum occurred, but it does provide some information on the dispersion by indicating how far apart the extremes are found.

> The range identifies the maximum and minimum values in a set of numbers.

Standard Deviation The **standard deviation** indicates the degree of variation or diversity in the values in such a way as to be translatable into a normal or bell-shaped curve distribution. Marketing researchers often rely on the standard deviation when performing basic analyses, and they usually report it in their tables. So it is worthwhile to digress for a moment to describe this statistical concept.

> A standard deviation indicates the degree of variation in a way that can be translated into a bell-shaped curve distribution.

Figure 12.1 shows the properties of a bell-shaped or normal distribution of values. As we have indicated in our chapter on sample size determination, the usefulness of this model is apparent when you realize that it is a symmetric distribution: Exactly 50% of the distribution lies on either side of the midpoint (the apex of the curve). With a normal curve, the midpoint is also the mean, signified by μ, the population mean, in the figure. Standard deviations are standardized units of measurement that are located on the horizontal axis. They relate directly to assumptions about the normal curve. For example, the range of 1.64 standard deviations above and 1.64 standard deviations below the midpoint includes 90% of the total area underneath that curve. Because the bell-shaped distribution is a theoretical or ideal concept, this property never changes. Moreover, the proportion of area under the curve and within plus or minus any number of standard deviations from the mean is perfectly known. For the purposes of this presentation, normally only two or three of these values are of interest to marketing researchers. Specifically, ±2.58 standard deviations describes the range in which 99% of the area underneath the curve is found, ±1.96 standard deviations is associated with 95% of the area underneath the curve, and ±1.64 standard deviations corresponds to 90% of the bell-shaped curve's area. Remember, we must assume that the shape of the frequency distribution of the numbers approximates a normal curve, so keep this in mind during our following examples.

> The standard deviation embodies the properties of a bell-shaped distribution of values.

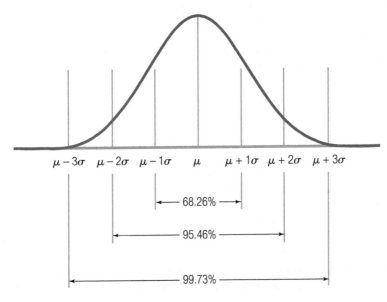

FIGURE 12.1 Normal Curve Interpretation of Standard Deviation

It is now time to review the calculation of the standard deviation. The equation typically used for the standard deviation is as follows:

Formula for a standard deviation

$$\text{Standard deviation } (s) = \sqrt{\dfrac{\displaystyle\sum_{i-1}^{n} (x_i - \bar{x})^2}{n - 1}}$$

where

n = the number of cases

x_i = each individual value

$\bar{x}$ = the mean (average)

$\sum$ signifies that all the x_i values are summed

The standard deviation is a measure of the differences of all observations from the mean, expressed as a single number. To compute the standard deviation, you must begin with the mean, and then compare each observation to the mean by subtracting and squaring the difference. It may seem strange to square differences, add them up, divide them by $(n - 1)$ and then take the square root. If we did not square the differences, we would have positive and negative values; if we summed them, there would be a cancellation effect. That is, large negative differences would cancel out large positive differences, and the numerator would end up being close to zero. But this result is contrary to what we know is the case with large differences: There is variation, which should be expressed by the standard deviation. The formula remedies this problem by squaring the subtracted differences before they are summed. Squaring converts all negative numbers to positives and, of course, leaves the positives positive. Next, all of the squared differences are summed and divided by 1 less than the number of total observations in the string of values; 1 is subtracted from the number of observations to achieve what is typically called an "unbiased" estimate of the standard deviation. But we now have an inflation factor to worry about because every comparison has been squared. To adjust for this, the equation specifies that the square root be taken after all other operations are performed. This final step adjusts the value back down to the original measure (e.g., units rather than squared units). By the way, if you did not take the square root at the end, the value would be referred to as the **variance**. In other words, the variance is the standard deviation squared.

Now, whenever a standard deviation is reported along with a mean, a specific picture should appear in your mind. Assuming that the distribution is bell shaped, the size of the standard deviation number helps you envision how similar or dissimilar the typical responses are to the mean. If the standard deviation is small, the distribution is greatly compressed. With a large standard deviation value, the distribution is consequently stretched out at both ends.

The squaring operation in the standard deviation formula is used to avoid the cancellation effect.

With a bell-shaped distribution, 95% of the values lie within ±1.96 times the standard deviation away from the mean.

Marketing Research on YouTube™ To learn about measures of central tendency, launch **www.youtube.com**, and search for "Summarizing Distributions: Measures of Variability."

12-3   When to Use a Particular Descriptive Measure

In Chapter 8, you learned that the level of measurement for a scale affects how it may be statistically analyzed. Remember, for instance, that nominal question forms contain much less information than do those questions with interval scaling assumptions. Recall that in Chapter 8, we defined and gave examples of interval and ratio scales. SPSS allows users to identify scale types, and it uses "scale" as the label to refer to either an interval or a ratio scale. We will use the SPSS label from this point on. Similarly, the amount of information provided by each of the various measures of central tendency and dispersion differs. As a general rule, statistical measures that communicate the most amount of information should be used with scales that contain the most amount of information, and measures that communicate the least amount of information should be used with scales that contain the

TABLE 12.2   What Descriptive Statistic to Use When

Example Question	Measurement Level	Central Tendency (Most Typical Response)	Variability (Similarity of Responses)
What is your gender?	Nominal scale	Mode	Frequency and/or percentage distribution
Rank these five brands from your first choice to your fifth choice.	Ordinal scale	Median	Cumulative percentage distribution
On a scale of 1 to 5, how does "Starbucks" rate on variety of its coffee drinks?	Interval scale	Mean	Standard deviation and/or range
About how many times did you buy fast food for lunch last week?	Ratio scale	Mean	Standard deviation and/or range

least amount of information. The level of measurement determines the appropriate measure; otherwise, the measure cannot be interpreted.

At first reading, this rule may seem confusing, but on reflection it should become clear that the level of measurement of each question dictates the measure that should be used. It is precisely at this point that you must remember the arbitrary nature of coding schemes. For instance, if on a demographic question concerning religious affiliation, "Catholic" is assigned a "1," "Protestant" is assigned a "2," "Jewish" is assigned a "3," and so forth, a mean could be computed. But what would be the interpretation of an average religion of 2.36? It would have no practical interpretation because the mean assumes interval or ratio scaling (SPSS's "scale"), whereas the religion categories are nominal. The mode would be the appropriate central tendency measure for these responses.

Table 12.2 indicates how the level of measurement relates to each of the three measures of central tendency and measures of variation. The table should remind you that a clear understanding of the level of measurement for each question on the questionnaire is essential because the researcher must select the statistical procedure and direct the computer to perform the procedure. The computer cannot distinguish the level of measurement because we typically store and handle our data as numbers as matters of convention and convenience.

© Eric Isselee/Shutterstock

Don't monkey around! Use the guide in Table 12.2 to decide which is the appropriate descriptive analysis to use.

12-4   The Auto Concepts Survey: Obtaining Descriptive Statistics with SPSS

INTEGRATED CASE

Beginning with this chapter and all subsequent chapters dealing with statistical analyses, we provide illustrations with the use of SPSS in two ways. First, in your textbook descriptions, we indicate step-by-step procedures used with SPSS to obtain the statistical analyses being described. Plus, we have included examples of SPSS output in these sections. The second way is with the use of your SPSS Student Assistant. By now, you are well acquainted with the Student Assistant. We prompt you to look at the statistical analysis sections that illustrate how to operate SPSS, as well as how to find specific statistical results in SPSS output.

The scaling assumptions underlying a question determine which descriptive measure is appropriate.

Descriptive statistics are needed to see the Auto Concepts survey's basic findings.

 **Active Learning**

Compute Measures of Central Tendency and Variability

This chapter has described measures of central tendency (mean, median, and mode) as well as measures of variability (percentage distribution, range, and standard deviation). At the same time, you should realize that certain measures are appropriate for some scales but inappropriate for other scales. In the table that follows is a dataset of respondents who answered questions on a survey about the propane gas grills they own.

For each question, determine what measure(s) of central tendency and what measures of variability are appropriate and compute them. We have identified the relevant measures under the "Respondent" column of the dataset, and your task is to write in the proper answer (or "not appropriate") under each of the three questions in the survey.

Respondent	For how many years have you owned your gas grill?	Where did you purchase your gas grill?	About how much did you pay for your gas grill?
1	2	Department store	$200
2	7	Hardware store	$500
3	8	Department store	$300
4	4	Specialty store	$400
5	2	Specialty store	$600
6	1	Department store	$300
7	3	Department store	$400
8	4	Department store	$300
9	6	Specialty store	$500
10	8	Department store	$400
Mean	____	____	____
Standard Deviation	____	____	____
Range: maximum	____	____	____
Range: minimum	____	____	____
Median	____	____	____
Mode	____	____	____

IBM **SPSS**   USE SPSS TO OPEN UP AND USE THE AUTO CONCEPTS DATASET

For your information and as a quick review, the questionnaire was posted online, and with the aid of a panel company qualified respondents answered the questions and submitted their questionnaires in the time period allotted for the online survey. Certain questions, such as demographics and automobile ownership, were purchased from the panel company's database. The survey and database data were combined and set up in SPSS with variable names and value labels and cleaned. The final dataset has a total of 1,000 respondents and 32 variables, and it exists as an SPSS data file called "**Auto Concepts.sav**." At your earliest convenience, you should download the "**Auto Concepts.sav**" file and use SPSS to examine the questions and response formats that were used in the Auto Concepts survey. We will refer to some of these as we instruct you on the use of SPSS for various types of analyses described in this chapter and other chapters that follow.

From now on, you are going to "watch over the shoulder" of the marketing researcher confronted with analyzing this dataset. As you should know, an SPSS dataset is made up of rows and columns (in the "Data View" window). The columns are the variables that correspond to the questions and parts of questions on the questionnaire, and the individual rows represent each respondent. To review the response categories and scales used in the survey, use the "Variable View" window and/or the Utilities-Variables feature of SPSS.

OBTAINING A FREQUENCY DISTRIBUTION AND THE MODE WITH SPSS

Many questions on the Auto Concepts survey had categorical response options and, thus, embodied nominal scaling assumptions. With a nominal scale, the mode is the appropriate measure of central tendency, and variation must be assessed by looking at the distribution of responses across the various response categories.

To illustrate how to obtain a frequency distribution and a percentage distribution and to determine the mode of our 1,000-respondent Auto Concepts dataset, we will use the size of the hometown variable, as it is a nominal scale. Figure 12.2 shows the clickstream sequence to find a mode for the size of hometown using the entire Auto Concepts survey dataset. As you can see, the primary menu sequence is ANALYZE-DESCRIPTIVE STATISTICS-FREQUENCIES. This sequence opens up the variable selection window where you specify the variable(s) to be analyzed, and the Statistics … button opens up the Statistics window, which has several statistical concepts as options. Since we are working only with the mode, click in the check mark box beside the Mode. Click Continue to close this window and OK to close the variable selection and cause SPSS to create a frequency distribution and to identify the mode. You can see this output in Figure 12.3 where the code number "4" is specified as the mode response, and the frequency distribution shows that "500K to 1 million" is the largest hometown/city size represented with 396 respondents selecting it, or 39.6% of the total.

As you look at the output, you should notice that the variable labels and value labels were defined, and they appear on the output. The DESCRIPTIVE STATISTICS-FREQUENCIES procedure creates a frequency distribution and associated percentage distribution of the responses for each question. Its output includes a statistics table and a table for each variable that includes the variable label, value labels, frequencies, percent, valid percent, and cumulative percent.

IBM SPSS

A frequency distribution and mode are appropriate for nominal scales.

Use the ANALYZE-DESCRIPTIVE STATISTICS-FREQUENCIES procedure to produce descriptive statistics for variables with nominal or ordinal scaling.

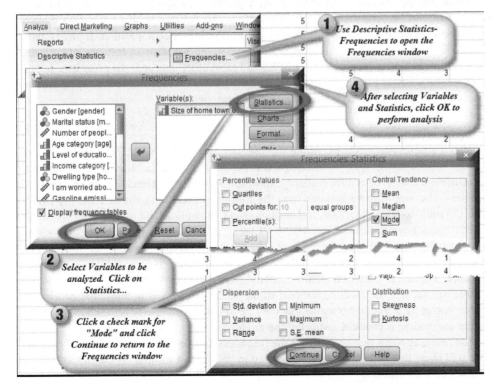

FIGURE 12.2
IBM SPSS Clickstream to Obtain a Frequency Distribution and the Mode

Source: Reprint Courtesy of International Business Machines Corporation, © International Business Machines Corporation.

FIGURE 12.3
IBM SPSS Output for a Frequency Distribution and the Mode

Source: Reprint Courtesy of International Business Machines Corporation, © International Business Machines Corporation.

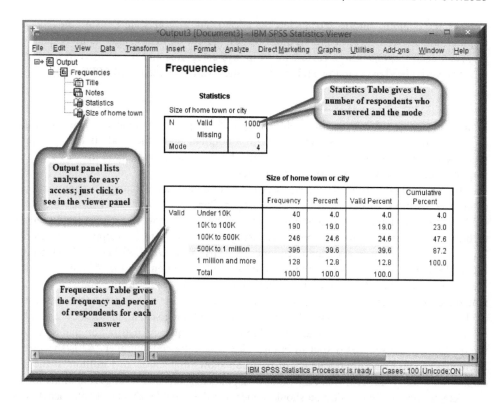

IBM SPSS
IBM SPSS Student Assistant Element
Descriptive Statistics for Nominal Data: Frequencies, Percents, Mode

Our Auto Concepts survey dataset is *not* typical because there are no missing answers. There are no missing responses because the dataset was purchased from a consumer panel company that guaranteed 100% response. However, as you learn in Chapter 14, it is not uncommon for respondents to refuse to answer a question in a survey or for them to be unable to answer a question. Alternatively, a respondent may be directed to skip a question if his or her previous answer does not qualify him or her for the subsequent question. If any of these occurs, and the respondent is still included in the dataset, we have an instance of "missing data." This is absolutely no problem for SPSS and most other data analysis programs, but the output will be adjusted to compensate for the missing data. Do the following Active Learning exercise to learn how SPSS recognizes and handles missing data.

IBM SPSS   **FINDING THE MEDIAN WITH SPSS**

It is also a simple matter to determine the median using the ANALYZE-DESCRIPTIVE STATISTICS-FREQUENCIES menu sequence. As we indicated, in order for the median to be a sensible measure of central tendency, the values must, at minimum, have ordinal scale properties. The size of town variable uses the following codes: (1) Under 10K, (2) 10K to 100K, (3) 100K to 500K, (4) 500K to 1 million, and (5) 1 million and more.

The codes have ordinal properties: A "1" size is smaller than a "2" size, and so on, through a "5" size city. It is a simple matter to use the Auto Concepts dataset to obtain the size of hometown median from the full dataset. The procedure is very similar to the mode procedure as, first, the "size of hometown or city" variable is selected in the variable selection window, but, second, the median, rather than the mode, is checked in the statistics window. Refer to Figure 12.3, and just imagine that the size of hometown or city is the chosen variable and that the median is checked instead of the mode.

The resulting SPSS output will have the frequency distribution of our likelihood variable, and it will show that code number 4, pertaining to "500K to 1 million" is the 50/50 location in the scale, or the median.

 Active Learning ─────────────────────────────────────

IBM **SPSS**

How SPSS Handles Missing Data

Use your SPSS Auto Concepts dataset to compute the frequency distribution and percentage distribution and to identify the mode as we have just described. Use Figure 12.2 to direct your mouse clicks and selections using the hometown size variable in the dataset. Compare the SPSS output that you obtain with Figure 12.3 and make sure that you can identify the mode of 5 (1 million and more). Also, if you want to understand the "valid percent" output provided by SPSS for its Frequencies analysis, use your cursor and block the first 10 respondents on the Data View of the SPSS Data Editor. With a right-click of your mouse, use the "clear" function to set these 10 town size numbers to blanks. Then rerun the frequencies for the hometown size variable.

You will now see that the SPSS frequencies table reports the 10 "Missing System" respondents because their responses were blanks. While missing data are not a concern in the Auto Concepts survey dataset, you most certainly will encounter this issue if your marketing research course includes an actual survey that you perform as part of the course requirements. Wait! Don't save your Auto Concepts dataset with the missing data unless you give it a new SPSS dataset name such as AutoConceptswithMissingData.sav.

FINDING THE MEAN, RANGE, AND STANDARD DEVIATION WITH SPSS

As we have mentioned, computer statistical programs cannot distinguish the level of measurement of various questions. Consequently, it is necessary for the analyst to discern the level of measurement and to select the correct procedure(s). There are some questions in the Auto Concepts survey that asked respondents to use a 7-point Likert (very strongly disagree to very strongly agree) response scale, so we have an interval scale.

For quick data analysis of these variables, we do not want frequency tables for two reasons. First, the Likert scale variables are interval scaled and, second, the frequency tables would be full of percents of all sizes, and their modes and medians would be very confusing, to say the least. But we can turn to the mean and other summarization statistics for interval or ratio data for help here. Specifically, we will use the ANALYZE-DESCRIPTIVE STATISTICS-DESCRIPTIVES commands, and click on the Options button after we have selected "Gasoline emissions contribute to global warming" as the variable for analysis. In the Options panel, you can select the mean, standard deviation, range, and so forth. Refer to Figure 12.4 for the SPSS clickstream sequence.

Figure 12.5 presents the output generated from this option. In our Auto Concepts survey, the output reveals that the average reaction to the statement "Gasoline emissions contribute to global warming" is 4.62. Recalling the interval scale used (1=Very strongly disagree, 2=Strongly disagree, 3=Disagree, 4=Neither disagree nor agree, 5=Agree, 6=Strongly agree, and 7=Very strongly agree), a 4.62 rounds to "5," meaning that, on average, our survey

IBM **SPSS**

IBM **SPSS**

IBM SPSS Student Assistant Element
Obtaining Descriptive Statistics for Scaled Data: Mean, Standard Deviation, Median, Range

When using SPSS DESCRIPTIVES, always bear in mind the variables being analyzed should be interval or ratio scaled.

 Active Learning ─────────────────────────────────────

Find a Median with SPSS

Use your SPSS Auto Concepts dataset to find the median size of hometown variable in the Auto Concepts survey. Again, use Figure 12.2 as your clickstream guide, but select the "number of people in household" variable for the analysis and place a check mark in the median checkbox. If you do not find that the code number 3 is the 50/50 location in the scale, or the median, redo your work carefully to correct any errors you may have made.

FIGURE 12.4
IBM SPSS Clickstream to Obtain a Mean, Standard Deviation, and Range

Source: Reprint Courtesy of International Business Machines Corporation, © International Business Machines Corporation.

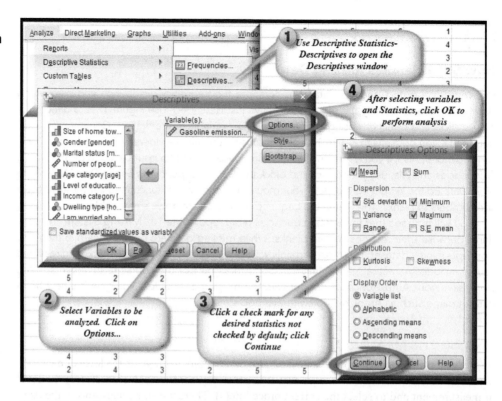

FIGURE 12.5
IBM SPSS Output for a Mean, Standard Deviation, and Range

Source: Reprint Courtesy of International Business Machines Corporation, © International Business Machines Corporation.

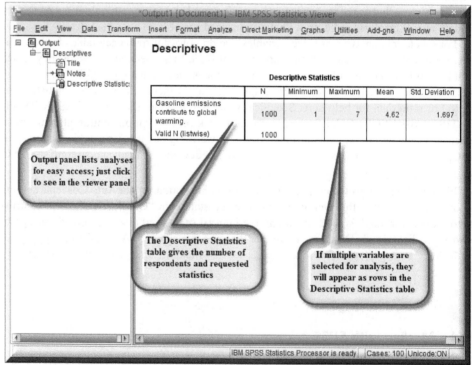

respondents "agree" with this statement. The standard deviation is 1.7 (rounded), meaning there was much variability, and you can also see that the lowest response (minimum) was 1, and the highest (maximum) was 7, meaning that the entire range of the scale was used by the sample of respondents.

 **Active Learning** ——————————————————————————————————————— IBM **SPSS**

Using SPSS for a Mean and Related Descriptive Statistics

In this Active Learning exercise, you are being asked to stretch your learning a bit, for instead of simply repeating what has just been described for how to obtain the mean, range, and standard deviation with SPSS and comparing it to the SPSS output in this chapter, we want you to find the mean, range, and standard deviation for a different variable. Specifically, use the clickstream shown in Figure 12.4, but select the question that pertains to "Number of people in household" and direct SPSS to compute these descriptive statistics.

You should find that the mean is 2.61, the standard deviation is 0.958, and the range has a minimum of 1 and a maximum of 6.

12-5   Reporting Descriptive Statistics to Clients

How does a marketing researcher report the findings of the various descriptive statistics used to summarize the findings of a survey? It is the researcher's responsibility to build tables or other presentation methods, such as graphs, to efficiently and effectively communicate the basic findings to the manager. For instance, the researcher may use a table format to show the means, standard deviations, and perhaps the ranges that have been found for a variable or a group of related variables. If percentages are computed, the researcher can develop or "lift" a percentages table from the statistical output. We have prepared Marketing Research Insight 12.1, which relates guidelines and gives examples of tables for data analysis findings.

To what extent do consumers agree that fuel emissions contribute to global warming?

REPORTING SCALE DATA (RATIO AND INTERVAL SCALES)

Scale data are summarized with the following descriptive measures: average, median, mode, standard deviation, minimum, and maximum. Typically, the researcher works with several variables or questions in the survey that are related either by the research objectives or logically. Often these questions have the same underlying response scales. For example, there may be a dozen attitude-related questions or several frequencies of product usage questions. It is often natural and efficient to combine the findings of related questions into a single table. Recommendations for what to include in standard scale variable tables are as follows:

Descriptive Measure	For a Standard Scale Variable Table...	Comment
Average (mean)	Absolutely include, as averages are the most commonly used central tendency measure for scale data.	Place averages in a column very close to the variable descriptions and arrange variables in ascending or descending order of the averages.
Median, mode	Do not include.	Managers do not relate to medians or modes of scale data.
Standard deviation	Typically include in the table.	If most standard deviations are approximately equal, do not include as redundancy would result.
Minimum, Maximum	Include if the data have several different values.	Reporting the same value several times is redundant.

© Bart Everett/Shutterstock

MARKETING RESEARCH INSIGHT 12.1

Practical Research

Guidelines for the Presentation of Data Analysis

A table is the most common vehicle for presenting summarizations of data. The most useful tables are ones where quick inspection will reveal the basic pattern(s) or the essence of the findings. Here are some table organization guidelines.[6]

- Keep tables as simple as possible.
- Use rows for the variables (scale data) or the categories (categorical data) presented in the table.
- Use columns for measures of central tendency and variability.
- Use highly descriptive and self-explanatory labels.
- Typically, use variables with identical response scales in a single table.
- If appropriate, arrange the variables (rows) in logical order, usually ascending or descending, based on the descriptive measure being used.
- Highlight key measures.

Beyond organization, there are guidelines that will ensure that the table strongly implies that it is credible and should be taken very seriously.

- Use one decimal place unless convention demands otherwise (e.g., currency requires two decimal places for cents).
- With scales, include a table footnote that describes the scale.
- Do not report measures that are largely redundant.
- Only report findings that are meaningful or useful.
- Use a conservative, professional format.

Here is an example of a scale variables table. Notice that the labels are self-explanatory and the averages are highlighted to indicate their importance. The features are arranged in descending order of the averages so it is easy to identify the highest-performing feature (assortment of breads) and the lowest performer (distinctive taste). The standard deviations are reported, as they vary, but the minimum and maximum values are not reported, as they are "1" or "5" in almost all cases. You should also note that an informative table footnote describes the scale used in these ratings.

Performance of the Subshop

Feature of the Subshop	Average*	Standard Deviation
Assortment of breads	4.5	0.5
Variety of subs	4.3	0.7
Variety of toppings	4.0	0.8
Freshness of bread	3.9	0.8
Freshness of toppings	3.8	0.7
Promptness of service	3.7	1.0
Cleanliness of facility	3.7	0.9
Value for the price	3.6	1.1
Generosity of toppings	3.5	1.0
Distinctive taste	3.2	1.3

*Based on a scale where 1 = "poor" and 5 = "excellent."

REPORTING NOMINAL OR CATEGORICAL DATA

Nominal data are summarized with the following descriptive measures: frequencies, frequency distribution, percents, percent distribution, and mode. It is important to note that usually only one categorical variable is summarized in each table because the categories are unique to the variable (such as male and female for gender or buyer and nonbuyer for type of customer). Recommendations for what to put in standard categorical data tables are as follows:

Descriptive Measure	For a Standard Categorical Variable Table...	Comment
Frequencies, frequency distribution	Include if the researcher wants the reader to note something about the sample, such as a very small sample in which percentages are greatly affected by a few respondents.	Place frequencies in a column very close to the variable group labels (such as male, female). If appropriate, arrange the categories in ascending or descending order of the percentages. Include a total of the frequencies at the bottom.
Percents, percent distribution	Absolutely include, as percentages are the most commonly used descriptive measure for nominal data.	Place percentages in a column close to the variable group labels (such as male, female) and beside the frequencies, if used. If appropriate, arrange the categories in ascending or descending order of the percentages. Include a 100% total at the bottom.
Mode	Highlight, but if obvious do not report in the table.	The largest percentage group is usually readily apparent in a percent distribution, especially if ascending or descending order can be used.

Here is a sample nominal (or categorical) variable table. The frequencies are not included, as a large number of respondents answered this question. Each time period is listed chronologically, and the mode is identified with the percentage in bold. The 100% total is included to indicate that all time periods are included in this table.

What Time in the Day Do You Typically Visit the Subshop?

Time Period	Percent
Before 12 p.m.	5.3%
Between 12 p.m. and 3 p.m.	**56.8%**
Between 3 p.m. and 6 p.m.	24.2%
After 6 p.m.	<u>13.7%</u>
Total	100.0%

12-6   Statistical Inference: Sample Statistics and Population Parameters

As you have just learned, descriptive measures of central tendency and measures of variability adequately summarize the findings of a survey. However, whenever a probability sample is drawn from a population, it is not enough to simply report the sample's descriptive statistics, for these measures contain a certain degree of error due to the sampling process. Every sample provides some information about its population, but there is always some sample error that must be taken into account. Values that are computed from information provided by a sample are referred to as the sample's **statistics**, whereas values that are computed from a complete census, which are considered to be precise and valid measures of the population, are referred to as **parameters**. Statisticians use Greek letters (alpha, beta, etc.) when referring to population parameters and Roman letters (a, b, etc.) when referring to statistics. Every sample statistic has a corresponding population parameter. For example, the notation used for a percentage is p for the statistic and π (pi) for the parameter, and the notations for the mean are $\bar{x}$ (statistic) and μ (parameter mu). Because a census is impractical, the sample statistic is used to estimate the population parameter. We will next describe the procedures used when estimating various population parameters.

Statistics are sample values, whereas parameters are corresponding population values.

Statistical inference takes into account that large random samples are more accurate than are small ones.

Statistical inference is based on sample size and variability, which then will determine the amount of sampling error.

Inference is a form of logic in which you make a general statement (a generalization) about an entire class based on what you have observed about a small set of members of that class. When you infer, you draw a conclusion from a small amount of evidence, such as a sample. **Statistical inference** is a set of procedures in which the sample size and sample statistic are used to make an estimate of the corresponding population parameter. That is, statistical inference has formal steps for estimating the population parameter (the generalization) based on the evidence of the sample statistic and taking into account the sample error based on sample size. For now, let us concentrate on the percentage, p, as the sample statistic we are using to estimate the population percentage, π, and see how sample size enters into statistical inference. Suppose that Dodge suspected that there were some dissatisfied customers, and it commissioned two independent marketing research surveys to determine the amount of dissatisfaction that existed in its customer group. (Of course, our Dodge example is entirely fictitious. We don't mean to imply that Dodge cars perform in an unsatisfactory way.)

In the first survey, 100 customers who had purchased a Dodge in the last six months are surveyed and it is found that 30 respondents (30%) are dissatisfied. This finding could be inferred to be the total population of Dodge owners who had bought one in the last six months, and we would say that there is 30% dissatisfaction. However, because we know that our sample, which was a probability sample, must contain some sample error, we would have to say that there was *about* 30% dissatisfaction in the population. In other words, it might actually be more or less than 30% if we did a census because the sample provided us with only an estimate.

The second survey utilized 1,000 respondents—that's 10 times more than in the first survey—and this survey found that 35% of the respondents are "dissatisfied." Again, we know that the 35% is an estimate that contains sampling error, so now we would also say that the population dissatisfaction percentage was *about* 35%. This means that we have two estimates of the degree of dissatisfaction with Dodges. One is *about* 30%, whereas the other is *about* 35%.

How do we translate our answers (remember they include the word *about*) into more accurate numerical representations? We could translate them into ballpark ranges. That is, we could translate them so we could say "30% plus or minus x%" for the sample of 100 and "35% plus or minus y%" for the sample of 1,000. How would x and y compare? To answer this question, consider that more evidence makes for stronger inferences. That is, with a larger sample (or more evidence), you would be more certain that the sample statistic was accurate with respect to estimating the true population value. In other words, with a larger sample size you should expect the range used to estimate the true population value to be smaller. Actually, the range for y is smaller than the range for x because you have a larger sample and less sampling error.

So, with statistical inference for estimates of population parameters such as the percentage or mean, the sample statistic is used as the beginning point, and then a range is computed in which the population parameter is estimated to fall. The size of the sample, or n, plays a crucial role in this computation, as you will see in all of the statistical inference formulas we present in this chapter.

Two types of statistical inference are parameter estimation and hypothesis tests.

Two types of statistical inferences often used by marketing researchers are described in this chapter: parameter estimates and hypothesis tests. A **parameter estimate** is used to approximate the population value (parameter) through the use of confidence intervals. **Hypothesis testing** is used to compare the sample statistic with what is believed (hypothesized) to be the population value prior to undertaking the study.

12-7 Parameter Estimation: Estimating the Population Percent or Mean

Parameter estimation is the process of using sample information to compute an interval that describes the range of a parameter such as the population mean (μ) or the population percentage (π). It involves the use of three values: the sample statistic (such as the mean or the percentage), the standard error of the statistic, and the desired level of confidence (usually 95% or 99%). A discussion of how each value is determined follows.

SAMPLE STATISTIC

The mean is the average of a set of scale variable numbers. For example, you might be working with a sample of golfers and researching the average number of golf balls they buy per month. Or you might be investigating how much high school students spend, on average, on fast foods between meals. For a percentage, you could be examining what percentage of golfers buy only Titleist balls, or you might be looking at what percentage of high school students buy from Taco Bell between meals. In either case, the mean or percentage is derived from a sample, so it is the sample statistic.

In parameter estimation, the sample statistic is usually a mean or a percentage.

STANDARD ERROR

There usually is some degree of variability in the sample. That is, our golfers do not all buy the same number of golf balls per month and they do not all buy Titleist. Not all of our high school students eat fast food between meals and not all of the ones who do go to Taco Bell. Earlier in this chapter, we introduced you to variability with a mean by describing the standard deviation. We used the percentage distribution as a way of describing variability with a mean by describing the standard deviation, and we used the percentage distribution as a way of describing variability when percentages are being used. Also, we described how, if you theoretically took many, many samples and plotted the mean or percentage as a frequency distribution, it would approximate a bell-shaped curve called the sampling distribution. The **standard error** is a measure of the variability in the sampling distribution based on what is theoretically believed to occur were we to take a multitude of independent samples from the same population. We described the standard error formulas in Chapter 10 on sample size, but we repeat them here because they are vital to statistical inference, as they tie together the sample size and its variability.

The standard error is a measure of the variability in a sampling distribution.

The formula for the standard error of the mean is as follows:

Formula for standard error of the mean

$$s_{\bar{x}} = \frac{s}{\sqrt{n}}$$

where

$s_{\bar{x}}$ = standard error of the mean

s = standard deviation

n = sample size

The formula for the standard error of the percentage is as follows:

Formula for standard error of the percentage

$$s_p = \sqrt{\frac{p \times q}{n}}$$

where

s_p = standard error of the percentage

p = the sample percentage

$q = (100 - p)$

n = sample size

© Monkey Business Images/Shutterstock

Statistical inference can be used to estimate how many minutes people read their daily newspaper.

The formula for mean standard error differs from a percentage standard error.

The standard error takes into account sample size and the variability in the sample.

Notice how sample variability affects the standard error in these two examples.

With a 50–50 split there is great variability.

A 50–50 split has a larger standard error than a 90–10 split when sample size is the same.

In both equations, the sample size n is found in the denominator. This means that the standard error will be smaller with larger sample sizes and larger with smaller sample sizes. At the same time, both of these formulas for the standard error reveal the impact of the variation found in the sample. Variation is represented by the standard deviation s for a mean and by $(p \times q)$ for a percentage. In either equation, the variation is in the numerator, so the greater the variability, the greater the standard error. Thus, the standard error simultaneously takes into account both the sample size and the amount of variation found in the sample. The following examples illustrate this fact.

Let's take two cases: *New York Times* surveys on the amount of daily time spent reading the *Times* have determined (1) a standard deviation of 20 minutes, and (2) a standard deviation of 40 minutes. Both surveys used a sample size of 100. The resulting standard error of the mean calculations would be as follows:

	Std. dev. = 20	**Std. dev. = 40**
Calculations of standard error of the mean with standard deviation = 20 and with standard deviation = 40	$s_{\bar{x}} = \dfrac{s}{\sqrt{n}}$ $s_{\bar{x}} = \dfrac{20}{\sqrt{100}}$ $= \dfrac{20}{10}$ $= 2$ minutes	$s_{\bar{x}} = \dfrac{s}{\sqrt{n}}$ $s_{\bar{x}} = \dfrac{40}{\sqrt{100}}$ $= \dfrac{40}{10}$ $= 4$ minutes

As you can see, the standard error of the mean from a sample with little variability (20 minutes) is smaller than the standard error of the mean from a sample with much variability (40 minutes), as long as both samples have the same size. In fact, you should have noticed that when the variability was doubled from 20 to 40 minutes, the standard error also doubled, given identical sample sizes. Refer to Figure 12.6.

The standard error of a percentage mirrors this logic, although the formula looks a bit different. In this case, as we indicated earlier, the degree of variability is inherent in the $(p \times q)$ aspect of the equation. Very little variability is indicated if p and q are very different in size. For example, if a survey of 100 McDonald's breakfast buyers determined that 90% of the respondents ordered coffee with their Egg McMuffin and 10% of the respondents did not, there would be very little variability because almost everybody orders coffee with breakfast. On the other hand, if the sample determined that there was a 50–50 split between those who had and those who had not ordered coffee, there would be a great deal more variability because any two customers would probably differ in their drink orders. The computations show that greater variability in responses results in a larger standard error of the percentage at a given sample size.

	$p = 90, q = 10$	**$p = 50, q = 50$**
Calculation of standard error of the percent with (1) $p = 90$ and $q = 10$ and (2) $p = 50$ and $q = 50$	$s_p = \sqrt{\dfrac{p \times q}{n}}$ $= \sqrt{\dfrac{(90)(10)}{100}}$ $= \sqrt{\dfrac{900}{100}}$ $= \sqrt{9}$ $= 3\%$	$s_p = \sqrt{\dfrac{p \times q}{n}}$ $= \sqrt{\dfrac{(50)(50)}{100}}$ $= \sqrt{\dfrac{2500}{100}}$ $= \sqrt{25}$ $= 5\%$

CONFIDENCE INTERVALS

Because there is always some sampling error when a sample is taken, it is necessary to estimate the population parameter with a range. We did this in the Dodge owners' example earlier. One factor affecting the size of the range is how confident the researcher wants to be that the range includes the true population percentage (parameter). Normally, the researcher first decides on how confident he or she wants to be; that is, the researcher formally selects a level of confidence. The sample statistic is the beginning of the estimate, but because there is sample error present, a "plus" amount and an identical "minus" amount is added and subtracted from the sample statistic to determine the maximum and minimum, respectively, of the range. **Confidence intervals** are the degree of accuracy desired by the researcher and stipulated as a level of confidence in the form of a range with a lower boundary and an upper boundary.

Typically, marketing researchers rely only on the 99%, 95%, or 90% levels of confidence, which correspond to ±2.58, ±1.96, and ±1.64 standard errors, respectively. They are designated z_α, so $z_{0.99}$ is ±2.58 standard errors. By far, the **most commonly used level of confidence** in marketing research is the 95% level,[7] corresponding to 1.96 standard errors. In fact, the 95% level of confidence is usually the default level found in statistical analysis programs such as SPSS. Now that the relationship between the standard error and the measure of sample variability—be it the standard deviation or the percentage—is apparent, it is a simple matter to determine the range in which the population parameter will be estimated. We use the sample statistics, $\bar{x}$ or p, compute the standard error, and then apply our desired level of confidence. In notation form these are as follows:

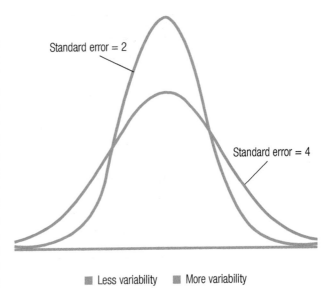

Standard error = 2

Standard error = 4

■ Less variability ■ More variability

FIGURE 12.6 Variability Found in the Sample Directly Affects the Standard Error

Population parameters are estimated with the use of confidence intervals.

The range of your estimate of the population mean or percentage depends largely on the sample size and the variability found in the sample.

Confidence intervals are estimated using these formulas.

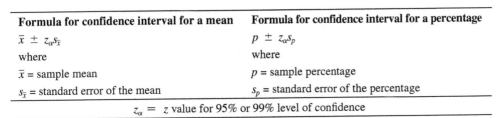

Formula for confidence interval for a mean	Formula for confidence interval for a percentage
$\bar{x} \pm z_\alpha s_{\bar{x}}$	$p \pm z_\alpha s_p$
where	where
$\bar{x}$ = sample mean	p = sample percentage
$s_{\bar{x}}$ = standard error of the mean	s_p = standard error of the percentage
z_α = z value for 95% or 99% level of confidence	

How do these formulas relate to inference? Recall that we are estimating a population parameter. That is, we are indicating a range into which it is believed that the true population parameter falls. The size of the range is determined by those pieces of information we have about the population on hand as a result of our sample. The final ingredient is our level of confidence or the degree to which we want to be correct in our estimate of the population parameter. If we are conservative and wish to assume the 99% level of confidence, then the range would be more encompassing than if we are less conservative and assume only the 95% level of confidence because 99% is associated with ±2.58 standard errors and 95% is associated with ±1.96 standard errors.

Marketing researchers typically use only the 95% or 99% confidence interval.

Using these formulas for the sample of 100 *New York Times* readers with a mean reading time of 45 minutes and a standard deviation of 20 minutes, the 95% confidence (z = 1.96) interval estimate would be calculated as shown in the following table on the left. Similarly, if 50% of the 100 McDonald's customers order coffee, the 95% confidence (z = 1.96) interval would be computed using the percentage formula on the right.

Here are examples of confidence interval computation with a mean and with a percentage.

Calculation of a 95% Confidence Interval for a Mean	Calculation of a 95% Confidence Interval for a Percentage
$\bar{x} \pm 1.96 \times s_{\bar{x}}$	$p \pm 1.96 \times s_p$
$\bar{x} \pm 1.96 \times \dfrac{s}{\sqrt{n}}$	$p \pm 1.96 \times \sqrt{\dfrac{p \times q}{n}}$
$45 \pm 1.96 \times \dfrac{20}{\sqrt{100}}$	$50 \pm 1.96 \times \sqrt{\dfrac{50 \times 50}{100}}$
$45 \pm 1.96 \times 2$	$50 \pm 1.96 \times 5$
45 ± 3.9	50 ± 9.8
$41.1 - 48.9$ minutes	$40.2\% - 59.8\%$
where	where
mean = 45	$p = 50$
std. dev. = 20	$q = 50$
	$n = 100$

Of course, if we use the 99% confidence interval, the computations would necessitate the use of 2.58 standard errors. The confidence interval is always wider for 99% than it is for 95% when the sample size is the same and the variability is equal. The five steps involved in computing confidence intervals for a mean or a percentage are listed in Table 12.3.

There are five steps to computing a confidence interval.

TABLE 12.3   How to Compute a Confidence Interval for a Mean or a Percentage

Step 1. Find the sample statistic, either the mean, $\bar{x}$, or the percentage, p.

Step 2. Identify the sample size, n.

Step 3. Determine the amount of variability found in the sample in the form of standard error of the mean, $s_{\bar{x}}$,

$$s_{\bar{x}} = \frac{s}{\sqrt{n}}$$

or standard error of the percentage, s_p.

$$s_p = \sqrt{\frac{p \times q}{n}}$$

Step 4. Decide on the desired level of confidence to determine the value for z: $z.95$ (1.96) or $z.99$ (2.58).

Step 5. Compute your (95%) confidence interval as $\bar{x} \pm 1.96s_{\bar{x}}$ or $p \pm 1.96s_p$.

Marketing Research on YouTube™
To learn about confidence intervals, launch **www.youtube.com**, and search for "Confidence Intervals Part 1 YouTube."

HOW TO INTERPRET AN ESTIMATED POPULATION MEAN OR PERCENTAGE RANGE

How are these ranges interpreted? The interpretation is quite simple when you remember that the sampling distribution notion is the underlying theoretical concept. If we were using a 95% level of confidence, and if we repeated the sampling process and computed the sample statistic many times, their frequency distribution (the sampling distribution) would comprise a bell-shaped curve. A total of 95% of these repeated sample results would produce a range that includes the population parameter.

Obviously, a marketing researcher would take only one sample for a particular marketing research project, and this restriction explains why estimates must be used. Furthermore, it is the conscientious application of probability sampling techniques that allows us to make use of the sampling distribution concept. So, statistical inference procedures are the direct linkages between probability sample design and data analysis. Do you remember that you had to grapple with confidence levels when we determined sample size? Now we are on the other

 **Active Learning**

Calculate Some Confidence Intervals

This Active Learning section will give you practice in calculating confidence intervals. For this set of exercises, you are working with a survey of 1,000 people who responded to questions about satellite radio. The questions, sample statistics, and other pertinent information are listed below. Compute the 95% confidence interval for the population parameter in each case. Be certain to follow the logic of the questions, as it has implications for the sample size pertaining to each question.

| | | 95% Confidence Interval | |
		Lower Boundary	Upper Boundary
Question	**Sample Statistic(s)**		
Have you heard of satellite radio?	500/1,000 = 50% responded "yes"		
If yes, do you own a satellite radio?	150/500 = 30% responded "yes"		
If you own satellite radio, about how many minutes of satellite radio did you listen to last week?	Average of 100.7 minutes; standard deviation of 25.0 minutes for the 150 satellite radio owners		

side of the table, so to speak, and we must use the sample size for our inference procedures. Confidence intervals must be used when estimating population parameters, and the size of the random sample used is always reflected in these confidence intervals.

12-8   The Auto Concepts Survey: How to Obtain and Use a Confidence Interval for a Mean with SPSS

Fortunately, because the calculations are a bit more complicated and tedious, your SPSS program will calculate the confidence interval for a mean. To illustrate this feature, we will look at the evidence that the general public is of the opinion that gasoline usage is detrimental. You should recall that in our descriptive analysis example of a mean (page 327), we found that the average disagree–agree response to the statement "Gasoline emissions contribute to global warming" was 4.6, or "agree."

To determine the 95% confidence interval for this average, examine Figure 12.7, which shows the clickstream sequence to accomplish a 95% confidence interval estimate using SPSS. As you can see, the correct SPSS procedure is a "One-Sample T Test," and you use the ANALYZE-COMPARE MEANS-ONE SAMPLE T TEST menu clickstream sequence to open up the proper window. Refer to Figure 12.7 to see that all you need to do is to select the "Gasoline emissions contribute to global warming" variable in the Test Variables area, and then click OK.

Figure 12.8 shows the results of ANALYZE-COMPARE MEANS-ONE SAMPLE T TEST for our "Gasoline emissions contribute to global warming" variable. As you can see, the average is 4.62, and the 95% confidence interval is 4.51–4.72. Although a "5" is the code for "Agree," this confidence interval is sufficiently close so we can claim that it amounts to "Agree." Our interpretation of this finding: If we conducted a great many replications of this survey using the same sample size, we would find that 95% of the sample average agreement with the statement "Gasoline emissions contribute to global warming."

IBM **SPSS**

IBM **SPSS**

IBM SPSS Student Assistant:
The Advanced Automobile Concepts Survey: Establishing Confidence Intervals for Means

FIGURE 12.7 IBM SPSS Clickstream to Obtain a 95% Confidence Interval for a Mean

Source: Reprint Courtesy of International Business Machines Corporation, © International Business Machines Corporation.

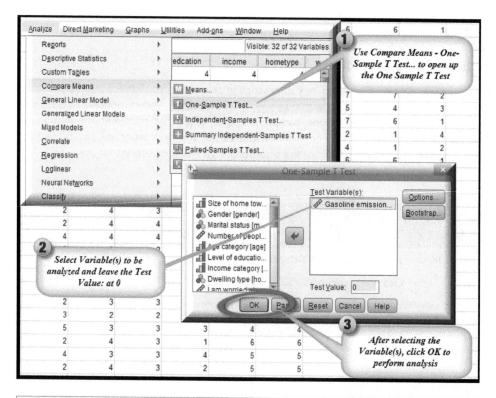

FIGURE 12.8 IBM SPSS Output for a 95% Confidence Interval for a Mean

Source: Reprint Courtesy of International Business Machines Corporation, © International Business Machines Corporation.

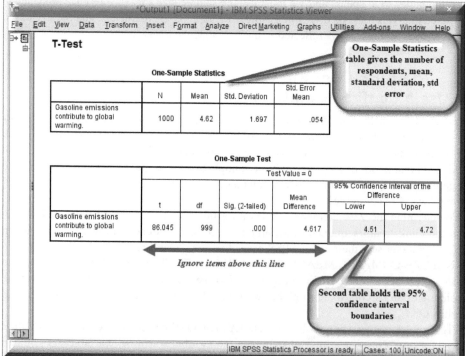

12-9 Reporting Confidence Intervals to Clients

How do marketing researchers report confidence intervals to their clients? It may surprise you to learn that detailed confidence intervals are typically not reported. Just think about all of the numbers that would have to be computed and reported to clients if confidence intervals

 **Active Learning**

Use SPSS for a Confidence Interval for a Mean

You have just learned that the 95% confidence interval for "Gasoline emissions contribute to global warming" variable would include an average of 4.62, with a lower boundary of 4.51 and an upper boundary of 4.72. What about the statement "I am worried about global warming"?

To answer this question, you must use SPSS to compute the 95% confidence interval for the mean of this variable. Use the clickstream identified in Figure 12.7 and use the annotations in Figure 12.8 to find and interpret your 95% confidence interval for the public's opinion on this topic. How do you interpret this finding, and how does this confidence interval compare to the one we found for "Gasoline emissions contribute to global warming"?

were reported for every finding—it would require two more numbers per finding: the lower boundary and the upper boundary. So there is a dilemma: Clients do not want to wade through so much detail, yet researchers must somehow inform clients that there is sample error in the findings. The solution to this dilemma is really quite simple, and you will learn about it by reading Marketing Research Insight 12.2.

 MARKETING RESEARCH INSIGHT 12.2   *Practical Research*

Guidelines for the Presentation of Confidence Intervals

Researchers have two options when it comes to reporting confidence intervals to clients or readers of their marketing research reports. These options are (1) the general case and (2) findings-specific confidence intervals.

The General Case

This is the industry standard; it is used almost unanimously with opinion polling, and it is by far the most popular approach used by marketing researchers. The general case is merely to state the sampling error associated with the survey sample size. For example, the report may say "findings are accurate to ±4%," or "the survey has an error of ±3.5%." This sample error, of course, is calculated using the sample error formula (refer to Chapter 13), typically at the 95% level of confidence with $p = q = 50\%$, and $z = 1.96$.

Sample error formula

$$\pm \, Sample \; Error \; \% \; = \; 1.96 \, \times \, \sqrt{\frac{p \times q}{n}}$$

The Findings-Specific Case

To decide whether or not to use the findings-specific approach, the researcher must answer the following question, "Are there findings that require more than the general case of reporting sample error?" For instance, there may be findings that the client will use to answer critical questions or on which to base important decisions. If the answer is no, the researcher will just

report the general case. If yes, the next step is to identify all the findings that he or she believes absolutely require the reporting of findings-specific confidence intervals. To present the confidence intervals for each relevant finding, the researcher can provide a table that lists the 95% confidence interval lower and upper boundaries, which must be computed either by the researcher's statistical analysis program or the use of some other computational aid in the researcher's tool kit. The following table illustrates how a researcher can efficiently accommodate the confidence intervals for diverse variables in a single table. Most likely, these findings will have been reported elsewhere in the report with other informative summary statistics, such as standard deviations and sample sizes for respondents answering various questions.

95% Confidence Intervals for Key Findings

	Sample Finding	Lower Boundary	Upper Boundary
Used the Subshop in the past 60 days	*30%*	*26.0%*	*34.0%*
Used a Subshop coupon in the past 30 days	*12%*	*9.2%*	*14.8%*
Number of Subshop visits in the past 60 days	*1.5*	*1.4*	*1.6*
Overall satisfaction with the Subshop*	*5.6*	*5.4*	*5.8*

*Based on a scale where 1 = Very dissatisfied and 7 = Very satisfied.

12-10   Hypothesis Tests

In some cases, the marketing researcher or marketing manager may offer an expectation about the population parameter (either the mean or the percentage) based on prior knowledge, assumptions, or intuition. This expectation, called a **hypothesis**, most commonly takes the form of an exact specification as to what the population parameter value is.

A **hypothesis test** is a statistical procedure used to "accept" or "reject" the hypothesis based on sample evidence.[8] With all hypothesis tests, you should keep in mind that the sample is the only source of current information about the population. Because our sample is random and representative of the population, the sample results are used to determine if the hypothesis about the population parameter is accepted or rejected.[9]

All of this might sound frightfully technical, but it is a form of inference that you do every day. You just do not use the words *hypothesis* or *parameter* when you do it. Here is an example to show how hypothesis testing occurs naturally. Your friend Bill does not use an automobile seat belt because he thinks only a few drivers actually wear them. But Bill's car breaks down, and he has to ride with his coworkers to and from work while it is being repaired. Over the course of a week, Bill rides with five different coworkers, and he notices that four out of the five buckle up. When Bill begins driving his own car the next week, he begins fastening his seat belt because he did not find support for his hypothesis that few drivers buckle up. Consequently, Bill changes his belief to be consistent with reality.

A hypothesis is what the manager or researcher expects the population mean (or percentage) to be.

TEST OF THE HYPOTHESIZED POPULATION PARAMETER VALUE

Here are formulas used to test a hypothesized population parameter.

The **hypothesized population parameter** value can be determined using either a percentage or a mean. The equations used to test the hypothesis of a population percentage and a hypothesis about a mean are as follows:

Formula for test of a hypothesis about a percent

$$z = \frac{p - \pi_H}{s_{\bar{x}}}$$

where

  p = sample percentage

  π_H = hypothesized population percentage

  s_p = standard error of the percentage

Formula for test of a hypothesis about a mean

$$z = \frac{\bar{x} - \mu_H}{s_{\bar{x}}}$$

where

  $\bar{x}$ = sample mean

  μ_H = hypothesized population mean

  $s_{\bar{x}}$ = standard error of the mean

Note that the equation used to test the hypothesis of a mean is identical in logic, except it uses the mean and standard error of the mean.

Tracking the logic of these equations, one can see that the sample mean ($\bar{x}$) is compared to the hypothesized population mean (μ_H). Similarly, the sample percentage (p) is compared to the hypothesized percentage (π_H). In this case, "compared" means "take the difference." This difference is divided by the standard error to determine how many standard errors away from the hypothesized parameter the sample statistic falls. The standard error, you should remember, takes into account the variability found in the sample as well as the sample size. A small sample with much variability yields a large standard error, so our sample statistic could be quite far away from the mean arithmetically but still less than one standard error away in certain circumstances. All the relevant information about the population as found by our sample is included in these computations. Knowledge of areas under the normal curve then comes into play to translate this distance into a probability of support for the hypothesis: If the computed z value is greater than 1.96 or less than -1.96, we are 95% confident that the sample evidence does not support the hypothesized parameter value.

To a statistician, "compare" means to "take the difference."

Here is a simple illustration using Bill's hypothesis that only 10% of drivers use seat belts. Let's suppose that Bill reads that a Harris poll finds that 80% of respondents in a national sample of 1,000 drivers wear their seat belts. The hypothesis test would be computed as follows (notice we substituted the formula for s_p in the second step):

An example of no support for Bill's seat belt hypothesis.

Calculation of a test of Bill's hypothesis that only 10% of drivers "buckle up"	

$$z = \frac{p - \pi_H}{s_p}$$

$$= \frac{p - \pi_H}{\sqrt{\frac{p \times q}{n}}}$$

Notes:
Hypothesized percent = 10
Sample percent (p) = 80
Sample $q = 100 - p = 20$
$n = 1,000$

$$= \frac{80 - 10}{\sqrt{\frac{80 \times 20}{1000}}}$$

$$= \frac{70}{\sqrt{\frac{1600}{1000}}}$$

$$= \frac{70}{\sqrt{1.6}}$$

$$= 55.3$$

The crux of statistical hypothesis testing is the **sampling distribution concept**. Our actual sample is one of the many theoretical samples comprising the assumed bell-shaped curve of possible sample results using the hypothesized value as the center of the bell-shaped distribution. If the person who stated the hypothesis is correct, there is a greater probability of finding a sample result close to the hypothesized number than of finding one that is far away. So, if our sample value turns out to

Bill found that his hypothesis about seat belts was not supported, so he started buckling up.

be within $\pm1.96/\pm2.58$ standard errors of the hypothesized mean, it supports the hypothesis maker at the 95%/99% level of confidence because it falls within 95%/99% of the area under the curve.

The sampling distribution concept says that our sample is one of many theoretical samples that comprise a bell-shaped curve with the hypothesized value as the mean.

But what if the sample result is found to be outside this range? Which is correct—the hypothesis or the researcher's sample results? The answer to this question is always the same: Sample information is invariably more accurate than a hypothesis. Of course, the sampling procedure must adhere strictly to probability sampling requirements and assure representativeness. As you can see, Bill was greatly mistaken because his hypothesis of 10% of drivers wearing seat belts was 55.3 standard errors away from the 80% finding of the poll of nationally representative drivers.

You always assume the sample information to be more accurate than any hypothesis.

The following example serves to describe the hypothesis testing process with a mean. Northwestern Mutual Life Insurance Company has a college student internship program that allows college students to participate in a training program and to become field agents in one academic term. Rex Reigen, district agent, hypothesizes, based on his knowledge of the program, that the typical college agent will be able to earn about $2,750 in his or her first semester of participation in the program. To check Rex's hypothesis, a survey was taken of 100 current college agents. The sample mean is determined to be $2,800, and the standard deviation is $350.

A hypothesis test gives you the probability of support for your hypothesis based on your sample evidence and sample size.

The amount of $2,800 found by the sample differs from the hypothesized amount of $2,750 by $50. Is this amount a sufficient enough difference to cast doubt on Rex's estimate?

Does the sample support Rex's hypothesis that student interns make $2,750 in the first semester?

Or, in other words, is it far enough from the hypothesized mean to reject the hypothesis? To answer these questions, we compute as follows (note that we have substituted the formula for the standard error of the mean in the second step):

Calculation of a test of Rex's hypothesis that Northwestern Mutual interns make an average of $2,750 in their first semester of work.	
Notes:	$z = \dfrac{\bar{x} - \mu_H}{s_{\bar{x}}}$
Hypothesized mean = 2,750	$= \dfrac{\bar{x} - \mu_H}{\dfrac{s}{\sqrt{n}}}$
Sample mean = 2,800	$= \dfrac{2,800 - 2,750}{\dfrac{350}{\sqrt{100}}}$
Std. dev. = 350	$= \dfrac{50}{35}$
$n = 100$	$= 1.43$

A computed z value of 1.43 is less than 1.96, so the hypothesis is supported.

The sample variability and the sample size have been used to determine the size of the standard error of the assumed sampling distribution. In this case, one standard error of the mean is equal to $35 (standard error of the mean formula: $350/\sqrt{100}$). When the difference of $50 is divided by $35 to determine the number of standard errors from the hypothesized mean that the sample statistic falls, the result is 1.43. As illustrated in Figure 12.9, 1.43 standard errors is within ±1.96 standard errors of Rex's hypothesized mean. It also reveals that the hypothesis is supported because it falls in the acceptance region.

It is handy to just recall the two numbers, 1.96 and 2.58; as we have said, these two are directly associated with the 95% and 99% confidence levels, respectively, which are the "standards" of the marketing research industry. Anytime that the computed z value falls outside ±2.58/1.96, the resulting probability of support for the hypothesis is 0.01/0.05 or less. Of course, computer statistical programs such as SPSS will provide the exact probability because they are programmed to look up the probability in the z table just as you would have to do if you did the test by manual calculations and you wanted the exact probability. The five basic steps involved in hypothesis testing are listed in Table 12.4.

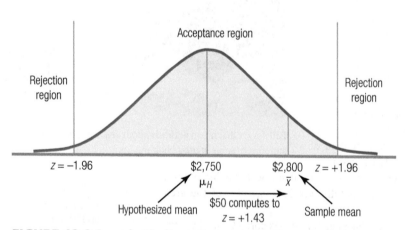

FIGURE 12.9 Sample Findings Support the Hypothesis in This Example

IBM **SPSS**

AUTO CONCEPTS: HOW TO USE SPSS TO TEST A HYPOTHESIS FOR A MEAN

We can test the hypothesized mean of any scale variable (interval or ratio scale) in our Auto Concepts survey. As an illustration, we will hypothesize that the general public is neutral to the statement "I am worried about global warming." You should recall that on our scale the "neutral" position corresponds to the value code of "4." Your SPSS software can be easily directed to make a mean estimation or to test a hypothesis for a mean.

To perform a mean hypothesis test, SPSS provides a Test Value box in which the hypothesized mean can be entered. As you can see in Figure 12.10, you get to this box by using the ANALYZE-COMPARE MEANS-ONE SAMPLE T TEST command sequence. You then

TABLE 12.4   The Five Basic Steps Involved in Hypothesis Testing

Here are five steps in hypothesis testing.

Step 1. Begin with a statement about what you believe exists in the population, that is, the population mean (μ_H) or percentage (π_H).

Step 2. Draw a random sample and determine the sample mean ($\bar{x}$) or percent (p).

Step 3. Compare the statistic to the hypothesized parameter; divide by standard error to compute z.

$$z = \frac{\bar{x} - \mu_H}{s_{\bar{x}}} \qquad\qquad z = \frac{p - \pi_H}{s_p}$$

Step 4. If z is within $\pm1.96/\pm2.58$ standard errors, it supports the hypothesis at the 95%/99% level of confidence. (Alternatively, the exact degree of support can be assessed on SPSS output.)

Step 5. If the sample does not support the hypothesis, revise the hypothesis to be consistent with the sample's statistic using the confidence interval formula.

select the variable, "I am worried about global warming." Next, enter "4" as the Test Value and click the OK button.

The resulting output is contained in Figure 12.11. The information layout for the output is identical to the previous output table. The output indicates our test value is equal to 4, and the bottom table contains 95% confidence intervals for the estimated population parameter (the population parameter is the difference between the hypothesized mean and the sample mean, expected to be 0). There is a mean difference of 0.880, which was calculated by subtracting the hypothesized mean value (4) from the sample mean (4.88), and the standard error is provided in the upper half (1.329). A t value of 20.932 is determined by dividing 0.880 by 0.042. It is associated with a two-tailed significance level of 0.000. (For now, assume t value is the z value we have used in our formulas and explanations.) In other words, our Auto Concepts sample finding of an average of about 4.88 does not support the hypothesis of 4.

To test a hypothesis about a mean with SPSS, use the ANALYZE-COMPARE MEANS-ONE SAMPLE T TEST command sequence.

IBM SPSS

IBM SPSS Student Assistant:
The Advanced Automobile Concepts Survey: Testing a Hypothesis for a Mean

Marketing To learn about hypothesis **Research** tests, launch **on YouTube™** www.youtube. com, and search for "Hypothesis tests, *p*-value – Statistics Help."

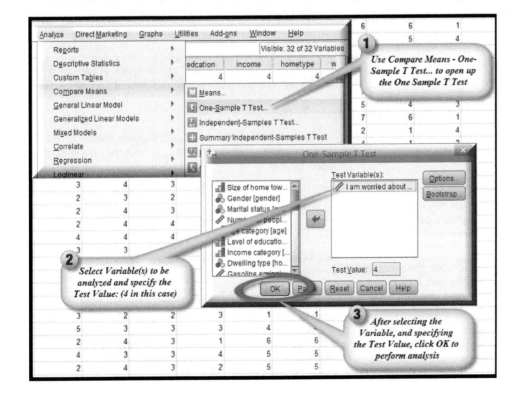

FIGURE 12.10

IBM SPSS Clickstream to Test a Hypothesis About a Mean

Source: Reprint Courtesy of International Business Machines Corporation, © International Business Machines Corporation.

FIGURE 12.11
IBM SPSS Output for the Test of a Hypothesis About a Mean

Source: Reprint Courtesy of International Business Machines Corporation, © International Business Machines Corporation.

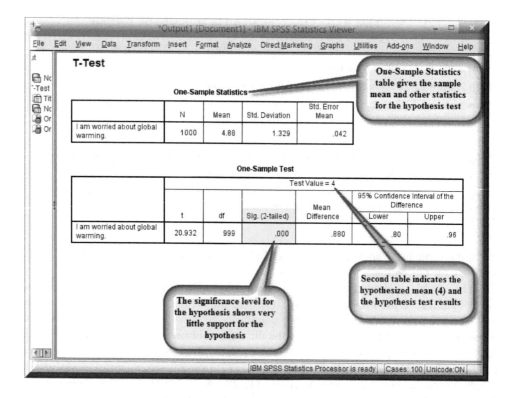

12-11 Reporting Hypothesis Tests to Clients

Explicit hypotheses are sometimes encountered by marketing researchers. When this happens, the marketing researcher performs the appropriate hypothesis test and interprets the findings. The steps involved are straightforward and listed in Marketing Research Insight 12.3.

MARKETING RESEARCH INSIGHT 12.3   *Practical Research*

Guidelines for the Presentation of Hypothesis Tests

The step-by-step approach to the presentation of hypothesis tests is as follows.

Step 1: State the hypothesis.

Step 2: Perform appropriate hypothesis test computations. That is, if the hypothesis test is stated as a percent, the percent formula should be used; if it is stated as an average, the average formula should be used.

Step 3: Determine if the hypothesis is supported or not supported by comparing the computed *z* value to the critical *z* value (normally 1.96 for a 95% level of confidence).

Step 4: If the hypothesis is not supported, compute confidence intervals to provide the client with the appropriate confidence intervals.

These steps are followed for each explicitly stated hypothesis. An example of how to present hypothesis tests in a research report follows:

Results of Hypothesis Tests

Hypothesis	Result of Test
Hypothesis 1: *60% of consumers buy from a fast-food location at least one time per month.*	*This hypothesis was supported at the 95% level of confidence by the findings of the survey.*
Hypothesis 2: *In a typical month, those consumers who purchase from a fast-food outlet spend about $45 for food, drinks, snacks, etc.*	*The average was found to be $31.87, and the hypothesis of $45 was not supported. The 95% confidence interval computations determined the range to be between $28.50 and $35.24.*

Summary

This chapter introduced you to the descriptive statistics researchers use to inspect basic patterns in datasets. We previewed the five types of statistical analysis: descriptive, inference, difference, association, and relationships. Descriptive analysis is performed with measures of central tendency such as the mean, mode, or median, each of which portrays the typical respondent or the typical answer to the question being analyzed. The chapter contained formulas and examples of how to determine these central tendency measures. Measures of variability, including the frequency distribution, range, and standard deviation, provide bases for envisioning the degree of similarity of all respondents to the typical respondent. The chapter also contained instructions and formulas of key variability measures. Basically, descriptive analysis yields a profile of how respondents in the sample answered the various questions in the survey. The chapter also provided information on how to instruct SPSS to compute descriptive analyses with SPSS using the Auto Concepts survey dataset. Both clickstream sequences for setting up the analyses and the resulting output were shown.

The chapter then distinguished a sample statistic from its associated population parameter. We then introduced you to the concept of statistical inference, which is a set of procedures for generalizing the findings from a sample to the population. A key factor in inference is the sample size, n. It appears in statistical inference formulas because it expresses the amount of sampling error: Large samples have less sampling error than do small samples given the same variability. We described how a population parameter, such as a mean or a percent, can be estimated by using confidence intervals computed by application of the standard error formula. We then related how a researcher can use the sample findings to test a hypothesis about a mean or a percentage.

We used SPSS and the Auto Concepts data to illustrate how you can direct SPSS to calculate 95% confidence intervals for the estimation of a mean as well as how to test a hypothesis about a mean. Both are accomplished with the SPSS One-Sample T Test procedure. For parameter estimation or test of a hypothesis with a percent, you can use SPSS to determine the percent, but you must use the formulas in this chapter to calculate the confidence interval or perform the significance test.

Key Terms

Data analysis (p. 317)
Descriptive analysis (p. 317)
Inference analysis (p. 318)
Difference analysis (p. 318)
Association analysis (p. 318)
Relationships analysis (p. 318)
Measures of central tendency (p. 319)
Mode (p. 319)
Median (p. 319)
Mean (p. 320)
Measures of variability (p. 320)

Frequency distribution (p. 320)
Percentage distribution (p. 320)
Range (p. 321)
Standard deviation (p. 321)
Variance (p. 322)
Statistics (p. 331)
Parameters (p. 331)
Inference (p. 332)
Statistical inference (p. 332)
Parameter estimate (p. 332)
Hypothesis testing (p. 332)

Parameter estimation (p. 332)
Standard error (p. 333)
Confidence intervals (p. 335)
Most commonly used level of
    confidence (p. 335)
Hypothesis (p. 340)
Hypothesis test (p. 340)
Hypothesized population parameter
    (p. 340)
Sampling distribution concept
    (p. 341)

Review Questions/Applications

12-1. Indicate what data analysis is and why it is useful.

12-2. Explain any four types of statistical analysis and their underlying statistical concepts. Describe how each of them has a unique role in the data analysis process.

12-3. What are the two popular types of descriptive measures? How are they related?

12-4. Explain the concept of variability and relate how it helps in the description of responses to a particular question on a questionnaire.

12-5. Using examples, illustrate how a frequency distribution (or a percentage distribution) reveals the variability in responses to a Likert-type question in a lifestyle study. Use two extreme examples of much variability and little variability.

12-6. What does a bell-shaped curve distribution show you? How is it used?

12-7. With explicit reference to the formula for a standard deviation, show how it measures how different respondents are from one another.

12-8. Explain why the mean is an inappropriate measure of central tendency in each of the following cases: (a) gender of respondent (male or female); (b) marital status (single, married, divorced, separated, widowed, other); (c) a taste test in which subjects indicate their first, second, and third choices of Miller Lite, Bud Light, and Coors Light.

12-9. For each of the cases in question 8, what is the appropriate central tendency measure?

12-10. In a survey on productivity apps, respondents write in the number of apps they have installed in the past six months. What measures of central tendency can be used? Which is the most appropriate and why?

12-11. If you use the standard deviation as a measure of the variability in a sample, what statistical assumptions have you implicitly adopted?

12-12. What essential factors are taken into consideration when statistical inference takes place?

12-13. What is meant by "parameter estimation," and what function does it perform for a researcher?

12-14. How does parameter estimation for a mean differ from that for a percentage?

12-15. List the steps in statistical hypothesis testing and the steps in intuitive hypothesis testing. How are they similar? How are they different?

12-16. What does it mean when a researcher says that a hypothesis has been supported at the 95% confidence level?

12-17. Here are several computation practice exercises to help you identify which formulas pertain and learn how to perform the necessary calculations. In each case, perform the necessary calculations and write your answers in the column identified by "Your Confidence Intervals" or "Your Test Results."

a. Determine Confidence Intervals for Each of the Following

Sample Statistic	Sample Size	Confidence Level	Your Confidence Intervals
Mean: 150	200	95%	
Standard Deviation: 30			_____

Sample Statistic	Sample Size	Confidence Level	Your Confidence Intervals
Percent: 67%	300	99%	_____
Mean: 5.4	250	99%	
Standard Deviation: 0.5			_____
Percent: 25.8%	500	99%	_____

b. Test the Following Hypothesis and Interpret Your Findings

Hypothesis	Sample Findings	Confidence Level	Your Test Results
Mean = 7.5	Mean: 8.5	95%	
Standard Deviation: 1.2			
$n = 670$			_____
Percent = 86%	$p = 95$	99%	
$n = 1000$			_____
Mean = 125	Mean: 135	95%	
Standard Deviation: 15			
$n = 500$			_____
Percent = 33%	$p = 31$	99%	
$n = 120$			_____

12-18. Alamo Rent-A-Car executives believe that Alamo accounts for about 50% of all Cadillacs that are rented. To test this belief, a researcher randomly identifies 20 major airports with on-site rental car lots. Observers are sent to each location and instructed to record the number of rental-company Cadillacs observed in a four-hour period. About 500 are observed, and 30% are observed being returned to Alamo Rent-A-Car. What are the implications of this finding for the Alamo executives' belief?

CASE 12.1

L'Experience Félicité Restaurant Survey Descriptive and Inference Analysis   IBM **SPSS**

In addition to the Auto Concepts survey, Cory Rogers of CMG Research was working with Jeff Dean, who believed that there was an opportunity to build an upscale restaurant, possibly to be called L'Experience Félicité (for "Delightful Experience") somewhere in the metropolitan area. The proposed restaurant was described as follows...

A restaurant with a very elegant decor, offering very personal service in a spacious, semi-private atmosphere, featuring both traditional and unusual menu items prepared by a chef with an international reputation. The atmosphere, food, and service at this restaurant meet the standards of the finest restaurants. Menu items are priced separately, known as "à la carte," and the prices are what one would expect for a restaurant meeting the highest restaurant standards.

Cory's team had designed an online questionnaire and gathered a representative sample. The code book for the SPSS dataset follows.

Question	Codes	Labels
Do you eat at an upscale restaurant at least once every two weeks?	1,2	Yes, No (If No, terminate the survey)
How many total dollars do you spend per month in restaurants (for your meals only)?	Actual dollars	No labels
How likely would it be for you to patronize this proposed new upscale restaurant?	1,2,3,4,5	Very unlikely, ... , Very likely
What would you expect an average evening meal entrée item alone to be priced in the proposed new restaurant? (If not "very unlikely" in previous question)	Actual dollars	No labels
Would you describe yourself as one who listens to the radio?	1,2	Yes, No
(If yes) To which type of radio programming do you most often listen?	1,2,3,4,5	Country, Easy listening, Rock, Talk/news, No preference
Would you describe yourself as a viewer of TV local news?	1,2	Yes, No
(If yes) Which newscast do you watch most frequently?	1,2,3,4	7:00 a.m., Noon, 6:00 p.m., 10:00 p.m.
Do you read the newspaper?	1,2	Yes, No
(If yes) Which section of the local newspaper would you say you read most frequently?	1,2,3,4,5	Editorial, Business, Local, Classifieds, Life-Health-Entertainment
Do you subscribe to *City Magazine*?	1,2	Yes, No
How often have you used online reviews to choose products and services?	0,1,2,3,4	Never, 1–2 times, 3–4 times, 5–7 times, more than 7 times per month
In this proposed new restaurant how much would you prefer... • Waterfront view • Drive less than 30 minutes • Formal waitstaff wearing tuxedos • Unusual desserts • Large variety of entrées • Unusual entrées • Simple decor • Elegant decor • String quartet • Jazz combo	1,2,3,4,5	Very strongly not prefer, Somewhat not prefer, Neither prefer nor not prefer, Somewhat prefer, Very strongly prefer
Year you were born	Actual year	No labels
What is your highest level of education?	1,2,3,4,5,6,7,8	Less than high school, Some high school, High school graduate, Some college, Associate degree, Bachelor's degree, Master's degree, Doctorate degree
What is your marital status?	1,2,3	Single, Married, Other
Including children under 18 living with you, what is your family size?	# children	No labels
Please check the letter that includes the ZIP code in which you live (designated by letter by combining ZIPs using the last two digits).	1,2,3,4	A (01 & 02), B (03, 04, & 05), C (07, 08, & 09), D (10, 11 & 12)
Which of the following categories best describes your before-tax household income?	1,2,3,4,5,6,7	Under $15,000; $15,000 to $24,999; $25,000 to $49,999; $50,000 to $74,999; $75,000 to $99,999; $100,000 to $149,999; $150,000 and above
What is your gender?	1,2	Male, Female

Cory had other marketing research projects and meetings scheduled with present and prospective clients, so he called in his marketing intern, Christine Yu. Christine was a senior marketing major at Able State University, and she had taken marketing research in the previous semester. Cory said, "Christine, it is time to do some analysis on the survey we did for Jeff Dean. For now, let's just get a feel for what the data look like. I'll leave it up to your judgment as to what basic analysis to run. Let's meet tomorrow at 2:30 p.m. and see what you have found."

Your task is to take the role of Christine Yu, marketing intern. The file name is L'Experience.sav and it is in SPSS data file format. Your instructor will provide this SPSS data file to you or indicate how you can obtain it.

1. Determine what variables are categorical (either nominal or ordinal scales), perform the appropriate descriptive analysis, and interpret it.
2. Determine what questions are scale variables (either interval or ratio scales), perform the appropriate descriptive analysis, and interpret it.

3. What are the population estimates for each of the following?
   a. Preference for "easy listening" radio programming
   b. Viewing of 10 p.m. local news on TV
   c. Subscribe to *City Magazine*
   d. Average age of heads of households
   e. Average price paid for an evening meal entrée
4. Because this restaurant will be upscale, it will appeal to high-income consumers. The investors hope that 15% of the households represented in the survey have an income level of $100,000 or higher. Test this hypothesis.
5. With respect to those who are "very likely" to patronize L'Experience Félicité Restaurant, Jeff believes that they will either "very strongly" or "somewhat" prefer each of the following: (a) waitstaff with tuxedos, (b) unusual desserts, (c) large variety of entrées, (d) unusual entrées, (e) elegant decor, and (f) jazz combo music. Does the survey support or refute Jeff's hypotheses? Interpret your findings.

CASE 12.2 INTEGRATED CASE

Auto Concepts Descriptive and Inference Analysis IBM **SPSS**

Cory Rogers of CMG Research was happy to call Nick Thomas to inform him that Auto Concepts survey data were collected and ready for analysis. Of course, Cory had other marketing research projects and meetings scheduled with present and prospective clients, so he called in his data analyst, Celeste Brown. Cory said, "Celeste, it is time to do some analysis on the survey we did for Nick Thomas of Auto Concepts. I am going to assign you primary responsibility for all data analysis on this important project. For now, let's just get a feel for what the data look like, so do some descriptives in order to reveal the basic patterns and to gain an understanding of the nature of the variability in

the data. Let's meet tomorrow at 3:30 p.m. and see what you have found."

Your task in Case 12.2 is to take the role of Celeste Brown, data analyst. The dataset for the Auto Concepts survey is now ready for descriptive analysis. The file name is Auto Concepts.sav, and it is in SPSS data file format. The instructor of your marketing research course will tell you how to access this SPSS dataset. The dataset sample represents American households, and it includes owners as well as nonowners of vehicles because any new vehicles to be developed will not "hit" the market for another 3 to 5 years.

Question Description	Codes	Value Labels
Size of hometown or city	1,2,3,4,5	Under 10K, 10K to 100K, 100K to 500K, 500K to 1 million, 1 million and more
Gender	0,1	Male, Female
Marital status	0,1	Unmarried, Married
Number of people in family	Actual number	No labels
Age category	1,2,3,4,5	18 to 24, 25 to 34, 35 to 49, 50 to 64, 65 and older
Education category	1,2,3,4,5	Less than high school, High school diploma, Some college, College degree, Postgraduate degree
Income category	1,2,3,4,5	Under $25K, $25K to 49K, $50K to $74K, $75K to $125K, $125K and more
Dwelling type	1,2,3,4	Single family, Multiple family, Condominium/townhouse, Mobile home

Question Description	Codes	Value Labels
I am worried about global warming. Gasoline emissions contribute to global warming. We need to do something to slow global warming. We should be looking for gasoline substitutes.	1,2,3,4,5,6,7	Very strongly disagree, Strongly disagree, Disagree, Neither disagree nor agree, Agree, Strongly agree, Very strongly agree
Desirability: 1-seat motorcycle electric Desirability: 2-seat runabout sport electric Desirability: 2-seat runabout hatchback gasoline hybrid Desirability: 4-seat economy diesel hybrid Desirability: 5-seat economy gasoline	1,2,3,4,5,6,7	Very undesirable, Undesirable, Somewhat desirable, Neutral, Somewhat desirable, Desirable, Very desirable
Lifestyle: Novelist Lifestyle: Innovator Lifestyle: Trendsetter Lifestyle: Forerunner Lifestyle: Mainstreamer Lifestyle: Classic	1, …,7	Does not describe me at all, …, Describes me perfectly
Favorite television show type	1,2,3,4,5,6,7	Comedy, Drama, Movies/mini-series, News/documentary, Reality, Science fiction, Sports
Favorite radio genre	1,2,3,4,5,6	Classic pop & rock, Country, Easy listening, Jazz & blues, Pop & chart, Talk
Favorite magazine type	1,2,3,4,5,6,7,8	Business & Money, Music & Entertainment, Family & Parenting, Sports & Outdoors, Home & Garden, Cooking-Food & Wine, Trucks-Cars & Motorcycles, News-Politics & Current Events
Favorite local newspaper section	1,2,3,4,5,6, 7	Editorial, Business, Local news, National news, Sports, Entertainment, Do not read
Use of online blogs Use of content communities Use of social network sites Use of online games Use of virtual worlds	0,1,2,3	Never, 1–2 times per day, 3–4 times per day, 5+ times per day

For each question below, it is your task to determine the type of scale for each variable, conduct the proper descriptive analysis with SPSS, and interpret it.

1. What is the demographic composition of the sample?
2. How do respondents feel about (1) global warming and (2) gasoline emissions?
3. What type of automobile model is the most desirable to people in the sample? What type is the least desirable?
4. Describe the "traditional" media usage of respondents in the sample.
5. Describe the social media usage of the respondents in the sample.
6. The Auto Concepts principals believe that the desirability on the part of the American public for each of the automobile models under consideration is the following:

Vehicle Model Type	Desirability*
Desirability: 1-seat motorcycle electric	3
Desirability: 2-seat runabout sport electric	4
Desirability: 2-seat runabout hatchback gasoline hybrid	4
Desirability: 4-seat economy diesel hybrid	3
Desirability: 5-seat economy gasoline	2

*Measured on 1–7 scale.

Test these hypotheses with the findings from the survey.

13

Implementing Basic Differences Tests

"WHERE WE ARE"

1 Establish the need for marketing research.

2 Define the problem.

3 Establish research objectives.

4 Determine research design.

5 Identify information types and sources.

6 Determine methods of accessing data.

7 Design data collection forms.

8 Determine the sample plan and size.

9 Collect data.

10 Analyze data.

11 Prepare and present the final research report.

20|20 Research

Jim Bryson, founder and CEO, 20|20 Research

20|20 Research is a global leader in the development, support, and service of online qualitative market research and the software and technology that sustain it. The company helps market research and advertising firms around the world perform better research for their clients.

Launched in 1986 by Jim Bryson, founder and CEO, the firm began as an in-person focus group facility in Nashville, Tennessee, later expanding to include similar centers in other parts of the nation. With the rapid growth of technology in the market research industry, in 2003 Bryson led a major pivot for the firm from leading in-person focus groups to specializing in emerging innovative technologies for researchers. The firm is now the global leader for online qualitative research software and services and the preferred provider for seven of the top 10 research companies in the world. It currently has projects in more than 122 countries and 30+ languages.

Some of 20|20's innovations include the following:

■ a threaded bulletin board platform that allows participants to join focus groups at times and locations convenient to them.

■ a tool that uses webcam technology and streaming video to provide real-time face-to-face research.

■ markup software that allows respondents to provide pointed feedback on ads, design concepts, new product ideas, storyboards, and other visual stimuli.

- the first real-time, fully integrated human translation tool for global online qualitative research that quickly translates any of 24 languages.
- facial coding technology that provides researchers insights into the true emotions of respondents, which can be implemented anywhere in the world where there is a computer, a webcam, and the Internet.
- a platform that harnesses virtual/augmented reality to place respondents in almost any setting, measure their responses, and better understand their reactions and purchasing behavior.

20|20

Visit 20|20 Research at www.2020research.com

In the past five years the company has been named one of the top 15 most innovative research firms worldwide by GreenBook Research Industry Trends, a principal arbiter of the market research industry. The firm's operations are headquartered in Nashville and the company continues to maintain traditional focus group facilities in Nashville, Charlotte, and Miami as well as a European office in London, England.

Bryson sits on the Market Research Association board of directors, has served three terms as president of Qualitative Research Consultants Association, and was named Market Research Executive of the Year in 2013 by *Research Business Report.* He holds an M.B.A. from Vanderbilt University.

Source: Text and photos courtesy of Jim Bryson and 20|20 Research.

In this chapter, we describe the logic of differences tests, and we show you how to use SPSS to conduct various types of differences tests.[1] Whereas meaningful insights are common with qualitative research, such as those described for 20|20 Research, differences tests also provide very useful findings; however, they require the use of quantitative data from a sizeable sample of survey participants. We begin this chapter discussing why differences are important to marketing managers. Next, we introduce differences (percentages or means) between two independent groups, such as a comparison of high-speed cable versus DSL telephone Internet users on how satisfied they are with their Internet connection service. Next, we introduce ANOVA, a scary name for a simple way to compare the means of several groups simultaneously and to quickly spot patterns of significant differences. We provide numerical examples and share examples of SPSS procedures and output using the Auto Concepts survey data. Finally, we establish that it is possible to test for a difference between the averages of two similarly scaled questions. For instance, do buyers rate a store higher in "merchandise selection" than they rate its "good values"?

13-1 Why Differences Are Important

Perhaps one of the most useful marketing management concepts is market segmentation. Basically, market segmentation holds that different types of consumers have different requirements, and these differences can be the bases of marketing strategies. As an example, the Iams Company that markets pet foods has over 20 different varieties of dry dog food geared

Market segmentation strategy explicitly recognizes differences between groups of consumers.

Market segmentation is based on differences between groups of consumers.

to the dog's age (puppy, adult, senior), weight situation (small, medium, large), and activity level (reduced, normal, moderate, high). Toyota Motors has 20 models including five car models, two truck models, seven SUV/van models, and eight hybrid/crossover models. Even Boeing Airlines has six different types of commercial jets plus a separate business jets division for corporate travel. Let's look at differences from the consumer's side. Everyone washes his or her hands, but the kind of soap required differs for weekend gardeners with potting soil under their fingernails, factory workers whose hands are dirty with solvents, preschoolers who have sticky drink residue on their hands and faces, or aspiring beauty princesses who wish their hands to look absolutely flawless. The needs and requirements of each of these market segments differ greatly from the others, and an astute marketer will customize his or her marketing mix to each target market's unique situation.[2]

These differences, of course, are quite obvious, but as competition becomes more intense with prolific market segmentation and target marketing being the watchword of most companies in an industry, there is a need to investigate differences among consumer groups for consumer marketers and business establishments for B2B (business-to-business) marketers. One commonly used basis for market segmentation is the discovery of (1) statistically significant, (2) meaningful, (3) stable, and (4) actionable differences. We will discuss each requirement briefly. In our comments, we will assume that we are working with a pharmaceuticals company that markets cold remedies.

To be potentially useful to the marketing researcher or manager, differences must, at minimum, be statistically significant.

The differences must be significant. As you know, the notion of statistical significance underpins marketing research.[3] **Statistical significance of differences** means that the differences found in the sample(s) truly exist in the population(s) from which the random samples are drawn. The differences that are apparent between and among market segments must be subjected to tests that assess the statistical significance of those differences. We will endeavor to teach you how to perform and interpret tests of the statistical significance of differences. With our cold remedy marketer, we could ask cold sufferers, "How important is it that your cold remedy relieves your ____?" The respondents would use a scale from 1 = "Not important" to 10 = "Very important" for each cold symptom such as fever, sore throat, congestion, and aching muscles, and statistical tests such those described in this chapter would determine if the responses were significantly different. With those in the grip of a cold virus, we might find two groups that have statistically significant differences: (1) *congestion sufferers*, who greatly desire breathing congestion relief, and (2) *muscle aches and pains sufferers*, who instead greatly desire relief from musculoskeletal aches and pains associated with their colds.

To be useful to the marketing researcher or manager, differences must, if statistically significant, be meaningful.

The differences must be meaningful. A finding of statistical significance in no way guarantees "meaningful" difference. In fact, with the proliferation of data mining analysis due to scanner data with tens of thousands of records, online surveys that garner thousands of respondents, and other ways to capture very large samples, there is a very real danger of finding a great deal of statistical significance that is not meaningful. The reason for this danger is that statistical significance is determined in large part by the sample size.[4] You will see in this chapter by examining the formulas we provide that the sample size, n, is instrumental in the calculation of z, the determinant of the significance level. Large samples, those in excess of 1,000 per sample group, often yield statistically significant results when the absolute differences between the groups are quite small. A **meaningful difference** is one that the marketing manager can potentially use as a basis for marketing decisions.

© Ljupco Smokovski/Shutterstock

In our common cold example, there are meaningful implications that those in one group cannot breathe easily while those in the other group have aches and pains, and thankfully there are cold remedy ingredients that reduce congestion and other ingredients that diminish pain. Should the pharmaceuticals company include both ingredients in one remedy? Research shows that the congestion sufferers do not want an ingredient that might make them drowsy due to the strong pain relief ingredient, and the aches and pains sufferers do not want their throats and nasal passages to feel dry and uncomfortable due to the decongestant ingredient. Thus these differences are meaningful both to the customer groups and to the pharmaceuticals manufacturer.

The differences should be stable. Stability refers to the requirement that we are not working with a short-term or transitory set of differences. Thus, a **stable difference** is one that will be in place for the foreseeable future. The persistent problem experienced by *congestion sufferers* is most probably due to some respiratory weakness or condition. They may have preconditions such as allergies or breathing problems, or they may be exposed to heavy pollution or some other factor that affects their respiration in general. *Muscle aches and pains sufferers* may be very active people who do not have respiration weaknesses but who value active lifestyle practices such as regular exercise, or their occupations may require a good deal of physical activity. In either case, there is a very good possibility that when a cold strikes, the sufferer will experience the same discomfort, either congestion or muscle aches, time and time again. That is, the differences between the two groups are stable. The pharmaceuticals company can develop custom-designed versions of a cold relief product because managers know from experience and research that certain consumers will be consistent (stable) in seeking certain types of relief or specific product benefits when they suffer from colds.

> To be useful to the marketing researcher or manager, differences must, if statistically significant and meaningful, be stable.

The differences must be actionable. Market segmentation requires that standard or innovative market segmentation bases are used, and that these bases uniquely identify the various groups so they can be analyzed and put in the marketer's targeting mechanisms. An **actionable difference** means that the marketer can focus various marketing strategies and tactics, such as product design or advertising, on the market segments to accentuate the differences between the segments. There are a great many segmentation bases that are actionable such as demographics, lifestyles, and product benefits. In our example, among the many symptoms manifested by cold sufferers, we have identified two meaningful and stable groups, so a cold remedy product line that concentrates on each one of these groups separately is possible. A quick glance at the cold remedies section of your local drugstore will verify the actionability of these cold symptoms market segments.

> To be useful to the marketing researcher or manager, differences must be statistically significant, meaningful, stable, and actionable.

You may be confused about meaningful and actionable differences. Recall that we used the phrase "potentially use" in our definition of a meaningful difference. With our cold remedies example, a pharmaceutical company could potentially develop and market a cold remedy that was specific to every type of cold symptom as experienced by every demographic group and further identified by lifestyle differences. For example, there could be a cold medicine to alleviate the runny noses of teenage girls who participate in high school athletics, and a different one for the sniffles in teenage boys who play high school sports. But it would be economically unjustifiable to offer so many different cold medicines, so all marketers must assess actionably based on market segment size and profitability considerations. Nevertheless, the fundamental differences are based on statistical significance, meaningfulness, and stability assessments.

To be sure, the bulk of this chapter deals strictly with statistically significant differences because it is the beginning point for market

Because cold suffers consistently have different symptoms such as runny noses, congestion, and achy muscles, pharmaceutical companies have identified different market segments.

© Subbotina/123rf

segmentation and savvy target marketing. Meaningfulness, stability, and actionability are not statistical issues; rather, they are marketing manager judgment calls.

IBM SPSS ## 13-2 Small Sample Sizes: The Use of a *t* Test or a *z* Test and How SPSS Eliminates the Worry

Most of the equations related in this chapter will lead to the computation of a *z* value. As we pointed out in the previous chapter, the computation of the *z* value makes the assumption that the raw data for most statistics under scrutiny have normal or bell-shaped distributions. However, statisticians have shown that this normal curve property does not occur when the sample size is 30 observations or fewer.[5] In this instance, a *t* value is computed instead of a *z* value. The **t test** is defined as the statistical inference test to be used with small samples sizes ($n \leq 30$). Any instance when the sample size is 30 or greater requires the use of a *z* **test**.

The *t* test should be used when the sample size is 30 or fewer.

Most computer statistical programs report only the *t* value because it is identical to the *z* value with large samples.

The great advantage to using statistical analysis routines on a computer is that they are programmed to compute the correct statistic. In other words, you do not need to decide whether you want the program to compute a *t* value, a *z* value, or some other value. With SPSS, the analyses of differences are referred to as *t tests*, but now that you realize that SPSS will always determine the correct significance level whether it is a *t* or a *z*, you do not need to worry about which statistic to use. The talent you need to acquire is how to interpret the significance level that is reported by SPSS. We have provided Marketing Research Insight 13.1 to introduce you to a "stoplight" analogy that students have told us is helpful in this regard.

MARKETING RESEARCH INSIGHT 13.1 *Practical Application*

Green Stoplight Signals and Significance in Statistical Analysis

The output from statistical procedures in all software programs can be envisioned as "green light" devices. When the green signal light is on, statistical significance is present. Then, and only then, is it warranted to look more closely to determine the pattern of the findings; if the light is not green, your time will be wasted by looking any further. To read statistical stoplight signals, you need to know two things. First, where is the stoplight located? Second, what color light is illuminated?

Where Is the Light?

Virtually every statistical test or procedure involves the computation of some critical statistic, and that statistic is used to determine the statistical significance of the findings. The critical statistic's name changes depending on the procedure and its underlying assumptions, but usually the statistic is identified as a letter, as in *z*, *t*, or *F*. Statistical analysis computer programs will automatically identify and compute the correct statistic, so although it is helpful to know ahead of time what statistic will be computed, it is not essential to know it. Moreover, the statistic is not the signal light; rather it is just a computation necessary to determine what color light to illuminate.

The computer program will also contain the stoplight, but its name changes a bit depending on the procedure. Often

called "*p* values" by statisticians, they are identified on computer output by the term *significance* or *probability*. Sometimes abbreviations such as "Sig." or "Prob." are used to economize on the output. To find the stoplight, locate the "Sig." or "Prob." designation in the analysis and look at the number that is associated with it. The number will be a decimal perhaps as low as .000 and ranging as high as 1.000. When you locate it, you have found the statistical significance stoplight.

What Is the Color of the Stoplight Signal?

Whenever you encounter a stoplight while driving your car, a green lights signals that you can advance forward. For purposes of this textbook, we have adopted the 95% level of confidence. That is, if you were 95% confident that the green light is on, you would proceed by stepping on your gas pedal. As we noted previously, the significance or probability values reported in statistical analysis output range from .0000 to 1.000, and they indicate the degree of support for the null hypothesis (no differences). If you take 1 minus the reported significance level—for example, if the significance level is .03, you take 1 minus .03 to come up with .97, or 97%—it is the level of confidence for our finding. Any time this value is 95% or greater, you should know that you have the green light to start your interpretation of the findings.

13-3   Testing for Significant Differences Between Two Groups

Often, as we have done in our cold remedy example, a researcher will want to compare two groups of interest. That is, the researcher may have two independent groups such as first-time versus repeat customers, and he or she may want to compare their answers to the same question. The question may use either a nominal or a scale measure. A nominal variable requires that the researcher compare percentages; a scale variable requires comparing means. As you know by now, the formulas differ depending on whether percentages or means are being tested.

Statistical tests are used when a researcher wants to compare the means or percentages of two different groups or samples.

DIFFERENCES BETWEEN PERCENTAGES WITH TWO GROUPS (INDEPENDENT SAMPLES)

When a marketing researcher is interested in making comparisons between two groups of respondents to determine whether or not there are statistically significant differences between them, in concept, he or she is considering them as two potentially different populations. The question to be answered then becomes whether or not their respective population parameters are different. But, as always, a researcher can only work with the sample results. Therefore, the researcher must fall back on statistical significance to determine whether the difference that is found between the two sample statistics is a true population difference. You will shortly discover that the logic of differences tests is very similar to the logic of hypothesis testing that you learned about in the previous chapter.

Independent samples are treated as representing two potentially different populations.

To begin, we will refer to an intuitive approach you use every day when comparing two things to make an inference. Let us assume you have read a *Business Week* article about college recruiters that quotes a Harris poll of 100 randomly selected companies, indicating that 65% of them will be visiting college campuses to interview business majors. The article goes on to say that a similar poll taken last year with 300 companies found that only 40% would be recruiting at college campuses. This is great news: More companies will be coming to your campus this year with job interviews. However, you cannot be completely confident of your joyous conclusion because of sampling error. If the difference between the percentages was very large, say 80% for this year and 20% for last year, you would be more inclined to believe that a true change had occurred. But if you found out the difference was based on small sample sizes, you would be less confident of your inference that last year's college recruiting and this year's college recruiting are different. Intuitively, you have taken into account two critical factors in determining whether statistically significant differences exist between a percentage or a mean compared between two samples: the magnitude of the difference between the compared statistic (65% versus 40%) and sample sizes (100 versus 300).

To test whether a true difference exists between two group percentages, we test the **null hypothesis**, or the hypothesis that the difference in their population parameters is equal to zero. The alternative hypothesis is that there is a true difference between them. To perform the test of **significance of differences between two percentages**, each representing a separate group (sample), the first step requires a comparison of the two percentages. The comparison is made by finding the arithmetic difference between them. The second step requires that this difference be translated into a number of standard errors away from the hypothesized value of zero. Once the number of standard errors is known, knowledge of the area under the normal curve will yield an assessment of the probability of support for the null hypothesis.

With a differences test, the null hypothesis states there is no difference between the percentages (or means) being compared.

For a difference between two percentages test, the equation is as follows:

Formula for significance of the difference between two percentages

$$z = \frac{p_1 - p_2}{s_{p_1 - p_2}}$$

where

p_1 = percentage found in sample 1

p_2 = percentage found in sample 2

$s_{p_1-p_2}$ = standard error of the difference between two percentages

The standard error of the difference between two percentages combines the standard error of the percentage for both samples, and it is calculated with the following formula:

Formula for the standard error of the difference between two percentages

> With a differences test, you test the null hypothesis that no differences exist between the two group means (or percentages).

$$s_{p_1-p_2} = \sqrt{\frac{p_1 \times q_1}{n_1} + \frac{p_2 \times q_2}{n_2}}$$

where

$q_1 = 100 - p_1$

$q_2 = 100 - p_2$

n_1, n_2 = sample sizes for sample 1 and 2, respectively

Again, if you compare these formulas to the ones we used in hypothesis testing in Chapter 12, you will see that the logic is identical. First, in the numerator, we subtract one sample's statistic (p_2) from the other sample's statistic (p_1) just as we subtracted the hypothesized percent from the sample percent in hypothesis testing. You should have noticed that we use the subscripts 1 and 2 to refer to the two different sample statistics. Second, the sampling distribution is expressed in the denominator. However, the sampling distribution under consideration now is the assumed sampling distribution of the differences between the percentage rather than the simple standard error of a percentage used in hypothesis testing. That is, the assumption has been made that the differences have been computed for comparisons of the two sample statistics for many repeated samplings. If the null hypothesis is true, this distribution of differences follows the normal curve with a mean equal to zero and a standard error equal to one. Stated somewhat differently, the procedure requires us, as before, to accept the (null) hypothesis as true until it lacks support from the statistical test. Consequently, the differences of a multitude of comparisons of the two sample percentages generated from many, many samplings would average zero. In other words, our sampling distribution is now the distribution of the difference between one sample and the other, taken over many, many times.[6] The following example will walk you through the point we just made.

Here is how you perform the calculations for the Harris poll on companies coming to campus to hire college seniors. Recall that last year's poll with 300 companies reported 40% were coming to campuses, whereas this year's poll with 100 companies reported that 65% were visiting campuses.

Computation of the significance of the difference between two percentages	$z = \dfrac{p_1 - p_2}{s_{p_1-p_2}}$
Notes:	$= \dfrac{65 - 40}{\sqrt{\dfrac{65 \times 35}{100} + \dfrac{40 \times 60}{300}}}$
$p_1 = 65\%$	
$p_2 = 40\%$	
$n_1 = 100$	$= \dfrac{25}{\sqrt{22.75 + 8}}$
$n_2 = 300$	$= \dfrac{25}{5.55}$
	$= 4.51$

We compare the computed z value with our standard z of 1.96 for the 95% level of confidence, and the computed z of 4.51 is larger than 1.96. A computed z value that is larger than the standard z value of 1.96 amounts to *no support* for the null hypothesis at the 95% level of confidence. Thus there is a statistically significant difference between the two percentages and we are confident that if we repeated this comparison many, many times with a multitude of independent samples, we would conclude that there is a significant difference in at least 95% of these replications. Of course, we would never do so many replications, but this is the statistician's basis for the level of significance.

It is a simple matter to apply the formulas to percentages to determine the significance of their differences, for all that is needed is the sample size of each group. We provide Marketing Research Insight 13.2, which relies on differences between percentages for two different groups. This feature highlights how U.S. Hispanic consumers have become and will continue to be a major market segment.

MARKETING RESEARCH INSIGHT 13.2 *Digital Marketing Reseach*

Do U.S. Hispanics Differ from Non-Hispanics in Digital Media Use?

In the past decade, a quiet revolution of sorts has occurred with respect to consumers in the United States. For a number of reasons, the Hispanic segment of the U.S. population has made very significant gains, and it is estimated that there are now well over 50 million Hispanic consumers living in the United States. At the current rate of growth the Hispanic segment may account for one-third of all U.S. consumers in the next 30 to 50 years.

While it is well known that U.S. consumers are heavy digital media users, is this also the case for the Hispanic segment in the United States? An article was recently published by executives[7] at comScore, a large digital metrics company, contrasting U.S. Hispanics from non-Hispanics. For anyone who has not kept up with U.S. Hispanic market segment trends, the findings are probably quite surprising. As can be seen in the accompanying figure, the percentages of Hispanic consumers' uses of all types of digital media surpass those of non-Hispanics. In particular, in the case of use of mobile phones, Hispanics are twice as active as non-Hispanics for photo and/or video posting; they are one-third more active for social networking uses, and almost twice as active for status updating. It can also be seen that Hispanics are more active than non-Hispanics in all measured digital multimedia and entertainment uses: games, music, streaming, video, and multiple types of television uses. You might ask about English- versus Spanish-speaking Hispanics. The authors report that almost one-half of U.S. Hispanic consumers speak primarily English, while another one-quarter speaks both English and Spanish. The incidence of Spanish-only speakers among U.S. Hispanics will diminish over the near term due to a younger population and a higher birthrate among U.S. Hispanics.

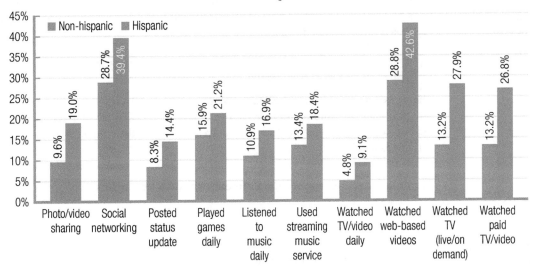

Differences in U.S. Hispanic and Non-Hispanic Consumers' Use of Digital Media

 Active Learning

Calculations to Determine Significant Differences Between Percentages

You can now perform your own tests of the differences between two percentages using the formulas we have provided and described. A local health club has just finished a media blitz (newspaper, television, radio, etc.) for new memberships. Whenever a prospective new member visited one of the health club's facilities, he or she was asked to fill out a short questionnaire. One question asked the person to indicate what ads he or she saw in the past month. Some of these prospects joined the health club, while some did not, which gave us two populations: those who joined the health club and those who did not. At the end of 30 days, a staff member performed the following tabulations.

	Joined the Health Club	Did Not Join the Health Club
Total visitors	100	30
Recalled newspaper ads	45	15
Recalled FM radio station ads	89	20
Recalled Yellow Pages ads	16	5
Recalled local TV news ads	21	6

Marketing Research on YouTube™ To learn about proportion differences tests, launch **www.youtube.com**, and search for "Hypothesis Test Comparing Population Proportions."

Use your knowledge of the formula and the test of the significance of the difference between two percentages to ascertain if there are any significant differences in the data. What are the implications of your findings with respect to the effectiveness of the various advertising media used during the membership recruitment ad blitz?

IBM SPSS

HOW TO USE SPSS FOR DIFFERENCES BETWEEN PERCENTAGES OF TWO GROUPS

SPSS does not perform tests of the significance of the difference between the percentages of two groups, but you can use SPSS to generate the relevant information and perform a hand calculation.

As is the case with most statistical analysis programs, SPSS does not perform tests of the significance of the difference between the percentages of two groups. You can, however, use SPSS to determine the sample percentage on your variable of interest along with its sample size. Use the SPSS command FREQUENCIES. Repeat this descriptive analysis for the other sample, and you will have all the values required (p_1, p_2, n_1, and n_2) to perform the calculations by hand or in a spreadsheet program. (Recall that you can compute q_1 and q_2, based on the "$p + q = 100\%$" relationship.)

DIFFERENCES BETWEEN MEANS WITH TWO GROUPS (INDEPENDENT SAMPLES)

The procedure for testing **significance of difference between two means** from two different groups (either two different samples or two different groups in the same sample) is identical to the procedure used in testing two percentages. However, the equations differ because a scale variable is involved.

Here is the equation for the test of difference between two sample means:

Formula for significance of the difference between two means

$$z = \frac{\bar{x}_1 - \bar{x}_2}{s_{\bar{x}_1 - \bar{x}_2}}$$

If the null hypothesis is true, when you subtract one group mean from the other, the result should be about zero.

where
$$\bar{x}_1 = \text{mean found in sample 1}$$
$$\bar{x}_2 = \text{mean found in sample 2}$$
$$s_{\bar{x}_1 - \bar{x}_2} = \text{standard error of the difference between two means}$$

The standard error of the difference is easy to calculate and again relies on the variability that has been found in the samples and their sizes. Because we are working with means, we use the standard deviations in the formula for the standard error of a difference between two means:

Formula for the standard error of the difference between two means

$$s_{\bar{x}_1 - \bar{x}_2} = \sqrt{\frac{s_1^2}{n_1} + \frac{s_2^2}{n_2}}$$

where

s_1 = standard deviation in sample 1

s_2 = standard deviation in sample 2

n_1 = size of sample 1

n_2 = size of sample 2

© Warren Goldswain/Shutterstock

Is there a difference in the average number of sports drinks consumed by males versus the average number of sports drinks consumed by females?

To illustrate how significance of difference computations are made, we use the following example that answers the question "Do male teens and female teens drink different amounts of sports drinks?" In a recent survey, teenagers were asked to indicate how many 20-ounce bottles of sports drinks they consume in a typical week. The descriptive statistics revealed that males consume 9 bottles on average and females consume 7.5 bottles of sports drinks on average. The respective standard deviations were found to be 2 and 1.2. Both samples were of size 100. Applying this information to the formula for the test of statistically significant differences, we get the following:

Here is the formula for the standard error of the difference between two means.

Computation of the significance of the difference between two means	
Notes:	$z = \dfrac{\bar{x}_1 - \bar{x}_2}{\sqrt{\dfrac{s_1^2}{n_1} + \dfrac{s_2^2}{n_2}}}$
$\bar{x}_1 = 9.0$	
$\bar{x}_2 = 7.5$	$= \dfrac{9.0 - 7.5}{\sqrt{\dfrac{2^2}{100} + \dfrac{1.2^2}{100}}}$
$s_1 = 2.0$	
$s_2 = 1.2$	
$n_1 = 100$	$= \dfrac{1.5}{\sqrt{.04 + 0.144}}$
$n_2 = 100$	
	$= \dfrac{1.5}{0.233}$
	$= 6.43$

Here are the calculations for a test of the difference between the means of two groups.

Figure 13.1 indicates how these two samples compare on the sampling distribution assumed to underlie this particular example. In the bottom of the figure, we have provided the standard error of the difference bell-shaped curve with 0 as its mean (the null hypothesis). By looking at the computed z value labeled on the graph, you know the probability of support for the null hypothesis of no difference between the two means is less than .05 because the large number of standard errors (6.43) calculated to exist for this example is much greater than 1.96.

How do you interpret this test for significance of differences? As always, the sampling distribution concept underlies our interpretation. If the null hypothesis is true, and we drew many, many samples and did this explicit comparison each time, then 95% of differences would fall within ±1.96 standard errors of zero. Of course, only one comparison can be made,

FIGURE 13.1 A Significant Difference Exists Between the Two Means Because z Is Calculated to Be Greater Than 1.96 (95% Level of Confidence)

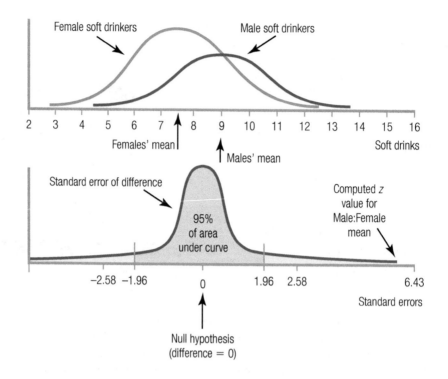

and you have to rely on the sampling distribution concept and its attendant assumptions to determine whether this one particular instance of information supports or refutes the hypothesis of no significant differences found between the means of your two groups.

INTEGRATED CASE

IBM **SPSS**   *The Auto Concepts Survey: How to Perform an Independent Sample Significance of Differences Between Means Test with SPSS*

To demonstrate an independent samples significance test, we will take up the question of whether or not market segmentation is relevant to Auto Concepts. We will begin by looking at gender as a possible segmentation variable and the desirability of the five-seat economy gasoline model. We have two groups: males and females. We can test the mean of the desirability of the five-seat economy gasoline model, which was measured on a 7-point scale where 1 = Very undesirable and 7 = Very desirable.

To determine the significance of the difference in the means of two groups with SPSS, use the ANALYZE-COMPARE MEANS-INDEPENDENT SAMPLES T-TEST ... menu sequence.

The clickstream that directs SPSS to perform an independent samples *t* test of the significance of the difference between means is displayed in Figure 13.2. As you can see, you begin with the ANALYZE-COMPARE MEANS-INDEPENDENT SAMPLES T-TEST ... menu sequence. This sequence opens up the selection menu, and the "Desirability: 5 Seat Economy Gasoline" model variable is clicked into the "Test variable" area, while the "Gender" variable is clicked in the "Grouping Variable" box. Using the "Define Groups" button, a window opens to let us identify the codes of the two groups (0 = male and 1 = female). This sets up the *t* test, and a click on OK executes it.

The annotated output is found in Figure 13.3. The first table reveals that the mean of the 560 males is 3.51, while the mean for the 440 females is 2.83.

The statistical test for the difference between the two means is given next. However, SPSS computes the results two different ways. One is identified as the "equal variances assumed," and the other is called the "equal variances not assumed." In our previous descriptions, we omitted a detail involved in tests for the significance of difference between two means.

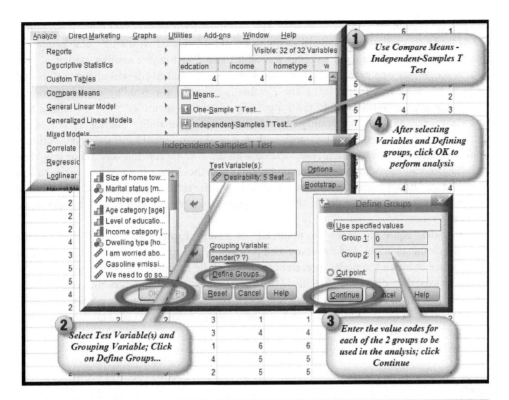

FIGURE 13.2

IBM SPSS Clickstream to Obtain an Independent Samples *t* Test

Source: Reprint Courtesy of International Business Machines Corporation, © International Business Machines Corporation.

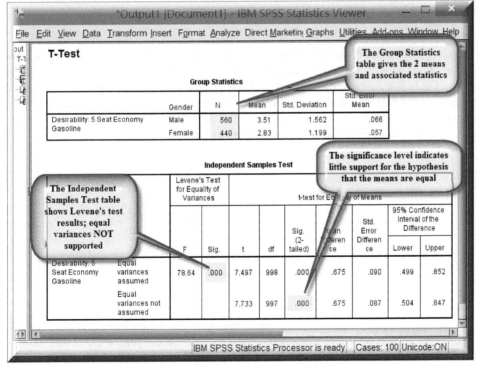

FIGURE 13.3

IBM SPSS Output for an Independent Samples *t* Test

Source: Reprint Courtesy of International Business Machines Corporation, © International Business Machines Corporation.

In some cases, the variances (standard deviations) of the two samples are about the same; that is, they are not significantly different. If so, you can use the formula pertaining to the equal variances (same variance for both samples), but if the standard deviations are statistically significant in their differences, you should use the unequal variances line on the output.

IBM SPSS

IBM SPSS Student Assistant:
Assessing Differences Between Means for 2 Groups (Independent)

To learn about differences between means tests, launch **www.youtube.com**, and search for "Hypothesis Test for Difference of Means."

How do you know which one to use? The null hypothesis here is that there is no difference between the variances (standard deviations), and it is tested with an F value printed in the top row of the independent samples test table. The F test is just another statistical test, and it is the proper one here. (Recall that we stated earlier that SPSS will always select and compute the correct statistical test.) The F value is based on a procedure called "Levene's Test for Equality of Variances." In our output, the F value is identified as 78.64 with a Sig. (probability) of .000. The probability reported here is the probability that the variances are equal, so anytime the probability is greater than, say .05, you would use the equal variance line on the output. If the probability associated with the F value is small, say .05 or less, then the variances null hypothesis is not supported, and you should use the unequal variance line (identified as "Equal variances not assumed"). If you forget this rule, look at the standard deviations. Try to remember that if they are about the same size, you would use the equal variances t value.

Using the "equal variances not assumed" estimate information, you will find that the computed t value is 7.733, and the associated probability of support for the null hypothesis of no difference between the males' preference mean and the females' preference mean is .000. In other words, they differ significantly. Males prefer the standard-size gasoline model more than do females, and Auto Concepts can segment this model's market using gender. However, one should bear in mind that the male mean is essentially "neutral," so perhaps other segmentation bases will derive more useful findings.

 Active Learning

Perform Means Differences Analysis with SPSS

You have just observed how to perform an independent samples t test with SPSS using your Auto Concepts survey data. For this Active Learning exercise, determine if there is a difference in preferences for the various possible electric or hybrid models based on gender. That is, redo the five-seat economy gasoline analysis to make sure that you can find and execute the analysis. Then use the clickstream instructions in Figure 13.2 to direct SPSS to perform this analysis for each of the four other possible models. Use the annotations on the independent samples t test output provided in Figure 13.3 to interpret your findings.

Synthesize Your Learning

The following case study will serve to synthesize your knowledge of material covered in the following chapters.

Chapter 11	Dealing with Fieldwork and Data Quality Issues
Chapter 12	Using Descriptive Analysis, Performing Population Estimates, and Testing Hypotheses
Chapter 13	Implementing Basic Differences Tests

A survey was recently conducted for a store called Pets, Pets, & Pets (PPP). The store has a list of 10,000 customers who have made a purchase there in the last year, and a random sample of 400 of these customers participated in the survey. Following are some of the relevant findings.

PPP Survey Table 1

What type of pet do you own?	Dog	Cat	Other	Total
	45%	34%	21%	100%

PPP Survey Table 2

	Sample Yes	Dog Owner	Cat Owner
Do you use PPP quite often?	44%	50%	38%
Would you recommend PPP to a friend?	82%	91%	75%
Do you recall a PPP newspaper ad in past month?	53%	50%	55%
Do you recall a PPP coupon in the past month?	47%	53%	40%

PPP Survey Table 3

Rate each of the following aspects of PPP.*	Sample		Dog Owner		Cat Owner	
	Average	Std Dev	Average	Std Dev	Average	Std Dev
Assortment of merchandise	4.6	2.1	4.9	1.6	4.5	1.9
Friendliness of employees	4.6	2.1	4.7	1.3	4.5	2.2
Speed of check-out	4.4	1.9	4.6	0.9	4.2	1.8
Convenience of parking	4.1	1.9	4.5	1.6	3.8	2.4
Competitive prices	4.0	2.0	4.3	1.9	4.0	1.9
Store layout	3.8	2.1	4.3	1.6	3.6	1.6
Helpfulness of employees	3.4	1.9	3.7	1.8	3.3	2.1
Variety of cat/dog food brands	3.4	2.1	3.4	1.8	3.4	1.9
Convenient location	2.8	1.9	3.3	1.5	2.8	1.6
Overall satisfaction with PPP	4.6	1.5	4.9	1.2	4.2	2.2

*Based on a scale where 1 = Very unsatisfied, ... 5 = Very satisfied.

PPP Survey Table 4

What is your household income level?	Sample	Dog Owner	Cat Owner
Refused	5%	0%	25%
Between $60,000 and $80,000	10%	15%	10%
Between $80,000 and $100,000	20%	25%	10%
Greater than $100,000	65%	60%	55%
Total	100%	100%	100%

1. Perform appropriate differences tests (95% level of confidence) to answer this question: "Do PPP dog owners differ from PPP cat owners with respect to their answers in PPP Table 1?" If so, how do they differ?

2. Perform appropriate differences tests (95% level of confidence) to answer this question: "Do PPP dog owners differ from PPP cat owners with respect to their answers in PPP Table 2?" If so, how do they differ?

3. PPP management believes that 75% of its customers are dog owners. Test this hypothesis, and if not supported at the 95% level of confidence, compute the confidence interval.

4. PPP management believes that all of its customers are overall "very satisfied" with PPP. Test this hypothesis, and if not supported at the 95% level of confidence, compute the confidence interval.

5. PPP Table 4 suggests that if PPP targets customers with household income of greater than $100,000 per year, it should emphasize its dog merchandise. Consider the data quality of the information contained in the table and assess if this conclusion is correct or incorrect. Be sure to do the appropriate statistical tests at the 95% level of confidence.

13-4 Testing for Significant Differences in Means Among More Than Two Groups: Analysis of Variance

As you have learned, it is fairly easy to test for the significance of the difference between means for two groups. But sometimes a researcher will want to compare the means of three, four, five, or more different groups. Analysis of variance, sometimes called ANOVA, should be used to accomplish such multiple comparisons.[8] The use of the word *variance* is misleading, for it is not an analysis of the standard deviations of the groups. To be sure, the standard deviations are taken into consideration, and so are the sample sizes, as you just saw in all of our differences between means formulas. Fundamentally, **ANOVA (analysis of variance)** is an investigation of the differences between the group means to ascertain whether sampling errors or true population differences explain their failure to be equal.[9] That is, the word *variance* signifies for our purposes differences between two or more groups' means—do they vary from one another significantly? Although a term such as *analysis of variance* or *ANOVA* sounds frightfully technical, it is nothing more than a statistical procedure that allows you to compare the means of several groups. As we noted in our discussion on market segmentations, markets are often comprised of a number of market segments, not just two, so ANOVA is a valuable tool for discovering differences between and among multiple market segments. The following sections explain the basic concepts involved with analysis of variance and how it can be applied to marketing research situations.

> ANOVA is used when comparing the means of three or more groups.

BASICS OF ANALYSIS OF VARIANCE

In using analysis of variance there is a desire on the part of a researcher to determine whether a statistically significant difference exists between the means for *any two groups* in a sample with a given variable regardless of the number of groups. The end result of analysis of variance is an indication to the marketing researcher as to whether a significant difference at some chosen level of statistical significance exists between *at least* two group means. Significant differences may exist between all of the group means, but analysis of variance results alone will not communicate how many pairs of means are statistically significant in their differences.

> ANOVA will "signal" when at least one pair of means has a statistically significant difference, but it does not tell which pair.

To elaborate, ANOVA is a **green light procedure**, meaning that if at least one pair of means has a statistically significant difference, ANOVA will signal this by indicating significance. Then it is up to the researcher to conduct further tests (called *post hoc tests*) to determine precisely how many statistically significant differences actually exist and which ones they are. If the green light is not illuminated, the researcher can conclude that no significant differences exist.

Let us elaborate just a bit on how ANOVA works. ANOVA uses some complicated formulas, and we have found from experience that market researchers do not memorize them. Instead, a researcher understands the basic purpose of ANOVA and is adept in interpreting ANOVA output. Let's assume that we have three groups, A, B, and C. In concept ANOVA performs all possible independent samples *t* tests for significant differences between the means, comparing, in our example, A:B, A:C, and B:C. ANOVA is very efficient, as it makes these comparisons simultaneously, not individually as you would need to do if you were running independent samples *t* tests. ANOVA's null hypothesis is that no single pair of means is significantly different. Because multiple pairs of group means are being tested, ANOVA uses the *F* test statistic, and the significance level (sometimes referred to as the *p* value) that appears on the output in this *F* test is the probability of support for the null hypothesis.

Here is an example that will help you to understand how ANOVA works and when to use it. A major department store conducts a survey. One of the

ANOVA is a "green light" procedure that signals when at least one pair of means is significantly different.

questions on the survey is "In what department did you last make a purchase for over $250?" There are four departments where significant numbers of respondents made these purchases: (1) electronics, (2) home and garden, (3) sporting goods, and (4) automotive. Another question on the survey is "How likely are you to purchase another item for over $250 from that department?" The respondents indicate how likely they are to do this on a 7-point scale where 1 = Very unlikely to 7 = Very likely. It is easy to calculate the mean of how likely each group is to return to the department store and purchase another major item from that same department.

The researcher who is doing the analysis decides to compare these means statistically, so six different independent samples *t* tests of the significance of the differences are performed. A summary of the findings is found in Table 13.1. On examining the table, you will see that the automotive department's mean is significantly different and lower than the repurchase likelihood means of the other three departments. Also, there is no significant difference in the other three department buyers' means. In other words, there is a good indication that the customers who bought an item for more than $250 from the department store's automotive department are not as satisfied with the purchase as are customers who bought large-ticket items from any of the other departments.

Now, look at Table 13.2. It is an abbreviated ANOVA output. Instead of looking at several significance values as in Table 13.1, all the researcher needs to do is to look at the significance level (Sig.) for the *F* test, our signal light. It is .000, which is less than .05, meaning that there is at least one pair of means with a significant difference, so the researcher has the green light to spend time and effort to look at the next table to find the significant difference(s). This table is arranged so the means that are not significantly different fall in the same column, while those that are significantly different fall in separate columns, and each column is identified as a unique subset. The means are arranged in the second table from the lowest mean to the highest mean, and it is immediately apparent that the automotive department has a problem.

> The Sig. value in the ANOVA table indicates the level of significance.

TABLE 13.1 Results of 6 Independent Samples *t* Tests of How Likely Customers Are to Return to Make Their Next Major Purchase

Groups Compared	Group Means*	Significance	
Electronics: Home and Garden	5.1: 5.3	.873	
Electronics: Sporting Goods	5.1: 5.6	.469	Significant difference between the two compared groups
Electronics: Automotive	5.1: 2.2	.000	
Home and Garden: Sporting Goods	5.3: 5.6	.656	
Home and Garden: Automotive	5.3: 2.2	.000	
Sporting Goods: Automotive	5.6: 2.2	.000	

*Based on a scale where 1 = Very unlikely to 7 = Very likely.

TABLE 13.2 Results of ANOVA of How Likely Customers Are to Return to Make Their Next Major Purchase

F	Sig.		
226.991	.000		There is a significant difference between at least two groups
Department	Subsets*		
	1	2	
Automotive	2.2		We have a problem with the Automotive Department!
Electronics		5.1	
Home and Garden		5.3	
Sporting Goods		5.6	

*Means in the same column are not significantly different; means in different columns are significantly different.

Using ANOVA is much more advantageous than running multiple *t* tests of the significance of the difference between means.

ANOVA has two distinct advantages over performing multiple independent sample *t* tests of the significance of the difference between means. First, it immediately notifies the researcher if there is any significant difference, because all he or she needs to do is to look at the Sig. value, our green signal light. Second, in our example, it arranges the means so the significant differences can be located and interpreted easily.

To elaborate, this Sig(nificance) value is the green light that we referred to earlier. When the light is green, the researcher is then justified at looking at the second table to find which means are significantly different. Once you learn how to read SPSS ANOVA output, it is quite easy to identify these cases. Of course, if the *F* statistic *p* value stoplight is not green, meaning that the *p* value is greater than .05, it is a waste of time to look at the differences between the pairs of means, as no difference will be statistically significant at the 95% level of confidence.

POST HOC TESTS: DETECT STATISTICALLY SIGNIFICANT DIFFERENCES AMONG GROUP MEANS

Duncan's multiple range test is our preferred post hoc test because its presentation is easy to interpret.

As we mentioned earlier, **post hoc tests** are options that are available to determine where the pair(s) of statistically significant differences between the means exist(s). As you will soon see in our SPSS example, there are over a dozen of these to choose from, including Scheffe's and Tukey's that you may recognize from your statistics course. It is beyond the scope of this book to provide a complete delineation of the various types of tests. Consequently, only one test, **Duncan's multiple range test,** will be shown as an illustration of how the differences may be determined. Duncan's multiple range test provides output that is mostly a "picture" of what means are significantly different, and it is much less statistical than most of the other post hoc tests, so we have chosen to use it here for these reasons. The picture provided by the Duncan's post hoc test is the arrangement of the means as you saw them in Table 13.2.

To illustrate how running ANOVA is much more efficient and convenient than performing successive independent sample differences tests, we have composed Marketing Research Insight 13.3, which describes a survey that measured how accepting consumers in 15 different countries are of six types of innovative new products.

INTEGRATED CASE

IBM **SPSS** *Auto Concepts: How to Run Analysis of Variance on SPSS*

In the Auto Concepts survey, there are several categorical variables that have more than two groups. For example, there are five education categories: less than high school diploma, high school diploma, some college, college degree, and postgraduate degree.

To run analysis of variance with SPSS, use the ANALYZE-COMPARE MEANS-ONE-WAY ANOVA menu command sequence.

One-way ANOVA uses only one grouping variable and, in this case, is done under the ANALYZE-COMPARE MEANS-ONE-WAY ANOVA menu command sequence illustrated in Figure 13.4. A window opens to set up the ANOVA analysis. The "Dependent list" is where you click in the variable(s) pertaining to the means, while the "Factor" variable is the grouping variable. In our example, the preference for the five-seat economy gasoline model is our dependent variable, and the "Age category" is the grouping variable. Figure 13.4 also shows how to select Duncan's Multiple Range option under the Post Hoc … Tests menu. Returning to the selection window and clicking OK commences the ANOVA procedure.

IBM **SPSS**
IBM SPSS Student Assistant:
Applying ANOVA (Analysis of Variance)

Figure 13.5 is an annotated ANOVA output. The first table contains a number of intermediate and additional computational results, but our attention should be focused on the "Sig." column. Here is the support for the null hypothesis that not one pair of means is significantly different. Since the Sig. value is .000, we are assured that there is at least one significantly different pair. The next table is the Duncan's test output. Specifically, the table is arranged so the means ascend in size from top left to right bottom, and the columns represent subsets of groups that are significantly different from groups in the other columns. You can immediately see that "18 to 24" (1.80) is the lowest group average, and it is significantly different from all other age groups because it occupies a column by itself. Similarly, looking at the next column,

MARKETING RESEARCH INSIGHT 13.3 — *Global Application*

ANOVA to the Rescue: How Accepting of Innovative Products Are Consumers in Different Countries?

No doubt you have become accustomed to encountering new, improved, and sometimes radically different products on a regular basis. Perhaps you are an eager adopter of such innovations; however, not everyone welcomes change or desires to learn and adopt new products and services. Researchers suspected that acceptance of innovative products differed by country because some countries, such as India and Japan, have long histories and deeply ingrained traditions while other countries, such as the United States and Australia that have been in existence for a much shorter time, have cultural values that favor progress and change. These researchers[10] conducted a very ambitious survey that took place in 15 different countries and sampled 5,569 respondents, or about 370 in each country. A key measure in the study was the degree of openness to innovative products or "eagerness to adopt" new products and services. However, the study was complicated by the fact that different product categories were used. Thus, for each country, the researchers determined the average eagerness to adopt home appliances, automobiles, cosmetics, food products, sporting goods, and financial services. The following figure is very busy, but it communicates all of the averages computed in the study—15 countries with six product categories plus an overall average.

For any one product category, such as home appliances, determining significant differences in the eagerness to adopt measure between countries would require a total of 105 separate independent samples tests (e.g., Brazil:Australia; Brazil:Canada, etc.). For the six product categories plus the overall average, there would need to be 7 × 105, or 735, separate independent samples average differences tests! Now, you might ask why not just use the country average measure and keep it down to 105, but by looking at the figure, it is apparent that some products such as food items tend to have high eagerness averages across all countries, while other products such as cosmetics tend to have low eagerness to adopt averages, and these important product differences would be lost by just looking at the country averages. Thus, all 735 comparisons are necessary. It is easy to see that ANOVA is a huge time saver and a much more convenient analysis to use here because it takes only seven ANOVAs (one per product category and one more for the country total) to accomplish the 735 different comparisons of each country average to all other country averages.

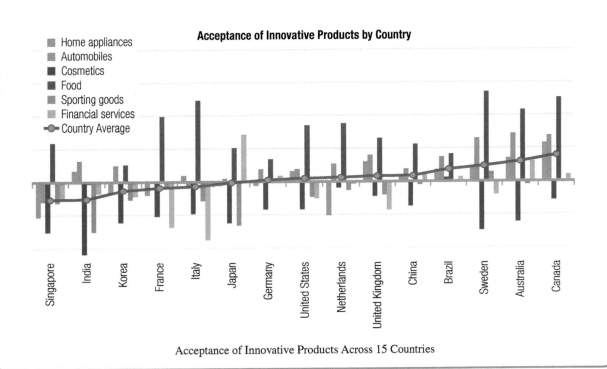

Acceptance of Innovative Products Across 15 Countries

FIGURE 13.4

IBM SPSS Clickstream to Perform Analysis of Variance (ANOVA)

Source: Reprint Courtesy of International Business Machines Corporation, © International Business Machines Corporation.

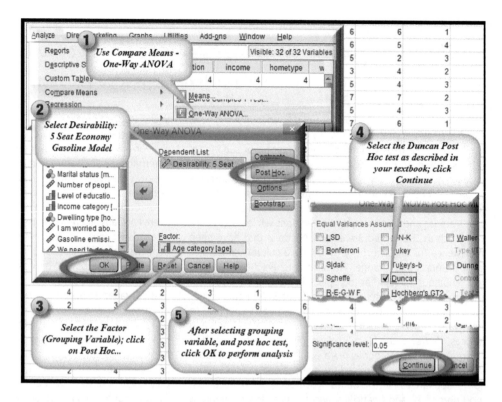

FIGURE 13.5

IBM SPSS Output for Analysis of Variance (ANOVA)

Source: Reprint Courtesy of International Business Machines Corporation, © International Business Machines Corporation.

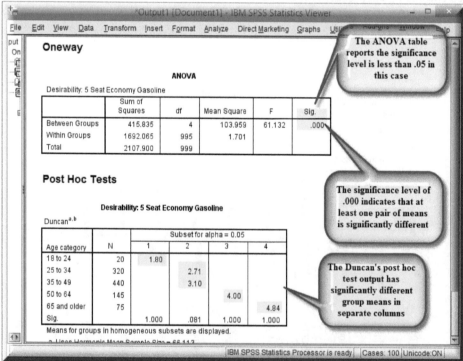

you can see two age groups have means that are not significantly different: 25 to 34 (2.71) and 35 to 49 (3.10). Next, the 50 to 64 (4.00) age group is in a column by itself, so it is significantly different from all other age groups, and finally we can see that the mean of the "65 and older" age is significantly different from all other education groups, and its mean is 4.84. Plus, since this column is the one on the far right, it is the one with the highest average. We have found that the people in the highest age group market segment most prefer the five-seat economy gasoline model. Now, let's think about this finding a bit. Most likely the consumers in the oldest age group are suspicious of the power of an electric or a hybrid fuel vehicle and/or they are resistant to changing from gasoline power, which they have used for several decades.

INTERPRETING ANOVA (ANALYSIS OF VARIANCE)

How do we interpret this finding? The answer lies in our knowledge that if we replicated this survey hundreds of times, we would find these age group differences exactly as we have found them with this one survey. Granted, the averages' values might shift slightly up or down, but the pattern portrayed in the Duncan's multiple range test table in Figure 13.5 would appear in at least 95% of these replications. Further, we can say that we have discovered a meaningful differences finding with the "65 and older" age group's mean of 4.84, which is on the positive side of the preference scale and quite a bit higher than the 1.80–4.00 range of the four youngest groups.

Marketing Research on YouTube™ To learn about analysis of variance, launch www.youtube.com, and search for "One-Way ANOVA Using SPSS."

Of several possible post hoc tests with ANOVA, we have used Duncan's multiple range test as an illustration with the Auto Concepts survey data.

Active Learning

Perform Analysis of Variance with SPSS

IBM **SPSS**

Let's investigate age group means differences across all of the models under consideration at this time by Auto Concepts. We recommend that you use the Auto Concepts.sav dataset and run the ANOVA just described. Make sure that your SPSS output looks like that in Figure 13.5. Then investigate the preference mean differences for the other hybrid models by age group.

13-5 Reporting Group Differences Tests to Clients

Finding significant differences is exciting to marketing researchers because it means that the researcher will have something that is potentially very useful to report to the client. Remember, market segmentation is very prevalent, and whenever significant differences are found, they may represent important market segmentation implications. However, in the bowels of a long marketing research report, differences may not be obvious to the client, especially if the researcher does not take care to highlight them. Marketing Research Insight 13.4 describes how researchers can use table organization and arrangement to present differences findings in a succinct and useful manner.

The reporting of findings has a significant ethical burden for the marketing researcher, as he or she cannot choose to report only "good news" to the client. Read the MRA ethical code section in Marketing Research Insight 13.5. You will find that researchers are charged with the responsibility of reporting "bad news" if it is discovered in the findings.

13-6 Differences Between Two Means Within the Same Sample (Paired Sample)

There is a final difference test to describe that is not used for market segmentation purposes. Occasionally, a researcher will want to test for differences between the means for two variables within the same sample. For example, in our pharmaceuticals company cold remedy situation described earlier in this chapter, a survey can be used to determine "How important is it that your cold remedy relieves your _____?" using a scale of 1 = Not important to 10 = Very important for each cold symptom. The question then becomes whether any two average importance levels are significantly different. To determine the answer to this question, we must perform a **paired samples test for the difference between two means**, which is a test to determine if two means of two different questions using the same scale format and answered by the same respondents in the sample are significantly different. Of course, the variables must be measured on the same scale; otherwise, the test would be analyzing differences

MARKETING RESEARCH INSIGHT 13.4 — *Practical Application*

Guidelines for the Reporting of Differences Tests

In reporting group differences to clients, marketing researchers usually construct a **group comparison table** that summarizes the significant differences in an efficient manner. In the case of two-group comparison tables, the presentation is made side by side where the groups are columns and the rows are the variables where significant differences are found. Depending on the objectives of the research, it is perfectly acceptable to combine percentage differences and mean differences in the same table. Of course, it is incumbent on the marketing researcher to design a table that communicates the differences with a minimum of confusion. Study the following example of two group differences found in a survey for the Subshop.

Differences Between Female and Male Customers of the Subshop*

Item	Females	Males
Menu Items Typically Purchased		
Alcoholic beverage	14%	37%
Large size sandwich	24%	59%
Salad	53%	13%
*Rating of the Subshop***		
Value for the price	5.2	6.1
Fast service	4.5	5.2
*Overall Satisfaction with the Subshop****	4.9	5.5
Use Subshop Promotions		
Use Subshop coupons	23%	5%
Belong to Subshop frequent buyer club	33%	12%

*Statistically significant at 95% level of confidence.
**Based on a rating scale where 1 = Poor to 7 = Excellent.
***Based on a rating scale where 1 = Very unsatisfied to 7 = Very satisfied.

In this group comparison table, it can be immediately seen that male and female customers of the Subshop are being compared and that there are four areas of comparison: menu items purchased, ratings of the Subshop's features, overall satisfaction, and use of promotions.

When the researcher is reporting differences found from ANOVA, the table presentation becomes more challenging, as there can be overlap of nonsignificant differences and significant differences. For the purposes of this textbook, we recommend that the researcher use a modification of Duncan's multiple range post hoc table.

Subshop Performance Differences Between Customer Types*

Subshop Feature**	Sit-Down Customers	Take-Out Customers	Drive-Through Customers
Fast service	5.4	|----------6.2------------|	
Value for the price	6.2	5.5	5.0
Friendly employees	5.1	|----------4.0------------|	

*Statistically significant at 95% level of confidence.
**Based on a rating scale where 1 = Poor to 7 = Excellent.

In this group comparison table, three types of customers are being compared, and the researcher has found significant differences for three different Subshop features. With the fast service rating, the take-out and drive-through customer groups are not different, but the sit-down customers rate the service slower than either of the other groups. With value for the price, all three group means are significantly different, while the sit-down customers' average rating for friendly employees is higher than the average for the take-out and drive-through customers, which are not significantly different. Notice that where nonsignificant differences are reported, the group cells are merged and the average of the two groups combined is indicated so the client will not focus on nonsignificant arithmetic differences.

MARKETING RESEARCH INSIGHT 13.5 — *Ethical Consideration*

Marketing Research Association Code of Ethics: Reporting Findings

37. Report research results accurately and honestly.
During data analysis and presentation of findings, researchers must strive for objectivity so that the data "speak for themselves." Such objectivity need not preclude the formation of researchers' own opinions or recommendations regarding findings. Instead, objectivity means that researchers analyze data impartially and let their opinions and recommendations be guided by the results of those analyses, rather than tailoring analyses to support preconceived agendas or biases.

Source: Used courtesy of the Marketing Research Association.

between variables that are logically incomparable, such as the number of dollars spent versus the number of miles driven.

Because the same respondents answered both questions, you do not have two independent groups. Instead, you have two independent questions with one group. The logic and equations we have described still apply, but there must be an adjustment factor because there is only one sample involved. We do not provide the equations, but in the following SPSS section we describe how to perform and interpret a paired samples *t* test.[11]

> You can test the significance of the difference between two means for two different questions answered by the same respondents using the same scale.

INTEGRATED CASE

The Auto Concepts Survey: How to Perform a Paired Samples t Test Significance of Differences Between Means Test with SPSS

IBM **SPSS**

With the paired samples test, we can test the significance of the difference between the mean of any two questions by the same respondents in our sample. Let's consider a critical question that Auto Concepts may have to address: Are worries about global warming and gasoline emissions contributing to global warming the same? If they are not statistically significant in their differences, the difference will evaporate in the face of a single replication of the survey. Using a paired samples difference test, you can determine the statistical significance.

The SPSS clickstream sequence to perform a paired samples *t* test of the significance of the difference between means is displayed in Figure 13.6. As you can see, you begin with the ANALYZE-COMPARE MEANS-PAIRED SAMPLES T-TEST ... menu sequence. This sequence opens up the selection menu, and via cursor clicks, you can select "I am worried about global warming" and "Gasoline emissions contribute to global warming" as the variable pair to be tested. This sets up the *t* test, and a click on OK executes it.

The resulting annotated output is found in Figure 13.7. You should notice that the table is similar, but not identical, to the independent samples output. The relevant information includes (1) 1,000 respondents gave answers to each statement and were analyzed; (2) the

> To test the significance of difference between two means for questions answered by the same respondents, use the SPSS ANALYZE-COMPARE MEANS-PAIRED SAMPLES T-TEST ... menu sequence.

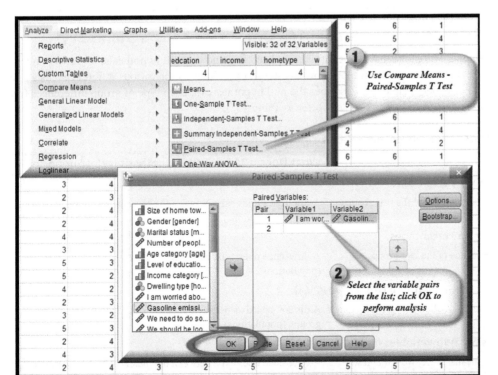

FIGURE 13.6
IBM SPSS Clickstream to Obtain a Paired Samples *t* Test

Source: Reprint Courtesy of International Business Machines Corporation, © International Business Machines Corporation.

FIGURE 13.7
**IBM SPSS Output
for a Paired Samples
t Test**

Source: Reprint Courtesy
of International Business
Machines Corporation,
© International Business
Machines Corporation.

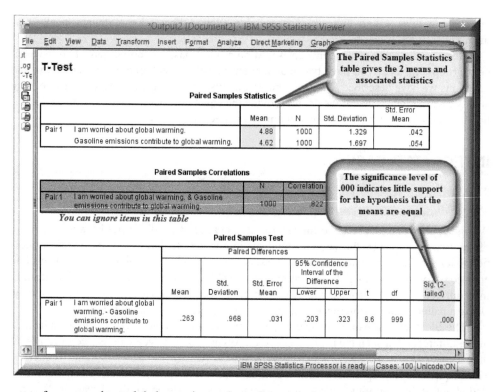

IBM SPSS

**IBM SPSS Student
Assistant:**
Assessing Differences
Between Means for Two
Questions (Paired)

means for worry about global warming and gasoline emissions contributing to global warming are 4.88 and 4.62, respectively; (3) the computed *t* value is 8.6; and (4) the two-tailed significance level is 0.000. In words, the test gives almost no support for the null hypothesis that the means are equal. So, on average, people agree with both statements, but they have stronger agreement with their worry about global warming than with a belief that gasoline emissions contribute to global warming.

13-7 Null Hypotheses for Differences Tests Summary

Because we realize that it is confusing to keep in mind the null hypothesis, to understand all the equations, and to figure out how to interpret the findings for various differences tests, we have provided a table that describes the null hypothesis for each type of group differences test that is described in this chapter. Refer to Table 13.3.

TABLE 13.3   Null Hypotheses for Differences Tests

Null Hypothesis	What Does It Mean If the Hypothesis Is Not Supported?
Differences Between Two Group Percentages	
No difference exists between the percentages of the two groups (populations).	A difference does exist between the percentages of the two groups (populations).
Differences Between Two Group Percentages	
No difference exists between the means of the two groups (populations).	A difference does exist between the means of the two groups (populations).
Differences in Means Among More Than Two Groups (ANOVA)	
No difference exists among the means of all paired groups (populations).	A difference exists between the means of at least one pair of groups (populations).
Differences Between Means for Two Variables (Paired Sample)	
No difference exists between the means of the two variables.	A difference does exist between the means of the two variables.

Summary

Differences matter to marketing managers. Basically, market segmentation implications underlie most differences analyses. It is important that differences are statistically significant, but it is also vital that they are meaningful and stable as well as an actionable basis of marketing strategy.

Differences between two percentages or means in two samples can be tested for statistical significance. The chapter illustrates how to determine if two percentages drawn from two different samples are significantly different. The *t* test procedure in SPSS is used to test the significance of the difference between two means from two independent samples. This chapter presented an illustration of how to use SPSS for this analysis using the Auto Concepts dataset.

When a researcher has more than two groups and wishes to compare their various means, the correct procedure involves analysis of variance (ANOVA). ANOVA is a signaling technique that tests all possible pairs of means for all the groups involved and indicates via the Sig. (significance) value in the ANOVA table if at least one pair is statistically significant in its difference. If the Sig. value is greater than .05, the researcher will inspect the means for differences. But if the Sig. value is .05 or less, the researcher can use a post hoc procedure such as Duncan's multiple range test to identify the pair or pairs of groups where the means are significantly different. Finally, you learned about a paired samples test and how to perform and interpret it using SPSS.

Key Terms

Statistical significance of differences (p. 352)
Meaningful difference (p. 352)
Stable difference (p. 353)
Actionable difference (p. 353)
t test (p. 354)
z test (p. 354)

Null hypothesis (p. 355)
Significance of differences between two percentages (p. 355)
Significance of difference between two means (p. 358)
ANOVA (analysis of variance) (p. 364)

Green light procedure (p. 364)
Post hoc tests (p. 366)
Duncan's multiple range test (p. 366)
One-way ANOVA (p. 366)
Group comparison table (p. 370)
Paired samples test for the difference between two means (p. 369)

Review Questions/Applications

13-1. What are differences and why should market researchers be concerned with them? Why are marketing managers concerned with them?

13-2. What is meant by *statistical significance of differences*? How does this notion underpin marketing research?

13-3. When a market researcher compares the responses of two identifiable groups with respect to their answers to the same question, what is this called?

13-4. With regard to differences tests, briefly define and describe each of the following:

    a. Null hypothesis
    b. Sampling distribution
    c. Significant difference

13-5. Relate the formula and identify each formula's components in the test of significant differences between two groups when the question involved is

    a. A "yes/no" type
    b. A scale variable question

13-6. For each of the following three cases (a–c), are the two sample results significantly different?

Sample One	Sample Two	Confidence Level	Your Finding
a. Mean: 10.6	Mean: 11.7	95%	
Std. dev:1.5	Std. dev: 2.5		
n = 150	*n* = 300		
b. Percent: 45%	Percent: 54%	99%	
n = 350	*n* = 250		
c. Mean: 1500	Mean: 1250	95%	
Std. dev: 550	Std. dev: 500		
n = 1200	*n* = 500		

13-7. When should one-way ANOVA be used and why?

13-8. When a researcher finds a significant *F* value in an analysis of variance, why may it be considered a "green light" device?

13-9. Why should a market researcher use a paired samples test? What does it show?

13-10. The circulation manager of the *Daily Advocate* newspaper commissions a market research study to determine what factors underlie its circulation attrition. Specifically, the survey is designed to compare current *Daily Advocate* subscribers with those who dropped their subscriptions in the past year. A telephone survey is conducted with both sets of individuals. Following is a summary of the key findings from the study. Interpret these findings for the circulation manager.

Item	Current Subscribers	Lost Subscribers	Significance
Length of residence in the city	20.1 yr	5.4 yr	.000
Length of time as a subscriber	27.2 yr	1.3 yr	.000
Watch local TV news program(s)	87%	85%	.372
Watch national news program(s)	72%	79%	.540
Obtain news from the Internet	13%	23%	.025
Satisfaction* with...			
Delivery of newspaper	5.5	4.9	.459
Coverage of local news	6.1	5.8	.248
Coverage of national news	5.5	2.3	.031
Coverage of local sports	6.3	5.9	.462
Coverage of national sports	5.7	3.2	.001
Coverage of local social news	5.8	5.2	.659
Editorial stance of the newspaper	6.1	4.0	.001
Value for subscription price	5.2	4.8	.468

*Based on a 7-point scale where 1 = Very dissatisfied to 7 = Very satisfied.

13-11. A researcher is investigating different types of customers for a sporting goods store. In a survey, respondents are asked to use their Fitbit devices to indicate how much they exercised last week using categories of "Less than 1 hour," "Between 1 and 2 hours," "Between 2 and 3 hours," and so on. These respondents have also rated the performance of the sporting goods store across 12 different characteristics, such as good value for the price, convenience of location, helpfulness of the sales clerks, and so on. The researcher used a 7-point rating scale for these 12 characteristics where 1 = Poor performance to 7 = Excellent performance. How can the researcher investigate differences in the ratings based on the amount of exercise reported by the respondents?

13-12. A marketing manager of *newegg,* a web-based electronic products sales company, uses a segmentation scheme based on the incomes of target customers. The segmentation system has four segments: (1) low income, (2) moderate income, (3) high income, and (4) wealthy. The company database holds information on customers' purchases over the past several months. Using Microsoft Excel on this database, the marketing manager finds that the average total dollar purchases for the four groups are as follows.

Market Segment	Average Total Dollar Purchases
Low income	$101
Moderate income	$120
High income	$231
Wealthy	$595

Construct a table that is based on the Duncan's multiple range test table concept discussed in the chapter that illustrates that the low- and moderate-income groups are not different from each other, but the other groups are significantly different from one another.

CASE 13.1

L'Experience Félicité Restaurant Survey Differences Analysis IBM **SPSS**

(For necessary background on this case, read Case 12.1 on page 346.)

Cory Rogers of CMG Research called a meeting with Jeff Dean, the client who needed research on the demand for a new, upscale restaurant to possibly be called L'Experience Félicité, with marketing intern, Christine Yu, attending. Cory began the meeting with a review of the research objectives agreed to by Jeff. After about 20 minutes, Christine listed the six following questions in which Jeff was especially interested.

Your task in this case is to take Christine's role. Using the L'Experience Félicité Restaurant survey SPSS dataset, perform the proper analysis and interpret the findings for each of the following questions.

1. Jeff wonders if L'Experience Félicité Restaurant is more appealing to women than it is to men or vice versa. Perform the proper analysis, interpret it, and answer Jeff's question.

2. With respect to the location of L'Experience Félicité Restaurant, is a waterfront view preferred more than a drive of less than 30 minutes?

3. With respect to the restaurant's atmosphere, is a string quartet preferred over a jazz combo?

4. What about unusual entrées versus unusual desserts?

5. In general, upscale establishments are more appealing to higher-income households than they are to lower-income households. Is this pattern the case for L'Experience Félicité Restaurant?

6. Jeff and Cory speculated that the different geographic areas that they identified by ZIP codes would have different reactions to the prospect of patronizing a new upscale restaurant. Are these anticipated differences substantiated by the survey? Perform the proper analysis and interpret your findings.

CASE 13.2 INTEGRATED CASE

The Auto Concepts Survey Differences Analysis IBM **SPSS**

Cory Rogers of CMG Research called a meeting with Nick Thomas, and Celeste Brown, CMG analyst, attended it. After meeting for about 20 minutes, Celeste understood that the Auto Concepts principals were encouraged by the findings of the survey, which indicate that there is substantial demand for the various types of futuristic high-mileage automobiles under consideration. Depending on development costs, prices, and other financial considerations, it seems that any one model or any combination of the new automobile models could be a viable option. The next step in their planning is to identify the target market for each automobile model type under consideration. This step is crucial to market strategy because the more precise the target market definition is, the more specific and pinpointed the marketing strategy can be. For a first cut at the market segment descriptions, the survey included the following commonly used demographic factors:

- Hometown size category
- Gender
- Marital status
- Age category
- Education category
- Income category

Your task is to apply appropriate differences analysis using the survey's desirability measures in your Auto Concepts SPSS dataset to determine the target market descriptions for each of the five possible automobile models.

1. "Super Cycle," One-Seat All Electric, mpg-e rating 125; estimated MSRP (manufacturer's suggested retail price) $30,000; range 200 miles.

2. "Runabout Sport," Two-Seat All Electric, mpg-e 99; estimated MSRP $35,000; range 150 miles.

3. "Runabout Hatchback," Two-Seat Gasoline Hybrid, mpg-e 50; runs on battery for 50 miles and then switches to gas engine; estimated MSRP $35,000; range 250 miles.

4. "Economy Hybrid," Four-Seat Diesel Hybrid, mpg-e 75; runs on battery for 75 miles and then switches to efficient diesel engine; estimated MSRP $38,000; range 300 miles.

5. "Economy Gasoline," Five-Seat Economy Gasoline, mpg 36; runs on gasoline with computer control for maximum efficiency; estimated MSRP $37,000; range 350 miles.

14

Making Use of Associations Tests

"WHERE WE ARE"

1 Establish the need for marketing research.
2 Define the problem.
3 Establish research objectives.
4 Determine research design.
5 Identify information types and sources.
6 Determine methods of accessing data.
7 Design data collection forms.
8 Determine the sample plan and size.
9 Collect data.
10 Analyze data.
11 Prepare and present the final research report.

iModerate

Adam Rossow, partner, head of marketing, iModerate

iModerate is a consumer insights firm that helps clients become fluent in their audiences through a deeper understanding of consumers' motivations, needs, and language. Most companies today are employing some combination of listening, asking, and observing to learn more about their consumers. Whether that means monitoring what consumers say on social networks, looking at the reviews left on websites, employing surveys, or crunching behavioral data, there is no shortage of information streams and feedback mechanisms. However, the information gathered is often incomplete and difficult to tie together.

At iModerate, they believe that without understanding the "why" behind consumer behavior, it's challenging to pinpoint how to move forward. Without a complete picture of the consumer, companies often attend to the wrong problem, misread the market, and push forward haphazardly.

Using solutions ranging from next-generation text analytics to one-on-one consumer engagements, iModerate helps clients get to know their consumers inside and out. The more companies know about their consumers, the better they can cater to them, the more loyalty they can build, and the more impact they can have on the bottom line.

A cognitive framework called ThoughtPath informs the way that the firm engages with its clients at each step of the research process, from design through reporting. Rooted in key elements of cognitive psychology—perception, experience, and identity—and informed by results from more than 200,000 consumer conversations, ThoughtPath is the backbone of everything they do at iModerate. Because it taps into how people naturally think, it's a useful guide to asking smarter, more engaging questions and the key to discovering deeper, more relevant insights.

The firm's products include the following:

(iM)pact One-On-Ones are professionally moderated individual conversations conducted online, which enable talking to consumers with complete anonymity, thereby creating an ideal environment for unveiling honest responses. The one-on-one setting allows moderators to utilize ThoughtPath, prompting richer, more relevant consumer responses to bring hidden knowledge to the forefront.

Whether conducted as a survey add-on or as a stand-alone, in-depth interview, these online, text-based conversations help clients fill the holes created by big data and other noncontextual information sources. Used on an ongoing basis, they help establish consumer intimacy, spot buying and acceptance trends, predict product receptivity, observe how outside factors—seasons, competitor moves, news events—impact consumers, and even anticipate behavior changes.

(iM)merge Analytics helps clients collect, analyze, and distill consumer commentary into answers rich with context. Consumers' social chatter, open-end survey responses, reviews, and call center transcripts can provide a starting point for understanding, but this commentary is often difficult to distill into meaningful insights. In other cases, the feedback clients need to answer questions isn't accessible or simply doesn't exist yet.

Whether the goal is to extract value from existing feedback streams or generate thoughtful questions and walk away with an answer, (iM)merge can help. This advanced text solution takes in all forms of consumer feedback and marries human storytelling with software's unbiased, scalable appeal.

(iM)merse Longitudinal gives clients a continual and flexible insights solution built on qualitative engagements with a broad swath of their target audience. A combination of one-on-one conversations and carefully crafted open-end questions allows iModerate to achieve both the depth and the scale clients need to make informed decisions. (iM)merse differs from other traditional longitudinal activities in that it offers clients the ability to explore, assess, and generate ideas without barriers. Unlike trackers, (iM)merse is agile due to the ability to shift topics and areas of focus. Unlike communities, the individuals in the target audience are different every month, thereby reducing bias and fatigue.

(iM)merse keeps a finger on the pulse of an audience. Whether it's identifying the most recent needs of the home cook as the basis for a new small kitchen appliance, keeping up to speed with the language of Gen Z so tweets sound authentic, or understanding that a hotel-sponsored wine and cheese hour might be the perfect way to engender traveler loyalty, the benefits of an ongoing dialogue with consumers cannot be overstated.

Source: Text and photos courtesy of iModerate.com

This chapter illustrates the usefulness of statistical analyses beyond simple descriptive measures, statistical inference, and differences tests. Just as iModerate is a company that collects and analyzes hundreds of qualitative comments for insights, the analyses in this chapter are applied to hundreds or thousands of quantitative data points gathered in a survey. Often, as we have described in the opening comments of this chapter, marketers are interested in relationships among variables. For example, Frito-Lay wants to know what kinds of people and under what circumstances these people choose to buy Cheetos, Fritos, Lay's potato chips, and any of the other items in the Frito-Lay line. The Pontiac Division of General Motors wants to know what types of individuals would respond favorably to the various style changes proposed for the Solstice. A newspaper wants to understand the lifestyle characteristics of its subscribers so that it is able to modify or change sections in the newspaper to better suit its audience. Furthermore, the newspaper desires information about various types of subscribers so as to communicate this information to its advertisers, helping them in copy design and advertisement placement within the various newspaper sections. For all of these cases, there are statistical procedures available, termed *associative analyses*, which determine answers to these questions.

As you learned in Chapter 8, every scale has unique descriptors, sometimes called levels or labels, that identify the different demarcations of that scale. The term *levels* implies that the scale is interval or ratio, whereas the term *labels* implies that the scale is, typically, nominal. A simple label is a "yes" or "no," for instance, if a respondent is labeled as a buyer (yes) or nonbuyer (no) of a particular product or service. **Associative analyses** determine whether a stable relationship exists between two variables; they are the central topic of this chapter. We begin the chapter by describing the four different types of relationships possible between two variables. Then we describe correlation coefficients, and we illustrate the use of Pearson product moment correlations. From correlations, we move to a discussion of cross-tabulations and indicate how a cross-tabulation can be used to determine whether a statistically significant association exists between the two variables. As in our previous analysis chapters, we show the SPSS steps to perform these analyses and the resulting output.

> Associative analyses determine whether stable relationships exist between two variables.

14-1   Types of Relationships Between Two Variables

> A relationship is a consistent and systematic linkage between the levels or labels for two variables.

A **relationship** is a consistent and systematic linkage between the levels for two scale variables or between the labels for two nominal variables. We use the words *relationship* and *association* interchangeably. This linkage is statistical, not necessarily causal. A causal linkage is one in which you are certain one variable affected the other one, but with a statistical linkage you cannot be certain because some other variable might have had some influence. Nonetheless, statistical linkages or relationships often provide us with insights that lead to understanding even though they are not cause-and-effect relationships. For example, if we found a relationship that most daily exercisers purchased some brand of sports drink, we understand that the ingredients of sports drinks are important to those who want to keep fit. Associative analysis procedures are useful because they determine if there is a consistent and systematic relationship between the presence (label) or amount (level) of one variable and the presence (label) or amount (level) of another variable. There are four basic types of relationships between two variables: linear, curvilinear, monotonic, and nonmonotonic. A discussion of each follows.

LINEAR AND CURVILINEAR RELATIONSHIPS

> A linear relationship means the two variables have a "straight-line" relationship.

First, we turn to a precise form of relationship, and one that is very easy to envision. A **linear relationship** is a "straight-line association" between two scale variables. Here, knowledge of the amount of one variable will automatically yield knowledge of the amount of the other variable as a consequence of applying the linear or straight-line formula that is known to exist between them. In its general form, a **straight-line formula** is as follows:

Formula for a straight line

$$y = a + bx$$

where

y = the dependent variable being estimated or predicted

a = the intercept

b = the slope

x = the independent variable used to predict the dependent variable

The terms intercept and slope should be familiar to you, but if they are a bit hazy, do not be concerned as we describe the straight-line formula in detail in the next chapter. It should be apparent to you that a linear relationship is precise and contains a good deal of information. By simply substituting the values of a and b, an exact amount can be determined for y given any value of x. For example, if Jack-in-the-Box estimates that every customer will spend about $9 per lunch visit, it is easy to use a linear relationship to estimate how many dollars of revenue will be associated with the number of customers for any given location. The following equation would be used:

Straight-line formula example

$$y = \$0 + \$9 \times \text{number of customers}$$

where x is the number of customers. So if 100 customers come to a Jack-in-the-Box location, the associated expected total revenue would be $0 plus $9 times 100, or $900. If 200 customers are expected to visit the location, the expected total revenue would be $0 plus $9 times 200, or $1,800. To be sure, the Jack-in-the-Box location would not derive exactly $1,800 for 200 customers, but the linear relationship shows what is expected to happen on average.

Linear relationships are quite precise.

In a **curvilinear relationship** one variable is again associated with another variable, but in this case the relationship is described by a curve rather than a straight line. In other words, the formula for a curved relationship is used rather than the formula for a straight line. Many curvilinear patterns are possible. For example, the relationship may be an S-shape, a J-shape, or some other curved-shape pattern. Curvilinear relationships are beyond the scope of this text; nonetheless, it is important to list them as a type of relationship that can be investigated through the use of special-purpose statistical procedures.

A curvilinear relationship means some smooth curve pattern describes the association.

MONOTONIC RELATIONSHIPS

In **monotonic relationships**, the researcher can assign a general direction to the association between the two variables. There are two types of monotonic relationships: increasing and decreasing. Monotonic increasing relationships are those in which one variable increases as the other variable increases. As you would guess, monotonic decreasing relationships are those in which one variable increases as the other variable decreases. You should note that in neither case is there any indication of the exact amount of change in one variable as the other changes. *Monotonic* means that the relationship can be described only in a general directional sense. Beyond this, precision in the description is lacking. For example, if a company increases its advertising, we would expect its sales to increase, but we do not know the amount that the sales would increase. Monotonic relationships are also not in the scope of this textbook, so we will simply mention them here as a type of relationship that can be investigated.

A monotonic relationship means you know the general direction (increasing or decreasing) of the relationship between two variables.

A nonmonotonic relationship means two variables are associated but only in a very general sense.

NONMONOTONIC RELATIONSHIPS

Finally, a **nonmonotonic relationship** is one in which the presence (or absence) of the label for one variable is systematically associated with the presence (or absence) of the label for another variable. The term *nonmonotonic* means essentially that although there is no discernible direction to the relationship, a relationship does exist. For example, managers at McDonald's, Burger King, and Wendy's all know from experience that morning customers typically purchase coffee whereas noon customers typically purchase soft drinks. The relationship is in no way exclusive—there is no guarantee that a morning customer will always order a coffee or that an afternoon customer will always order a soft drink. In general, though, this relationship exists, as can be seen in Figure 14.1. The nonmonotonic relationship is simply that the morning customer tends to purchase breakfast foods such as eggs, biscuits, and coffee, and the afternoon customer tends to purchase lunch items such as burgers, fries, and soft drinks. So, the "morning" label is associted with the "coffee" label while the "noon" label is associated with the "soft drink" label. In other words, with a nonmonotonic relationship, when you find the presence of one label for a variable, you will tend to find the presence of a specific label of another variable: Breakfast customers typically order coffee. But the association is very general, and we must state each one by spelling it out verbally. In other words, we know only the general pattern of presence or absence with a nonmonotonic relationship.

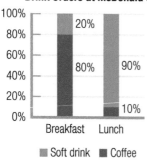

Drink Orders at McDonald's

FIGURE 14.1 Example of a Nonmonotonic Relationship Between Drink Orders and Meal Type at McDonald's

The presence of a relationship between two variables is determined by a statistical test.

14-2 Characterizing Relationships Between Variables

Depending on its type, a relationship can usually be characterized in three ways: by its presence, direction, and strength of association. We need to describe these before taking up specific statistical analyses of associations between two variables.

PRESENCE

Presence refers to the finding that a systematic relationship exists between the two variables of interest in the population. Presence is a statistical issue. By this statement, we mean that the marketing researcher relies on statistical significance tests to determine if there is sufficient evidence in the sample to support the claim that a particular association is present in the population. The chapter on statistical inference introduced the concept of a null hypothesis. With associative analysis, the null hypothesis states there is no association (relationship) present in the population and the appropriate statistical test is applied to test this hypothesis. If the test results reject the null hypothesis, then we can state that an association (relationship) is present in the population (at a certain level of confidence). We describe the statistical tests used in associative analysis later in this chapter.

DIRECTION (OR PATTERN)

You have seen that in the cases of monotonic and linear relationships, associations may be described with regard to direction. For a linear relationship, if b (slope) is positive, then the linear relationship is increasing; if b is negative, then the linear relationship is decreasing. So the direction of the relationship is straightforward with linear relationships.

For nonmonotonic relationships, positive or negative direction is inappropriate, because we can only describe the pattern verbally,[1] as, for example, the relationship that breakfast buyers tend to purchase coffee. Later in this chapter, it will become clear to you that the scaling assumptions

That most tourists at sunny beach resorts use sun block is a nonmonotonic relationship.

of variables having nonmonotonic association negate the directional aspects of the relationship. Nevertheless, we can verbally describe the pattern of the association as we have in our examples, and that statement substitutes for direction.

Direction means that you know if the relationship is positive or negative, whereas *pattern* means you know the general nature of the relationship.

STRENGTH OF ASSOCIATION

Finally, when present, that is, statistically significant, the association between two variables can be envisioned as to its strength, commonly using words such as "strong," "moderate," "weak," or some similar characterization. That is, when a consistent and systematic association is found to be present between two variables, it is then up to the marketing researcher to ascertain the strength of association. Strong associations are those in which there is a high probability that the two variables will exhibit a dependable relationship, regardless of the type of relationship being analyzed. A low degree of association, on the other hand, is one in which there is a low probability that the two variables will exhibit a dependable relationship. The relationship exists between the variables, but it is less evident.

Strength means you know how consistent the relationship is.

There is an orderly procedure for determining the presence, direction, and strength of a relationship, which is outlined in Table 14.1. As can be seen in the table, you must first decide what type of relationship can exist between the two variables of interest: nonmonotonic or linear. As you will learn in this chapter, the answer to this question depends on the scaling assumptions of the variables; as we will illustrate further, nominal scales can embody only imprecise, pattern-like, relationships, but scale variables (interval or ratio) can incorporate very precise and linear relationships. Once you identify the appropriate relationship type as either nonmonotonic or linear, the next step is to determine whether that relationship actually exists in the population you are analyzing. This step requires a statistical test, and we will describe the use of correlation (for scale variables, a linear relationship) and cross-tabulation (for nominal variables, a nonmonotonic relationship) beginning with the next section of this chapter.

Based on scaling assumptions, first determine the type of relationship, and then perform the appropriate statistical test.

When you determine that a true relationship does exist in the population by means of the correct statistical test, you then establish its direction or pattern. Again, the type of relationship dictates how you describe its direction. You might have to inspect the relationship in a table or graph, or you might need only to look for a positive or negative sign before the computed statistic. Finally, the strength of the relationship remains to be judged. Some associative analysis statistics, such as correlations, indicate the strength in a very straightforward manner—that is, just by their absolute size. With nominally scaled variables, however, you must inspect the pattern to judge the strength. We describe this procedure, the use of cross-tabulations, after we describe correlation analysis next in this chapter.

TABLE 14.1   Step-by-Step Procedure for Analyzing the Relationship Between Two Variables

Step	Description
Step 1. Choose variables to analyze.	Identify two variables you think might be related.
Step 2. Determine the scaling assumptions of the chosen variables.	For purposes of this chapter, both must be either scale (interval or ratio) or categorical (nominal) variables.
Step 3. Use the correct relationship analysis.	For two scale (interval and/or ratio scale) variables, use correlation; for two nominal variables, use cross-tabulation.
Step 4. Determine if the relationship is present.	If the analysis shows the relationship is statistically significant, it is present.
Step 5. If present, determine the direction of the relationship.	A linear (scale variables) relationship will be either increasing or decreasing; a nonmonotonic relationship (nominal scales) will require looking for a pattern.
Step 6. If present, assess the strength of the relationship.	With correlation, the size of the coefficient denotes strength; with cross-tabulation, the pattern is subjectively assessed.

14-3 Correlation Coefficients and Covariation

A correlation coefficient standardizes the covariation between two variables into a number ranging from −1.0 to +1.0.

Because you have no doubt heard about and perhaps used it, we will now describe the use of correlation analysis. The **correlation coefficient** is an index number, constrained to fall between −1.0 and +1.0, that communicates both the strength and the direction of a linear relationship between two scale variables. The strength of association between two variables is communicated by the absolute size of the correlation coefficient, whereas its sign communicates the direction of the association. Stated in a slightly different manner, a correlation coefficient indicates the degree of covariation between two variables. **Covariation** is defined as the amount of change in one variable systematically associated with a change in another variable. The greater the absolute size of the correlation coefficient, the greater is the covariation between the two variables, or the stronger is their relationship.[2]

Let us take up the statistical significance of a correlation coefficient first. Regardless of its absolute value, a correlation that is not statistically significant has no meaning at all. This is because of the null hypothesis, which states that the population correlation coefficient is equal to zero. If this null hypothesis is rejected (statistically significant correlation), then you can be assured that a correlation other than zero will be found in the population. But if the sample correlation is found to be not significant, the population correlation will be zero. Here is a question. If you can answer it correctly, you understand the statistical significance of a correlation. If you repeated a correlational survey many, many times and computed the average for a correlation that was not significant across all of these surveys, what would be the result? (The answer is zero because if the correlation is not significant, the null hypothesis is true, and the population correlation is zero.)

To use a correlation, you must first determine that it is statistically significant from zero.

Step 4, "Determine if the relationship is present," in our "Procedure for Analyzing Relationships" in Table 14.1, requires a statistical test, but how do you determine the statistical significance of a correlation coefficient? Although tables exist that give the lowest value of the significant correlation coefficients for given sample sizes, most computer statistical programs will indicate the statistical significance level of the computed correlation coefficient. Your SPSS program provides the significance in the form of the probability that the null hypothesis is supported. In SPSS, this is a Sig. value that we will identify for you when we show you SPSS correlation output.

RULES OF THUMB FOR CORRELATION STRENGTH

After we have established that a correlation coefficient is statistically significant, we can talk about some general rules of thumb concerning the strength of association. Correlation coefficients that fall between the absolute values of 1.00 and .81 are generally considered to be "very strong." Those correlations that fall between the absolute values of .80 and .61 generally indicate a "strong" association. Those that fall between the absolute values of .60 and .41 are typically considered to be "moderate." Any correlation that falls between the absolute value range of .21 and .40 is usually considered indicative of a "weak" association between the variables. Finally, any correlation that is equal to or less than the absolute value of .20 is typically uninteresting to marketing researchers because it rarely identifies a meaningful association between two variables. Of course, this range includes a correlation coefficient of 0, or no association whatsoever, so we characterize the +.20 to −.20 range as "very weak."

We provide Table 14.2 as a reference on these rules of thumb. As you use these guidelines, remember two things: First, we are assuming that the statistical significance of the correlation has been established. Second, researchers make up their own rules of thumb, so you may encounter someone whose guidelines differ slightly from those in the table.[3]

Rules of thumb exist concerning the strength of a correlation based on its absolute size.

In any case, it is helpful to think in terms of the closeness of the correlation coefficient to zero or to ±1.00. Statistically significant correlation coefficients that are close to zero show that there is no systematic association between the two variables, whereas those that are closer to +1.00 or −1.00 express that there is some systematic association between the variables.

TABLE 14.2   Rules of Thumb About Correlation Coefficient Size*

Coefficient Range	Strength of Association*
+.81 to +1.00; −.81 to −1.00	Very strong
+.61 to +.80; −.61 to −.80	Strong
+.41 to +.60; −.41 to −.60	Moderate
+.21 to +.40; −.21 to −.40	Weak
+.20 to −.20	Very weak

*Assuming the correlation coefficient is statistically significant

THE CORRELATION SIGN: THE DIRECTION OF THE RELATIONSHIP

But what about the sign of the correlation coefficient? The sign indicates the direction of the relationship. A positive sign indicates a positive direction; a negative sign indicates a negative direction. For instance, if you found a significant correlation of .83 between years of education and hours spent viewing *National Geographic Digital* magazine, it would mean that people with more education spend more hours viewing this magazine. But if you found a significant negative correlation between years of education and frequency of cigarette smoking, it would mean that more educated people smoke less.

A correlation indicates the strength of association between two variables by its size. The sign indicates the direction of the association.

GRAPHING COVARIATION USING SCATTER DIAGRAMS

We addressed the concept of covariation between two variables in our introductory comments on correlations. It is now time to present covariation in a slightly different manner. Here is an example: A marketing researcher is investigating the possible relationship between total company sales for Novartis, a leading pharmaceuticals sales company, in a particular territory and the number of salespeople assigned to that territory. At the researcher's fingertips are the sales figures and number of salespeople assigned for each of 20 different Novartis territories in the United States.

It is possible to depict the raw data for these two variables on a scatter diagram such as the one in Figure 14.2. A **scatter diagram** plots the points corresponding to each matched pair of *x* and *y* variables. In this figure, the vertical axis is Novartis sales for the territory and the horizontal axis contains the number of salespeople in that territory. The arrangement or scatter of points appears to fall in a long ellipse. Any two variables that exhibit systematic covariation will form an ellipse-like pattern on a scatter diagram. Of course, this particular scatter diagram portrays the information gathered by the marketing researcher on sales and the number of salespeople in each territory and only that information. In actuality, the scatter diagram could have taken any shape, depending on the relationship between the points plotted for the two variables concerned.[4]

Covariation can be examined with use of a scatter diagram.

A number of different types of scatter diagram results are portrayed in Figure 14.3. The results of each of these scatter diagrams are indicative of a different degree of covariation. For instance, you can see that the scatter diagram depicted in Figure 14.3(a) is one in which there is no apparent association or relationship between the two variables; the points fail to create any identifiable pattern. Instead, they are clumped into a large, formless shape. Those points in Figure 14.3(b) indicate a negative relationship between variable *x* and variable *y*;

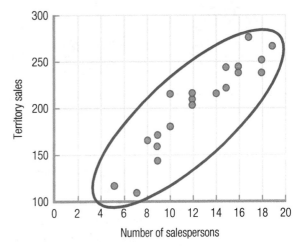

FIGURE 14.2 A Scatter Diagram Showing Covariation

FIGURE 14.3
Scatter Diagrams Illustrating Various Relationships

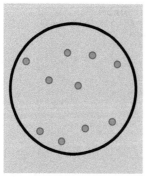

(a) No association

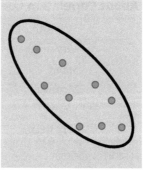

(b) Negative association

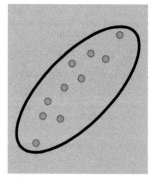

(c) Positive association

The success of a prescription drug pharmaceutical company may be related to how many salespersons it has in the field to talk with doctors.

Two highly correlated variables will appear on a scatter diagram as a tight ellipse pattern.

higher values of x tend to be associated with lower values of y. Those points in Figure 14.3(c) are fairly similar to those in Figure 14.3(b), but the angle or the slope of the ellipse is different. This slope indicates a positive relationship between x and y because larger values of x tend to be associated with larger values of y.

What is the connection between scatter diagrams and correlation coefficients? The answer to these questions lies in the linear relationship described earlier in this chapter. Look at Figures 14.3(b) and 14.3(c). Both form ellipses. Imagine taking an ellipse and pulling on both ends. It would stretch out and become thinner until all of its points fall on a straight line. If you happened to find some data that formed an ellipse with all points falling on the axis line and you computed a correlation, you would find it to be exactly 1.0 (+1.0 if the ellipse went up to the right and −1.0 if it went down to the right). Now imagine pushing the ends of the ellipse until it became the pattern in Figure 14.3(a). There would be no identifiable straight line. Similarly, there would be no systematic covariation. The correlation for a ball-shaped scatter diagram is zero because there is no discernable linear relationship. In other words, a correlation coefficient indicates the degree of covariation between two variables, and you can envision this relationship as a scatter diagram. The form and angle of the scatter pattern are revealed by the size and sign, respectively, of the correlation coefficient.

14-4 The Pearson Product Moment Correlation Coefficient

The **Pearson product moment correlation** measures the linear relationship between two interval- and/or ratio-scaled variables (scale variables) such as those depicted conceptually by scatter diagrams. The correlation coefficient that can be computed between the two variables is a measure of the "closeness" of the scatter points to the straight line. You already know that in a case in which all of the points fall exactly on the straight line, the correlation coefficient indicates this as a plus or minus 1.00. In the case in which it was impossible to discern an ellipse, such as in scatter diagram Figure 14.3(a), the correlation coefficient approximates zero. Of course, it is extremely unlikely that you will find perfect 1.00 or .00 correlations. Usually, you will find some value in between that, if statistically significant, can be interpreted as "strong," "moderate," "weak," and so on, using the rules of thumb given earlier.

The computational formula for Pearson product moment correlations is as follows:

Formula for Pearson product moment correlation

$$r_{xy} = \frac{\sum\limits_{n}^{i=1}(x_i - \bar{x})(y_i - \bar{y})}{ns_x s_y}$$

where

x_i = each x value

$\bar{x}$ = mean of the x values

y_i = each y value

$\bar{y}$ = mean of the y values

n = number of paired cases

s_x, s_y = standard deviations of x and y, respectively

We briefly describe the components of this formula to help you see how the concepts we just discussed fit in. In the statistician's terminology, the numerator represents the cross-products sum and indicates the covariation or "covariance" between x and y. The cross-products sum is divided by n to scale it down to an average per pair of x and y values. This average covariation is then divided by both standard deviations to adjust for differences in units. The result constrains r_{xy} to fall between -1.0 and $+1.0$.

Here is a simple computational example. You have some data on population and retail sales by county for 10 counties in your state. Is there a relationship between population and retail sales? You do a quick calculation and find the average number of people per county is 690,000, and the average retail sales are $9.54 million. The standard deviations are 384.3 and 7.8, respectively, and the cross-products sum is 25,154. The computations to find the correlation are the following:

Calculation of a correlation coefficient	
	$r_{xy} = \dfrac{\sum\limits_{i-1}^{n}(x_i - \bar{x})(y_i - \bar{y})}{ns_x s_y}$
Notes:	
Cross-products sum = 25,154	$= \dfrac{25{,}154}{10 \times 7.8 \times 384.4}$
$n = 10$	
Standard deviation of x = 7.8	$= \dfrac{25{,}154}{29{,}975.4}$
Standard deviation of y = 384.3	
	$= .84$

A correlation of .84 is a high positive correlation coefficient for the relationship. This value reveals that the greater the number of citizens living in a county, the greater the county's retail sales.

To summarize, Pearson product moment correlation and other linear association correlation coefficients indicate not only the degree of association but the direction as well because, as we described in our introductory comments on correlations, the sign of the correlation coefficient indicates the direction of the relationship. Negative correlation coefficients reveal that the relationship is opposite: As one variable increases, the other variable decreases. Positive correlation coefficients reveal that the relationship is increasing: Larger quantities of one variable are associated with larger quantities of another variable.

The Pearson product moment correlation coefficient measures the degree of linear association between two variables.

MARKETING RESEARCH INSIGHT 14.1   *Digital Marketing Research*

Brand Fans and Music Preferences

Social media contain vast stores of data, and it is possible to find correlations and other associations that have marketing strategy implications. Specifically, it is possible to find "brand fans," consumers who avidly follow brands on Facebook, Twitter, Instagram, Spotify, and other social media sites, and then to trace their online searches for favorite music lyrics, concerts, or other platforms. Two companies, Cellfish and Echo Nest, recently divulged some of these correlation findings.[5] In the listing that follows, see if you can correctly match the "brand" with the preferred music of its fans. Match each brand or topic with a line just as you did with the matching questions on your tests in grammar school. The correct answers appear at the end of this chapter.

What is the value of these correlations? Just think about the fact that consumers are hit with thousands upon thousands of visual, audio, and other commercial impressions daily. Consequently, consumers are "tuning" out many of these impressions because they are not relevant. However, when a consumer hears or sees a favorite music performer, something called "selective perception" kicks in, and the consumer immediately stops and pays attention to the stimulus. So, if a company knows the favorite music artists of its fans, it can pair its advertising or other promotions with that music to increase the likelihood that its fans will attend to the message.

Fans of This Brand or Topic	Have Which Musical Preference?
Ciroc vodka	*American Idol alt-rocker Chris Daughtry*
Craft beers	*Andrew Lloyd Webber*
EA's console sports games	*Bruce Springsteen and Pink Floyd*
Harrods	*Classic rock stars such as the Beatles, Jimi Hendrix, etc.*
Motorola	*Hip-hop and rap artists*
NHL	*Jam bands (Phish, Umphrey's McGee)*
NPR	*Hip-hop and rap artists (Ice Cube, Nas)*
Travel Channel	*Rock and country rock artists, like Meat Loaf, Kid Rock*
Victoria's Secret Pink brand	*Younger artists like Miley Cyrus, the Jonas Brothers*

A positive correlation signals an increasing linear relationship, whereas a negative correlation signals a decreasing one.

It is important to note that the angle or the slope of the ellipse has nothing to do with the size of the correlation coefficient. Everything hinges on the width of the ellipse. (The slope will be considered in Chapter 15 under regression analysis.) To learn how correlations were used to discover the relationships among certain brand fans and their music preferences, see the findings of companies that analyze social media in Marketing Research Insight 14.1.

Active Learning

Date.net: Male Users' Chat Room Phobia

Date.net is an online meeting service that competes with other dating sites such as Match, eHarmony, and ChristianMingle. Date.net operates a virtual meeting place for men seeking women and women seeking men. Date.net's public chat room is where its members first become aquainted and, if a couple wants to move into its own private chat room, Date.net creates one and assesses a fee for each minute that the couple is chatting in this private chat room. Recent internal analysis has revealed that women chat room users are considerably less satisfied with Date.net's public chat room than are its male chat room users. This is frustrating to Date.net principals, as they know that disappointing public chats will not lead to private chats.

Managers at Date.net commission an online marketing research company to design a questionnaire that is posted on the Date.net website. The survey asks a number of questions covering demographics, online chatting, Date.net services usage, and personal satisfaction measures, and over 3,000 Date.net users fill it out. Date.net executives request a separate analysis of men members who use the public chat room. The research company reports all correlations that are significant at the .01 level. Here is a summary of the correlation analysis findings:

Factor		Correlation with Amount of Date.net Chat Room Use
Demographics:	Age	−.68
	Income	−.76
	Education	−.78
	Number of years divorced	+.57
	Number of children	+.68
	Years at present address	−.90
	Years at present job	−.85
Satisfaction with:	Relationships	−.76
	Job/career	−.86
	Personal appearance	−.72
	Life in general	−.50
Online behavior:	Minutes online daily	+.90
	Online purchases	−.65
	Other chatting time/month	+.86
	Number of email accounts	+.77
Use of Date.net (where 1 = Not important and 5 = Very important):	Meet new people	+.38
	Only way to talk to women	+.68
	Looking for a life partner	−.72
	Not much else to do	+.59

For each factor, use your knowledge of correlations and provide a statement of how it characterizes the typical Date.net male chat room user. Given your findings, what tactics do you recommend to Date.net to address the low satisfaction with Date.net's public chat room that has been expressed by its female members?

INTEGRATED CASE

Auto Concepts: How to Obtain Pearson Product Moment Correlation(s) with SPSS   IBM **SPSS**

With SPSS, it takes only a few clicks to compute correlation coefficients. Once again, we will use the Auto Concepts survey case study, as you are familiar with it. In the survey, we measured preferences for each of the five possible automobile models on a 7-point interval scale. CMG Research also purchased the lifestyle measures of the respondents. There are six different lifestyles: Novelist, Innovator, Trendsetter, Forerunner, Mainstreamer, and Classic. Each lifestyle type is measured with a 7-point interval scale where 1 = Does not describe me

With SPSS, correlations are computed with the CORRELATE-BIVARIATE feature.

A correlation matrix is symmetric with 1s on the diagonal.

at all to 7 = Describes me perfectly. Correlation analysis can be used to find out what lifestyle profile is associated with a particular automobile model preference. That is, high positive correlations would indicate that consumers wanted a particular model and that they scored high on the lifestyle type. Conversely, low or negative correlations would signal that they did not match up well at all. We'll only do one of the model preferences here, and you can do the rest in your SPSS integrated case analysis work specified at the end of the chapter.

We need to perform correlation analysis with the preference for the five-seat, economy gasoline automobile model and the six lifestyle types to determine which, if any, lifestyle type is associated with preference for this model. The clickstream sequence is ANALYZE-CORRELATE-BIVARIATE that leads, as can be seen in Figure 14.4, to a selection box to specify which variables are to be correlated. Note that we have selected the desirability of the standard size gasoline model and all six lifestyle types. Different types of correlations are optional, so we have selected Pearson's, and the two-tailed test of significance is the default.

The output generated by this command is provided in Figure 14.5. As can be seen in the figure, whenever you instruct SPSS to compute correlations, its output is a symmetric correlation matrix composed of rows and columns that pertain to each of the variables. Each cell in the matrix contains three items: (1) the correlation coefficient, (2) the significance level, and (3) the sample size. Figure 14.5 sets out the computed correlations between "Desirability: 5 Seat Economy Gasoline" and the six lifestyles of Novelist, Innovator, Trendsetter, Forerunner, Mainstreamer, and Classic.

If you look at our correlation printout, you will notice that a correlation of 1 is reported where a variable is correlated with itself. This reporting may seem strange, but it serves the purpose of reminding you that the correlation matrix that is generated with this procedure is symmetric. In other words, the correlations in the matrix above the diagonal 1s are identical to those correlations below the diagonal 1s. With only a few variables, this fact is obvious;

FIGURE 14.4
IBM SPSS Clickstream to Obtain Correlations

Source: Reprint Courtesy of International Business Machines Corporation, © International Business Machines Corporation.

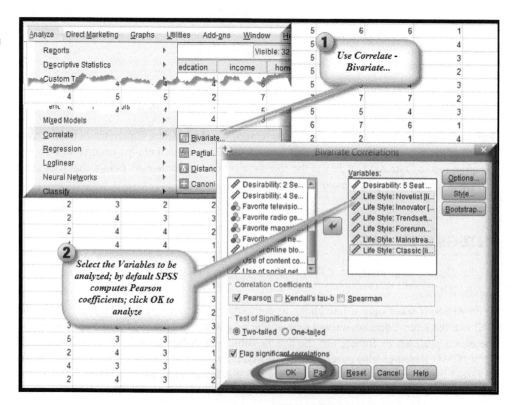

FIGURE 14.5
IBM SPSS Output for Correlations

Source: Reprint Courtesy of International Business Machines Corporation, © International Business Machines Corporation.

*Output1 [Document1] - IBM SPSS Statistics Viewer

File   Edit   View   Data   Transform   Insert   Format   Analyze   Direct Marketing   Graphs   Utilities   Add-ons   Window   Help

Correlations

The Correlations table has correlations, significance levels, and sample size for each pair

The table is symmetric with 1's on the diagonal meaning you use only one-half of it.

Correlations

		Desirability: 5 Seat Economy Gasoline	Life Style: Novelist	Life Style: Innovator	Life Style: Trendsetter	Life Style: Forerunner	Life Style: Mainstreamer	Life Style: Classic
Desirability: 5 Seat Economy Gasoline	Pearson Correlation	1	.090	-.116	.026	.220	-.008	.634
	Sig. (2-tailed)		.004	.000	.409	.000	.795	.000
	N	1000	1000	1000	1000	1000	1000	1000
Life Style: Novelist	Pearson Correlation	.090	1	-.061	.093	.119	.020	.070
	Sig. (2-tailed)	.004		.056	.003	.000	.536	.026
	N	1000	1000	1000	1000	1000	1000	1000
Life Style: Innovator	Pearson Correlation	-.116	-.061	1	-.173	-.005	-.023	-.070
	Sig. (2-tailed)	.000	.056		.000	.877	.467	.027
	N	1000	1000	1000	1000	1000	1000	1000
Life Style: Trendsetter	Pearson Correlation	.026	.093	-.173	1	.007	-.035	.071
	Sig. (2-tailed)	.409	.003	.000		.823	.263	.025
	N	1000	1000	1000	1000	1000	1000	1000
Life Style: Forerunner	Pearson Correlation	.220	.119	-.005	.007	1	.111	.106
	Sig. (2-tailed)	.000	.000	.877	.823		.000	.001
	N	1000	1000	1000	1000	1000	1000	1000
Life Style: Mainstreamer	Pearson Correlation	-.008	.020	-.023	-.035	.111	1	-.043
	Sig. (2-tailed)	.795	.536	.467	.263	.000		.177
	N	1000	1000	1000	1000	1000	1000	1000
Life Style: Classic	Pearson Correlation	.634	.070	-.070	.071	.106	-.043	1
	Sig. (2-tailed)	.000	.026	.027	.025	.001	.177	
	N	1000	1000	1000	1000	1000	1000	1000

**. Correlation is significant at the 0.01 level (2-tailed).
*. Correlation is significant at the 0.05 level (2-tailed).

IBM SPSS Statistics Processor is ready   Cases: 100   Unicode:ON   H: 566, W: 975 pt.

however, sometimes several variables are compared in a single run, and the 1s on the diagonal are handy reference points. They all have a Sig. value of .000 that translates into a .001 or less probability that the null hypothesis of zero correlation is supported.

With correlation analysis, each correlation will have a unique significance level.

Since we now know that the correlations are statistically significant, or significantly different from zero, we can assess their strengths. Searching the first column of statistics, we find only one correlation of appreciable size. It is .634 for Classic. In other words, we only have one lifestyle-type relationship that is positive, stable, and strong. The interpretation of this finding is that those who prefer the five-seat economy gasoline model are people who tend to be traditional and reluctant to change their ways.

14-5   Reporting Correlation Findings to Clients

We again remind you that in step 4 of the "Procedure for Analyzing Relationships" outlined in Table 14.1, the researcher must test to determine that a significant correlation has been found before reporting it. Losing sight of this step is entirely possible when a statistical analysis program issues a great many correlations often in a layout that is confusing to first-time data analysts. To our knowledge, there is no marketing research industry standard on how to report statistically significant correlations to clients. But we do have a recommended approach that takes into account correlation signs and sizes. Our recommendation is offered in Marketing Research Insight 14.2.

To learn how to compute a Pearson product moment correlation, launch **www.youtube.com**, and search for "Product Moment Correlation Coefficient: Exam Solutions."

14-6   Cross-Tabulations

We now turn to cross-tabulation and the associated Chi-square value used to assess if a non-monotonic relationship exists between two nominally scaled variables. Recall that nonmonotonic relationships are those in which the presence of the label for one nominally scaled

MARKETING RESEARCH INSIGHT 14.2   *Practical Application*

Guidelines for the Reporting of Correlation Findings

To begin, marketing researchers usually have a "target" or a "focal" variable in mind, and they look at correlations of other variables of interest with this target variable. As an illustration, we will say that in our fictitious Subshop survey, the researcher decides that the target variable is the number of times Subshop customers used the Subshop in the past two months. This is a ratio scale variable where respondents have given a number such as "0," "3," "10," and so on. The researcher has found six other scale variables with statistically significant correlations with the target in the analysis of the Subshop survey data. Naturally, some of these have negative correlations, and the correlations range in size or strength. Study how these findings are arranged in the following table.

Notice in the table that the target variable is clearly indicated, and the positive and negative correlations are identified and separated. Also, in each case, the correlations are reported in descending order based on the absolute size. In this way, the client's attention is drawn first to the positively related variables, and he or she can see the pattern from strong to weak positive correlations. Next, the client's attention is drawn to the negatively associated variables, and, again, he or she can see the pattern from strong to weak negative correlations. If the

researcher thinks it appropriate, a third column can be added to the table, and the designations of "Strong," "Moderate," "Weak," and so on can be placed beside each correlation according to the rules of thumb regarding strength labels listed in Table 14.2. Alternatively, these designations can be specified as asterisks with a table footnote or otherwise noted in the text.

Variables Correlated with Subshop Patronage

Variable	Correlation
*Variables positively correlated with patronage:**	
*I tend to use the same sandwich shop.***	.76
*I worry about calories.***	.65
Age	.55
Number of years with present company	.40
*Variables negatively correlated with patronage:**	
*I "do" lunch at the place closest to my work.***	−.71
Years of education	−.51

*Subshop patronage (number of times used in past two months)
** Based on a 7-point scale where 1 = Strongly disagree to 7 = Strongly agree

variable coincides with the presence of the label for another nominally scaled variable such as lunch buyers ordering soft drinks with their meals. (Actually, cross-tabulation can be used for any two variables with well-defined labels, but it is best demonstrated with nominal variables.)

CROSS-TABULATION ANALYSIS

When a researcher is investigating the relationship between two nominally-scaled variables, he or she typically uses "cross-tabs," or the use of a **cross-tabulation table**, defined as a table in which data are compared using a row and column format. A cross-tabulation table is sometimes referred to as an "$r \times c$" (*r*-by-*c*) table because it is comprised of rows by columns. The intersection of a row and a column is called a **cross-tabulation cell**. As an example, let's take a survey in which there are two types of individuals: buyers of Michelob Ultra beer and nonbuyers of Michelob Ultra beer. There are also two types of occupations: professional workers who might be called "white-collar" employees, and manual workers who are sometimes referred to as "blue-collar" workers. There is no requirement that the number of rows and columns are equal; we are just using a 2 × 2 cross-tabulation to keep the example as simple as possible. Cross-tabulation tables for our Michelob Ultra beer survey are presented in Table 14.3A and Table 14.3B. The columns are in vertical alignment and are indicated in the tables as either "Buyer" or "Nonbuyer" of Michelob Ultra, whereas the rows are indicated as "White Collar" or "Blue Collar" for occupation. Additionally, there is a "Totals" column and row.

A cross-tabulation consists of rows and columns defined by the categories classifying each variable.

TYPES OF FREQUENCIES AND PERCENTAGES IN A CROSS-TABULATION TABLE

Look at the frequencies table in Table 14.3A. There are annotations and "+" and "=" signs in the table to help you learn the terminology and to understand how the numbers are computed.

TABLE 14.3A **Cross-Tabulation Frequencies Table for a Michelob Ultra Survey**

Observed Frequencies Table

		Type of Buyer		
		Buyer	Nonbuyer	Totals
Buyer/White Collar Cell Frequency →	White Collar	152 +	8 =	**160** ← Row Totals
		+	+	+
Occupational Status	Blue Collar	14 +	26 =	**40**
		=	=	=
	Totals	**166** +	**34** =	**200**

Column Totals ↗   Grand Total ↗

TABLE 14.3B **Cross-Tabulation Percentages Tables for a Michelob Ultra Survey**

Raw Percentages Table

		Buyer		Nonbuyer		Totals
Buyer/White Collar Cell Raw Percent →	White Collar	76% (152/200)	+	4% (8/200)	=	80% (160/200)
		+		+		+
Occupational Status	Blue Collar	7% (14/200)	+	13% (26/200)	=	20% (40/200)
		=		=		=
	Totals	83% (166/200)	+	17% (34/200)	=	**100%** (200/200)

Column Percentages Table

		Buyer	Nonbuyer	Totals
Buyer/White Collar Column Percent →	White Collar	92% (152/166)	24% (8/34)	80% (160/200)
		+	+	+
Occupational Status	Blue Collar	8% (14/166)	76% (26/34)	20% (40/200)
		=	=	=
		100%	**100%**	**100%**
	Totals	(166/166)	(34)	(200/200)

Row Percentages Table

		Buyer		Nonbuyer		Totals
Buyer/White Collar Row Percent →	White Collar	95% (152/160)	+	5% (8/160)	=	**100%** (160/160)
Occupational Status	Blue Collar	35% (14/40)	+	65% (26/40)	=	**100%** (40/40)
	Totals	83% (166/200)	+	17% (34/200)	=	**100%** (200/200)

The **frequencies table** (often referred to as the *observed frequencies table*) contains the raw numbers determined from the preliminary tabulation.[6] The upper left-hand cell number is a frequency cell that counts people in the sample who are both white-collar workers and buyers of Michelob Ultra (152), and the cell frequency to its right identifies the number of individuals who are white-collar workers who do not buy Michelob Ultra (8). These cell numbers represent raw counts or frequencies; that is, the number of respondents who possess the quality indicated by the row label as well as the quality indicated by the column label. The cell frequencies can be summed to determine the row totals and the column totals. For example, Buyer/White Collar (152) and Nonbuyer/White Collar (8) sum to 160, while Buyer/White Collar (152) and Buyer/Blue Collar (14) sum to 166. Similarly, the row and column totals sum to equal the grand total of 200. Take a few minutes to be familiar with the terms and computations in the frequencies table, as they will be referred to in the following discussion.

> A cross-classification table can have four types of numbers in each cell: frequency, raw percentage, column percentage, and row percentage.

Table 14.3B illustrates how at least three different sets of percentages can be computed for cells in the table. These three percentages tables are the raw percentages table, the column percentages table, and the row percentages table.

> Raw percentages are cell frequencies divided by the grand total.

The first table in Table 14.3B shows that the raw frequencies can be converted to raw percentages by dividing each by the grand total. The **raw percentages table** contains the percentages of the raw frequency numbers just discussed. The grand total location now has 100% (or 200/200) of the grand total. Above it are 80% and 20% for the raw percentages of white-collar occupational respondents and blue-collar occupational respondents, respectively, in the sample. Divide a couple of the cells just to verify that you understand how they are derived. For instance, $152 \div 200 = 76\%$. Our "+" and "=" signs indicate how the totals are computed.

Two additional cross-tabulation tables can be presented, and these are more valuable in revealing underlying relationships. The **column percentages table** divides the raw frequencies by the column total raw frequency. That is, the formula is as follows:

Formula for a column cell percent

$$\text{Column cell percent} = \frac{\text{Cell frequency}}{\text{Total of cell frequencies in that column}}$$

For instance, it is apparent that of the nonbuyers, 24% are white-collar respondents and 76% are blue-collar respondents. Note the reverse pattern for the buyers group: 92% of Michelob Ultra buyers are white-collar respondents and 8% are blue-collar. You are beginning to see the nonmonotonic relationship.

The **row percentages table** presents the data with the row totals as the 100% base for each. That is, a row cell percentage is computed as follows:

Formula for a row cell percent

$$\text{Row cell percent} = \frac{\text{Cell frequency}}{\text{Total of cell frequencies in that row}}$$

> Row (column) percentages are row (column) cell frequencies divided by the row (column) total.

Now it is possible to see that, of the white-collar respondents, 95% are buyers and 5% are nonbuyers. As you compare the row percentages table to the column percentages table, you should detect the relationship between occupational status and Michelob Ultra beer preference. Can you state it at this time?

Unequal percentage concentrations of individuals in a few cells, as we have in this example, illustrate the possible presence of a nonmonotonic association. If we had found that approximately 25% of the sample had fallen in each of the four cells, no relationship would be found to exist—it would be equally probable for any person to be a Michelob Ultra buyer or nonbuyer and a white- or a blue-collar worker. However, the large concentrations of individuals in two particular cells here suggest that there is a high probability that a buyer of Michelob Ultra beer is also a white-collar worker, and there is also a tendency for nonbuyers to work in blue-collar occupations. In other words, there is probably an association between occupational status and the beer-buying behavior of individuals in the population represented by this sample. However, as noted in step 4 of our procedure for analyzing relationships (Table 14.1), we must test the statistical significance of the apparent relationship before we can say anything more about it.

14-7 Chi-Square Analysis

Chi-square (χ^2) analysis is the examination of frequencies for two nominally scaled variables in a cross-tabulation table to determine whether the variables have a statistically significant nonmonotonic relationship.[7] The formal procedure for Chi-square analysis begins when the researcher formulates a statistical null hypothesis that the two variables under investigation are not associated in the population. Actually, it is not necessary for the researcher to state this hypothesis in a formal sense, for Chi-square analysis always implicitly takes this hypothesis into account. In other words, whenever we use Chi-square analysis with a cross-tabulation, we always begin with the assumption that no association exists between the two nominally scaled variables under analysis.[8]

Chi-square analysis assesses the statistical significance of nonmonotonic associations in cross-tabulation tables.

OBSERVED AND EXPECTED FREQUENCIES

The statistical procedure is as follows. The cross-tabulation table in Table 14.3A contains **observed frequencies**, which are the actual cell counts in the cross-tabulation table. These observed frequencies are compared to **expected frequencies**, which are defined as the theoretical frequencies that are derived from this hypothesis of no association between the two variables. The degree to which the observed frequencies depart from the expected frequencies is expressed in a single number called the *Chi-square test statistic*. The computed Chi-square test statistic is then compared to a table Chi-square value (at a chosen level of significance) to determine whether the computed value is significantly different from zero.

Expected frequencies are calculated based on the null hypothesis of no association between the two variables under investigation.

The expected frequencies are those that would be found if there were no association between the two variables. Remember, this is the null hypothesis. About the only "difficult" part of Chi-square analysis is in the computation of the expected frequencies. The computation is accomplished using the following equation:

Formula for an expected cross-tabulation cell frequency

$$\text{Expected cell frequency} = \frac{\text{Cell column total} \times \text{Cell row total}}{\text{Grand total}}$$

The application of this equation generates a number for each cell that would occur if no association existed. Returning to our Michelob Ultra beer example in which 160 white-collar and 40 blue-collar consumers were sampled, it was found that there were 166 buyers and

34 nonbuyers of Michelob Ultra. The expected frequency for each cell, assuming no association, calculated with the expected cell frequency is as follows:

Calculations of expected cell frequencies using the Michelob Ultra example	
Notes:	White-collar buyer $= \dfrac{160 \times 166}{200} = 132.8$
Buyers total = 166	White-collar nonbuyer $= \dfrac{160 \times 34}{200} = 27.2$
Nonbuyers total = 34	Blue-collar buyer $= \dfrac{40 \times 166}{200} = 33.2$
White-collar buyers total = 160	
Blue-collar buyers total = 40	Blue-collar nonbuyer $= \dfrac{40 \times 34}{200} = 6.8$
Grand total = 200	

THE COMPUTED χ^2 VALUE

Next, compare the observed frequencies to these expected frequencies. The **Chi-square formula** for this computation is as follows:

Chi-square formula

$$\chi^2 = \sum_{i-1}^{n} \frac{(\text{Observed}_i - \text{Expected}_i)^2}{\text{Expected}_i}$$

where

   Observed_i = observed frequency in cell i

   Expected_i = expected frequency in cell i

   n = number of cells

Applied to our Michelob Ultra beer example,

The computed Chi-square value compares observed to expected frequencies.

Calculation of Chi-square value (Michelob Ultra example)	
Notes:	$\chi^2 = \dfrac{(152 - 132.8)^2}{132.8} + \dfrac{(8 - 27.2)^2}{27.2}$
Observed frequencies are in Table 14.3A	$\quad + \dfrac{(14 - 33.2)^2}{33.2} + \dfrac{(26 - 6.8)^2}{6.8} = 81.64$
Expected frequencies are computed above	

The Chi-square test statistic summarizes how far away from the expected frequencies the observed cell frequencies are found to be.

   You can see from the equation that each expected frequency is compared (via subtraction) to the observed frequency and squared to adjust for any negative values and to avoid the cancellation effect. This value is divided by the expected frequency to adjust for cell size differences, and these amounts are summed across all the cells. If there are many large deviations of observed frequencies from the expected frequencies, the computed Chi-square value will increase. But if there are only a few slight deviations from the expected frequencies, the computed Chi-square number will be small. In other words, the computed Chi-square value is really a summary indication of how far away from the expected frequencies the observed frequencies are found to be. As such, it expresses the departure of the sample findings from the null hypothesis of no association.

THE CHI-SQUARE DISTRIBUTION

Now that you've learned how to calculate a Chi-square value, you need to know if it is statistically significant. In previous chapters, we described how the normal curve or z distribution, the F distribution, and Student's t distribution, all of which exist in tables, are used by a computer statistical program to determine level of significance. Chi-square analysis requires the use of a different distribution. The **Chi-square distribution** is skewed to the right and the rejection region is always at the right-hand tail of the distribution. It differs from the normal and *t* distributions in that it changes its shape depending on the situation at hand, and it does not have negative values. Figure 14.6 shows examples of two Chi-square distributions.

The Chi-square distribution's shape is determined by the number of degrees of freedom. The figure shows that the greater the degrees of freedom, the more the curve's tail is pulled to the right. Or, in other words, the greater the degrees of freedom, the larger the Chi-square value must be to fall in the rejection region for the null hypothesis.

It is a simple matter to determine the number of degrees of freedom. In a cross-tabulation table, the degrees of freedom are found through the following formula:

For doing a great job, do these blue-collar workers want their boss to buy them a Michelob Ultra? Cross-tabulation can answer this question.

Formula for Chi-square degrees of freedom

$$\text{Degrees of freedom} = (r - 1)(c - 1)$$

where

  r = the number of rows

  c = the number of columns

The Chi-square distribution's shape changes depending on the number of degrees of freedom.

A table of Chi-square values contains critical points that determine the break between the acceptance and rejection regions at various levels of significance. It also takes into account the number of degrees of freedom associated with each curve. That is, a computed Chi-square value says nothing by itself—you must consider the number of degrees of freedom in the cross-tabulation table because more degrees of freedom indicate higher critical Chi-square

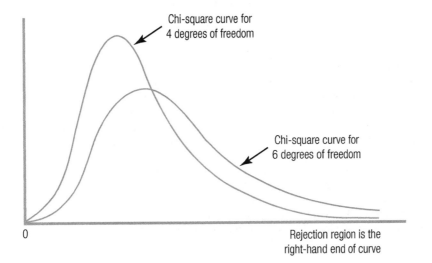

Chi-square curve for 4 degrees of freedom

Chi-square curve for 6 degrees of freedom

0

Rejection region is the right-hand end of curve

FIGURE 14.6 The Chi-Square Curve's Shape Depends on Its Degrees of Freedom

The computed Chi-square value is compared to a table value to determine statistical significance.

table values for the same level of significance. The logic of this situation stems from the number of cells. With more cells, there is more opportunity for departure from the expected values. The higher table values adjust for potential inflation due to chance alone. After all, we want to detect real nonmonotonic relationships, not phantom ones.

Computer statistical programs look up table Chi-square values and display the probability of support for the null hypothesis.

SPSS and virtually all computer statistical analysis programs have Chi-square tables in memory and display the probability of the null hypothesis. Let us repeat this point: The program itself will take into account the number of degrees of freedom and determine the probability of support for the null hypothesis. This probability is the percentage of the area under the Chi-square curve that lies to the right of the computed Chi-square value. When rejection of the null hypothesis occurs, we have found a statistically significant nonmonotonic association existing between the two variables.[9] With our Michelob Ultra example, the degrees of freedom is 1, and the critical Chi-square value is 3.841, so because 81.64 is greater, there is less than 5% support for the null hypothesis. A statistically significant association does exist.

HOW TO INTERPRET A CHI-SQUARE RESULT

How does one interpret a Chi-square result? Chi-square analysis yields the amount of support for the null hypothesis if the researcher repeated the study many, many times with independent samples. By now, you should be well acquainted with the concept of many, many independent samples. For example, if the Chi-square analysis yielded a .02 significance level for the null hypothesis, the researcher would conclude that only 2% of the time would he or she find evidence to support the null hypothesis. Since the null hypothesis is not supported, this means there is a significant association.

A significant Chi-square means the researcher should look at the cross-tabulation row and column percentages to "see" the association pattern.

It must be pointed out that Chi-square analysis is simply a method to determine whether a statistically significant nonmonotonic association exists between two variables. Chi-square does not indicate the nature of the association, and it indicates only roughly the strength of association by its size. It is best interpreted as a prerequisite to looking more closely at the two variables to discern the nature of the association that exists between them. That is, the Chi-square test is another one of our "signal lights" telling us whether or not it is worthwhile to inspect all those rows and columns percentages. Read Marketing Research Insight 14.3 to see how cross-tabulation findings are used to identify the demographic profiles of Indian hypermarket shoppers.

MARKETING RESEARCH INSIGHT 14.3   *Global Application*

Cross-Tabulation Discovers Indian Hypermarket Shopper Segment Profiles

In India, as in many countries experiencing modernization and growth in the retail sector, one of the fastest-growing retail formats is the hypermarket. A hypermarket, popularly known as a "superstore" in the United States, is a very large department store–supermarket facility where shoppers can buy a very wide variety of merchandise as well as groceries without having to travel or otherwise patronize several stores on the same shopping trip. The growth rate of Indian hypermarkets is nothing short of phenomenal, and the competition is intense as several national and multinational retail companies are locked in battle for shares of the immense Indian consumer market.

An interesting aspect of the Indian consumer market is that many shoppers are distrustful of giant and impersonal grocery markets. That is, they prefer traditional, small, local food vendors where they can fully inspect the items and engage in bargaining and bartering as have taken place for generations in India. As with other countries that have experienced rapid transition from agrarian to urban venues, hypermarkets are replacing local food vendors, but not all consumers have completely embraced the hypermarket concept, even though they are being forced to shop in them. To better understand Indian hypermarket shoppers and to identify important demographic segments, researchers[10] recently surveyed shoppers patronizing a typical Indian hypermarket as well as shoppers patronizing traditional grocery stores. These researchers discovered four shopper segments that they labeled as follows: Utilitarian,

Maximizer, Enthusiast, and Browser. The Utilitarian shopper segment is comprised of shoppers who just want to buy items without any fanfare whatsoever and with minimal effort. Maximizer shoppers are similar to Utilitarian shoppers in that they want the one-stop, easy access aspects of hypermarkets, but they enjoy their shopping trips and consider them recreational and entertaining as well as functional. Enthusiast shoppers are like Maximizers, but they also seek social aspects such as being in shopper crowds and just watching other shoppers. Finally, Browser shoppers greatly enjoy the social aspects of being with and observing other shoppers, but they are not on purchasing missions as are the other segment shoppers. With respect to the total hypermarket shopper population, Utilitarians account for about 25%, Maximizers account for about 33%, Enthusiasts are about 12%, and Browsers constitute the last 33%.

The researchers then used cross-tabulations and Chi-square analysis to determine distinct demographic profiles of these shopper segments. They found significant associations with four demographic variables: gender, marital status, age, and education. The stacked bar graphs for gender and marital status reveal that Utilitarians tend to be married females, Maximizers are married males or females, Enthusiasts tend to be married males, and Browsers are largely single males.

The two bar graphs reveal the age and education profiles of these hypermarket shopper segments. Utilitarians tend to have college degrees and are 30 years old or more; Maximizers also have college degrees but are more likely to be in the 30–49 age range. Enthusiasts are quite similar to Utilitarians with respect to age and education, whereas Browsers are somewhat lower in education and younger in age than other segments.

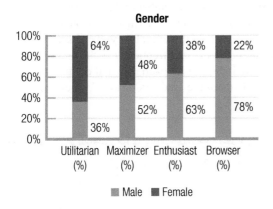

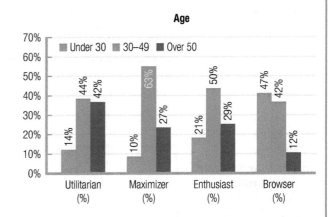

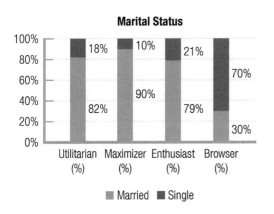

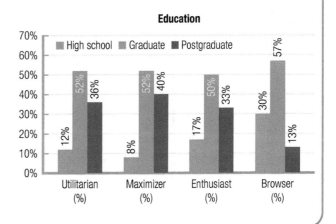

INTEGRATED CASE

IBM SPSS *Auto Concepts: Analyzing Cross-Tabulations for Significant Associations by Performing Chi-Square Analysis with SPSS*

We are going to use our Auto Concepts survey data to demonstrate how to perform and interpret cross-tabulation analysis with SPSS. You should recall that we have several demographic variables including gender and marital status. We will take gender as one of the nominal variables. For the second nominal variable, we will take the preferred magazine type. Thus, we are investigating the possible association of gender (male versus female) and favorite magazine type (Business & Money; Music & Entertainment; Family & Parenting; Sports & Outdoors; Home & Garden; Cooking, Food & Wine; Trucks, Cars & Motorcycles; or News, Politics & Current Events).

The clickstream command sequence to perform a Chi-square test with SPSS is ANALYZE-DESCRIPTIVE STATISTICS-CROSSTABS, which leads to a dialog box in which you can select the variables for Chi-square analysis. In our example in Figure 14.7, we have selected Gender as the column variable, and Favorite magazine type as the row variable. There are three option buttons at the bottom of the box. The Cells ... option leads to the specification of observed frequencies, expected frequencies, row percentages, column percentages, and so forth. We have opted for just the observed frequencies (raw counts) and the row percents. The Statistics ... button opens up a menu of statistics that can be computed from cross-tabulation tables. Of course, the only one we want is the Chi-square option.

The resulting output is found in Figure 14.8. In the top table, you can see that we have variable and value labels, and the table contains the raw frequency as the first entry in each cell. Also, the row percentages are reported along with each row and column total. In the second table, there is information on the Chi-square analysis result. For our purposes, the

> With SPSS, Chi-square is an option under the "Crosstabs" analysis routine.

FIGURE 14.7
IBM SPSS Clickstream to Create Cross-Tabulations with Chi-Square Analysis

Source: Reprint Courtesy of International Business Machines Corporation, © International Business Machines Corporation.

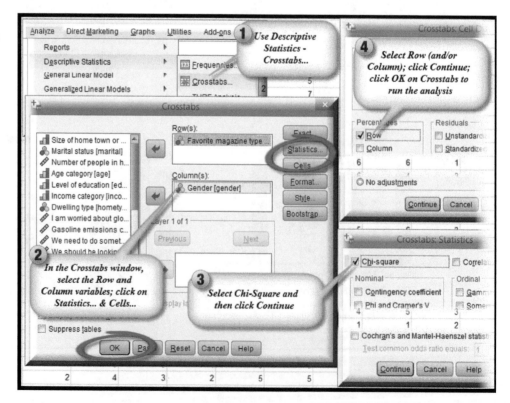

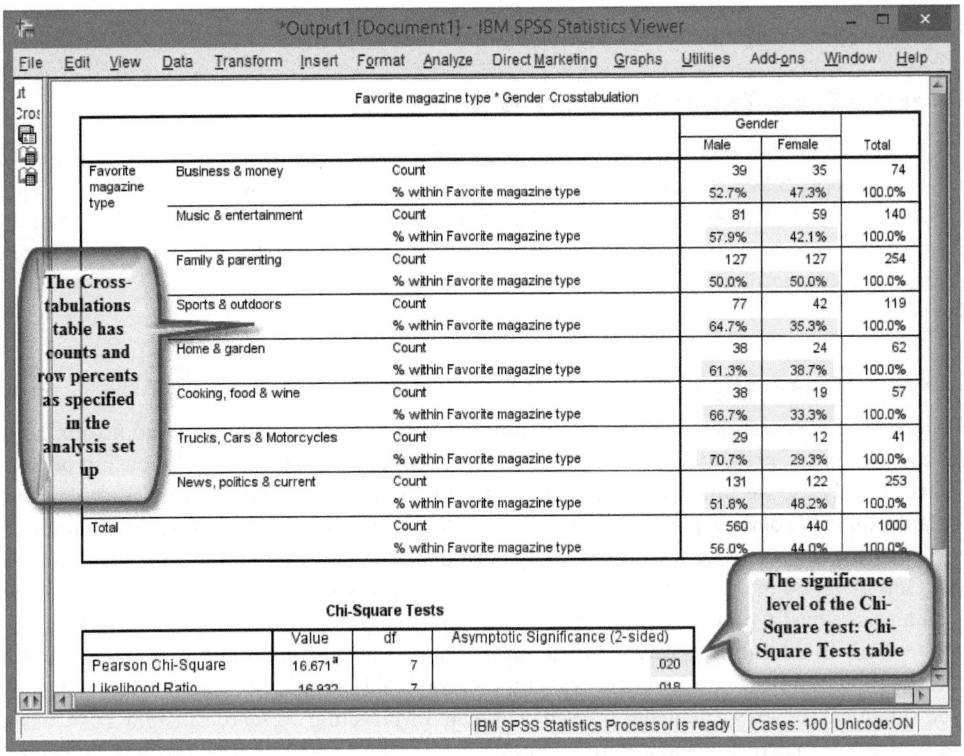

Favorite magazine type * Gender Crosstabulation

			Gender		Total
			Male	Female	
Favorite magazine type	Business & money	Count	39	35	74
		% within Favorite magazine type	52.7%	47.3%	100.0%
	Music & entertainment	Count	81	59	140
		% within Favorite magazine type	57.9%	42.1%	100.0%
	Family & parenting	Count	127	127	254
		% within Favorite magazine type	50.0%	50.0%	100.0%
	Sports & outdoors	Count	77	42	119
		% within Favorite magazine type	64.7%	35.3%	100.0%
	Home & garden	Count	38	24	62
		% within Favorite magazine type	61.3%	38.7%	100.0%
	Cooking, food & wine	Count	38	19	57
		% within Favorite magazine type	66.7%	33.3%	100.0%
	Trucks, Cars & Motorcycles	Count	29	12	41
		% within Favorite magazine type	70.7%	29.3%	100.0%
	News, politics & current	Count	131	122	253
		% within Favorite magazine type	51.8%	48.2%	100.0%
Total		Count	560	440	1000
		% within Favorite magazine type	56.0%	44.0%	100.0%

Chi-Square Tests

	Value	df	Asymptotic Significance (2-sided)
Pearson Chi-Square	16.671[a]	7	.020
Likelihood Ratio	16.932	7	.018

FIGURE 14.8
IBM SPSS Output for Cross-Tabulations with Chi-Square Analysis

Source: Reprint Courtesy of International Business Machines Corporation, © International Business Machines Corporation.

only relevant statistic is the "Pearson Chi-square," which you can see has been computed to be 16.671. The df column pertains to the number of degrees of freedom, which is 7; and the Asymp. Sig. corresponds to the probability of support for the null hypothesis. Significance in this example is .020, which means that there is practically no support for the hypothesis that Gender and Favorite magazine type are not associated. In other words, they are related.

IBM **SPSS**

IBM SPSS Student Assistant:
Setting Up and Analyzing Cross-Tabulations

SPSS has effected the first step in determining a nonmonotonic association. Through Chi-square analysis, it has signaled that a statistically significant association actually exists. The next step is to fathom the nature of the association. Remember that with a nonmonotonic relationship, you must inspect the pattern and describe it verbally. We can ask the question, "Which gender is reading what magazine type?" Remember that the pattern is a matter of degree, not "on versus off." Look at the column percents in Figure 14.8, and you will see some magazine types that garner proportionally more male readers: Trucks, Cars & Motorcyles; Cooking, Food & Wine; and Sports & Outdoors. The other magazine types have somewhat balanced readership profiles with respect to gender. You can interpret this finding in the following way: If Auto Concepts wants to communicate to prospective male automobile buyers, it should use the magazine types they prefer; if it desires to communicate to prospective female buyers, it should not use these types, as women do not prefer to read them.

With Chi-square analysis, interpret the SPSS significance level as the amount of support for *no* association between the two variables being analyzed.

In other words, because the significance is less than .05, it is worthwhile to inspect and interpret the percentages in the cross-tabulation table. By doing this, we can discern the pattern or nature of the association, and the percentages indicate its relative strength. More importantly, because the relationship was determined to be statistically significant, you can be assured that this association and the relationship you have observed will hold for the population that this sample represents.

 **Active Learning**

IBM **SPSS**   **Practice Cross-Tabulation Analysis with SPSS**

To make certain that you can perform SPSS cross-tabulation with Chi-square analysis, use the Auto Concepts SPSS dataset and replicate the Gender–Favorite magazine type analysis just described. When you are convinced that you can do this analysis correctly and interpret the output, use it to see if there is an association between marital status and favorite magazine type. What about marital status and newspaper reading habits?

Marketing Research on YouTube™ | To learn about cross-tabulation and Chi-square analysis, launch **www.youtube.com**, and search for "Interpreting the SPSS Output for a Chi Square Analysis."

14-8   Reporting Cross-Tabulation Findings to Clients

Whenever the researcher finds a statistically significant cross-tabulation relationship, he or she moves to the presentation phase. When we introduced the notion of relationship or association analysis, we noted that characterizing the direction and strength of nonmonotonic relationships is not possible because nominal scales are involved. Nominal scales do not have order or magnitude; they are simply categories or labels that uniquely identify the data. As you have learned in our descriptions of the various tables possible with cross-tabulations, percentages are easily prepared, and percentages can usually depict nonmonotonic relationships quite well. In addition, to reveal the nonmonotonic relationships found to be significant in cross-tabulation tables, researchers often turn to graphical presentations, as pictures will show the relationships very adequately. We have created Marketing Research Insight 14.4, which describes alternative ways to present the findings of cross-tabulation relationships analyses to clients.

14-9   Special Considerations in Association Procedures

Bar charts can be used to "see" a nonmonotonic relationship.

While *cross-tab* is not common, it is unfortunate that the word *correlation* is used in everyday language, because statistical correlations are sometimes misunderstood by clients.[11] We will discuss each of four cautions to keep in mind when working with associations—either correlations or cross-tabulations. First, we will reiterate that the correlation coefficient discussed in this section assumes that both variables share interval-scaling assumptions at minimum. If the two variables have nominal-scaling assumptions, the researcher would use cross-tabulation analysis. Second, the association analyses in this chapter take into consideration only the relationship between two variables. They do not take into consideration interactions with any other variables. In fact, you must explicitly assume that all other variables do not have any bearing on the relationship with the two variables of interest. All other factors are considered to be constant or "frozen" in their bearing on the two variables under analysis.

Association does not demonstrate cause and effect.

Third, association analysis and especially the correlation coefficient explicitly do not assume a **cause-and-effect relationship**, which is a condition of one variable bringing about the other variable. For instance, although you might be tempted to believe that more company salespeople cause more company sales or that an increase in the competitor's sales force in a territory takes away sales, correlation should not be interpreted to demonstrate such cause-and-effect relationships.[12] Just think of all of the other factors that affect sales: price, product quality, service policies, population, advertising, and more. It would be a mistake to assume that just one factor causes sales. Instead, a correlation coefficient merely investigates the presence, strength, and direction of a linear relationship between two variables. Similarly, cross-tabulation investigates only the presence and pattern of a nonmonotonic relationship between two variables.

Fourth and finally, the Pearson product moment correlation expresses only linear relationships. Consequently, a correlation coefficient result of approximately zero does not

MARKETING RESEARCH INSIGHT 14.4 *Practical Application*

Guidelines for the Reporting of Cross-Tabulation Findings

Using Column and Row Percents

A question that quickly arises whenever a researcher finds a statistically significant relationship in a cross-tabulation analysis is "Should I report the row percents, or should I report the column percents?" The answer to this question depends on the research objective that fostered the nominal questions on the survey. Take, for instance, the following significant cross-tabulation finding for the Subshop.

Column Percents Table

Size of Sandwich Ordered	Males	Females
Jumbo size	**50%**	5%
Large size	**40%**	20%
Regular size	10%	**75%**
Total	100%	100%

Rows Percents Table

Size of Sandwich Ordered	Males	Females	Total
Jumbo size	**90%**	10%	100%
Large size	**67%**	33%	100%
Regular size	13%	**87%**	100%

If the research question is "Who orders what size of sandwich?" the rows percents table is appropriate as it indicates that males tend to order the Jumbo size and the Large size (90% and 67%, respectively), while females tend to be the ones who order the Regular size (87%). However, if the research question is "What do males versus females order?" then the column percents table is appropriate, as it indicates that males order Jumbo and Large sizes (50% and 40%), while females order the Regular size (75%). You should remember that we described a nonmonotonic relationship as an identifiable association where the presence of one variable is paired with the presence (or absence) of another, so the relationships are not 100% versus 0%; rather, it is a degree or relative presence that exists in the population. Study our two presentation tables, and you will notice that we have used shading to help you understand how the percents are computed. That is, the males and females columns are different shades, as they express percents within each gender. Similarly, the sandwich size rows are different shades, as they represent percents within each sandwich size. We have also used bold font to emphasize where the percents reveal especially strong relationships.

Using Stacked Bar Charts

A handy graphical tool that illustrates a nonmonotonic relationship is a stacked bar chart. With a stacked bar chart, two variables are accommodated simultaneously in the same bar graph. Each bar in the stacked bar chart stands for 100%, and it is divided proportionately by the amount of relationship that one variable shares with the other variables. You saw stacked bar charts in the graphs for gender and marital status in Marketing Research Insight 14.3. Thus, a stacked bar chart is an excellent visual display of row or column percents in a cross-tabulation table. For instance, you can see in the following figures that the two Subshop cross-tabulation percents tables have been used to create the visual displays.

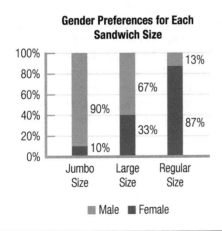

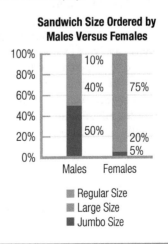

Correlation will not detect nonlinear relationships between variables.

necessarily mean that the scatter diagram that could be drawn from the two variables defines a formless ball of points. Instead, it means that the points do not fall in a well-defined elliptical pattern. Any number of alternative, curvilinear patterns such as an S-shape or a J-shape pattern are possible, and the linear correlation coefficient would not be able to communicate the existence of these patterns to the marketing researcher. Only those cases of linear or straight-line relationships between two variables are identified by the Pearson product moment correlation. In fact, when a researcher does not find a significant or strong correlation, but still believes some relationship exists between two variables, he or she may resort to running a scatter plot. This procedure allows the researcher to visually inspect the plotted points and possibly to spot a systematic nonlinear relationship. Your SPSS program has a scatter plot option that will provide a scatter diagram that you can use to obtain a sense of the relationship, if any exists, between two variables.

Summary

This chapter deals with instances in which a marketing researcher wants to see if there is a relationship between the responses to one question and the responses to another question in the same survey. Four different types of relationship are possible. First, a linear relationship is characterized by a straight-line appearance if the variables are plotted against one another on a graph. Second, a curvilinear relationship means the pattern has a definite curved shape. Third, a nonmonotonic relationship indicates that the presence (or absence) of a label for one nominal variable is sytematically associated with the presence (or absence) of a label for another nominal variable. Fourth and finally, a monotonic relationship indicates the direction of one variable relative to the direction of the other variable. In the cases of linear relationships and nonmonotonic relationships in this chapter, association analyses to assess these relationships statistically are described.

Associations can be characterized by presence, direction, and strength, depending on the scaling assumptions of the questions being compared. These characteristics are readily seen in correlation analysis. A correlation coefficient is an index number, constrained to fall between +1.0 and −1.0, that communicates both the strength and the direction of association between two variables. The sign indicates the direction of the relationship, and the absolute size indicates the strength of the association. Normally, correlations in excess of ±.8 are considered high. With two questions that are interval and/or ratio in their scaling assumptions, the Pearson product moment correlation coefficient is appropriate as the means of determining the underlying linear relationship. A scatter diagram can be used to inspect the pattern.

With Chi-square analysis, a cross-tabulation table is prepared for two nominally scaled questions, and the Chi-square test statistic is computed to determine whether the observed frequencies (those found in the survey) differ significantly from what would be expected if there were no nonmonotonic relationship between the two. If the null hypothesis of no relationship is rejected, the researcher then looks at the cell percentages to identify the underlying pattern of association.

With correlations as well as cross-tabulations, it is important to keep in mind that only two variables are being examined and that all other variables are explicitly assumed to not have influence in the relationship. Also, while it is tempting to do so, one should not infer any "cause-and-effect" relationship exists between the two variables. Correlations should be envisioned within the context of the linear relationship assumptions that underpin them, and cross-tabulation relationships should be interpreted with the appropriate percentages, using tables or helpful bar charts to display the patterns that have been discovered.

Key Terms

Associative analyses (p. 378)
Relationship (p. 378)
Linear relationship (p. 378)
Straight-line formula (p. 379)
Curvilinear relationship (p. 379)
Monotonic relationships (p. 379)
Nonmonotonic relationship (p. 380)
Correlation coefficient (p. 382)

Covariation (p. 382)
Scatter diagram (p. 383)
Pearson product moment correlation (p. 384)
Cross-tabulation table (p. 390)
Cross-tabulation cell (p. 390)
Frequencies table (p. 392)
Raw percentages table (p. 392)

Column percentages table (p. 392)
Row percentages table (p. 392)
Chi-square (χ^2) analysis (p. 393)
Observed frequencies (p. 393)
Expected frequencies (p. 393)
Chi-square formula (p. 394)
Chi-square distribution (p. 395)
Cause-and-effect relationship (p. 400)

Correct Answers for Marketing Research Insight 14.1

Fans of This Brand or Topic	Have What Musical Preference?
Ciroc vodka	Hip-hop and rap artists
Craft beers	Jam bands (Phish, Umphrey's McGee)
EA's console sports games	Rap and hip-hop artists (Ice Cube, Nas)
Harrods	Andrew Lloyd Webber
Motorola	Younger artists like Miley Cyrus, the Jonas Brothers
NHL	Bruce Springsteen and Pink Floyd
NPR	Classic rock stars such as the Beatles, Jimi Hendrix, etc.
Travel Channel	Rock and country rock artists, like Meat Loaf, Kid Rock
Victoria's Secret Pink brand	*American Idol* alt-rocker Chris Daughtry

Review Questions/Applications

14-1. Explain the distinction between a statistical relationship and a causal relationship.

14-2. Define and provide an example for each of the following types of relationship: (a) linear, (b) curvilinear, (c) nonmonotonic, and (d) monotonic.

14-3. Relate the three different aspects of a relationship between two variables.

14-4. Do association analysis and the correlation coefficient explicitly assume a cause-and-effect relationship? State the reasons for your answer.

14-5. Briefly describe the connections among the following: covariation, scatter diagram, correlation, and linear relationship.

14-6. Indicate, with the use of a scatter diagram, the general shape of the scatter of data points in each of the following cases: (a) a strong positive correlation, (b) a weak negative correlation, (c) no correlation, (d) a correlation of −.98.

14-7. What must be determined before using correlation? Why is it essential?

14-8. What are the scaling assumptions assumed by Pearson product moment correlation?

14-9. What is the advantage of reporting cross-tabulation findings through a stacked bar chart?

14-10. With respect to Chi-square analysis, describe or identify each of the following: (a) $r \times c$ table, (b) frequencies table, (c) observed frequencies, (d) expected frequencies, (e) Chi-square distribution, (f) significant association, (g) scaling assumptions, (h) row percentages versus column percentages, and (i) degrees of freedom.

14-11. Listed here are various factors that may have relationships that are interesting to marketing managers. With each one, (1) identify the type of relationship, (2) indicate its nature or direction, and (3) specify how knowledge of the relationship could help a marketing manager in designing marketing strategy.

a. The amount (number of minutes per day) of time spent reading certain sections of the Sunday newspaper and age of the reader for a sporting goods retail store.

b. Subscription to the local television cable company versus online TV viewing and household income (low or high) for a telemarketing service being used by a public television broadcasting station soliciting funds.

c. Number of miles driven in company cars and need for service such as oil changes, tune-ups, or filter changes for a quick auto service chain attempting to market fleet discounts to companies.

d. Plans to take a five-day vacation to Jamaica and the exchange rate of the Jamaican dollar to that of other countries for Sandals, an all-inclusive resort located in Montego Bay.

e. Homeowners opting for do-it-yourself home repairs and state of the economy (for example, a recession or a boom) for Ace Hardware stores.

14-12. Indicate the presence, nature, and strength of the relationship involving purchases of intermediate-size automobiles and each of the following factors: (a) price, (b) fabric versus leather interior, (c) exterior color, and (d) size of rebate.

14-13. With each of the following examples, compose a reasonable statement of an association you would expect to find existing between the factors involved, and construct a stacked bar chart expressing that association.

a. Wearing braces to straighten teeth by children attending expensive private schools versus those attending public schools.

b. Having a Doberman pinscher as a guard dog, use of a home security alarm system, and ownership of rare pieces of art.

c. Adopting MyPlate eating style recommended by the U.S. Department of Argiculture and family history of heart disease.

d. Purchasing toys as gifts during the Christmas buying season versus other seasons of the year by parents of preschool-aged children.

14-14. Following is some information about 10 respondents to a mail survey concerning candy purchases. Use SPSS to construct the four different types of cross-tabulation tables that are possible. Label each table and indicate what you perceive to be the general relationship apparent in the data.

Respondent	Buy Plain M&Ms	Buy Peanut M&Ms
1	Yes	No
2	Yes	No
3	No	Yes
4	Yes	No
5	No	No
6	No	Yes
7	No	No
8	Yes	No
9	Yes	No
10	No	Yes

14-15. Morton O'Dell is the owner of Mort's Diner, which is located in downtown Atlanta, Georgia. Mort's opened up about 12 months ago, and it has experienced success. But Mort is always worried about what food items to order on a weekly basis because, on some weeks, Mort has excess inventory, such as too much fish that must be discarded. Mort's daughter, Mary, is an M.B.A. student at Georgia State University, and she offers to help her father. She asks him to provide sales data for the past 10 weeks in terms of total pounds of food bought by customers. With some difficulty, Mort comes up with the following numbers.

Week	Meat	Fish	Fowl	Vegetables	Desserts
1	100	50	150	195	50
2	91	55	182	200	64
3	82	60	194	209	70
4	75	68	211	215	82
5	66	53	235	225	73
6	53	61	253	234	53
7	64	57	237	230	68
8	76	64	208	221	58
9	94	68	193	229	62
10	105	58	181	214	62

Mary uses these sales figures to construct scatter diagrams that illustrate the basic relationships among the various types of food items purchased at Mort's Diner over the past 10 weeks. She tells her father that the diagrams provide some help in his weekly inventory ordering problem. Construct Mary's scatter diagrams with SPSS to indicate what assistance they are to Mort. Perform the appropriate associated analysis with SPSS and interpret your findings.

CASE 14.1

L'Experience Félicité Restaurant Survey Associative Analysis IBM **SPSS**

(For necessary background, read Case 12.1 on page 346, and Case 13.1 on page 375.)

Cory Rogers calls in his marketing intern, Christine Yu, and says, "I am going to be in San Francisco attending the AMA Marketing Research Event for three days, but I need you to make progress on the L'Experience Félicité Restaurant survey. I know you might be a bit lost with this project, but why don't you take a look at the proposal, and see if there is any further analysis that you can do while I am out. Have Tonya pull the proposal from the file." Christine immediately looks at the research proposal, and she jots down some notes with respect to research questions that need to be addressed. Her notes follow.

Your task in Case 14.1 is to use the L'Experience Félicité Restaurant SPSS dataset and perform the proper analysis. You will also need to interpret the findings.

1. Perform the correct analysis and interpret your findings with regard to the L'Experience Félicité Restaurant menu, décor, and atmosphere for those people who prefer to drive less than 30 minutes to get to the restaurant.

2. Do older or younger people want unusual desserts and/or unusual entrées?

3. Use the variable that distinguishes the "Probable patrons" of L'Experience Félicité Restaurant (Likely to patronize = 1 or 2) from the "Not probable patrons" (Likely to patronize = 3, 4, or 5). If the probable

patrons constitute L'Experience Félicité Restaurant's target market, what is the demographic makeup of this target market? Use the demographics of household income, education level, gender, and ZIP code.

4. Is *City Magazine* a viable advertising medium for Jeff Dean to use? Apart from this question, are there other viable promotion vehicles that Jeff should know about?

CASE 14.2　INTEGRATED CASE

The Auto Concepts Survey Associative Analysis

IBM **SPSS**

Cory Rogers of CMG Research was very pleased with the way the Auto Concepts project was shaping up. Celeste Brown, the CMG data analyst, had applied differences analysis using the desirability measures for the various alternative automobile models that might be developed, and she had found a unique demographic target market profile for each model. Celeste had summarized her findings into a professional PowerPoint presentation that Cory and Celeste presented to Nick Thomas and his assembled managers just yesterday. The presentation was one of the smoothest possible, and Nick's development team members became very excited and animated when they realized that Auto Concepts had a possibility of multiple "winner" model vehicles to work with. In fact, at the end of the meeting, Nick had decided to go ahead with a preliminary marketing plan for each model.

Nick informed Cory and Celeste that all automobile companies place a huge amount of emphasis on communications, investing millions of dollars every year in many different types of advertising to convince prospective customers that their models are the best possible choices. Nick explained, "Everything is based on solid marketing research that reveals the media usage characteristics of each target market. That is why I insisted on including the media usage information in our Auto Concepts survey. My superiors will most certainly shoot us down if we come to it with any preliminary marketing plan for any proposed automobile model that does not have advertising recommendations based on media usage research. I did not realize at the time that we would be working on all five models, but each of my development teams will need whatever media usage findings you can come up with for its particular model."

Cory and Celeste are in a meeting the following day to discuss further analysis for the Auto Concepts project. Cory says, "I recall that we have a lot of detail on the media habits of the survey respondents. Let's see, it includes favorite television show type, radio genre, magazine type, and local newspaper section as well as four different types of social marketing media. Nick Thomas called this morning and asked if we could have our findings to him inside of a week, so I guess he and his team are moving very fast. Nick also told me that the advertising agency they use has strong preferences as to which demographic factors should be used for the different media. Nick says that for radio

they prefer to use age; for newspaper and television, they prefer to use education; and for magazines, they prefer to use income. Social media are somewhat new, so if you could find distinct profiles for these, it would be like icing on the cake."

Celeste says, "I can get to it by the end of this week and have it ready to present early next week, assuming no glitches." Cory concludes the meeting by saying, "Great, just let me know on Friday morning how it is coming, as I told Nick I will call him on that day to set up the presentation."

Your task in Case 14.2 is to revisit Case 13.2 where Celeste used differences analyses to find the unique demographic profiles for each of the five possible new models.

  a. "Super Cycle," One-Seat All Electric, mpg-e rating 125; estimated MSRP (manufacturer's suggested retail price) $30,000; range 200 miles.
  b. "Runabout Sport," Two-Seat All Electric, mpg-e 99; estimated MSRP $35,000; range 150 miles.
  c. "Runabout Hatchback," Two-Seat Gasoline Hybrid, mpg-e 50; runs on battery for 50 miles and then switches to gas engine; estimated MSRP $35,000; range 250 miles.
  d. "Economy Hybrid," Four-Seat Diesel Hybrid, mpg-e 75; runs on battery for 75 miles and then switches to efficient diesel engine; estimated MSRP $38,000; range 300 miles.
  e. "Economy Standard," Five-Seat Standard Gasoline, mpg 36; runs on gasoline with computer control for maximum efficiency; estimated MSRP $37,000; range 350 miles.

1. Use each unique automobile model demographic profile to determine whether or not statistically significant associations exist, and if they do, recommend the specific media vehicles for radio, newspaper, television, and magazines. Do not forget to use the advertising division's preferred demographic for each medium.
2. What is the social media profile of each of the possible target markets, and what are the implications of this finding for the placement of advertising messages that would "speak" to this market segment when the automobile model is introduced?

15 Understanding Regression Analysis Basics

"WHERE WE ARE"

1 Establish the need for marketing research.

2 Define the problem.

3 Establish research objectives.

4 Determine research design.

5 Identify information types and sources.

6 Determine methods of accessing data.

7 Design data collection forms.

8 Determine the sample plan and size.

9 Collect data.

10 Analyze data.

11 Prepare and present the final research report.

MESH Experience

Fiona Blades, chief experience officer, MESH Experience

In 2006 MESH was set up to help clients make quicker and smarter decisions about their marketing and trade investment. Brand growth is driven by *all* experiences people have with brands, yet half or more typically go unmeasured. By taking an experience-driven marketing approach and capturing how people come into contact with brands in real time (real-time experience tracking—RET), MESH helps clients measure and create experiences that grow brands, people, and society. With over a million experiences collected across many countries during the last decade, MESH has a rich dataset to mine to understand how people experience brands today.

MESH operates globally out of offices in New York, London, Sao Paulo, and Singapore (entity and virtual team) servicing annual and ad hoc contracts for clients across a variety of sectors including financial services, the automotive industry, airlines, electronics, utilities, mobile networks, and packaged goods. Major clients include LG Electronics, Delta Air Lines, Diageo, General Motors, Unilever, Heineken, PepsiCo, and Latin American Airlines.

What sets MESH apart is its development of innovative and bespoke tools to help CEOs and marketers have the right information at their fingertips just when they need it. Experience-driven marketing provides a human-centered approach in a complex world. It can unlock new opportunities for brand growth.

MESH's state-of-the-art Experience Intelligence Unit has developed proprietary tools and interfaces to provide clients with data today that predict customers' behavior tomorrow. New experience metrics transform a marketer's ability to take action. For instance, *share of experience* is much more predictive of brand growth than *share of voice*.

Pioneering the Real-time Experience Tracking (RET)™ market, MESH captures every way customers come into contact with a client's brand and its competitors' brands. *Harvard Business Review* (September 2012) described RET as "a new tool (that) radically improves marketing research."

Sustainable research offers companies a unique way of getting a deeper customer understanding while building sustainability credentials. This award-winning work with PepsiCo in Brazil acted as a change agent for Pepsi stakeholders to understand the emerging middle class. MESH business strategists work with researchers to provide robust information that clearly signals the actions needed by a client's team.

Source: Text and photos courtesy of Fiona Blades, President and Chief Experience Officer, MESH.

M ESH
The Experience Agency

Visit the MESH Experience at
www.meshexperience.com

This chapter takes up the subject of multiple regression analysis. Undoubtedly, your reading of Fiona Blades's company clued you into the fact that an important goal of marketing research is insight, the deeper the better. Your own perceptive insight should alert you to the fact that we are going to describe a very complex analytical technique. We will endeavor to describe multiple regression analysis in a slow and methodical manner, and when we end our description, we will warn you that, while you have learned to run it and interpret its findings, we have barely scratched the surface of this complicated analysis.

15-1 Bivariate Linear Regression Analysis

In this chapter, we will deal exclusively with linear regression analysis, a predictive model technique often used by marketing researchers. However, regression analysis is a complex statistical technique with a large number of requirements and nuances.[1] Because this chapter is basically an introduction to this area, we will remind you toward the end of the material that there are a great many aspects of regression analysis that are beyond the scope of this textbook.

We first define **regression analysis** as a predictive analysis technique in which one or more variables are used to predict the level of another by use of the straight-line formula. **Bivariate regression** means only two variables are being analyzed, and researchers sometimes refer to this case as "simple regression." We will review the equation for a straight line and introduce basic terms used in regression. We also describe some basic computations and significance with bivariate regression.

A straight-line relationship underlies regression, and it is a powerful predictive model. Figure 15.1 illustrates a straight-line relationship, and you should refer to it as we describe the elements in a general straight-line formula. The formula for a straight-line relationship is shown here:

Formula for a straight-line relationship

$$y = a + bx$$

With bivariate regression, one variable is used to predict another variable using the formula for a straight line.

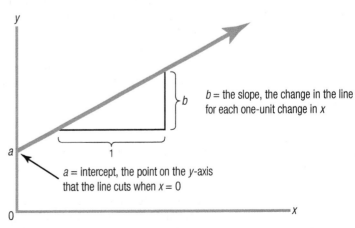

b = the slope, the change in the line for each one-unit change in x

a = intercept, the point on the y-axis that the line cuts when $x = 0$

FIGURE 15.1 General Equation for a Straight Line in Graph Form

The straight-line equation is the basis of regression analysis.

where

y = the predicted variable

x = the variable used to predict y

a = the **intercept**, or point where the line cuts the y axis when $x = 0$

b = the **slope** or the change in y for any one-unit change in x

Regression is directly related to correlation by the underlying straight-line relationship.

You should recall the straight-line relationship we described underlying the correlation coefficient: When the scatter diagram for two variables appears as a thin ellipse, there is a high correlation between them. Regression is directly related to correlation.

BASIC CONCEPTS IN REGRESSION ANALYSIS

We now define the variables and show how the intercept and slope are computed. Then we use SPSS output to show how tests of significance are interpreted.

In regression, the independent variable is used to predict the dependent variable.

Independent and Dependent Variables As we indicated, bivariate regression analysis is a case in which only two variables are involved in the predictive model. When we use only two variables, one is termed *dependent* and the other is termed *independent*. The **dependent variable** is that which is predicted, and it is customarily termed y in the regression straight-line equation. The **independent variable** is that which is used to predict the dependent variable, and it is the x in the regression formula. We must quickly point out that the terms *dependent* and *independent* are arbitrary designations and are customary to regression analysis. There is no cause-and-effect relationship or true dependence between the dependent and independent variables. It is strictly a statistical relationship, not causal, that may be found between these two variables.

Computing the Slope and the Intercept To compute a (intercept) and b (slope), you must work with a number of observations of the various levels of the dependent variable paired with different levels of the independent variable, identical to the scatter diagrams we illustrated previously when we were demonstrating how to perform correlation analysis.

The formulas for calculating the slope (b) and the intercept (a) are rather complicated, but some instructors are in favor of their students learning these formulas, so we have included them in Marketing Research Insight 15.1.

The least squares criterion used in regression analysis guarantees that the "best" straight-line slope and intercept will be calculated.

When SPSS or any other statistical analysis program computes the intercept and the slope in a regression analysis, it does so on the basis of the least squares criterion. The **least squares criterion** is a way of guaranteeing that the straight line that runs through the points on the scatter diagram is positioned so as to minimize the vertical distances away from the line of the various points. In other words, if you draw a line where the regression line is calculated and calculate the distances of all the points away from that line (called *residuals*), it would be impossible to draw any other line that would result in a lower sum of all of those distances. The least squares criterion guarantees that the line is the one with the lowest total squared residuals. Each residual is squared to avoid a cancellation effect of positive and negative residuals.

Marketing Research on YouTube™ To learn about linear regression, launch **www. youtube. com**, and search for "Intro to Linear Regression."

HOW TO IMPROVE A REGRESSION ANALYSIS FINDING

When a researcher wants to improve a regression analysis, the researcher can use a scatter diagram to identify outlier pairs of points. An **outlier**[2] is a data point that is substantially outside the normal range of the data points being analyzed. As one author has noted, outliers "stick out like sore thumbs."[3] When using a scatter diagram to identify outliers,[4] draw an ellipse that encompasses most of the points that appear to be in an elliptical pattern.[5] Then eliminate outliers from the data and rerun the regression analysis. Generally, this approach will improve the regression analysis results.

MARKETING RESEARCH INSIGHT 15.1   *Practical Application*

How to Calculate the Intercept and Slope of a Bivariate Regression

In this example, we are using the Novartis pharmaceuticals company sales territory and number of salespersons data found in Table 15.1. Intermediate regression calculations are included later in the chapter in Table 15.2.

TABLE 15.1   Bivariate Regression Analysis Data and Intermediate Calculations

Territory (l)	Sales ($ millions) (y)	Number of Salespersons (x)	xy	x^2
1	102	7	714	49
2	125	5	625	25
3	150	9	1,350	81
4	155	9	1,395	81
5	160	9	1,440	81
6	168	8	1,344	64
7	180	10	1,800	100
8	220	10	2,200	100
9	210	12	2,520	144
10	205	12	2,460	144
11	230	12	2,760	144
12	255	15	3,825	225
13	250	14	3,500	196
14	260	15	3,900	225
15	250	16	4,320	256
16	275	16	4,400	256
17	280	17	4,760	289
18	240	18	4,320	324
19	300	18	5,400	324
20	310	19	5,890	361
Sums	**4,325**	**251**	**58,603**	**3,469**
	(Average = 216,25)	(Average = 12.55)		

The formula for computing the regression parameter b is:

Formula for b, the slope, in bivariate regression

$$b = \frac{n\sum_{i=1}^{n} x_i y_i - \left(\sum_{i=1}^{n} x_i\right)\left(\sum_{i=1}^{n} y_i\right)}{n\sum_{i=1}^{n} x_i^2 - \left(\sum_{i=1}^{n} x_i\right)^2}$$

where

x_i = an x variable value
y_i = a y value paired with each x_i value
n = the number of pairs

The calculations for b, the slope, are as follows:

Calculation of b, the slope, in bivariate regression using Novartis sales territory data

$$b = \frac{n\sum_{i=1}^{n} x_i y_i - \left(\sum_{i=1}^{n} x_i\right)\left(\sum_{i=1}^{n} y_i\right)}{n\sum_{i=1}^{n} x_i^2 - \left(\sum_{i=1}^{n} x_i\right)^2}$$

$$= \frac{20 \times 58603 - 251 \times 4325}{20 \times 3469 - 251^2}$$

$$= \frac{1172060 - 1085575}{69380 - 63001}$$

$$= \frac{86485}{6379}$$

$$= 13.56$$

Notes:

$n = 20$
Sum $xy = 58.603$
Sum of $x = 251$
Sum of $y = 4.325$
Sum of $x^2 = 3.469$

The formula for computing the intercept is:

Formula for a, the intercept, in bivariate regression

$$a = \bar{y} - b\bar{x}$$

The computations for a, the intercept, are as follows:

Calculation of a, the intercept, in bivariate regression using Novartis sales territory data

$$a = \bar{y} - b\bar{x}$$
$$= 216.25 - 13.56 \times 12.55$$
$$= 216.25 - 170.15$$
$$= 46.10$$

Notes:

$\bar{y} = 216.25$
$\bar{x} = 12.55$

In other words, the bivariate regression equation has been found to be:

Novartis sales regression equation

$$y = 46.10 + 13.56x$$

The interpretation of this equation is as follows: Annual sales in the average Novartis sales territory are $46.10 million, and they increase $13.56 million annually with each additional salesperson.

15-2 Multiple Regression Analysis

We follow up our introduction to bivariate regression analysis by discussing multiple regression analysis. You will find that all of the concepts in bivariate regression apply to multiple regression analysis, except you will be working with multiple independent variables.

AN UNDERLYING CONCEPTUAL MODEL

A *model* is a structure that ties together various constructs and their relationships. It is beneficial for the marketing manager and the market researcher to have some sort of model in mind when designing the research plan. The bivariate regression equation that you just learned about is a model that ties together an independent variable and its dependent variable. The dependent variables that interest market researchers are typically sales, potential sales, or some attitude held by those who make up the market. For instance, in the Novartis example, the dependent variable was territory sales. If Dell computers commissioned a survey, it might want information on those who intend to purchase a Dell computer, or it might want information on those who intend to buy a competing brand as a means of understanding these consumers and perhaps dissuading them. The dependent variable would be purchase intentions for Dell computers. If managers at Maxwell House Coffee were considering a line of gourmet iced coffee, they would want to know how coffee drinkers feel about gourmet iced coffee; that is, their attitude toward buying, preparing, and drinking iced coffee would be the dependent variable.

Figure 15.2 provides a general conceptual model that fits many marketing research situations, particularly those that are investigating consumer behavior. A **general conceptual model** identifies independent and dependent variables and shows their expected basic relationships to one another. In Figure 15.2, you can see that purchases, intentions to purchase, and preferences are in the center, meaning they are dependent. The surrounding concepts are the possible independent variables. That is, any one could be used to predict any dependent variable. For example, intentions to purchase an expensive automobile like a Lexus could depend on income. It could also depend on friends' recommendations (word of mouth), personal opinion about how a Lexus would enhance one's self-image, or experiences riding in or driving a Lexus.

In truth, consumers' preferences, intentions, and actions are potentially influenced by a great number of factors, as would be very evident if you listed all of the subconcepts that make up each concept in Figure 15.2. For example, there are probably a dozen different demographic variables; there could be dozens of lifestyle dimensions; and a person is exposed to a great many types of advertising media every day. Of course, in the problem definition stage, the researcher and manager reduce the myriad of independent variables down to a manageable number to be included on the questionnaire. That is, they have the general model structure in Figure 15.2 in mind, but they identify and measure specific variables that pertain to the problem at hand. Because bivariate regression analysis treats only dependent–independent pairs, it would take a great many bivariate regression analyses to account for all the possible relevant dependent–independent pairs of variables in a general model such as Figure 15.2. Fortunately, there is no need to perform a great many bivariate regressions, as there is a much better tool called *multiple regression analysis*, a technique we will describe in some detail.

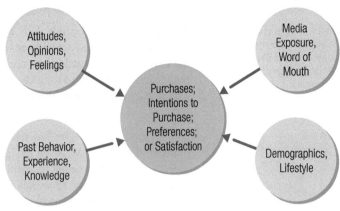

FIGURE 15.2 A General Conceptual Model for Multiple Regression Analysis

There is an underlying general conceptual model in multiple regression analysis.

The researcher and the manager identify, measure, and analyze specific variables that pertain to the general conceptual model in mind.

 **Active Learning**

The General Conceptual Model for Auto Concepts

Understandably, Nick Thomas, CEO of Auto Concepts, wants everyone to intend to purchase a new gasoline alternative technology automobile; however, this will not be the case due to different beliefs and predispositions in the driving public. Regression analysis will assist Nick by revealing what variables are good predictors of intentions to buy the various new technology automobile models under consideration at Auto Concepts. What is the general conceptual model apparent in the Auto Concepts survey dataset?

In order to answer this question and to portray the general conceptual model in the format of Figure 15.2, you must inspect the several variables in this SPSS dataset or otherwise come up with a list of the variables in the survey. A handy list of all these variables is found in Case 12.2 on page 348. Using the "Desirability" variable as the dependent variable, diagram the general types of independent or predictor variables that are apparent in this study. Comment on the usefulness of this general conceptual model to Nick Thomas; that is, assuming that the regression results are significant, what marketing strategy implications will become apparent?

MULTIPLE REGRESSION ANALYSIS DESCRIBED

Multiple regression means that you have more than one independent variable to predict a single dependent variable.

Multiple regression analysis is an expansion of bivariate regression analysis in that more than one independent variable is used in the regression equation. The addition of independent variables complicates the conceptualization by adding more dimensions or axes to the regression situation. But it makes the regression model more realistic because, as we have just explained with our general model discussion, predictions normally depend on multiple factors, not just one.

Basic Assumptions in Multiple Regression Consider our Novartis example with the number of salespeople as the independent variable and territory sales as the dependent variable. A second independent variable such as advertising levels can be added to the equation. The addition of a second variable turns the regression line into a regression plane because there are three dimensions if we were to try to graph it: territory sales (y), number of sales people (x_1), and advertising level (x_2). A **regression plane** is the shape of the dependent variable in multiple regression analysis. If other independent variables are added to the regression analysis, it would be necessary to envision each one as a new and separate axis existing at right angles to all other axes. Obviously, it is impossible to draw more than three dimensions at right angles. In fact, it is difficult to even conceive of a multiple-dimension diagram, but the assumptions of multiple regression analysis require this conceptualization.

With multiple regression, you work with a regression plane rather than a line.

Everything about multiple regression is largely equivalent to bivariate regression except you are working with more than one independent variable. The terminology is slightly different in places, and some statistics are modified to take into account the multiple aspects, but for the most part, concepts in multiple regression are analogous to those in the simple bivariate case. We note these similarities in our description of multiple regression.

The equation in multiple regression has the following form:

Multiple regression equation

$$y = a + b_1x_1 + b_2x_2 + b_3x_3 + \ldots + b_mx_m$$

where

A multiple regression equation has two or more independent variables (x's).

y = the dependent, or predicted, variable

x_i = independent variable i

a = the intercept

b_i = the slope for independent variable i

m = the number of independent variables in the equation

As you can see, the addition of other independent variables has done nothing more than to add b_ix_i's to the equation. We still have retained the basic $y = a + bx$ straight-line formula, except now we have multiple x variables, and each one is added to the equation, changing y by its individual slope. The inclusion of each independent variable in this manner preserves the straight-line assumptions of multiple regression analysis. This is sometimes known as **additivity** because each new independent variable is added on to the regression equation.

Let's look at a multiple regression analysis result so you can better understand the multiple regression equation. Here is a possible result using our Lexus example.

Lexus purchase intention multiple regression equation example	Intention to purchase a Lexus = 2 + 1.0 × attitude toward Lexus (1–5 scale) − .5 × attitude toward current auto (1–5 scale) + 1.0 × income level (1–10 scale)	*Notes:* $a = 2$ $b_1 = 1.0$ $b_2 = -.5$ $b_3 = 1.0$

This multiple regression equation says that you can predict a consumer's level of intention to buy a Lexus if you know three variables: (1) attitude toward the Lexus brand,

(2) attitude toward the automobile the consumer owns now, and (3) income level using a scale with 10 income grades. Further, we can see the impact of each of these variables on Lexus purchase intentions. Here is how to interpret the equation. First, the average person has a 2 intention level, or some small propensity to want to buy a Lexus. Attitude toward Lexus is measured on a 1–5 scale, and with each attitude scale point, intention goes up one point. That is, an individual with a strong positive attitude of 5 will have a greater intention than one with a strong negative attitude of 1. With attitude toward the current automobile he or she owns (for example, a potential Lexus buyer may currently own a Cadillac or a BMW), the intention *decreases* by .5 for each level on the 5-point scale. Of course, we are assuming that these potential buyers own automobile models other than a Lexus. Finally, the intention increases by 1 with each increasing income grade.

Here is a numerical example for a potential Lexus buyer whose Lexus attitude is 4, current automobile model attitude is 3, and income is 5.

Calculation of Lexus purchase intention using the multiple regression equation	Intention to purchase a Lexus = 2 + 1.0 × 4 − .5 × 3 + 1.0 × 5 = 9.5	*Notes:* *Intercept = 2* *Attitude toward Lexus (x_1) = 4* *Attitude toward current auto (x_2) = 3* *Income level (x_3) = 5*

Multiple regression is a very powerful tool because it tells us what factors are related to the dependent variable, how each factor influences the dependent variable (the sign), and how much each factor influences it (the size of b_i).

It is possible to inspect the strength of the linear relationship between the independent variables and the dependent variable with multiple regression. Multiple R, also called the **coefficient of determination**, is a handy measure of the strength of the overall linear relationship. Just as in bivariate regression analysis, the multiple regression analysis model assumes that a straight-line (plane) relationship exists among the variables. Multiple R ranges from 0 to +1.0 and represents the amount of the dependent variable "explained," or accounted for, by the combined independent variables. High multiple R values indicate that the regression plane applies well to the scatter of points, whereas low values signal that the straight-line model does not apply well. At the same time, a multiple regression result is an estimate of the population multiple regression equation and, just as is the case with other estimated population parameters, it is necessary to test for statistical significance.

Multiple R indicates how well the independent variables can predict the dependent variable in multiple regression.

Multiple R is like a lead indicator of the multiple regression analysis findings. As you will see soon, it is one of the first pieces of information provided in a multiple regression output. Many researchers mentally convert the multiple R value into a percentage. For example, a multiple R of .75 means that the regression findings will explain 75% of the dependent variable. The greater the explanatory power of the multiple regression finding, the better and more useful it is for the researcher.

Before we show you how to run a multiple regression analysis using SPSS, consider this caution. The **independence assumption** stipulates that the independent variables must be statistically independent and uncorrelated with one another. The independence assumption is very important because, if it is violated, the multiple regression findings are untrue. The presence of moderate or stronger correlations among the independent variables is termed **multicollinearity** and will violate the independence assumption of multiple regression analysis results when it occurs.[6] It is up to the researcher to test for and remove multicollinearity if it is present.

With multiple regression, the independent variables should have low correlations with one another.

The way to avoid multicollinearity is to use warning statistics issued by most statistical analysis programs to identify this problem. One commonly used method is the **variance inflation factor (VIF)**. The VIF is a single number, and a rule of thumb is that as long as VIF is less than 10, multicollinearity is not a concern. With a VIF greater than 10 associated with any independent variable in the multiple regression equation, it is prudent to remove that

Multicollinearity can be assessed and eliminated in multiple regression with the VIF statistic.

variable from consideration or to otherwise reconstitute the set of independent variables.[7] In other words, when examining the output of any multiple regression, the researcher should inspect the VIF number associated with each independent variable that is retained in the final multiple regression equation by the procedure. If VIF is greater than 10, the researcher should remove that variable from the independent variable set and rerun the multiple regression.[8] This iterative process is used until only independent variables that are statistically significant and that have acceptable VIFs are in the final multiple regression equation.

Although you have not learned how to run multiple regression analysis on SPSS, you have sufficient knowledge to realize that this analysis can provide interesting insights into consumer behavior. We have prepared Marketing Research Insight 15.2 to demonstrate an application of multiple regression analysis in the social media marketing research arena.

MARKETING RESEARCH INSIGHT 15.2 — *Digital Marketing Research*

Multiple Regression Reveals Why Fans Post Likes and Comments on Facebook

Of the several social media platforms, Facebook is perhaps the oldest and most widely used. For many companies, Facebook is the premier social media promotional vehicle, and companies have a number of tactics or aspects of their posts on Facebook available to engage followers. With Facebook, there are two measures of such engagement: (1) likes and (2) comments. Fans may click a "like" icon on a post to indicate that they feel positive about the post. Company posts with a large number of likes are successful, whereas posts with few or no likes are considered unsuccessful at garnering fan engagement. Alternatively, fans may post comments that are different with respect to engagement. Comments require fans to think about the post and to compose some phrase or statement about it. Thus, a comment requires more cognitive and physical effort than a like, so presumably the fan who comments on a company post has a deeper and longer-lasting engagement with the company than the fan who simply likes it.

Social media researchers recently sought to use multiple regression as a means of understanding what aspects of company posts are related to likes and comments.[9] They identified the following six aspects of company posts that qualified as independent variables.

- Followers—the number of followers of the brand
- Characters—the number of words in the company post
- Links—the number of links in the post
- Images—the number of images within the post
- Videos—the number of videos in the post
- Time—time of day of the post, measured by a 24-hour clock

The dependent variables for the two multiple regression analyses were number of likes and number of comments. These analyses found statistically significant independent variables that differed. Since this was not an attempt to predict the number of likes or comments, only the signs of the significant betas are relevant. A summary of the findings appears in the following table.

Facebook Post Aspect	Likes	Comments
Followers	+	+
Characters	+	
Links		−
Images	+	+
Videos	+	
Time of day		+

As can be seen, likes are strongly influenced by the number of followers, length of the post, number of images, and videos. Comments, on the other hand, are related to the number of followers, number of images, and time of day of the post. Also comments are dampened or discouraged by the number of links in the post.

These findings make it clear that companies should strive for large numbers of followers because more followers are associated with both more likes and more comments on any given company Facebook post. Longer Facebook posts with more images and videos are highly "likable" or otherwise associated with a greater number of like votes. More images and posting later in the day tend to garner more comments; however, links are apparently distracting and perhaps pull fans off the Facebook site and onto other sites before they take the time to write a comment to the post.

INTEGRATED CASE

Auto Concepts: How to Run and Interpret Multiple Regression Analysis on SPSS

IBM **SPSS**

Running multiple regression first requires specification of the dependent and independent variables. Let's select the desirability of the five-seat, standard-size gasoline automobile model as the dependent variable, and think about a general conceptual model that might pertain to Auto Concepts. We already know from basic marketing strategy that demographics are often used for target marketing, and we have hometown size, age, income, education, and household size. Also, beliefs are often useful for predicting market segments, and we have some variables that pertain to beliefs about gasoline usage and global warming. To summarize, we have determined our conceptual model: the desirability of a standard-size gasoline automobile related to (1) household demographics and (2) beliefs about global warming and gasoline usage. Where appropriate, we have recoded the ordinal demographic variables with midpoints to convert them to ratio scales. If you wish to perform this analysis, use the dataset called *Auto Concepts.Recoded.sav.*

The ANALYZE-REGRESSION-LINEAR command sequence is used to run a multiple regression analysis, and the variable Desirability: 5-seat economy gasoline model is selected as the dependent variable, while the other 11 are specified as the independent variables. You will find this annotated SPSS clickstream in Figure 15.3.

The SPSS ANALYZE-REGRESSION-LINEAR command is used to run multiple regression.

As the computer output in Figure 15.4 shows, the multiple R value (Adjusted R Square in the Model Summary table) indicating the strength of relationship between the independent variables and the dependent variable is .249, signifying that there is some linear relationship present. Next, the printout reveals that the ANOVA F is significant, signaling that the null hypothesis of no linear relationship is rejected, and it is justifiable to use a straight-line relationship to model the variables in this case.

It is necessary in multiple regression analysis to test for statistical significance of the b_i (beta) determined for each independent variable. In other words, you must determine whether

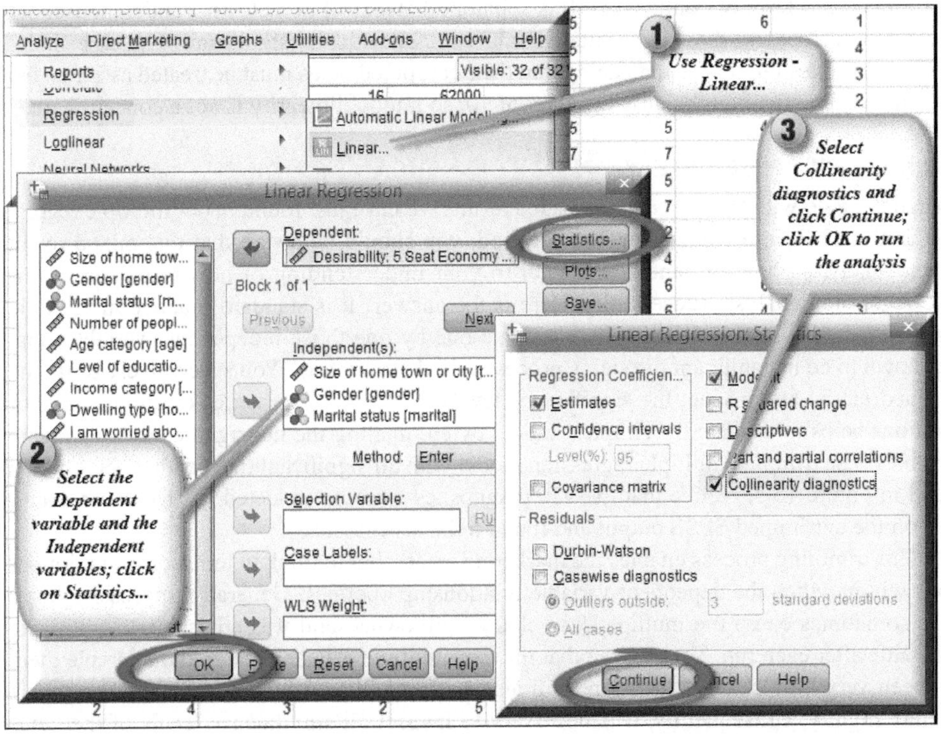

FIGURE 15.3 IBM SPSS Clickstream for Multiple Regression Analysis

Source: Reprint Courtesy of International Business Machines Corporation, © International Business Machines Corporation.

FIGURE 15.4
IBM SPSS Output for Multiple Regression Analysis

Source: Reprint Courtesy of International Business Machines Corporation, © International Business Machines Corporation.

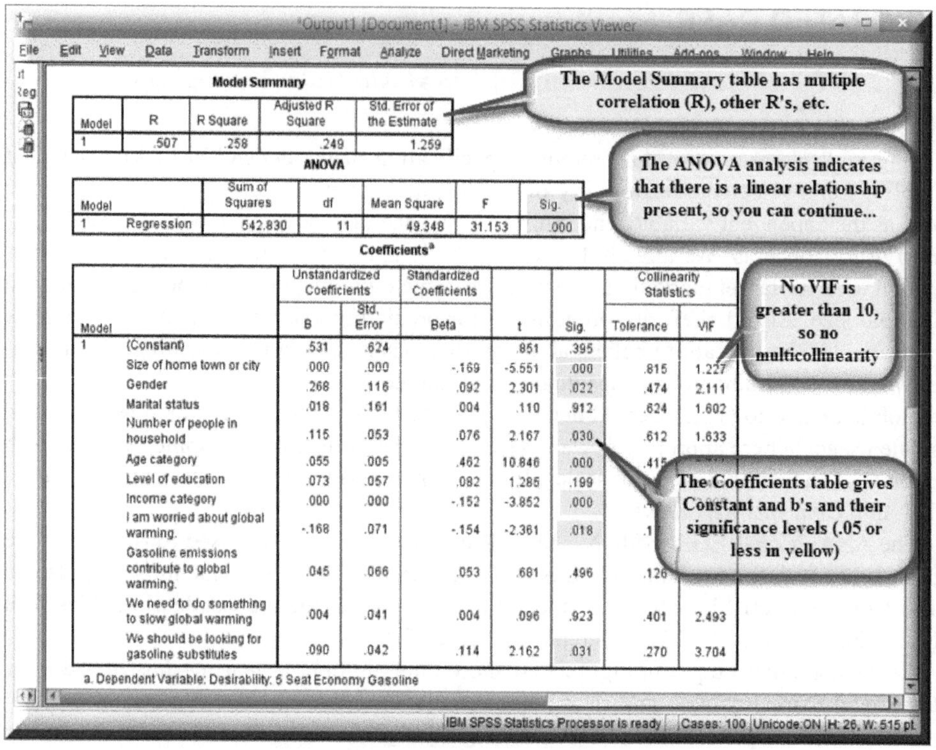

With multiple regression, look at the significance level of each calculated beta.

sampling error is influencing the results and giving a false reading. One must test for significance from zero (the null hypothesis) through the use of separate *t* tests for each b_i. The SPSS output in Figure 15.4 indicates the levels of statistical significance in the Coefficients table in the Sig. column, and we have highlighted in yellow the cases where the significance level is .05 or less (95% level of confidence). It is apparent that size of hometown, gender, household size, age, income, and the two attitude variables are statistically significant. The other independent variables fail this test, meaning that their computed betas must be treated as zeros. No VIF value is greater than the problem level of 10, so multicollinearity is not a concern here.

"TRIMMING" THE REGRESSION FOR SIGNIFICANT FINDINGS

What do you do with the mixed significance results we have just found in our multiple regression analysis? Before we answer this question, you should be aware that this mixed result is very likely, so how to handle it is vital to your understanding of how to perform multiple regression analysis successfully. Here is the answer: It is standard practice in multiple regression analysis to systematically eliminate one by one those independent variables that are shown to be insignificant through a process called "trimming." You successively rerun the trimmed model and inspect the significance levels each time. This series of eliminations or iterations helps to achieve the simplest model by eliminating the nonsignificant independent variables. The trimmed multiple regression model with all significant independent variables is found in Figure 15.5. Notice that the VIF diagnostics were not selected, as they were examined on the untrimmed SPSS output and found to be acceptable.

A trimmed regression means that you eliminate the nonsignificant independent variables and rerun the regression.

This trimming process enables the marketing researcher to think in terms of fewer dimensions within which the dependent variable relationship operates. Generally, successive iterations sometimes cause the multiple *R* to change somewhat, and it is advisable to scrutinize this value after each run. You can see that the new multiple *R* is .250, so in our example there has been very little change. Iterations will also cause the beta values and the intercept value to shift slightly; consequently, it is necessary to inspect all significance levels of the betas

FIGURE 15.5
IBM SPSS Output for Trimmed Multiple Regression Analysis

Source: Reprint Courtesy of International Business Machines Corporation, © International Business Machines Corporation.

Model Summary

Model	R	R Square	Adjusted R Square	Std. Error of the Estimate
1	.505	.255	.250	1.258

The Model Summary table has multiple correlation (R), other R's, etc.

ANOVA

Model		Sum of Squares	df	Mean Square	F	Sig.
1	Regression	537.913	7	76.845	48.555	.000

The ANOVA analysis indicates that there is a linear relationship present, so you can continue...

The Coefficients table gives Constant and b's and their significance levels (all less than .05)

Coefficients[a]

Model		Unstandardized Coefficients B	Std. Error	Standardized Coefficients Beta	t	Sig.	Collinearity Statistics Tolerance	VIF
1	(Constant)	1.222	.302		4.049	.000		
	Size of home town or city	-7.532E-7	.000	-.175	-5.905	.000	.855	1.170
	Gender	.275	.113	.094	2.439	.015	.505	1.978
	Number of people in household	.131	.044	.086	2.948	.003	.873	1.146
	Age category	.055	.005	.465	11.050	.000	.423	2.362
	Income category	-6.185E-6	.000	-.128	-3.463	.001	.552	1.812
	I am worried about global warming.	-.087	.044	-.080	-1.993	.047	.467	2.141
	We should be looking for gasoline substitutes	.120	.032	.152	3.770	.000	.463	2.160

a. Dependent Variable: Desirability: 5 Seat Economy Gasoline

IBM SPSS Statistics Processor is ready   Cases: 100 Unicode:ON H: 321, V6 pt.

once again. Through a series of iterations, the marketing researcher finally arrives at the final regression equation expressing the salient independent variables and their linear relationships with the dependent variable. A concise predictive model has been found. Using the signs of the betas, the findings predict that people who prefer the five-seat economy gasoline model reside in smaller cities, have larger families, are older with less income, are less concerned about global warming, and agree that we should be looking for gasoline substitutes. Gender is also significant, but it is a "dummy" variable, which will be explained next.

Run trimmed regressions iteratively until all betas are significant.

IBM **SPSS**

IBM SPSS Student Assistant:
Running and Interpreting Multiple Regression

SPECIAL USES OF MULTIPLE REGRESSION ANALYSIS

We will return to our findings in Figure 15.5 shortly, but first we need to describe some special uses and considerations to keep in mind when running multiple regression analysis. These include using a "dummy" independent variable, examining standardized betas to compare the importance of independent variables, and using multiple regression as a screening device.

Using a "Dummy" Independent Variable A **dummy independent variable** is defined as one that is scaled with a nominal 0-versus-1 coding scheme. The 0-versus-1 code is traditional, but any two adjacent numbers might be used, such as 1-versus-2. The scaling assumptions that underlie multiple regression analysis require that the independent and dependent variables both be at least intervally scaled. However, there are instances in which a marketing researcher may want to use an independent variable that does not embody interval-scaling assumptions. It is not unusual, for instance, for the marketing researcher to wish to use a dichotomous or two-level variable as an independent variable in a multiple regression analysis. Some commonly used dummy variables are gender (males

Gender can be used as a dummy variable in multiple regression analysis.

The interval-at-minimum scaling assumption requirement of multiple regression may be relaxed by use of a dummy variable.

versus female), purchasing behavior (buyer versus nonbuyer), advertising exposure (recalled versus not recalled), and purchase history (first time buyer versus repeat buyer). For instance, with gender, a researcher may want to use a "0" for male and "1" for female as an independent variable. In these instances, it is usually permissible to go ahead and slightly violate the assumption of interval or ratio scaling (called "metric") for the independent variable to come up with a result that is in some degree interpretable. In our Auto Concepts multiple regression example, we used two dummy variables: Gender and Marital status. The other variables were metric or assumed to be metric (recall midrange recoding of the ordinal demographic variables). In Figure 15.4, gender is significant, and it has a positive beta sign, so since the dummy coding is 0 = male and 1 = female, females find the five-seat economy gasoline model more desirable than do males.

Using Standardized Betas to Compare the Importance of Independent Variables

Regardless of the application intentions of the marketing researcher, it is usually of interest to determine the relative importance of the independent variables in the final multiple regression result. Because independent variables are often measured with different units, it is erroneous to make direct comparisons between the calculated betas. For example, it is improper to directly compare the beta coefficient for family size to another for money spent per month on personal grooming because the units of measurement are so different (people versus dollars). The most common approach is to standardize the independent variables through a quick operation that involves dividing the difference between each independent variable value and its mean by the standard deviation of that independent variable. This results in what is called the **standardized beta coefficient**. In other words, standardization translates each independent value into the number of standard deviations away from its own mean. Essentially, this procedure transforms these variables into a set of values with a mean of 0 and a standard deviation equal to 1.0.

The researcher can compare standardized beta coefficients' sizes directly, but comparing unstandardized betas is like comparing apples and oranges.

Standardized, direct comparisons may be made among the resulting betas. The larger the absolute value of a standardized beta coefficient, the more relative importance it assumes in predicting the dependent variable. SPSS and most other statistical programs provide the standardized betas automatically. In Figure 15.5, we have highlighted the standardized betas with light green, and we will discuss how to interpret them shortly. You probably need a break from all of this technical information, so do so by reading about road rage exhibited by Chinese drivers in Marketing Research Insight 15.3.

Using Multiple Regression as a Screening Device A final important application of multiple regression analysis is as an identifying or **screening device**. That is, the marketing researcher may be faced with a large number and variety of prospective independent variables in a general conceptual model, and he or she may use multiple regression as a way of spotting the salient (statistically significant) independent variables for the dependent variable at hand. In this instance, the intent is *not* to determine some sort of a prediction of the dependent variable; rather, it may be to search for clues as to what factors help the researcher understand the behavior of this particular dependent variable. For instance, the researcher might be seeking market segmentation bases and could use regression to spot which demographic variables are related to the consumer behavior variable under study. The true purpose is to identify segments of the car-buying public that are more likely to purchase various vehicle models in the future; this goal is usually well served when multiple regression is used as a screening device to identify the salient

Used as a screening device, multiple regression analysis identifies independent variables that qualify to be part of the final equation.

MARKETING RESEARCH INSIGHT 15.3   *Global Application*

Multiple Regression Applied to Stressed-Out, Angry, Drunk Drivers: Chinese Road Ragers

"Road rage" occurs when vehicle drivers act out in dangerous and irrational ways. Wikipedia[10] lists the following manifestations of road rage:

- Generally driving aggressively, including suddenly accelerating or braking and close tailgating
- Cutting others off in a lane or deliberately preventing someone from merging
- Chasing other motorists
- Flashing lights and/or sounding the horn excessively
- Yelling or exhibiting disruptive behavior at roadside establishments
- Driving at high speeds in the median of a highway to terrify drivers in both lanes
- Gesturing rudely
- Shouting verbal abuses or threats
- Intentionally causing a collision between vehicles
- Hitting other vehicles
- Assaulting other motorists, their passengers, cyclists, or pedestrians
- Exiting the car to attempt to start confrontations, including striking other vehicles with an object
- Threatening to use or using a firearm or other deadly weapon
- Throwing projectiles from a moving vehicle with the intent of damaging other vehicles

As can be seen in this list, road rage ranges from vulgar and rude gestures to dangerous, life-threatening driving. Moreover, road rage is not isolated to a single country; just as automobiles are driven in every country in the world, rude and dangerous driving is found universally.

Compared to Western and European countries, the People's Republic of China has only recently joined the road rage club, but it has caught up quickly. Researchers recently studied the psychological makeup and other aspects of Chinese drivers in an attempt to understand Chinese road rage.[11] They measured the propensity for road rage with a "dangerous driving index" that has four components: emotional driving, aggressive driving, risky driving, and drunk driving. They also measured personality traits such as anger, sensation seeking, and

the like. Finally, they measured drivers' perceived stress levels. In the accompanying figure, the check marks indicate statistical significance at the .01 level or less.

	Dangerous Driving	Emotional Driving	Aggressive Driving	Risky Driving	Drunk Driving
Stressed	✓	✓			✓
Angry	✓		✓		
Sensation seeking	✓		✓	✓	
Altruistic			✓ *(minus)*		✓ *(minus)*

In general, dangerous Chinese drivers are stressed-out, angry, and sensation-seeking individuals. However, emotional driving occurs under stress regardless of internal anger or other personality factors. Aggressive driving that is not especially risky tends to occur with Chinese drivers who are angry, sensation seeking, and not altruistic. Risky Chinese drivers are not necessarily under stress or angry, but they are sensation seekers. Finally, drunk Chinese driving is most likely with stressed-out and nonaltruistic drivers who are not angry or sensation seekers.

Although the sample used in this research was composed strictly of Chinese drivers, the findings are intuitive and may apply to all raging drivers. Here are some tag lines that concerned organizations, such as the American Automobile Association, might consider using to quell road rage:

- Stressed? Don't take a drink to calm your nerves, and take the bus, the train, or car pool.
- Angry? Get a grip before getting behind the wheel.
- Need a thrill? Go to an amusement park or play an exciting video game instead of driving around.
- Don't like your coworkers or neighbors? Don't drown your sorrows in alcohol.

---

segmentation factors. We have included Marketing Research Insight 15.4 to illustrate the use of multiple regression analysis as a screening device.

Interpreting the Findings of Multiple Regression Analysis By now, you probably realize that our Auto Concepts multiple regression analysis example showed the use of multiple regression analysis to identify the significant demographic and/or attitudinal

MARKETING RESEARCH INSIGHT 15.4 — *Practical Application*

Using Multiple Regression Analysis as a Screening Device Simplifies Marketing Competition in the Optical Centers Industry

According to the Vision Council of America, about 75% of adults use some sort of vision correction. Many of these individuals use optical or vision centers for eye testing, diagnosis, and making purchases. Eyeglass purchasing is a unique phenomenon. Often vision is directly affected by age. That is, people with 20/20 vision almost invariably experience deterioration in vision, normally nearsightedness, as they age. It is quite common for individuals in their forties and fifties to realize that reading regular-sized print is difficult, so they turn to optical centers or other eye-testing alternatives for diagnosis and prescriptions for reading glasses. However, the decision to wear eyeglasses or contact lens is subject to a number of considerations. For instance, there are social influence factors, such as the advice of opinion leaders, family members, coworkers, or other acquaintances. There are psychological factors such as motivations, perceptions, and self-concept. Finally, there are individual differences such as gender or income.

Researchers[12] listed 13 possible competitive factors that might affect a consumer's decision to purchase eyeglasses and used multiple regression analysis to determine which ones were significant to the age-related eyeglasses purchase decision. These factors included the following:

- Design of the frame
- Lens brand
- Price
- Weight of the frame
- Warranty
- Treatment of the lens (such as scratch resistance, etc.)
- Materials making up the lens (glass, plastic, etc.)
- Lens type (such as polarized, bifocals, etc.)
- Lens accessories
- Purchase promotion
- Eye exam
- Point-of-sale service
- Advertising

Due to the several independent variables identified, the researchers used multiple regression analysis as a screening device to identify the statistically significant ones. Three variables were found to be significant at the 95% level of confidence, while a fourth one was significant at the 90% level of confidence. To be more precise, price, warranty, and advertising comprise the first three statistically significant independent variables, and point-of-sale service was the fourth one. Interestingly, advertising was found to have a negative beta coefficient, whereas the other three exhibited positive relationships.

Interpretation of these findings gives marketing strategy recommendations for optical centers: (1) offer competitive prices, (2) incorporate attractive warranties, (3) ensure that point-of-sale purchase employees and systems are top-notch, and (4) do not engage in advertising battles with other optical centers.

---

independent variables. That is, it was used as a screening device. Now, let's look at the standardized beta values (green highlight in Figure 15.5) to interpret our findings. Interpretation is facilitated by the relative sizes of the standardized betas and their signs. A positive value means that there is a positive relationship, so people who prefer the five-seat economy gasoline automobile model are males (dummy coded with 0 = female and 1 = male), have more people in their households, are older, and tend to believe that we should be looking for gasoline substitutes. A negative sign means that there is a negative relationship, so desire for the five-seat economy gasoline automobile model tends to be higher for individuals living in smaller hometowns, with lower income, and with people who are less worried about global warming. Because it has the highest absolute standardized beta (.465), age is the most important variable in identifying people desiring the five-seat economy gasoline model, and hometown size is the next most important, with belief that we should be looking for gasoline substitutes falling in third place. When you examine the standardized betas and take into consideration their relative sizes and signs, you can develop a mental market segment picture of the kind of individual who would comprise the target market if Auto Concepts develops a standard-size gasoline automobile model. You can also begin to understand these consumers' desires for a gasoline-powered automobile: They are not worried about global warming.

Standardized betas indicate the relative importance of alternative predictor variables.

 **Active Learning**

Segmentation Associates, Inc.

Segmentation Associates, Inc., is a marketing research company that specializes in market segmentation studies. It has access to large and detailed databases on demographics, lifestyles, asset ownership, consumer values, and a number of other consumer descriptors. It has developed a reputation for reducing these large databases into findings that are managerially relevant to its clients. That is, Segmentation Associates is known for its ability to translate its findings into market segmentation variables for its clients to use in their marketing strategies.

In the past year, Segmentation Associates has conducted a great many market segmentation studies for a number of automobile manufacturers. The company has agreed to provide disguised findings of some of its work. In the following table segmentation variables are identified, and each of three different automobile buyer types is identified. For each segmentation variable, Segmentation Associates has provided the results of its multiple regression findings. The values are the standardized beta coefficients of those segmentation variables found to statistically significant. Where "—" appears, the regression coefficient was not statically significant.

Segmentation Variable	Economy Auto Buyer	Sports Car Buyer	Luxury Auto Buyer
Demographics			
Age	−.28	−.15	+.59
Education	−.12	+.38	—
Family Size	+.39	−.35	—
Income	−.15	+.25	+.68
Lifestyle/Values			
Active	—	+.59	−.39
American Pride	+.30	—	+.24
Bargain Hunter	+.45	−.33	—
Conservative	—	−.38	+.54
Cosmopolitan	−.40	+.68	—
Embraces Change	−.30	+.65	—
Family Values	+.69	—	+.21
Financially Secure	−.28	+.21	+.52
Optimistic	—	+.71	+.37

Here are some questions to answer.

1. What is the underlying conceptual model used by Segmentation Associates that is apparent in these three sets of findings?
2. What are the segmentation variables that distinguish economy automobile buyers and in what ways?
3. What are the segmentation variables that distinguish sports car buyers and in what ways?
4. What are the segmentation variables that distinguish luxury automobile buyers and in what ways?

15-3 Stepwise Multiple Regression

When the researcher is using multiple regression as a screening tool or is otherwise faced with a large number of independent variables in the conceptual model to be tested by multiple regression, it can become tedious to narrow down the independent variables by successive manual trimming. Fortunately, a type of multiple regression called *stepwise multiple regression* does the trimming operation automatically.

Here is a simple explanation. With **stepwise multiple regression**, the statistically significant independent variable that explains the most variance in the dependent variable is determined and entered into the multiple regression equation. Then the statistically significant independent variable that contributes most to explaining the remaining unexplained variance in the dependent variable is determined and entered. This process is continued until all statistically significant independent variables have been entered into the multiple regression equation.[13] In other words, all the insignificant independent variables are eliminated from the final multiple regression equation based on the level of significance stipulated by the researcher in the multiple regression options. The final output contains only statistically significant independent variables. Stepwise regression is used by researchers when they are confronted with a large number of competing independent variables and they want to narrow down the analysis to a set of statistically significant independent variables in a single regression analysis. With stepwise multiple regression, there is no need to trim and rerun the regression analysis because SPSS does the trimming automatically based on the stepwise method selected by the researcher.

> Stepwise regression is useful if a researcher has many independent variables and wants to narrow the set down to a smaller number of statistically significant variables.

IBM SPSS

HOW TO DO STEPWISE MULTIPLE REGRESSION WITH SPSS

A researcher executes stepwise multiple regression by using the ANALYZE-REGRESSION-LINEAR command sequence precisely as described for multiple regression. The dependent variable and many independent variables are selected into their respective windows as before. To direct SPSS to perform stepwise multiple regression, one uses the "Method:" drop-down menu to select "Backward." The findings will be the same as those arrived at by a researcher who uses the iterative trimmed multiple regressions that we described earlier. Of course, with stepwise multiple regression output, information on those independent variables is taken out of the multiple regression equation based on nonsignificance and, if the researcher wishes, SPSS stepwise multiple regression will also take into account the VIF statistic to assure that multicollinearity is not an issue.

We do not have screenshots of stepwise multiple regression, as this technique is quite advanced. In fact, there are four different stepwise regression methods available on SPSS. We do not recommend that you use stepwise multiple regression unless you gain a good deal more background on multiple regression, as you may encounter findings that are difficult to understand or are even counterintuitive.[14]

> **Marketing Research on YouTube™** To learn about performing stepwise multiple regression with SPSS, launch **www.youtube.com**, and search for "Multiple Regression – SPSS (Brief)."

STEP-BY-STEP SUMMARY OF HOW TO PERFORM MULTIPLE REGRESSION ANALYSIS

While we have attempted to move slowly, you are no doubt overwhelmed by all the facets of multiple regression analysis that we have covered. Nonetheless, you realize that every statistical analysis beyond simple descriptive ones involves some sort of statistical test, and the complexity of regression analysis requires multiple such tests. These tests are considered in a step-by-step manner by the marketing researcher, and we have listed and described these steps in Table 15.2 as a way of summarizing how to perform multiple regression analysis.

TABLE 15.2   Step-by-Step Procedure for Multiple Regression Analysis Using SPSS

Step	Description
Step 1. **Choose the dependent variable and independent variables to analyze.**	The dependent variable (y) is the predicted variable, and the independent variables (x_i's) are used to predict y. Typically, both y and x variables are scale variables (interval or ratio scales), although some dummy independent variables are allowable.
Step 2. **Determine if a linear relationship exists in the population (using 95% level of confidence).**	From the initial SPSS output, the ANOVA table reports a computed F value and associated Sig. level. a. If the Sig. value is .05 or less, there is a linear relationship among the chosen variables in the population. Go to Step 3. b. If the Sig. value is more than .05, there is no linear relationship among the chosen variables in the population. Return to Step 1 with a new set of variables, or stop.
Step 3. **Determine if the chosen independent variables are statistically significant (using 95% level of confidence).**	Also look at the Sig. level for the computed beta coefficient for each associated independent variable. a. If the Sig. level is .05 or less, it is permissible to use the associated independent variable to predict the dependent variable with the $y = a + bx$ linear equation. b. If the Sig. level is more than .05, it is not permissible to use the associated independent variable to predict the dependent variable. c. If you find a mixture of a. and b., you should do "trimmed" or stepwise multiple regression analysis (see the text on these techniques).
Step 4. **Determine the strength of the relationship(s) in the linear model.**	In the SPSS output Model Summary table, R Square is the square of the correlation coefficient, and the Adjusted R Square reduces the R^2 by taking into account the sample size and number of parameters estimated. Use Adjusted R Square as a measure of the "percent variance explained" in the y variable using the linear equation to predict y.
Step 5. **Interpret the findings.**	With a result where only statistically significant independent variables are used in the analysis, use the standardized betas' magnitudes and signs. Then assess each independent variable's relative importance and relationship direction with the dependent variable.

15-4   Warnings Regarding Multiple Regression Analysis

Before leaving our description of multiple regression analysis, we must issue warnings about your interpretation of regression. First, we all have a natural tendency to think in terms of causes and effects, and regression analysis invites us to think in terms of a dependent variable resulting from or being caused by an independent variable's actions. This line of thinking is absolutely incorrect: Regression analysis is nothing more than a statistical tool that assumes a linear relationship between two variables. It springs from correlation analysis, which is, as you will recall, a measure of the linear association and not the causal relationship between two variables. Consequently, even though two variables, such as sales and advertising, are logically connected, a regression analysis does not permit the marketing researcher to make cause-and-effect statements because other independent variables are not controlled.

> Regression is a statistical tool, not a cause-and-effect statement.

Our other warning is that the amount of knowledge about multiple regression analysis presented in this chapter is indeed rudimentary. There is a great deal more to multiple regression analysis that is beyond the scope of this textbook. Our coverage in this chapter introduces you to regression analysis, and it provides you with enough information about it to run uncomplicated regression analyses on SPSS, to identify the relevant aspects of the SPSS output, and to interpret the findings. As you will see when you work with the SPSS regression analysis procedures, we have only scratched the surface of this topic.[15] There are many more options, statistics, and considerations involved.[16] In fact, there is so much material that whole textbooks on regression exist. Our purpose has been to teach you the basic concepts and to help you interpret the statistics associated with these concepts as you encounter them as statistical analysis program output. Our descriptions are merely an introduction to multiple regression analysis to help you comprehend the basic notions, common uses, and interpretations involved with this predictive technique.[17]

Despite our simple treatment, we fully realize that even simplified regression analysis is very complicated and difficult to learn and that we have showered you with a great many regression statistical terms and concepts in this chapter. Seasoned researchers are intimately knowledgeable with them and very comfortable in using them. However, as a student encountering them for the first time, you undoubtedly feel very intimidated. While we may not be able to reduce your anxiety, we have created Table 15.3 that lists all of the regression analysis concepts we have described in this chapter, and it provides an explanation of each one. At least, you will not need to search through the chapter to find these concepts when you are trying to learn or use them.

TABLE 15.3 Regression Analysis Concepts

Concept	Explanation
Regression analysis	A predictive model using the straight-line relationship of $y = a + bx$
Intercept	The constant, or a, in the straight-line relationship that is the value of y when $x = 0$
Slope	The b, or the amount of change in y for a one-unit change in x
Dependent variable	y, the variable that is being predicted by the x(s) or independent variable(s)
Independent variable(s)	The x variable(s) used in the straight-line equation to predict y
Least squares criterion	A statistical procedure that assures that the computed regression equation is the best one possible
R Square	A number ranging from 0 to 1.0 that reveals how well the straight-line model fits the scatter of points; the higher, the better
Multiple regression analysis	A powerful form of regression where more than one x variable is in the regression equation
Additivity	A statistical assumption that allows the use of more than one x variable in a multiple regression equation: $y = a + b_1x_1 + b_2x_2 \ldots + b_mx_m$
Independence assumption	A statistical requirement that when more than one x variable is used, no pair of x variables has a high correlation
Multiple R	Also called the coefficient of determination, a number that ranges from 0 to 1.0 that indicates the strength of the overall linear relationship in a multiple regression; the higher, the better
Multicollinearity	The term used to denote a violation of the independence assumption that causes regression results to be in error
Variance inflation factor (VIF)	A statistical value that identifies what x variable(s) contribute to multicollinearity and should be removed from the analysis to eliminate multicollinearity. Any variable with VIF of 10 or greater should be removed.
Trimming	Removing an x variable in multiple regression because it is not statistically significant, rerunning the regression, and repeating until all remaining x variables are significant
Beta coefficients and standardized beta coefficients	Beta coefficients are the slopes (b values) determined by multiple regression for each independent variable x. These are normalized to be in the range of .00 to .99 so they can be compared directly to determine their relative importance in y's prediction.
Dummy independent variable	Use of an x variable that has a 0, 1, or similar coding, used sparingly when nominal variables must be in the independent variables set
Stepwise multiple regression	A specialized multiple regression that is appropriate when there is a large number of independent variables that need to be trimmed down to a small, significant set and the researcher wishes the statistical program to do this automatically

15-5 Reporting Regression Findings to Clients

The objective of a screening mechanism is to identify the relevant or meaningful variables as they relate to some dependent variable of interest. For most clients, the dependent variable of interest is sales, purchases, intentions to purchase, satisfaction, or some other variable that translates in some way to how customers regard or behave toward the company or brand. Normally, the researcher is faced with a large number of possible factors, any combination of which might relate to the dependent variable. When regression is used as a screening device, the items to report are (1) the dependent variable, (2) statistically significant independent variables, (3) signs of beta coefficients, and (4) standardized beta coefficients for the significant variables. Following is a table that reports the use of regression analysis to determine the target market profile of the Subshop.

Factors Related to Number of Visits to the Subshop (Stepwise Regression Analysis Results)

Dependent Variable		
How many times have you eaten at the Subshop in the past 30 days?	288 Total Cases	
Independent Variable(s)	Coefficient*	Standardized
Demographic Factors		
Gender**	−3.02	−.43
Age	4.71	.35
Education	−7.28	−.12
Lifestyle Factors		
I typically go to restaurants that have good prices.***	0.32	.35
Eating at restaurants is a large part of my diet.	−0.21	−.27
I usually buy the "special of the day" at lunch.	−0.17	−.20
Intercept	2.10	

*95% level of confidence
**(Dummy variable coded 0 = female and 1 = male)
***Based on a scale where 1 = Strongly disagree to 7 = Strongly agree

In the presentation table, there are a number of nuances that we will point out. First, the method of multiple regression (stepwise) is reported. Second, only the statistically significant (95% level of confidence) independent variables are reported. Third, the types of independent variables (demographics and lifestyle, here) are separated. Fourth, within each type, the independent variables are arranged in descending order according to the absolute values of their standardized beta coefficients. Fifth, where the coding of the independent variable is pertinent to proper interpretation, the measurement scale is reported as a footnote to the table. Note, in particular, that gender was used as a dummy variable, so it is important that the reader know the code in order to realize that the finding denotes that the Subshop's target market is skewed toward women.

 Synthesize Your Learning

This exercise will require you to take into consideration concepts and material from these three chapters.

Alpha Airlines uses marketing research to decide on service improvements.

Alpha Airlines

In the middle of the second decade of the 21st century, many airlines found themselves in a very unfortunate situation. On the supply side, costs rose at an unusually high rate. Aviation fuel, despite a slight dip, continued to rise, and other costs—employee wages and salaries, supplies, services, rent, and repair—rose faster than ever before. Unable to counter these cost increases, most airlines slowly instituted price increases and unbundled some of their services, such as charging $15 per checked-in bag. On the demand side, as the result of rising costs of many goods and services, business flyers reduced their flying and consumers cut back on their travel plans or turned to less expensive travel methods such as traveling by train or personal automobile. Reports by ticket sales agencies confirmed that many international vacationers and tourists had canceled or indefinitely postponed their plans due to high airline costs and concerns about personal safety.

Alpha Airlines, a major international airline, felt the squeeze on both sides of the equation during this time as passenger miles and revenues began to fall in what some airline industry analysts characterized as a "death spiral." However, marketing executives at Alpha Airlines vowed to not give up without putting up a very good fight, and they designed a questionnaire to obtain some baseline data as well as to assess the reactions of customers to possible changes in the airline's services and prices. An abbreviated version of the questionnaire follows.

1. Approximately how many of the following trips have you taken on Alpha Airlines this year?

    a. Domestic business _____
    b. Domestic tourist _____
    c. International business _____
    d. International tourist _____

2. Do you … (check all that apply)

    _____ Belong to Alpha Airlines' frequent flyer program?
    _____ Belong to Alpha Airlines' Prestige Club (private lounge areas in some airports)?
    _____ Typically use Alpha Airlines' website to book most of your flights?
    _____ Usually travel business class (including first class) on Alpha Airlines?

3. Indicate how desirable each of the following potential new Alpha Airlines' services is to you from 1 to 7 where 1 = Do not want at all to 7 = Desire very much.

    _____ Double Alpha Airlines frequent flyer miles for any trips after you have earned 25,000 miles in that year
    _____ From 33% to 50% savings on airfare for a second family member on any international flight with you
    _____ No $15 checked-in bag charge if you belong to the Alpha Airlines Prestige Club
    _____ Priority boarding on international Alpha Airlines flights if you belong to the Alpha Airlines Frequent Flyer program
    _____ Free wireless Internet service while in flight

In addition to the answers to these questions, the questionnaire also gathered information on the following: gender, education level (highest level in years), income level (in $10,000 increments), age (actual years), marital status, approximate number of air flight trips (any airline) taken for each of the past three years, and some lifestyle dimensions.[18] (From my experience, I have found that the larger the airline company the lower the actual cost of travel has been; I generally call several airlines or travel agents to get price quotes and routing before I decide on a particular airline; the price I pay for my ticket is more important to me than the service I receive prior to and during the flight; I choose to travel by airline because my time is very valuable to me; I feel that the services I receive during the flight are good; I feel that the pre-flight services, such as baggage handling and ticket processing, are good; and normally, I fly with one particular airline company.)

The self-administered questionnaire is handed out by flight attendants to all Alpha Airlines passengers traveling on domestic or international flights during the first week of the month, resulting in over 20,000 completed and usable questionnaires. The Alpha Airlines marketing executives have a number of questions that they hope will be answered by this survey.

For each question that follows, indicate the specific questions or variables in the survey that should be analyzed, paying close attention to the scale properties of each variable. Specify the type of statistical analysis that is appropriate and how SPSS output would indicate whether or not statistically significant findings are present.

1. What is the target market profile of each of the following types of Alpha Airlines traveler? That is, what demographic and lifestyle factors are related to the number of miles traveled on Alpha Airlines for each of the following types?

    a. Domestic business traveler
    b. Domestic tourist traveler
    c. International business traveler
    d. International tourist traveler

2. Are there differences in the desirabilities of each of the five potential new Alpha Airlines services with respect to the following?

    a. Gender
    b. Belonging (or not) to Alpha Airlines' frequent flyer program
    c. Belonging (or not) to Alpha Airlines' Prestige Club (private lounge areas in some airports)
    d. Use or nonuse of Alpha Airlines' website to book most flights
    e. Usual class of seating (business versus economy class) on Alpha Airlines

3. Do relationships exist for estimated number of air flight trips in each of the past three years on any airline with each of the following charateristics?

    a. Age
    b. Income
    c. Education
    d. Any of the lifestyle dimensions

4. Do associations exist for (1) participating or not in Alpha Airlines' frequent flyer program, (2) membership or not in Alpha Airlines Prestige Club (private lounge areas in some airports), and/or (3) use or not of Alpha Airlines website to book most flights with the following variables?

    a. Gender
    b. Marital status
    c. Usual class of seating (business versus economy class) on Alpha Airlines

Source: Cano, Lucila Zarraga, Sandoval, Enrique Corona, and Miguel Angel Olivares Urbina (2012), *Proposals for Marketing Strategies for Optical Centers Based on the Consumer, Global Conference on Business and Finance Proceedings,* Vol. 7, No 1, 601-606.

Summary

Market researchers use regression analysis to make predictions. The basis of this technique is an assumed straight-line relationship existing between the variables. With bivariate regression, one independent variable, *x*, is used to predict the dependent variable, *y*, using the straight-line formula of $y = a + bx$. A high R^2 and a statistically significant slope indicate that the linear model is a good fit. With multiple regression analysis, the underlying conceptual model specifies that several independent variables are to be used, and it is necessary to determine which ones are significant. Multiple regression analysis allows for the use of several independent variables (additivity) that are not highly correlated with one another. Multicollinearity, or the condition of high correlations among the independent variables, violates this necessary condition, and statistical analysis programs can be programmed to report variance inflation factors (VIFs) that will warn the researcher of this violation and prompt him or her to eliminate some of the offending independent variables.

By systematically eliminating the nonsignificant independent variables in an iterative manner in a process called trimming, a researcher will ultimately derive a set of significant independent variables that yields a significant predictive model. While the dependent and independent variables should be scale variables (interval or ratio), it is permitted to use a few dummy independent variables that are nominally coded for two categories such as male/female. With surveys, it is common for market researchers to use multiple regression analysis as a screening device to determine the statistically significant independent variables that emerge from a large set of possible independent variables. Interpretation of a multiple regression analysis finding is facilitated by examining the standardized beta coefficients that indicate the relative importance and the direction of the relationship of the variables.

Because the process of trimming nonsignificant independent variables is tedious and time consuming, seasoned researchers may opt to use stepwise multiple regression analysis if faced with a large number of candidate independent variables, such as several demographic, lifestyle, and buyer behavior characteristics. With stepwise multiple regression, independent variables are entered by the program until the multiple regression equation contains only statistically significant independent variables.

Key Terms

Regression analysis (p. 407)
Bivariate regression (p. 407)
Intercept (p. 408)
Slope (p. 408)
Dependent variable (p. 408)
Independent variable (p. 408)
Least squares criterion (p. 408)

Outlier (p. 408)
General conceptual model (p. 411)
Multiple regression analysis (p. 412)
Regression plane (p. 412)
Additivity (p. 412)
Independence assumption (p. 413)
Multicollinearity (p. 413)

Variance inflation factor (VIF) (p. 413)
Dummy independent variable (p. 417)
Standardized beta coefficient (p. 418)
Screening device (p. 418)
Stepwise multiple regression (p. 422)

Review Questions/Applications

15-1. Use an *x-y* graph to construct and explain a reasonably simple linear model for each of the following cases:

   a. What is the relationship between gasoline prices and distance traveled for family automobile touring vacations?

   b. How do hurricane-force wind warnings (e.g., Category 1, Category 2, etc.) relate to purchases of flashlight batteries in the expected landfall area?

   c. What is the relationship between passengers with carry-on luggage and charges for checking luggage on airlines?

15-2. Indicate what the scatter diagram and probable regression line would look like for two variables that are correlated in each of the following ways (in each instance, assume a negative intercept): (a) −0.89 (b) +0.48, and (c) −0.10.

15-3. Circle K runs a contest, inviting customers to fill out a registration card. In exchange, they are eligible for a grand-prize drawing of a trip to Alaska. The card asks for the customer's age, education, gender, estimated weekly purchases (in dollars) at that Circle K, and approximate distance the Circle K is from his or her home. Identify each of the following if a multiple regression analysis were to be performed: (a) independent variable, (b) dependent variable, (c) dummy variable.

15-4. Explain what is meant by the independence assumption in multiple regression. How can you examine your data for independence, and what statistic is issued by most statistical analysis programs? How is this statistic interpreted? That is, what would indicate the presence of multicollinearity, and what would you do to eliminate it?

15-5. What is a *general conceptual model*? With respect to multiple regression analysis, in what ways can a general conceptual model help marketing researchers and managers?

15-6. If one uses the "enter" method for multiple regression analysis, what statistics on an SPSS output should be examined to assess the result? Indicate how you would determine each of the following:
   a. Variance explained in the dependent variable by the independent variables
   b. Statistical significance of each of the independent variables
   c. Relative importance of the independent variables in predicting the dependent variable

15-7. Explain what is meant by the notion of "trimming" a multiple regression result. Use the following example to illustrate your understanding of this concept.

A bicycle manufacturer maintains records over 20 years of the following: retail price in dollars, cooperative advertising amount in dollars, competitors' average retail price in dollars, number of retail locations selling the bicycle manufacturer's brand, and whether or not the winner of the Tour de France was riding the manufacturer's brand (coded as a dummy variable where 0 = no and 1 = yes).

The initial multiple regression result determines the following:

Variable	Significance Level
Average retail price in dollars	.001
Cooperative advertising amount in dollars	.202
Competitors' average retail price in dollars	.028
Number of retail locations	.591
Tour de France winner	.032

Using the "enter" method in SPSS, what would be the trimming steps you would expect to undertake to identify the significant multiple regression result? Explain your reasoning.

15-8. Using the bicycle example in question 7, what do you expect would be the elimination of variables sequence using stepwise multiple regression? Explain your reasoning with respect to the operation of each step of this technique.

15-9. Using SPSS graphical capabilities, diagram the regression plane for the following variables.

Number of Gallons of Gasoline Used per Week	Miles Commuted to Work per Week	Number of Riders in Carpool
5	50	4
10	125	3
15	175	2
20	250	0
25	300	0

15-10. The Maximum Amount is a company that specializes in making fashionable clothes in large sizes for plus-size people. A survey was performed for the Maximum Amount, and a regression analysis was run on some of the data. Of interest in this analysis was the possible relationship between self-esteem (dependent variable) and number of Maximum Amount articles purchased last year (independent variables). Self-esteem was measured on a 7-point scale in which 1 signifies very low and 7 indicates very high self-esteem. Below are some items that have been taken from the output.

Pearson product moment correlation = +0.63
Intercept = 3.5
Slope = +0.2

All statistical tests are significant at the .01 level or less. What is the correct interpretation of these findings?

15-11. Wayne LaTorte is a safety engineer who works for the U.S. Postal Service. For most of his life, Wayne has been fascinated by UFOs. He has kept records of UFO sightings in the desert areas of Arizona, California, and New Mexico over the past 15 years and he has correlated them with earthquake tremors. A fellow engineer suggests that Wayne use regression analysis as a means of determining the relationship. Wayne does this and finds a "constant" of 30 separate earth tremor events and a slope of 5 events per UFO sighting. Wayne then writes an article for the *UFO Observer*, claiming that earthquakes are largely caused by the subsonic vibrations emitted by UFOs as they enter Earth's atmosphere. What is your reaction to Wayne's article?

CASE 15.1

L'Experience Félicité Restaurant Survey Regression Analysis   IBM **SPSS**

(For necessary background, refer to Case 12.1 on page 346, Case 13.1 on page 375, and Case 14.1 on page 404.)

Jeff Dean, the aspiring restaurant owner, was a very happy camper. He had learned that his dream of L'Experience Félicité Restaurant could be a reality. Through the research conducted under Cory Rogers's expert supervision and Christine Yu's SPSS analysis, Jeff had a good idea of what features were desired, where the restaurant should be located, and even what advertising media to use to promote it. He believed he had all the information he needed to obtain the financing necessary to design and build L'Experience Félicité Restaurant.

Jeff called Cory on Friday morning and said, "Cory, I am very excited about everything that your work has found about the good prospects of L'Experience Félicité Restaurant. I want to set up a meeting with my banker next week to pitch it to him for the funding. Can you get me the final report by then?"

Cory was silent for a moment, and then he said, "Christine is doing the final figures and dressing up the tables so we can paste them into the report document. But I think you have forgotten about the last research objective. We still need to address the target market definition with a final set of analyses. I know Christine just finished some exams at school, and she has been asking if there is any work she can do over the weekend. I'll give her this task. Why don't you plan on coming over at 11:00 a.m. on Monday. Christine and I will show you what we have found, and then we can take Christine to lunch for giving up her weekend."

Your task in Case 15.1 is to take Christine Yu's role, use the L'Experience Félicité Restaurant SPSS dataset, and perform the proper analysis. You will also need to interpret the findings.

1. What is the demographic target market definition for L'Experience Félicité Restaurant?
2. What is the restaurant spending behavior target market definition for L'Experience Félicité Restaurant?
3. Develop a general conceptual model of market segmentation for L'Experience Félicité Restaurant. Test it using multiple regression analysis and interpret your findings for Jeff Dean.

CASE 15.2   INTEGRATED CASE

Auto Concepts Segmentation Analysis   IBM **SPSS**

It is Monday, and today is your first day in your new marketing internship. After a rigorous application and review process including two grueling interviews with Cory Rogers and Celeste Brown, you have been hired by CMG Research. It is 9:00 a.m., and you are in Rogers's office along with Brown. Cory says, "We know that it is just your first day as the CMG Research marketing intern, but we are getting bogged down with a lot of work that must be completed very quickly or our clients will be unhappy. As I indicated to you a few days ago when I let you know that we chose you to be this year's marketing intern, Celeste and I were very impressed with your command of SPSS and your understanding of more advanced statistical analyses such as regression and analysis of variance. So, we are going to let you show us your stuff right away."

Cory continues, "We are in the final stages of a major survey that we conducted for Auto Concepts. They have five automobile models under consideration for multimillion-dollar development. We have provided them with a great deal of analysis, and they are in the process of narrowing down the development list. I would like to give them one more set of findings. Specifically, I would like to give them target market definitions for each of the possible models. That is, using multiple regression analysis as a screening device, we need to identify the significant demographic and attitudes about global warming that uniquely define these preference segments."

Celeste then says, "We can go to the office where I can give you a copy of the SPSS dataset, and, as you know, you can use SPSS Variable View or Utilities-Variables to see the code book for this survey." Cory ends the meeting by saying, "Great. I am sure that you will do a fantastic job with this assignment. Celeste and I have to catch a flight in a couple of hours, and we will be out of town for the next three days. But you can call, text, or email. Let's set a meeting for 9:00 a.m. on Thursday, and you can show us what you have found."

Your task as the new CMG marketing intern: Use the *AutoConcepts.Recoded.sav* data file. The dataset is "recoded" with midpoint values for town size, education, and so on, so these variables are now scale variables that conform to the requirements for regression analysis. Perform the proper analyses to identify the salient demographic and/or attitude factors that are related to preferences for each of the automobile models under consideration. With each automobile model, prepare a summary that:

1. Lists the statistically significant independent variables (use 95% level of confidence).
2. Interprets the direction of the relationship of each statistically significant independent variable with respect to the preference for the automobile model concerned.
3. Identifies or distinguishes the relative importance of each of the statistically significant independent variables.
4. Assesses the strength of the statistically significant independent variables as they join to predict the preferences for the automobile model concerned.

16

The Research Report

"WHERE WE ARE"

1 Establish the need for marketing research.
2 Define the problem.
3 Establish research objectives.
4 Determine research design.
5 Identify information types and sources.
6 Determine methods of accessing data.
7 Design data collection forms.
8 Determine the sample plan and size.
9 Collect data.
10 Analyze data.
11 Prepare and present the final research report.

Tableau: Modern Marketers: It's Never Too Late to Start Your Analytics Journey

Elissa Fink, Global Chief Marketing Officer, Tableau Software.

Marketers have come a long way even in recent years; once known primarily for logos, brochures, and pretty websites, modern marketers are not only expected to build the brand, spread awareness, and drive sales of products and services, but they're expected to justify all expenses with proven return on investment (ROI) as well. Furthermore, the majority of marketers today are using and tracking the performance of at least nine different channels, digital and offline, to target customers.

Because the days of go-with-your-gut-style marketing tactics are long gone, the successful multichannel marketers are able to integrate and understand all their data to help drive decision making for faster, better results. Never before have data and analytics played a more crucial role in marketing.

That being said, data visualization dashboards are one of the most important and often overlooked tools for marketers. Top-tier employers expect all marketers, leaders and entry level alike, to ask and answer their own questions of the data and to waste no time in acting on those insights. With the world's volume of data growing exponentially by the day, analytical skills are no longer optional.

The good news: Tableau Software, Inc., has created an easy-to-use, drag-and-drop analytics platform to help marketers see and understand what's happening across their many channels, campaigns, and business goals in real time.

If you haven't yet embraced data, you may find the whole idea intimidating. Here are three tips to help you get started today:

1. Start with a Small Database

The first step is to stop procrastinating. It's not about having the perfect dataset. Start with what you have. Look to Google Analytics data to better understand website traffic. Play with social media data to measure engagement. Dig into campaign data to see which efforts are resonating with your customers. Nothing begets success like success, and even small achievements will encourage you to push further. Students at accredited schools anywhere in the world can start learning these crucial analytics skills today with a free license of Tableau Desktop. Learn more at http://www.tableau.com/academic.

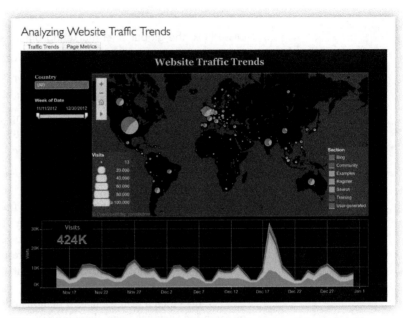

This dashboard is connected directly with Google Analytics. It is easy to see traffic trends by country, section of website visited, and number of visits in a given time period. Click into the visualization to interact with this dataset (link: http://www.tableau.com/learn/gallery/website-traffic-trends).

2. Visualize Your Data

If you thought spreadsheets were powerful, try on visualization for size. Because our brains are wired to process information visually, we're much faster at spotting trends, identifying correlations, and honing in on outliers when our data are visualized. With visual marketing dashboards, your insights become easier to absorb, whether through a map capturing geographic information, height variations within a bar chart, or a trend line aggregating millions of data points.

3. Interact with Your Data

Marketing dashboards are important because they get teams looking at the same data visualizations. But once users are interacting with the same datasets, different viewers will have unique questions about what they see. Marketers and agency clients alike will both interact with the same data to get answers to specific questions they each have.

Interactive dashboards enable basic analytical tasks, such as filtering views, adjusting parameters, making quick calculations, and drilling down to examine underlying data. Because interactivity transforms stockpiles of data into actionable insights, marketers and business leaders throughout an organization become engaged in problem solving and decision making instead of struggling to understand datasets.

—Elissa Fink

About Elissa Fink

Elissa Fink, the global chief marketing officer at Tableau Software since 2007, believes that human intelligence is a key part of making data work for marketing decisions. The Tableau Software marketing department uses its own tool every day to execute across hundreds of campaigns and business goals. "Marketing is about recognizing where you are and knowing where you want to be. It's all about measuring progress," Fink says.

Source: Text and photos courtesy of Elissa Fink and Tableau Software, Inc.

The importance of communicating the findings from a marketing research project with clarity, accuracy, and style cannot be overemphasized. Quite simply, no matter how competently a research project has been conducted—from the problem definition stage to the data analysis stage—if the results are not presented well, the project is a failure. A researcher's work is often judged solely on the basis of the quality of the marketing research report.

As this chapter's introduction demonstrates, one of the many ways that the marketing research industry has been changing is in the new and innovative ways that are being used to communicate results. Research results are now often displayed through animations, videos, photographs, and other visual tools. Innovative research firms use storytelling and other emotion-inducing techniques to present results so that their research clients will be drawn into the findings.[1] Marketing research results can even be presented in the form of documentary videos or theater.

Another trend is the growing expectation that marketing researchers will not just present statistical findings but also recommend actionable strategies that stem from the results. To be seen as relevant, researchers must demonstrate to their clients that acting on their findings will have a positive impact on their business.[2] Researchers who simply present table after table of results without explaining why these data are important offer limited value to managers. Researchers are increasingly being asked not only to collect data but also to serve in the role of trusted advisor.

A related trend is an increased emphasis on getting data into the hands of the client-side users across multiple departments in an organization, called the "democratization" of marketing research. As explained in the introduction, software platforms such as Tableau allow users throughout a firm to have access to data in real time to perform their own analyses and create their own graphics. Tableau specializes in **data visualization**, or the visual display of information in graphical or pictorial form. Increasingly, marketing research firms are being asked to support end users in managing their own data.[3]

Data visualization is the visual display of information in graphical or pictorial form.

It is important for you to be aware of these new trends, tools, and techniques that are transforming the marketing industry. Yet none of these changes mitigate the importance of knowing how to present research results clearly and accurately in both oral and written forms. In this chapter, you will learn the basics of preparing written and oral reports. You will learn the important elements that compose a report. You will be introduced to guidelines and principles for the written report. You will be shown how to develop visuals, such as tables and figures, to clearly display your findings. And you will be provided with guidelines for presenting oral reports. To end the chapter, we will introduce other tools that can be used to communicate results in effective, easy-to-understand, and impactful ways.

16-1 The Importance of the Marketing Research Report

The **marketing research report** is a written and/or oral presentation that transmits research results, conclusions, recommendations, and other important information to the client, who in turn bases his or her decision making on the contents of the report. The importance of the research report was addressed by the marketing research director at Kodak, who stated that even the best research will not drive the appropriate action unless the audience understands the results and their meaning.[4] Marketing researcher James A. Rohde notes that the presentation is important in demonstrating that the findings are relevant to the client because these decision makers base their judgments on what they can accomplish with the information in the final report. They are less concerned about the method and analytical tools used by the researcher.[5] This places greater importance on writing a report that is relevant to the decisions the client must make. The ultimate result of all the work on the research project is communication with the client.

The marketing research report is the product that represents the efforts of the marketing research team. It is often the only part of the project that the client will see. If the report is poorly written, riddled with grammatical errors, sloppy, or inferior in any way, the quality of the research (including its analysis and information) becomes suspect and its credibility is reduced. If organization and presentation are faulty, the reader may never reach the intended conclusions. The time and effort expended in the research process are wasted if the report does not communicate effectively.

If, on the other hand, all aspects of the report are done well, the report will not only communicate properly, but also it will serve to build credibility. Many managers will not be involved in any aspect of the research process but will use the report to make business decisions. Effective reporting is essential and includes careful attention to organization, formatting, good writing, and good grammar.

> The marketing research report is a written and/or oral report that transmits research results, conclusions, vital recommendations, and other important information to the client, who in turn bases his or her decision making on the contents of the report.

IMPROVING THE EFFICIENCY OF REPORT WRITING

Assuming that you have written a term paper (or several!), you realize that report writing is not easy. Still, electronic tools can aid in some processes. Word processing software typically includes many features that increase writing efficiency. Features such as automatic referencing coupled with automated citation formatting, available on many of today's online databases, have reduced much of the tedious time spent on report writing. Most of today's statistical analysis packages, such as SPSS, include sophisticated tools that offer ease of presentation in tables, pie charts, bar graphs, and other visuals that allow for customization to suit the writer's purpose.

Computer-assisted questionnaire design tools, such as SurveyMonkey or Qualtrics, often generate automatic reports, including tables and graphs, with the survey results (see Chapter 8). These reports generally present only descriptive statistics. To conduct higher-level statistical tests, you need access to the raw data of your survey. Computer-assisted questionnaire design tools often allow you to download survey results to data analysis software such as Excel or SPSS, although that capability is typically only available on a long-term basis if you pay a higher price for the service. Your university may provide free access for students to a professional version of an electronic survey.

16-2 Know Your Audience

Marketing research reports are tailored to specific audiences and purposes, and you must consider both in all phases of the research process, including planning the report. Before you begin writing, you must answer some questions:

- What message do you want to communicate?
- What is your purpose?

© Rawpixel/Shutterstock

Know your audience.

- Who is the audience?
- If there are multiple audiences, who is your primary audience? Your secondary audience?
- What does your audience know?
- What does your audience need to know?
- Are there cultural differences you need to consider?
- What biases or preconceived notions of the audience might serve as barriers to your message?
- What strategies can you use to overcome these negative attitudes?

- Do demographic and lifestyle variables of your audience affect their perspective of your research?
- What are your audience's interests, values, and concerns?

These and other questions must be addressed before you can determine how best to structure your report.

When you are preparing the final report, it is often helpful "to get on the other side of the desk." Assume you are the reader instead of the writer. Doing so will help you see things through the eyes of your audience and increase the success of your communication. This is your opportunity to ask that basic (and critical) question from the reader's point of view: "What's in it for me?" Once you have answered these questions, you need to organize your report.

16-3 Avoid Plagiarism!

Plagiarism refers to representing the work of others as your own. It is a serious offense to plagiarize; people lose their jobs due to this ethical lapse.

Marketing | To learn
Research | more about
on YouTube™ | the perils of plagiarism, go to **www. youtube.com** and type in "Understanding Plagiarism" and "York St. John University."

Make sure you understand what plagiarism means. If in doubt, provide a reference to the source and put the citation in the proper format.

Before we introduce the major elements of a marketing research report, it is important to discuss the importance of carefully referencing sources. If you use secondary information, you will need to document your sources (provide enough information so that your sources can be located). You do not need to document facts that are common knowledge or can be easily verified. But if you are in doubt, document! **Plagiarism** refers to representing the work of others as your own. Citing the work of others not only allows you to avoid charges of plagiarism but also adds credibility to your message. All sources, including information that is found online, should be accurately referenced.

Students often underestimate what a serious offense it is to commit plagiarism. Plagiarism can cost you your job. Detecting plagiarism is much easier today than it was in the past. To check a document for plagiarism, all you need to do is to put the suspected part of a document into a search engine and see what matches appear. In addition, specialized software such as Turnitin can be used to check for plagiarism.

Take the opportunity to learn more about plagiarism by watching the YouTube video cited in the following feature. You can also explore the Internet for examples of how serious plagiarism is: Students have lost their college degrees, top-level professionals have lost their jobs, and well-known celebrity writers have been defamed. Marketing Research Insight 16.1 offers more information about this important topic.

MARKETING RESEARCH INSIGHT 16.1   *Ethical Consideration*

Properly Reference Your Sources

Referencing sources is essential in the business world.

Plagiarism is derived from a Latin word for kidnapping a Roman citizen's slave.[6] Words can be thought of as property. Avoiding plagiarism involves respect for the original author's work and respect for your audience's needs or desire to trace data and learn more from the source.

Just as all printed sources must be documented, so must information found online. In a letter to the *New York Times*, Marilyn Bergman, president of the American Society of Composers, Authors, and Publishers, expressed a disturbing trend of online theft of words when she said that Americans are prompted by a "free for the taking" feeling of information on the web.[7] The Internet is not public domain. Proper documentation of all sources helps a writer avoid public humiliation and maintain professional integrity.

APA (American Psychological Association) and MLA (Modern Language Association) are two styles that offer formats for citation. Many online databases offer a "Cite This" option that automatically gives you the reference in a format of your choice. In terms of formats, APA is used in business fields, and MLA is used in the humanities. Style books and university websites offer examples of documentation for a range of sources, including electronic formats.

Sample Format:

Author, I., Author, I., & Author, I. (Year, month date). Title, [Type of medium]. Available: Site/Path/File [Access date].

16-4 Elements of the Report

Reports are organized in sections, or elements. If the organization for which you are conducting the research has specific guidelines for preparing the document, you should follow them. If no specific guidelines are provided, certain elements must be considered when you are preparing the report. These elements can be grouped into three sections: front matter, body, and end matter. Table 16.1 displays these three sections along with elements covered in each section.

FRONT MATTER

The **front matter** consists of all pages that precede the first page of the report: the title page, letter of authorization (optional), letter/memo of transmittal, table of contents, list of illustrations, and abstract/executive summary.

Front matter consists of all pages that precede the first page of the report.

TABLE 16.1   The Elements of a Marketing Research Report

A. Front Matter

    1. Title Page

    2. Letter of Authorization

    3. Letter/Memo of Transmittal

    4. Table of Contents

    5. List of Illustrations

    6. Abstract/Executive Summary

B. Body

    1. Introduction

    2. Research Objectives

    3. Method

    4. Results

    5. Limitations

    6. Conclusions or Conclusions and Recommendations

C. End Matter

    1. Appendices

    2. Endnotes

Title Page The **title page** (Figure 16.1) contains four major items of information: (1) the title of the document, (2) the organization/person(s) for whom the report was prepared, (3) the organization/person(s) who prepared the report, and (4) the date of submission. If names of individuals appear on the title page, they may be in either alphabetical order or some other agreed-upon order; each individual should also be given a designation or descriptive title.

The document title should be as informative as possible. It should include the purpose and content of the report, such as "An Analysis of the Demand for a Branch Office of the Law Firm of Dewey, Cheatam, and Howe" or "Alternative Advertising Copy to Introduce the New M&M/Mars Low-Fat Candy Bar." The title should be centered and printed in all uppercase (capital) letters. Other items of information on the title page should be centered and printed in uppercase and lowercase letters. The title page is counted as page i of the front matter; however, no page number is printed on it. See Figure 16.1. On the page following the title page, the printed page number will be ii.

Some experts recommend that you change the title to be brief and understandable if you are making a presentation on the survey results.[8] For example, "An Analysis of the Demand for a Branch Office of the CPA Firm of Dean and Allen" would be simplified to "Demand for a Branch Office of Dean and Allen." Additional insights on preparing for an oral presentation are provided later in the chapter.

Letter of Authorization The **letter of authorization** is the marketing research firm's certification to do the project. This element is optional. It includes the name and title of the persons authorizing the research to be performed, and it may also include a general description of the nature of the research project, completion date, terms of payment, and any special conditions of the research project requested by the client or research user. If you allude to the conditions of your authorization in the letter/memo of transmittal, the letter of authorization is not necessary in the report. However, if your reader may not know the conditions of authorization, inclusion of this document is helpful.

FIGURE 16.1
Title Page

NEW PRODUCTS DIVISION

OF HOGER CHOCOLATIERS:

A MARKETING RESEARCH STUDY OF
SHOPPERS' REACTIONS TO NEW PACKAGING
OF GIFT CHOCOLATES

Prepared for
Ms. Ola Hoger, CEO

Prepared by
Jonathan Yu, Vice President
CMG Research, Inc.

July 2016

Letter/Memo of Transmittal Use a **letter of transmittal** to release or deliver the document to an organization for which you are not a regular employee. Use a **memo of transmittal** to deliver the document within your organization. The letter/memo of transmittal describes the general nature of the research in a sentence or two and identifies the individual who is releasing the report. The primary purpose of the letter/memo of transmittal is to orient the reader to the report and to build a positive image of the report. It should establish rapport between the writer and receiver. It gives the receiver a person to contact if questions arise.

Writing style in the letter/memo of transmittal should be personal and slightly informal. Some general elements that may appear in the letter/memo of transmittal are a brief identification of the nature of the research, a review of the conditions of the authorization to do the research (if no letter or authorization is included), comments on findings, suggestions for further research, and an expression of interest in the project and further research. It should end

Use a letter of transmittal outside your organization and a memo within your organization.

FIGURE 16.2
Letter of Transmittal

CMG Research, Inc.
1100 St. Louis Place
St. Louis, MO

July 14, 2016

Ms. Ola Hoger
Gift Chocolate Division
Hoger Chocolatiers
Cocoa, USA 00000

Dear Ms. Hoger:

With your letter of authorization, dated April 25, 2016, you authorized CMG to conduct a research project for Hoger Chocolatiers. With this letter, I am hereby transmitting to you the report of that project, entitled "A MARKETING RESEARCH STUDY OF SHOPPERS' REACTIONS TO NEW PACKAGING OF GIFT CHOCOLATES."

The method used to generate the findings of this report is described in detail in the report. Moreover, the method follows that described in our proposal to you. We believe the report accomplishes the research objectives we set out at the beginning of this process and, therefore, you should be able to use the information contained herein to make the important decisions needed for Hoger Chocolatiers.

My colleagues and I have been pleased to work with you on this project. We are prepared to make a presentation of the report at your convenience. Do not hesitate to call me at (877) 492-2891 should you have any questions.

Sincerely,

Jonathan Yu

Jonathan Yu

---

with an expression of appreciation for the assignment, acknowledgment of assistance from others, and suggestions for following up. Personal observations, unsupported by the data, are appropriate. Figure 16.2 presents an example of a letter of transmittal.

Table of Contents The **table of contents** helps the reader locate information in the research report. The table of contents (Figure 16.3) should list all sections of the report that follow. Each heading should read exactly as it appears in the text and should identify the number of the page on which it appears. If a section is longer than one page, list the page on which it begins. Indent subheadings under headings. All items except the title page and the table of contents are listed with page numbers in the table of contents. Front-matter pages are numbered with lowercase Roman numerals: i, ii, iii, iv, and so on. Arabic numerals (1, 2, 3) begin with the introduction section of the body of the report.

FIGURE 16.3
Table of Contents

Table of Contents

List of Illustrations If the report contains tables and/or figures, include in the table of contents a **list of illustrations** with page numbers on which they appear. All tables and figures should be included in this list, which helps the reader find specific illustrations that graphically portray the information. **Tables** are words and/or numbers arranged in rows and columns; **figures** are graphs, charts, maps, pictures, and so on. Because tables and figures are numbered independently, you may have both a Figure 1 and a Table 1 in your list of illustrations. Give each a name, and list each in the order in which it appears in the report.

Abstract/Executive Summary Your report may have many readers. Some of them will need to know the details of your research, such as the supporting data on which you base your conclusions and recommendations. Others will not need as many details but will want

Abstracts are summaries of reports.

to read the conclusions and recommendations. Still others with a general need to know may read only the executive summary. Therefore, the **abstract** or **executive summary** is a "skeleton" of your report. It serves as a summary for the busy executive or a preview for the in-depth reader. It provides an overview of the most useful information, including the conclusions and recommendations. The abstract or executive summary should be very carefully written, conveying the information as concisely as possible. It should be single-spaced and should briefly cover the general subject of the research, the scope of the research (what the research covers/does not cover), identification of the methods used (e.g., an electronic survey of 1,000 homeowners), conclusions, and recommendations.

BODY

The **body** is the bulk of the report. It contains an introduction to the report, an explanation of your method, a discussion of your results, a statement of limitations, and a list of conclusions and recommendations. Generally, only a few people will read a traditional marketing research report in its entirety. Most will read the executive summary, conclusions, and recommendations. Therefore, formal reports are repetitious. For example, you may specify the research objectives in the executive summary and refer to them again in the findings section as well as in the conclusions section. Researchers often choose to use the same terminology to introduce the tables and/or figures. In many lengthy reports, repetition actually enhances reader comprehension.

The first page of the body contains the title, such as "Introduction." Whatever title you select should be centered on the top of the page; this page is counted as page 1, but no page number is printed on it. All other pages throughout the document are numbered consecutively.

Introduction The **introduction** to the marketing research report orients the reader to its contents. It may contain a statement of the background situation leading to the problem, the statement of the problem, and a summary description of how the research process was initiated. It should contain a statement of the general purpose of the report and also the specific objectives for the research.

Research Objectives **Research objectives** may be listed either as a separate section or within the introduction. The listing of research objectives should follow the statement of the problem, since the two concepts are closely related. The list of specific research objectives often serves as a good framework for organizing the results section of the report.

The method describes in detail how the research was conducted, who (or what) the subjects were, and what tools or methods were used to achieve the objectives.

Method The **method** describes, in as much detail as necessary, how you conducted the research, who (or what) your subjects were, and what tools or methods were used to achieve your objectives. In most cases, the method section does not need to be long. It should, however, provide the essential information that your reader needs to understand how the data were collected and how the results were achieved. It should be detailed enough that the data collection could be replicated by others for purposes of reliability. In other words, the method section should be clear enough that other researchers could conduct a similar study. In some cases, the needs of the research user may dictate an extensive method section. A client may, for example, want the researcher to not only thoroughly describe the method that was used but also discuss why other methods were not selected. For example, in situations in which research information will be provided in litigation, where there is certain to be an adversary, a researcher may be asked to provide an exhaustive description of the methods used in conducting the study as well as the methods that were not chosen.

Method or Methodology? The method section describes the details of the procedures and tools used in the study. Some reports may instead use *methodology* as the title for this section, but we recommend sticking with *method*. Why? The two terms have different meanings. Because so many people use them interchangeably does not mean that such usage is correct. **Methodology** refers to the science of determining appropriate methods to conduct research. It has been defined as the theoretical analysis of the methods appropriate to a field of study or to the body of methods and principles particular to a branch of knowledge.[9] Therefore, it would be appropriate to say that there are *objections to the methodology of a consumer survey* (that is, objections dealing with the appropriateness of the methods used in the survey) or to refer to the *methodology of modern marketing research* (that is, the principles and practices that underlie research in the field of marketing research).[10] Consequently, there is an important conceptual distinction between methodology and method. *Method* refers to the tools of scientific investigation (and the tools used in a marketing research project are described in detail in the method section of the report). *Methodology* refers to the principles that *determine how* such tools are deployed and interpreted. Marketing research *methodology* prescribes, for example, that we must use probability samples if we desire to have a sample that is representative of some population. Researchers would describe their use of a probability sample for a particular study in the *method* section of their paper. In short, use *method,* not *methodology.*

> Methodology refers to the science of determining appropriate methods to conduct research.

Results The **results** section is the main body of your report. Some researchers prefer to use the term *findings.* This section should logically present the findings of your research and may be organized around the research objectives for the study. The results should be presented in narrative form and accompanied by tables, charts, figures, and other appropriate visuals that support and enhance the explanation of results. Tables and figures are supportive material; they should not be overused or used as filler. Each should contain a number and title and should be referred to in the narrative.

> The results section is the most important portion of your report and should logically present the findings of the research.

Outline your results section before you write the report. The survey questionnaire itself can serve as a useful aid in organizing your results because the questions are often grouped in a logical order or in purposeful sections. Another useful method for organizing your results is to individually print all tables and figures and arrange them in a logical sequence. Once you have the results outlined properly, you are ready to write the introductory sentences, definitions (if necessary), review of the findings (often referring to tables and figures), and transition sentences to lead into the next topic.

Limitations No research is flawless. Do not attempt to hide or disguise problems in your research. Always be above board and open regarding all aspects of your research. Reporting all important limitations can actually add credibility to your research. Avoiding discussion of limitations may render suspect your integrity and your research, and not reporting research results accurately and honestly is against the Marketing Research Association's Code of Marketing Research Standards.[11] Suggest what the limitations are or may be and what impact they have on the results.

You might also suggest opportunities for further study based on the limitations. Typical **limitations** in research reports often focus on but are not limited to factors such as constraints of time, the size and composition of the sample, and biases that may have been introduced into the research process. Consider the following example: "The reader should note that this study was based on a survey of graduating students at a midsized public university in the Southeast United States. Care should be exercised in generalizing these findings to other populations."

> Limitations of research, such as constraints of time, the size and composition of the sample, and biases that may have been introduced into the research process, should always be reported.

Conclusions and Recommendations Conclusions and recommendations may be listed together or in separate sections, depending on the amount of material you have to report. In any case, you should note that conclusions are not the same as recommendations. **Conclusions** are the outcomes and decisions you have reached based on your research results. For example, if the data show the order of preference for five car models, a conclusion would be "Model C had the highest preference."

> Conclusions are the outcomes and decisions you have reached based on your research results.

Recommendations are suggestions for how to proceed based on the conclusions. For example, "The company should produce and market Model C." The researcher and the

> Recommendations are suggestions for how to proceed based on the conclusions.

client should determine prior to the study to what extent the report is to contain recommendations. A clear understanding of the researcher's role will result in a smoother process and will help avoid conflict. As stated in the introduction, an emerging trend in the marketing research industry is the expectation that researchers will perform a consulting role with their clients. That is, researchers are increasingly expected to become knowledgeable about their clients' businesses and offer recommendations that have strategic value (see Chapter 3).

END MATTER

End matter contains additional information to which the reader may refer for further reading but that is not essential to reporting the data.

The **end matter** comprises the **appendices**, which contain additional information to which the reader may refer for further reading but that is not essential to reporting the data; references list; and endnotes. Any information that is critical to the reader should be included in the report itself. Appendices contain "nice to know" information—not "need to know." Therefore, that information should not clutter the body of the report but should instead be inserted at the end for the reader who desires or requires additional information. Tables, figures, additional reading, technical descriptions, data collection forms, and appropriate computer printouts are some elements that may appear in an appendix. Each appendix should be labeled with both a letter and a title, and each should appear in the table of contents.

A reference page or endnotes (if appropriate) should precede the appendix. A **reference list** contains all of the sources from which information was collected for the report. The references should be complete so that a reader could retrieve the source if needed. **Endnotes** are notes at the end of a document that provide supplementary information or comments on ideas provided in the body of the report.

16-5   Guidelines and Principles for the Written Report

In addition to understanding the purpose of the parts of the research report, you should also consider their form, format, and style.

HEADINGS AND SUBHEADINGS

A well-organized report, with appropriate headings and subheadings, will substantially improve readability.

In a long report, your reader needs signals and signposts that serve as a road map. Headings and subheadings perform this function. **Headings** indicate the topic of each section. All information under a specific heading should relate to that heading, and **subheadings** should divide that information into segments. A new heading should introduce a change of topic. Choose the kind of heading that fits your purpose—single word, phrase, sentence, question—and consistently use that form throughout the report. If you use subheadings within the divisions, the subheadings must be parallel to one another but not to the main headings.

You should begin by organizing your report into sections. This requires time on the front end of the process, but it is time well spent. A well-organized report, with appropriate headings and subheadings, will substantially improve readability. Then find any communications book and organize your headings using one of the standard formats. For example, a Level 1 heading is centered and all caps; a Level 2 heading is left justified with upper- and lowercase. Alternatively, use the professional format contained in a word processing program such as Microsoft Word. Learning how to use headings and subheadings will improve your writing skills. Be sure that all of the sections of a report follow a consistent format, particularly if different people have responsibility for different sections.

VISUALS

Visuals are tables, figures, charts, diagrams, graphs, and other graphic aids that concisely present information that might otherwise be difficult to comprehend.

Visuals are tables, figures, charts, diagrams, graphs, and other graphic aids. Used properly, they can dramatically and concisely present information that might otherwise be difficult to comprehend. Tables systematically present numerical data or words in columns and rows. Figures translate numbers into visual displays so that relationships and trends become comprehensible. Examples of figures are graphs, pie charts, and bar charts.

Visuals should tell a story; they should be uncluttered and self-explanatory. Even though they are self-explanatory, the key points of all visuals should be explained in the text. Refer to visuals by number: "...as shown in Figure 1." Each visual should be titled and numbered. If possible, place the visual immediately below the paragraph in which its first reference appears. Or, if sufficient space is not available, continue the text and place the visual on the next page. Visuals can also be placed in an appendix. Additional information on preparing visuals in SPSS is presented later in this chapter.

STYLE

Proper grammar and sentence construction are essential in report writing. Sentences should be constructed for the reader's ease of reading and understanding, and the rules of grammar should be observed. Readers will make assumptions about your knowledge of other subjects based on your knowledge of grammar.

Good paragraph construction is essential to a well-written report. A good paragraph has one main idea, and a **topic sentence** should state that main idea. For example: "To assess whether residents would patronize an upscale restaurant, respondents were asked their likelihood of patronizing an upscale restaurant." Next, the **body of the paragraph** provides the main idea of the topic sentence by giving more information, analysis, or examples. For example, continuing from the topic sentence example: "A description of an upscale restaurant was read to all respondents. The description was as follows: ... The respondents were then asked to indicate their likelihood of patronizing an upscale restaurant by selecting a choice on a 5-point response rating scale ranging from 'Very likely to patronize' to 'Very unlikely to patronize.' The actual scale was as follows: ...."

Paragraphs should close with a sentence that signals the end of the topic and indicates where the reader is headed. For example: "How respondents answered the likelihood-to-patronize scale is discussed in the following two paragraphs." Note this last sentence is a **transitional sentence**, which tells readers where they are headed. This helps readers' comprehension.

Controlling for the length of paragraphs should encourage good communication. As a rule, paragraphs should be short. Business communication experts believe most paragraphs should be under or around the 100-word range.[12] This is long enough for the topic sentence and three or four sentences in the body of the paragraph. The paragraph should never cover more than one main topic. Complex topics should be broken into several paragraphs.

Other guidelines for improving the style of your report include the following:

- Use jargon sparingly.
- Use strong verbs (for example, say "recommend" instead of "making a recommendation").
- Favor the active voice (the subject of the verb is doing the action).
- Remove extra words.
- Avoid changes in tense.
- Keep the subject and the verb close together.

Overall, edit and proofread your report carefully. Proofread a report multiple times to be sure it is without errors, and then ask somebody else to read the report and report problems to you. Often professionals rewrite reports several times until they are confident that their writing is clear and then ask somebody else in the company to review the report and note any problems.

16-6   Using Visuals: Tables and Figures

Visual representations of data and ideas assist in the effective presentation of findings. The key to a successful visual is a clear and concise presentation that conveys the message of the report. The selection of the visual should match the presentation purpose for the data. Common visuals include the following:[13]

Tables, which identify exact values (see Marketing Research Insight 16.2)

Graphs and *charts*, which illustrate relationships among items

> *Pie charts*, which compare a specific part of the whole to the whole (see Marketing Research Insight 16.3)
>
> *Bar charts* (see Marketing Research Insight 16.4) and *line graphs*, which compare items over time or show correlations among items

Flow diagrams, which introduce a set of topics and illustrate their relationships (useful when the sequence of events or topics is important)

Maps, which define geographical locations

Photographs, which visually display and provide live examples of findings

Drawings, which illustrate details of findings to provide clarity

A discussion of some of these visuals follows.

TABLES

Tables allow the reader to compare numerical data.

Tables allow the reader to compare numerical data. Effective table guidelines are as follows:

- Do not allow computer analysis to imply a level of accuracy that is not achieved. Limit your use of decimal places (12% or 12.2% instead of 12.223%).
- Place items you want the reader to compare in the same column, not the same row.
- If you have many rows, darken alternating entries or double-space after every few (five) entries to assist the reader in accurately lining up items.
- Total columns and rows when relevant.

In practice, researchers commonly report the sum of the two highest rating points (or the bottom two rating scores) from a scale in a table. This is called the **top-two box scores**.[14] For example, instead of showing an entire table, only the "Very likely" and "Somewhat likely" scores are shown. Top-two box scores refer to the sum of percentages in the top two boxes (e.g., "Agree" and "Strongly agree") on a 5-point or 7-point scale. Clients often request top-two box, top box, and (sometimes) bottom-two box scores. Clients sometimes find these easier to interpret than mean scores. Marketing Research Insight 16.2 lists the necessary keystroke instructions to create tables using SPSS.

PIE CHARTS

Pie charts are useful to illustrate the relative sizes or proportions of categories of data.

When you want to illustrate the *relative* sizes or *proportions* of one component versus others, pie charts are useful. For example, if you wanted to illustrate the proportions of consumers that prefer different types of radio programming, a pie chart would be an excellent tool for showing the relative sizes of each type of programming preference. The **pie chart** is a circle divided into sections. Each section represents a percentage of the total area of the circle associated with one category of data. Today's data analysis programs easily and quickly make pie charts. SPSS, for example, allows you to build customized pie charts.

MARKETING RESEARCH INSIGHT 16.2   *Practical Application*

How to Create a Table Using IBM SPSS

We will use the integrated case Auto Concepts dataset (AutoConcepts.sav), which we have used for statistical analysis examples in previous chapters, to demonstrate creating a table with SPSS. Let's say we want to find out education levels of respondents. To do this, we create a simple frequency table for responses to the "Level of education" question in our SPSS dataset. Refer to Figure 16.4.

1. Create a frequency table for responses to the "Level of education" question on the questionnaire. After opening the data file, use ANALYZE-DESCRIPTIVE STATISTICS-FREQUENCIES and select the variable corresponding to education level. The resulting frequency table is displayed in the SPSS Output Viewer.
2. To edit the table, put the cursor anywhere on the table and double-click. This activates the table editor, which is indicated by a black table label and a red arrow pointing to the selected table.
3. Right-click on the table, and select "TableLooks" from the drop-down menu that appears.
4. To select a particular table format, browse through the directory and select one that suits your needs. In this

case, we used AvantGarde format. However, because we want to change the fonts, we have to edit the format we had selected.

5. To edit an already available format, click "Edit Look" while in TABLELOOKS. To change the fonts, alignment, margins, and so on, click on Cell Formats. Change the fonts, size, style, and so on to suit your needs. To change borders, click on Borders and select appropriate borders. You can hide categories by shading all the data in a column, right-clicking, and selecting CLEAR. You can also do this by moving your cursor to the right side of the border of a column and dragging the border to close the column.
6. After adjusting the table properties for the attributes you want, save your customized table format by clicking on SAVE AS within the TABLELOOKS dialog box and saving the table under a new file name.
7. You are now back in the table edit mode. The next step is to change the text in specific cells if you so desire. To do this, double-click on the cell in which you want to change the text. The selected text will be highlighted. Simply type over the text and press Enter when you are done.

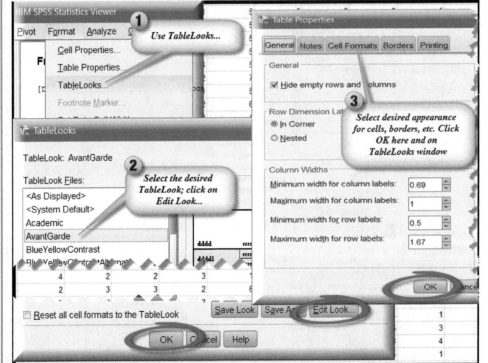

FIGURE 16.4 How to Use IBM SPSS Table-Looks Feature to Create a Table

Source: Reprint Courtesy of International Business Machines Corporation, © International Business Machines Corporation

Most experts agree that the pie chart should have a limited number of segments (four to eight, at most). If your data have many small segments, consider combining the smallest or the least important into an "other" or "miscellaneous" category. Because internal labels are difficult to read for small sections, labels for the sections should be placed outside the circle.

Marketing Research Insight 16.3 lists the keystroke instructions for creating pie charts using SPSS.

MARKETING RESEARCH INSIGHT 16.3   *Practical Application*

How to Create a Pie Chart Using IBM SPSS

We again use data from the Auto Concepts survey (AutoConcepts.sav) to demonstrate the creation of a simple pie graph using SPSS. Let's say we want to show responses to the "Level of education" question in the form of a pie chart.

1. Create a pie chart for responses to the "Level of education" question on the questionnaire. As Figure 16.5 demonstrates, use the Command sequence of the GRAPHS-LEGACY DIALOGS-PIE. Click Summaries for Groups of Cases and then Define.

   The next screen allows you to choose the variable you want to graph. Select the variable corresponding to the question on the questionnaire; click the button for Define Slices By, and the variable will be entered. You can choose what you want your slices to represent. In this case, we selected the slices to represent % of cases.

2. Enter the titles and footnotes for the chart by clicking on TITLES and entering the appropriate labels. Using the command OPTIONS, you can decide how you want missing values to be treated. Click OK and the resulting pie chart will appear in the SPSS Viewer. SPSS displays a legend with the pie chart. You are now ready to edit the chart. (If you have an existing template of a pie graph, you can request the output to be formatted according to template specifications by double-clicking anywhere on the chart; go to FILE-APPLY CHART TEMPLATE and select the saved file name.)

3. Scroll down to the pie chart. To edit the chart, double-click anywhere on the chart. This takes you to the SPSS Chart Editor screen. You will do all your editing in this screen. Refer to Figure 16.6.

FIGURE 16.5 How to Make a Pie Chart with IBM SPSS

Source: Reprint Courtesy of International Business Machines Corporation, © International Business Machines Corporation

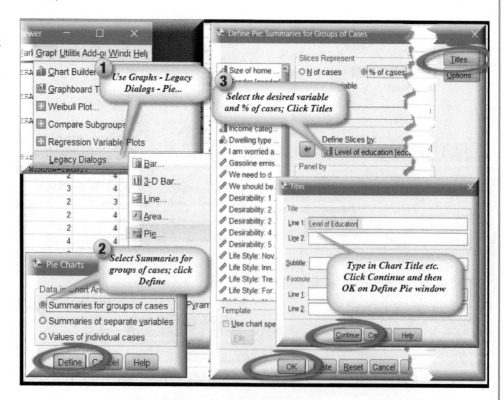

4. In the Chart Editor screen, click on the area you wish to edit. This puts a border around the area to be edited. It also changes the editing tools available to you in the Chart Editor. Click once on the title. You can now edit the font. Right-click once on the pie. Go to SHOW DATA LABELS. A Properties prompt screen will appear. To place a descriptive label on each slice as well as the value, click on the description under Not Displayed and click the green upward arrow. Click Apply and Close. This places values and corresponding descriptive labels within each slice. Click once on any slice so that only that slice is highlighted with a border. Right-click and go to EXPLODE SLICE.

5. Still in Chart Editor, right-click on the pie chart, as shown in Figure 16.6. Choose PROPERTIES WINDOW. Select DEPTH & ANGLE-3-D for EFFECT, move the slide bar down to –60 for *ANGLE*, 3 for DISTANCE. Apply and Close.

6. You can add text *anywhere* on the chart in SPSS. Click the *TEXT* icon in Chart Editor (or go OPTIONS-TEXT BOX).

7. After making all the changes, save your customized chart by using the command options FILE-SAVE CHART TEMPLATE. For future charts, you can call up the customized template, saving the need for you to edit every pie chart you create.

8. The chart is now ready to be transferred to a word processing document.

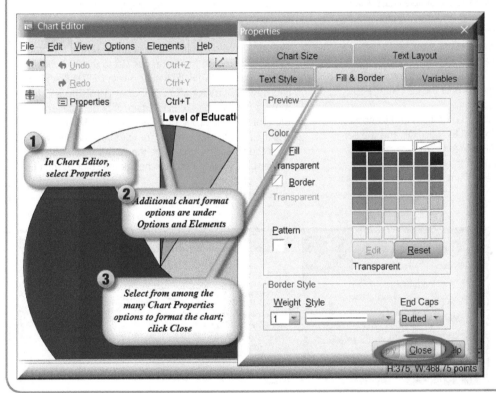

FIGURE 16.6 Use the IBM SPSS Chart Editor to Improve Your Pie Chart's Appearance

Source: Reprint Courtesy of International Business Machines Corporation, © International Business Machines Corporation

BAR CHARTS

Bar charts are used often in reporting survey data because they are easy to interpret. They are useful to report the magnitude of responses or to compare magnitudes among groups. They are also useful for illustrating change over time. Several types of bar charts can be used. Marketing Research Insight 16.4 lists the keystroke instructions for creating bar charts of various types using SPSS. Study the types of bar charts available to you in SPSS. Your selection of the type of bar chart will depend on what you are trying to communicate to your readers.

Bar charts are useful to report the magnitude of responses, to compare magnitudes among groups, and to illustrate change over time.

LINE GRAPHS

Line graphs are easy to interpret if they are designed properly. Line graphs may be drawn in SPSS using the *graphs* option. You will notice there are several options in types of line graphs.

MARKETING RESEARCH INSIGHT 16.4 *Practical Application*

How to Create a Bar Chart Using IBM SPSS

We use data from the Auto Conceptss dataset (AutoConcepts. sav) to demonstrate the creation of a simple bar graph using SPSS. Let's say we want to show graphically the frequency distribution of the level of education.

1. Create a bar chart for responses for "Level of Education." As you can see in Figure 16.7, after opening the data file, use the command GRAPHS-LEGACY DIALOGS-BAR. You have the option of choosing from three different styles of bar charts. In this case, we used the Simple chart. Click Summaries for Groups of Cases and then Define.

   The next screen allows you to choose the variable you want to graph. Enter "Level of Education" in Category Axis. You can choose what you want your bars to represent. In this case, we selected the bars to represent % of cases because we want to know the percentages of respondents' level of education.

2. At this stage, you can also enter the titles and footnotes for the chart by clicking on TITLES. Click OK and the bar chart will appear in the SPSS Viewer. You are now ready to edit the chart. (If you have an existing template of a bar graph while in the Define Simple Bar Summaries for

Groups of Cases box, you can request the output to be formatted according to template specifications by clicking on Use Chart Specifications From and selecting the saved file name.)

3. To edit the chart, double-click anywhere on the chart. This opens the SPSS Chart Editor screen. You will do all your editing in this screen. Figure 16.8 shows the operation of the SPSS Chart Editor screen with our bar chart.

4. In the Chart Editor screen, right-click and select Properties Window. This window allows size, fill and border, 3-D elements, and Variables selections.

5. Click once on one of the bars. All the bars should now be highlighted with a border around them. Notice the tools available to you on the menu bar. Go to the PROPERTIES icon (or go to EDIT-PROPERTIES). Select DEPTH & ANGLE, choose SHADOW for EFFECT, and set OFFSET to +15 by moving the slide bar. APPLY. Again, click on a bar and then the PROPERTIES icon. Select FILL & BORDER and select a pattern and fill color for your bars. APPLY. *Note:* Click the fill button to change the color of the bars. The border button allows you to change the color of the border line of the bars.

FIGURE 16.7 How to Make a Bar Chart with IBM SPSS

Source: Reprint Courtesy of International Business Machines Corporation, © International Business Machines Corporation

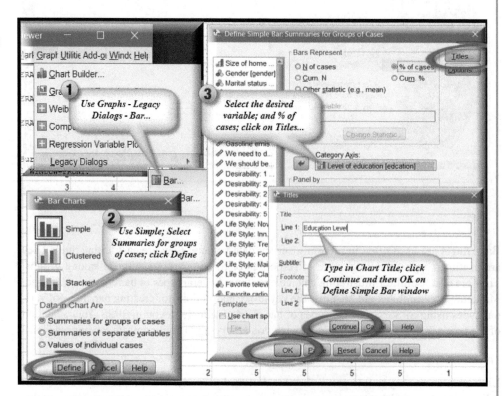

6. Still in Chart Editor, click anywhere other than a bar. Select PROPERTIES WINDOW-FILL & BORDER. Change the color of the background. Click APPLY

7. To edit the textual content of the chart, select the TEXT icon in the Chart Editor (or go to OPTIONS-TEXT BOX). A box and a set of markers will appear. Insert your text and then drag the box where you want the text to appear.

8. After making all the changes, you can save your customized chart by using the command FILE-SAVE CHART TEMPLATE. For future charts, you can call up the customized template, saving the need for you to edit every bar chart you create.

9. The chart is now ready to be transferred to a word processing document.

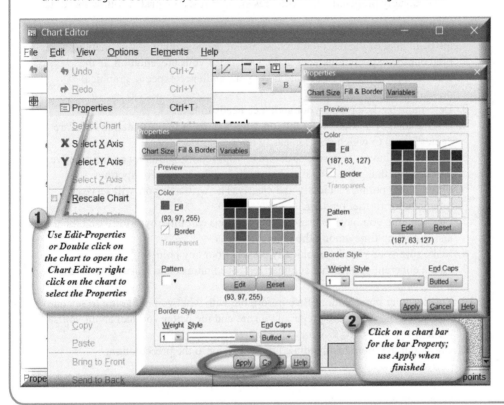

FIGURE 16.8 Use the SPSS Chart Editor to Improve Your Bar Chart's Appearance

Source: Reprint Courtesy of International Business Machines Corporation, © International Business Machines Corporation

FLOW DIAGRAMS

Flow diagrams introduce a set of topics and illustrate their relationships. Flow diagrams are particularly useful to illustrate topics that are sequential (for example, step 1, step 2, and so on).

16-7 Producing an Appropriate Visual

A marketing researcher should always provide visuals that accurately demonstrate the data and avoid misrepresenting the information. Sometimes misrepresenting information is intentional (as when a client asks a researcher to misrepresent the data to promote his or her "pet project") or it may be unintentional. In the latter case, those preparing a visual are sometimes so familiar with the material being presented that they falsely assume the graphic message is apparent to all who view it.

To ensure that you have accurately and objectively prepared your visuals, you should do the following:

- Double- and triple-check all labels, numbers, and visual shapes. A faulty or misleading visual discredits your report and work.
- Make sure all parts of the scales are presented. Truncated graphs (having breaks in the scaled values on either axis) are acceptable only if the audience is familiar with the data.

16-8 Presenting Your Research Orally

The purpose of the oral presentation is to succinctly present the recommendations and conclusions of research and to provide an opportunity for questions and discussion.

Marketing researchers are often asked to present an oral summary of the conclusions and recommendations of their research. The purpose of the **oral presentation** is to succinctly present the information and to provide an opportunity for questions and discussion. The presentation may be accomplished through a simple conference with the client, or it may be a formal presentation to a roomful of people.

To be adequately prepared when you present your research orally, follow these steps:

1. Identify and analyze your audience. Consider the same questions you addressed at the beginning of the research process and at the beginning of this chapter.
2. Find out the expectations your audience has for your presentation. Is the presentation formal or informal? Does your audience expect a graphical presentation?
3. Determine the key points your audience needs to hear.
4. Outline the key points, preferably on 3-by-5 cards or in presentation software "notes" areas to which you can easily refer.
5. Be sure you have a cohesive structure to your report, including an informative introduction that explains why what you are about to say is important.
6. Present your points succinctly and clearly. The written report will serve as a reference for further reading.
7. Plan the time you have to present your findings carefully by prioritizing the points and allocating time among the points.
8. Make sure your visuals graphically portray your key points.
9. Plan a coherent ending that summarizes your findings and leaves a final strong impression.
10. Practice your presentation. Be comfortable with what you are going to say and how you look. The more prepared you are and the better you feel about yourself, the less you will need to worry about jitters.
11. Check out the room and media equipment prior to the presentation.
12. Arrive early.
13. Be positive and confident. You are the authority; you know more about your subject than anyone else.
14. Speak loudly enough for all in the room to hear. Enunciate clearly. Maintain eye contact and good posture.
15. Look engaged while other members of your team are presenting.
16. Dress appropriately.

16-9 Alternative Ways to Present Findings

Marketing Research on YouTube™ To see how one marketing research firm incorporates storytelling when presenting results, go to **www.youtube.com** and type in "Unforgettable Story Writing in 6 Easy Steps."

It is important for you to know the standard practices of reporting data as presented in this chapter. However, you should also know that there are a number of alternative innovative and effective ways to present findings. Using an example of its research on Latino consumers, the marketing research firm Gongos demonstrates how researchers present findings in ways that bring data to life for their clients in Marketing Research Insight 16.5. In another example, MTV used an entire floor of offices to create an exhibit called "High School Hallways." Parts of the exhibit included a high school bedroom, a party room, and a social media detox tent (see Chapter 6). While Gongos and MTV take communicating results to a whole new level, there are a number of tools that all researchers can use to present results in interesting and potent ways, such as videos and infographics. Keep in mind, however, that no matter what techniques you use, it is up to you—not your tools—to bring meaning to the data that you present.[15]

Reporting in the World of Market Research: The New Dimensionality of Learning

There was a time when an 80+-page research report was commonplace. Nearly every question market researchers asked of their consumer subjects landed either in a chart, an executive summary, or both. Those deliverables, often found in PowerPoint, were eventually dispersed on a shared drive and archived into growing terabytes of proprietary knowledge.

But today a new imperative—one that serves to empower frontline and C-suite executives—exists inside insight organizations within *Fortune 500* and *Global 1000* companies: *Storytelling. Synthesis. Insight Curation. Video Documentaries.* And the ever-important *IWIK-SIC ("I wish I knew, so I could")*. These are the new buzzwords in "reporting." And the students of today and researchers of tomorrow will not only become intimately acquainted with these tools but work swiftly and strategically as well to create new generations of information-gathering techniques and knowledge-centric platforms.

The Industry's Stance

Peer-to-peer industry presentations and feature articles exclaiming "Is PowerPoint dead?" have filled the blogosphere since 2012. Soon after, the onslaught of "big data" and other impending sources of consumer knowledge changed the way we take in information. Beyond dashboards and other digital visualization platforms, insight professionals had to find a way to cut through the fray of information to truly garner the attention of time-constrained decision makers. With real-time information feeds and the mandate to gut check those against

primary research findings, conventional reporting was neither the quickest nor the most impactful way to distribute information that would ultimately empower decision makers to do their job well.

Besides presenting compelling and immersive insights packaged inside a headline or two, this information needs to reach a broader corporate audience while being accessible, consumable, and memorable. In theory, research findings of today must find ways to reach readers at a visceral level. They need to inform and inspire people at all levels of an organization to make faster and better decisions on behalf of their peers and their organization.

Insights in Action: One Client's Story

So, what does this actually look like inside an organization?

As an industry, health care had experienced a marketplace shift brought on, in part, by the Affordable Care Act (ACA) of 2010. As a result, this shift prompted the need for a prominent health insurer in the Midwest to recalibrate its customer-minded strategies to create more reciprocal relationships with Latinos living in Michigan. In its vast customer base, Latinos are a critical, growing, underinsured population deserving to be understood both from a cultural and community-driven perspective.

This client entrusted Gongos' insight curation practice, Arti|fact, to create an immersive experience at its corporate headquarters to enable key executives and decision makers to

Visit Gongos at http://www.gongos.com.

"walk in the shoes" of Latino families. Instead of *presenting* the research insights and subsequent marketing and business implications within the staid walls of a boardroom, researchers leveraged the senses of sight, sound, and touch to empower company stakeholders to truly understand—and empathize with—this growing population. In place of an 80+-page report, the research findings *came to life* inside of an 800+-square-foot space.

LATINO IMMERSION SPACE

STATION 1

Immerse in the most uninsured demographic with life-size information panels that set the stage for understanding why Latinos are an imperative focus for this company.

STATION 2

Discover frictions between Latinos and the U.S. health care system in the doctor's office waiting room, complete with a video story, interactive tablet activity and competitive intelligence booklet!

STATION 3

Dive into Latino values including family, friends, faith and diversity in this 3D exhibit space highlighting Latino culture. Learn what matters most to their identity and how it must translate into messaging and communication.

STATION 4

Reflect on your experience at the wrap-up station, featuring a board to share learnings and inspiration. Dive deeper into the dynamic report, which showcases insights from the initiative in an immersive and interactive web-based platform.

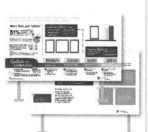

Gongos replaced a research report with an immersive experience to make research findings come to life.

Source: Text and photos courtesy Gongos Research

VIDEOS

Many marketing research firms and advertising agencies supplement their written and oral research reports with videos showing "in-the-moment" clips (sometimes called "vox pops" or "voice of the people"). Videos can be embedded in electronic reports or incorporated into oral presentations. A written and oral report can be replaced by a documentary-style video.[16] Video footage that is gathered through observation or ethnographic methods can be used to illustrate key takeaways from research studies. For example, when Pittsburgh advertising agency MARC USA presented research for repositioning a cable television network, the agency illustrated its findings by incorporating video clips of opinions from the target audience.[17] When BP conducted a segmentation study, the research report was supplemented with an eight-minute video that featured footage of a person from each segment.[18] Seeing real people speaking with emotion can be a very powerful tool in support of recommended directions.

INFOGRAPHICS

Infographics are visual reports designed to make key research results understood quickly and easily. Infographics are part of a trend to keep results simple and actionable. Like written reports, infographics display findings through graphs, tables, figures, and other visuals with written explanations reduced to their essential meanings. Infographics can take a physical form, as in a brochure or a newsletter-style document, or be solely electronic.

Infographics are visual reports designed to make key research results understood quickly and easily.

Well-designed infographics can summarize or even replace lengthy written reports—and can take just as long to create. Creating a short and effective document that avoids "chartjunk" takes skill and time.[19] A demand exists in the marketing field for employees who are not only knowledgeable about marketing research techniques but who also have the graphic skills to create attractive and informative visual representations of information.[20] Excellent examples of infographics can be found online at websites such as http://www.teradata.com, http://www.dailyinfographic.com, http://www.coolinfographics.com, and http://www.mashable.com.

16-10 Disseminating Results Throughout an Organization

Whatever method is used to present research findings, results uncovered from a marketing research study will ultimately have little or no effect on how a company conducts its business if the insights gained from the project are not disseminated across a firm to all the essential operating units and become part of the "lifeblood" of the organization.[21] Tom De Ruyck, managing partner of InSites Consulting, advocates for "the memefication of insights" in which insights about consumer behavior and emotions are spread through "key ambassadors" in a company. In one example, InSites used multiple methods to increase the knowledge that 1,000 Unilever employees working in research and development had of consumers, including administering mini-quizzes on consumers' habits and attitudes over a period of several weeks.[22] In another example, Northstar Research created and distributed coasters with customer-inspired avatars throughout the Land Rover automobile manufacturer to develop awareness of consumer characteristics in all departments of the organization.[23] Research updates can be disseminated on an ongoing basis to managers through regular newsletters or through social media tools such Twitter. Whatever the method, it is important that research findings are communicated throughout a company.

DASHBOARDS

Web-based platforms, often called "dashboards," are an increasingly popular means of disseminating research throughout an organization. As featured in the introduction, Tableau and other brands of dashboards allow users to visualize and interact with their data. **Dashboards** provide digital interfaces that allow users to quickly and easily see information that is presented in a simplified manner. Dashboards are part of the "democratization" of marketing research that was referred to in the introduction. They allow companies to gather and integrate data from several different sources and then exhibit the data automatically with tables, graphs, and other numerical displays. Dashboards can be used for tracking a number of marketing activities, such as performance of web pages, responses to advertising campaigns, and geographical buying behavior.

Dashboards provide digital interfaces that allow users to quickly and easily see information that is presented in a simplified manner.

Firms such as Tableau and Burke, Inc., provide clients with access to dashboards that allow clients to monitor data on an ongoing basis. Readers can examine total results or conduct their own subgroup analysis, even down to examining the results of individual respondents. Because the reports are available online, different client users can access the reports and conduct analyses that are important to their unit or division. Online reporting software electronically distributes marketing research reports to selected managers in an interactive format that allows users to conduct their own analyses. To give you a "close encounter" with Burke's dashboard concept, we provide an Active Learning exercise.

 **Active Learning**

Take a Tour of an Online Marketing Research Report Service

To take a closer look at Burke's online reporting writing software, Digital Dashboard, go to http://www.digitaldashboard.com. Click on "About Digital Dashboard®." Read about the features and take a look at the example output pages. (Don't run the demonstration yet!) Note the features of "In the Customer's Words," "Individual Reports," and "Data Collection Status Report." When you have read all the features, it is time to take the tour, noted at the bottom of the screen. (The program will run automatically—just give it a few seconds.) Watch for features such as the data filter, executive summary, trends over time, and comparison of the results of significant subgroups; the ability to filter to examine any subgroup results desired; the option to search for verbatim comments; the ability to conduct statistical testing using the report software; and the utility to create your own charts and titles and transfer data to spreadsheets. Can you see how such tools can make the reporting process more efficient and the report more usable for clients?

The use of dashboards is an important development in the reporting of marketing research data for two important reasons. First, dashboards put research results into the hands of nontechnical users, allowing managers to explore data on their own. Second, research analysts may use dashboards to replace slide presentations of data, such as PowerPoint slides. The dashboard can be projected, allowing a researcher to use just one dynamic computerized interface to display data. An advantage of this method is that it eliminates the time needed to develop static slides, along with the mistakes that can result when data are copied. In addition, the data used in a presentation will always be the latest data, with no need to update slides. When questions arise during a presentation (for example, "How did lower-income consumers respond to this question?" or "Which retailers showed the best response to these promotions?"), the researcher is able to answer the queries on the spot.

Summary

Just as technology has changed the way we do many things, it has also affected report writing and presentations. The marketing research report is a factual message that transmits research results, vital recommendations, conclusions, and other important information to the client, who in turn bases his or her decision making on the contents of the report. The client's decisions may depend on how well the report communicates the research results. Regardless of the care in the design and execution of the research project itself, if the report does not adequately communicate the project to the client, all of the hard work in conducting the project is meaningless.

While preparing and writing the report may be time consuming, advances are being made to make report writing more efficient. Tools are available that automatically provide citations for sources of information used in a report. Statistical packages, such as SPSS, have features that allow for ease of preparation of tables and visuals such as bar charts and pie charts. Technology will continue to improve report writing, presentation preparation, and distribution of reports.

Marketing research reports should be tailored to their audiences. They are typically organized into the elements of front matter, body, and end matter. Each element has subparts that serve a specific purpose.

Plagiarism refers to representing the work of others as your own. It is a serious offense in the real world to plagiarize; people lose their jobs due to this ethical lapse. Proper referencing of source materials not only allows writers to avoid charges of plagiarism but offers other advantages as well.

Conclusions are based on the results of the research, and recommendations are suggestions on how to proceed based on conclusions. Increasingly, researchers are expected to add strategic value to their reports.

Guidelines for writing the marketing research report include proper use of headings and subheadings, which serve as signposts to the reader, and proper use of visuals, such as tables and figures. Style considerations include beginning paragraphs with topic sentences, using transitional sentences, and keeping paragraphs short. Style also includes spare use of jargon, strong verbs, active voice, consistent tense, and proofreading.

Care should be taken to ensure that all presentations are clear and objective to the reader. Many visual aids may be distorted so that they have a different meaning to the reader. Researchers must adhere to ethical guidelines when preparing research reports. Reports rely on tables, figures, and graphical displays of various types. SPSS includes routines for creating report tables and graphs. We describe step-by-step commands on how to use SPSS to make professional-appearing tables and graphs.

In some cases, marketing researchers are required to present the findings of their research project to the client orally. Guidelines for making an oral presentation include knowing the audience and their expectations and the key points you wish to make; correctly preparing visuals; practicing; checking out presentation facilities and equipment prior to the presentation; and being positive.

In addition to traditional written and oral reports, there are a number of alternative and innovative ways to present research results. Some research firms emphasize storytelling techniques to bring data to life. An example by Gongos Research shows how the company created a room-sized physical space to provide clients with an immersive and interactive understanding of the research findings. Many marketing research suppliers and advertising firms use videos to show "in-the-moment" clips. Infographics are used to make key research results understood quickly and easily.

Online reporting software is an efficient tool that assists marketing researchers in monitoring data collection and disseminating research results. It also allows data users to interact with the reports and to manage data. Tableau is a good example of an online reporting system that allows clients to interact with the report.

Key Terms

Data visualization (p. 434)
Marketing research report (p. 435)
Plagiarism (p. 436)
Front matter (p. 437)
Title page (p. 438)
Letter of authorization (p. 438)
Letter of transmittal (p. 439)
Memo of transmittal (p. 439)
Table of contents (p. 440)
List of illustrations (p. 441)
Tables (p. 441)
Figures (p. 441)
Abstract/executive summary (p. 442)
Body (p. 442)

Introduction (p. 442)
Research objectives (p. 442)
Method (p. 442)
Methodology (p. 443)
Results (p. 443)
Limitations (p. 443)
Conclusions (p. 443)
Recommendations (p. 443)
End matter (p. 444)
Appendices (p. 444)
Reference list (p. 444)
Endnotes (p. 444)
Headings (p. 444)
Subheadings (p. 444)

Visuals (p. 444)
Topic sentence (p. 445)
Body of the paragraph (p. 445)
Transitional sentence (p. 445)
Tables (p. 446)
Top-two box scores (p. 446)
Pie charts (p. 446)
Bar charts (p. 449)
Line graphs (p. 449)
Flow diagrams (p. 451)
Oral presentation (p. 452)
Infographics (p. 455)
Dashboards (p. 455)

Review Questions/Applications

16-1. Discuss the relative importance of the marketing research report to the other stages in the marketing research process.

16-2. What is the derivation of the word *plagiarism*?

16-3. What are the components of the marketing research report?

16-4. When should you write a memo? When should you write a letter?

16-5. Should you use *method* or *methodology* to describe how the research was conducted? Why?

16-6. Distinguish among results, conclusions, and recommendations.

16-7. When should you acknowledge you have limitations in your report?

16-8. When should you use a subheading?

16-9. What are the components of a readable, logical paragraph?

16-10. What are some elements of good style in report writing?

16-11. What are the key features of a table?

16-12. What visual would be the best at displaying the relative changes in spending between four promotion mix variables over time?

16-13. What tool can be used to present lengthy findings in a shorter form?

16-14. What is the purpose of an oral presentation?

16-15. Go online and search for examples of marketing research reports. Chances are good that you will be able to find several reports of various kinds. Examine the reports. What commonalities do they have in terms of the sections the authors have created? Look at the sections carefully. What types of issues were addressed in the introduction section and the method section? How did the authors organize all of the information reported in the results section? How are recommendations different than conclusions?

16-16. Describe what may be in the future for reporting data, based on the example provided by Gongos Research.

16-17. How can videos be utilized in marketing research reports?

16-18. What are *dashboards*? How can they be used by marketing researchers and clients?

CASE 16.1 INTEGRATED CASE

Auto Concepts: Report Writing IBM **SPSS**

Cory Rogers is ready to write the first draft of the final report for Auto Concepts. Nick Thomas of Auto Concepts has told Cory that ZEN Motors has its own marketing research department and that researchers there are eager to read his report. Cory knows they will be particularly interested in technical issues such as determination of sample size and margin of error. Cory has also had a frank discussion with Nick about conclusions and recommendations. Nick told him, "Cory, I want to know what the numbers say. What are the conclusions based on those numbers? In terms of how to proceed, I will meet with my top staff members, and we will make those decisions. We have to factor in many constraints to make final decisions."

As an experienced marketing researcher, Cory is very familiar with the steps in the marketing research process. Knowledge of these steps is useful in writing the method section of his marketing research reports. For example, Cory knows he should address the types and sources of information used in the report; he should also address the research design and why it was chosen over other designs. The sampling plan and sample size should also be included in this section. Cory makes a list of topics he should cover and starts organizing these topics in terms of headings and subheadings that will be used in the final report.

Cory reminds himself, "I have to properly cite every source I have used in this report." He dreads this step. As many times as he has written reports, remembering every detail that goes in a reference is just something that will not stay in Cory's memory bank. Still, he understands how important it is to use the proper form for his reference list.

1. What should Cory consider doing with the information in this case before he actually begins to write the report? Name some specific issues Cory should address.

2. Should Cory include the standard "Conclusions and Recommendations" section of the report? Why or why not?

3. What tools can Cory use to be sure he is properly citing the secondary sources used in the marketing research report?

CASE 16.2 INTEGRATED CASE

Auto Concepts: Making a PowerPoint Presentation

Cory Rogers of CMG Research completes the report for Auto Concepts and decides to make some PowerPoint slides to use in his presentation of the findings. Working in Microsoft Word, he writes a title to his presentation: "Auto Concepts: A Marketing Research Study to Determine Car Model Preferences and Profile Market Segments." Then he writes several other comments he wants to include in the beginning of his presentation, such as the research objectives and several issues dealing with the method used, including the sample plan and sample size. After Cory writes a number of the statements that he thinks might help him communicate the purpose and method of the study, he turns his attention to presenting the findings.

Cory decides to begin his presentation of the study with a description of the sample, often referred to as a "profile of the sample." He notices that for gender and marital status, there are only two categories (male, female and married, unmarried) for each question. He decides to orally report the percentages of these categories. However, for some of the other variables, there are several categories of response, and he decides the best way to communicate the results is by showing the frequency distribution table. He prepares a frequency distribution of the responses to these questions using SPSS and then continues to make several key analyses of the data using SPSS.

1. Using a word processing program, write several of the statements you think would be appropriate to present to the client in an oral presentation.
2. Import the statements you prepared in question 1 into PowerPoint using copy and paste. Experiment with different color text and font sizes and styles.
3. For each statement, using SPSS, run the appropriate frequency distribution. Using TABLELOOKS, select the format you like. Copy and paste your tables into PowerPoint.
4. Using SPSS, make a bar chart of the answers to the question regarding the variable "I am worried about global warming." Experiment with the different options of bar charts available to you in SPSS. Select a bar chart and copy and paste that chart into PowerPoint using copy and paste. Experiment with making edits on your slide.

Endnotes

Chapter 1

1. Wasserstrom, J. (2011, February 24). Media and revolution 2.0: From Tiananmen to Tahrir. Retrieved from Miller-McCune, http://www.miller-mccune.com/media/media-and-revolution-2-0-tiananmen-to-tahrir-28595

2. Kotler, P., & Keller, K. L. (2006). *Marketing management* (12th ed.). Upper Saddle River, NJ: Prentice Hall, p. 5.

3. Kindle Fire is the most successful product we've ever launched. (2011, December 11). *Time Techland*. Retrieved from http://techland.time.com/2011/12/15/amazon-kindle-fire-is-the-most-successful-product-weve-ever-launched

4. American Marketing Association. (2007, October). Definition of marketing. Retrieved from https://www.ama.org/AboutAMA/Pages/Definition-of-Marketing.aspx

5. Shostack, G. L. (1977). Breaking free from product marketing. *Journal of Marketing, 41*(2), 74. Shostack's original example used General Motors.

6. Schneider, J., & Hall, J. (2011, April). Why most product launches fail. *Harvard Business Review*, 21–23.

7. 25 biggest product flops of all time. (2012, January 21). *Daily Finance*. Retrieved from http://www.dailyfinance.com/photos/top-25-biggest-product-flops-of-all-time

8. Jargon, J. (2014, April 13). Burger King drops lower-calorie fry 'satisfries.'" *Wall Street Journal*. Retrieved from http://www.wsj.com/articles/burger-king-drops-lower-calorie-fries-1407964129

9. These philosophies epitomize the product concept and the selling concept. See Kotler, P., & Armstrong, G. (2001). *Principles of marketing* (9th ed.). Upper Saddle River, NJ: Prentice Hall, p. 18.

10. Kotler, P. (2003). *Marketing management* (11th ed.). Upper Saddle River, NJ: Prentice Hall, p. 19.

11. Kotler, P. (2003). *Marketing management* (11th ed.). Upper Saddle River, NJ: Prentice Hall, p. 19.

12. Some scholars have added the concept of holistic marketing, which includes four components: relationship marketing, integrated marketing, internal marketing, and social responsibility marketing. For additional reading on this topic, see Kotler & Keller, *Marketing management*, pp. 15–23.

13. Bennett, P. D. (Ed.) (1995). *Dictionary of marketing terms* (2nd ed.). Chicago: American Marketing Association, p. 169.

14. See the Marketing Research Association website for a glossary of these and other terms used in the marketing and opinion research industry. (2012, June 29). Retrieved from http://www.marketingresearch.org/glossary

15. Pimley, S. (2008, August). Looking to increase their (s)miles per gallon. *Quirk's Marketing Research Review*, p. 32.

16. Berstell, G. (2011, December) Listen and learn—and sell. *Quirk's Marketing Research Review*, 48.

17. Monllos, K. (2015, September 28). Chobani extends its "Flip" Campaign after sales increase by 300%. *Adweek*. Retrieved from http://www.adweek.com/news/advertising-branding/chobani-extends-its-flip-campaign-after-sales-increase-300-167186

18. Dahab, D., O'Gara, L., & Vermass, J. (2007, October). As banks strive to build relationships, a national tracking study finds that good service is still key for customers. *Quirk's Marketing Research Review*, 52.

19. Janakiraman, N., Meyer, R., & Hoch, S. (2011). The psychology of decisions to abandon waits for service. *Journal of Marketing Research, 48*(6), 970. Retrieved from ABI/INFORM Global (Document ID: 2548456281)

20. Personal communication with the authors from Vincent P. Barabba, General Motors Corp, 1997.

21. Market research: Pre-testing helps ad effectiveness. (2003, May 8). *Marketing*, 27.

22. Tracy, K. (1998). *Jerry Seinfeld: The entire domain.* Secaucus, NJ: Carol, pp. 64–65.

23. Hodock, C. L. (2007). *Why smart companies do dumb things.* Amherst, NY: Prometheus, p. 157.

24. The description of MIS is adapted from Kotler & Keller, *Marketing management.*

25. Ibid.

Chapter 2

1. *U.S. News & World Report.* (2015). Best business jobs. Retrieved from http://money.usnews.com/careers/best-jobs/market-research-analyst

2. Lockley, L. C. (1950). Notes on the history of marketing research. *Journal of Marketing, 14*(5), 733–736.

3. Gallup, G., & Rae, S. F. (1940). *The pulse of democracy.* New York: Simon & Schuster, p. 35.

4. Hower, R. M. (1939). *The history of an advertising agency.* Cambridge, MA: Harvard University Press, pp. 88–90.

5. You can see a list of past Parlin Award winners going back to 1945 at http://themarketingfoundation.org/parlin_recipients.html

6. Hardy, H. (1990). *The politz papers: Science and truth in marketing research.* Chicago: American Marketing Association.

7. Bartels, R. (1976). *The history of marketing thought.* Cleveland, OH: Grid Publishing, p. 125.

8. Much of this section is based on Honomichl, J. (2006). Jack J. Honomichl on the marketing research industry. In Burns, A. C., & Bush, R. F. (2006). *Marketing research* (5th ed.). Upper Saddle River, NJ: Pearson/Prentice Hall, pp. 40–41.

9. *GreenBook.* (2015). *GreenBook Industry Trends Report*, 17th ed., New York, p. 40.

10. Murphy, L. (2015, July 21). Microsoft aims to disrupt market research: Here is the scoop and what it means for the future. *GreenBook*. Retrieved from www.greenbookblog.org/2015/07/21/microsoft-aims-to-disrupt-market-research-here-is-the-scoop-and-what-it-means-for-the-future

11. ESOMAR Industry Report. (2014). *Global market research 2014.* Amsterdam, The Netherlands: ESOMAR, p. 6.

12. Bowers, D., & Brereton, M. (2015). The 2015 AMA gold global top 50 report. *Marketing News,* 13.

13. Ibid.

14. Ibid.

15. ESOMAR (2015). *Global market research 2015*, p. 6.

16. Poynter, R. (2010). *The handbook of online and social media research: Tools and techniques for market researchers.* West Sussex, UK: Wiley, pp. xiv–xix.

17. ESOMAR (2015). *Global market research 2015*, p. 59.

18. ESOMAR (2015). *Global market research 2015*, p. 64.

19. ESOMAR (2011). *Global market research 2011*, pp. 22–29.

20. ESOMAR (2015). *Global market research 2015*, p. 64.

21. Rydholm, J. (2015). Client-side researchers offer dos and don'ts for MR vendors. *Quirk's Marketing Research Media*. Retrieved from http://www.quirks.com/articles/2015/20151025-1.aspx

22. *Quirk's Marketing Research Media* (2015). *Quirk's Corporate Research Report*. http://www.quirks.com/PDF/CorporateResearch Report.pdf

23. *GreenBook*. (2015). *GreenBook Industry Trends Report*, 17th ed., New York, p. 46.

24. Rydholm, J. (2015). Client-side researchers offer dos and don'ts for MR vendors. *Quirk's Marketing Research Media*. Retrieved from http://www.quirks.com/articles/2015/20151025-1.aspx

25. *GreenBook*. (2015). *GreenBook Industry Trends Report*, 17th ed., New York, pp. 43–45.

26. *GreenBook*. (2015). *GreenBook Industry Trends Report*, 17th ed., New York, p. 46.

27. ESOMAR. (2015). *Global market research 2015*, p. 59.

28. ESOMAR. (2015). *Global market research 2015*, p. 61.

29. See http://www.marketingresearch.org/issues-policies/best-practice

30. What is a push poll? AAPOR defines it as a form of negative campaigning disguised as a political poll. "Push polls" are actually political telemarketing—phone calls disguised as research that aim to persuade large numbers of voters and affect election outcomes rather than measure opinions. Retrieved from http://www.aapor.org/What_is_a_Push_Poll_1.htm, accessed March 10, 2012.

31. Council of American Survey Research Organizations. (2015, July 1). *What survey participants need to know*. Retrieved from http://www.casro.org/?page=participantstoknow&hhSearchTerms=%22Survey+and+Participants+and+Need+and+Know%22

32. American Association for Public Opinion Research. (2015, July 1). *Transparency Initiative*. Retrieved from https://www.aapor.org/AAPORKentico/Transparency-Initiative.aspx

33. ESOMAR. (2015). *Global market research 2015*, pp. 60–65.

34. Riviera, E. (2015). *Market research in the U.S.* Retrieved from http://www.ibisworld.com/industry/default.aspx?indid=1442

Chapter 3

1. Others have broken the marketing research process down into different numbers of steps. Regardless, there is widespread agreement that using a step process approach is a useful tool for learning marketing research.

2. Malhotra, N. (2010). *Marketing research: An applied orientation* (6th ed.). Upper Saddle River, NJ: Pearson/Prentice Hall, p. 14.

3. Hagins, B. (2010, May). The ROI on calculating research's ROI. *Quirk's Marketing Research Review, 14*, 52–58.

4. Adapted from Adler, L. (1979, September 17). Secrets of when and when not to embark on a marketing research project. *Sales & Marketing Management Magazine, 123*, 108.

5. Gibson, L. D. (1998, Spring). Defining marketing problems: Don't spin your wheels solving the wrong puzzle. *Marketing Research, 10*(4), 7.

6. Retrieved from www.dictionary.com, accessed November 13, 2003.

7. Muthalyan, S. (2011, November 15). Maximizing retail promotions using smart alerts. *Marketing News*, 13.

8. For example, see Gordon, G. L., Schoenbachler, D. D., Kaminski, P. F., & Brouchous, K. A. (1997). New product development: Using the salesforce to identify opportunities. *Business and Industrial Marketing, 12*(1), 33; Ardjchvilj, A., Cardozo, R., & Ray, S. (2003, January). A theory of entrepreneurial opportunity identification and development. *Journal of Business Venturing, 18*(1), 105.

9. Drummond-Dunn, D. (2015, May 6). Why marketing doesn't always get the research it needs, but usually what it deserves. *GreenBook*. Retrieved from http://www.greenbookblog.org/2015/05/06/why-marketing-doesnt-always-get-the-research-it-needs-but-usually-what-it-deserves

10. Semon, T. (1999, June 7). Make sure the research will answer the right question. *Marketing News, 33*(12), H30.

11. Adapted from Merriam-Webster online at http://www.merriam-webster.com/dictionary/hypothesis and dictionary.com/hypothesis

12. "Students may be surprised to learn that there is little agreement in the advertising industry as to what constitutes a 'better' advertising claim at the testing stage. The researcher is often saddled with the task of measuring the quality of the claims and with defining what a better claim should be. It would be helpful if the firm has a history of testing claims and has reached agreement on what constitutes a 'better' claim. In the end the definition of 'better' must be based on consensus or the decision cannot be made." Quote provided to the authors by Ron Tatham, Ph.D.

13. Smith, S. M., & Albaum, G. S. (2005). *Fundamentals of marketing research*. Thousand Oaks, CA: Sage, p. 349.

14. American Marketing Association. (n.d.). Dictionary. Retrieved from www.marketingpower.com, December 10, 2003.

15. Bearden, W. O., Netemeyer, R. G., & Mobley, M. F. (1993). *Handbook of marketing scales*. Newberry Park, CA: Sage; Bearden, W. O., & Netemeyer, R. G. (1999). *Handbook of marketing scales: Multi-item measures for marketing and consumer behavior research*. Thousand Oaks, CA: Sage; and Bruner, G. C., Hensel, P. J., & James, K. E. (2005). *Marketing scales handbook: A compilation of multi-item measures for consumer behavior and advertising*. Chicago: American Marketing Association.

16. Moser, A. (2005). Take steps to avoid misused research pitfall. *Marketing News, 39*(15), 27.

17. See Burns, A. C., & Bush, R. F. (2006). Insights based on 30 years of defining the problem and research objectives, *Marketing research* (5th ed.). Upper Saddle River, NJ: Pearson/Prentice Hall, pp. 92–93.

18. Kane, C. (1994, November 28). New product killer: The research gap. *Brandweek, 35*(46), 12.

19. Mariampolski, H. (2000, December). A guide to writing and evaluating qualitative research proposals. *Quirk's Marketing Research Review*.

Chapter 4

1. Singleton, D. (2003, November 24). Basics of good research involve understanding six simple rules. *Marketing News*, 22–23.

2. For an excellent in-depth treatment of research design issues, see Creswell, J. (2003). *Research design: Qualitative, quantitative, and mixed methods approaches*. Thousand Oaks, CA: Sage.

3. Boitnott, J. (2014, September 22). 40 young people who became millionaires before they were 20. *Inc.* Retrieved from http://www.inc.com/john-boitnott/40-young-people-who-became-millionaires-before-they-were-20.html

4. Company test marketing water bottle kiosks at WVU. (2012, April 9). *The Marietta Times*. Retrieved from http://www.wvgazettemail.com/Business/201204080024

5. For one example, see Parasuraman, A., Berry, L. L., & Zeithaml, V. A. (1991, Winter). Refinement and reassessment of the SERVQUAL scale. *Journal of Retailing, 67*(4), 420ff. A small effort of exploratory research on this topic will find many references on measuring service quality.

6. Stewart, D. W. (1984). *Secondary research: Information sources and methods*. Newbury Park, CA: Sage; Davidson, J. P. (1985,

April). Low cost research sources. *Journal of Small Business Management, 23,* 73–77.

7. Malhotra, N. K. (2010). *Marketing research: An applied orientation* (6th ed.). Upper Saddle River, NJ: Pearson Prentice Hall, p. 40.

8. Bonoma, T. V. (1984). Case research in marketing: Opportunities, problems, and a process. *Journal of Marketing Research, 21,* 199–208.

9. Chen, C., Zhang, J., & Delaurentis, T. (2014). Quality control in food supply chain management: An analytical model and case study of the adulterated milk incident in China. *International Journal of Production Economics, 152,* 188–199.

10. Bowen, S. A., & Zheng, Y. (2015). Auto recall crisis, framing, and ethical response: Toyota's missteps. *Public Relations Review, 41*(1), 40–49.

11. Thomas, J. (2015, April 2). Rams fans make plea, express concern to NFL over team's possible move. *McClatchy-Tribune Business News.* ProQuest.

12. Sudman, S., & Wansink, B. (2002). *Consumer panels* (2nd ed.). Chicago: American Marketing Association. This book is recognized as an authoritative source on panels.

13. Esterl, M., & Vranica, S. (2015, August 7). Pepsi starts shipping aspartame-free soda. *Wall Street Journal.* Retrieved from http://www.wsj.com/articles/pepsi-starts-shipping-aspartame-free-soda-1438948840

14. Esterl, M. (2015, October 8). New Diet Pepsi leaves some loyalists with bad taste. *Wall Street Journal.* Retrieved from http://www.wsj.com/articles/new-diet-pepsi-leaves-some-loyalists-with-bad-taste-1444327691

15. In fact, the Affordable Care Act signed into law in March 2010 by President Obama requires the FDA to develop standards requiring restaurant chains with 20 or more outlets to provide food labeling.

16. See, for example, Montgomery, D. (2001). *Design and analysis of experiments.* New York: Wiley; Kerlinger, F. N. (1986). *Foundations of behavioral research* (3rd ed.). New York: Holt, Rinehart, and Winston.

17. Campbell, D. T., & Stanley, J. C. (1963). *Experimental and quasi-experimental designs for research.* Chicago: Rand McNally.

18. Calder, B. J., Phillips, L. W., & Tybout, A. M. (1992, December). The concept of external validity. *Journal of Consumer Research, 9,* 240–244.

19. Gray, L. R., & Diehl, P. L. (1992). *Research methods for business and management.* New York: Macmillan, pp. 387–390.

20. Brennan, L. (1988, March). Test marketing. *Sales Marketing Management Magazine, 140,* 50–62.

21. Chavez, J. (2015, May 14). Taco Bell's Quesalupa to be served nationwide. *Toledo Blade.* Retrieved from http://www.toledoblade.com/Retail/2015/05/14/Taco-Bell-s-Quesalupa-to-be-served-nationwide.html

22. Churchill, G. A., Jr. (2001). *Basic marketing research* (4th ed.). Fort Worth, TX: Dryden Press, pp. 144–145.

23. Spethmann, B. (1985, May 8). Test market USA. *Brandweek, 36,* 40–43.

24. Melvin, P. (1992, September). Choosing simulated test marketing systems. *Marketing Research, 4*(3), 14–16.

25. Ibid. Also see Turner, J., & Brandt, J. (1978, Winter). Development and validation of a simulated market to test children for selected consumer skills. *Journal of Consumer Affairs,* 266–276.

26. Greene, S. (1996, May 4). Chattanooga chosen as test market for smokeless cigarette. *Knight-Ridder/Tribune Business News.* Retrieved from Lexis-Nexis.

27. Power, C. (1992, August 10). Will it sell in Podunk? Hard to say. *Business Week,* 46–47.

28. Murphy, P., & Laczniak, G. (1992, June). Emerging ethical issues facing marketing researchers. *Marketing Research,* 6.

29. Much of the content of this case was taken from a discussion with marketing researcher Doss Struse.

Chapter 5

1. Lohr, S. (2013, January 1). The origins of "Big Data": An etymological detective story. *New York Times.* Retrieved from http://bits.blogs.nytimes.com/2013/02/01/the-origins-of-big-data-an-etymological-detective-story/?_r=0.

2. Rosenbush, S., & Totty, M. (2013, March 11). From a molehill to a mountain. *Wall Street Journal,* p. B1.

3. *GreenBook.* (2015). *GreenBook Industry Trends Report,* 17th ed. New York, p. 44.

4. Survey monitor: Boomers and gen X the most spend-happy; Millennials buy more per trip. (2010, May). *Quirk's Marketing Research Review, 14,* 10, 59.

5. Short, K. (2015, February). Brands, prepare to engage with Generation Z. *Quirk's Marketing Research Media.* Retrieved from http://www.quirks.com

6. Tootelian, D. H., & Varshney, S. B. (2010). The grandparent consumer: A financial "goldmine" with gray hair? *The Journal of Consumer Marketing, 27*(1), 57–63. Retrieved May 5, 2010, from ABI/INFORM Global (Document ID: 1945854611).

7. Senn, J. A. (1988). *Information technology in business: Principles, practice, and opportunities.* Upper Saddle River, NJ: Prentice Hall, p. 66.

8. Grisaffe, D. (2002, January 21). See about linking CRM and MR systems. *Marketing News, 36*(2), 13.

9. Drozdenko, R. G., & Drake, P. D. (2002). *Optimal database marketing.* Thousand Oaks, CA: Sage.

10. Berman, B., & Evans, J. R. (2010). *Retail management: A strategic approach.* Upper Saddle River, NJ: Pearson Prentice Hall, p. 235.

11. Kotler, P., & Keller, K. L. (2016). *Marketing management* (15th ed.). Upper Saddle River, NJ: Pearson Prentice Hall, p. 640.

12. McKim, R. (2001, September). Privacy notices: What they mean and how marketers can prepare for them. *Journal of Database Marketing, 9*(1), 79–84.

13. *Economist.* (2015, November 21). Out of the box, pp. 56–57.

14. Data.gov. (2015). Retrieved from http://www.data.gov/

15. For a discussion of these and other similar situations, see Crosen, C. (1994). *Tainted truth: The manipulation of fact in America.* New York: Simon & Schuster, p. 140.

16. America's experience with Census 2000. (2000, August). *Direct Marketing, 63*(4), 46–51.

17. Accuracy of the census is measured by Census Coverage Measurement (CCM). CCM for the 2010 Census showed that it had an error of 0.01 percent overcount, meaning that an estimated 36,000 extra people were counted. Retrieved on May 24, 2012, from http://www.census.gov.

18. Lange, K. E. (2009, November). The big idea: Electric cars. *National Geographic*, p. 24.

19. Database of personalities (living and dead). (n.d.). Retrieved on May 30, 2012, from http://www.qscores.com/Web/personalities.aspx

20. Based on information provided to the authors by Marketing Evaluations, Inc., on May 31, 2012. These were the top two celebrities in the 2012 Performer Q study.

21. Television measurement. (2012). Retrieved on May 30, 2012, from http://www.nielsen.com/us/en/measurement/television-measurement.html

22. Actually, virtually all these firms offer some customization of data analysis, and many offer varying methods of collecting data. Still, while customization is possible, these same companies provide standardized processes and data.

23. Lifestyles-Esri Tapestry Segmentation. (n.d.). Retrieved on May 30, 2012, from http://www.esri.com/data/esri_data/tapestry.html

24. Murphy, L. (2015). The top 10 most innovative supplier companies in market research. *GreenBook Blog*. Retrieved from http://www.greenbookblog.org/2015/04/28/the-top-10-most-innovative-supplier-companies-in-market-research-grit-spring-2015-sneak-peek

25. ESOMAR. (2015). *Global market research 2015*, p. 35.

26. Fitzsimmons, C. (2013, October 10). Big Data: Forget the "big" and make better use of the data you already have. *Business Review Weekly*. Retrieved from http://www.brw.com.au/p/tech-gadgets/data_data_forget_already_have_and_cY0C3L5M9N1dYkVrsOFeuK

27. ESOMAR. (2014, June 10). The future of market research. *RW Connect*. Retrieved from https://rwconnect.esomar.org/the-future-of-market-research

28. Campbell, S., & Swigarts, S. (2015, April 17). 10 things marketing research needs to know about the Internet of Things. *Marketing Research Association*. Retrieved from http://www.marketingresearch.org/article/10-things-market-researchers-need-know-about-internet-things

29. Smith, R. (2015, August 19). Ralph Lauren to sell wearable-tech shirt timed for US Open. *Wall Street Journal*. Retrieved from http://www.wsj.com/articles/ralph-laurens-new-wearable-shirt-for-us-open-1439999079?alg=y

30. Inspired by a project by Robert Bellon, Steven Moser, Alec Pearson, Marissa Pertler, and Daniel Stropes.

Chapter 6

1. Ezzy, D. (2001, August). Are qualitative methods misunderstood? *Australian and New Zealand Journal of Public Health, 25*(4), 294–297.

2. Clark, A. (2001, September 13). Research takes an inventive approach. *Marketing*, 25–26.

3. *GreenBook*. (2015, Q3-4). *GreenBook Research Industry Trends Report* (18th ed.). New York: New York, p. 10.

4. Rydholm, J. (2011, May). A clearer picture. *Quirk's Marketing Research Review, 25*(5), 30–33.

5. Cusumano, L. (2010, April). How Big Pharma is misusing qualitative marketing research. *Quirk's Marketing Research Review, 24*(4), 18–20.

6. Smith, S. M., & Whitlark, D. B. (2001, Summer). Men and women online: What makes them click? *Marketing Research, 13*(2), 20–25.

7. Piirto, R. (1991, September). Socks, ties and videotape. *American Demographics*, 6.

8. Fellman, M. W. (1999, Fall). Breaking tradition. *Marketing Research, 11*(3), 20–34.

9. Modified from Tull, D. S., & Hawkins, D. I. (1987). *Marketing research* (4th ed.). New York: Macmillan, p. 331.

10. Rust, L. (1993, November/December). How to reach children in stores: Marketing tactics grounded in observational research. *Journal of Advertising Research, 33*(6), 67–72; Rust, L. (1993, July/August). Parents and children shopping together: A new approach to the qualitative analysis of observational data. *Journal of Advertising Research, 33*(4), 65–70.

11. Rydholm, J. (2010, May). Steering in the right direction. *Quirk's Marketing Research Review, 24*(5), 26–32.

12. See http://www.instituteofhomescience.com/

13. Viles, P. (1992, August 24). Company measures listenership in cars. *Broadcasting, 122*(35), 27.

14. Mariampolski, H. (1988, January 4). Ethnography makes comeback as research tool. *Marketing News, 22*(1), 32, 44; Peñaloza, L. (1994, June). Atravesando Fronteras/Border Crossings: A critical ethnographic study of the consumer acculturation of Mexican immigrants. *Journal of Consumer Research, 21*, 32–53; Peñaloza, L. (2006). Researching ethnicity and consumption. In Russell W. Belk (Ed.), *Handbook of qualitative research techniques in marketing*. Cheltenham, England: Edward Elgar, 547–549; Carlon, M. (2008, April). Evolving ethnography. *Quirk's Marketing Research Review, 22*(4), 18, 20.

15. Kephart, P. (1996, May). The spy in aisle 3. *American Demographics Marketing Tools*. Retrieved from http://www.marketingtools.com/Publications/MT/96_mt/9605MD04.htm

16. Del Vecchio, E. (1988, Spring). Generating marketing ideas when formal research is not available. *Journal of Services Marketing, 2*(2), 71–74.

17. Hellebursch, S. J. (2000, September 11). Don't read research by the numbers. *Marketing News, 34*(19), 25.

18. Greenbaum, T. I. (1988). *The practical handbook and guide in focus group research*. Lexington, MA: D. C. Heath.

19. Knutson, R. (2015, September 19). How a Silicon Valley project to reimagine TV became a Verizon app. *Wall Street Journal*. Retrieved from http://www.wsj.com/articles/verizons-go90-video-service-targets-millennials-1441906523

20. Stoltman, J. J., & Gentry, J. W. (1992). Using focus groups to study household decision processes and choices. In R. P. Leone and V. Kumar (Eds.), *AMA Educator's Conference Proceedings*, Vol. 3. Enhancing knowledge development in marketing (pp. 257–263). Chicago: American Marketing Association.

21. Quirk's Marketing Research Media. (2015). *Quirk's Corporate Research Report*, 8.

22. Greenbaum, T. L. (1993, March 1). Focus group research is not a commodity business. *Marketing News, 27*(5), 4.

23. Greenbaum, T. L. (1991, May 27). Answer to moderator problems starts with asking right questions. *Marketing News, 25*(11), 8–9; Fern, E. F. (1982, February). The use of focus groups for idea generation: The effects of group size, acquaintanceship, and moderator on response quantity and quality. *Journal of Marketing Research*, 1–13.

24. Greenbaum, T. L. (1991). Do you have the right moderator for your focus groups? Here are 10 questions to ask yourself. *Bank Marketing, 23*(1), 43.

25. For guidelines for "backroom observers," see Langer, J. (2001, September 24). Get more out of focus group research. *Marketing News, 35*(20), 19–20.

26. Grinchunas, R., & Siciliano, T. (1993, January 4). Focus groups produce verbatims, not facts. *Marketing News, 27*(1), FG-19.

27. Lonnie, K. (2001, November 19). Combine phone, Web for focus groups. *Marketing News, 35*(24), 15–16.

28. For interesting comments, see DeNicola, N., & Kennedy, S. (2001, November 19). Quality Inter(net)action. *Marketing News, 35*(24), 14.

29. Jarvis, S., & Szynal, D. (2001, November 19). Show and tell. *Marketing News, 35*(24), 1, 13.

30. Langer, J. (2001). The mirrored window: Focus groups from a moderator's viewpoint. New York: Paramount Market, 11.

31. Quinlan, P. (2000, December). Insights on a new site. *Quirk's Marketing Research Review, 15*(11), 36–39.

32. Hines, T. (2000). An evaluation of two qualitative methods (focus group interviews and cognitive maps) for conducting research into entrepreneurial decision making. *Qualitative Market Research, 3*(1), 7–16; Quinlan, P. (2008, June). Let the maps be your guide. *Quirk's Marketing Research Review, 22*(6), 74, 76, 77.

33. Berlamino, C. (1989, December/January). Designing the qualitative research project: Addressing the process issues. *Journal of Advertising Research, 29*(6), S7–S9; Johnston, G. (2008, June). Qualitatively speaking. *Quirk's Marketing Research Review, 22*(6), 18, 20; *Alert! Magazine.* (2007, September). Special expanded qualitative research issue, *45*(9); Brownell, L. (2008, April). Chief executive column. *Alert! Magazine, 46*(4), 11, 23.

34. Perez, R. (2010, May). Shaping the discussion. *Quirk's Marketing Research Review*, 24(5), 34–40.

35. See, for example, Seidler, S. (2010, May). Qualitative research panels: A new spin on traditional focus groups. *Quirk's Marketing Research Review, 25*(5), 18–20.

36. American Marketing Association. (n.d.). Dictionary. Retrieved from http://www.marketingpower.com

37. Taylor, C. (2003, December). What's all the fuss about? *Quirk's Marketing Research Review, 17*(11), 40–45.

38. Brogdon, T. (2011, February). A bit more personal. *Quirk's Marketing Research Review, 25*(2), 50–53.

39. Davis, J. (2015, September/October). 10 minutes with Mike Mickunas. *Marketing Insights, 27*(5), 28–31.

40. Burns, A., & Bush, R. (2010). *Marketing research* (6th ed.). Upper Saddle River, NJ: Prentice Hall, p. 231.

41. Rodriguez, L. (2014, February). Qualitatively speaking: Mobile, yes; ethnography, not so much. *Quirk's Marketing Research Review, 28*(2), 20–23.

42. Kozinets, R. V. (2015). *Netnography: Redefined.* Thousand Oaks, CA: Sage.

43. Are marketers losing control of fashion brands? (2014). *Strategic Direction, 30*(6), 20–22.

44. de la Pena, A., & Quintanilla, C. (2015). Share, like and achieve: The power of Facebook to reach health-related goals. *International Journal of Consumer Studies, 39*(5), 495–505.

45. *GreenBook.* (2015). *GreenBook Industry Trends Report* (17th ed.). New York: New York, p. 44.

46. Conon, J. (2014, April). 12 strategies for keeping your Gen Z community engaged. *Quirk's Marketing Research Review, 28*(4), 56–59.

47. Austin, M. (2013, May). More than an activity: How passive "shopping" is changing the path to purchase. *Quirk's Marketing Research Review, 27*(5). Retrieved from http://www.quirks.com/articles/2013/20130526-2.aspx?searchID=1437330499&sort=5&pg=1

48. Based on a table in Goon, E. (2011, May). Need research? Won't travel. *Quirk's Marketing Research Review, 25*(5), 22–28.

49. Davies, H. (2014). Online communities vs. focus groups—who wins? *Quirk's Marketing Research Review.* Retrieved from http://researchindustryvoices.com/2014/03/13/online-communities-vs-focus-groups-who-wins/

50. Flores Letelier, M., Spinosa, C., & Calder, B. (2000, Winter). Taking an expanded view of customers' needs: Qualitative research for aiding innovation. *Marketing Research, 12*(4), 4–11.

51. Grapentine, T. (2010, December). Does more time equal more insights? *Quirk's Marketing Research Review, 24*(10), 34–37.

52. Donnely, T. (2011, May). Marrying phone and web. *Quirk's Marketing Research Review, 25*(5), 42–46.

53. Kahan, H. (1990, September 3). One-on-ones should sparkle like the gems they are. *Marketing News, 24*(18), 8–9.

54. Roller, M. R. (1987, August 28). A real in-depth interview wades into the stream of consciousness. *Marketing News, 21*(18), 14.

55. Kahan, One-on-ones should sparkle like the gems they are.

56. An interesting article on developments in in-depth interviewing is Wansink, B. (2000, Summer). New techniques to generate key marketing insights. *Marketing Research, 12*(2), 28–36.

57. Kates, B. (2000, April). Go in-depth with depth interviews. *Quirk's Marketing Research Review, 14*(4), 36–40.

58. Mitchell, V. (1993, First Quarter). Getting the most from in-depth interviews. *Business Marketing Digest, 18*(1), 63–70.

59. Reynolds, T. J., & Gutman, J. (1988). Laddering, method, analysis, and interpretation. *Journal of Advertising Research, 28*(1), 11–21.

60. Qualitative Research Services. (n.d.). Word association tests. Retrieved on May 20, 2015, from http://www.decisionanalyst.com

61. These techniques are provided by Holly M. O'Neill, President, Talking Business.

62. Pich, C., & Dean, D. (2015). Qualitative projective techniques in political brand image research from the perspective of young adults. *Qualitative Market Research: An International Journal 2015 18*(1), 115–144.

63. Singer, N. (2010, November 13). Making ads that whisper to the brain. *New York Times.* Retrieved from http://www.nytimes.com/2010/11/14/business/14stream.html?_r=0

64. Crupi, A. (2015, May 27). Nielsen buys neuromarketing research company Innerscope: Ratings giant wants to get inside your head. *Advertising Age.* Retrieved from http://adage.com/article/media/nielsen-buys/298771/

65. Eisenberger, N., Lieberman, M., & Williams, K. (2003). Does rejection hurt? An fMRI study of social exclusion. *Science, 302*(5643), 290–292.

66. Marshall, S., Drapeau, T., & DiSciullo, M. (2001, July/August). An eye on usability. *Quirk's Marketing Research Review, 15*(7), 20–21, 90–92.

67. Zapata, C. (2012). What caught their eye? *Quirk's Marketing Research Review, 26*(5), 32–37.

68. Hille, D., & Levin, A. (2013, March). Applying facial coding to ad testing. *Quirk's Marketing Research Review, 27*(3), 46–51.

69. Randall, K. (2015, November 3). Neuropolitics: Where campaigns try to read your mind. *New York Times.* Retrieved from http://www.nytimes.com/2015/11/04/world/americas/neuropolitics-where-campaigns-try-to-read-your-mind.html?_r=0

70. Jarrett, J. (2015, October 14). Has the age of neuromarketing finally arrived? *New York Magazine.* Retrieved from http://nymag.com/scienceofus/2015/10/has-the-age-of-neuromarketing-finally-arrived.html

71. Dooley, R. (2015, June 3). Nielsen doubles down on neuro. *Forbes.* Retrieved from http://www.forbes.com/sites/rogerdooley/2015/06/03/nielsen-doubles-down-on-neuro/

Chapter 7

1. Malhotra, N. (1999). *Marketing research: An applied orientation* (3rd ed.). Upper Saddle River, NJ: Prentice Hall, p. 125.

2. Tourangeau, R. (2004). Survey research and societal change. *Annual Review of Psychology, 55*(1), 775–802.

3. Blyth, B. (2008). Mixed mode: The only 'fitness' regime. *International Journal of Market Research, 50*(2), 241–266.

4. Curtin, R., Presser, S., & Singer, E. (2005, Spring). Changes in telephone survey nonresponse over the past quarter century. *Public Opinion Quarterly, 69*(1), 87–98.

5. Macer, T., & Wilson, S. (2015, April). FocusVision Annual Market Research Technology Report, meaning ltd, London, p. 17.

6. Couper, M. P. (2011). The future of modes of data collection. *Public Opinion Quarterly, 75*(5), 889–908.

7. See Oishi, S. M. (2003). *How to conduct in-person interviews for surveys*. Thousand Oaks, CA: Sage, p. 6.

8. Bronner, F., & Kuijlen, T. (2006, June). The live or digital interviewer. *International Journal of Market Research, 49*(2), 167–190.

9. Bourque, L., & Fielder, E. (2003*). How to conduct self-administered and mail surveys* (2nd ed.). Thousand Oaks, CA: Sage.

10. Jang, H., Lee, B., Park, M., & Stokowski, P. A. (2000, February). Measuring underlying meanings of gambling from the perspective of enduring involvement. *Journal of Travel Research, 38*(3), 230–238.

11. Mavletova, A. (2015). A gamification effect in longitudinal web surveys among children and adolescents. *International Journal of Market Research, 57*(3), 413–438.

12. Maronick, T. (2011, March). Pitting the mall against the Internet in advertising-research completion. *Journal of Advertising Research, 51*(1), 321–331.

13. See, for example, Dudley, D. (2001, January). The name collector. *New Media Age*, 18–20; Kent, R., & Brandal, H. (2003). Improving email response in a permission marketing context. *International Journal of Market Research, 45*(4), 489–540; Agrawal, A., Basak, J., Jain, V., Kothari, R., Kumar, M., Mittal, P. A., et al. (2004, September/October). Online marketing research. *IBM Journal of Research & Development, 48*(5/6), 671–677.

14. Bronner, F., & Kuijlen, T. (2007). The live or digital interviewer. *International Journal of Market Research, 49*(2), 167–190.

15. Haynes, D. (February 2005). Respondent goodwill is a cooperative activity. *Quirk's Marketing Research Review, 19*(2), 30–32.

16. Macer, T., & Wilson, S. (February 2007). Online makes more inroads. *Quirk's Marketing Research Review, 23*(2), 50–55; Westergaard, J. (2005, November). Your survey, our needs. *Quirk's Marketing Research Review, 19*(10), 64–66.

17. Some authors restrict the definition to only cases where two or more data collection methods are used in the same phase of the study. See Hogg, A. (2002, July). Multi-mode research dos and don'ts. *Quirk's Marketing Research Review*. Retrieved from http://www.quirks.com.

18. Cuneo, A. Z. (2004, November). Researchers flail as public cuts the cord. *Advertising Age, 75*(46), 3.

19. Townsend, L. (2010, November). Hit 'em where they surf. *Quirk's Marketing Research Review, 24*(11), 40–43.

20. Katz, M., & Mackey, P. (2010, April). Positive, negative, or neutral. *Quirk's Marketing Research Review*, 24(4), 26–31.

21. Mora, M. (2011, July). Understanding the pros and cons of mixed-mode research. *Quirk's Marketing Research Review, 25*(7), 50–54.

22. Lugtig, P., Gerty, J. L. M., Lensvelt-Mulders, R. F., & Greven, A. (2011). Estimating nonresponse bias and mode effects in a mixed-mode survey. *International Journal of Market Research, 53*(5), 669–686.

23. Fricker, S., Galesic, M., Tourangeau, R., & Ting, Y. (2005, Fall). An experimental comparison of web and telephone surveys. *Public Opinion Quarterly, 69*(3), 370–392.

24. Hsu, J. W., & McFall, B. H. (2015). Mode effects in mixed-mode economic surveys: Insights from a randomized experiment. *Finance and Economics Discussion Series 2015-008*. Washington: Board of Governors of the Federal Reserve System. Retrieved from http://www.federalreserve.gov/econresdata/feds/2015/files/2015008pap.pdf.

25. See Roy, A. (2003). Further issues and factors affecting the response rates of e-mail and mixed-mode studies. In M. Barone et al. (Eds.), *Enhancing knowledge development in marketing*. Proceedings of the American Marketing Association Educators' Conference, Chicago, pp. 338–339; Bachmann, D., Elfrink, J., & Vazzana, G. (1999). E-mail and snail mail face off in rematch. *Marketing Research, 11*(4), 11–15.

26. Hogg, Multi-mode research dos and don'ts.

27. Roy, S. (2004, July). The littlest consumers. *Display & Design Ideas, 16*(7), 18–21.

28. Trott, D. L., & Simpson, A. M. (2005). Computer assisted personal interviewing—The Bermuda experience. *Statistical Journal of the United Nations*, ECE 22, 133–145.

29. Caeyers, B., Chalmers, N., & De Weerdt, J. (2012). Improving consumption measurement and other survey data through CAPS: Evidence of a randomized experiment. *Journal of Development Economics, 98*, 19–33.

30. See Jacobs, H. (1989, Second Quarter). Entering the 1990s: The state of data collection–From a mall perspective. *Applied Marketing Research, 30*(2), 24–26; Lysaker, R. L. (1989, October). Data collection methods in the U.S. *Journal of the Market Research Society, 31*(4), 477–488; Gates, R., & Solomon, P. J. (1982, August/September). Research using the mall intercept: State of the art. *Journal of Advertising Research*, 43–50; Bush, A. J., Bush, R. F., & Chen, H. C. (1991). Method of administration effects in mall intercept interviews. *Journal of the Market Research Society, 33*(4), 309–319.

31. See, for example, Ghazali, E., Mutum, A. D., & Mahbob, N. A. (2006). Attitude towards online purchase of fish in urban Malaysia: An ethnic comparison. *Journal of Food Products Marketing, 12*(4), 109–128; Yun, W., & Heitmeyer, J. (2006, January). Consumer attitude toward US versus domestic apparel in Taiwan. *International Journal of Consumer Studies, 30*(1), 64–74.

32. Frost-Norton, T. (2005, June). The future of mall research: Current trends affecting the future of marketing research in malls. *Journal of Consumer Behavior, 4*(4), 293–301.

33. Hornik, J., & Eilis, S. (1989, Winter). Strategies to secure compliance for a mall intercept interview. *Public Opinion Quarterly, 52*(4), 539–551.

34. At least one study refutes the concern about shopping frequency. See DuPont, T. D. (1987, August/September). Do frequent mall shoppers distort mall-intercept results? *Journal of Advertising Research, 27*(4), 45–51.

35. Bourque, L., & Fielder, E. (2003). *How to conduct telephone interviews* (2nd ed.). Thousand Oaks, CA: Sage.

36. Holbrook, A. L., Green, M. C., & Krosnick, J. A. (2003, Spring). Telephone versus face-to-face interviewing of national probability samples with long questionnaires. *Public Opinion Quarterly, 67*(1), 79–126.

37. Brennan, M., Benson, S., & Kearns, Z. (2005). The effect of introductions on telephone survey participation rates. *International Journal of Market Research, 47*(1), 65–75.

38. At the extreme, it is reported that Chinese research companies monitor at least 50% of all telephone interviews; see Harrison, M. (2006, Winter). Learning the language. *Marketing Research, 18*(4), 10–16.

39. Bos, R. (1999, November). A new era in data collection. *Quirk's Marketing Research Review, 12*(10), 32–40.

40. Fletcher, K. (1995, June 15). Jump on the omnibus. *Marketing,* 25–28.

41. Bronner, F., & Kuijlen, T. (2007). The live or digital interviewer: A comparison between CASI, CAPI, and CATI with respect to difference in response behavior. *International Journal of Market Research, 49*(2), 167–190.

42. DePaulo, P. J., & Weitzer, R. (1994, January 3). Interactive phone technology delivers survey data quickly. *Marketing News, 28*(1), 15.

43. Jones, P., & Palk, J. (1993). Computer-based personal interviewing: State-of-the-art and future prospects. *Journal of the Market Research Society, 35*(3), 221–233.

44. For a "speed" comparison, see Cobanouglu, C., Warde, B., & Moeo, P. J. (2001). A comparison of mail, fax and Web-based survey methods. *International Journal of Market Research, 43*(3), 441–452.

45. See De Bruijne, M., & Wijnant, A. (2014, Winter). Improving response rates and questionniare design for mobile web surveys. *Public Opinion Quarterly, 78*(4), 951–962; Fine, B., & Menictas, C. (2012, December). The who, when, where and how of smartphone research. *Australasian Journal of Market & Social Research, 20*(2), 29–46.

46. See Singh, A., Taneja, A., & Mangalaraj, G. (2009, June). Creating online surveys: Some wisdom from the trenches tutorial. *IEEE Transactions on Professional Communication, 52*(2), 197–212; Costa de Silva, S., & Duarte, P. (2014). Suggestions for international research using electronic surveys. *The Marketing Review, 4*(3), 297–309.

47. Not all observers agree that this trend is positive. See Lauer, H. (2005, July/August). You say evolution, I say devolution. *Quirk's Marketing Research Review, 19*(7), 82–88.

48. Miles, L. (2004, June 16). Online market research panels offer clients high response rates at low prices. *Marketing,* 39.

49. Grecco, C. (2000, July/August). Research non-stop. *Quirk's Marketing Research Review, 14*(7), 70–73.

50. Greenberg, D. (2000, July/August). Internet economy gives rise to real-time research. *Quirk's Marketing Research Review, 14*(7), 88–90.

51. Frazier, D., & Rohmund, I. (2007, July/August). The real-time benefits of online surveys, *Electric Perspectives, 32*(4), 88–91.

52. Noh, M., Runyan, R., & Mosier, J. (2014). Young consumers' innovativeness and hedonic/utilitarian cool attitudes. *International Journal of Retail & Distribution Management, 42*(4), 267–280.

53. Brown, S. (1987). Drop and collect surveys: A neglected research technique? *Journal of the Market Research Society, 5*(1), 19–23.

54. See Ibeh, K. I., & Brock, J. K. (2004). Conducting survey research among organizational populations in developing countries. *International Journal of Market Research,* (3), 375–383; Ibeh, K. I., Brock, J. K., & Zhou, Y. J. (2004, February). The drop and collect survey among industrial populations: Theory and empirical evidence. *Industrial Marketing Management, 33*(2), 155–165.

55. Bourque & Fielder, *How to conduct self-administered and mail surveys.*

56. American Statistical Association. (1997). More about mail surveys. *ASA Series: What is a survey?* Alexandria, VA: Author.

57. Anderson, R. C., Fell, D., Smith, R. L., Hansen, E. N., & Gomon, S. (2005, January). Current consumer behavior research in forest products. *Forest Products Journal, 55*(1), 21–27.

58. Grandcolas, U., Rettie, R., & Marusenko, K. (2003). Web survey bias: Sample or mode effect? *Journal of Marketing Management, 19,* 541–561.

59. See, for example, McDaniel, S. W., & Verille, P. (1987, January). Do topic differences affect survey nonresponse? *Journal of the Market Research Society, 29*(1), 55–66; Whitehead, J. C. (1991, Winter). Environmental interest group behavior and self-selection bias in contingent valuation mail surveys. *Growth & Change, 22*(1), 10–21.

60. Radder, L., Malder, A., & Han, X. (2013). Motivations and socio-demographic characteristics of safari hunters: A South African perspective. *Academy of Marketing Studies Journal, 17*(1), 3–4.

61. Fulgoni, G. (2014, June). Uses and misuses of online-survey panels in digital research. *Journal of Advertising Research, 54*(2), 133–137.

62. Lusk, J. L., & Brooks, K. (2011). Who participates in household scanning panels? *American Journal of Agricultural Economics, 93*(1), 226–240.

63. Sellers, R. (2009). Dirty little secrets of online panels. Grey Matter Research & Consulting, Phoenix, AZ. Retrieved from http://affluenceresearch.org/Dirty-Little-Secrets-of-Online-Panels.pdf.

64. Kanyal, A. (2014, May 14). Top 20 most valuable companies in the online panel industry. Retrieved from http://www.onlinemr.com/2012/05/14/top-20-most-valuable-companies-in-the-online-panel-industry/.

65. Murphy, L. F. (Ed.), (2014, Fall). Greenbook Research Industry Trends. Greenbook, GRIT greenbook.org/GRIT, New York, 24.

66. An industry study identified effectiveness, demand for a specific modality, cost, speed of data collection, and available resources as the top five selection criteria when selecting a data collection modality. Pioneer Marketing Research. (2004, April). *Research industry trends: 2004 report.* Retrieved from http://www.dialtek.com.

67. Philpott, G. (2005, February). Get the most from Net-based panel research. *Marketing News, 39*(2), 58.

68. Gerlotto, C. (2003, November). Learning on the go: Tips on getting international research right. *Quirk's Marketing Research Review,* 44.

Chapter 8

1. For an example of formal, academically sound scale development, see Sung, Y., Choi, S. M., Ahn, H., & Song, Y. (2015, January). Dimensions of luxury brand personality: Scale development and validation. *Psychology and Marketing, 32*(1), 121–132.

2. In some cases, it is recommended to use "Don't know" instead of "No opinion." See Dolnicar, S., & Grun, B. (2012, September). Including don't know answer options in brand image surveys improves data quality. *International Journal of Marketing Research, 56*(1), 33–50.

3. See, for example, Yoon, S., & Kim, J. (2001, November/December). Is the Internet more effective than traditional media? Factors affecting the choice of media. *Journal of Advertising Research, 41*(6), 53–60; Donthu, N. (2001, November/December). Does your web site measure up? *Marketing Management, 10*(4), 29–32; Finn, A., McFadyen, S., Hoskins, C., & Hupfer, M. (2001, Fall). Quantifying the sources of value of a public service. *Journal of Public Policy & Marketing, 20*(2), 225–239.

4. For research on the number of categories, see Wakita, T., Ueshima, N., & Noguchi, H. (2012). Psychological distance between categories in the Likert scale: Comparing different numbers of options. *Educational and Psychological Measurement, 72*(4), 533–546.

5. Edmondson, D., Edwards, Y., & Boyer, S. (2014, Fall). Likert scales: A marketing perspective. *International Journal of Business, Marketing, and Decision Sciences, 5*(2), 73–85.

6. See, for example, Wellner, A. S. (2002, February). The female persuasion. *American Demographics, 24*(2), 24–29; Wasserman, T.

(2002, January 7). Color me bad. *Brandweek, 43*(1), 2; Wilke, M., & Applebaum, M. (2001, November 5). Peering out of the closet. *Brandweek, 42*(41), 26–32.

7. Kaplanidou, K., & Vogt, C. (2010, September). The meaning and measurement of a sport event experience among active sport tourists. *Journal of Sport Management, 24*(5), 544–566.

8. Other methods of brand image measurement have been found to be comparable. See Driesener, C., & Romaniuk, J. (2006). Comparing methods of brand image measurement. *International Journal of Market Research, 48*(6), 681–698.

9. Another way to avoid the halo effect is to have subjects rate each stimulus on the same attribute and then move to the next attribute. See Wu, B. T. W., & Petroshius, S. (1987). The halo effect in store image management. *Journal of the Academy of Marketing Science, 15*(1), 44–51.

10. The halo effect is real and used by companies to good advantage. See, for example, Moukheiber, Z., & Langreth, R. (2001, December 10). The halo effect. *Forbes, 168*(15), 66; Sites seeking advertising (the paid kind). (2002, March 11). *Advertising Age, 73*(10), 38.

11. Some authors recommend using negatively worded statements with Likert scales to avoid the halo effect; however, recent evidence argues convincingly against this recommendation. See Swain, S. D., Weathers, D., & Niedrich, R. W. (2007, February). Assessing three sources of misresponse to reversed Likert items. *Journal of Marketing Research, 45*(1), 116–131.

12. Garg, R. K. (1996, July). The influence of positive and negative wording and issue involvement on responses to Likert scales in marketing research. *Journal of the Marketing Research Society, 38*(3), 235–246.

13. See, for example, Bishop, G. F. (1985, Summer). Experiments with the middle response alternative in survey questions. *Public Opinion Quarterly, 51,* 220–232; Schertizer, C. B., & Kernan, J. B. (1985, October). More on the robustness of response scales. *Journal of the Marketing Research Society, 27,* 262–282.

14. See also Duncan, O. D., & Stenbeck, M. (1988, Winter). No opinion or not sure? *Public Opinion Quarterly, 52,* 513–525; Durand, R. M., & Lambert, Z. V. (1988, March). Don't know responses in survey: Analyses and interpretational consequences. *Journal of Business Research, 16,* 533–543.

15. Semon, T. T. (2001, October 8). Symmetry shouldn't be goal for scales. *Marketing News, 35*(21), 9.

16. Semon, Symmetry shouldn't be goal for scales.

17. Elms, P. (2000, April). Using decision criteria anchors to measure importance among Hispanics. *Quirk's Marketing Research Review, 15*(4), 44–51.

18. Ashley, D. (2003, February). The questionnaire that launched a thousand responses. *Quirk's Marketing Research Review.* Retrieved from http://www.quirks.com.

19. Scale development requires rigorous research. See, for example, Churchill, G. A. (1979, February). A paradigm for developing better measures of marketing constructs. *Journal of Marketing Research, 16,* 64–73; Ram, S., & Jung, H. S. (1990). The conceptualization and measurement of product usage. *Journal of the Academy of Marketing Science, 18*(1), 67–76.

20. The topic of internal consistency of multiple-item measures is too advanced for this basic textbook. Also, recent research touts single-item measures in certain instances. See Bergkvist, L., & Rossiter, J. (2007, May). The predictive validity of multiple-item versus single-item measures of the same constructs. *Journal of Marketing Research, 44*(2), 175–184.

21. For example, bogus recall was found negatively related to education, income, and age but positively related to "yea-saying" and attitude toward the slogan. See Glassman, M., & Ford, J. B. (1988, Fall). An empirical investigation of bogus recall. *Journal of the Academy of Marketing Science, 16*(3–4), 38–41; Singh, R. (1991). Reliability and validity of survey research in marketing: The state of the art, in R. L. King (Ed.), *Marketing: Toward the twenty-first century, Proceedings of the Southern Marketing Association* (pp. 210–213); Pressley, M. M., Strutton, H. D., & Dunn, M. G. (1991). Demographic sample reliability among selected telephone sampling replacement techniques, in R. L. King (Ed.), *Marketing: Toward the twenty-first century, Proceedings of the Southern Marketing Association* (pp. 214–219); Babin, B. J., Darden, W. R., & Griffin, M. (1992). A note on demand artifacts in marketing research, in R. L. King (Ed.), *Marketing: Perspectives for the 1990s, Proceedings of the Southern Marketing Association* (pp. 227–230); Dunipace, R. A., Mix, R. A., & Poole, R. R. (1993). Overcoming the failure to replicate research in marketing: A chaotic explanation, in Tom K. Massey, Jr. (Ed.), *Marketing: Satisfying a diverse customerplace, Proceedings of the Southern Marketing Association* (pp. 194–197); Malawian, K. P., & Butler, D. D. (1994). The semantic differential: Is it being misused in marketing research? in R. Achrol & A. Mitchell (Eds.), *Enhancing knowledge development in marketing, A.M.A. Educators' Conference Proceedings,* 19.

22. Susan, C. (1994). Questionnaire design affects response rate. *Marketing News, 28,* H25; Sanchez, M. E. (1992). Effects of questionnaire design on the quality of survey data. *Public Opinion Quarterly, 56*(2), 206–217.

23. For a more comprehensive coverage of this topic, see Baker, M. J. (2003, Summer). Data collection: Questionnaire design. *Marketing Review, 3*(3), 343–370.

24. Babble, E. (1990). *Survey research methods* (2nd ed.). Belmont, CA: Wadsworth, pp. 131–132.

25. Hunt, S. D., Sparkman, R. D., & Wilcox, J. (1982, May). The pretest in survey research: Issues and preliminary findings. *Journal of Marketing Research, 26*(4), 269–273.

26. Lietz, P. (2010). Research into questionnaire design: A summary of the literature. *International Journal of Market Research, 52*(2), 249–272.

27. Dillman, D. A. (1978). *Mail telephone surveys: The total design method.* New York: Wiley.

28. Interested readers may wish to read Wood, R. T., & Williams, R. J. (2007, February). 'How much money do you spend on gambling?' The comparative validity of question wordings used to assess gambling expenditure. *International Journal of Social Research Methodology, 10*(1), 63–77.

29. Loftus, E., & Zanni, G. (1975). Eyewitness testimony: The influence of the wording of a question. *Bulletin of the Psychonomic Society, 5,* 86–88.

30. For an alternative set of guidelines, see Webb, J. (2000, Winter). Questionnaires and their design. *The Marketing Review, 1*(2), 197–218.

31. Several other marketing research textbooks advocate question focus. See Baker, M. J. (2008, February). Data collection: Questionnaire design do's and don'ts. *CRM Magazine, 12*(2), Special section, 13.

32. Webb, Questionnaires and their design.

33. Ibid.

34. Question clarity must be achieved for respondents of different education levels, ages, socioeconomic strata, and even intelligence; see Noelle-Neumann, E. (1970, Summer). Wanted: Rules for wording structured questionnaires. *Public Opinion Quarterly, 34*(2), 191–201.

35. Webb, Questionnaires and their design.

36. For memory questions, it is advisable to have respondents reconstruct specific events. See, for example, Cook, W. A. (1987, February–March). Telescoping and memory's other tricks. *Journal of Advertising Research, 27*(1), RC5–RC8.

37. Baker, Data collection: Questionnaire design.

38. Ibid.

39. Peterson, R. A. (2000). *Constructing effective questionnaires.* Thousand Oaks, CA: Sage, p. 58.

40. Webb, Questionnaires and their design.

41. Baker, Data collection: Questionnaire design.

42. Webb, Questionnaires and their design.

43. See, for example, More ways to build a better survey. (2008, May). *HR Focus, 85*(5), 13–14.

44. Brennan, M., Benson, S., & Kearns, Z. (2005). The effect of introductions on telephone survey participation rates. *International Journal of Market Research, 47*(1), 65–74.

45. There is some evidence that mention of confidentiality has a negative effect on response rates, so the researcher should consider not mentioning it in the introduction even if confidentiality is in place. See Brennan, Benson, & Kearns, The effect of introductions on telephone survey participation rates.

46. Screens can be used to quickly identify respondents who will not answer honestly. See Waters, K. M. (1991, Spring–Summer). Designing screening questionnaires to minimize dishonest answers. *Applied Marketing Research, 31*(1), 51–53.

47. The Marketing Research Association offers recommendations and model introduction, closing, and validation scripts on its website (http://cmor.org/resp_coop_tools.htm).

48. For recommended guidelines for introductions in B2B surveys, see Durkee, A. (2005, March). First impressions are everything in b-to-b telephone surveys. *Quirk's Marketing Research Review, 19*(3), 30–32.

49. While we advocate common sense, researchers are mindful of question order effects. See, for instance, Laflin, L., & Hansen, M. (2006, October). A slight change in the route. *Quirk's Marketing Research Review, 20*(9), 40–44.

50. Smith, R., Olah, D., Hansen, B., & Cumbo, D. (2003, November/December). The effect of questionnaire length on participant response rate: A case study in the U.S. cabinet industry. *Forest Products Journal, 53*(11/12), 33–36.

51. Webb, Questionnaires and their design.

52. Bethlehem, J. (1999/2000, Winter). The routing structure of questionnaires. *International Journal of Market Research, 42*(1), 95–110.

53. Baker, Data collection: Questionnaire design.

54. At least one group-administered survey found that question sequence had no effect on cooperation rate. See Roose, H., De Lange, D., Agneessens, F., & Waege, H. (2002, May). Theatre audience on stage: Three experiments analysing the effects of survey design features on survey response in audience research. *Marketing Bulletin, 13*, 1–10.

55. They also represent new presentation and format considerations that need to be researched. See, for example, Healey, B., Macpherson, T., & Kuijten, B., (2005, May). An empirical evaluation of three web survey design principles. *Marketing Bulletin, 2005, 16*, Research Note 2, 1–9; Christian, L. M., Dillman, D. A., & Smyth, J. D. (2007, Spring). Helping respondents get it right the first time: The influence of words, symbols, and graphics in web surveys. *Public Opinion Quarterly, 71*(1), 113–125.

56. Highly sophisticated questionnaire design systems have a great many question formats and types in their libraries, and they sometimes have algorithms built into them to arrange the questions into a logical format. See Jenkins, S., & Solomonides, T. (1999/2000, Winter). Automating questionnaire design and construction. *International Journal of Market Research, 42*(1), 79–95.

57. While very effective, "check all that apply" questions have recently been found to be slightly less effective than forced choice or yes/no question formats. See Smyth, J. D., Christian, L. M., & Dillman, D. A. (2008). Does yes or no on the telephone mean the same as check-all-that-apply on the web? *Public Opinion Quarterly, 72*(1), 103–113.

58. At least one author says to not pretest is foolhardy; see Webb, Questionnaires and their design.

59. Some authors refer to pretesting as piloting the questionnaire, meaning pilot testing the questionnaire. See Baker, Data collection: Questionnaire design.

60. Normally pretests are done individually, but a focus group could be used. See Long, S. A. (1991, May 27). Pretesting questionnaires minimizes measurement error. *Marketing News, 25*(11), 12.

61. For a detailed description of the goals and procedures used in pretesting, see Czaja, R. (1998, May). Questionnaire pretesting comes of age. *Marketing Bulletin, 9*, 52–64.

62. For a comprehensive article on pretesting, see Presser, S., Couper, M. P., Lessler, J. T., Martin, E., Martin, J., Rothgeb, J. M., & Singer, E. (2004, Spring). Methods for testing and evaluating survey questions. *Public Opinion Quarterly, 68*(1), 109–130.

63. Berman, A. (2013, November). Tips for effective mobile surveying. *Quirk's Marketing Research Review, 24*(11), 38–41.

Chapter 9

1. Statement by deputy U.S. commerce secretary Rebecca Blank on release of data measuring 2010 census accuracy. (2012). Lanham, United States, Lanham: Retrieved from http://ezproxy.lib.uwf.edu/login?url=http://search.proquest.com/docview/1015154014?accountid=14787.

2. Wyner, G. A. (2001, Fall). Representation, randomization, and realism. *Marketing Research, 13*(3), 4–5.

3. Jackson, A., Pennay, D., Dowling, N., Coles-Janess, B., & Christensen, D. (2014). Improving gambling survey research using dual-frame sampling of landline and mobile phone numbers. *Journal of Gambling Studies, 30*, 291–307.

4. Sample frame error is especially a concern in business samples. See, for example, Macfarlene, P. (2002). Structuring and measuring the size of business markets. *International Journal of Market Research, 44*(1), 7–30.

5. Wyner, G. A. (2007, Spring). Survey errors. *Marketing Research, 19*(1), 6–8.

6. Bradley, N. (1999, October). Sampling for Internet surveys: An examination of respondent selection for Internet research. *Journal of the Market Research Society, 41*(4), 387.

7. Hall, T. W., Herron, T. L., & Pierce, B. J. (2006, January). How reliable is haphazard sampling? *CPA Journal, 76*(1), 26–27.

8. The RANDBETWEEN (bottom, top) function in Microsoft Excel returns a random integer number between 2 numbers that define the bottom and the top of the range.

9. See Tucker, C., Brick, J. M., & Meekins, B. (2007, Spring). Household telephone service and usage patterns in the United Stated in 2004: Implications for telephone samples. *Public Opinion Quarterly, 71*(1), 3–22; Link, M. W., Battaglia, M. P., Frankel, M. R., Osborn, L., & Mokdad, A. H. (2008, Spring). A comparison of address-based sampling (ABS) versus random-digit dialing (RDD) for general population surveys. *Public Opinion Quarterly, 72*(1), 6–27.

10. Random digit dialing is used by the major web traffic monitoring companies. See Fatth, H. (2000, November 13). The metrics system. *Adweek, 41*(46), 98–102.

11. Tucker, C., Lepkowski, J. M., & Piekarski, L. (2002). The current efficiency of list-assisted telephone sampling designs. *Public Opinion Quarterly, 66*(3), 321–338.

12. Huang, E., Liu, T., & Wang, J. (2014). E-health videos on Chinese hospitals' websites. *International Journal of Healthcare Management, 7*(4), 273–280.

13. Economy is dependent on the number of clusters. See Zelin, A., & Stubbs, R. (2005). Cluster sampling: A false economy? *International Journal of Market Research, 47*(5), 503–524.

14. See also Sudman, S. (1985, February). Efficient screening methods for the sampling of geographically clustered special populations. *Journal of Marketing Research, 22,* 20–29.

15. Cronish, P. (1989, January). Geodemographic sampling in readership surveys. *Journal of the Market Research Society, 31*(1), 45–51.

16. For a somewhat more technical description of cluster sampling, see Carlin, J. B., & Hocking, J. (1999, October). Design of cross-sectional surveys using cluster sampling: An overview with Australian case studies. *Australian and New Zealand Journal of Public Health, 23*(5), 546–551.

17. Academic global business researchers often use nonprobability samples for cost savings. See Yang, Z., Wang, X., & Su, C. (2006, December). A review of research methodologies in international business. *International Business Review, 15*(6), 601–617.

18. Thomas, J. S., Reinartz, W., & Kumar, V. (2004, July/August). Getting the most out of all your customers. *Harvard Business Review, 82*(7/8), 116–124.

19. Academic marketing researchers often use convenience samples of college students. See Peterson, R. A. (2001, December). On the use of college students in social science research: Insights from a second-order meta-analysis. *Journal of Consumer Research, 28*(3), 450–461.

20. Wyner, G. A. (2001, Fall). Representation, randomization, and realism. *Marketing Research, 13*(3), 4–5.

21. A variation of the snowball sample is found in Eaton, J., & Struthers, C. W. (2002, August). Using the Internet for organizational research: A study of cynicism in the workplace. *CyberPsychology & Behavior, 5*(4), 305–313; university students were required to return surveys completed by family, friends, or coworkers.

22. Browne, K. (2005, February). Snowball sampling: Using social networks to research non-heterosexual women. *Journal of Social Research Methodology, 8*(1), 47–60.

23. For an application of referral sampling, see Moriarity, R. T., Jr., & Spekman, R. E. (1984, May). An empirical investigation of the information sources used during the industrial buying process. *Journal of Marketing Research, 21*(2), 137–147.

24. For an historical perspective and prediction about online sampling, see Sudman, S., & Blair, E. (1999, Spring). Sampling in the twenty-first century. *Academy of Marketing Science, 27*(2), 269–277.

25. Internet surveys can access hard-to-reach groups. See Pro and con: Internet interviewing. (1999, Summer). *Marketing Research, 11*(2), 33–36.

26. Sample plans are useful wherever someone desires to draw a representative group from a population. For an auditing example, see Martin, J. (2004, August). Sampling made simple. *The Internal Auditor, 61*(4), 21–23.

Chapter 10

1. One author refers to these attributes as "quality" and "quantity." See Hellebusch, S. J. (2006, September). Know sample quantity for clearer results. *Marketing News, 40*(15), 23–26.

2. Lenth, R. (2001, August). Some practical guidelines for effective sample size determination. *The American Statistician, 55*(3), 187–193.

3. Williams, G. (1999, April). What size sample do I need? *Australian and New Zealand Journal of Public Health, 23*(2), 215–217.

4. Cesana, B. M., Reina, G., & Marubini, E. (2001, November). Sample size for testing a proportion in clinical trials: A "two-step" procedure combining power and confidence interval expected width. *The American Statistician, 55*(4), 288–292.

5. This chapter simplifies a complex topic. See, for example, Williams, What size sample do I need?

6. This chapter pertains to quantitative marketing research samples. For qualitative research situations, see, for example, Christy, R., & Wood, M. (1999). Researching possibilities in marketing. *Qualitative Market Research, 2*(3), 189–196.

7. Frendberg, N. (1992, June). Increasing survey accuracy. *Quirk's Marketing Research Review.* Retrieved from http://www.quirks. com.

8. Frendburg (1992) states it simply: "Sampling error has the unique distinction of being a measurable source of error in survey research."

9. We realize that some researchers prefer to always use the sample size formula that includes *N*; however, since *N* does not affect sample size unless *N* is small (or *n* is large relative to *N*), we have opted for simplicity in using the sample size formula without *N*.

10. Xu, G. (1999, June). Estimating sample size for a descriptive study in quantitative research. *Quirk's Marketing Research Review.* Retrieved from http://www.quirks.com

11. For a similar but slightly different treatment, see Sangren, S. (1999, January). A simple solution to nagging questions about survey, sample size and validity. *Quirk's Marketing Research Review.* Retrieved from http://www.quirks.com

12. For a different formula that uses the difference between two means, see Minchow, D. (2000, June). How large did you say the sample has to be? *Quirk's Marketing Research Review.* Retrieved from http://www.quirks.com

13. For a caution on this approach, see Browne, R. H. (2001, November). Using the sample range as a basis for calculating sample size in power calculations. *The American Statistician, 55*(4), 293–298.

14. See Shiffler, R. E., & Adams, A. J. (1987, August). A correction for biasing effects of pilot sample size on sample size determination. *Journal of Marketing Research, 24*(3), 319–321.

15. For more information, see Lenth, Some practical guidelines for effective sample size determination.

16. Other factors affect the final sample size; see, for example, Sangren, S. (2000, April). Survey and sampling in an imperfect world. *Quirk's Marketing Research Review.* Retrieved from http://www.quirks.com

17. See, for example Cesana, Reina, & Marubini, Sample size for testing a proportion in clinical trials.

18. To see how simple cross-tabulations can increase the required sample size, see Sangren, Survey and sampling in an imperfect world.

19. Kupper, L. L., & Hafner, K. B. (1989, May). How appropriate are popular sample size formulas? *American Statistician, 43*(2), 101–195.

20. Bartlett, J., Kotrlik, J., & Higgins, C. (2001, Spring). Organizational research: Determining appropriate sample size in survey research. *Information Technology, Learning, and Performance Journal, 19*(1), 43–50.

21. Hunter, J. E. (2001, June). The desperate need for replications. *Journal of Consumer Research, 28*(1), 149–158.

22. A different statistical analysis determination of sample size is through use of estimated effect sizes. See, for example, Semon, T. T. (1994). Save a few bucks on sample size, risk millions in opportunity cost. *Marketing News, 28*(1), 19.

23. Ball, J. (2004, February). Simple rules shape proper sample size. *Marketing News, 38*(2), 38.

24. Ibid.

25. There are some emerging guidelines to sample size in qualitative research. See Marshall, B., Cardon, P., Poddar, A., & Fontenot, R. (2013, Fall). Does sample size matter in qualitative research: A review of qualitative interviews in IS research. *Journal of Computer Information Systems, 54*(1), 11–22; Fugard, A., & Potts, H. (2015). Supporting thinking on sample sizes for thematic analyses: A quantitative tool. *International Journal of Social Research Methodology, 18*(6), 669–684.

26. See, for example, Hall, T. W., Herron, T. L., Pierce, B. J., & Witt, T. J. (2001, March). The effectiveness of increasing sample size to mitigate the influence of population characteristics in haphazard sampling. *Auditing, 20*(1), 169–185.

27. Savage, J. (2014). By the numbers: 10 online sample integrity tips. *Quirk's Marketing Research Review, 28*(3), 26–28.

Chapter 11

1. In Chapter 10 you learned how to control sampling error by using a sample size formula that determines the sample size required to control for the amount of sample error (e) you are willing to accept.

2. For a breakdown of the types of nonsampling errors encountered in business-to-business marketing research studies, see Lilien, G., Brown, R., & Searls, K. (1991, January 7). Cut errors, improve estimates to bridge biz-to-biz info gap. *Marketing News, 25*(1), 20–22.

3. Interviewer errors have been around for a long time. See Snead, R. (1942). Problems of field interviewers. *Journal of Marketing, 7*(2), 139–145.

4. Intentional errors are especially likely when data are supplied by competitors. See Croft, R. (1992). How to minimize the problem of untruthful response. *Business Marketing Digest, 17*(3), 17–23.

5. To better understand this area, see Barker, R. A. (1987, July). A demographic profile of marketing research interviewers. *Journal of the Market Research Society, 29*, 279–292.

6. For some interesting theories on interviewer cheating, see Harrison, D. E., & Krauss, S. I. (2002, October). Interviewer cheating: Implications for research on entrepreneurship in Africa. *Journal of Developmental Entrepreneurship, 7*(3), 319–330.

7. Peterson, B. (1994, Fall). Insight into consumer cooperation. *Marketing Research, 6*(4), 52–53.

8. These problems are international in scope. For an example from the United Kingdom, see Kreitzman, L. (1990, February 22). Market research: Virgins and groupies. *Marketing,* 35–38.

9. Collins, M. (1997, January). Interviewer variability: A review of the problem. *Journal of the Market Research Society, 39*(1), 67–84.

10. See Flores-Macias, F., & Lawson, C. (2008, Spring). Effects of interviewer gender on survey responses: Findings from a household survey in Mexico. *International Journal of Public Opinion Research, 20*(1), 100–110; Oksenberg, L., Coleman, L., & Cannell, C. F. (1986, Spring). Interviewers' voices and refusal rates in telephone surveys. *Public Opinion Quarterly, 50*(1), 97–111.

11. Conrad, F. G., Broome, J. S., Benkí, J. R., Kreuter, F., Groves, R. M., Vannette, D., & McClain, C. (2013). Interviewer speech and success of survey invitations. *Journal of the Royal Statistical Society, 176*(1), 191–210.

12. See, for example, Pol, L. G., & Ponzurick, T. G. (1989, Spring). Gender of interviewer/gender of respondent bias in telephone surveys. *Applied Marketing Research, 29*(2), 9–13 or Dykema, J., Diloreto, K., Price, J. L., White, E., & Schaeffer, N. C. (2012, June). ACASI gender-of-interviewer voice effects on reports to questions about sensitive behaviors among young adults. *Public Opinion Quarterly, 76*(2), 311–325.

13. See Hansen, K. M. (2007, Spring). The effects of incentive, interview length, and interviewer characteristics on response rates in a CATI study. *International Journal of Public Opinion Research, 19*(1), 112–121; Olson, K., & Peytchev, A. (2007, Summer). Effect of interviewer experience on interview pace and interviewer attitudes. *Public Opinion Quarterly, 71*(2), 273–286.

14. Guéguen, N., Stefan, J., Jacob, C., & Sobecki, M. (2014). She wore a red/white flower in her hair: The effect of hair ornamentation on compliance with a survey request. *Marketing Bulletin, 25*(1), 1–5.

15. McKendall, M., Klein, H., Levenburg, N., & de la Rosa, D. (2010, Fall). College student cheating and perceived instructor fairness. *Journal of the Academy of Business Education, 11*, 14–32.

16. Sanchez, M. E. (1992, Summer). Effects of questionnaire design on the quality of survey data. *Public Opinion Quarterly, 56*(2), 206–217.

17. Kiecker, P., Nelson, J. E. 1996, April). Do interviewers follow telephone survey instructions? *Journal of the Market Research Society, 38*(2), 161–173.

18. Loosveldt, G., Carton, A., & Billiet, J. (2004). Assessment of survey data quality: A pragmatic approach focused on interviewer tasks. *International Journal of Market Research, 46*(1), 65–82.

19. Epstein, W. M. (2006, January). Response bias in opinion polls and American social welfare. *Social Science Journal, 43*(1), 99–110.

20. Tourangeau, R., & Yan, T. (2007). Sensitive questions in surveys. *Psychological Bulletin, 133*(5), 859–883.

21. Preisendörfer, P., & Wolter, F. (2014, Spring). Who is telling the truth? A validation study on determinants of response behavior in surveys. *Public Opinion Quarterly, 78*(1), 126–146.

22. Honomichl, J. (1991, June 24). Legislation threatens research by phone. *Marketing News, 25*(13), 4; Webster, C. (1991). Consumers' attitudes toward data collection methods, in R. L. King (Ed.), *Marketing: Toward the twenty-first century, Proceedings of the Southern Marketing Association,* 220–224.

23. The Pew Research Center for the People & the Press (2012). Assessing the representativeness of public opinion surveys. Retrieved from http://www.people-press.org/files/legacy-pdf/Assessing%20the%20Representativeness%20of%20Public%20Opinion%20Surveys.pdf

24. Arnett, R. (1990). Mail panel research in the 1990s. *Applied Marketing Research, 30*(2), 8–10.

25. Lind, L. H., Schober, M. F., Conrad, F. G., & Reichert, H. (2013, Winter). Why do survey respondents disclose more when computers ask the questions? *Public Opinion Quarterly, 77*(4), 888–935.

26. One author refers to responses to questions on a survey as "hearsay," which includes potential for misunderstanding. See Semon, T. (2003). Settle for personal truth vs. facts in surveys. *Marketing News, 37*(2), 17.

27. Lynn, P., & Kaminska, O. (2012, Summer). The impact of mobile phones on survey measurement error. *Public Opinion Quarterly, 77*(2), 586–605.

28. Of course, eliminating the interviewer entirely may be an option. See Horton, K. (1990, February). Disk-based surveys: New way to pick your brain. *Software Magazine, 10*(2), 76–77.

29. For early articles on interviewers and supervision, see Clarkson, E. P. (1949, January). Some suggestions for field research supervisors. *Journal of Marketing, 13*(3), 321–329; Reed, V. D., Parker, K. G., & Vitriol, H. A. (1948, January). Selection, training, and supervision of field interviewers in marketing research. *Journal of Marketing, 12*(3), 365–378.

30. See Fowler, F., & Mangione, T. (1990). *Standardized survey interviewing: Minimizing interviewer-related error.* Newbury Park, CA: Sage.

31. There are advocates for interviewer certification in the United Kingdom. See Hemsley, S. (2000, August 17). Acting the part. *Marketing Week, 23*(28), 37–40.

32. For an argument against interviewer standardization, see Gobo, G. (2006, October). Set them free: Improving data quality by broadening the interviewer's tasks. *International Journal of Social Research Methodology, 9*(4), 279–301.

33. Tucker, C. (1983, Spring). Interviewer effects in telephone surveys. *Public Opinion Quarterly, 47*(1), 84–95.

34. See Childers, T., & Skinner, S. (1985, January). Theoretical and empirical issues in the identification of survey respondents. *Journal of the Market Research Society, 27*, 39–53; Finlay, J. L., & Seyyet, F. J. (1988). The impact of sponsorship and respondent attitudes on response rate to telephone surveys: An exploratory investigation, in D. L. Moore (Ed.), *Marketing: Forward motion, Proceedings of the Atlantic Marketing Association,* 715–721; Goldsmith, R. E. (1987). Spurious response error in a new product survey, in J. J. Cronin, Jr., & M. T. Stith (Eds.), *Marketing: Meeting the Challenges of the 1990s, Proceedings of the Southern Marketing Association,* 172–175; Downs, P. E., & Kerr, J. R. (1982). Recent evidence on the relationship between anonymity and response variables, in J. H. Summey, B. J. Bergiel, & C. H. Anderson (Eds.), *A spectrum of contemporary marketing ideas, Proceedings of the Southern Marketing Association*, 258–264; Glisan, G., & Grimm, J. L. (1982). Improving response rates in an industrial setting: Will traditional variables work? in J. H. Summey, B. J. Bergiel, & C. H. Anderson (Eds.), *A spectrum of contemporary marketing ideas, Proceedings of the Southern Marketing Association,* 265–268; Taylor, R. D., Beisel, J., & Blakney, V. (1984). The effect of advanced notification by mail of a forthcoming mail survey on the response rates, item omission rates, and response speed, in D. M. Klein & A. E. Smith (Eds.), *Marketing comes of age, Proceedings of the Southern Marketing Association,* 184–187; Friedman, H. H. (1979, Spring). The effects of a monetary incentive and the ethnicity of the sponsor's signature on the rate and quality of response to a mall survey. *Journal of the Academy of Marketing Science,* 95–100; Goldstein, L., & Friedman, H. H. (1975, April). A case for double postcards in surveys. *Journal of Advertising Research,* 43–49; Hubbard, R., & Little, E. L. (1988, Fall). Cash prizes and mail response rates: A threshold analysis. *Journal of the Academy of Marketing Science,* 42–44; Childers, T. L., & Ferrell, O. C. (1979, August). Response rates and perceived questionnaire length in mail surveys. *Journal of Marketing Research,* 429–431; Childers, T. L., Pride, W. M., & Ferrell, O. C. (1980, August). A reassessment of the effects of appeals on response to mail surveys. *Journal of Marketing Research,* 365–370; Steele, T., Schwendig, W., & Kilpatrick, J. (1992, March/April). Duplicate responses to multiple survey mailings: A problem? *Journal of Advertising Research,* 26–33; Wilcox, J. B. (1977, November). The interaction of refusal and not-at-home sources of nonresponse bias. *Journal of Marketing Research,* 592–597.

35. An opposite view is expressed by Pruden and Vavra, who contend that it is important to identify participants and provide some sort of follow-up acknowledgment of their participation in the survey. Pruden, D. R., & Vavra, T. G. (2000, Summer). Customer research, not marketing research. *Marketing Research, 12*(2), 14–19.

36. See, for example, Lynn, P. (2002, Autumn). The impact of incentives on response rates to personal interview surveys: Role and perceptions of interviewers. *International Journal of Public Opinion Research, 13*(3), 326–336.

37. A comparison on nonresponse errors under different incentives is offered by Barsky, J. K., & Huxley, S. J. (1992, December). A customer-survey tool: Using the "quality sample." *The Cornell Hotel and Restaurant Administration Quarterly, 33*(6), 18–25.

38. Derham, P. (2006, October). Increase response rates by increasing relevance. *Quirk's Marketing Research Review, 20*(9), 26–30.

39. Screening questionnaires can also be used. See Waters, K. M. (1991, Spring/Summer). Designing screening questionnaires to minimize dishonest answers. *Applied Marketing Research, 31*(1), 51–53.

40. Coleman, L. G. (1991, January 7). Researchers say nonresponse is single biggest problem. *Marketing News, 25*(1), 32–33.

41. Landler, M. (1991, February 11). The "bloodbath" in market research. *Business Week, 72,* 74.

42. Baim, J. (1991, June). Response rates: A multinational perspective. *Marketing & Research Today, 19*(2), 114–119.

43. Dutwin, D., Loft, J. D., Darling, J. E., Holbrook, A. L., Johnson, T. P., Langley, R. E., Lavrakas, P. J., Olson, K., & Peytcheva, E. (2015, Summer). Current knowledge and considerations regarding survey refusals: Executive summary of the AAPOR task force report on survey refusals. *Public Opinion Quarterly, 79*(2), 411–419.

44. Groves, R. M., Couper, M. P., Presser, S., Singer, E., Tourangeau, R., Acosta, G. P., & Nelson, L. (2006). Experiments in producing nonresponse bias. *Public Opinion Quarterly, 70*(5), 720–736.

45. Tourangeau, R., & Yan, T. (2007, September). Sensitive questions in surveys. *Psychological Bulletin, 133*(5), 859–883.

46. For an interesting attempt to explain participation in surveys, see Heerwegh, D., & Loosveldt, G. (2009, July). Explaining the intention to participate in a web survey: A test of the theory of planned behavior. *International Journal of Social Research Methodology, 12*(3), 181–195.

47. Eisenfeld, B. (2011, January). Play it forward. *Quirk's Marketing Research Review, 25*(1), 58–61.

48. Vogt, C. A., & Stewart, S. I. (2001). Response problems in a vacation panel study. *Journal of Leisure Research, 33*(1), 91–105.

49. Suresh, N., & Conklin, M. (2009, July). Designed to engage. *Quirk's Marketing Research Review, 24*(7), 34–41. See also Peytchev, A. (2009, Spring). Survey break-off. *Public Opinion Quarterly, 73*(1), 74–97.

50. Some authors use the term *unit nonresponse* to refer to item omissions. See, for example, Hudson, D., Seah, L., Hite, D., & Haab, T. (2004). Telephone presurveys, self-selection, and nonresponse bias to mail and Internet surveys in economic research. *Applied Economics Letters, 11*(4), 237–240.

51. Shoemaker, P. J., Eichholz, M., & Skewes, E. A. (2002, Summer). Item nonresponse: Distinguishing between don't know and refuse. *International Journal of Public Opinion Research, 14*(2), 193–201.

52. Vicente, P., Reis, E., & Santos, M. (2009). Using mobile phones for survey research: A comparison with fixed phones. *International Journal of Market Research, 51*(5), 613–633.

53. The American Association for Public Opinion Research (2015). *Standard Definitions; Final Dispositions of Case Codes and Outcome Rates for Surveys,* 14.

54. Frankel, L. R. (1982). *Special report on the definition of response rates.* Port Jefferson, NY: Council of American Survey Research Organizations.

55. The CASRO formula pertains to telephone surveys. For web-based surveys, see Bowling, J. M., Rimer, B. K., Lyons, E. J., Golin, C. E., Frydman, G., & Ribisl, K. M. (2006, November). Methodologic challenges of e-health research. *Evaluation and Program Planning, 29*(4), 390–396.

56. Data quality issues endemic in marketing. (2007, October). *Data Strategy, 3*(8), 10.

57. For yea-saying and nay-saying, see Bachman, J. G., & O'Malley, P. M. (1985, Summer). Yea-saying, nay-saying, and going to extremes: Black–white differences in response styles. *Public Opinion Quarterly, 48*, 491–509; Greenleaf, E. A. (1992, May). Improving rating scale measures by detecting and correcting bias components in some response styles. *Journal of Marketing Research, 29*(2), 176–188.

58. Fisher, S. (2007). How to spot a fake. *Quirk's Marketing Research Review, 21*(1), 44.

59. Speeders are not necessarily straightliners. See Professional test takers (2008, Spring). *Marketing Research, 20*(1), 4.

60. Tellis, G. J., & Chandrasekaran, D. (2010). Extent and impact of response biases in cross-national survey research. *International Journal of Research in Marketing, 27*, 329–341.

61. ESOMAR. (2012). 28 questions to help buyers of online samples. Retrieved from https://www.esomar.org/knowledge-and-standards/research-resources/28-questions-on-online-sampling.php.

Chapter 12

1. It is important for the researcher and client to have a partnership during data analysis. See, for example, Fitzpatrick, M. (2001, August). Statistical analysis for direct marketers—in plain English. *Direct Marketing, 64*(4), 54–56.

2. The use of descriptive statistics is sometimes called "data reduction," although some authors term any appropriate analysis that makes sense of data "data reduction." See Vondruska, R. (1995, April). The fine art of data reduction. *Quirk's Marketing Research Review*, online archive.

3. Some authors argue that central tendency measures are too sterile. See, for example, Pruden, D. R., & Vavra, T. G. (2000, Summer). Customer research, not marketing research. *Marketing Research, 12*(2), 14–19.

4. For an illustrative article on central tendency measures used in business valuation, see Sellers, K., Yingping, H., & Campbell, S. (2008, January/February). Measures of central tendency in business valuation. *Value Examiner*, 7–18.

5. Gutsche, A. (2001, September 24). Visuals make the case. *Marketing News, 35*(20), 21–23.

6. Some guidelines are drawn from Ehrenberg, A. (2001, Winter). Data, but no information. *Marketing Research, 13*(2), 36–39.

7. The 95% level is standard in academic research and commonly adopted by practitioners; however, some authors prefer to use the "probability" of 1 minus the discovered significance level of a finding being true. See Zucker, H. (1994). What is significance? *Quirk's Marketing Research Review*, electronic archive.

8. It has been well documented that tests of statistical significance are often misused in the social sciences, including the field of marketing research. Critics note that researchers endow the tests with more capabilities than they actually have and rely on them as the sole approach for analyzing data (Sawyer & Peter, 1983). Other critics note that combining *p* values with alpha levels in the often used model $p \leq \alpha$ = significance is inappropriate since the two concepts arise from incompatible philosophies (Hubbard & Bayarri, 2003). Users of statistical tests should be familiar with these arguments and other writings noting misinterpretations of statistical significance testing (Carver, 1978). See Sawyer, A. G., & Peter, J. P. (1983, May). The significance of statistical significance tests in marketing research. *Journal of Marketing Research, 20*, 122–133; Hubbard, R., & Bayarri, M. J. (2003, August). Confusion over measures of evidence (*p*'s) versus errors (α's) in classical statistical testing (with comments). *The American Statistician, 57*, 171–182; and Carver, R. P. (1978, August). The case against statistical significance testing. *Harvard Educational Review, 48*, 278–399.

9. Some disciplines, such as psychology and medicine, encourage their researchers to refrain from performing hypothesis testing and to report confidence intervals instead. See Fidler, F., Cumming, G., Burgman, M., & Thomason, N. (2004, November). Statistical reform in medicine, psychology and ecology. *Journal of Socio-Economics, 33*(5), 615–630; or Fidler, F., Thomason, N., Cumming, G., Finch, S., & Leeman, J. (2004, February). Research article editors can lead researchers to confidence intervals, but can't make them think: Statistical reform lessons from medicine. *Psychological Science, 15*(2), 119–126.

Chapter 13

1. One author considers *t* tests (differences tests) to be one of the most important statistical procedures used by marketing researchers. See Migliore, V. T. (1996). If you hate statistics … *Quirk's Marketing Research Review*. Retrieved from http://www.quirks.com

2. For a contrary view, see Mazur, L. (2000, June 8). The only truism in marketing is they don't exist. *Marketing, 20*.

3. Unfortunately, the nature of statistical significance is not agreed to: See Hubbard, R., & Armstrong, J. S. (2006). Why we don't really know what statistical significance means: Implications for educators. *Journal of Marketing Education, 28*(2), 114–120.

4. Meaningful difference is sometimes called "practical significance." See Thompson, B. (2002, Winter). "Statistical," "practical," and "clinical": How many kinds of significance do counselors need to consider? *Journal of Counseling and Development, 30*(1), 64–71.

5. This is common but controversial. See Ozgur, C., & Strasser, S. (2004). A study of the statistical inference criteria: Can we agree on when to use *z* versus *t*? *Decision Sciences Journal of Innovative Education, 2*(2), 177–192.

6. For some cautions about differences tests, see Helgeson, N. (1999). The insignificance of significance testing. *Quirk's Marketing Research Review*, electronic archive.

7. Fulgoni, G., & Lella, A. (2014). Is your digital marketing strategy in sync with Latino-user behavior? *Journal of Advertising Research, 54*(3), 255–258.

8. Hellebusch, S. J. (2001, June 4). One chi square beats two *z* tests. *Marketing News, 35*(12), 11, 13.

9. For illumination, see Burdick, R. K. (1983, August). Statement of hypotheses in the analysis of variance. *Journal of Marketing Research, 20*(3), 320–324.

10. Tellis, G. J., Yin, E., & Bell, S. (2009). Global consumer innovativeness: Cross-country differences and demographic commonalities. *Journal of International Marketing, 2*(17), 1–22.

11. For an example of the use of paired samples *t* tests, see Ryan, C., & Mo, X. (2001, December). Chinese visitors to New Zealand demographics and perceptions. *Journal of Vacation Marketing, 8*(1), 13–27.

Chapter 14

1. For elaboration and an example, see Semon, T. (1999, August). Use your brain when using a Chi-square. *Marketing News, 33*(16), 6.

2. Garee, M. (1997, September). Statistics don't lie if you know what they're really saying. *Marketing News, 31*(9), 11.

3. Correlation is sensitive to the number of scale points, especially in instances when variables have fewer than 10 scale points. See Martin, W. (1978, May). Effects of scaling on the correlation coefficient: Additional considerations. *Journal of Marketing Research, 15*(2), 304–308.

4. For a more advanced treatment of scatter diagrams, see Goddard, B. L. (2000, April). The power of computer graphics for comparative analysis. *The Appraisal Journal, 68*(2), 134–141.

5. Pathak, S. (2013, September 30). Fans and brands. *Advertising Age, 84*(34), 18.

6. It is not advisable to use cross-tabulations analysis with Chi-square when there are cases of cell frequencies of fewer than five cases. See Migliore, V. (1998). *Quirk's Marketing Research Review*, electronic archive.

7. For advice on when to use Chi-square analysis, see Hellebush, S. J. (2001, June 4). One chi square beats two *z* tests. *Marketing News, 35*(12), 11, 13.

8. An alternative view is that the researcher is testing multiple cases of percentage differences (analogous to multiple independent group means tests) in a cross-tabulation table, and use of the Chi-square test compensates for Type I error that reduces the confidence level. See Neal, W. (1989, March). The problem with multiple paired comparisons in crosstabs. *Marketing Research, 1*(1), 52–54.

9. For a more technical explanation of contingency table analysis, see Anawis, M. (2013, August). Contingency tables: A special class of analysis. *Scientific Computing*, 23–25.

10. Mehta, R., Sharma, N. K., & Swami, S. (2013). A typology of Indian hypermarket shoppers based on shopping motivation. *International Journal of Retail and Distribution Management, 42*(1), 40–55.

11. See also Gibson, L. (2007). Irreverent thoughts: Just what are correlation and regression? *Marketing Research, 19*(2), 30–33.

12. For a great many such "spurious" correlations that illustrate the absurdity of attributing cause and effect, see http://www.tylervigen.com/spurious-correlations

Chapter 15

1. At least one marketing researcher thinks that regression analysis is so complex that it actually clouds reality. See Semon, T. T. (2006). Complex analysis masks real meaning. *Marketing News, 40*(12), 7.

2. There are, of course, other and more acceptable ways of identifying outliers. However, our approach relates to the graphical presentation we have used for visualizing linear relationships existing in correlations and regression. At best, our approach simply introduces students to outlier analysis and helps them identify the most obvious cases.

3. Semon, T. (1999, June 23). Outlier problem has no practical solution. *Marketing News, 31*(16), 2.

4. A well-known marketing academic has recommended graphing to researchers: Zinkhan, G. (1993). Statistical inference in advertising research. *Journal of Advertising, 22*(3), 1.

5. For more sophisticated handling of outliers, see Clark, T. (1989, June). Managing outliers: Qualitative issues in the handling of extreme observations in marketing research. *Marketing Research, 2*(2), 31–48.

6. For more information, see, for example, Grapentine, T. (1997, Fall). Managing multicollinearity. *Marketing Research, 9*(3), 11–21, and Mason, R. L., Gunst, R. F., & Webster, J. T. (1986). Regression analysis and problems of multicollinearity in marketing models: Diagnostics and remedial measures. *International Journal of Research in Marketing, 3*(3), 181–205.

7. For a graphical presentation, see Stine, R. (1995, February). Graphical interpretation of variance inflation factors. *The American Statistician, 49*(1), 53–56.

8. For alternatives see Wang, G. (1996, Spring). How to handle multicollinearity in regression modeling, *The Journal of Business Forecasting, 14*(4), 23–27.

9. Sabate, F., Bergegal-Mirabent, J., Canabate, A., & Levherz, P. R. (2014). Factors influencing popularity of branded content in Facebook fan pages, *European Management Journal, 32*(6), 1001–1011.

10. https://en.wikipedia.org/wiki/Road_rage

11. Ge, Y., Qu, W., Jiang, C., Du, F., Sun., X., & Xhang, K. (2014). The effect of stress and personality on dangerous driving behavior among Chinese drivers. *Accident Analysis and Prevention, 73*, 34–40.

12. Cano, L. Z., Sandoval, E. C., & Urbina, M. (2012). Proposals for marketing strategies for optical centers based on the consumer, *Global Conference on Business and Finance Proceedings, 7*(1), 601–606.

13. Our description pertains to "forward" stepwise regression. We admit that this is a simplification of stepwise multiple regression.

14. See, for example, Kennedy, P. (2005, Winter). Oh no! I got the wrong sign! What should I do? *Journal of Economic Education, 36*(1), 77–92.

15. We admit that our description of regression is introductory. Two books that expand our description are Lewis-Beck, M. S. (1980). *Applied regression: An introduction*. Sage Publications, Newbury Park, CA; Schroeder, L. D., Sjoffquist, D. L., & Stephan, P. E. (1986). *Understanding regression analysis: An introductory guide*. Sage Publications, Newbury Park, CA.

16. For readable treatments of problems encountered in multiple regression applied to marketing research, see Mullet, G. (1994, October). Regression, regression. *Quirk's Marketing Research Review*, electronic archive; Mullet, G. (1998, June). Have you ever wondered…. *Quirk's Marketing Research Review*, electronic archive; Mullet, G. (2003, February). Data abuse. *Quirk's Marketing Research Review*, electronic archive.

17. Regression analysis is commonly used in academic marketing research. Here are some examples: Callahan, F. X. (1982, April/May). Advertising and profits 1969–1978. *Journal of Advertising Research, 22*(2), 17–22; Dubinsky, A. J., & Levy, M. (1989, Summer). Influence of organizational fairness on work outcomes of retail salespeople. *Journal of Retailing, 65*(2), 221–252; Frieden, J. B., & Downs, P. E. (1986, Fall). Testing the social involvement model in an energy conservation context. *Journal of the Academy of Marketing Science, 14*(3), 13–20; and Tellis, G. J., & Fornell, C. (1988, February). The relationship between advertising and product quality over the product life cycle: A contingency theory. *Journal of Marketing Research, 25*(1), 64–71. For an alternative to regression analysis, see Quaintance, B. S., & Franke, G. R. (1991). Neural networks for marketing research. In Robert L. King, ed., Marketing: Toward the twenty-first century. *Proceedings of the Southern Marketing Association* (1991), 230–235.

18. Taken from Bruning, E. R., Kovacic, M. L., & Oberdick, L. E. (1985). Segmentation analysis of domestic airline passenger markets. *Journal of the Academy of Marketing Science, 13*(1), 17–31.

Chapter 16

1. Ewing, T. (2015, June). Why the research industry has reasons to be cheerful. *Quirk's Marketing Research Review*. Retrieved from http://www.quirks.com/articles/2015/20150610.aspx?searchID=1430763919&sort=7&pg=2

2. De Ruyck, T., & Willems, A. (2015, July 27). The memefication of insights. Retrieved from http://www.greenbookblog.org/2015/07/27/the-memefication-of-insights

3. Macer, T., & Wilson, S. (2015, July). Highlights from the FocusVision 2014 Annual MR Technology Report. *Quirk's Marketing Research Review*. Retrieved from http://www.quirks.com/articles/2015/20150609.aspx?searchID=1430763919&sort=7&pg=2

4. Based on personal communications with the authors and Michael Lotti. Originally published in Burns, A., & Bush, R. (2005). *Marketing research: Online research applications* (4th ed.). Upper Saddle River, NJ: Prentice Hall, p. 580.

5. Rohde, J. A. (2012, May). Three steps to better research presentations. Retrieved from Quirk's e-newsletter at http://www.quirks.com

6. Jameson, D. A. (1993, June). The ethics of plagiarism: How genre affects writers' use of source materials. *The Bulletin, 2,* 18–27.

7. Imperiled copyrights. (1998, April 15). *New York Times*, A24.

8. Fink, A. (2003). *How to report on surveys* (2nd ed.). Thousand Oaks, CA: Sage, p. 35.

9. *The American Heritage Dictionary of the English Language* (4th ed.) (2000). Boston: Houghton-Mifflin. Retrieved May 24, 2005, from http://www.dictionary.com

10. *American Heritage Dictionary*. Retrieved May 24, 2005, from http://www.dictionary.com

11. See Section A.7, Marketing Research Association's Code of Marketing Research Standards. Retrieved June 7, 2012, from http://www.marketingresearch.org/standards

12. Ober, S. (1998). *Contemporary business communication* (3rd ed.). Boston: Houghton Mifflin, p. 121.

13. Tufte, E. R. (1983). *The visual display of quantitative information*. Cheshire, CT: Graphics Press.

14. Based on personal conversation with the authors and *Research Now's* Kartik Pashupati following a discussion of terms used by marketing research practitioners on March 9, 2012.

15. Donaldson, C. (2015, April). Dear PowerPoint. *Quirk's Marketing Research Review*. Retrieved from http://www.quirks.com/articles/2015/20150426-1.aspx

16. Kelly, B. (2015). Want foresight from Insight? Part 2: An interview with Gongos' Greg Heist. Retrieved from http://www.innovationexcellence.com/blog/2015/07/05/foresight-from-isight/?utm_campaign=Innovate+%40TBD+Festival&utm_content=17857989&utm_medium=social&utm_source=twitter&Itemid=92

17. Personal communication with Jim McConnell, Director of Consumer Insights, MARC USA, October 25, 2015.

18. Chakravarty, R., & Gudding, L. (2013, May). Activating segmentation through storytelling. *Quirk's Marketing Research Review*. Retrieved from http://www.quirks.com/articles/2013/20130507.aspx?searchID=1431741196&sort=7&pg=1

19. Tufte, E. (2001). *The visual display of quantitative information* (2nd ed.). Cheshire, CT: Graphics Press.

20. Macer, T., & Wilson, S. (2015, July). Highlights from the FocusVision 2014 Annual MR Technology Report. *Quirk's Marketing Research Review*. Retrieved from http://www.quirks.com/articles/2015/20150609.aspx?searchID=1430763919&sort=7&pg=2

21. Kelly, B. (2015). Pulling wisdom from abundant data—Part 1: An interview with Gongos' Greg Heist. Retrieved from http://www.innovationexcellence.com/blog/2015/06/01/pulling-wisdom-from-abundant-data-part-1-an-interview-with-gongos%E2%80%99-greg-heist

22. De Ruyck, T., & Willems, A. (2015, July 27). The memefication of insights. *GreenBook*, Retrieved from http://www.greenbookblog.org/2015/07/27/the-memefication-of-insights

23. Middlemiss, M. (2015). Sharing good ideas. Retrieved from http://www.aqr.org.uk/a/20150415-sharing-good-ideas

Name Index

Subject Index